Praise for *Uncommon Fruits and Vegetables*

". . . a masterly volume that every good cook and culinary savant deserves for Christmas this year. . . . It is a must for anyone who has ever been in a quandary about how to buy and how to cook the crop of exotic vegeteria that is changing America's gastronomic landscape."

—*New York Daily News*

" . . . destined to become a classic . . . an indispensable reference for home cooks and professional chefs."

—*Good Food*

"This is a wonderful introduction to everything from anise and arugula to yautia and yams, literally. It is well and clearly written and jam-packed with valuable information."

—*San Francisco Chronicle*

" . . . a must have."

—*Bon Appétit*

"Anyone who has wandered through today's produce markets and felt in need of a glossary will appreciate Schneider's scholarly but no-nonsense approach to the exotics that have pushed their way into the 1980s marketplace."

—*Miami Herald*

". . . a fascinating encyclopedia/cookbook that succeeds in making the unknown sound delicious. . . . The recipes . . . are upbeat and tempting. . . . The reader—and this is a book to read—will not only come away with first-time knowledge about these foods, but will also have a new idea about familiar ones."

—*Garden*

"A treat to read and cook from."

—*Food & Wine*

". . . terrific . . . if there were Emmys or Oscars for cookbooks, Elizabeth Schneider would surely receive one for *Uncommon Fruits and Vegetables*."

—*Boston Globe*

"A fabulous compendium of facts and recipes."

—*Health & Living*

"Finally, what to look for, how to prepare each item for cooking and excellent recipes to bring out their best . . . a must."

—*Chocolatier*

"Elizabeth Schneider's *Uncommon Fruits and Vegetables* is a real cooks' cookbook and reference source. . . . A fine work in every particular, the book has extremely clear, complete recipes that not only work but excite."

—*Cook's*

"The recipes are imaginative and delicious, yet easy to prepare . . . very useful to anyone who wants to take best advantage of today's rare fruit explosion."

—Indoor Citrus and Rare Fruit
Society Newsletter

"Schneider has included a wealth of facts about cultivation, selection and storage, use, preparation, and nutritional value as well as tempting recipes."

—The Pleasures of Cooking

"What a treat—to be able to cook and serve all the exciting, uncommon fruits and vegetables that I didn't know what to do with. . . . It has changed the way I shop—and the way we eat."

—Maida Heatter

"The more good information that's made available about these unusual ingredients, the greater are our cooking possibilities."

—Alice Waters

"At last, someone has taken pity on the poor cook who needs a Bible and Baedeker just to go food shopping! . . . It's a garden of delights no food lover should do without."

—Bert Greene

"A landmark book to those who want expert knowledge, fine reading, and good food."

—Paula Wolfert

"I'm delighted to have another book by Elizabeth Schneider. It's a pleasure to read work that's so concise, friendly, candid, helpful, and well-presented."

—M. F. K. Fisher

"It fills a gap in the cookbook realm. The material is interesting, well-presented, and useful, qualities synonymous with all good cookbooks."

—Jacques Pépin

"Elizabeth Schneider displays a very special talent: She is a most exacting researcher, and her unrestrained curiosity for food and food history is positively infectious. As well, she's an accomplished cook and author, writing in a style that's at once personal, friendly, and generous."

—Patricia Wells

"Elizabeth Schneider, the scientist, the linguist, the sleuth, the tenacious researcher, the literate, passionate cook, has cooked up a fine feast for us."

—Irena Chalmers

UNCOMMON
FRUITS & VEGETABLES
A COMMONSENSE GUIDE

ELIZABETH SCHNEIDER

Illustrations by Soun Vannithone

PERENNIAL LIBRARY

HARPER & ROW, PUBLISHERS, NEW YORK
GRAND RAPIDS, PHILADELPHIA, ST. LOUIS, SAN FRANCISCO, LONDON, SINGAPORE, SYDNEY, TOKYO, TORONTO

Portions of this work previously appeared in *Food & Wine* and *Gourmet*.

A hardcover edition of this book was published by Harper & Row, Publishers, Inc., in 1986.

First PERENNIAL LIBRARY edition published in 1989.

DESIGNED BY JOEL AVIROM

The Library of Congress has catalogued the hardcover edition as follows:

Schneider, Elizabeth.
  Uncommon fruits & vegetables: a commonsense guide.

  Bibliography: p.
  Includes index.
  1. Cookery (Fruit) 2. Cookery (Vegetables) 3. Fruit. 4. Vegetables. I. Title.
  TX811.S35 1986   641.6′4   85-45659
  ISBN 0-06-015420-9

ISBN 0-06-091669-9 (pbk.)
89 90 91 92 93 MPC 10 9 8 7 6 5 4 3 2 1

CONTENTS

ACKNOWLEDGMENTS

This book is mined from experts in many areas: research scientists in the fields of horticulture, genetics, taxonomy, chemistry, plant pathology; farmers and growers; produce distributors; buyers for supermarket chains; agricultural economists; and cooperative extension agents. Help has also come from writers, editors and teachers in the food field; chefs, nutritionists, restaurateurs, language and food historians, storekeepers, amateur cooks; and friends, who offered advice, ingredients, recipes, tales, and meals.

Rick Kot edited precisely and wisely, refining these pages with grace and understanding; Alan Davidson's generous participation made practicable the execution of long-distance artwork; Frieda Caplan, Carol Bowman-Williams, and Judi Greening of Frieda's Finest Specialty Produce went out of their way to obtain out-of-the-way produce.

Of the hundreds who have offered information and assistance, I would particularly like to thank the following: from the United States Department of Agriculture at Beltsville, Maryland, Dr. Raymon Webb, Chief of Vegetable Laboratories, Dr. James Duke, Research Leader of the Germplasm Resources Laboratory, Dr. Edward E. Terrell of the Plant Exploration and Taxonomy Laboratory, and Dr. Miklos Faust, Chief of Fruit Laboratories; Janell Smith, nutritionist; Bill Schaefer of J. R. Brooks & Son; Peggy Kenney of No Bananas; Dr. Robert J. Knight, Jr., of the Subtropical Horticulture Research Station of the USDA in Miami; Dr. Robert E. Berry of the Citrus and Subtropical Products Laboratory of the USDA in Winter Haven; from the Institute of Food and Agricultural Sciences of the University of Florida, Dr. William Stall, Dr. Robert T. McMillan, Dr. D. N. Maynard, Carl Campbell, Seymour Goldweber, Stephen K. O'Hair; Dr. Paul Williams of the University of Wisconsin; Dr. Thomas W. Whitaker; Dr. George Markle of Rutgers University; Jim Fobel; Annabel Langbein; Maricel Presilla;

Joan Nathan; Elisabeth Lambert Ortiz; Grace Kirschenbaum; Nancy Tucker and Rita M. Beasley of the Produce Marketing Association; Mary Pitts of Seald-Sweet Growers; Kate Alfriend of the Media Liaison Center of the USDA; Sherry Vance of the Bailey Hortorium at Cornell University; Geraldine C. Kaye of the Farlow Reference Library and Herbarium of Cryptogamic Botany at Harvard University; Beverly Berkley of Fowler Nurseries; Peter Nichols of California Tropics; Chris B. Rollins of Preston B. Bird and Mary Heinlein Fruit & Spice Park; Tad Thompson; Dr. Marylou Arpaia of the University of California at Riverside; John Pehrson and Ray Copeland of the University of California at the Lindcove Field Station; Members of the Institute of Economic Botany at the New York Botanical Garden; Stephen Tim of the Brooklyn Botanic Garden; Robert Chambers of the California Rare Fruit Growers; Glenn Drowns; Noel Vietmeyer of the National Academy of Sciences; Ted C. Torrey and Steve Frowine of the W. Atlee Burpee Company; Calvin Lamborn; Lamar Timmons of the California Citrus Nurseymen's Association; Dr. John C. Bouwkamp of the University of Maryland; Dr. Wayne Bidlack of the Pharmacology and Nutrition Department of the University of Southern California; Kara Noble of Merriam-Webster, Inc.; Millie Chan; Marva Taylor; Joseph Dohnert of the Puerto Rico Tourism Company; John Gottfried; Bonnie Slotnick; Mrs. Hoang Phan of Vietnam Food & Drink; Adriana Robba; Jeff Imoto of the Ito Packing Company; Nahum Waxman of Kitchen Arts & Letters; Dr. Phillip Crandall of the Citrus Research Education Center at Lake Alfred, Florida; Emil Demartini of Jewel Food Stores; George Michalak of Weis Markets; Richard M. Bird of Safeway Stores; E. C. Godwin of Tom Thumb Supermarkets; Lee Grimsbo of Dean & De Luca; Paul Kang of Green Village; Linda Shoaf-Blinn of Multimate International; Joel Avirom, the extraordinary designer of this book; Richard Levy, who photographed the exquisite jacket; and Maggie Cheney, copy editor supreme.

Those who contributed recipes have been acknowledged on the pages on which their work appears.

Books frequently consulted are listed on page 525.

Gratitude without measure goes to my parents, Herman and Nina Schneider, whose scientific, culinary, artistic, and literary teachings continue to be both inspiring and useful. Without the sustaining help of Carter Jones, Barbara Spiegel, Ronald Christ, and Dennis Dollens, this book could not have been written.

INTRODUCTION

Amerca the melting pot is now also America the wok, the steamer, the pasta machine, the tortilla press, and the food processor. Over the last ten years we have seen a phenomenal increase in our range of cooking techniques, styles, and ingredients. Foods that were once available only in little "ethnic" shops now compete for shelf space in nationwide supermarket chains. Vegetables that were the province of home gardeners and nature buffs have moved into specialty shops. Exotic fruits have traveled from steamy shores and landed in neighborhood groceries. Consider these changes:

Chinese cabbage, bok choy, and snow peas have quit Chinatowns to go national. Fresh chili-peppers have departed from the Southwest and are to be found at all points of the compass.

Foods gathered from the forest, such as chanterelles, fiddlehead ferns, and oyster mushrooms, appear in the wilds of the city; some are even cultivated by giant corporations.

Sour cherries, squash blossoms, and other delicate, hard-to-ship items are trucked by local farmers to roadside stands and greenmarkets, increasing the variety of strictly seasonal produce.

Passion fruit has been tamed, and is making regular appearances around the country. Radicchio (red chicory), recently unknown outside Italy, now flaunts its brilliant red head all over town.

Once again, America is restocking the melting pot to suit her newest immigrants, who are increasing in diversity and number. Mexicans bring jícama, Thais want lemon grass, Japanese ask for daikon, and Cubans love calabaza. Every day the larder grows. Foods that look strange now (as ginger, shallots, bean sprouts, and even avocados did not so long ago) may soon be common in our culinary vocabulary.

The influx of people from other countries has had another vitalizing effect: it has encouraged us to examine our own national identity, our regional distinctions. We have begun to share and enjoy foods that were formerly geographically and culturally isolated. Morels no longer belong solely to the fortunate foragers of Michigan, nor are okra and mustard greens confined to the Deep South. Once local specials, the big sweet onions of Vidalia and Walla Walla have found new homes, and Floridians send off their guavas and lychees.

Another cause of the explosion in the produce aisle: our increased attention to nutrition and health. Since 1977, beginning with the publication of new nutritional guidelines for Americans, many of us have changed the balance of our diet (salad bars are a recent phenomenon for much of the country). We are increasing our intake of complex carbohydrates and dietary fiber, while lowering our intake of fat—which means enlarging the repertoire of fruits and vegetables.

An unprecedented increase in restaurant dining has expanded our awareness of this fresh palette of produce. Chefs, always in the culinary avant-garde, rush to acquire exciting, unfamiliar ingredients from all over the world. Stimulated by the abundance available to them, they never cease interpreting the new flavors, which they then pass on to us.

Not the least significant factor in the new cosmopolitanism of our cuisine is that methods for harvesting, cooling, and transporting edibles have kept up with the jet age, allowing new food for thought to be delivered daily. Cool from trucks, trains, and airplane and ship containers, the ever-increasing quantities of exotica spill forth for everyday meals: Clementines from Morocco and Spain, papayas from Hawaii, chayotes from Costa Rica, tamarillos and feijoas from New Zealand.

This book is an attempt to guide you through the burgeoning produce sections of our markets. It includes the in-depth information you'll need to select, store, clean, and cook the fruits and vegetables that pique your curiosity. Simple recipes should help you turn specialty items into regulars, for it is less trouble to cook Chinese cabbage than "American"; more intriguing at times to sliver jícama or Asian pear into your salad than apple; no more time-consuming to sauté fennel or kohlrabi than onions. Nutritional highlights will help you incorporate these foods most beneficially in your menus. Here, as well, should you wish to know the characters more intimately, is the background story for each of the fruit and vegetable players.

Beyond nutrition and the pleasures of the table you may find an additional bonus, as I have. You'll get to meet some of the nicest people in the world without an introduction. Take tomatillos to the check-out counter and listen to the Mexican cashier tell you about the special way her sister makes *salsa verde*. Carry your groceries so that the yard-long beans or cactus pears are visible and see what happens to conversation in the parking lot or apartment elevator. Mention at a dinner party with Greeks or Iranians that you breakfasted on stewed quinces. Offer cherimoyas to anyone who has lived in Central or South America. People share their stories, recipes, and heritage when you introduce the common denominator of an uncommon fruit or vegetable.

Fruit and vegetable names change from region to region, depending more or less upon the provenance of the residents of the area. They even vary from one grocery chain to another, and from store to store. Usage may be determined by distributors and produce dealers, who "simplify" names of time-honored species by shortening them to fit on signs or replacing them with catchy cognomens. The poor feijoa is called *pineapple guava* in parts of the country, and even *guava* (a different species) in others. *Sunchokes* have replaced *Jerusalem artichokes* in many areas, and *kiwifruit* (or *kiwi*), an invented marketing name, is never called anything else. Fennel is not anise (a different plant), although some distributors call it that. In Puerto Rican neighborhoods cassava is called *yuca* and malanga is called *yautia*—but malanga isleña is *taro* to Cubans, and taro is *dasheen* to an equal number of customers. *Arugula*, *rucola*, and *rocket* (and even some fancy misspellings in between) refer to the same leaf in different markets. What you see is what you get, which is why we have supplied drawings of the most usual market version of each, as well as the most accepted and prevalent common names (the *most* commonly accepted is the first, in capitals), according to a consensus of scientists, produce buyers, and growers.

In the end, the only way to be fairly sure you are talking about the same fruit or vegetable that someone else is (short of both looking at it together) is to use the binomial classification established by the Linnaean system, in which genus (always capitalized), then species is indicated, as has been done here. But don't think for a minute that even this venerable system remains fixed. Taxonomic classification changes as the science does: the appearance of a chromosome or two, the discovery of a hidden ovule will move a plant from one grouping to another. What was *Brassica rapa* this year may be *Brassica campestris* the next, as scientific equipment and methods become more specialized. The binomials in this book were reviewed by a dozen specialists—who often disagreed on the classification of a fruit or vegetable. Nevertheless, with common names a dime a dozen there is still nothing as solid as the Latin one.

Another variable to consider is that the season in which produce may show up in the market does not necessarily remain fixed. What came from New Zealand last year during our winter may now be planted in the United States, which adds a summer season. What was successfully test-marketed for a month one year will reappear for three months the next. A crop failure in Florida (sadly, not an uncommon event) may mean that there will be none of a certain fruit. Radicchio from Italy, once an occasional import, became so popular that American growers planted it, making it available all year. The important thing to remember is that *you* determine what happens to our produce marketplace by what you buy, what you complain about, and what you request. If papaya has no taste, say so; if pomegranates are dried out, object. If you would like to have mustard greens and oyster mushrooms, ask for them. Your voice keeps up demand and maintains quality.

RECIPES BY CATEGORY

A

ANISE (OR SWEET ANISE)
See Fennel

ARUGULA, ROCKET
(Eruca vesicaria subspecies *sativa)*
also Rucola, Rugula, Roquette, Mediterranean Rocket, Rocket-Salad

A friend from the South cannot believe that catfish is virtually unknown in New York City (neither can I). When I leave the city I am astonished to find that the nippy leaf I dote on is often a curiosity. Raised in Greenwich Village, where most greengrocers were Italian during the time I was growing up, I never realized that arugula

(pronounced ah-ROO-guh-lah) was a specialty grown nearby for my neighbors in Little Italy. Although it has finally done some spreading out in this country, arugula has never really traveled far from the Mediterranean area and western Asia where it originated, except to accompany those who grew up on it.

The tender, mustard-flavored, bitterish green is standard salad-bowl fare in Italy, the South of France, and Greece, where it is used as the old herbals specified, as "a seasoning leaf." Arugula resembles the leaves of the radish (a close relative) in flavor and appearance. Like watercress, it is more than a leafy green, less than a strong herb. The combination of new American cuisine and a national interest in nutritious greens has moved this member of the vast Crucifer pack out of the shadows of small Italian restaurants and into the California sunlight.

Like fresh chili-peppers, it has one of those tastes that you crave once you've adopted it—or it, you.

SELECTION AND STORAGE: Arugula is usually available year round. If your market doesn't stock it, ask the grocer to order some, as it is widely distributed. Arugula is sold in small bunches, with roots attached, and should be bright emerald, with no sign of yellowing or limpness. Nor should it appear waterlogged, which it will become if kept too long on ice.

Arugula is most perishable. Wrap the roots in damp toweling, enclose the bunch in plastic, and refrigerate for a day or two, if you must.

USE: Taste arugula before you prepare it. Like radishes, it can be quite hot, especially during the summer, and you may want to use it sparingly.

Arugula is one of the most vervy and attractive leaves (somewhere between oak-leaf lettuce and dandelion in shape) that you can add to your repertoire. It really *makes* a salad. In Italy it is commonly, and beautifully, tossed with radicchio and a softer pale lettuce. In Provence it appears as one of the small flavorful leaves in the celebrated mesclun salad, a toss of baby and bitter lettuces and mild herbs. In nouvelle French and American cooking it shows up as the perfect foil for mild, creamy goat cheese, whether marinated, fried or baked, warm or cold. Arugula is particularly delicious with the citrus sweetness of oranges (especially blood oranges). It contrasts eloquently with creamy avocado, sweetened with a touch of balsamic vinegar and nut oil, and adds a welcome edge to potato salad, when used as a surrounding or cradling leaf for the mixture.

Although cooked arugula loses some bite, it has much flavor. Toss in hot oil and garlic, then with pasta or potatoes. Add to stir-fries at the last minute. Purée in soups and sauces.

PREPARATION: Candid, clean-faced arugula leaves hide sand no matter how pristine they may appear. Do not be tempted to rinse the leaves casually under running water. Instead, cut off the roots and any thick stems, then dunk the leaves up and down in a bowl of cold water. Let stand a moment, then gently lift them out, so sand is left at the bottom. Rinse out the bowl and repeat; a third time may be necessary. Spin the leaves dry, then wrap in toweling and chill until serving time.

NUTRITIONAL HIGHLIGHTS: Arugula is source of vitamin A, vitamin C, calcium, and fiber.

WARM ARUGULA TOSSED WITH DICED RED ONION AND TOMATO

This brilliantly colored first course is light and simple, but unusual enough to pave the way for an elegant meal. Although the few ingredients must be prepared just before serving, cooking time is under 4 minutes.

4 servings

2 large bunches (½ pound) arugula, trimmed, washed, and dried (see Preparation)

2 large plum tomatoes

3 tablespoons cider vinegar

2 teaspoons brown sugar

¼ teaspoon salt, or to taste

1 medium-large red onion cut in ½-inch dice (1 cup)

3 tablespoons full-flavored olive oil (or 1½ tablespoons each imported walnut oil and olive oil, for variation)

1. Cut or tear arugula in large mouthful-sized pieces. Place a tomato on a fork and hold directly in gas flame, turning until skin bubbles and splits, about 15 seconds. Repeat. (Alternatively, drop tomatoes into boiling water and let water return to a full boil; lift out immediately and run cold water over them.) Peel and halve crosswise; squeeze out seeds, then cut out stem ends. Cut into ½-inch squares.

2. In nonaluminum skillet combine vinegar, sugar, and salt; bring to a boil. Add onion and cook over moderate heat until onion softens slightly and vinegar almost evaporates, about 2 minutes. Add tomato dice and boil until juice begins to exude—about 1 minute. Do not overcook; vegetables should retain texture and shape. Set aside.

3. Immediately heat oil in wide skillet over moderate heat. Add arugula and toss until just hot, but not wilted through—about 20 seconds. Divide at once among 4 serving plates.

4. Top with tomato-onion mixture and serve.

ARUGULA, POTATO, AND LEEK SOUP

As watercress changes potato soup into something that doesn't taste quite like any of the individual ingredients, so arugula transforms this traditional soup base.

Flexible, the soup can be puréed to a chunky or a smooth texture, and served hot, as a main dish, or chilled, as a first course.

Makes about 6 cups

1½ tablespoons safflower or other light vegetable oil
2 medium leeks, trimmed, cleaned thoroughly, and chopped (1½ cups)
1 medium onion, sliced (1 cup)
1 teaspoon ground fennel seeds
1¼ pounds potatoes, peeled and coarsely cubed (3 cups)
3 cups chicken broth
1½ cups water
About 10 ounces arugula, washed, trimmed, to yield 4 cups packed (see Preparation)
Pepper and salt, as needed
About 2 tablespoons Ricard or Pernod
Yogurt, about 2 tablespoons per serving
Garnish: 4 arugula leaves, finely slivered

1. Heat oil in large pot. Add leeks and onion; cook over moderately low heat, stirring often, until softened—about 10 minutes. Sprinkle with fennel and stir 30 seconds.

2. Add potatoes, broth, and water. Simmer 25 minutes, until soft. Add arugula and cook about 10 minutes longer, or until stems are soft. Add salt, pepper, and liquor to taste.

3. Purée to rough or smooth texture, as you like. Adjust seasoning. Serve hot or chilled, topped with yogurt and garnished with arugula slivers.

SALAD OF ARUGULA, ENDIVE, RADICCHIO

Although there is a brisk touch of orange in this combination, the effect of the whole is bitter, crisp, with a peppery arugula bite: altogether clean and refreshing.
4 servings

1 healthy bunch arugula (3–4 ounces), cleaned (see Preparation)

1 small radicchio rosso, about 4 ounces (or substitute redleaf lettuce)

3 small Belgian endive, about ½ pound

1 large navel orange, all peel and pith removed

1 tablespoon balsamic vinegar

1 tablespoon white wine vinegar

Salt to taste

Pepper to taste

2 tablespoons olive oil

2 tablespoons corn oil

1. Cut arugula in bite-size pieces. Cut out cores from radicchio and endive; separate leaves. Rinse, and dry thoroughly. Cut to size desired. Wrap and chill.

2. At serving time combine leaves in bowl. Cut between membranes of orange to section closely, working over salad to catch juices.

3. Combine vinegars, salt, and pepper; mix. Add oils and blend thoroughly. Pour dressing over salad; toss. Serve at once.

PASTA WITH ARUGULA, PROSCIUTTO, AND TOMATOES

When sautéed, arugula loses much of its bite, while the color and flavor are intensified. The bitter green, softened by its brief toss in the pan, is balanced by the bright acid-sweet tomato and chewy bits of salty prosciutto.
2 or 3 servings as a main course

2 large bunches (½ pound) arugula, washed, dried and trimmed (see Preparation)

½ pound narrow egg pasta (fettuccine or linguine) or egg noodles

2 tablespoons butter

1 tablespoon olive oil

1 large garlic clove, minced

4 ounces prosciutto (2 thick slices), cut in ¼-inch dice (⅓ cup)

2 meaty plum tomatoes, peeled (p. 23) and cut in ½-inch dice (⅔ cup)

1. Coarsely slice arugula. There should be about 3 cups, lightly packed. Drop pasta into a very large pot of salted water and stir until water returns to a boil.

2. Heat 1 tablespoon butter and the olive oil over moderate heat in a wide skillet. Stir in garlic and prosciutto and toss until garlic is slightly softened, about 2 minutes. Reserve.

3. Drain pasta and combine in heated serving bowl with remaining tablespoon butter. Toss.

4. Heat garlic-prosciutto to sizzling on high heat. Add tomatoes and toss. Add arugula and toss until not quite wilted, about 1 minute.

5. Scoop over the pasta. Season to taste and serve at once.

🐌 *Substitute arugula for dandelions in the Salad of Dandelion and Fresh Goat Cheese (page 164) or Felipe Rojas-Lombardi's Dandelions with Penn Dutch dressing (page 165).*

ASIAN PEAR
(*Pyrus ussuriensis* and *Pyrus pyrifolia*)
also Nashi (Japanese for pear), Apple Pear, Sand Pear, Salad Pear, Chinese Pear, Oriental Pear (also called, incorrectly, Pear Apple)

*E*ach time you meet up with an Asian pear in the market it seems to look little like the last. You'll find a wide range of seemingly disparate fruits, from petite and chartreuse to mammoth and brown. They may be smooth-skinned and lacquer-like, or, more commonly, sprinkled with a confetti of russeting. While there is much varia-

tion among the types of the fruit, the basic characteristics are as follows: Asian pears *are* crunch and juice, so crisp-firm they can be cut paper-thin, their nectar welling up and pouring off each slice. They are lightly sweet, low in acid and aroma, mild to bland in flavor, and granular in texture. If you cook them, they will take longer than "regular" pears. Asian pears are ready to eat when you buy them, and can be stored for a long period. With the exception of Ya Li and Tsu Li, two Chinese varieties (both yellow-green), Asian pears sold in the United States are round.

There are more than 25 varieties of Asian pear known in this country (many were planted by Chinese prospectors during the Gold Rush, as they passed through the Sierra Nevada), and more than 100 in Japan. There are also crosses of both, to confuse things further. Thus, it seems a shame to refer to them collectively, which is the present marketing practice, as each has distinctive characteristics (imagine the difference between a Comice and a Seckel pear, for instance). Pomologists at the main

United States experimental station, the University of California at Davis, confirm that the variety of Asian pear now most commonly enjoyed in both Japan and the United States is Twentieth Century (also called Nijisseiki), a smoothly round, fairly large, green-to-yellow fruit with sweet, mild, very juicy flesh. Running a close second in popularity is Shinseiki, which has many of the same qualities but is more yellowed, like a Bartlett pear, and has slightly sweeter flesh and less gushing juice. Developers agree that the most important future market varieties will soon be: Hosui, a large matte gold-bronze, rather thick-skinned fruit that is low in acid and splashingly juicy; and Kikusui, a large, rounded and lopsided yellow-green fruit that spurts freshets of light, tart juice.

SELECTION AND STORAGE: You're most likely to come across Asian pear varieties in the early summer through early spring. They will be expensive, so select a sample of each kind as it appears, to enable you to snatch up your favorites in quantity the next time they come to town. Choose the most fragrant pears you can find. They will be hard when ripe—unlike the pears we are accustomed to, which have considerable give. Store them in the refrigerator, like apples, but expect them to last considerably longer, if not bruised.

USE: Orientals eat Asian pears peeled, cut horizontally in thin rounds to expose the pretty flowerlike core (virtually every bit but this slim center is edible). I like them chilled, sliced by each diner, to be savored as an icy-clean dessert or a between-course refresher, as cool and crisp as cucumbers. At their best, few fruits are as refreshing.

Or incorporate slivers of peeled pear in a dainty fruit mélange free of strong flavors (they are easily overwhelmed by aggressive aromas and liqueurs). Dip iced rounds of Asian pear in raspberry, strawberry, kiwi, or apricot sauce.

Cooked, they resemble our pears (which are European) in flavor; but they do not become meltingly tender. As a matter of fact, in my experience there is no way to overcook these fruits. When they are poached, baked, or sautéed the taste is intensified while the flesh remains slightly firm, meaty. For any method, allow a much longer cooking time than you would for other pears.

NUTRITIONAL HIGHLIGHTS: Asian pears are a good source of vitamin C and provide a modest amount of fiber.

SAUTÉED ASIAN PEARS WITH HAZELNUTS

Utterly simple, this alternative to sautéed apple slices is delicate and unusual in flavor and texture, an ideal complement to chicken, ham, duck, or a grain or legume entrée. I keep a pepper grinder filled with coriander seeds to aromatize whatever suits my taste. If you do not wish to devote a mill to them, crush whole seeds in a mortar instead. If you have only the commercially ground coriander, sprinkle the cooked slices with a little of the spice, then turn and cook for a few seconds.

4 servings

2 large Asian pears, each about ¾ pound
About 3 tablespoons butter
Pinch of salt
Squeeze of lemon juice
Freshly ground coriander seeds, to taste
2 tablespoons coarsely sliced roasted, skinned hazelnuts (or almonds)

1. Peel pears. Remove stems and blossom ends; cut crosswise into ¼-inch-thick slices. (There is no need to core.)

2. Heat butter in 2 large skillets; add pears in a single layer and cook over moderate heat until lightly browned—about 3 minutes. Turn and lightly brown the other side, cooking until fruit has just barely lost its raw crunch in the center. Sprinkle with salt and lemon juice to taste. Grind (or sprinkle) over coriander to taste.

3. Transfer slices to a hot platter and sprinkle with nuts.

SMALL ASIAN PEARS IN GINGER-VINEGAR SYRUP

Small Asian pears retain their shape and firm texture when long-cooked in a sharp, gingery syrup that tints the fruit a rich caramel color. Serve as you would a condiment fruit—with hot or cold roasted ham, duck, turkey, pork loin, or chicken.

About 8 servings

8 small Asian pears, ¼ pound each
6 cups water acidulated with 3 tablespoons lemon juice
4 cups white grape juice, or part apple juice, part white grape juice
⅔ cup cider vinegar
½ cup brown sugar
⅓ cup thinly sliced fresh ginger

1. Peel and halve pears, removing stems. With melon-ball cutter carefully remove cores. Drop into acidulated water to prevent browning.

2. Combine grape juice, vinegar, brown sugar, and ginger in a nonaluminum pan; simmer, covered, for 10 minutes. Drain pears and add. Uncover pan and simmer gently, turning pears occasionally until tender—which may be as long as an hour.

3. With slotted spoon transfer fruits to a serving dish. Boil syrup briefly to thicken and reduce to about ¾ cup. Pour over pears. Let cool, then chill.

ASIAN PEAR CLAFOUTIS

This fragrant dessert is similar to the French clafoutis of the Limousin area in which fresh, soft fruits (traditionally cherries) are baked in an eggy pancake batter. You can prebake the pear slices, then cover them with the custardy, puffy topping about 35 minutes before you're ready to serve dessert.

6 servings

About 2 pounds large sweet-smelling
    Asian pears
4 tablespoons sugar
1 tablespoon butter, cut into tiny bits
3 tablespoons pine nuts (pignolia)
About 3 tablespoons pear brandy or
    liqueur
1 cup milk
2 eggs plus 1 egg yolk
⅛ teaspoon salt
2 tablespoons melted butter
Scant ⅔ cup flour
Powdered sugar
Optional: Heavy (or whipping) cream, to
    pour, or lightly whipped

1. Peel pears and halve lengthwise; scoop out cores with a melon-ball cutter. Cut halves crosswise, on a slant, to make slices about ¼ inch thick. Arrange them, closely overlapping, in a buttered baking-serving dish of about 2-quart capacity, about 2 inches high (an oval dish looks pretty). Sprinkle with 3 tablespoons sugar and dot with butter.

2. Cover with foil and bake on lowest level of preheated 375-degree oven until tender, about 45 minutes, basting 2 or 3 times. Remove foil and bake about 10–15 minutes, until a small amount of juice evaporates. Set aside until ready to bake dessert.

3. Combine remaining tablespoon sugar and nuts in processor. Whirl to a paste, scraping down sides. Drain juice from pears into measuring cup. Add pear brandy to equal ¼ cup. Add this liquid and milk to nuts, processing to blend. Add eggs and egg yolk, salt, and butter; whirl to just mix. Sift in flour and blend to barely combine.

4. Pour batter over pears. Bake in lower level of preheated 400-degree oven until lightly browned and puffed—about 30–35 minutes. Sift powdered sugar over top; serve at once, with cream if desired.

ATEMOYA
(Annona Hybrid)
**cross between the Cherimoya *(Annona cherimola)* and the Sugar Apple or
Sweetsop *(Annona squamosa)***

*T*his is one of a genus *(Annona)* of pudding-like fruits that are indigenous to tropical America and the West Indies. Atemoya's appearance on the scene is recent. It was "invented" by an employee of the United States Department of Agriculture, P. J. Wester, in 1907—but, as it turned out, nature had already come up with the same cross in 1850 in Australia, and did so again in Israel in 1930. The tough-skinned, gray-green fruit, which resembles in size and shape a distorted, slightly melted, Stone Age artichoke, is presently cultivated in Florida, from where it is shipped commercially on a limited basis.

Cut open the fruit and you will find a creamy, ivory flan-like expanse of rich, sweet, virtually acid-free pulp studded with slippery, dark, watermelon-like seeds—fewer than are found in most cherimoyas. The dense pulp, at its best, tastes astonishingly like cooked vanilla custard with a hint of mango, with a real milk flavor. Less than perfect, it can be rather starchy, like winter squash blended with pear.

SELECTION AND STORAGE: Look for atemoya from late August through November. Choose pale green ones, relatively thin-skinned and somewhat tender, if available. If not, simply look for unblemished fruits that have not cracked open. Although atemoyas often split slightly at the stem end as they ripen, it is best to buy whole fruits at the market to avoid bacterial invasion. But, once at home, there is no harm if the fruit opens. Simply cover the ripening atemoya with a clean towel or napkin. Keep at room temperature, checking often: tropical fruits ripen very quickly—from a baseball to a cream puff in 2 days. Do not refrigerate before the fruit is tender or it will be ruined. Once it is ripened, you can hold the atemoya for a few days in the refrigerator. Although the skin darkens, like a banana, the flesh is not affected.

USE: The best way to enjoy a properly ripened atemoya is to chill it, halve, and serve it straight. Spoon out the creamy pulp (I find a grapefruit spoon makes for tidy scooping), then savor, spitting out the seeds (daintily, of course) as you go. You might gild the lily with some cream as you spoon away. Or cut the atemoya into small pieces, seed them, and combine with other mild fruits for an exotic fruit cup: papaya, mango, soft melon, and toasted coconut seem to suit. For an easy, subtle sauce sieve the fruit and serve as is (or sparked with a little lime, orange, or tangerine juice), over delicate sponge cake, poached fruit, or pudding.

NUTRITIONAL HIGHLIGHTS: Atemoya is relatively high in calories. It is an excellent source of vitamin C. It is high in fiber and low in sodium.

—

ATEMOYA CREAM DESSERT

Although I prefer to savor the supersweet, pudding-like atemoya (or cherimoya) right from the skin, I have found that I may be in the minority. This whipped-cream concoction retains the flavor of the lush fruit, but lightens its somewhat dense texture. You might think of this as a luxurious (and generous) midnight snack for two, or a post-meal delicacy for four. In either case, know your company: the fruit is so expensive that you will want to be sure of its reception.

Fully ripe atemoya, about ¾ pound
2 tablespoons fresh orange juice
½ cup chilled heavy (or whipping) cream

Halve the atemoya and pick out all the seeds (they are fairly central) with a small fork. Scoop out every bit of the pulp and combine with the juice in a processor or blender. Work to a fine purée. Whip the cream to form peaks; fold in the purée with a rubber spatula. Cover and chill for a few hours.

—

ATEMOYA WITH SOUR CREAM AND BROWN SUGAR

One of those easy treats that just plain works. Halve the atemoya lengthwise; with a knife tip, pick out the seeds. With a blunt knife, spread the soft pulp evenly to fill in the gaps left by the seeds (as you would spread peanut butter). Spoon a thick, even layer of sour cream onto this; top with a thick layer of brown sugar. Refrigerate for ½ hour (but no longer, or the atemoya skin darkens and the sugar turns syrupy).

ᏉᎡ *Atemoya can be substituted for cherimoya in the recipes on pages 117–118.*

B

BLOOD ORANGE
(Citrus sinensis)
also Pigmented Orange

*T*his beauty is one of the many members of the huge sweet orange group, but certainly not to be lost in the crowd. The orange flesh of the memorably flavorful fruit may be flecked with (or completely colored) rust, scarlet, garnet, or purple and may yield a dramatically sanguine juice: hence the name. Although yet to win large-scale

appreciation in the United States, blood oranges are enormously popular all over Europe. (In hotels in Sicily, for example, the tart burgundy juice is served at breakfast as a matter of course.)

While domestic commercial production is quite small—many blood oranges that do turn up in East Coast markets are imported —five kinds of blood oranges did flourish here in the 1930s, brought from their homeland by Italian and Spanish immigrants. But it turned out that the fruits were unpredictable for American-sized production, with pigmentation, seed count, and sweetness dependent upon too many uncontrollable factors. However, with the renewed interest in specialty fruit crops of late, nurserymen and agricultural spokesmen have cited a sizable increase in plantings of Ruby Blood and Moro varieties during the last few years, mainly in food-wise California (with a very few in Florida). Although I have found most blood orange varieties to be zesty and full-bodied, having tasted Moros (the most deeply colored of all) this year, I can say they are among the most perfect fruits I've savored, bursting with rich citrus flavor and a deep raspberry aftertaste. The seedless pulp is juicy but firm, and the membranes separating the segments are downy and soft—unless stored too long.

SELECTION AND STORAGE: Look for blood oranges beginning in December, but don't be surprised if they show up in March—or not at all. Depending upon their place of origin, they may be available into June. Gauge freshness as you would for any orange, by hefting for the weightiest. The skin may be as monochromatically orange as that of a perfect navel, or flushed with red; the fruit may be small (more often than not) or medium-sized; the skin may be smooth or pitted. In my experience, redder pulp and more pungently orangy taste belong to the imported varieties (with the exception of the marvelous Moros), but this may change as a result of the new plantings. Store in the refrigerator.

USE: Enjoy blood oranges as you would any sweet oranges, but reserve the rather pricy beauties for simple dishes in which their color can be admired. You may have to remove seeds from some varieties, so be warned. In others (the least delicious, so far) the membrane may be tougher than that of our common sweet oranges; so cut into an orange before you plan a dish around it. Blood-orange sections will enliven any fruit mixture or salad. As a garnish the fruit is unbeatable, whether for savory or sweet dishes. Or prepare a vivid water ice. Don't forget the juice, straight or in mixed drinks, or as a base for sauces. Or make a glowing marmalade.

NUTRITIONAL HIGHLIGHTS: Blood oranges are a very good source of vitamin C and a fair source of fiber.

COMPOTE OF BLOOD ORANGES WITH CANDIED PEEL

This vivid dessert combines the pungency of peel with the tart sweetness of citrus flesh and perfume of orange flowers.

6 servings

1½ cups water
¼ cup sugar
¼ cup honey, preferably orange-flower
7 medium blood oranges, rinsed
2–3 tablespoons orange liqueur
About 1 teaspoon orange-flower water

1. Combine water, sugar, and honey in a nonaluminum pan and bring to a boil; skim off froth. Meanwhile, peel thin rind from 3 oranges; cut into very fine julienne strips. Add to syrup; simmer, partly covered, for 15 minutes, until tender.

2. Pare all white pith from peeled oranges. Remove both peel and pith from remaining 4 oranges. Halve them lengthwise, then cut across into semicircles about ¼ inch wide. Arrange in a 1-quart heatproof dish, preferably glass.

3. Strain and reserve cooking syrup; place peel in a small heavy pot. Add ⅓ cup syrup and cook gently until peel is transparent (no liquid should remain). Spread strips on a sheet of waxed paper.

4. Add liqueur and orange-flower water to remaining syrup, adjusting to taste. Pour over oranges; cover. Cool; then refrigerate.

5. At serving time, strew candied peel over the oranges.

CHICKEN SAUTÉ WITH BLOOD ORANGES

Simple, subtle, beautiful, and quick to prepare, this dish is right for a speedy weekday meal or an elegant dinner party. Look for the deepest-colored oranges you can find so there will be a color contrast for the chicken. If you increase the recipe, you'll need to brown the chicken in several batches.

2 servings

2 or 3 blood oranges

2-pound chicken, cut into 8 pieces (giblets reserved for another use)

2 tablespoons butter

1 tablespoon vegetable oil

¼–½ teaspoon salt, to taste

White pepper

Scant ½ teaspoon dried rosemary, very finely crumbled

1½ tablespoons minced shallot

⅓ cup dry white wine or dry vermouth

1. Grate slightly less than ½ teaspoon orange rind and reserve. Halve 1 orange and squeeze juice; if there is less than about ⅓ cup, squeeze more to make that amount. Peel remaining orange (or orange plus the cut half), removing all white pith. With sharp knife cut between membranes to release orange sections. Reserve.

2. Remove bits of loose fat from under chicken skin. Dry pieces. Heat 1 tablespoon butter and the oil in a wide skillet. Sauté chicken over moderate heat until golden—about 4 minutes on each side. Sprinkle with salt and pepper to taste. Set aside breast pieces.

3. Add grated rind, rosemary, and shallot to chicken in pan. Cover tightly and cook over low heat for 8 minutes. Turn pieces, then add reserved breast pieces to pan. Re-cover and cook about 10 minutes, until cooked through, turning breast pieces halfway through. Place on serving dish in a warm oven.

4. Pour out most fat from pan. Add wine; boil, stirring and scraping, until reduced to about 2 tablespoons. Add orange juice; boil briefly, stirring, until sauce reaches the desired consistency. Taste and season. Off heat swirl in remaining tablespoon butter.

5. Arrange orange with chicken. Pour sauce over all; serve at once.

TART OF BLOOD ORANGES

With its cooky crust, almond-butter filling, and glistening fruit sections, this is a splendid finale for a late-winter meal. It is important that you place the jewel-like orange on the tart filling just before eating, or the whole will become too moist. This last step takes only minutes and has no risky aspects, so don't worry that you'll be fussing during the meal.

8 servings

PASTRY
1¼ cups flour
4 teaspoons sugar
¼ teaspoon salt
8 tablespoons chilled unsalted butter cut into tiny pieces
1 egg yolk
2 tablespoons orange juice

FILLING
2 egg yolks plus 1 egg
½ cup sugar
6 tablespoons unsalted butter, softened
¾ cup blanched almonds, finely ground
¼ teaspoon almond extract
1 tablespoon tangerine or orange liqueur

TOPPING
Approximately 6 medium blood oranges (about 5 ounces each)
About ¼ cup blood orange jelly (see recipe) or ¼ cup strained bitter-orange marmalade

1. Make pastry: Combine flour, sugar, and salt in processor container and whirl to mix. Add chilled butter pieces and pulse machine on and off until mixture resembles oatmeal. Scrape into a bowl and squeeze any conspicuous butter bits to break up. Blend together egg yolk and orange juice. Sprinkle into flour mixture, tossing with fork to incorporate evenly. Mass together into a ball. If the dough does not hold together, add a few drops of water. Flatten to a thick disk, dust with flour, wrap, and refrigerate for an hour, or up to 2 days.

2. Roll pastry on lightly floured surface to form 13-inch circle. Set loosely in 9½-inch fluted tart ring with removable bottom. Trim dough to make a 1-inch overhang. Turn this inward and press against the side to make an even wall. Freeze 15 minutes.

3. Line shell with foil, covering rim. Fill with dried beans or other weights. Place in center of preheated 375-degree oven for 15 minutes. Lift out foil and weights. Prick with skewer in several places on side and bottom. Bake 10 minutes longer. Set on rack.

4. Whirl eggs in a processor; with motor running add sugar. Process until very pale and fluffy. Beat in butter; add almonds, extract, and liqueur. Scrape into prepared shell.

5. Bake in oven center (still at 375 degrees) until evenly browned—about 20 minutes. Let cool completely on rack.

6. Remove peel and pith from oranges (reserve last one; you may not need it). Cut between membranes to remove each section neatly. Set on paper toweling.

7. Heat jelly and brush a little over the almond filling. Place the orange sections on this to form concentric circles. Spoon over the warmed jelly. Serve within an hour.

Blood Orange Jelly

This tender jelly adds gloss, color, and a bittersweet taste to a tart—or to morning toast. Choose the darkest-skinned oranges for the most vivid hue.

Makes about 1 cup

Peel from 3 blood oranges, coarsely cut
About 3 cups water
¼ cup fresh lemon juice
¼ cup blood orange juice
1¼ cups sugar

1. Combine peel and water to cover in small, heavy nonaluminum pot. Boil gently until peel is tender—about 40 minutes. Drain liquid and measure; there should be a little less than 1 cup. If there is more, boil a few minutes to reduce. Discard solids.

2. Return liquid to pot with lemon and orange juice and sugar. Bring to a boil, stirring. Boil until mixture reaches jelly stage; large, heavy bubbles will roil and pop. Test as follows: Dip a clean metal spoon in syrup. Move it away from the steam, then tilt so jelly runs off. If it forms a stream or falls in 2 distinct drops, continue boiling. If 2 drops travel slowly along the rim and merge, remove pot from heat at once. Pour into a clean jar. Cool, cover, and refrigerate.

Note: Clementines can be substituted for blood oranges in the above recipe. Use the peel of 5 for the jelly. For the topping, pull off the peel and pith from 6–8 fruits; slice in rounds, then halve these to place on tart filling.

BOK CHOY, PAK CHOI
(*Brassica rapa* subspecies *chinensis*)
also Baak Choi, Chinese White Cabbage, Chinese Mustard Cabbage, White Celery Mustard, Taisai

*O*f the myriad members of the Crucifer family (cabbages, radishes, turnips, mustards, cress) that distinguish the cuisine of China (where half of the pound of fresh vegetables consumed per capita each day comes from this group), bok choy is among the mildest, most versatile, and prettiest. Long a best-seller throughout the Orient and

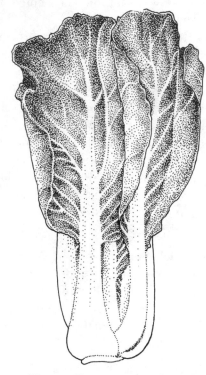

Asia, it has recently become a regular item in many North American markets, much as Chinese cabbage did a while earlier—which brings us at once to a problem. Both *Brassica* varieties, *chinensis* (bok choy) and *pekinensis* (Chinese cabbage, see p. 134) are commonly called *Chinese cabbage*—as are a number of their other relatives. I suggest that you give up on names and become familiar with the appearance of each, lest you request one kind and wind up with a shopping bag filled with green leafy things that are *all* called Chinese cabbage in one market or another.

Although bok choy may be of several types—long-stemmed, thick-stemmed, short and fat, flowering, green- or pearly-stalked—it is always shaped more or less like its beautiful illustration (left)—and never like a head cabbage. Packed upright in a bin, the bunched vegetables resemble a grove of moonlit silver trees with dark leaves. The stalks are smooth and rounded and bear a vague resemblance to Swiss chard or celery minus grooves or strings. Also chard or spinach-like in appearance are the leaves, but the flavor is not earthy-green, like chard, spinach, beets, but rather, cabbage-like. The crunchy stalks have a mild, juicy sweetness that suggests romaine lettuce; the leaves are soft and more cabbagy.

SELECTION AND STORAGE: Bok choy is available all year at Oriental markets and many greengrocers and supermarkets. Select large-leaved types for soup making, narrower and longer stems for stir-frying. If you want to incorporate large pieces into a dish, or serve the vegetable alone, choose the very small "baby bok choy" or "hearts" to be halved or quartered.

Store unwashed bok choy in a perforated plastic bag in the vegetable crisper for a few days; it wilts much more rapidly than head cabbage.

USE: Although you can eat bok choy raw, cooking enhances it considerably. I prefer Chinese cabbage (page 134) for slaws and other crunchy salads.

No matter how you'll be using it, bok choy takes just a few minutes to cook to a lovely crisp-tender texture. Almost all dishes will benefit from cooking stems and leaves separately as the latter take only seconds to soften.

Bok choy is the most satisfying of stir-fry vegetables: easy (requires no peeling), crunchy, nutritious, quick-cooking—and you get two different vegetables (leaf and stem) for the effort of one. The celery-like quality of the stalks complements quick-seared seafood, pork, duck, chicken, beef, or lamb slivers. Add cooked rice and toss until hot through for a fried rice meal-in-one.

In Japan, China, and Korea, a standard part of meals is a simple salted and spiced pickle made from bok choy and Chinese cabbage—whether sweet, fresh, and lightly vinegary, or peppery-hot and long-fermented.

Simple and tasty soups can be assembled in minutes by combining stock, meat shreds, ribbons of bok choy leaves (halve lengthwise, stack, then cut in very thin slices), and a snippet of ginger, then simmering for 5 minutes. Or add soft tofu dice during the last minute of simmering. Bok choy leaves, by the way, are the familiar green in wonton and other similar Chinese broths. Dice the stalks for a celery-like contribution.

The leaves can be made into an unusual nest that looks like Eastertime excelsior: Halve lengthwise, shred fine, drop into deep fat, fry momentarily, then drain. Sprinkle sparingly with salt, sugar, and pepper. Serve at once, as a bed for a special appetizer.

For tender stalks cooked in the Cantonese style: using ½ teaspoon baking soda for each 4 cups water boil for a moment to get the puffy-soft, authentic texture (even though it means losing vitamins and minerals); drain. Stir-fry for a moment in oil, then coat lightly with a delicate egg, Chinese crab or shrimp or cream sauce. Or braise the stalks, then bake in a cream or cheese sauce, as on p. 41.

PREPARATION: Trim off the heavy base (if not too tough or tired, slice and include along with the stalks). Discard blemished or tough leaves. Separate stalks from the base, as you would celery. Slice leaves neatly from stalks, leaving as little green as possible on stalks (the tiny central "heart" need not have stems and leaves separated). If cooking both parts, rinse separately. If storing one, do not rinse first; simply bag and refrigerate.

NUTRITION HIGHLIGHTS: Bok choy is very low in calories—about 15 per ½ cup. It supplies plenty of vitamin C and vitamin A and a fair quantity of calcium.

BASIC BOK CHOY STIR-FRY

The next time you're planning your green vegetable dish for dinner, think of this. Bright, healthy, flavorful, crunchy, quick-cooking: What more can you ask? Although I like to use a wok to toss quick-cooked vegetables, you can use a large skillet.

3 or 4 servings

1½ pounds bok choy, cleaned (see Preparation)
1–2 tablespoons peanut oil, to taste
1 teaspoon sugar
¼ teaspoon minced garlic
Salt to taste

1. Cut stems at an angle into 1-inch pieces. Slice leaves separately. Have other ingredients ready.
2. Heat wok; pour oil around the edge, then tip to distribute. Add stems and toss over moderately high heat until somewhat softened, but still crispy inside —about 3 minutes.
3. Add sugar, garlic, salt, and reserved leaves, and toss until bok choy is crisp-tender, about 2 minutes.

Note: This basic formula lends itself to additions of just about any vegetable that can be stir-fried—onion, scallion, carrot, red pepper, asparagus, mushrooms, corn, peas, or squash.

BOK CHOY WITH APPLE AND GINGER

Another basic dish that can stand plenty of adjustment and substitution. If you can't find Smithfield ham or prosciutto, use 1 tablespoon oil and 1 tablespoon bacon fat; if you want to double the recipe, fine.

3 servings

1 pound bok choy, cleaned (see Preparation)
1 medium apple
1 tablespoon peanut oil
1½ ounces thinly slivered Smithfield ham or other firm country ham, or fatty prosciutto
Rounded tablespoon coarsely grated peeled ginger
Salt and pepper

1. Slice bok choy stems from leaves. Cut widest part of stalks in half lengthwise; then cut stalks across on a slant to make ½-inch wide slices. Halve leaves lengthwise, then slice across ½ inch wide. Quarter and core the apple (do not peel). Cut each quarter crosswise into ⅛-inch slices.
2. Heat oil in large skillet; add ham and toss for a minute. Add bok choy stems, apples, and ginger, and toss over moderately high heat until tender—about 5 minutes.
3. Add leaves and toss over high heat until leaves are tender and most liquid has evaporated—about a minute. Season with salt and pepper.

INDIA JOZE INDONESIAN STIR-FRIED VEGETABLES

A thoroughly versatile mélange (*tumis*), this dish complements both Eastern and Western entrées, like so many of the dishes from this Santa Cruz restaurateur. It is a gala and complex stir-fry that takes only 3–4 minutes to cook, but you must have completely prepared all ingredients for the wok before you begin to toss. The *tumis* becomes soggy if even slightly overcooked or allowed to stand.

4 servings

1 pound bok choy, well washed (see Preparation)
2 small zucchini (6 ounces)
3 ounces snow peas
2 teaspoons minced garlic
1 teaspoon minced, seeded fresh jalapeño or serrano pepper (or to taste)
2 tablespoons soy sauce
Ground white pepper to taste
2 tablespoons peanut oil
2 medium plum tomatoes, diced
¼ pound (1½ cups) mung-bean sprouts

1. Cut apart bok choy leaves and stems. Cut stems across in ¼-inch diagonals. Chop leaves in coarse pieces. Cut zucchini into strips about 2 inches long and ⅛ inch thick. Zip strings from snow-pea pods and halve pods diagonally. Combine garlic, chili, soy sauce, and white pepper in small container.

2. Heat wok; drizzle oil around rim; tip to distribute. On moderately high heat toss bok choy stems, zucchini, and snow peas for 2 minutes.

3. Add soy mixture and bok choy leaves and toss just to wilt leaves. Add tomatoes and sprouts and toss on highest heat just to warm through. Transfer to heated dish and serve immediately.

BOK CHOY FRIED RICE WITH BACON

Crunchy bok choy stems, smoky bacon dice, scallions, and tender rice (cold, leftover can be substituted) combine in a dish that can be part of a Chinese-style multi-dish meal, or can serve as a vegetable-starch side dish alongside roast meat in a Western meal.

4 servings

1 cup long-grain white rice
1¾ cups water
About ½ teaspoon coarse kosher salt
1–1¼ pounds bok choy (or ¾ pound bok choy stems), cleaned (see Preparation)
¼ pound slab bacon, cut in ¼–½-inch dice
2 tablespoons vegetable oil
¼ teaspoon sugar
Optional: 1 medium clove garlic, minced
1 egg, beaten
⅓ cup sliced scallion greens
Pepper to taste

1. Combine rice, water, and ½ teaspoon salt in heavy 1-quart saucepan. Bring to rolling boil, stirring. Reduce heat to its lowest point, cover pot, and cook 20 minutes. Remove from heat and let stand, covered, 15–20 minutes. Fluff into bowl to cool at least an hour, preferably more. (Can be prepared ahead and chilled; or substitute 3½ cups cooked rice.)

2. Trim leaves from bok choy stems and refrigerate for another use. Rinse stems well, then cut in pieces about 1 by ½ inch; you should have about 3 generous cups. Cook bacon in heavy pan over moderately low heat until browned and almost crisp. Drain and reserve fat.

3. Heat wok; pour ½ tablespoon each bacon fat and vegetable oil around rim. Toss stems in fat over moderate heat until they become lightly green and tender throughout—about 5 minutes. Transfer to a dish; sprinkle with sugar and salt to taste.

4. Heat remaining 1½ tablespoons vegetable oil and 1 tablespoon bacon fat in wok. Add optional garlic. Toss rice in this to coat. With chopstick form hole in center of rice; pour in egg and stir against wok for a few seconds until almost set (do not blend with rice). Add scallions, bok choy, and bacon. Toss for a minute, until hot through. Season to taste and serve.

STIR-FRIED BOK CHOY AND CARROTS

A bright green and orange stir-fry that is a fine all-purpose vegetable dish to serve with chops, steaks, or burgers.

3 or 4 servings

1 pound tender, small bok choy, cleaned
 (see Preparation)
3 medium carrots, peeled
2 tablespoons peanut oil
1 teaspoon brown sugar
1 tablespoon soy sauce

1. Slice apart leaves and stems. Cut stems across in ½-inch slices on a slant. Cut leaves in ½-inch slices. Slice carrots very thin on a slant.

2. Heat a wok and pour oil around the rim. Add bok choy stems and carrot slices and toss over moderately high heat until almost tender—4–5 minutes. Add leaves, sugar, and soy sauce; toss until most of liquid evaporates and the vegetables are tender—about a minute. Serve at once.

BARBARA SPIEGEL'S BAKED BOK CHOY WITH GRUYÈRE

A lovely example of cross-cultural cuisine: traditional European oven-braising, plus crispy Oriental cabbage, plus French cheese and mustard yield a mellow, useful hybrid side dish. Barbara (best friend and cookbook editor) reminds me that there is no reason to be strict about the 400-degree temperature. Between 350 and 425 degrees will do fine, to agree with whatever else you may be baking or roasting.

4 servings

1½ pounds bok choy, cleaned, stalks and
 leaves separated (see Preparation)
1 cup chicken broth
1 tablespoon butter
1½ tablespoons flour
2 teaspoons Dijon mustard
1 cup (about 2 ounces) grated Gruyère
 cheese
Salt to taste
Few drops hot pepper sauce

1. Cut bok choy stalks in ½-inch slices (you should have 4 cups). Combine in large, shallow baking dish with broth. Cover and bake 35 minutes in 400-degree oven. (Vegetable will still be quite crisp.)

2. Chop leafy tops roughly. Add to stalks and stir. Bake 10 minutes longer, until leaves are wilted.

3. Heat butter in small saucepan. Add flour and stir 1 minute over moderately low heat. Whisk in mustard. Pour broth from bok choy into pan. Whisk on high heat until sauce thickens slightly. Add cheese and stir until smooth. Add salt and pepper sauce to taste.

4. Pour sauce over bok choy and fold in gently. Return to oven for 10 minutes, until hot and bubbling.

🖝 *Bok choy can be substituted for Chinese Cabbage in Richard Sax's Hot and Sour Soup-Stew, page 136.*

BOLETE, PORCINO (PORCINI, PLURAL), CEP, CÈPE
(Boletus edulis)
also King Bolete, Steinpilz

*O*h for the day when these firm, piny-earthy treasures are cultivated! Or at least when they are treated with the respect due such magical creations, as they are in a good part of Europe. In Italy, for example, when porcini (por-CHEE-nee) are gathered, they are fêted and honored in restaurants, served gloriously alone as a main course,

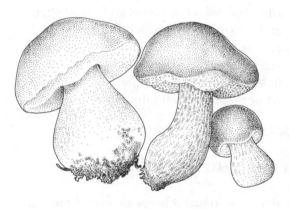

cooked with nothing other than limpid olive oil (and optional garlic and parsley). The pale, meaty but silken flesh—filet mignon-like in texture, but with considerably more character and pungency—speaks eloquently for itself.

While strictly speaking the words *cèpes* and *porcini* should refer only to *Boletus edulis*, many other unforgettable *Boletus* species (more often dried than fresh) travel under these names. In most general terms, the fresh mushroom looks like an outsize, tan to brown-topped common mushroom with a bulbous stem; caps range from one to ten inches in diameter and weights vary from an ounce to a pound. Like all Boletus family members, this one will have a sponge-like mass of tubes or tiny holes beneath the cap, not gills. The stem is usually light-colored, as is the underside of the cap (if fresh—otherwise it may be yellowy brown), and the flesh inside is creamy white and remains the same when cooked.

Although the choice fungus pushes through blankets of pine needles and the mossy floors of birch and aspen forests in the United States and Canada, the domestic boletus is so prone to insect infestation and mold that it is rarely marketed outside the West. More often (though not exactly frequently) you'll find French and Italian imports for a spectacular sum, either in fancy groceries or in fine restaurants.

SELECTION AND STORAGE: If you should encounter real, live bolete specimens in your market in late spring (fleetingly) or in the fall, your choice will be minimal. John Gottfried, authority on wild foods, recommends gauging freshness by firmness. His experience suggests that although cèpes of any size can be heavenly, ones with caps six to seven inches in diameter are predictably best. Check the stems carefully for insects, which are usual in this species, but do not toss away perfectly good specimens if some minuscule characters are discreetly ensconced in the base; just trim away. If there is a choice, pick caps with the palest undersides. Other than that, my advice is take the mushrooms and run, unless they are loathsomely over the hill.

Don't wrap or store; cèpes pick up other flavors and lose their own—and spoil very rapidly. If they are in superb condition, they can last for a few days in the refrigerator, spread in a single layer and covered with a towel.

USE: There are slow-cooked French cèpes (*cèpe* is a Gascon word: slow-cooking is the usual Gascon manner)—braised, incorporated into sauces, or cooked over very low heat with shallots, garlic, and oil. There are speedily grilled or sautéed Italian porcini, richly anointed with olive oil. For whole caps or wide slices I like to warm a fairly delicate olive oil with a sliced garlic clove in it over low heat for about 5 minutes. Then thickly daub the mushrooms with the seasoned oil, reserving a little in the pan. (If very large whole caps are used, lightly score both sides.) Allow to rest briefly before cooking. Preheat the oven to high, set the pan in it until the oil sizzles, then add the mushrooms. Cook for a few minutes, until just cooked through. (If you have a grill, let the flame die down, then roast the mushroom caps near the coals, turning once.)

However you decide to cook these gems, keep it simple, or their meaning will be lost. Accompany with bland dishes based on pasta, rice, cornmeal, eggs, potatoes, or cracked wheat.

PREPARATION: Except when very small, caps are traditionally detached from the stems so the tops can be grilled whole. But, because stems are usually as flavorful and tender as the caps (if somewhat more fibrous), there is really no need for this; simply cut mushrooms vertically, through cap and stem, in wide slices. Or slice the stems (across or lengthwise), cook, and serve as a separate dish. The mushrooms are usually quite clean, except at the base, where they need brushing or trimming. If necessary, pare and peel bad spots.

If the spongy underside of the cap is deep yellow, brownish, or slimy, trim off this discolored part, which may taste bitter.

NUTRITIONAL HIGHLIGHTS: Boletes are very low in calories and a good source of vitamin D. They also contain a goodly amount of fiber and a small amount of the B vitamins thiamine, niacin, and riboflavin.

PORCINI PERFECTION (Oven-Sautéed or Broiled)

Plain and simple is the way to enjoy most mushrooms, but particularly creamy-textured, fragrant boletes.

I find that oven-roasted or broiled boletes (all kinds, native or imported, small or large) absorb less oil and have a purer taste than sautéed. You can choose either method, or combine—oven-roasting the stems and broiling the caps.

4 servings, as a side dish or appetizer

¼ cup very finest olive oil, rather light in flavor and texture

1 large garlic clove, quartered

1¼ pounds porcini or other boletus mushrooms, preferably medium-sized, brushed and trimmed as necessary

Salt

Optional: Finely minced parsley

1. Combine oil and garlic in a wide skillet with an ovenproof handle. Cook over very low heat for about 5 minutes, until oil is well flavored but the garlic not browned; discard garlic.

2. Trim base of mushroom caps. Cut the stem across or lengthwise into slices about ⅛ inch thick. Cut cap into slices about ¼ inch wide and 2 inches long.

3. In preheated 450-degree oven heat flavored oil to sizzling. Toss mushrooms until coated; salt to taste. Return to the oven and cook until tender throughout—about 5–10 minutes—tossing once.

4. Serve with parsley, as desired.

GRILLED PORCINI CAPS

Using same ingredients as above, remove stems from mushrooms (slice and cook as above, or reserve for another use). Coat a wide flameproof pan with the seasoned oil. Set cleaned caps in a single layer, spongy side up. Drizzle oil on each, using about a teaspoon for each 3-inch cap. Sprinkle with salt. Set under a preheated broiler, close to the heat. Checking often, broil until tender throughout, but not deeply browned, turning down flame if necessary; timing varies from 3 to 10 minutes. Let stand a moment, then very carefully transfer to a heated plate, spongy side down. Sprinkle with parsley and let stand for a few minutes before serving.

PAULA WOLFERT'S PORCINI WITH TOMATOES AND MINT

In *The Cooking of South-West France*, Paula Wolfert describes the use of the cèpe (the Gascon word for *Boletus edulis*) in that area—but this dish (from her book in progress, *Paula Wolfert's World of Food*) is Corsican in origin. Curiously, the day she gave me the recipe (we had both merrily mushroomed through the well-stocked pine and scrub oak forests of Martha's Vineyard) I received a letter from my uncle Julian Zimet, a fine cook with a fondness for wild mushrooms. He suggested that I try a recipe from *Leaves from Our Tuscan Kitchen* (originally published in 1899, reissued by Vintage books in 1975) that incorporates the same unusual combination—mushrooms, anchovies, and mint—but substitutes lemon juice for the tomatoes. That makes three of us who recommend the intriguing mélange.

2 generous servings

¾ pound porcini (cèpes, boletes), cleaned and trimmed

3 tablespoons olive oil

2 teaspoons puréed anchovy (or 2 fillets, rinsed, drained, puréed)

1½ teaspoons crushed garlic

1½ tablespoons mint leaves (preferably peppermint), slivered

Salt and pepper to taste

1 tablespoon mild vinegar, such as cider or rice wine

1 medium plum tomato, peeled (see page 23), seeded, and cubed

Toasted French bread

1. Cut stems of mushrooms level with caps; reserve for soups or stews. (See Note.) Slice caps in strips ¼ inch wide. If mushrooms are large, cut these in half.

2. Heat oil over moderate heat in wide skillet; add mushrooms (if stems are used, cook these for a few minutes before adding the caps), anchovies, and garlic and toss until mushrooms are well coated. Reduce heat and cover; cook until tender, about 10 minutes.

3. Uncover and cook until juices are reduced by half. Add mint, salt and pepper, vinegar, and tomato. Bring to a boil. Remove from heat; let cool to room temperature.

4. Serve with toasted bread as a first course.

Note: I have had better luck with mushroom stems than Paula; I have almost always been able to add them to cooked dishes with little trimming and peeling. For this dish I sliced them thin.

BONIATO
(Ipomoea batatas)
also Batata, Batata Dulce, White Sweet Potato, Cuban Sweet Potato, Camote

*N*ow here's a pretty mess: In the 1930s a very sweet, orange-fleshed sweet potato was introduced as a Louisiana "yam," a marketing ploy that was intended to distinguish it from the similar, but firmer variety that was grown in New Jersey, Maryland, and Virginia. That orange variety is not in any respect a true yam (see page 506), nor

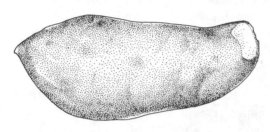

is it what most of the world recognizes as a sweet potato (nor, for that matter, is a sweet potato related to what we call a potato, if you want to really tear out your hair). In the tropics and subtropics, where almost all sweet potatoes grow, the vegetable that most people would identify by this name is white- or yellow-fleshed, rather dry, and slightly sweet, with a chestnut-like flavor. This is the rule world-wide; our sweet potato is an exception. Now, thanks to the same growers that brought us malanga, yuca, and calabaza, we have a large crop of these light-fleshed varieties growing in Dade County, Florida. Because the growers and immediate audience are Cuban, the light-colored sweet potato is being marketed as a boniato, adding another name to the confusion.

Although all forms of the sweet potato originated in Central America, it traveled at an early date to South America (being cultivated in Peru and Colombia as early as 1000 B.C.). The most unusual aspect of its history (and still a source of scholarly debate) is that it may have found its way to Polynesia before going to Spain with Columbus. This is reflected in the names *kumar* and *kumara* (and similar words) by which it is known in the Pacific islands, names that are thought to have come directly from the aboriginal Quechua language. *Camote*, the word now used in most of Spanish-speaking Latin America, derives from the Nahuatl *camotli* (first recorded in 1560). The Cuban *boniato* was first recorded in the Antilles, in 1537, and is thought to have been used as an adjective to mean something sweet and harmless, as opposed to hot (*picante*) or poisonous. *Aji boniato* (sweet pepper) and *yuca boniato* (nontoxic cassava) are examples of such usage. By the eighteenth century *boniato* had become a noun and referred exclusively to the sweet potato. Although there is still some doubt about the *patatas*, *patates*, and *batatas* of Romance languages, they may come from a Carib or neighboring language. *Batatas*, its scientific name, reveals it as the lone edible tuber in a genus of 400-odd morning glories. I shall not add to this the myriad names that accompanied the obliging sweet potato when it spread throughout Asia, where an astonishing 90 percent of the world's considerable production (it is sixth among the world's principal food crops) is raised.

It is not difficult to understand why the vegetable is a staple from Vietnam to

Mexico. Sweetly aromatic (freshly cut, it has a surprising violet scent), creamy-textured, much less sweet than our orange potato, it is fluffier and feels drier in the mouth. You might imagine it to be a cross between a sweet potato and a baking potato, but with more delicacy than either. To my taste, it is a superb and useful vegetable, considerably more versatile than the rich, very sweet (however delicious) orange sweet potato, which is considered a dessert dish in these same countries.

SELECTION AND STORAGE: Available year round, generally at Hispanic markets, boniato is scarce during February and March, or thereabouts. Because freshly harvested boniato can be marketed almost all the time, the crop is not cured for storage in the way that our common sweet potato is. It is therefore prone to bruising and *rapid* spoilage. Choose carefully, being sure that the tuber (which is irregularly shaped) is rock-hard, with no soft or moldy spots. The skin may be pinkish, purplish, cream, reddish, and patchier-looking than what you may be accustomed to. Do not seek monochromatic, smooth perfection.

Do not refrigerate white (or any) sweet potatoes. Keep at room temperature in a ventilated spot (a basket in a single layer is good) for as short a time as possible, no more than a few days.

USE: You can do anything with boniato that you would with a common North American sweet potato, taking into consideration its comparative fluffiness, pallor, and lack of sweetness. Bake, boil, roast, fry, steam, sauté, mash, purée, cream, combine in custards and flans, puddings, pies, muffins—the works. Boniato has a subtle flavor of its own, so go easy on the additions: it is easily overwhelmed with heavy seasoning.

PREPARATION: I love the flavor of the skin of a baked boniato, which gets as crusty and hard as pretzels. For boiling or steaming, the question of peeling will depend upon the specific potato, as boniatos have a tendency to be shabbily clothed or blemished. Peeled potatoes must be dropped into cold water immediately, as the flesh discolors at once. When cooking, keep completely covered with water for the same reason, or you may have grayish or purplish blotches where the air affected the potato.

NUTRITIONAL HIGHLIGHTS: Boniato is moderately high in calories at about 115 per ½-cup serving. Nutritional information is incomplete at this time.

BAKED BONIATO, BASIC

Nothing could be simpler and more delicious than any good baked potato, but fine boniatos are particularly special.

For each person choose a dry, firm boniato weighing 8–12 ounces. Scrub and dry (rub with butter if you want a slightly softer skin). Bake at 400 degrees for about 1 hour. Test with a knife or cake tester, being sure you have checked the dead center, which should be creamy soft. Because the skin becomes so crunchy hard, you will not be able to gauge doneness by pressing the potato as you would other varieties.

STUFFED BAKED BONIATOS

For a fancier baked boniato, enrich the pulp with cream, butter, honey, rum, and spices, then sprinkle with nuts and reheat. You may want to spend some time selecting the neatest, longest potatoes available, as boniatos tend to be rounded and scruffy—which does not make for an appealing presentation.

4 servings

4 small boniatos, about 10 ounces each, scrubbed and dried
About 2 tablespoons butter
About ¼ cup heavy (or whipping) cream
1–2 tablespoons flowery honey
1–2 tablespoons light rum
About ½ teaspoon ground cardamom
About ¼ teaspoon ground coriander
Salt and white pepper to taste
3–4 tablespoons pecans or macadamia nuts, chopped fine

1. Rub potatoes with butter. Bake in 400-degree oven until soft inside when pierced with knife tip (check center), about 50 minutes.

2. Slice top third off each lengthwise. Scrape pulp from top and bottom into a food mill fitted with a medium disk; leave a neat shell about ¼ inch thick to refill.

3. Press pulp through mill into bowl. Gradually beat in butter, cream, honey, rum, adjusting amount of cream so that mixture will pipe nicely. Beat in seasonings to taste.

4. With wide star tube, pipe potato mixture into shells. Sprinkle with nuts. Arrange potatoes on baking sheet. Bake in upper third of preheated 450-degree oven until nuts brown and potatoes heat through, about 10 minutes. Serve at once.

BOILED BONIATO

Simple as can be, and absolutely delicious, especially served along with stews or roast meats with gravies or pan juices. It is best to skin the potatoes before boiling as the often blotchy peel discolors the flesh. The aroma of roses or violets and tea that wafts up as you peel is very slightly retained after cooking. The cooked potato is creamy, close-textured, and lightly sweet.

Two caveats: Keep the potatoes well submerged as they boil, or they turn gray. Serve them as soon as they are cooked: held, they become dry, klutzy, and vague.

Figure about 8 ounces per person. Scrub the boniatos well with a brush. Peel one quickly and immediately submerge in water. Continue until all are peeled, then cut the potatoes into pieces about the size of medium new potatoes. Drop into a large kettle of boiling, salted water. Boil until completely cooked through (test carefully in center), about 25 minutes, or slightly longer than "ordinary" potatoes. Drain well, arrange in a warmed dish (with butter, if you like) and serve at once.

—

FRIED BONIATOS

Experimenting with this delicious pale, semisweet potato, I found that it dries out when cooked french-fry fashion but keeps its tender interior and delicate flavor when cut in larger chunks and cooked at a slightly lower temperature. If cooked at a higher temperature the sugar scorches before the flesh cooks through.

Figuring about 6–8 ounces per person, peel the boniatos and place in cold water until ready to fry. Heat about 1 inch corn oil, preferably in an electric fry pan, to 325 degrees. Slice enough potato to almost cover the surface, cutting it into pieces about 1½ inches square and ¼–½ inch thick. Drop into the hot oil and fry until golden and tender, about 2 minutes per side. Drain on toweling. Sprinkle lightly with salt and sugar and serve at once: or keep warm briefly in a warm oven while you fry the remaining boniatos.

—

BONIATO AND APPLE PURÉE

Simple, easily embellished or varied, this purée reheats for company and family. If you wish, add a topping of dried crumbs and pecans ground together (half and half), then dot with butter to warm up. Or dust with a combination of coriander, cinnamon, and anise. To increase or decrease, figure on 12 ounces potato and 1 medium apple per person. For fancy presentations, the mixture can be piped through a wide star tube.

4 servings

4 smallish boniatos (about 12 ounces each)
4 medium apples, preferably several varieties
About 2½ tablespoons butter
Salt and white pepper

1. Arrange boniatos and apples in a roasting pan. Bake at 400 degrees until apples are soft—about 35 minutes. Pick up apples by stems and remove them. Continue baking potatoes until very soft, about 20–25 minutes longer.

2. Remove apple peels and stems. Remove potato skins (eat them!). Press apples and potatoes together, in batches, through medium disk of food mill. Stir in 1½–2 tablespoons butter, or to taste, and salt and pepper.

3. Scoop into buttered baking dish. Dot with tiny bits of butter. (Can be cooled, covered, and refrigerated at this point.)

4. At serving time, heat in upper level of 425-degree oven until slightly browned and bubbling at the edges, about 15–20 minutes.

❧ *ADDITIONAL RECIPE*
Malanga-Yam Pancakes, page 294

BREADFRUIT
(Artocarpus altilis)
also Panapen, Pana de Pepita, Fruit à Pain

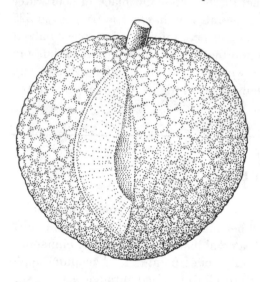

*M*ajestic to behold, the breadfruit tree yields considerable shade and food for those who live in the Pacific islands, the Caribbean, and Brazil. So monumental and beautiful is the huge-leafed tree, so strange is the green fruit (the size of a baby's head and covered with a reticulated pattern of small protrusions), so vital are all the parts of the tree to the general welfare of many, that countless myths and legends have grown up around the breadfruit.

Yet few compare with the "real story" of the tree's ill-fated first voyage to the New World from Tahiti. Championed by the British naturalist Joseph Banks, who had joined Captain Cook in a major South Pacific research voyage to determine breadfruit's value, it was elected as the crop that would best and most cheaply nourish the slaves of the British West Indies. In 1789 one thousand seedlings were packed into the hold of H.M.S. *Bounty*, supervised by Captain William Bligh. The rest, as they say, is history. Put to sea by his crew in this best-known of mutinies, Bligh survived a 4,000-mile trip and returned to England. Once again he sailed to Tahiti, filled a ship with breadfruit trees, and headed for Jamaica, this time arriving successfully (in 1793). But the slaves refused the food, which was used chiefly as animal fodder for close to sixty years thereafter. It was not until some time after the emancipation of slaves in the Caribbean that breadfruit became part of the diet.

No one tasting breadfruit for the first time is likely to dispute that it is an acquired taste (and texture), although fifty to sixty years to become habituated may seem excessive. But a couple of samplings might be par. Breadfruit is used almost exclusively as a vegetable, generally when wholly or partly green. When completely green, the raw breadfruit is hard and starchy, like a raw potato; when slightly ripe, the raw pulp resembles both eggplant and partly baked bread. Cooked at this later stage, breadfruit acquires a texture that might be likened to that of an extremely starchy potato mixed with a plantain, but is much stickier than either. It has a slightly musky, fruity flavor, but at the same time it is very bland. Fully ripened (it is rarely available this way when received in this country), the flesh becomes rather sweet and tacky; it may be as soft and creamy as an avocado, or runny as ripe Camembert, or tender as rising yeast batter, with an aroma that matches. In fact, the fruit, which has no staying power, is fermented for use in much of the tropics.

SELECTION AND STORAGE: Breadfruit may appear in stores year round, being subject to import regulations which vary from month to month in this country. It is available in United States markets primarily in areas where there is a Caribbean population. The fruit is sold whole—it can weigh from 2 to 5 pounds—usually from a bucket or drum of water. Most will be speckled with a gummy white or gray dried latex-like substance.

Breadfruit is tricky to select. If you want to keep it for a few days, select a fruit that is all green, evenly colored, hard, with large, well-developed scales (they're not exactly scales, but when you see them you'll recognize what I mean) of more or less the same size; if they are small, or very different in size, the fruit has not fully matured. Neither green nor ripe fruit should have dents, hard knotty areas, or dark spots, which signify spoilage. The fruit should feel dense and heavy for its size, not spongy. If you plan to use it immediately, choose breadfruit as your recipe requires. For some dishes, you'll want to have a specimen that is mottled with brown and evenly tender (like a not-quite-ripe avocado). For others, you may want it rock hard. For some, creamy.

All breadfruits store poorly. Hold at room temperature until the degree of ripeness you want is reached (this happens very quickly). Once at this stage, the fruit can be refrigerated for a day, or two at most.

Green breadfruit freezes well. Peel it, placing the chunks immediately in water acidulated with lemon juice. Blanch in salted boiling water for a minute. Cool in ice water, drain. Then wrap tightly and freeze.

USE: In the countries that cultivate them, the breadfruit is cooked in all the ways that Europeans and North Americans do both white and sweet potatoes: boiled, baked, roasted, fried, steamed, mashed, creamed, puréed, and turned into smooth soups, puddings, cakes, and pies. It is also cored, then stuffed and baked with a rich filling of meat or cheese.

Plain-cooked, the green fruit is served *piping* hot—or it is inedibly waxy—to accompany highly seasoned stews and meats with peppery sauces. Although it can be peeled and boiled for this use, I find its flavor and texture are best suited to roasting in the peel (about an hour in a 375-degree oven for a smallish one), which yields an extremely dry (yes, bread-like), firm-textured side dish that is slightly nutty, fruity, and altogether unique.

Once cooked, the vegetable can be sliced and deep-fried or combined with a creamy (or, most often, coconutty), spicy, piquant, or cheesy sauce and baked to heat up and absorb the sauce (which it does, like a sponge). To make a soup or purée, use considerably more liquid than you would for potatoes; breadfruit's swelling and absorbing capacities are limitless.

Very ripe breadfruit that is soft and creamy can be sieved, then mixed with whipped cream and a touch of liqueur for a quick, uncooked mousse—but it is very much an acquired taste. Chill before serving. Or use it as the base for a sweet or savory quickbread.

PREPARATION: To peel a fairly hard breadfruit, quarter it lengthwise and cut out the darker core. Pare off the skin, rinsing as you go; place the pieces in water as you continue to pare. For softer fruit, score the peel, then pull it off gently; the core should pull out like a plug.

NUTRITIONAL HIGHLIGHTS: Breadfruit is fairly high in calories—about 230 per cup. It is low in sodium, and an excellent source of vitamin C and potassium. It supplies a fairly good amount of iron.

SALAD OF BREADFRUIT, TOMATO, CUCUMBER, AND HERBS

The breadfruit is a mystery ingredient here, unidentifiable but appealing—somewhere between eggplant and potato. It holds its shape nicely and absorbs most of the liquid which keeps the tomatoes and cucumbers firm, and makes the salad a good candidate for picnics and barbecues.

4 servings

1 pound green breadfruit
¼ cup white wine vinegar
½ teaspoon salt, or to taste
6 tablespoons olive oil
¼ cup diced, peeled Anaheim or poblano peppers (see page 125 to peel)
2 tablespoons slivered scallion greens
2 large plum tomatoes, diced (1 cup)
1 medium cucumber, peeled and diced
Basil, dill, thyme, or cilantro to taste

1. Peel and core breadfruit (see Preparation). Cut into narrow wedges about ¼ inch wide; place in cold salted water as you slice. Drain and drop into boiling salted water. Cook until tender, about 25 minutes. Drain.

2. Blend vinegar, salt, olive oil. Toss half of the dressing with hot breadfruit. Add chilies and scallions. Toss now and then until cooled completely.

3. Add tomatoes, cucumber, and herbs to taste. Add remaining dressing; toss gently. Cover and chill until serving time.

CREAM OF BREADFRUIT SOUP

When Sandra Allen, teacher of Brazilian cooking, came to help me understand breadfruit basics, she brought along a recipe that was almost identical to one I thought I had "invented" that week—and had thrown in the garbage because it was thicker than wallpaper paste. She suggested I blanch the breadfruit, which was just the trick needed to produce this smooth, rich soup. The tropical-musky soup is a bit like vichyssoise, but stickier and fruitier.

6 servings as a first course

2-pound breadfruit, medium-ripe
3 tablespoons butter
White part of 2 medium leeks, cleaned and sliced (2 cups)
2 teaspoons grated fresh ginger
About 6 cups chicken stock or broth
¼ teaspoon white pepper
About 1 cup heavy (or whipping) cream
Salt to taste
½ cup toasted peanuts, macadamia nuts, or almonds, chopped

1. Peel and core breadfruit (see Preparation), dropping into cold water as you work. Cut flesh in 1-inch cubes. Drain, then drop into a large pot of boiling water; boil 2 minutes. Drain.

2. Heat butter in flameproof casserole; stir in leeks and cook on moderately low heat until softened, about 5 minutes. Add breadfruit and ginger and cook a minute. Add 6 cups stock and pepper; simmer, covered, until very tender, about 35 minutes.

3. Press through a food mill, then through a fine sieve. Return to pot. Add cream, and broth if necessary, for desired consistency. Season. Heat through, then ladle into bowls and garnish with nuts.

SANDRA ALLEN'S BREADFRUIT PUDDING

Sandra Allen also gave me a recipe for *Pudim de Fruta Pão*, which appears below with minor changes. The not-too-sweet pudding is thick but light, and has a pleasantly coconutty texture and fruity, buttery aroma.

As a considerable bonus, the dessert can be baked up to two days before you need it, refrigerated with a foil covering, then reheated in a 350-degree oven for twenty minutes before serving.

6 servings

¾–1 pound chunk partly ripe breadfruit
2 small very ripe bananas
1 tablespoon lime juice
¼ teaspoon salt
2 eggs, lightly beaten
2 tablespoons port (or use another sweet wine)
⅓ cup plus 1 tablespoon sugar
½ cup freshly grated coconut
½ cup fresh coconut milk (see Note)
¼ cup milk
¾ teaspoon ground cinnamon
¼ cup Brazil nuts (or use 1 tablespoon pine nuts and 3 tablespoons blanched almonds)
3 tablespoons melted butter
Whipped cream
Garnish: Slivered toasted nuts and tiny shreds preserved ginger

1. Cut core and peel from breadfruit (see Preparation). Cut flesh in 1-inch cubes (you should have 1¾ cups), placing in bowl of cold water as you cut. Drain and drop into boiling lightly salted water. Boil until very tender, about 35 minutes.

2. Drain; mash to a lumpy consistency. Mash bananas (there should be about ½ cup) and add with lime juice and salt. Mix lightly. Add eggs; blend. Add port, ⅓ cup sugar, coconut, coconut milk, milk, and cinnamon.

3. Grind nuts and remaining 1 tablespoon sugar in processor to medium-fine texture. Paint six ¾-cup custard dishes or ramekins with some of the melted butter. Coat lightly with nuts, adding remainder to pudding mixture. Add remaining melted butter.

4. Pour pudding into dishes and shake each to settle. Arrange in pan to hold dishes with plenty of room. Place a round of waxed paper on each. Pour in hot water to come about halfway up dishes. Set in center of preheated 375-degree oven.

5. Bake 25 minutes. Lower heat to 325 degrees and bake 20–25 minutes longer, until pudding is almost firm in center. Cool about 15 minutes, then remove paper.

6. Run butter knife around each dish, then unmold puddings on warm plates. (Or serve lukewarm, if you prefer.) Serve with whipped cream and garnish of nuts and ginger.

Note: You can use unsweetened canned or bottled coconut milk, or make your own, as follows:

To Prepare Coconut Milk

Makes about 2–2½ cups

With clean nail or pick, tap holes in 2 eyes of coconut; drain and reserve liquid. Bake 10 minutes in 375-degree oven. Holding with towel, hit around equator with hammer until cracked all round. Pry out flesh and cut in chunks. Add enough water to reserved coconut juice to make 2 cups; bring to a boil. Combine half boiling liquid with half coconut meat in blender or processor; grind as fine as possible.

Pour into sieve lined with dampened cheesecloth and let drain. Repeat. Press and twist cloth to extract all liquid from coconut shreds.

For a thinner coconut milk, repeat process with ground coconut and additional 1 cup boiling water.

Store for a day or two in the refrigerator, or for months in the freezer.

BROAD BEAN
See Fava Bean

BROCCOLI RAAB, RAPINI
(*Brassica rapa* subspecies *parachinensis*)
also Broccoli Rabe, Brocoletti di Rape, Brocoletto, Choy Sum,
Chinese Flowering Cabbage

*R*esembling thin, leafy, sparsely budded broccoli stalks, broccoli raab might easily go unrecognized in the market. Turnip-related (*raab* is from *rapa*, Latin for turnip), it is, in fact, a kind of broccoli, but a nonheading variety. The similarity is skin-deep. If you chance upon it casually, anticipating a mild green vegetable to serve

as a string-bean or spinach replacement, you might be taken off guard, for it packs an assertive wallop. But if you meet it head on, expecting a ferocious pungent-bitter taste, quite unlike that of any other vegetable, you might be happily surprised.

Because bitterness has seldom been a characteristic esteemed by Americans, the vegetable has not traveled far beyond the Italians and Chinese, who esteem it and other related tastes in their cooking. (The choy sum from Chinese markets is milder and sweeter than others.) However, once it becomes part of your repertoire, as it has mine, you will find it invaluable. Nothing else has quite the presence of this aggressive green, which can add a zesty lift to bland foods, such as mild potato and pasta dishes, or hold its own with highly seasoned foods, such as hot sausage.

SELECTION AND STORAGE: Choose broccoli raab that is firm, with small stems and relatively few buds and open flowers. It is available all year round, but is most plentiful from late fall to spring. It will keep in the vegetable crisper, wrapped, for a few days.

USE: Cook broccoli raab more or less as you would broccoli, remembering that it is considerably more pungent and cooks through more rapidly, becoming soft all of a sudden. Very little cooking time is needed—only 2 to 6 minutes, for my taste (Italians would scorn this as raw). Quick-cooking is the rule no matter how you cook the green, whether boiled, steamed, stir-fried, braised, or sautéed. If you like the flavor, but find it a bit much, blanch the vegetable for a minute in boiling salted water, then drain and dry before proceeding with one of the other cooking methods. Broccoli raab's intensity works in dishes that are hot or chilled, spiked with garlic and hot peppers, or soothed with cream, with an assortment of other foods, or all by itself—but not raw.

PREPARATION: Clean broccoli raab by rinsing it quickly, then shaking off the water. You can cut off the heavier base stems, as they usually do in Italy, or trim off the skin from this part and leave the stems intact. Depending upon how you'll use the vegetable, you can leave it whole or cut it into bite-sized pieces.

NUTRITIONAL HIGHLIGHTS: Broccoli raab is very low in calories—about 40 per cup. It is an excellent source of the vitamins A, C, and K, a good source of potassium, and a fairly good source of folic acid; it is low in sodium.

BROCCOLI RAAB AND ITALIAN SAUSAGES

It was not in sunny Italy that I first tasted this classic Tuscan dish, but in a bleak and unfashionable area of Long Island City, New York. There, at a casual restaurant called Manducatis, broccoli raab and homemade sausage were felicitously paired—as they have been often at my table since. The addition of quickly cooked pasta makes this a complete and delicious meal in minutes.

4 servings

1¾ pounds sweet or hot Italian sausage links

1¾–2 pounds broccoli raab, trimmed (see Preparation)

3 tablespoons water

1. Prick sausage here and there with a knife tip or needle. Arrange in a wide skillet in a scant ⅛ inch water. Cook over moderately low heat, covered, until no longer pink, about 5 minutes. Uncover, evaporate liquid, and cook over moderate heat, turning the sausages often until they are well browned—about 10 minutes.

2. Meanwhile, cut broccoli raab into 2-inch pieces, keeping the leaf and stem parts separate.

3. Pour off most fat from the sausages. Add broccoli raab stems and water and cook, covered, over moderate heat for 3–5 minutes, until not quite tender. Add leaf sections, cover, and cook until they wilt—about 2–4 minutes longer. Serve at once, with pasta or rice.

BROCCOLI RAAB VINAIGRETTE

Deep umber, aged balsamic vinegar from Italy adds just the right touch of sweetness to the earthy-bitter broccoli raab; the carrot supplies crunch and color. Watch the steaming carefully; the vegetable takes just a few minutes to cook, then quickly becomes soggy.

2 or 3 servings

1 pound small-stemmed, tender broccoli raab, trimmed

1 tablespoon balsamic vinegar

About ⅛ teaspoon salt

3 tablespoons full-flavored olive oil, or more to taste

1 medium-large carrot, peeled and coarsely grated or cut into very fine julienne strips

Pepper to taste

1. Cut broccoli raab stalks and flowers into bite-sized bunches or branchlets. Set on steaming rack over boiling water; cover and cook until not quite tender, 2–3 minutes. Transfer to a serving dish.

2. Blend vinegar and salt; add oil and mix well. Sprinkle the carrot over the broccoli raab, toss with the dressing; taste for seasoning. Serve hot, warm, or at room temperature.

PIQUANT ORIENTAL-STYLE BROCCOLI RAAB SALAD

An assertive spice (Szechuan peppercorns—available in all Oriental stores), hot pepper, sweet honey, salty soy sauce, and acid vinegar seem to both overrule and blend with broccoli raab's usually fierce bitterness.

3 servings

1 large bunch broccoli raab (¾ pound), trimmed

1 tablespoon peanut oil

1 medium red onion, in ½-inch dice

½–¾ teaspoon Szechuan peppercorns

1 tiny dried hot chili-pepper (or ⅛–¼ teaspoon crushed hot pepper flakes)

1 tablespoon Oriental sesame oil

2 tablespoons rice vinegar (or cider vinegar)

1 tablespoon honey

1 tablespoon soy sauce

1. Cut broccoli raab in 2-inch pieces. Drop into a large pot of salted boiling water. Return to a boil over highest heat; boil 1 minute, stirring down center stalks. Drain; refresh in cold water. Spread on towel to dry.

2. Heat peanut oil in skillet. Add onion and toss over moderate heat for about 3 minutes, or until it just loses its raw bite, but not its crunch. Scoop into a serving dish.

3. In a mortar crush peppercorns and hot pepper as fine as possible. Heat sesame oil in very small pan; add peppers. Stir for a few seconds, just long enough to release the lovely aroma, but not burn the peppers. Remove from heat and stir in vinegar, honey, and soy sauce.

4. Add broccoli raab to onion. Toss with dressing. Chill to serve.

BROCCOLI RAAB, NUTS, AND EGGS WITH BROWN RICE

When you're in the mood for an unusual, meatless one-dish meal, try this close relative of vegetable fried rice—except that the rice is not fried. I prefer to bake brown rice, which gives the grains a firm, chewy texture and separates them without additional oil. However, if you prefer the consistency or convenience of fried rice, let the rice cool completely (or prepare it a day ahead). When you have cooked the broccoli raab, scoop it out and toss the cold rice into the wok with 2 tablespoons oil; heat through, tossing. Return the broccoli raab to the wok with the scallions, nuts, and eggs and toss gently before serving.

3 servings as a single main dish

1 cup medium- or short-grain brown rice
1¾ cups plus 3 tablespoons water
2 eggs
⅛ teaspoon salt
3 tablespoons peanut oil
½–¾ cup (to taste) peanuts or cashews
¾ pound broccoli raab, trimmed (see Preparation), in bite-sized pieces
2 large garlic cloves, minced (about 1 teaspoon)
1 small hot chili-pepper (Fresno or jalapeño), seeded and minced
1 tablespoon soy sauce
1 teaspoon brown sugar
⅓ cup thinly sliced scallion greens

1. Pick over rice to remove bits of soil or pebbles; rinse. Combine in a heavy 1½-quart pot with 1¾ cups water. Bring to a full boil, stirring occasionally. Cover; place in center of preheated 350-degree oven for 45 minutes. Remove from the oven and let stand, covered, for 10–20 minutes before serving.

2. Blend eggs, 1 tablespoon water, and salt. Pour ½ tablespoon oil into a heated wok; add eggs and swirl to soft scramble. Transfer to a dish and break up. Wipe out wok, if necessary. Pour 1 tablespoon oil into the wok; add the nuts and toss until lightly colored; set aside.

3. Pour remaining 1½ tablespoons oil into heated wok. Add broccoli raab, garlic, and chili, and toss over medium heat until not quite tender—about 3 minutes. Blend together soy sauce, sugar, and remaining 2 tablespoons water, and add; toss until broccoli raab is tender—another minute or so.

4. Fluff the hot rice into a heated serving dish, toss gently with scallions, nuts, egg, and broccoli mixture.

BURDOCK
(Arctium lappa)
also Gobo, Great Burdock, Beggar's Button

*T*he very long, thin taproot of this Siberian native is the part of the plant for which it is cultivated, primarily in Japan; it is also a familiar market item in Taiwan and Hawaii. (I have read that burdock has long been admired in Scotland, as well, but have not been able to find recipes that corroborate the fact.) It is through Japanese and

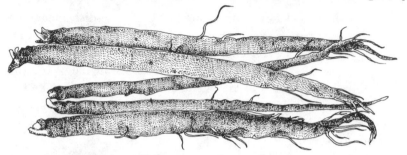

health-food markets that the root has become available in this country, or you can find it in quite a surprising number of seed catalogues, if you are a gardener.

Wild burdock grows throughout much of the United States and a good part of Europe as well, producing large leaves and, in the spring, tender green shoots—both edible. It also puts forth masses of sticky burrs, which has made it a well-known, if undesirable, lawn and garden pest.

Burdock roots are generally 1–2 feet long (they can be longer), preferably no thicker than a medium carrot. When scrubbed the peel is a rusty beige—the color of a scruffy parsnip. Inside, the flesh is a grayish white that quickly becomes brown on contact with the air. Although rather fibrous, when slivered or cut into chips and added to delicate soups, stews, braises, or plain grain dishes, it adds a pleasantly chewy texture and subtly sweet taste. Burdock's delicious, earthy flavor is very similar to that of artichoke hearts or salsify.

SELECTION AND STORAGE: Don't pass burdock by because of its limpish look. Irregularly available year round (it usually travels from Hawaii, California, and Japan), it has a humble exterior: muddy and rooty—which it should be if you want it in good shape. Choose soil-covered specimens that are firm and relatively crisp, not flabby.

Although I have read everywhere that burdock should be lightly wrapped, then refrigerated, it turns to rubbery flab within 2 days if treated that way. Instead, I find that wrapping in wet paper towels and plastic, then refrigerating, will keep it in good condition for a few days. For longer storage, refrigerate it in a shallow dish of water or be sure to keep the toweling damp.

USE: To my taste, burdock is best used as a flavoring vegetable, rather than as a side dish. It lends an earthy-sweet depth when cooked with grains or in stews or braises. If you have a great quantity, I imagine it would make an extremely subtle puréed soup. Shreds of the peeled root can also be added to stir-fried dishes.

PREPARATION: Depending upon how you will use the burdock, you have choices about how to handle it. If the flavorful skin is thin, it need not be peeled. Otherwise, scrub the mud from the roots, then peel as you cut up each piece, not beforehand, or the flesh will turn brown. To rid the vegetable of a slight bitter aftertaste, soak the pieces in salted water for 5 to 10 minutes before cooking.

For dishes in which you'll be using chunks or slices, rather than shreds, I find it preferable to tenderize the roots with a preliminary cooking in water and baking soda, Oriental-style (or pound them with a meat flattener or pestle to soften the fibers). Although the nutritional value is lessened by the precooking procedure, the eating qualities are improved, as the root becomes even-textured (not stringy, as larger pieces can be). Combine the burdock with cold water and baking soda (½ teaspoon per 2 cups water); bring it to a boil, then drain. Cover the burdock with fresh water and boil to the desired state of doneness, or add it to the stew or braise you're preparing.

NUTRITIONAL HIGHLIGHTS: Burdock is very high in fiber and modest in calories, as well as being a very good source of potassium. It is very very low in sodium and contributes small amounts of iron and calcium.

—

BROWN RICE BAKED WITH BURDOCK AND DRIED MUSHROOMS

Toasty brown rice, strips of shiitake, shreds of burdock, and tiny dots of carrot have a warm, sweet sylvan savor. Baking the mixture ensures firm, separate grains of rice and a subtle blending of tastes.

4 servings

4 medium dried shiitake (forest or
    Oriental mushrooms)
2 cups hot water
1 tablespoon vegetable oil
1 medium burdock root (about 4 ounces),
    scrubbed
2 cups cold water mixed with 1 teaspoon
    salt
1 cup long-grain brown rice
1 small carrot, cut into tiny dice
½ teaspoon salt, or to taste

1. Combine shiitake, hot water, and oil; let stand at least ½ hour, stirring occasionally. Drain and reserve liquid; strain through cheesecloth if sandy. Cut shiitake caps into thin strips (reserve stems to use in future stocks).

2. Peel burdock a little at a time; with a paring knife whittle off long, sharp, diagonal slivers, placing them in cold salted water as you proceed. Let soak 5 minutes.

3. Drain burdock; combine in heavy 1½-quart pot with mushrooms, reserved soaking liquid, rice, carrot, and salt. Bring to full boil; stir occasionally.

4. Cover and bake in center of preheated 350-degree oven 45 minutes. Let stand, covered, 15–30 minutes. Fluff into a heated serving dish.

CHICKEN WITH BURDOCK AND MUSHROOMS

Autumnal colors and flavor, slightly Japanese, this is a simple dish for those who enjoy mild, low-key, monochromatic dishes. It is subtle, with no bright contrasts in texture or taste; no sharp edges.

2 servings

1 burdock root, about 4 ounces

1 quart cold water mixed with 1 teaspoon baking soda

6 ounces small mushrooms, sliced ¼ inch thick

½ cup water mixed with ¼ teaspoon salt

1 pound chicken thighs (10 ounces boned, skinned thighs)

2 tablespoons peanut oil

1 tablespoon sugar

1 tablespoon sherry

1 tablespoon soy sauce

Pepper to taste

About 1 tablespoon each finely minced parsley and scallion green

1. Peel part of burdock, immediately slice in thin diagonals, and drop into water-baking-soda mixture in nonaluminum pot. Continue until all is peeled. Bring to a full, rolling boil; drain and rinse.

2. Combine burdock in small, heavy pot with sliced mushrooms and salted water; simmer, covered, until tender—about 10 minutes.

3. Meanwhile, skin and bone chicken. Cut into ½-inch pieces.

4. Heat oil in wide skillet; add chicken and toss until it loses its raw look. Add burdock and mushrooms, sugar, sherry, soy sauce, and pepper. Sauté over high heat until liquid is almost syrupy—about 2 minutes.

5. Scoop into a warm serving dish; toss with parsley and scallion.

BUTTERCUP SQUASH
(Cucurbita maxima)

*D*eveloped in 1932 at North Dakota Agricultural College (now the State University) by Dr. A. F. Yeager, this turban-shaped squash with its distinctive pale "beanie" has long been esteemed by many growers as the ideal winter squash, but it has just recently begun to be better distributed nationwide. The heavy rind is deep ivy-green

(but may be orange in several closely related varieties that are sold as buttercup) marked with uneven, narrow stripes the same color as the cap. Although generally about 3 pounds, the squash may be as light as 1½, or as heavy as 6. The medium-sweet orange flesh is fine-textured, creamy, and mild, very similar to that of butternut.

SELECTION AND STORAGE: Look for buttercup from late summer through the winter. It should be hard-shelled with no signs of pitting or soft spots, particularly in the cap, which is the first place to go. The stem (never buy one without) should be cork-like and rounded, not soft, blackened, or greenish—or the squash may be flavorless. The buttercup rind should be dull, not shiny. It stores for months, preferably at cool room temperature. Do not refrigerate.

USE: Buttercup becomes tender and custardy when steamed, a remarkable change from its raw state. Baked, it is denser and drier, which is preferable in some dishes, but the flesh may be slightly fibrous. I do not find the shape convenient for stuffing. Serve in chunks, or scrape from the shell and mash or purée, which suits this squash well. Use in any way you would butternut or acorn squash, particularly in purées, pies, and puddings.

PREPARATION: If you want to cut up the buttercup, a heavy cleaver or giant knife usually does the job. However, some tough-rinded specimens need extra attention: Place your biggest, sharpest knife lengthwise on the squash (off center, to avoid the stem). With a wooden mallet or rolling pin gently hammer the part of the blade that joins the handle. Keep going until the squash is cut in two. Scoop out and discard the seeds and fibers.

NUTRITIONAL HIGHLIGHTS: All winter-type squashes are excellent sources of vitamin A and have substantial amounts of vitamin C and potassium. They are modest in calories and low in sodium.

BUTTERCUP SQUASH, BASIC

Buttercup is transformed by steaming. Its dense texture becomes custard-smooth. Because the cavity is wastefully large and seeds usually plentiful and heavy, you'll need to figure about ¾ pound per person, cooked this way. Halve and seed, then place cut side down on a steamer rack. Cover and steam 15–20 minutes, until tender when pierced with a toothpick.

For a drier texture, preferred in the Orient, put a bit of butter and salt and pepper in the cavities; set in a pan with a little water, cover with foil, then bake about 45 minutes to an hour for a medium squash.

PURÉED BUTTERCUP SQUASH

For a golden all-purpose purée, buttercup will fill the bill. To serve as a savory side dish, add pinches of ground fennel seeds and thyme, or cook with sautéed garlic and onions. Or use the purée as the base for puddings, pies, soufflés, muffins—anything for which pumpkin would be appropriate. As a side dish, figure on 1 pound squash per person (which will give you about 1 cup per person).

For 3–4 cups purée

3-pound buttercup squash
About ¼ cup heavy (or whipping) cream
Salt and pepper to taste
Optional: Ground fennel seeds, thyme, cinnamon, or other seasonings

1. Place whole squash on steamer rack. Cover and steam until squash is soft when pierced deeply near the stem end, about 30 minutes. (Alternatively, halve the squash, seed, set cut side down, and steam for about half that time.)

2. Remove from heat, halve, and scoop out seeds. When cool enough to handle, scoop flesh into a saucepan. Mash with cream, adding salt and pepper to taste.

3. Cook over low heat, stirring, for about 10 minutes. Serve hot.

❧ *Buttercup can be substituted for calabaza in the recipes on pages 71–73.*

C

CACTUS PADS

See Nopales

CACTUS PEAR

(primarily *Opuntia ficus-indica* and *Opuntia tuna*)

also Prickly Pear, Tuna, Indian Fig, Indian Pear, Barbary Fig

*T*his barrel-shaped "pear," the size of a large egg, is the fruit of several varieties of Opuntia cactus and is actually a berry (check out the multitude of seeds). Enveloped in a slightly prickly, firm casing, the pulp is quite sweet, smells very like watermelon, and is soft and spongy—and a sensational color. In the United States, fruit skins

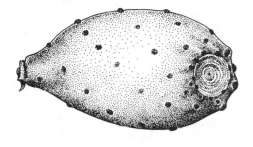

usually range from medium green to dark magenta, while the interior may be a brilliant red-violet or ruby-garnet. Other varieties, rarely available here, may be chartreuse or yellow-ocher, inside and out. A pale-green, small-seeded, flavorful variety from Chile has recently appeared in U.S. markets. (In Israel, the word *sabra*, which denotes the cactus fruit, is also used to describe the Israeli temperament—prickly on the outside, sweet on the inside.)

Because the fruit is somewhat bland and dotted with hard, black seeds, it is not a big seller in this country. However, it is enormously popular in a good part of the rest of the world. Around the Mediterranean—everywhere in southern Europe and northern Africa—as well as in Madeira, the Azores, Canary Islands, South Africa, southwestern Asia, Australia, and Central and South America the fruit flourishes and is marketed. All of the 300-odd species of *Opuntia* are native to the Americas, but most originated in northwest Mexico and the southwestern United States—both of which remain major suppliers of the fruit. Mexico's current production alone is double the current world production of apricots, and more than double the production of papayas, strawberries, and avocados. With the growing interest in Mexican and southwestern cooking, we have recently seen an increase in the availability of this unusual fruit.

SELECTION AND STORAGE: Look for cactus pears from summer through early spring, when they appear erratically in the market. Chilean fruit may appear in the fall.

Choose ones that are tender but not squishy, full and deep-colored, not faded. Beware of moldy spots, which warn of interior mush. If fruit is very firm, let it soften up a few days at room temperature. Once slightly tender, refrigerate. If purchased in good condition, the fruit will last a week or more.

USE: Serve cactus pears chilled, whichever guise you choose. If the seeds do not bother you (some are out of the question, some crispy and tolerable), use the pears cubed or thin-sliced in fresh fruit cups or salads. Serve chilled, peeled whole fruits for dessert (with knife and fork) along with strips of other soft fruits.

Sieve the garishly gorgeous flesh and mix into punches and cocktails, where the flavor and color work particularly well. Chef Felipe Rojas-Lombardi combines lemon juice, sugar, and cactus pears in a processor, purées them, then presses the mixture through a fine sieve to remove the seeds. This is chilled and enjoyed straight, or with vodka, gin, or rum to taste. Felipe also likes to slip small slices into sparkling wines.

If you have a generous number of cactus pears, use the sieved pulp to make a spectacular ice, sharpened with lemon or lime juice; or cook up a quantity of jam—which makes a splendid filling for tarts and cakes.

PREPARATION: Peeling cactus fruit is a necessity, no matter what you plan to do with it. Although the prickly pears in our market today have been mechanically de-prickled, there remain some stinging, invisible hairs to irritate the unwary. Here's how to avoid them: Jab a fork into the fruit; holding the cactus pear steady with this, slice ½ inch from each end, then cut a lengthwise slit about ¼ inch deep. Slip the tip of the knife under the cut, beneath the thick underlayer and skin. Pull off the outer and under layers of skin by holding them down on the work surface with the knife blade as you roll the fruit with the fork—or, more easily, with your hand, as the exposed fruit is graspable at this point. Or simply pull off this thick double layer with your fingers, once the skin is slit, if you're not sensitive. (Although it sounds complex, peeling a prickly pear is as easy as unwrapping toffee.)

NUTRITIONAL HIGHLIGHTS: Cactus pear is low in calories, about 45 per fruit. It is rich in fiber and supplies a goodly amount of vitamin C and potassium. It is very low in sodium.

CACTUS PEAR BREAKFAST SHAKE

This looks like a strawberry malted but has a delicate flavor, quite like watermelon.
2 servings

2 cactus pears, peeled (see Preparation), chunked
1 large banana, peeled and chunked
4 ice cubes
1½–2 tablespoons honey
1 cup milk

Press cactus pears through medium disk of food mill. Combine purée in blender or processor container with banana, ice, honey, and milk; whirl until no chunks of ice remain. Serve at once.

KIWI, BANANA, ORANGE, AND CACTUS PEAR FRUIT CUP

For a gaudily delightful change of pace for breakfast, brunch, or a fast and fresh dessert, combine this colorful quartet. Even those who remain unmoved by the rather bland, seedy cactus pear will probably be pleased by this festive presentation.

4 servings

3 large cactus pears, peeled (see Preparation)
About 1 tablespoon lime juice
1–2 tablespoons rum
1–2 tablespoons honey
1 large banana, peeled
1 large navel orange, rind and pith removed
2 large kiwifruits

1. Cut 2 cactus pears in chunks; press through medium disk of food mill. Add lime juice, rum, and honey to taste. Chill this sauce.

2. Halve banana lengthwise, then cut into thin diagonal slices. Quarter orange lengthwise, then cut across into very thin slices. Slice ends from kiwis, then remove skin with swivel peeler. Halve lengthwise; cut across into thin slices. Halve remaining cactus pear lengthwise and cut across into slices.

3. Pour sauce into shallow, wide serving dish and arrange the fruits across it; or distribute the sauce and fruit in 4 dishes.

CACTUS PEAR COCKTAIL

A wild, hot pink color and fruity flavor distinguish this delicious drink. While gin is my preference—particularly the aromatic Bombay gin—light rum, tequila, or vodka work equally well.

2 drinks

3 cactus pears, peeled (see Preparation), chunked
½ cup gin
½ cup grapefruit juice
Extra-fine sugar or pomegranate syrup (page 372) to taste
Lemon juice
2 slices lemon

Combine cactus pears in processor or blender with gin, grapefruit juice, and sugar; purée. Press through strainer. Add lemon juice to taste. Pour over ice in 2 highball glasses and serve with a slice of lemon.

MICHAEL ROSE'S CACTUS PEAR AND JÍCAMA SALAD

Michael Rose of the Ballroom Restaurant and Tapas Bar in New York City devised this acid-fresh dish to accompany apéritifs and fried appetizers. It is particularly right with his garlicky golden malanga fritters (page 292), but might also be served with roasted and salted cashews or macadamia nuts, or as an intermezzo between courses of a lengthy meal. Crunchy, *tart*-sweet, and flamboyantly fuchsia, ivory, and lime, it is an unusual refresher.

4 servings

1 pound jícama
2 cactus pears (preferably small-seeded), peeled (see Preparation)
1½ limes, approximately
1 lemon
Salt to taste
1 lemon, approximately
Splash of raspberry vinegar or another fruit vinegar
Small hot chili-pepper, preferably a red serrano or jalapeño

1. Cut the jícama in quarters, following lobes if possible. With paring knife remove skin and fibrous layer beneath it by pulling up, once you've cut under skin. Slice paper-thin. Place in ice water.

2. Slice cactus pears across in rounds. Arrange one-third of these in the center of a platter. Drain about three-quarters of the jícama slices and arrange around the cactus pears, alternating with the remaining cactus-pear slices. Squeeze about ½ each lime and lemon over both; salt lightly.

3. Cut remaining jícama in julienne strips. Squeeze ½ lime over them; salt to taste. Arrange on centered prickly pears. Sprinkle with vinegar. Slice remaining halves of lime and lemon thin. Arrange over jícama and cactus pears. Mince serrano to taste; strew over all. Serve.

CALABAZA
(Cucurbita moschata)
Identical and similar varieties may be variously called West Indian Pumpkin, Cuban Squash, Toadback, Crapaudback, Ahuyama, Zapallo, Abóbora, Giraumon

*H*uge crescent slices of glaringly bright orange calabaza (kah-lah-BAH-sa) are one of the memorable sights in vegetable markets throughout Central and South America and the Caribbean, where this versatile squash is daily fare. Though usually sold in hunks (since few could tote the entire large vegetable), the calabaza may also be as

small as a honeydew, round, or slightly pear-shaped. The mottled skin may be ever-green, sunset, or buff, speckled or striated, but is always relatively smooth and hard-shelled when mature.

Native to the Americas (a wild variety was a mainstay of Florida Indians and early settlers), the calabaza has only recently begun to reappear in North America. Migrations during the last decade have made Florida a home for many Latins and for calabaza (the word simply means squash in Spanish), where the hardy climbing vine creeps into more and more fields at a steady, slow rate. (There is calabaza being cultivated elsewhere, as well: a Cuban vegetable buyer told me, with a look of utter incomprehension, that the calabaza presently grown in New Jersey is as good as what is available in his homeland.) Other West Indians, too, demand a steady diet of the rich-colored pumpkin, which means it is also shipped to areas in the East and Midwest to which they have migrated.

Because it is not planted on a large commercial scale, the seeds that produce calabaza are simply culled from the previous year's crop—rather than being obtained from a seed company—resulting in a profusion of unpredictable strains and quality. Varietal recommendations are out of the question at this point, and even generalizations are hard to make—but here is one, nevertheless: Those who remember pumpkins as part of the American larder, not just a Halloween decoration, should be very pleased with this old newcomer. If you imagine a superior pumpkin, you have an idea of the cooking qualities of the best calabazas: fine-grained, sweet, moist (not watery), and ravishingly orange.

SELECTION AND STORAGE: Although calabaza and many of its relatives are referred to as "winter squash," this is a description that no longer has seasonal meaning. It generally refers, rather, to a hard-shelled squash that can be stored, as opposed to an immature "summer squash" (such as zucchini) that cannot. One form of calabaza or another will be available at any time during the year. Because the uncut vegetable stores admirably, when you see one with soft spots or dried cracked areas, you know it must be *really* ancient. A squash should be comparatively heavy for its size, with rind that is fairly dull (not shiny) and a solid stem attached. When buying chunks, it is easy to see what you're getting: Look for the least fibrous, most close-grained flesh, which should not be dry or watery looking.

Whole squash will keep for a month in a well-ventilated spot. Cut calabaza, covered tightly with plastic, should stay fresh for a week or so in the refrigerator. Cooked, puréed squash will keep well in the freezer for a year, packed airtight in 1-cup containers.

USE: Calabaza develops a pleasing flavor and texture when cooked with other foods or puréed; it does not do well alone (whether foil-baked or steamed, a chunk of calabaza on its own seems fibrous and watery, qualities that are not otherwise apparent). It is at home in chunky or smooth soups, salads, stews, purées, sauces, cakes, pies, custards, quick breads, cookies, puddings. Any good recipe that calls for pumpkin, butternut, acorn, buttercup, or Hubbard squash will be fine for calabaza. Keep in mind that the most fine-grained varieties also fry well.

PREPARATION: If you have an uncut calabaza, a heavy cleaver or giant knife usually does the job of opening it. However, some tough-rinded specimens need extra attention: Cut off the stem end, then place your biggest, sharpest knife lengthwise on the squash. With a wooden mallet gently hammer the part of the blade that joins the handle. Keep going until the calabaza is cut in two. Scoop out and discard the seeds (see Note) and fibers. Cut the squash into smallish pieces, about 3 inches square. Remove the rind with a paring knife or vegetable peeler, then cut to suit the recipe.

NUTRITIONAL HIGHLIGHTS: Calabaza is very low in calories—about 35 in a cooked 1-cup serving. It is an excellent source of vitamin A and a fair source of potassium and folic acid. It is very low in sodium and contributes a good amount of fiber and of vitamin C.

Note: Or save the seeds for toasting: Boil each 2 cups seeds in 1 quart water with 2 tablespoons salt until somewhat tender—10 to 15 minutes. Drain, toss with a tablespoon of corn oil, and spread in a pan. Bake in a 350-degree oven until golden and crisp, about 30 minutes, tossing often.

CALABAZA PURÉE 1

This all-purpose squash purée can be used as is or dolled up with herbs, spices, eggs, cream, bread crumbs, nuts, sausage—whatever suits. It is a bland, orangy, soft mixture that closely resembles the best acorn squash. Figure on about ¾ pound per person.

Remove seeds and spongy fibers. Cut calabaza into manageable chunks, about 3 inches on a side. Peel off skin, then cut flesh into ½-inch slices. Combine with lightly salted stock or water to reach about three-quarters up the squash. Add a small amount of butter, or goose, pork, or bacon fat. Add spices or herbs, as desired. Simmer, covered, until tender—about ½ hour. Drain and reserve liquid. Press squash through medium disk of food mill (or simply mash). Return to pot; add salt, pepper, and butter or fat to taste. Reheat, adding cooking liquid, as needed.

CALABAZA PURÉE 2

This quickly assembled unseasoned purée is intended for use as an ingredient in other dishes—desserts, soups, sauces. Refrigerate up to a week, or freeze indefinitely. You can figure the cup yield to be the same as the number of pounds: that is, 1 pound untrimmed squash produces about 1 cup purée.

Cut calabaza into hearty chunks—about ½ pound each. Scrape out seeds and spongy fibers. Set on steamer rack over boiling water. Cover and steam until tender, about 20 minutes. Cool briefly. Pare off peel. Press through medium disk of a food mill. Cool, cover, then refrigerate or freeze.

RICHARD KOWALL'S PURÉED CALABAZA-APPLE SOUP

Richard Kowall, a gracious and erudite neighbor, is a conservator of paintings—and a perfectionist. Whether restoring a damaged portrait, or making dinner, he will be precise. I had the good fortune to taste this unusual thick, russet soup just as I began to work with calabaza. The cranberries lend mysterious tartness and color. Richard used butternut squash—as can you, if you find no calabaza about.

4 servings

2 medium onions, coarsely diced
2 tablespoons butter
4 cups chicken stock
2 pounds calabaza, peeled, seeded, and
    cut into 1–2-inch cubes
4 large, well-perfumed apples, peeled,
    cored, and coarsely diced
¾ cup cranberries
Salt and sugar to taste
6 tablespoons heavy (or whipping) cream
Optional: Nutmeg

1. Soften onions in butter in heavy nonaluminum pot set over moderately low heat, about 5 minutes. Add chicken stock and bring to a boil.

2. Add calabaza, apples, and cranberries. Simmer, partly covered, until very tender, about 45 minutes; check, as squash timing varies.

3. Let soup cool for about 10 minutes. Purée in batches in blender or processor. Return to pot; reheat gently. Soup should be quite thick; if it is too dense, add a little water. Season with salt and sugar to taste.

4. Ladle into bowls. Gently dip a tablespoon of cream into center of each bowl. Tip gently, to allow cream to flow into middle of bowl only. With knife tip, extend into flower shape. Dust with nutmeg, if desired.

CALABAZA GRATIN

Savory and usetul, this side dish is composed of garlicky, herbed orange squash cubes, cooked until creamy on the inside, crunchy on top. Depending on the accompanying dishes, you can substitute butter for oil, or use bacon or goose fat (my favorite). Vary the herbs, as well, and you have a dish that is as versatile as potato gratin. The dish reheats nicely.

4 servings

2½ pounds calabaza
1½ tablespoons flour
1 small garlic clove, minced
½ teaspoon dried savory, crumbled

1 teaspoon coarse kosher salt
Pepper to taste
2 tablespoons full-flavored olive oil

1. Scrape seeds and soft fibrous area from squash cavity and discard. Cut squash in easy-to-handle pieces, then peel. Cut in ¾-inch dice (you should have about 6 cups).

2. Combine flour, garlic, savory, salt, and pepper in small dish. Place calabaza in well-oiled shallow baking-serving dish of about 8-cup capacity. Add flour mixture and toss to coat. Drizzle with 1 tablespoon oil and toss again. Drip remaining oil over top. Cover closely with foil; cut a few slits in the foil.

3. Set in upper third of preheated 325-degree oven. Bake 40 minutes. Remove foil, then toss calabaza gently. Raise heat to 400 degrees and bake until crusty and browned—about 40 minutes.

CALABAZA STRIPS WITH WHOLE-WHEAT PASTA

Whole-wheat spaghetti dressed with sunny squash strips, herbal vinegar, and oil makes an appealing main course to satisfy vegetarians and carnivores alike.

4 or 5 servings

2½ pounds calabaza, seeded (see Preparation for whole squash)
About ⅔ cup full-flavored olive oil
2 medium onions, cut lengthwise into thin strips
1 teaspoon salt, or to taste
½ cup flour
½ cup wine vinegar
¼ cup water
6 cloves
¼ teaspoon fennel seeds
¼ teaspoon dried oregano
Generous handful of basil leaves, to taste
1 pound whole-wheat spaghetti
Pepper to taste
Freshly grated Parmesan cheese to taste

1. Cut squash in pieces 2–3 inches long; then peel. Cut into ¼-inch strips.

2. Heat 2 tablespoons oil in a large skillet. Add onions and cook over moderate heat until slightly softened, about 3 minutes. Transfer to a wide dish.

3. Pour half remaining oil into skillet, half into another similar one and heat (alternatively, you can fry the squash in batches in 1 skillet). Sprinkle squash with ½ teaspoon salt, then flour; toss to coat. Divide between pans and toss in oil. Fry gently over moderately low heat until golden brown on both sides and softened —but not mushy—throughout. If necessary, add oil during cooking so there will be a goodly amount in pan at all times to prevent burning. Add squash to onions.

4. In small nonaluminum pot, simmer vinegar, water, cloves, fennel, oregano, and remaining ½ teaspoon salt for 3 minutes. Strain over squash and onion. Cover tightly and let marinate at least an hour.

5. Just before serving, boil pasta in plenty of salted water until tender. Drain. Transfer to an oiled serving dish. Add basil, squash, onions, and all juice and oil; toss very gingerly, lest you break the calabaza. Season with salt and pepper; add oil, if desired. Sprinkle each portion with Parmesan.

🦐 *Substitute calabaza for other squash in Soup of Beans, Kale, and Squash (page 251).*

CAPE GOOSEBERRY
(Physalis species, particularly *Physalis peruviana* also called *Physalis edulis)*
also Physalis (New Zealand marketing name), Ground Cherry, Husk Tomato,
Strawberry Tomato, Golden Berry, Golden Husk, and Poha
(Note: The common names are shared by members of closely related species.)

*I*t is certainly a circuitous path that has led this intriguing berry to our door. A South American native, this member of the prolific Solanaceae family, sister to the tart little Mexican tomatillo *(Physalis ixocarpa)* has long been running wild far and wide. Finally settling down to cultivation in South Africa, Hawaii (as poha), India, New

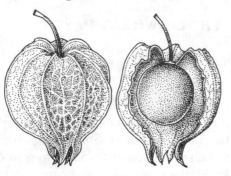

Zealand, Australia, and China, the golden berry has been sent to us (at a staggering price) by those same folks who brought us the kiwi.

More circuitous still is this writer's association with the berry, which I first saw in Italy, in a bakery window in Verona. It was so beautiful I had to ask in my creaky Italian what it could be. "Alkekengi" was the response. No cook that I queried in Italy seemed to know what that was, including master of Italian cuisine Giuliano Bugialli, to whose place I was headed at the time. British friends had spoken of a Cape gooseberry (so named because its cultivation at the Cape of Good Hope in the early nineteenth century was so well established that it was exported with that name), also known as *golden berry* when canned or conserved. I had tasted poha jam from Hawaii, but never knew that it had anything in common with the above fruits.

And all the while the same berry has been growing all around me and you, in almost all the states in the country, a fruit that has been happily gathered and eaten fresh and dried by just about every South and North American Indian tribe, as it grows wild in temperate, subtropical, and tropical areas.

If you haven't seen the ground cherry or one of its closest relatives, the red-orange Chinese lantern plant (which, incidentally, *is* the real *Physalis alkekengi*, not the one on the cake in Verona), as you walked along a country path, you've probably noticed it at a florist shop. The ground cherry (the American *Physalis pruinosa*) and imported Cape gooseberry have more or less the same structure: Each rustly-crisp parchment bladder (in Greek, *physalis*), twisted closed at the tip like a party favor, hides a firm, marble-sized, richly yellow, opaque fruit. Resembling a small cherry tomato in size and shape, it has a thin, waxy skin that surrounds a very juicy, dense pulp of the same brilliant color, whorled with soft, tiny edible seeds. Its unusual taste is part tomato, part strawberry, part gooseberry, part grape—and yet all its own: sweet and pleasantly acid, with a lightly bitter aftertaste.

SELECTION AND STORAGE: New Zealand distributors say Physalis comes to the United States from March to June. Depending on nature and the exporters, you may find it then—or perhaps another time. The small California crop usually arrives in early fall and lasts until Thanksgiving. Domestic ground cherries are erratically available at stands and greenmarkets during summer months, in very small volume. As long as the berries are yellow or orangy, they're fine and ripe; avoid greenish ones. If the balloony husks are clean and shiny, all the better, but a bit of dinginess won't hurt.

Storage is just plain unbelievable. Spread in a single layer in a dish, uncovered and unhusked, the berries last 4 weeks in the refrigerator. They would probably keep longer if not eaten.

USE: Unadorned is best of all, husks simply opened back like ghostly moth wings. Rinse and eat. Chilled Cape gooseberries make a spectacular palate freshener in lieu of ices, in the middle of a rich meal. Or offer as part of a crudité selection or hors d'oeuvre plate.

Combine halved Cape gooseberries with rice or cracked wheat for a stuffing or salad. Sample in combination with other salad ingredients, testing to your own taste, as the fruit and vegetable characteristics make for unusual and personal taste combinations.

Stew a small quantity of berries with pork slices, veal chops, or chicken: strain pan juices and berries for a richly tart-sweet sauce.

In Europe golden berries are dipped into chocolate or fondant, their opened calyxes used as handles, and served as bonbons or placed atop fancy cakes and tortes. I prefer a clear or caramel glaze that allows the lustrous color to show through (see recipe); and judging from the luscious cake filling in the next recipe, the berries make as good a jam as all texts promise.

Cape gooseberries add an intriguing flavor, texture, and color to apple pies, especially with the assistance of a little preserved ginger. Include quartered berries in cornbread, gingerbread, and muffins.

PREPARATION: To remove husks from berries, open them up, then twist the base to release the fruit. Rinse well. To keep the "wings" intact for serving or candy dipping, gently separate the sections, or snip open the calyx with scissors. Pull straight back, like the tail of a game bird or a comet.

NUTRITIONAL HIGHLIGHTS: Cape gooseberries are a source of vitamin C and fiber.

CHICKEN WITH CAPE GOOSEBERRY SAUCE

With only minutes of preparation, these ingredients produce an unusual, intensely flavorful dish. The Cape gooseberries, stewed with the cut-up chicken and spices, become a savory, curry-ish sauce (really more of a glaze) that is naturally sweet-sour. Decorated with a few whole berries, the quickly prepared chicken looks special.

2 or 3 servings

2½-pound chicken, cut into 8 serving pieces and trimmed of fat (reserve giblets for another use)
About 1 tablespoon lime juice
¾ teaspoon coarse kosher salt
2 tablespoons corn oil
7-ounce container Cape gooseberries, husked and rinsed (see Preparation)
1 large garlic clove, sliced
½ teaspoon ground coriander
⅛ teaspoon ground cloves
White pepper to taste
2 tablepoons medium-dry sherry

1. Sprinkle chicken with 1 tablespoon lime juice and ¼ teaspoon salt; let stand about 15 minutes, as convenient. Heat oil in 10–12-inch skillet. Slowly brown chicken pieces on both sides; set aside breast pieces.

2. Meanwhile, cut up enough berries to equal about ⅔ cup; save remainder (5 or 6) for garnish. Pour out all fat, leaving a thin slick in pan. (Dark meat remains in pan.) Add garlic and stir over medium heat for a minute. Add coriander, cloves, pepper, cut-up berries, and sherry; stir to distribute.

3. Cover and cook on low heat 10 minutes. Return breast pieces to pan, turn others. Cover and cook 15 minutes longer, until done.

4. Transfer chicken to serving dish; place in warm oven. Press sauce in pan through fine sieve; degrease, as desired. Return to pan and boil for a minute, stirring, to concentrate slightly and thicken. Season to taste, adding lime juice, if needed. Spoon sauce over chicken pieces. Pull back husks from remaining berries, twisting them slightly so tails stay in place; rinse berries. Arrange with chicken and serve.

SALAD OF AVOCADO, CAPE GOOSEBERRIES, AND CUCUMBER

Buttery avocados suit tart Cape gooseberries as they do tomatoes. Use the hothouse or English cucumber (or seedless, burpless—whatever they're called in your market) for the good texture its sweet-tasting skin and crisp flesh provide.

4–5 servings

½ large English cucumber

7-ounce container Cape gooseberries, husked and rinsed (see Preparation), halved

2 medium avocados

2 tablespoons lemon juice

½ teaspoon coarse kosher salt, or to taste

Pepper to taste

6 tablespoons olive oil

¼ cup finely chopped fresh cilantro

Small bunch watercress, well trimmed, rinsed, and dried

1. Trim off tips and quarter cucumber lengthwise. Cut across in thin slices. Combine in bowl with gooseberries.

2. Halve and seed avocados. With small melon-ball cutter remove flesh and add to bowl.

3. Mix lemon juice, salt, and pepper. Add oil and blend well. Pour over salad, add cilantro and mix well.

4. Serve on a bed of watercress.

CAPE SCALLOPS WITH CAPE GOOSEBERRIES

The two capes above are (1) Cape Cod, where Barbara Spiegel spends the summer, and from whence comes this recipe, and (2) the Cape of Good Hope, from whence comes the most common name (Cape gooseberry) of the fruit presently exported from New Zealand as Physalis.

It is difficult to capture in words the flavors of this curious berry, which works so well in savory dishes, but you can imagine the presentation of little round scallops and baby golden fruits flecked with green chili-peppers.

2 or 3 servings

3 tablespoons corn oil

½ cup finely chopped scallions

2 tablespoons finely chopped, seeded mild green chili-pepper (such as Anaheim)

2 medium garlic cloves, minced

7-ounce container Cape gooseberries, husked, washed, and halved (see Preparation), to equal 1 cup

1 pound bay scallops

Salt and pepper to taste

2 tablespoons lime juice

¼ cup heavy (or whipping) cream

2 tablespoons finely chopped mint

1. Heat oil in heavy skillet over moderate heat; add scallions, chili-pepper, and garlic. Cook, stirring, for 5 minutes.

2. Add Cape gooseberries and scallops and cook over high heat, stirring, until berries are soft (but not breaking) and scallops just opaque, about 2 minutes. Add salt, pepper, and lime juice.

3. With slotted spoon gently transfer berries and scallops from pan to a dish. Boil liquid in pan, as necessary, to reduce to syrupy consistency. Add cream and stir until slightly thickened.

4. Return gooseberries and scallops to pan to just barely heat through, mixing gently. Sprinkle with mint and serve at once.

GLACÉED GOLDEN BERRIES

This may be the most striking mouthful you have ever placed on a plate of petits fours. Glistening in its glaze, its shiny straw-colored calyx opened back like butterfly wings, each berry is a Fabergé jewel—but simple to make, requiring no more labor than a fast dip in hot hard-crack sugar syrup. For variety, coat berries in chocolate or fondant, as is more usual with this fruit.

Makes about 2 dozen bonbons

About 2 dozen Cape gooseberries
1 cup sugar
½ cup water
1/16 teaspoon cream of tartar

1. Divide husks in 3 or 4 lengthwise sections by tearing or snipping with scissors; do not pull from fruit. Open out, pulling straight back like tails. Rinse fruit without wetting husks; dry well. Lightly oil sheet of aluminum foil.

2. Combine sugar, water, and cream of tartar in small saucepan; bring to a boil, stirring. Cover pot; boil 2 minutes. Uncover and boil over moderately low heat until temperature reaches about 290 degrees and syrup is thickened and slightly yellowed; swirl for a moment until it turns pale golden, not brown. Set over pan of simmering water.

3. When syrup stops bubbling, dip in a berry, reaching almost, but not quite, to stem area, holding back-turned husk as handle; dip quickly in and out to coat lightly. Do not let fruit remain in the syrup for more than a moment or skin will crack. Let excess drip into pot. Place berry gently on foil to cool and harden.

4. Working rapidly, repeat until you have coated as many berries as you wish. Reheat syrup, if necessary, to keep glaze thin enough.

CAPE GOOSEBERRY–GINGER TEA CAKE

Light, but full of flavor, this sponge cake, based on the versatile *Génoise Électrique* in *Mastering the Art of French Cooking* (volume 2), takes on a new identity when filled and decorated with Cape gooseberries—beautiful as birds in flight with their husks opened. The intense fruitiness of the filling, a mingling of quince and tomato flavors, suits the ginger-scented génoise particularly well. If you like a moist cake, fill the halved sponge a day before serving and let mellow, wrapped in plastic. Although dubbed *tea cake*, it goes as well with fresh lemonade or madeira.

6–8 servings

½ stick unsalted butter
1 scant tablespoon grated drained ginger
    in syrup (preserved ginger)
⅔ cup cake flour

⅛ teaspoon salt

3 large eggs

½ cup sugar

¾ teaspoon lemon extract

¼ teaspoon almond extract

FILLING AND TOPPING

About 11 ounces Cape gooseberries (1½ containers), husked and rinsed (see Preparation)

2 teaspoons grated ginger in syrup

⅓ cup sugar

¼ cup water

Confectioners' sugar

About 3 tablespoons fruit jelly—orange, currant, apricot, or apple

8 Glacéed Golden Berries (preceding recipe)

1. Melt butter slowly over lowest heat; stir in ginger, separating shreds thoroughly. Cool. Butter 8-inch round cake pan. Set round of wax paper in this. Butter well, then coat lightly with flour.

2. Sift flour and salt; return to sifter. Beat eggs, sugar, and lemon and almond extracts in bowl of electric mixer on moderate speed until fluffy. Turn gradually to high speed and continue beating for about 5 minutes or longer, until firmly peaked, like softish meringue. Do not underbeat. When beaters are lifted, mixture that falls should form distinct ribbons on surface.

3. Remove bowl from beater stand. Gradually sift in flour, folding with rubber spatula; take care not to deflate batter. When you have folded in about two-thirds of the flour, alternate the remainder with spoons of the butter-ginger mixture, gently pouring against side of bowl. When butter and flour are well incorporated, gently scoop batter into pan. Delicately spread with spatula, drawing batter to reach rim of pan.

4. Bake in center of preheated 350-degree oven 25–30 minutes, or until center of cake no longer sounds wet and spongy when pressed; there will be a line of separation around edge of pan.

5. Cool 5 minutes on rack. Invert, remove pan, and cool slightly, then remove paper. Cool completely. (If storing, cool thoroughly, then wrap tightly.)

6. Make filling: Cut berries in quarters; you should have about 1⅓ cups. Combine in small, heavy saucepan with ginger, sugar, and water. Simmer until slightly thick and translucent, 10–15 minutes, keeping mixture syrupy, not jam-like. Cool completely, then cover and chill.

7. Delicately trim brown edges from cake so sides are evenly yellow and smooth. Halve cake horizontally, using long serrated knife. Spread both cut sides with berries and syrup. Sandwich together neatly, so that bottom (from which paper was peeled) is on top.

8. Place three 1½-inch-wide strips of waxed paper on cake, equidistant from each other. Sieve a thick coat of confectioners' sugar over surface. Carefully lift strips straight up to leave neat sugar bands.

9. Heat jelly in tiny pan. Paint stripes of this on cake, filling bands between sugared areas, taking care not to touch these. Apply a second coat to jelly bands. At serving time, arrange glazed berries on cake.

ANNABEL LANGBEIN'S APPLE AND
CAPE GOOSEBERRY PICNIC CAKE

Annabel Langbein, a beautiful and vivacious young woman from New Zealand, writes and teaches about the food specialties of her country. She bakes several versions (see Note) of the following portable sweet, a golden, tender, shortbread-like confection.

12–14 servings

PASTRY

½ pound softened unsalted butter

1 cup sugar

¼ teaspoon salt

1 teaspoon vanilla

1 tablespoon orange juice

4 egg yolks

2¾ cups all-purpose flour

FILLING AND ASSEMBLY

1 pound (4 medium) Golden Delicious apples

1¾ cups (about 13 ounces) husked and rinsed Cape gooseberries (see Preparation)

3 tablespoons butter

2 tablespoons lemon juice

2 tablespoons Scotch

½ cup sugar

1 egg beaten with 1 tablespoon water

1. Combine butter, sugar, and salt in small bowl of electric mixer. Beat until very light and creamy. Add vanilla and orange juice. Add egg yolks one at a time, beating a minute at high speed after each addition. On low speed add flour; mix until barely incorporated. Do not overbeat. Divide mixture into 2 slightly unequal parts. Form neat disks and wrap in floured waxed paper. Refrigerate for an hour or more.

2. Quarter, peel, and core apples. Slice crosswise ¼ inch thick. Cut up berries. Heat butter in wide pan. Add apples, berries, lemon juice, Scotch, and sugar; stir. Cover and cook on low heat until soft and juicy—10 minutes. Uncover and continue cooking until juices evaporate, about 15 minutes; stir occasionally. Cool.

3. Roll larger portion of dough between sheets of floured waxed paper to form rough circle 12–13 inches in diameter. Place in bottom of 10-inch springform pan (it will break; don't worry). Press and patch pastry into pan and up sides about 1¼ inches to form even shell.

4. Spoon cooled filling into pastry. Generously flour remaining dough; set on another 9½–10-inch springform or tart pan bottom. Roll out carefully to form 10-inch round, trimming edges neatly. Using pan bottom as you would a spatula, slide this soft dough onto filling, jiggling into place. (Or roll floured dough between sheets of waxed paper, then trim to make neat circle; remove paper and slip onto filling.) Press edges together (again, don't worry about breakage; you can patch). Paint cake lavishly with egg mixture, smoothing surface. With fork tines seal edge, then incise pattern on surface.

5. Bake 45–55 minutes in center of preheated 350-degree oven, until golden. Set on rack; cool 15 minutes. Remove sides of pan and cool completely.

Note: Try these equally delicious fillings: Substitute a combination of 1 pound each Golden Delicious apples and feijoas (peeled and sliced) *or* 6 medium tamarillos (peeled and sliced) and 4 large Granny Smith apples. For the latter increase the sugar to 1 cup, replace the Scotch with anise liqueur or rum, and omit lemon juice. Time for cooking the filling may be less for feijoas and will be longer for tamarillos.

GINGERBREAD WITH CAPE GOOSEBERRIES

Tart berries add moisture and a citrusy edge to this rich gingerbread. For a soft cake, wrap in plastic and let mellow a day before serving.

6–8 servings

5 tablespoons butter
7-ounce container Cape gooseberries
1¾ cups flour
1 tablespoon ground ginger
1 teaspoon ground coriander
½ teaspoon cinnamon
2 eggs plus 1 yolk
Big pinch salt
½ cup light molasses
½ cup brown sugar, lightly packed (remove all lumps)
¾ cup buttermilk
1 teaspoon baking soda
Crème fraîche or whipped cream

1. Melt butter on low heat; set aside to cool. Remove and discard husks from about ¾ container of berries. Rinse well, then quarter. You should have a bit more than ¾ cup fruit. Add more to make that amount, if necessary. Sift together flour, ginger, coriander, and cinnamon. Butter and flour 9-inch square pan.

2. In medium bowl of electric stand mixer beat eggs, yolk, and salt on high speed until pale, thick, and fluffy. Gradually add molasses, beating on moderate speed. Continue beating and gradually add sugar.

3. Blend buttermilk and soda thoroughly, mixing with whisk. With mixer at lowest speed add one-third flour mixture to batter. When barely mixed, add butter, then half remaining flour. With spatula fold in buttermilk, then remaining flour, mixing to not quite blend (do not overmix or cake will be tough). Fold in berries. Pour into pan.

4. Bake in center of preheated 350-degree oven until center is springy and cake shows slight separation from side of pan, about 40 minutes.

5. Cool slightly on rack. Run knife around edge, turn out, then set right side up to cool. Serve warm with cream. If you like a very moist cake, let it cool entirely, then wrap in plastic and allow to mellow 12–24 hours before serving.

CARAMBOLA
(Averrhoa carambola)
also Star Fruit, Five-Angled Fruit, Chinese Star Fruit

A show-stopper that lives up to its gorgeous appearance—sometimes—the carambola (kah-rahm-BO-la) may become the most important "new" fruit since the kiwi. As selected cultivars are planted in Florida, we have increasing opportunities to sample this exquisitely scented and stunning fruit. A carambola is easy to recognize, for

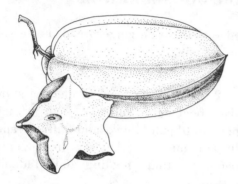

nothing else looks anything like it: a glossy yellow (sometimes white) ellipsoid decorated with five deeply delineated longitudinal ribs or wings that form star shapes when sliced. It has a thin, slightly waxy skin that in no way interferes with the quality of the very juicy, crisp, almost translucent flesh. For an apparently fragile fruit, it stores for an uncommonly long time. Carambola is easy to prepare, requiring no peeling or seeding. It is unusually versatile, as delicious and appealing in a shrimp sauté as it is in fruit or vegetable salad, an ice, or mousse.

At the time of this writing, carambola's only catch is figuring out if you're buying a fragrantly sweet one or a puckery-sour one. Both can be delightful, but if you're seeking a fruit for dessert, or to eat out of hand, you probably won't want to wind up with the acid variety. When sweet, the flesh has a flavor that combines the flowery best of plums, McIntosh apples, and Concord grapes with a citric edge. When sour, it is brightly sharp, as clean as a lemon, but less harsh, more fruity.

The carambola is no newcomer to cultivation. It flourishes as an important crop in Asia (Averrhoës, after whom the fruit was named, was a twelfth-century Arabic physician and philosopher; carambola is an Indian name for the fruit), South and Central America, the Caribbean, and Hawaii. Although it is nearly a hundred years since trees were acquired from this last island for the American mainland, it is only recently that the fruit has been marketed here. Earlier varieties bore both sweet and sour fruits, but now predictably sweet ones, notably the Arkin (unfortunately a rather bland variety), have been established and will become more common, along with the tart to semisweet varieties, particularly the Golden Star, a much more aromatic type.

SELECTION AND STORAGE: In the United States carambolas are a fall and winter fruit, generally appearing from August to mid-February. Look for full, firm fruits from 2 to 5 inches long, with juicy-looking ribs. Avoid fruits with browned, shriveled ribs—generally the result of customers who poke and pinch. But, even if browned, the fruit can taste quite fine, so don't give up if that is all you can find. If green-ribbed fruit is purchased, be sure to let it ripen until yellow. Most important, carambolas must have a full floral-fruity aroma: leave them at room temperature until you can smell the perfume, which indicates full development.

If carambolas are not marked "tart" or "sweet," you should at least *try* to convince your fruit man of the value of taste tests for sales. Ask him to sample the fruits so that he'll understand the difference. If all else fails, figure that most tart varieties have very narrow ribs, while the sweet yellow varieties have thick, fleshy ones. The two white varieties marketed are sweet.

Store the fruits at room temperature, if you'll be serving them in a day or two. If they are fully ripe and you wish to keep them longer than that, store in the refrigerator, in a place where they won't be bruised; they should last for at least 2 weeks (depending on their condition).

USE: Sour carambolas work well in place of lemon or lime slices, to garnish seafood, poultry, or mixed drinks. Sauté for a second as a garnish/accompaniment to delicate fish or poultry dishes, sprinkling with a touch of sugar to glaze briefly; serve at once. In the East sour carambolas are pickled for relish. While I do not recommend dousing them in vinegar, the taste, unadorned, suggests uses similar to those for a pickle or caper—as a tart component of composed meat or vegetable salads.

Because carambolas do not discolor, they are ideal for fruit and vegetable salads or fruit cups, used sparingly. They are particularly right with avocados in both fruit and vegetable combinations. Purée (alone or mixed with other fruits) and sieve to make vervy ices, sherbets, Bavarian creams, mousses.

Sweet carambolas work in all of the above but, because of their lesser acidity, can assume a primary role in fruit salads and other fresh desserts. Combine them with relatively soft, sweet fruits for a texture/flavor balance that particularly suits Indian, Oriental, and Southeast Asian meals.

PREPARATION: Generally speaking, carambolas need only be rinsed and thin-sliced to be enjoyed, or simply eat them whole, if that's your pleasure. (At my local vegetable market a three-year-old Korean boy chooses the biggest, juiciest blimps in the heap, sits down and devours them neatly—four or five at a sitting—starting at one tip and continuing breathlessly to the other end.) If the skin is not to your liking, simply pull it off each slice. Often, the appearance of the ribs is improved by a quick zip with a vegetable peeler to shave off the darker stripe of skin. You may have to pick out an occasional seed with the tip of a knife.

NUTRITIONAL HIGHLIGHTS: Carambola is low in calories—about 40 for a medium one. It is a good source of vitamin A, vitamin C, potassium, and fiber.

SIMPLEST CARAMBOLA-AVOCADO SIDE DISH

This dish takes moments to assemble. It can serve as the base for a composed summer main-dish salad—with chicken, or shrimp, or ham—or can stand alone as an unusual complement to an impromptu meal of cold meat or fowl. For this combination, the sourer varieties of carambola will do just fine, adding a pleasant acid lift to the creamy avocado.

Because carambolas store so well, keeping their grapy-lemony flavor for a long refrigerator stay, you can put this together spontaneously, whenever an avocado happens by. If you don't care about specifics, just figure on 2 small carambolas per medium avocado, plus the juice of half an orange. If an exact recipe is preferable, here 'tis:

4 servings

2 ripe medium avocados (about 1 pound)
4 very small carambolas (about ½ pound)
Salt and white pepper
1 juice orange

Halve avocados lengthwise; remove pit and skin. Cut into thin crosswise slices on a slant. Arrange on four plates. Shave the tips off the carambola fins, then cut the fruits across into very thin slices, placing one on each avocado piece. Sprinkle salt and white pepper over all, then squeeze the orange juice over that. Let stand at least 15 minutes before serving.

BREAKFAST OR BRUNCH FRUIT MÉLANGE

Carambolas make an eye-catching and refreshing contribution to a straightforward, fresh-tasting assortment of soft fruits.

6 servings

3 tablespoons fragrant honey
¼ cup lemon juice
1 tablespoon rum
¼ teaspoon vanilla extract
⅛ teaspoon almond extract
2 medium carambolas (sweet or medium-sweet), 3–4 ounces each
2 pounds soft-textured melon—such as Crenshaw, Canary, honeydew
½ pound seedless grapes, preferably red
2 medium bananas, or 6 tiny "apple" or "finger" bananas

1. Mix together honey, lemon juice, rum, vanilla and almond extract. With swivel peeler remove skin from carambola ribs. Cut fruit across in thin slices (you may want to halve lengthwise, depending on size); toss with honey mixture.

2. With melon-ball cutter form small balls of the melon flesh and place in serving bowl. Halve grapes and add. Slice bananas and add. Add carambolas and syrup and toss gently. Refrigerate for about ½ hour before serving.

SALAD OF AVOCADO, ENDIVE, AND CARAMBOLA

The acid freshness of carambola lends just the right edge to the oily avocado, while brightly complementing its color. If you cannot find sweet carambolas, sprinkle the fruit with sugar.

4 servings

2 tablespoons fruit-flavored vinegar
¼ teaspoon salt, or to taste
1 tablespoon hazelnut oil (see Note)
3 tablespoons peanut oil
3 medium Belgian endives, cored and cut into 2–3-inch julienne strips
1 medium avocado (preferably Hass variety)
1 large carambola (sweet or medium-sweet), about 5 inches long

1. Blend together vinegar and salt. Add both oils and mix well.

2. Arrange endive on a serving dish. Halve avocado lengthwise. Remove pit and peel. Cut across on slant to make thin slices; arrange over endive.

3. Cut a central slice from the carambola and reserve. Halve rest of fruit lengthwise, then cut across in very thin slice. Place these over avocado; center the reserved whole star slice.

4. Drizzle dressing over all and serve.

Note: Hazelnut oil imported from France is available in fancy shops all over the country. You may substitute ¼ cup light olive oil to replace both oils.

BAKED FISH FILLETS WITH CARAMBOLA

For a ridiculously simple, remarkably pretty, delicate dish that can be whipped together in seconds, try this. It may sound far out to combine fish with fruit if you're not accustomed to cooking with carambola, but the result is fresh, mild, and not at all strange to the taste buds. If you want to increase the recipe, it will behave properly as long as you bake the fish in a single layer.

2 servings

2 tablespoons softened butter
2 fairly lean fish fillets, about ½ pound each, about ½ inch thick
Salt and white pepper
2 very small carambolas, preferably slightly tart
Lime juice to taste

1. Select a baking-serving dish to hold fillets in a single layer. Spread a little less than half the butter in the dish. Set fillets on this. Add salt and pepper.

2. Cut off carambola tips. Slice fruit thin; arrange on fish. Dot with remaining butter. Taste carambola; if rather sweet, sprinkle with a healthy dose of lime juice; if tart, a smaller amount.

3. Bake in preheated 450-degree oven for about 8 minutes, until fish just becomes opaque in the center. It will continue to bake in the dish, so do not overcook. Serve at once.

SAUTÉED SHRIMPS AND CARAMBOLA

Golden stars, pink crescents, and a freshly fruity flavor make this dish a simple delight. It takes 2 minutes to cook, 15 minutes to prepare from start to finish, if you shell shrimp in leisurely fashion. If you have a choice, select narrow, long carambolas, which make smaller, prettier mouthfuls.

2 servings

1 pound shrimp, preferably small
3 small carambolas, preferably medium-sweet, about 2 ounces each
2½ tablespoons butter
Salt and white pepper to taste
Pinch sugar
1 tablespoon lemon juice, approximately

1. Shell shrimp; devein. If they are not small, halve lengthwise. Cut tips off carambolas, then slice ⅛ inch thick.

2. Heat 2 tablespoons butter over moderately high heat in large nonaluminum sauté pan. Add shrimp, carambola slices, salt, pepper, and sugar. Sauté for a minute or two, until shrimp are pink. Add lemon juice and toss.

3. Off heat stir in remaining butter. Taste and season. Serve at once.

CARAMBOLA COCKTAIL

Anyone who has visited the French West Indies will become dreamy-eyed when he sips this type of white rum and fruit drink, which instantly creates tropical nostalgia. Although I've not tasted this sunny yellow combination anywhere but in my own wintry New York City living room, it deserves a tropical home.

About 4 drinks

½ pound carambolas (3 medium)
2 tablespoons pale fruit liqueur—
    Cointreau, Triple Sec, banana
    liqueur, apricot liqueur
About 2 tablespoons lime juice
About 1½ tablespoons superfine sugar
¾ cup golden or white rum

1. Shave ribs off carambolas. Halve one fruit crosswise; wrap and refrigerate half. Quarter remaining fruit lengthwise; remove seeds (if any) which surround the central area. Purée seeded carambolas and liqueur. Press through a sieve. Add sugar and lime juice to taste; oversweeten slightly. Add rum.

2. Cover and refrigerate until serving time. To serve, cut 4 slices from the carambola half; make a slit in each and fit over the rim of a highball glass in which you've put crushed ice. Shake the drink to blend; pour and serve.

CARAMBOLA ICE

The idea for this elegant, perfumed sorbet comes from Richard Chirol, formerly pâtissier at the restaurant Jean-Louis in Washington, D.C. The intense taste and aroma of the carambola make it a prime candidate for a simple ice. Serve the smooth-textured, pale canary-yellow dessert as suggested below; or leave out the sugared fruit slices and nestle a scoop of Gingered Papaya Milk Sherbet (page 345) alongside.

Because carambola is quite pricey and very rich in flavor, I have developed the recipe for a small amount. However, you can double the quantities if you wish.

4 servings (about 3 cups)

1¼ pounds fragrant medium-sweet carambolas (choose deep-colored ones, if you have a choice), rinsed
1¼ cups sugar
1¾ cups plus 1 tablespoon water

1. Set aside ¼ pound carambolas (preferably 2 very small fruit) and cut remainder into dice.

2. Combine 1 cup sugar and 1¾ cups water in saucepan; boil for 2 minutes. Remove from heat and stir in diced fruit.

3. Purée in blender or processor to a smooth texture; press through a fine-meshed sieve. Let cool slightly, then chill thoroughly.

4. Pour into can of ice-cream maker. Freeze according to manufacturer's directions.

5. When frozen, scoop into a container and allow to mellow in the freezer for a few hours or more.

6. Shave brownish skin from ribs of remaining carambolas; cut fruit across into ⅛–¼-inch slices. Combine remaining ¼ cup sugar and 1 tablespoon water in a nonaluminum skillet; heat to boiling and add the fruit slices in a single layer. Cook on high heat for about 10 seconds. Turn over the slices and cook 10–15 seconds, to glaze slightly. With a slotted spoon transfer to a dish; cool and chill.

7. To serve, soften ice for about ½ hour in refrigerator. Place a tidy scoop on each chilled dessert plate and set a few slices of carambola alongside.

CARDOON
(Cynara cardunculus)
also Cardoons, Cardoni, Cardi

A blossoming cardoon resembles its relative the globe artichoke, a more popular edible thistle. Its name, whether derived from Latin *carduus* or the later French *chardon*, means thistle. (In Australia, it is called weed artichoke and has spread, weed-like, through the country, as it has in the Argentine pampas.) Unlike the artichoke, it

is not the flower of the cardoon that is eaten but the fleshy, silver-gray stalks. They grow in bunches, like celery, but are flattened, longer, and wider, with slightly notched sides and a brushed-suède finish. Cooked, the cardoon is soft and meaty. The flavor is complex, bitter and sweet, with hints of artichoke heart, celery, and oyster plant.

How sad that this lovely, subtle food has fallen out of favor except in its native Mediterranean region, where it still figures in the cuisines of France, Spain, and particularly Italy, a country that has honored it since Roman times. By the Middle Ages the cardoon was cultivated throughout Europe. Still popular in the 1796 edition of *The Art of Cookery Made Plain and Easy* by Hannah Glasse, the vegetable appeared as "Chardoons Fried and Buttered" and "Chardoons à la Fromage," the latter an unusual treatment with a medieval melding of red wine, pepper, butter, orange juice, and a grating of Parmesan or Cheshire cheese to brown it. Louis Eustace Ude, celebrated chef to nobility of the nineteenth century, wrote that to prepare Cardoons in Sauce Espagnole "requires great attention, and no small share of skill in the art of cookery. It is not much relished in England, but in France it is held in the highest estimation. It is always one of those selected for the trial of a cook."

But by 1911 the British culinary historian Frederick Hackwood, having described *cardo* as a "delicacy of the Italians in former times," goes on to remark hopefully that "the 'cardoon' is a most succulent and esculent vegetable which might find a welcome at English tables." Unfortunately, it found little. Although it was familiar to the American colonists and up through the early part of our century, it dwindled in popularity, becoming a specialty to be found in Italian markets only.

SELECTION AND STORAGE: Look for the vegetable, particularly in Italian markets, from winter through early spring. Although they vaguely resemble celery, cardoons are not crisp and bright, but supple and grayish. If you have a choice, head for smallish, comparatively firm stalks with little browning or wilting. Do not be dismayed at the severed discolored top of cardoons: prior to harvesting they sport huge fernlike plumes that are sliced off before shipping, and the browned area is the result of the vegetable's darkening immediately upon cutting.

Store cardoons wrapped at the base with damp toweling, then covered by a plastic bag. If in good condition when purchased, they should last for about 2 weeks.

USE: In Italy, *cardi* are offered raw in strips (as well as cooked) to dunk in fine olive oil, salt, and pepper *(in pinzimonio)* or in the hot, rich Piedmontese dip *bagna cauda.* The cardoons that I've experimented with in the United States have been too coarse and bitter for raw use, but if you are luckier than I, serve them this way, as well as chopped into salad.

If you think of the flavors and texture of celery and artichoke hearts (and oyster plant, if it's part of your repertoire), you'll be able to imagine how to dress cardoons: delicate cream and cheese sauces, light vinaigrettes, lemony emulsions—all suit. In addition, the meaty-textured vegetable lends itself, once precooked (see basic recipes following), to being dipped in batter or crumbs and pan-fried. Added to soups and pale stews, cardoons impart a subtle, mysterious flavor.

PREPARATION: Although I have yet to read a recipe for cardoons that does not require the application of lemon to cut stalks, I see no reason for it. Once the vegetable is cooked, it turns the same grayish color whether acid-treated or not. Although it does look a peculiar brown as you trim it, the color evens out when cooked.

For most dishes, you'll need to trim and precook the cardoons. The traditional *à blanc* treatment follows, as well as a more casual one that I use. However you cook cardoons, do not be tempted to ignore the precooking step, which removes the often considerable bitterness.

NUTRITIONAL HIGHLIGHTS: Cardoon is very low in calories, an excellent source of potassium, and a source of calcium and iron. It is, however, high in sodium at 300 milligrams per cup, if you are watching your intake.

BASIC PREPARATION 1 FOR CARDOONS

I don't know whether it's different tastes or different cardoons, but French and Italian cookbooks recommend an initial 2–3-hour cooking for this vegetable, while I have found that about ½ hour should do. The preliminary cooking will suit just about any preparation except one that requires lengthy secondary cooking.

For every 2–2½ pounds cardoons (about ½ bunch) you'll need:

3 tablespoons flour
6 cups water
3 tablespoons lemon juice
1 teaspoon salt

1. Place flour in nonaluminum pot; slowly whisk in water. Add lemon juice and salt and bring to a boil.

2. Meanwhile, trim off base of cardoons. Remove leaves and any wilted or damaged outside stalks; halve remaining stalks crosswise. With a paring knife zip off heavy strings, as you would from celery. Divide wider base section in half lengthwise. Cut stalks and leaves in diagonal slices to suit the dish you're preparing. (Generally, I find that pieces about 1 inch square are useful.)

3. Drop into the boiling liquid and simmer, partly covered, until barely tender. Timing can vary from 15 minutes to 45, so test frequently, unless you're an old hand with cardoons.

BASIC PREPARATION 2 (My Preference)

Although it is traditional and effective to precook cardoons as above, I have had good luck with this simple alternative procedure.

Halve the trimmed stalks crosswise (if you're not cooking them all, rub with lemon the cut side of those to be stored). Separate and carefully wash the stalks. Drop into a huge amount of boiling salted water—such as you would use for pasta. Boil until tender, from 15 to 30 minutes (keep testing). Drain, then cool in running water. Set in bowl of water. Removing a stalk at a time, zip off strings with aid of a paring knife, pulling first from one end of the stalk, then the other. Cut the stalks to suit your recipe.

To serve or to finish cooking cardoons prepared as in either Basic Preparation try these:

☐ Dress with vinaigrette, parsley, and chives.
☐ Toss with olive oil, salt, and pepper; bake in a moderate oven until very tender; remove from oven and sprinkle with Parmesan cheese.
☐ Combine in a shallow baking dish with mornay or béchamel sauce; bake in a moderate oven until bubbling.
☐ Stew in cream until very tender.

—

CARDOONS IN ONION CREAM SAUCE

The sweetness of butter-stewed onions and richness of cream offset the bitterness of this assertive yet elusive-flavored vegetable.

4 servings

2 pounds (about ½ bunch) cardoons, prepared as in Basic Preparation 1 or 2, cut in 1-inch pieces
2 medium onions, thinly sliced (to make 1½ cups)
3 tablespoons butter
2 tablespoons flour
1 cup light cream or half-and-half
Salt, pepper, and nutmeg to taste

1. Spread cardoons in a shallow baking dish about 9 inches in diameter or of a size to fit the vegetable fairly snugly.

2. Stew onions in butter in a heavy skillet, covered, over very low heat until extremely soft (but not browned), about 25 minutes, stirring occasionally. Raise heat slightly, add flour and stir 2–3 minutes.

3. Bring cream to a simmer. Remove onions from heat and whisk in half the cream; add remainder. Simmer, partly covered, for 5 minutes. Purée. Add salt, pepper, and nutmeg to taste.

4. Fold into cardoons and bake in upper third of 400-degree oven until lightly golden. (You can make this dish ahead. When you have combined the sauce and cardoons, allow to cool. Then cover and refrigerate.)

—

CARDOON-POTATO SALAD

The subtly artichoke-like, bitter flavor of cardoons is pleasantly softened by the sweet starchiness of potatoes. It is best to have just prepared and drained the cardoons before beginning the recipe.

4–6 servings

1½ pounds even-sized all-purpose potatoes, peeled
3 tablespoons beef broth
About 2¼ pounds cardoons, cooked by Basic Preparation 2 and cut in smallish pieces (you should have 4 cups)
2 tablespoons lemon juice
About ⅓ cup olive oil
Salt, if desired
2 tablespoons minced parsley

1. Boil potatoes in salted water until just tender—about 20 minutes; do not overcook.

2. Drain potatoes and let stand 5–10 minutes to firm up. Slice in half lengthwise, then across into ½-inch-thick slices. Mix with broth; let stand until cool.

3. Combine cardoons, lemon juice, 3 tablespoons olive oil, and optional salt in a serving dish. Add potatoes and minced parsley. Add olive oil to taste; mix lightly. Serve at room temperature.

DEEP-FRIED CARDOONS

It's difficult to gauge the amount of cardoons you'll need as an appetizer, but figure on about ½ pound per person. I like a wide electric skillet for deep-frying, as the surface area is generous and the oil temperature constant. Like so many deep-fried foods, this is rather messy to prepare—and scrumptious.

4 servings, as an appetizer

2 tablespoons lemon juice
½ teaspoon salt
¼ teaspoon ground coriander
⅛ teaspoon white pepper
1 tablespoon olive oil
2–2¼ pounds cardoons, cooked as in Basic Preparation 2, cut 1–1½ inches wide and 3 inches long
About 1 pound solid shortening
¾ cup flour
2 eggs, lightly beaten

1. Mix together lemon juice, salt, coriander, and pepper; add oil. Toss with cardoons in a wide dish. Let marinate at room temperature for at least ½ hour.

2. Heat shortening to 350 degrees. Toss cardoons in flour, removing excess. Dip quickly in beaten eggs. Drop into hot fat, leaving some space for the pieces to swim about. Fry until browned lightly, turning once—about 2 minutes per side.

3. Drain on paper toweling. If desired, set in a 200-degree oven until all the pieces are fried, then serve at once; or serve casually, offering the fried cardoons as you cook them.

—

BRAISED CARDOONS

An old-fashioned treatment for an old-fashioned vegetable. The chopped ham, tomato, and onion offset the bitterness of the cardoons. The dish can be prepared ahead (in fact it improves with reheating), making it a fine companion for a roast. Let the dish come to room temperature before placing in the oven with the meat or poultry. (The basic preparation is the first step of this recipe, which does not follow the same treatment as the others.)

5 or 6 servings

2½ pounds cardoons, trimmed
2 tablespoons olive oil
About 2 ounces (⅓ cup) finely chopped fatty, firm, flavorful ham, such as prosciutto, Smithfield or country ham, or Westphalian ham
1 medium onion, minced
1 pound ripe plum tomatoes, peeled, seeded, and diced
Pepper to taste, salt if desired
1 cup chicken, beef, or veal stock or broth

1. Halve stalks crosswise, then halve wider base parts lengthwise. Rinse well. Drop into a very large pot of boiling water. Boil, partly covered, until barely tender—about 15 minutes.

2. Meanwhile, heat oil in heavy skillet. Add ham and onion and sauté for a few minutes over moderate heat. Add tomatoes and toss. Cover and cook over low heat until softened, about 10 minutes.

3. Cool cardoons briefly. With paring knife zip strings from each stalk, working first from one end, then the other.

4. Spread half vegetable mixture in a shallow baking-serving dish that will just hold stalks closely (about 2-quart capacity). Arrange cardoons in dish, tightly packed. Top with remaining vegetables. Sprinkle with pepper (add salt if you like, but cardoons are unusually salty, as is ham). Pour stock into skillet in which vegetables cooked. Bring to boil, then pour over cardoons. Cover with sheet of oiled waxed paper to just fit inside dish. Cover tightly with foil or close-fitting lid.

5. Bake in 350-degree oven about 1½ hours, until very tender. Remove foil and paper, raise heat to 400 degrees, and bake about ½ hour longer, to evaporate some juices and concentrate flavors.

SOUP OF PURÉED CARDOONS

This delicate purée looks and tastes as though it were made from artichoke hearts —but it entails a fraction of the labor and expense. Even heavy, stringy cardoons emerge smooth and light after straining.

4 servings

2 pounds cardoons
4 cups veal stock or beef broth
4 cups water
4 small shallots, sliced
Few sprigs parsley
½ teaspoon coriander seeds, roughly crushed
6 tablespoons white rice, preferably medium- or short-grain
Salt, white pepper, and lemon juice to taste
2 tablespoons cold butter
2 tablespoons thinly slivered, toasted almonds

1. If the bunch of cardoons is large, divide it lengthwise to obtain the amount needed; rub the cut side with lemon. Cut off base and leaves, rinse stalks well, and cut crosswise into 1–2-inch slices. Cover with cold water; bring to a boil, then drain (to remove bitterness).

2. Add stock, water, shallots, parsley, coriander, and rice to the cardoons. Simmer, partly covered, until tender— about 45 minutes.

3. Purée mixture very thoroughly in a processor or blender in batches. Strain through a sieve.

4. Return to pot. Season with salt, white pepper, and lemon juice to taste. Reheat gently. Off heat, stir in the butter. Ladle into heated bowls and sprinkle with almonds.

CASSAVA
See Yuca

CELERIAC, CELERY ROOT
(*Apium graveolens*, variety *rapaceum*)
also Knob Celery and Turnip-Rooted Celery

*I*f you have ever been to a French bistro, chances are good you began your *prix fixe* supper with a chewy, vervy salad/appetizer of julienned or shredded celeriac dressed with a sharp mustard mayonnaise—the ubiquitous *céleri* (or *céleri-rave*) remoulade. Chances are also good that it was delicious, for it is a simple dish that

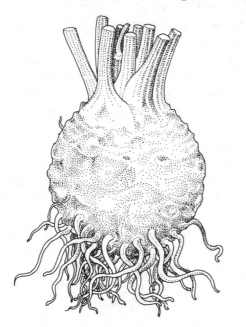

accentuates the herbaceous pungency and hardy texture of the root—and it is difficult to prepare badly. But there is more to celery root than remoulade (although that may be its finest hour), as purées, soups, braises, fritters, stuffings, and salads of Scandinavia, France, Russia, Germany, Holland, and Hungary demonstrate.

Celery root, not surprisingly, is a variety of branch celery that has been cultivated for its lowers, rather than its uppers. Although the gnarled beige vegetable has been a fixture in gardens and markets in the United States since the beginning of the nineteenth century, it is passed over by most cooks who were not raised with it on the table. Perhaps it is neglected because of its unglamorous appearance, for few who taste the zesty, parsley- and celery-scented

vegetable dislike it. The swollen form would be at home in the forest of a tale by the brothers Grimm. Between an apple and a cantaloupe in size, the lopsided sphere is embossed and channeled, decorated with whorls, crevices, and disorderly rootlets—often scruffy and muddy. But what a range of possibilities the strange creature possesses!

SELECTION AND STORAGE: Look for celery root in all markets, usually from fall through early spring. It is often stashed among parsnips, root parsley, and other similarly neutral-colored roots, which makes it difficult to locate. Sometimes it will sport celery-like leaves, often it is bald. Sniff if you're not sure; the fresh celery aroma will declare itself. Select the least convoluted exterior you can find: the smoother the skin, the easier to peel. Small- and medium-sized roots (up to a pound or so) that are comparatively heavy are firmer and smoother within, which is preferable. Press the stalk end of the root to be sure it is not soft, an indication of an undesirably spongy center.

To store the celeriac, trim off any stalks (they are fine for flavoring soups and stews, but more potent than celery, so beware). Wrapped in plastic the root will keep for more than a week in the refrigerator.

USE: You can do anything with celeriac that you can with turnips, and more. Raw, it is grated, shredded, or julienned, dressed with mayonnaise, vinaigrette, or a cream dressing, for a uniquely intense salad. For this treatment you must allow considerable mellowing, marinating time (I like to make the salad a day before I use it), so that the dense vegetable can absorb and blend with the sauce you've chosen.

For less "raw" flavor, toss the slivered root with salt and lemon juice (about 1 teaspoon salt and 1 tablespoon lemon juice per pound of celeriac) and let marinate about an hour; then rinse, drain, and dry thoroughly before dressing. Or blanch the sliced root (drop into plenty of boiling, salted water; return to a boil), then drain, freshen in cold water, drain again, and dry well for a milder, less crisp salad. Although celeriac tends to dominate, it works well in combination with watercress, beets, potatoes, carrots, walnuts, smoked meats, or sausages, in particular.

After salads, the next-best use for celeriac is in purées and soups, where it seasons, adds body, and blends, without being potently identifiable. All root vegetable soups and stews are transformed by its presence (especially in the company of members of the onion family). Peeled and sliced or cubed, celeriac needs 10–15 minutes' cooking time.

Although it is not uncommon to boil or steam celery root, I find these methods do not bring out the best in the vegetable, but rather accentuate its fibrous nature and flatten the taste. However, when the peeled and cut-up root is blanched briefly, then baked with a sauce, as in a gratin or creamed dish, the delicacy is retained. I do not find that cooking the vegetable whole (which takes considerably longer) has any virtues.

Celeriac, when braised, particularly alongside meat, tastes very different from the vegetable cooked in any other way: it lends a complex flavor to the meat juices (which it also absorbs) while retaining its own identity. In the same way, celery root makes a special poultry stuffing (all the aromas of poultry seasoning mix rolled into one vegetable). Cut into logs the size of small French fries, boil for a minute, then mix with whatever seasonings suit your bird; stuff and roast as usual.

However you decide to cook celeriac, be careful not to overcook it, for it changes rapidly from firm to mushy.

PREPARATION: Scrub celeriac thoroughly with a brush. With a very sharp knife cut off both top and bottom of the knob, hacking off all the roots as well. If you are very patient, you can use a vegetable peeler to remove all the skin, which makes for very little waste; generally it is easiest to remove the skin by cutting it off, more or less as you would from an orange. Drop the whole, or large pieces, into cold water acidulated with a little lemon juice to prevent darkening. Remember that the root absorbs the soaking water, however, so keep the pieces large and soaking time short.

NUTRITIONAL HIGHLIGHTS: Celery root is very low in calories—only about 20 per ½ cup. It contains small amounts of the B vitamins.

CELERIAC SALAD

This is a simplified, lightened version of the traditional French favorite *céleri-rave* remoulade. For variation, toss with walnuts or toasted hazelnuts; modify the flavor by sprinkling with tarragon, dill, thyme, or marjoram; add tiny cubes of smoked meat and capers; or use as part of an antipasto or appetizer plate, along with dry sausage, olives, pickles, hard-cooked eggs, and such.

4 servings

½ teaspoon coarse kosher salt, approximately
1 tablespoon sharp mustard
1½ tablespoons lemon juice
3 tablespoons olive oil
3 tablespoons sour cream
2 small celery roots, to equal about 1¼ pounds trimmed weight
1 tablespoon thin-sliced scallion greens
1 tablespoon finely minced parsley
Radicchio or red-leaf lettuce for serving

1. Blend together salt, mustard, and lemon juice in a small bowl; whisk in oil, a tablespoon at a time. Gradually add sour cream.

2. Peel and quarter celery roots. Cut out spongy core, if any. Cut in very fine julienne strips or shred in coarse pieces, using food processor or vegetable cutter.

3. With your hands, mix celeriac and dressing in a bowl, separating and tossing strands until thoroughly coated. Cover and refrigerate several hours, preferably longer; the more marinating, the better.

4. To serve, toss together celeriac, scallion, and parsley. Arrange on radicchio or lettuce.

RICHARDS' MASHED CELERIAC AND POTATOES

Richard Sax, co-author of *From the Farmers' Market*, learned this simple method of preparing aromatic celery root from Richard Olney, the chief consultant for the Time-Life Good Cook Series, when they worked together on those books. No milk, no cream, just full-strength good vegetable flavor. The butter, when added after the vegetables have cooked, binds, mellows, and softens the purée.

4–6 servings

2 medium-large celery roots (2 pounds, weighed without leaves)
3 medium all-purpose potatoes (1 pound)
2 medium garlic cloves, smashed and peeled
Salt and white pepper
Nutmeg
2 tablespoons cold unsalted butter

1. Trim, peel, and chunk celery roots (should equal about 4–5 cups). Peel and chunk potatoes (should equal 2½ generous cups).

2. Combine vegetables and garlic in saucepan with cold water to cover; salt lightly and bring to a boil, covered. Boil gently, covered, until very tender, 25–30 minutes.

3. Drain vegetables thoroughly, reserving cooking liquid. Press through food mill or sieve, using pestle or large wooden spoon. Season with salt, pepper, and nutmeg. Add cooking liquid gradually until purée has a fairly soft consistency—as much as 1–2 cups.

4. Reheat, stirring, over low heat. Remove from heat; stir in butter. Serve at once.

PURÉED CELERIAC AND POTATO SOUP

If you're one of those cooks who always use stock for soup, try water first this time: the frank celeriac and potato flavors are dandy in the foreground, instead of hidden.

If you like, serve this thick, homey family soup with a garnish—minced fresh herbs, croutons (whole-wheat are nice) sautéed in butter, snippets of ham or sausage, or whatever is on hand. The pleasing pottage is quickly assembled and, unlike most such purées, does not require mellowing time—although holding it doesn't hurt.

4 generous servings

2 tablespoons butter
2 medium onions, sliced
2 largish celery roots (2 pounds trimmed weight)
1 pound old (stored) potatoes, peeled and chunked

1¼ teaspoons salt, or to taste
Scant ½ teaspoon celery seed
3 cups water
2–3 cups milk
White pepper to taste

1. Heat butter in heavy flameproof casserole; stir in onions and toss. Cover and cook over moderately low heat, stirring occasionally, until golden—about 10 minutes.

2. Meanwhile, scrub and peel celeriac; perfect peel removal is not required, unless you object to beige soup. Cut celeriac into rough slices. Add to onions.

3. Add potatoes, salt, and celery seed; toss. Add water and 2 cups milk; simmer gently, covered, until vegetables are very tender—about 30 minutes.

4. Purée soup mixture in blender or processor in batches, keeping it chunky; it should be plumply lumpy, not refined. Return to the pot. Add milk to obtain desired consistency. Season with white pepper and salt, to taste.

GRATIN OF CELERIAC

This creamy gratin of cubed celeriac has plenty of room for variation: for a milder, starchier flavor, use half potatoes and half celeriac; for a sweeter taste, use one-third parsnip; for a main dish, add cubed smoked ham to what follows.

4 servings

2 medium-large celery roots (about 2¼ pounds)
1 cup beef broth
1 cup milk
1 cup water
½ teaspoon dried summer savory
About 1 teaspoon coarse kosher salt
2 tablespoons butter
2 tablespoons flour
½ teaspoon freshly grated nutmeg
⅔ cup finely shredded Parmesan

1. Trim and peel celeriac. Cut in ¾-inch cubes, placing them in a bowl of water as you proceed. Drain.

2. Combine in saucepan with broth, milk, water, savory, and 1 teaspoon salt; liquid should not quite cover. Gently simmer, covered, until barely tender—about 10 minutes.

3. With slotted spoon transfer cubes to buttered shallow baking dish of 1½-quart capacity. Strain and reserve liquid. Heat butter in rinsed-out saucepan. Add flour; stir on low heat until golden. Add 1½ cups cooking liquid. Whisk over moderate heat until liquid boils.

4. Sprinkle nutmeg on celeriac. Season sauce with salt and pepper to taste; pour over cubes. Sprinkle cheese to cover evenly. Bake in center of preheated 350-degree oven about 35 minutes, until lightly browned and bubbling.

RICHARD SAX'S CHICKEN WITH CELERIAC AND MUSHROOMS

Friend and author Richard Sax writes: "This is a good illustration of roasting by the method known in French as *poêler* or *en cocotte*—covered roasting on a bed of moist aromatics basted with butter. Although the bird roasts without liquid, it is essentially a moist cooking method, good for birds whose flesh could easily dry out during open roasting," such as pheasant, for which this recipe was originally developed. If you have not cooked celeriac in this way, it will be a revelation: tender, browned, rich-flavored, it also imparts its special herbal taste to the sauce.

4 servings

4 tablespoons butter

1 medium onion, chopped

1 medium carrot, in ¼-inch dice

1 small celery stalk, in ¼-inch dice

3 ounces ham, in ¼-inch dice (⅓ cup)

¼ teaspoon chopped thyme leaves plus 2 sprigs (or substitute ¼ teaspoon dried thyme for total)

6 ounces shiitake, or 8 ounces common mushrooms

3½-pound chicken and giblets (see Note)

Salt and pepper

2 small wedges onion

2 small garlic cloves, bruised and peeled

3 tablespoons olive oil

⅓ cup dry madeira

2 medium celeriac to equal about 1½ pounds (weighed without tops)

1 cup rich chicken broth

Lemon juice

2 tablespoons chopped parsley, plus sprigs for garnish

1. Heat 1 tablespoon butter in wide skillet over medum heat; add onion, carrot, celery, ham, and chopped thyme (or ⅛ teaspoon dried thyme). Chop mushroom stems and add. Sauté about 10 minutes, until softened. Transfer to Dutch oven or heavy flameproof casserole to fit chicken fairly closely, with just enough space for celeriac slices.

2. Pat chicken dry; season inside and out with salt and pepper. Tuck onion wedges, thyme sprigs (or ⅛ teaspoon dried thyme), and garlic in cavity. Truss chicken to make compact package.

3. Heat 1 tablespoon butter and 1 tablespoon oil in skillet.Place bird on its side in fat and tuck giblets around it. Cook over moderate heat, shaking skillet to prevent sticking, until golden, 3–4 minutes. Turn gently with wooden spoons and brown on all sides in same way. Place breast side up in casserole. Scatter giblets (minus liver, which is for the cook) around bird. Pour 1 tablespoon fat from skillet over breast; discard remainder (do not wash pan).

4. Cover casserole tightly and set in preheated 350-degree oven. Roast 50 minutes, basting once with pan juices. Meanwhile, pour madeira into skillet and bring to boil, stirring. Strain into a small cup and set aside.

5. Peel celeriac. Quarter lengthwise; remove any spongy pith. Cut into slices ¼ inch wide. Heat 1 tablespoon each butter and oil in pan. Add slices, sprinkle with salt and pepper, then cook over moderate heat until browned, about 5–7 minutes. Tuck celeriac slices around chicken; pour over madeira mixture. Roast, covered, until bird and celeriac are tender, 10–15 minutes longer.

6. Meanwhile, cut mushroom caps in wide slices or wedges. Heat 1 tablespoon each oil and butter in skillet and sauté until softened, 4–5 minutes. Add a few tablespoons broth and cook until evaporated. Cover skillet and set aside.

7. Carefully transfer bird to oval serving platter; remove string. With slotted spoon transfer celeriac (leaving chopped vegetables in casserole) to platter; add mushrooms. Cover lightly with foil and set in turned-off oven.

8. Place casserole over high heat and add remaining chicken broth. Boil to reduce by about half. Strain sauce and spoon off fat. Add drops of lemon juice to taste; correct seasonings. Sprinkle parsley over celeriac and mushrooms. Garnish bird with sprigs. Serve at once, passing sauce separately in heated pitcher.

Note: I find poultry browns better if dried for a day or more in the refrigerator: If you have time, remove giblets, pat bird dry with towel, then set on paper towel on a dish, uncovered. Turn a few times to dry evenly. Let come to room temperature before browning.

If you wish to prepare this dish with pheasant, cut the cooking time in step 4 to 25 minutes. A bird of 2½ to 2¾ pounds will feed 3.

SALAD OF SEAFOOD, CELERIAC, AND CELERY, SICILIAN-STYLE

When Sicilians cook seafood, they rarely add herbs or seasonings, but in this unusual salad the fragrant celeriac and celery add herbal depth, as well as a welcome crunch.

6 servings, as a main course

2 cups water
2 bay leaves
1 small onion, halved
2 peeled garlic cloves
1 teaspoon coarse kosher salt
½ cup lemon juice
½ cup full-flavored olive oil
1½ pounds cleaned small squid (see Note)
1 pound small shrimp in the shell, rinsed
¾ pound celeriac (weighed without tops)
3 or 4 tender celery stalks
2–3 tablespoons capers, rinsed
Thinly sliced scallion greens from ½ bunch (about ⅓ cup)
Radicchio rosso or red oakleaf lettuce for garnish

1. Combine water, bay leaves, onion, garlic, salt, ¼ cup lemon juice, and ¼ cup olive oil in 2–3-quart nonaluminum saucepan. Cover and boil gently 15–20 minutes.

2. Meanwhile, cut squid across into ⅛–¼-inch rings. Cut tentacles into bite-sized pieces, if large; place in mixing bowl.

3. Strain solids from stock; return liquid to saucepan. Add squid and simmer 1–2 minutes, until opaque. Remove with slotted spoon; reserve. Add shrimp to broth and bring to a boil, stirring. Remove from heat and let stand, covered, 3–4 minutes. With slotted spoon transfer to dish to cool.

4. Boil stock to reduce to ¾ cup. Pour into mixing bowl with squid. Peel shrimp and halve lengthwise, removing veins. Add to squid. Cool, cover, and chill, preferably overnight.

5. Peel celeriac; quarter lengthwise. Cut out and discard any spongy core. Cut celeriac in very fine julienne strips, using processor, vegetable cutter, or mandoline. Toss strips with remaining ¼ cup each lemon juice and oil.

6. Halve celery stalks along their length, then cut across on slant in narrow slices. Add to celeriac and toss.

7. About ½ hour before serving, add celeriac and celery to seafood. Add capers to taste, then scallions. Toss gently to mix. Season. Arrange radicchio around edge of platter and salad in center.

Note: If you are not familiar with squid cleaning, it is simple—more so than writing the directions, which follow: Holding body (mantle) with one hand and tentacle part with the other, pull to separate the two: the viscera and ink sac will come out attached to tentacle section. Cut tentacle section from head part and discard latter. Squeeze bony beak from center of tentacles; it will pop out. Pull out clear plastic-like pen or sword from mantle section and discard. Peel purplish membrane from this section, working under running water. Carefully wash mantle inside and out, emptying it of any remaining material.

CELERY ROOT
See Celeriac

CÈPE (OR CEP)
See Bolete

CERIMAN
See Monstera

CHANTERELLE
(Cantharellus cibarius)
also Girolle, Pfifferling

*T*he lovely chanterelle mushroom, pretty as its name, cannot be cultivated, only gathered—in this country, usually from the wilds of the Pacific Northwest and a few places on the East Coast. Although there are numerous delectables in the family of Cantharellaceae—most notably the black trumpet *(Craterellus fallax)* and white chan-

terelle *(Cantharellus subalbidus)*—it is the apricot-gold-to-orange variety shaped like a trumpet flower (usually called simply "chanterelle") that is most commonly marketed here. While the *succès fou* of the delightful fungus is relatively recent here, the chanterelle has long been a European favorite. As a matter of fact, we export a vast quantity to Europe, a good percentage of which returns to our country expensively and less than deliciously canned and dried. Fresh mushrooms, however, are predict-

ably tasty—although you cannot always tell what the taste will be. There is enormous variation in flavor (and size) among chanterelles from different locations: they can range from pleasantly mild and meaty to flowery, nutty, and softly cinnamony.

SELECTION AND STORAGE: Look for chanterelles from summer through winter, with a good deal of erratic activity during that period. Select by gently stroking the frilled edges to see that they are firm, plump, and spongy; of these, pick out the cleanest. Beware of broken, moist caps or shriveled, dry ones. Inhale the aroma: if it is fleeting, you will have a delicately flavored cooked dish; if the scent is intense, it generally remains that way. Store in a single layer in a basket or dish, lightly covered with a barely moist piece of cheesecloth. If purchased in peak condition, chanterelles should last about a week.

USE: Chanterelles have a natural affinity for chicken and other light meats, such as rabbit, veal, Cornish hen, quail, and pheasant—whether used as stuffing, a sauce component, or side dish. They also love cream, and starches and grains (as do most mushrooms) such as pasta, brown and white rice, cornmeal, millet, and kasha. Or sauté the fungi momentarily in olive oil for a warm composed salad. Whichever way you use them, keep it simple: the flavor is obscured by complex or assertive seasonings.

PREPARATION: If possible, it is best to clean chanterelles by brushing them with a soft paintbrush (not one of those abrasive "mushroom brushes"). While it is never desirable to immerse mushrooms in water, it is often impossible to find chanterelles that are clean. Therefore, quickly toss the mushrooms in a strainer under running water, bouncing lightly to remove soil. Immediately blot dry on a large, soft towel. Trim the heavy tips off the bases and discard. If large, cut mushrooms into bite-sized pieces; if small, leave whole.

NUTRITIONAL HIGHLIGHTS: Chanterelles are very low in calories. They also contribute thiamine, riboflavin, and niacin, and are a good source of fiber.

SAUTÉED-BRAISED CHANTERELLES

I find that most wild mushrooms respond best to a combination of sauté cooking and a short bath in hot broth and wine. While timing for each batch of mushrooms will vary, as will the amount of liquid needed, the basic technique allows the fresh flavor of the mushrooms to come through without their becoming oil- or butter-soaked.

4 servings

1 pound chanterelles, cleaned, as needed (see Preparation)

2–3 tablespoons butter

About 1 cup veal or chicken stock

About ⅓ cup dry white wine or ¼ cup dry vermouth

Salt and pepper to taste

Optional: Small amount of minced parsley and/or chives

1. Trim off base tips from chanterelles. Leave mushrooms whole, if tiny, or cut large ones into bite-size pieces.

2. Heat butter in a large skillet; stir in mushrooms and sauté over moderate heat until barely softened. Add stock and cook over high heat until most liquid has been absorbed. Add wine and toss until almost evaporated. Season and serve with herbs, if desired.

Note: The wine can be omitted for a different, less-diffuse flavor.

WARM SALAD OF TWO MUSHROOMS, CELERY, AND PARMESAN

For this luxurious dish, find the freshest *parmigiano-reggiano* available. The special nuttiness of this famed cheese adds depth to the mushrooms and tastes wonderful with wine, which you can enjoy wholeheartedly with this vinegar-free first course.

6 servings

1 tablespoon dry vermouth
1 tablespoon lemon juice
¼ teaspoon salt
7 tablespoons full-flavored olive oil
1 large garlic clove, halved
¾ pound medium-sized chanterelles, cleaned (see Preparation)
½ pound small button mushrooms
¾ pound soft red-leaf lettuce, rinsed and dried, torn in pieces
1 cup tender celery heart, cut into thin julienne strips
3 ounces soft, fresh Parmesan cheese, shredded with a vegetable peeler

1. Preheat oven to 450 degrees. Blend vermouth, lemon juice, salt, and 3 tablespoons oil in a small jar. Rub a serving bowl with ½ garlic clove.

2. Remove stems from chanterelles; reserve for another use. Cut caps into thin strips. Wipe the button mushrooms clean and cut both stems and caps into thin strips. Toss button mushrooms, lettuce, and dressing in the bowl. Arrange on 6 serving plates.

3. Heat remaining 4 tablespoons oil and garlic in medium skillet; when garlic is golden, discard it. Add chanterelles and celery and toss to coat with oil. Set at once in top level of oven and bake 2 minutes, until chanterelles just cook through. Divide over lettuce, top with Parmesan, and serve immediately.

Note: Oyster mushrooms or shiitake can replace chanterelles.

CHICKEN BREASTS WITH CHANTERELLES AND CREAM

Chicken and chanterelles have an affinity that is as strong as the one between chanterelles and cream: therefore, this is trebly delicious.

4 servings

2 large chicken breasts, bones in (about 2¼ pounds total weight)
2 celery stalks with leaves, sliced
2 carrots, sliced
2 cups water
3 tablespoons butter
3 tablespoons minced shallots
1 pound chanterelles, cleaned (see Preparation), trimmed, and cut into bite-size pieces
¼ cup dry white wine or dry vermouth
Salt and pepper to taste
⅓ cup heavy (or whipping) cream
Minced parsley

1. Remove chicken bones; break them up and combine in a pot with the celery, carrots, and water. Simmer, partly covered, for ¾–1 hour. Uncover; boil to reduce stock to 1 cup. Meanwhile, discard chicken skin and loose fat. Slice meat in julienne strips; reserve.

2. Melt butter in wide, heavy skillet; add shallots and stir over moderately low heat until slightly softened—about 2 minutes. Add chanterelles and toss to coat. Add the stock, then stir over high heat until about half of the liquid evaporates.

3. Add wine; stir until most boils off. Add salt and pepper. Add cream and stir until it is almost absorbed. Add chicken; toss until just cooked through—about 1 minute. Sprinkle with parsley, and serve.

CHANTERELLE-STUFFED ROCK CORNISH HENS WITH FETTUCCINE

Savory and satisfying, this meal of golden mushrooms and hens should feed 6 average eaters. A fresh Rock Cornish hen weighs about 1½ pounds (a minimum is bone; most is pure meat), which will be plenty for two diners, especially with the buttery chanterelles and fettuccine. But, because it has been customary to serve these birds whole, one to each diner, follow whatever your heritage dictates. Incidentally, do not view the spices in the ingredient list with suspicion: they do not overpower the gentle chanterelles, but serve to underscore their natural flavor. Sip a cool California Chardonnay or a Meursault.

6 servings

4 tablespoons butter

2 tablespoons minced shallots

¾ pound chanterelles, cleaned (see Preparation), in bite-sized pieces

1¼ teaspoons salt

3 large, fresh Rock Cornish hens, giblets reserved for another use

½ teaspoon ground cinnamon

¾ teaspoon ground cardamom

1 cup chicken or veal stock

Soft greens for the platter, such as Boston, Bibb, or mâche

1 pound fresh fettuccine

⅓ cup toasted or roasted almonds (not blanched), coarsely slivered

1. Melt 2 tablespoons butter in skillet over moderately low heat; stir in shallots. When slightly softened, add chanterelles. Stir over moderate heat until tender—about 5 minutes; do not sear, but cook gently, raising heat only at the end to evaporate some juices, if necessary. Transfer to a dish, toss with ¼ teaspoon salt; let cool.

2. Rinse hens and pat dry. Remove loose fat. Combine ¾ teaspoon salt, cinnamon, and cardamom. Sprinkle a scant ¼ teaspoon in each bird. Rub remaining mixture evenly over them; set them on a rack, and let stand 1–2 hours to season. (See Note.)

3. Fill cavities of hens with chanterelles. Sew openings closed with a needle and white thread. Truss birds and set breast down on a rack.

4. Roast in preheated 375-degree oven for 30 minutes. Turn birds over; smear breasts with 1 tablespoon butter. Sprinkle with remaining ¼ teaspoon salt. Raise heat to 400 degrees and roast birds, basting often, until golden, not dark brown—about 40 minutes.

5. Transfer to a cutting board. Add stock to roasting pan, place over high heat, and stir until reduced by about half. Cut birds in half lengthwise with a heavy knife; scrape stuffing and juices into roasting pan. Arrange hens on the lettuce-garnished platter.

6. Boil fettuccine in salted water for about 1½ minutes, or until barely tender. Drain, toss in a heated serving dish with last tablespoon butter, chanterelles, and sauce; check seasoning. Sprinkle with the almonds and serve at once.

Note: I find that poultry browns better if the skin dries for a while before roasting. If you have additional time, set the seasoned hens on a paper-towel-covered rack and refrigerate, turning occasionally, for a day or two. Let reach room temperature before roasting.

❧ *Chanterelles can be substituted for oyster mushrooms in the Puffy Mushroom Oven Pancake, page 335.*

CHARD
See Swiss Chard

CHAYOTE
(Sechium edule)
also Mirliton, Christophine, Chocho, Vegetable Pear, Sousous, Chuchu, Choko, Custard Marrow, Pepinella, Xuxu

*R*oughly pear-shaped and -sized, with uneven furrows running its length, the versatile chayote (chy-O-tay) may be celadon, alabaster-cream, or dark green in color. It may have a fairly smooth skin or a hairbrush-like array of nonsticking prickles covering it. The pale flesh is crisp and fine-textured, with a taste and consistency that

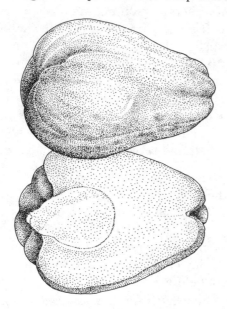

blend cucumber, zucchini, and a bit of kohlrabi. Although I have read about many different sizes and varieties of chayote, I have usually encountered the pale ice-green or apple-green ones, either deeply ridged or rather smooth-skinned. Free of soft, spiny protrusions, unlike many varieties, these generally weigh from ½ to 1 pound, with ¾ the average specimen.

The chayote grows on a hardy vine that has tangled itself irrevocably in the cuisines of lands as far-flung as the West Indies, South and Central America, India, North Africa, Indonesia, New Zealand, and Australia. In many countries its young shoots and flowers are eaten, as well as its tuberous roots. Horticulturists have rated its nectar-rich blossoms among the finest honey producers. It is difficult to imagine, therefore, why a simple, charming, unaffected member of the gourd family that was cultivated close by in Central America as far back as the ancient Aztecs and Mayans (the word *chayotli* is the name for the vegetable in the Aztec language, Nahuatl) could have traveled so far from home before being noticed in the rest of America.

The chayote (which although part of the Cucurbit clan is not of the same genus as squash and pumpkin) is grown only in pockets of this country: in Louisiana (as mirliton); in the Southwest, where it continues a Mexican tradition; and in Florida. It is also shipped from Costa Rica and Puerto Rico to a scattering of markets nationwide. The majority of the shipments find their way into the hands of newcomers to America who have been raised with the vegetable as a staple in their kitchens. This is good news for those of us who have not, because it means that the useful chayote is slowly becoming a supermarket standard in many cities.

SELECTION AND STORAGE: Supplies are most abundant in the winter, but, because chayotes may be shipped from various sources, you can find them year round, unpredictably. Sometimes they will appear in Oriental markets, sometimes in Spanish-American, sometimes in West Indian, sometimes in large supermarkets, depending upon their place of origin. Look for very firm, unblemished chayotes. Although most cooks agree that the smallest are most tender, French West Indians recommend the more mature fruit, in which the stem end has opened to reveal a germinating seed. I have found both closed and open specimens to be delicious, and smaller ones to be slightly more tender.

It's worth picking up a few chayotes even if you don't know just when you'll prepare them. Lightly wrapped and refrigerated, they store for weeks—even up to a month, if in good condition—unlike zucchini, pattypan, or other tender squashes.

USE: Chayote can be used in the same way that you would all summer squashes—and more. Because it has a firmer texture, it needs more cooking time (figure 20–25 minutes, in general), but holds up better than the others when stuffed or used in salads (always cooked, not raw). Although most recipes recommend jazzing up chayote's faint flavor with aggressive seasoning, I like to retain the delicacy—with the chayote puréed in cream soup, steamed and sliced in light salads, sautéed with butter and herbs, creamed in gratins, or simply steamed. In some countries, chayotes are favored for pickles and chutneys. They blend particularly well with seafood or ham, whether in soup, a stir-fry, a casserole, or a fried mixture.

In Latin America the vegetable is most commonly halved and stuffed—as either main course or dessert—with raisins, nuts, brown sugar, and eggs. (In Jamaica it is the fruit of "apple pie.") Although stuffing is traditionally accomplished without peeling the chayote, I prefer to peel and partly cook the shells, then bake the stuffed vegetable until tender.

PREPARATION: Unless you can get tiny chayotes you will need to peel them carefully; the skin is surprisingly tough, once cooked. Depending upon the dish (and how annoyingly furrowed or sweetly smooth the squash may be), this can be done before cooking, with a vegetable peeler, or afterward, by simply pulling off the skin. If the very slippery substance that oozes out as you peel is bothersome, oil your hands lightly or work under running water. It has been known to irritate and even numb the skin of some cooks. The mucilaginous material completely disappears in the cooking, by the way, although it lends a tiny bit of substance to clear soups. Don't discard the large edible seed; cook it along with the squash for a delicious nibble that tastes somewhere between a lima bean and an almond.

NUTRITIONAL HIGHLIGHTS: Chayote is very low in calories—about 40 per cup. It is very low in sodium, a good source of potassium, and a fairly good source of fiber.

BASIC CHAYOTE

To prepare chayotes as a simple side dish, you can either bake them or sauté them, depending upon what the rest of the meal will be. Unadorned, chayote has the sweet freshness of very firm cucumber, with a touch of yellow-summer-squash flavor. For variety you can add garlic, shallot, or onion to the general recipe that follows, then finish it off with a touch of fresh herbs (such as chives, chervil, marjoram) or toasted, buttered bread crumbs or grated cheese.

For each person allow about ½ pound chayote and 1 tablespoon butter or oil, decreasing the amount of fat as you increase the amount of chayote. Peel chayotes thoroughly (see Preparation). Cut crosswise into ¼-inch slices, halving large center cuts.

To bake, arrange pieces in a buttered baking dish, overlapping; sprinkle with salt and pepper and dot with butter or drizzle with oil. Cover with foil. Bake in preheated 350-degree oven until tender, 20–25 minutes. Uncover, baste; bake 10 minutes longer, until juices have evaporated somewhat. Add optional herbs if desired. Serve hot.

To pan-cook, heat large, heavy skillet and melt butter or heat oil. Add sliced chayote and cook over moderate heat, tossing often, until tender throughout—about 15 minutes; lower heat, if necessary, to prevent browning of slices, which affects delicate flavor. Sprinkle with salt, pepper, and optional herbs; scoop into a heated dish and serve at once.

CREAMY CHAYOTE SOUP WITH SHRIMP

Offer this pale, smooth soup for a first course. Although each serving contains a generous portion of succulent pink shrimp, the flavor is too delicate for a main course.
4 servings

½ pound small shrimp in the shell, rinsed
1 celery stalk with leaves, cut up
1 cup water
2 large chayotes (1¾ pounds) peeled (see Preparation)
2 tablespoons butter
2 large shallots, minced (¼ cup)
1½ tablespoons flour
2 cups veal or chicken stock (should be homemade for this)
White pepper
About 2 tablespoons finely minced dill

Salt
About ⅓ cup heavy (or whipping) cream
Few tablespoons dry white wine or sake to taste

1. Peel shrimp; combine shells in a saucepan with the celery and water. Simmer, covered, for 20 minutes. Meanwhile, devein shrimp and halve lengthwise. Cut chayotes into large chunks, reserving one-quarter of one. Strain shrimp stock.

2. Heat 1½ tablespoons butter in a casserole; add shallots and stir over low heat until somewhat softened. Add flour; stir for 2 minutes. Pour in shrimp stock and bring to a boil, stirring.

3. Add chayotes; add veal stock and white pepper to taste. Simmer, covered, until very tender—about 30 minutes. Meanwhile, cut the reserved chayote piece into very very fine julienne strips. Toss in a bowl with the shrimp, 1 tablespoon dill, and ¼ teaspoon salt.

4. Process soup in batches to a very smooth purée. Return to pot; stir in cream, salt and pepper to taste. Add wine; set over lowest heat.

5. Heat remaining ½ tablespoon butter in a skillet; stir in the shrimp mixture, cover, and steam on low heat until just cooked through—less than a minute. Divide the mixture among 4 heated bowls. Pour soup over, and top with remaining dill to taste.

HOT AND SOUR SOUP WITH CHAYOTE, SHRIMP, AND MUSHROOMS

A snappy, tart broth thick with chayote, mushrooms, and shrimp, this soup of East Asian origin makes an unusual first course for a simple meal. The authentic versions are assertively hot and sour, but you can adjust the balance slowly to your taste.

6 servings as a first course

½ pound small shrimp, rinsed
Rind of 1 small lemon
Optional: Thin, grassy top part of lemon-grass stalk (see page 275)
½ teaspoon allspice berries (whole allspice)
2 garlic cloves, sliced
About 3 tablespoons Chinese oyster sauce (see Note)
5 cups water
1 medium chayote (¾ pound), peeled and cut in ⅛–¼-inch dice (see Preparation)
6 ounces small mushrooms, sliced thin
About 2 teaspoons chili-garlic paste (see Note)
About ¼ cup lemon juice
Cilantro leaves to taste

1. Peel shrimp; combine shells in a pot with lemon rind, optional lemon grass, allspice, garlic, 2 tablespoons oyster sauce, and water. Simmer, covered, for 15–20 minutes.

2. Strain shrimp broth, discarding solids. Return to the pot with the chayote; simmer until not quite tender, 5–6 minutes.

3. Devein and halve shrimp lengthwise; add to soup with mushrooms and 1 teaspoon chili paste. Bring soup to a boil, stirring until shrimps turn pink. Slowly add lemon juice, chili paste, and oyster sauce to taste. Stir in cilantro and serve.

Note: Oyster sauce and chili-garlic paste are available in most Oriental groceries and in many specialty shops. Like so many Oriental supplies, they last for ages and are worth stocking, even for occasional use.

GRATIN OF CHAYOTES AND POTATOES

Traditional creamed potatoes—with a few twists. Potato dice are combined with pale green chayote cubes and baked in a creamy sauce that turns apricot from the minced red peppers. Although the nutmeg may sound excessive, it isn't, if you use fluffy, freshly grated nutmeg; in fact, it is quite delicate.

6 servings

1¼ pounds chayotes (2 medium), peeled (see Preparation)
1¼ pounds potatoes
4 tablespoons butter
¼ cup chopped shallots
1 medium red bell pepper, chopped fine
2½ tablespoons flour
1¼ cups milk
⅓ cup heavy (or whipping) cream
¾ teaspoon salt
¾ teaspoon freshly grated nutmeg
White pepper to taste
¾ cup grated Parmesan or Gruyère cheese

1. Cut chayotes (and seed) in ½-inch dice. Peel potatoes and cut in dice the same size. Drop potatoes into pot of boiling salted water. Boil about 2 minutes, until half-cooked. Add chayotes and boil about 3–4 minutes longer, until tender. Drain.

2. Melt 2 tablespoons butter in saucepan over low heat. Stir in shallots and pepper and cook until soft, about 10 minutes. Scoop into dish. In same pan melt remaining 2 tablespoons butter. Add flour and stir for a minute. Add milk and cream and stir with whisk over moderate heat until mixture boils and thickens. Lower heat and stir 2 minutes longer. Return shallots and pepper to pan with sauce; add salt, nutmeg, and white pepper. Bring to a simmer. Remove from heat and stir in ¼ cup cheese.

3. Spread potatoes and chayotes in shallow baking dish of about 8-cup capacity. Add sauce and mix gently with rubber spatula. Smooth top and sprinkle evenly with remaining ½ cup cheese. Cover with foil. (Can be made ahead, cooled and refrigerated; bring to room temperature and add 5–10 minutes to baking time if you do this.)

4. Bake in upper level of 350-degree oven until bubbling, about 20 minutes. Remove foil and bake about 10–15 minutes longer, until lightly browned. Serve hot.

CHAYOTES STUFFED WITH PORK, GINGER, AND MINT

Savory and satisfying, this combination of flavors may taste unusual, but not odd. You can present the dish as part of a large buffet or a traditional Asian meal; or serve it as a main course.

4 servings as a side dish or part of a large meal
2 servings as a main course

2 chayotes, about ¾ pound each, peeled (see Preparation), halved

1 tablespoon peanut oil

½ cup minced scallions (white part only)

1 piece ginger, about 1 inch wide and 1½ inches long, coarsely grated (no need to peel)

½ pound ground pork (preferably a coarse grind)

About 2 tablespoons fish sauce (*nuoc mam:* see Note)

2 very thin slices whole-wheat or white sandwich bread, cubed

½ teaspoon grated lemon rind (see Note)

About 3 tablespoons minced fresh mint

1 egg, beaten slightly

1. Place chayotes in skillet or saucepan of boiling salted water to just cover. Simmer until barely tender, about 10–15 minutes. Cool slightly. With melon-ball cutter (or teaspoon) scoop out flesh and soft seed, leaving a ¼-inch shell. Chop pulp and seed.

2. Heat oil in skillet; stir in scallions, ginger, and pork; stir and break up mixture over moderate heat until pork loses its pinkness. Add chopped chayotes and 1 tablespoon fish sauce; stir 2 minutes over high heat.

3. Scrape mixture into a bowl. Whirl bread in processor or blender to make fine crumbs; stir into stuffing mixture with lemon, 2 tablespoons mint, egg, and fish sauce to taste. Divide evenly among shells, heaping and packing to make a neat mound in each. Set in lightly oiled baking dish to fit closely.

4. Bake in preheated 400-degree oven until stuffing is browned and firm—about 30–35 minutes.

Note: Nuoc mam, a salty sauce often compared to soy sauce, is readily available in Oriental groceries. Vietnamese and Thai brands are recommended. If you have lemon grass (see page 274), chop ½ teaspoon and add to stuffing mixture, reducing lemon rind to ¼ teaspoon.

SALAD OF CHAYOTES, CORN, AND TOMATOES

This very pretty salad, mellow and slightly tart, should please summer diners (and lunchers).

6 servings as a side dish

2 medium chayotes, about ¾ pound each
3 medium ears of corn, husked
6 medium plum tomatoes (about 1 pound), peeled (see page 23), cut in ½-inch dice
3 tablespoons thinly sliced scallion greens
⅓ cup lime juice
½ teaspoon salt, or to taste
⅛ teaspoon crushed hot pepper flakes, or to taste
½ cup light olive oil
⅓ cup minced parsley

1. Quarter chayotes and set on a steamer rack over boiling water; cover and cook until not quite tender—about 20–25 minutes. Set corn on rack during the last 7–8 minutes. Let both cool briefly. Pull off all peel from the chayotes and cut flesh into ½-inch cubes.

2. Cut corn kernels from the cobs; combine in a bowl with chayotes, tomatoes, and scallions. Blend together lime juice, salt, and red pepper flakes. Beat in olive oil. Toss gently with vegetables, then add parsley. Chill until serving time.

SALAD OF CHAYOTES, SUGAR SNAP PEAS, AND RADICCHIO

A beautiful salad of tender chayote dice and crisp sugar snap peas nestled in leaves of striated maroon and white radicchio. Served around a sauced cold poached fish or chicken, it will make a handsome spring or summer dinner.

6 servings as side dish or first course

2 small chayotes, about ½ pound each
¾ pound sugar snap peas
2 tablespoons lemon juice
2 tablespoons white wine vinegar
¼ teaspoon salt, or to taste
About ⅛ teaspoon white pepper
⅓ cup light olive oil
3 tablespoons minced fresh basil
1 tablespoon finely minced scallion green
½ pound radicchio rosso (or variegated variety), rinsed and dried

1. Quarter chayotes and set on steamer rack over boiling water. Cover and cook until barely tender—from 15 to 25 minutes. Meanwhile, zip strings from both sides of each sugar snap pea with help of a paring knife. Add peas to chayotes during last 5 minutes of cooking.

2. Drop vegetables in ice water. Drain at once, then dry thoroughly. Peel chayotes carefully; cut into ¼–½-inch dice. Refrigerate peas.

3. Blend together lemon juice, vinegar, salt, and pepper; beat in oil. Reserve one-quarter; toss remainder with chayotes, basil, and scallion. Cool, then cover and refrigerate.

4. To serve, arrange a few radicchio leaves, cup-like, on each serving plate. Toss chayotes; season with salt, pepper, and vinegar. Heap into leaves, scatter peas over all, then drizzle over reserved dressing.

CHERIMOYA
(Annona cherimola)
sometimes called Custard Apple (which is properly *Annona reticulata*)

*A*lthough many consider this unusual fruit unattractive, I find it stunning—like a pre-Columbian jade pine cone, or the finial for a giant Inca four-poster bed. The word *cherimoya* (cheree-MOY-a), as a matter of fact, comes from the ancient Quechua (Incan) language. The fruit originated in the same area, the South American highlands,

and may be the earliest recorded New World fruit. For centuries it and other members of the Annonaceous family have been cultivated in South and Central America and the Caribbean, primarily for local use. Commercial plantings are increasing in South America, Spain, and Chile and are now being established in Australia and New Zealand. We have quite a substantial crop coming of age in California, as well. But, because the cherimoya is sensitive to extremes of heat and cold, requires complicated and time-consuming pollinating techniques, must be harvested by hand, and bruises extremely easily, its future, however heavenly its taste, may not be secure in this country.

Because there are a number of varieties being cultivated, it is somewhat misleading to generalize about the flavor of cherimoyas as a group. But a few characteristics will be common. When in prime condition, the sweet, low-acid flesh is silky smooth and juicy, cream-colored, with a slight granular finish, like a custard of fine pears. The flavor may touch on mango, pineapple, papaya, and vanilla custard, in varying proportions. If you do not fall in love at first bite, try again: chances are good that one of the varieties will delight—unless you are not a fancier of the very slightly fermented, musky taste of most tropical fruits. Even exquisite specimens of the fruit abound with fat, shiny-dark, watermelon-style seeds; so be warned, if you're a seed fusser. If the crops succeed, however, seedless or near-seedless varieties will not be far off.

SELECTION AND STORAGE: Finding cherimoyas in great shape is not an easy task. Despite its embossed leather-like exterior, the fruit is easily damaged, particularly by jostling and severe cold. Unfortunately, its season is winter through early spring, so it often risks being frozen in transport. Like the avocado, it is picked hard to ripen at room temperature. Also like the avocado, it deteriorates when chilled prior to ripening.

Select fruit of any size (the range is large, from ½ to about 2 pounds, but small and large taste the same) that is firm and slightly yellow-green, or with a little give if you want to eat it within a day or so. Avoid fruits that are dark or splotched with many dark areas, as they may have been subjected to cold in transit and will not ripen properly. (Surface scars, however—not generalized discoloration—are normal, caused by the fruit rubbing against a leaf or twig while growing.)

Store cherimoyas at room temperature until soft as an almost ripe avocado, not more. As they ripen, many varieties become more dull and grayish, sometimes speckled with tan, but some remain pale green. Do not let them become squishy-soft. Once ripened—which takes less time than you might imagine, a few days at most—cherimoyas can be refrigerated for 4–5 days, carefully protected from bumping, which will bruise them.

USE: Serve chilled (the difference between warm and cold fruit is amazing) cherimoya in the half-shell, to best savor it. Simply halve lengthwise, and offer spoons (I like the tidiness of grapefruit spoons). Although diners will have to wade through the heavy seeds, there is no other way to get the full effect. Or assemble an unusual fruit mélange: Quarter the cherimoya, cut out the central fiber, then peel; cut each quarter into thin lengthwise slices and pick out the seeds with a knife tip. Combine the pieces with delicate fruits, such as grapes, melon, tender-fleshed pears, or berries. Or sieve the cherimoya to make a custard-like sauce, adding a little cream and nutmeg, if you like; or sharpen with a few drops of lemon, lime, tangerine, or orange juice. Serve with delicate cakes, crêpes, or poached fruit, or in any way that you might a crème anglaise or pouring custard. Or incorporate into a mousse or Bavarian cream or custard or chiffon pie filling.

NUTRITIONAL HIGHLIGHTS: Cherimoya is moderately high in calories. It is high in fiber and provides a fair amount of vitamin C and niacin.

CHERIMOYA AND ORANGE WITH CHERIMOYA CREAM

If you're fortunate enough to acquire a windfall of cherimoyas and find that simply spooning the creamy pulp from its shell is no longer satisfying, try this slightly fancified fruit cup, which neither overwhelms the delicate flavor of the fruit nor hides its special texture.

2 servings

¾–1 pound cherimoya, chilled
1 large navel orange, chilled
About 1 tablespoon Cointreau, or other
　orange liqueur
¼ cup heavy (or whipping) cream, lightly
　whipped to soft peaks

1. Halve the cherimoya; pull off the skin. Cut half into small wedges, removing the seeds as you proceed; divide between 2 dessert dishes. Cut the skin and pith from the orange, then cut between the membrane sections to free the orange pulp. Cut these wedges into 2 or 3 pieces each. Divide the orange evenly between the serving dishes.

2. Pick the seeds out of the remaining cherimoya half. Combine the flesh and 1 tablespoon orange liqueur in the container of a blender; purée to a smooth, homogenized consistency. Add liqueur to taste. Pour the purée over the whipped cream and fold in gently but thoroughly. Spoon over the fruit and serve.

CHERIMOYA-MELON BASKET

For this easy, luxurious fruit cup (literally), you'll need one of the very small, very sweet melons—such as the Israeli Ogen melon or the Charentais or whatever baby hybrid is available in your market—that is just the right size for two portions. Serve for a gala breakfast or brunch, or as the finale to a rich meal.

2 servings

1 very small, perfectly ripe melon
1 medium cherimoya, about ¾ pound
Lime juice to taste
Tiny mint sprigs or lemon balm for
　garnish

1. Using a noncorrodible chef's knife, cut through the melon rind and flesh in a neat zigzag pattern around the equator of the fruit. Scoop out and discard seeds. Cut a thin sliver from the base of each half so melon "bowls" will not tip. Using a small melon-ball cutter, remove the flesh, leaving an even, pretty edge along the zigzags. Place balls in a wide dish.

2. Cut cherimoya in eighths lengthwise. Pick out all the seeds. Cut pulp into neat pieces, removing it from peel as you proceed. If there are few seeds (which is unlikely), use melon-ball cutter. Toss gently with melon and lime juice to taste. Refrigerate.

3. When fruit has chilled briefly—about 30 minutes will do—mound neatly in the melon shells, placing the tidier melon balls on top. Garnish with mint.

CHERIMOYA-PINEAPPLE MOUSSE

Creamy, with a very slightly granular texture (like that of ripe pears), this light dessert has a complex flavor—like a bouquet of exotic fruits.

I'm fond of the bit of tartness and perfume that pineapple lends, but others have preferred the slightly more bland, full creaminess of cherimoya alone. If you wish the latter, leave out the pineapple, double the amount of cherimoya, soak the gelatine in ¼ cup pineapple juice or orange juice instead of the reserved syrup, and add another tablespoon of superfine sugar. Taste for additional lime juice before chilling.

6 servings

1 tender-ripe cherimoya, about 1 pound
About 2 tablespoons lime juice
8¼-ounce can pineapple chunks in heavy syrup (1 cup)
1 envelope unflavored gelatine
About 2 tablespoons sugar
2 large eggs, separated, "strings" removed
Big pinch salt
1 tablespoon superfine sugar, approximately
½ cup heavy (or whipping) cream
Lime slivers for garnish

1. Halve cherimoya and scoop flesh into processor, carefully removing all seeds as you go. Add 2 tablespoons lime juice; purée. Scoop into a 2-cup measure. Drain pineapple and reserve juice; purée pineapple and add to cherimoya. There should be 2 cups fruit.

2. Sprinkle gelatine over pineapple syrup and let soften 5 minutes. Blend 2 tablespoons sugar and egg yolks in heavy pot. Blend in half the fruit purée and the gelatine mixture. Stir constantly over low heat until mixture almost begins to simmer and thickens slightly; do not boil.

3. Immediately scrape into mixing bowl set in large bowl half filled with ice and water. Add remaining fruit purée. Stir now and then until thickened and custardy. As mixture thickens, taste it, adding more lime juice and sugar, if necessary, so that there is a little bit too much of both.

4. When fruit mixture is sufficiently chilled, whip whites with salt to form soft peaks. Gradually beat in superfine sugar to form shiny but *not* stiff peaks. Whip cream to mound *softly*.

5. Whisk fruit mixture lightly to soften if it has firmed up. Fold in cream in 2 batches. Fold 1 cup of this mixture into the beaten whites, then fold into the fruit-cream mixture.

6. Gently spoon into 6 parfait glasses, cover with plastic, and chill 4 hours or more. Garnish each with a thin slice of lime.

🍃 *Cherimoya can be substituted for Atemoya in the recipes on page 30.*

CHERRY, SOUR
See Sour Cherry

CHICORY, RED-LEAF
See Radicchio

CHILI-PEPPER, CHILE, HOT PEPPER, CHILI
**(All peppers under this heading are *Capsicum annuum*.
See listings below for individual varieties.)**

*C*hili-peppers (the words selected by specialists in the study of capsicums to designate the pungent members of the *Capsicum* genus) belong to the same Nightshade family that includes among its two thousand species the tomato, potato, eggplant, tamarillo, tobacco, Cape gooseberry, pepino melon, mandrake, petunia, and a remark-

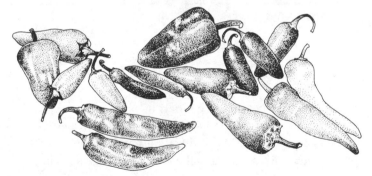

able number of other unlikely kin that make me glad I'm not a taxonomist. Chili-peppers, in particular, refuse to be tamed, codified, classified, and otherwise put in their place. Adventurous and spirited, they mix and match, reproduce unpredictably and prolifically, and generally run their own show. But, with the Mexican and Southeast Asian food explosions in this country of late, we had best begin to make an effort to understand which is which and how to use them.

Our historical connection with peppers is curious indeed. These delicious, promiscuous plants have been pleasing the world at large, flourishing in the Caribbean, Africa, India, the Far East, and Europe for centuries. Yet the pepper habit all started out right next door in Mexico, probably around 7000 B.C.(!) Picked up by Columbus in the West Indies, the capsicum traveled around the world before arriving in North America, with European colonists.

Once it does arrive anywhere, though, it sticks, transforming a cuisine. Can you imagine Hungary without paprika, Szechuanese or Thai dishes with no heat? Can you conceive of *no* nippy enchiladas or chili con carne? Just think about how dramatically our foods have been affected by the presence of chili-peppers in the last decade (unless you come from the Southwest, where hot pepper—called chile, from the Spanish—has been around for a much longer time). Once you develop a taste for the incendiary edibles, it is really quite impossible not to lust after them. Although many people (I once counted myself among them) think that heat overpowers subtle flavors and numbs the palate, more food lovers find that the piquancy (not overdone) enhances and expands tastes.

Now that we can buy the fresh beauties, as shiny and perfect as holiday ornaments, how do we make sense of the heaps of them that sit in grocery stores—labeled indiscriminately, not labeled, or perhaps labeled correctly without our knowing? We thank heaven that Jean Andrews came along with her exquisitely lovely, comprehensive, scholarly book, *Peppers: The Domesticated Capsicums* (University of Texas Press). With her help, the varieties are deciphered below.

The selection here is mine, based on the advice of produce buyers and distributors throughout the country. The numerous names of the dried forms have been avoided, for the most part, in order to focus on the fresh without creating even more confusion than already exists.

Note: All instructions for roasting, peeling, and freezing are on pages 125–126.

Anaheim
also Long Green or Red Chili, California Long Green, New Mexico Chili (and New Mexico Green or Red Chili), Chile Verde, Chile Colorado

*T*his long, narrow, slightly twisted pepper, usually a medium to light green, is the one most commonly available in this country. Named after the city in California where a pepper cannery was opened in 1900, it developed independently in that state and in New Mexico, where the same strain is called the *chile verde*, when green, and *chile*

colorado, when red. This is the familiar pepper that, when dried, makes up the graceful oxblood-colored string or wreath called a *ristra*. Generally mild (although its bite can be sharp) it is perhaps the most often used chili—whether fresh or from cans. Roasted and peeled, it becomes tender and succulent, with a pleasantly bitter-sweet, if relatively simple, fresh taste.

Anaheim is the chili that is frequently stuffed, and the same one that makes up the ubiquitous red or green sauce that accompanies or coats the food of New Mexico. Strips or dice stirred into a wide variety of foods add zip and color. Include it in egg, potato, cornmeal, chicken, and fish dishes, or in creamy or chunky soups and macaroni casseroles, or blended with soft cheeses for fillings and dips; or purée it with broth, soft crumbs and nuts, and herbs, to make a chunky and savory sauce.

Store Anaheims in a paper bag in the refrigerator for a week. Roasted Anaheims freeze well for up to a year (see Preparation).

Fresno

*P*ointed, tapering from broadish shoulders, this medium-short pepper is about the same size as the more familiar jalapeño. Lightish green, like the Anaheim, or cherry-red when mature, it looks very like the Santa Fe Grande, but unlike it, does not turn

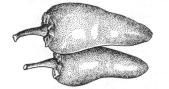

yellow or orange, going directly from green to red as it matures.

As hot as a jalapeño, the Fresno is best used as seasoning rather than a vegetable, in sauces (cooked and raw), or minced sparingly in dips and salads (such as gua-camole). I like the sweetness of the ripe chili, very finely chopped, for a piquant garnish on cooked vegetables (hot or marinated), particularly the Latin starchy vegetables, such as yuca, malanga, yam, or plantain.

Store Fresno chili-peppers in the refrigerator for about a week, enclosed in a paper bag. Blanch or roast peppers to be frozen, and wrap each separately.

Hungarian Wax, Banana Pepper
also Hungarian Yellow Wax, Sweet Banana, Hot Hungarian Wax

*L*ong, tapering, fairly narrow, a translucent, waxy, creamy yellow (some become red-orange when mature), this is one chili-pepper that must be labeled—and tasted. One form (usually called banana) has no heat at all; the other (usually Hungarian Wax) can be warm to moderately hot. Distributors have been miserably lax on this score,

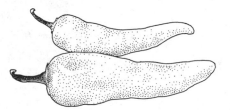

and storekeepers worse. A yellow pepper seems to be a yellow pepper, period—as if peppers were purchased solely to look upon.

Traditionally, these peppers are pickled (look for the gorgeous golden slabs in big jars, usually under Hungarian labels). Their relatively thin skin does not require peeling. Test their pungency, then sliver fresh into salads (they are particularly tasty and colorful in bean or grain dishes) or uncooked sauces, dips, or relishes. Mince plenty of Hungarian wax pepper into an oil-and-citrus dressing to pour over the starchy tropical tubers malanga, yuca, and yam. Or toss hair-thin strips on chilled or hot puréed soups.

Refrigerate Hungarian wax peppers in a paper bag for a week to ten days.

Jalapeño

*F*resh or pickled (*en escabeche,* as it is called in Mexico, where only the pickled form is called jalapeño—pronounced ha-la-PAY-nyo), the deep-green little jalapeño, a hot chili indeed, is probably second to the Anaheim in familiarity and popularity in this  country (perhaps because it has the best keeping qualities). Blunt-tipped, slightly tapered, it has unusually dense, rich flesh for a petite pepper. Occasionally it appears in the market in its mature red form, which, like the green, is prone to show a slight cracking or crazing along the length, particularly near the stem end.

The smooth, thick flesh of the jalapeño makes it ideal for slivered garnishes for soups, for salads (particularly meat), and for pickling. Its powerful bite has assured its place on nachos and other bland melted-cheese combos. Chop it to fire up a dip or purée or an uncooked sauce—particularly one for the tropical starches: plantain, yam, malanga, and yuca or cassava. A small amount in spoonbreads, cornbreads, cheese soufflés or pasta dough makes a snappy difference. I almost always prefer the jalapeños roasted and peeled, rather than raw, which makes them more concentrated in flavor and less hot.

Fiery jalapeño appetizers can be made by roasting and peeling the red or green pepper, slitting to remove the seeds, then stuffing to taste, or first marinating, then stuffing (as in Josefina's Jalapeños Stuffed with Sardines, page 131). For a hot and crunchy condiment, cut narrow circles of fresh jalapeño and *quickly* sauté with bits of carrot, cauliflower, string bean, and zucchini; marinate in a mixture of vinegar, oregano, peppercorns, and salt.

Store jalapeños in the refrigerator, wrapped in a paper bag, for a week or two. Jalapeños, roasted (leave on the peel) or blanched, can be frozen for about 6 months (see Preparation).

Poblano, Ancho

*T*he name *poblano* (poh-BLAH-no) refers to several similar cultivars that are used when green, ancho being the most common. To really confuse matters, the same kind of chili-pepper is called a pasilla (which is also a completely different variety) in parts  of California. Not widely available, but increasing in popularity, this glossy, rich-green fruit, shiny as patent leather, resembles a slightly flattened green bell pepper, but is pointed at the tip and rather heart-shaped. It is usually very mild, but can sometimes be quite pungent, with a remarkably full, herbal flavor and aroma.

Like most of the larger chilies, it should be cooked and peeled, which develops taste and tenderness. Its exceptionally thick flesh makes it perfect for stuffing (the Anaheim cannot compare with it on this score). Roasted, cut in strips (*rajas*, in Mexico), and stirred into a dish near the end of cooking time, the poblano adds a depth of flavor and piquancy. Like the Anaheim (and even more so, to my taste), it is an extremely versatile and delicious component to enliven corn and cornmeal mixtures, egg dishes, chicken, beef, and fish dishes, light soups, vegetable mélanges, sauces, stuffings, and cooked vegetable salads. Josefina Howard of the Rosa Mexicano restaurant in New York City places wide strips of peeled poblano on pompano fillets, then tops them with a few thin slices of white onion. She wraps this in parchment or foil and bakes in a moderate oven until barely cooked, about 15 minutes. She also adds pepper strips and onions to rice as it finishes cooking, and puts a thick layer of the same vegetables on grilled steaks.

Store in the refrigerator, in a paper bag, for about a week. Roasted but not peeled, the poblano can be frozen (with some loss of quality) for a few months, but in this form it becomes too soft for stuffing.

Santa Fe Grande
also Caloro, Caribe, Goldspike, and occasionally Yellow Wax

*J*ean Andrews says that, according to most authorities, the peppers in this category are virtually the same cultivar (she does not include the Yellow Wax, but many storekeepers do). They are tapered, conical, and look very like the Fresno, although they are generally marketed yellow (and hence may also be called *güeros*, meaning

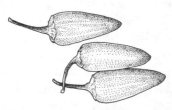

blonds, as is done in Mexico), but they can be orange to red, as well. They are moderately hot to hot, with a pleasant sweetness.

Use the Santa Fe Grande for pickles, uncooked sauces, and relishes; or roast and peel, then cut in tiny strips or mince for garnishing cooked vegetable salads or antipasto or to add to cornmeal muffins, bread, or soufflés. Purée the peeled roasted peppers in small amounts in sauces for bland vegetables, such as hominy, yuca or cassava, malanga, and plantain; or add to pasta dough. Add to beans as they finish cooking, keeping the pepper whole (cut slits in it) for easy removal.

Store in the refrigerator, wrapped in a paper bag, for a week. The Santa Fe Grande can be blanched and frozen for a few months.

Serrano

*S*mall (about 2 inches long), slightly pointed, fairly constant in its ½-inch diameter, this medium-green chili, smooth and sleek, packs a tremendous wallop—usually more than any above. The burn is intense and immediate, with a lasting bite.

Serrano is extremely popular in Mexico, where it is generally used fresh (veins, seeds, and all) in guacamole and uncooked salsas. Being quite thin and tiny, it is not suitable for peeling. Woven on skewers between chunks of meat and onion, serranos make a breathtaking barbecue. In Mexico green or red serranos are sometimes made into chunkily puréed cooked dipping sauces (for fire eaters). A tiny bit in pasta dough makes a stunning contribution, as it does in fresh tomato sauce and seafood salads. Or season dishes as they cook with whole serranos, then remove as the desired piquancy is achieved.

Store in the refrigerator, wrapped in a paper bag, for upward of a week. Although they can be blanched and frozen, they do not maintain their vigor and heat as well as some.

CHILI-PEPPER CAVEATS:

☐ Chili-peppers used carelessly can ruin a dish. Unless you have developed a terrific tolerance, do not combine them with other ingredients until they have been individually sampled; every single chili-pepper has a different bite, even ones that come from the same plant. To control heat, add whole peppers (cut slits in them) to whatever dish you are cooking. Taste at various stages, then remove as the correct amount of heat and seasoning is achieved. Or add chilies toward the end of the cooking period, a bit at a time.

☐ Despite what you may read, the fire in chilies is not contained in the seeds, although they can have some heat. Some 89 percent of the compound capsaicin, responsible for the incendiary quality, is located in the interior "ribs" (placental partitions) of the pepper; taste if you're a doubter. There are uneven deposits throughout the chili-pepper, but this is the main hot spot.

☐ Sample chili-peppers without their bite before deciding how you'll use them. To do this, halve the chili, carefully choose a section that does not contain ribs, then taste it. You'll be astonished. You can cut down on the heat, if you wish, by delicately shaving off the ribs and removing the seeds (wear gloves).

☐ If you overestimate the chili capacity of your diners (and it is an acquired tolerance), do not try to douse the flames with water, beer, or wine. Offer plain table sugar or hard candy. It *works*.

☐ Chili-peppers burn hands, noses, eyes, and anything else they touch—and the burn can develop gradually and last for days. This is no joke. Wear thin gloves unless you are callused. Do not interrupt chili-pepper preparation to answer the telephone, taste a custard, or clean your glasses—or you may find yourself burned by the next call, bitten by a hot dessert, or temporarily blinded. Scrub the cutting board with salt and cold water.

☐ When stocking up on chilies in the freezer, you will not have tasted the peppers beforehand. Uncharacteristically hot ones can creep into a batch and heat up all the others in the container. To avoid this, and to have useful quantities, keep the containers small. It is useful, as well, to place foil between layers so you can withdraw a small amount when you wish.

PREPARATION: Most green chili-peppers have the skin removed before they are added to a dish. This develops flavor and succulence, and improves their digestibility. There are as many ways to peel chilies as there are authentic chili recipes, but this works for me:

   To Peel Chili-Peppers: Wash chilies and make a small slit near the stem end of each. For a small quantity and quickest roasting, blister peppers directly in the flame on top of a gas stove, turning until the skin is blackened all over, but not the flesh. In a good flame, this is only a matter of a minute or so. *Or,* for a larger quantity, place on a baking sheet. Set in broiler in position closest to flame, keeping the door ajar. Broil, turning, until peppers are blistered on each side (but not blackened throughout), about 10 minutes in all. *Or* set the peppers on a piece of wire mesh or a small-gridded rack close to the flame on a barbecue or grill. *Or* for a very large batch, you can deep-fry the chilies, as they do in some restaurants.

When they are blistered all over, remove chili-peppers from the heat. Enclose in damp paper toweling for 10 minutes—which is my preference—or let stand 2 minutes, then slip into a plastic bag, close tightly, and let stand 10 minutes. Slide off the skins by pulling downward from the stem end to the tip. Finish cleaning by scraping with paring knife. Remove veins and seeds, if you like.

To Freeze Chili-Peppers: After roasting, cook the chilies *without peeling* (they stay firmer, tastier, and more nutritious), then stack in plastic containers and freeze. To use, defrost at room temperature for a few hours, pulling the pods apart when sufficiently thawed. The skins slip right off.

For chopped chilies, skin them, then chop with seeds and veins if you like them hot; or remove both for a mild flavor. Pack into small containers and freeze until needed.

Whole chili-peppers can be frozen up to a year. Chopped ones hold on for about 6 months.

NUTRITIONAL HIGHLIGHTS: Chili-peppers are extremely low in calories. They are excellent sources of the vitamins C and A, potassium, and folic acid. They also contribute a fair amount of fiber.

ROBBIE'S SALSA

My brother Robert Schneider is as calm and competent wielding a cleaver or grater as he is building a cabinet, amusing a group of five-year-olds, or managing a cast of hundreds—which he does in Hollywood. To make this simple salsa, he showed me a grating technique that is so reasonable that I am still embarrassed that I had never managed to come up with it myself. For a rough, fresh sauce of tomatoes or peppers you scrape them on the largest holes of a hand grater, holding your hand flat against the skin. There is no need for peeling or chopping.

We bathed a grilled swordfish with the pungent sauce, but you can use it for dipping tostadas or embellishing eggs, chicken, pork, or cornmeal preparations. When Robbie has leftover sauce—which he always does, since he never makes less than a cauldron of anything—he cooks pot roast in it.

Makes about 2 cups

4 firm medium tomatoes, halved	½–1 jalapeño or serrano, to taste
1 small green bell pepper, halved and seeded	2 medium garlic cloves, peeled and finely minced
2 small yellow onions, peeled	¼–⅓ cup finely minced cilantro
1 medium-hot large chili-pepper, such as Anaheim or poblano	2–3 tablespoons red wine vinegar
	Salt

1. Grate tomatoes on largest holes of a standing hand grater, pressing firmly to make large pieces; discard skin. Do the same with green peppers, holding the cut side against the grater. Grate the onions.

2. Remove stems and seeds from chilies; chop flesh very fine. Add to vegetables with garlic and cilantro and 2 tablespoons vinegar. Cover and refrigerate several hours or more. Season to taste at serving time, adding salt and vinegar if needed.

———

MARDEE REGAN'S CHUNKY POBLANO-TOMATO SALSA

Mardee (editor and friend) and her husband Gary are so crazy about this chunky, rich, colorful sauce that they eat bowls of it, soup-like. They also enjoy more moderate amounts on scrambled eggs, fried-egg sandwiches, nachos, tacos, enchiladas, cold meat loaf, fried potatoes, and pork chops.

Makes about 1½ quarts

3 tablespoons vegetable oil
1 very large onion, diced (2 cups)
3 large garlic cloves, minced
½ teaspoon whole cumin seeds
¼ teaspoon crushed hot pepper flakes (or to taste)
½ cup chopped cilantro
1 teaspoon salt
½ teaspoon ground cumin
4 medium poblanos, roasted, peeled, seeded, and diced (see Preparation), to make about 1 cup (or substitute Anaheims)
Optional: 1 jalapeño, seeded and minced
6 large very ripe tomatoes, peeled (page 23), seeded, coarsely chopped (6 cups)

1. Heat oil over moderate heat in large skillet. Add onion and garlic and sauté until softened but not browned, about 5 minutes.

2. In tiny pan stir cumin seeds and hot pepper flakes over low heat until they smell wonderful but are not smoking—a few seconds. Add to onion-garlic mixture with cilantro, salt, and ground cumin.

3. Sample poblanos and add to skillet: if not hot enough for your taste, add jalapeño. Add tomatoes. Simmer over low heat, stirring occasionally, for 20 minutes, until slightly thickened and mellowed and blended to taste. Serve hot, at room temperature, or chilled.

Note: Peeled tamarillos can be substituted for tomatoes in salsa, cooked or raw.

MEXI-MAGYAR HOT TABLE RELISH

There is nothing Hungarian about this mixture but the name of the chili-peppers —nor is it an authentic Mexican salsa—but it is tasty. Adjust the heat and sweetness of the brash and vivid combination by your selection of hot pepper varieties, or by using a judicious selection of hot and mild, such as jalapeño or Fresno mixed with Anaheim. For most hot salsas of this kind, the peppers are simply chopped—seeds and veins included—for maximum punch. The combination of herbs is nicely mysterious, not as outspoken as either one is alone. The piquant sauce makes a lively salad topping, accompaniment to cold meat or fish, or garnish for iced soup, as well as a Mexican-style dipping or seasoning sauce.

Makes about 1¾ cups

½ cup chopped Hungarian wax peppers (or substitute any other fresh chili-peppers to suit your taste)

¼ cup chopped onion (red onion is nice)

2 meaty, large plum tomatoes, diced small (¾ cup)

3 tablespoons lime juice

Salt to taste

About 2 tablespoons slivered cilantro leaves

About 1 tablespoon slivered basil leaves

2 teaspoons vegetable or olive oil

1 small avocado cut in very tiny dice (or ⅔ cup)

1. Combine the chili-peppers, onion, tomatoes, lime juice, salt, 2 tablespoons cilantro, 1 tablespoon basil, and olive oil. Cover and chill for ½ hour or so.

2. Shortly before serving, gently fold in the avocado. Season to taste with salt and additional herbs.

JIM FOBEL'S CHILES RELLENOS

Transplanted early to Southern California, food writer Jim Fobel has tasted his way through more than his fair share of chiles rellenos, a popular restaurant dish that gets dragged mercilessly through sauces and batters not worthy of the poblano that belongs therein. Neither neat nor easy to prepare, the rich-flavored peppers, filled with melting cheese and coated with a soufflé-like batter, demand attention and patience. This is the careful version he has refined over the years.

Makes 12 stuffed chili-peppers, to serve 6 as a main course

TOMATO SAUCE

2 pounds ripe tomatoes (6 medium)
1 tablespoon vegetable oil
1 small white onion, minced
2 medium cloves garlic, minced
1 cup water
¼ cup red wine
Salt and sugar to taste

CHILES RELLENOS

12 fresh poblanos (about 2 pounds) (see
    Note)
1 pound Monterey jack cheese
5 eggs, separated
¼ teaspoon salt
¼ cup flour
Vegetable oil for frying

1. Prepare sauce: Peel tomatoes, preferably by flame-peeling method (see page 23), then core, seed, and chop them. Heat oil in medium saucepan; add onion and cook over moderately low heat until somewhat softened, about 5 minutes. Add garlic and stir. Add water; simmer until soft, 5 minutes. Add tomatoes and wine and simmer, stirring occasionally, until most liquid evaporates, 15–20 minutes. Sauce should be thick. Add seasoning.

2. Carefully char and peel poblanos (see To Roast and Peel Chili-Peppers, page 125). With paring knife make slit from stem end to point of each pepper, working slowly to avoid tearing flesh. Cut through core under base of stem (do not remove stem); remove and discard along with seeds. Scrape off veins, if desired. Rinse gently and drain on paper towels.

3. Cut cheese in strips about ¼ inch wide and 2 inches long. Carefully stuff each poblano with enough cheese to fill it, but retain its shape.

4. Beat egg whites and salt until soft peaks form. Continue beating for a moment or two longer, but do not form stiff peaks. Lightly stir yolks; fold into whites along with flour to blend evenly.

5. Pour vegetable oil into a large skillet (preferably electric) to a depth of ¼ inch. Heat to 360 degrees.

6. Holding it by the stem, dip a stuffed pepper into batter to coat, then place in oil. Repeat the procedure, frying several peppers at once, but taking care not to crowd skillet. Turn with spatula, fry on each side 3–4 minutes, until batter is browned and cheese has melted (the center will be soft when pressed). You may need to lower temperature so peppers do not brown before cheese melts. As peppers are finished, drain on paper towels, then place in pan in 250-degree oven to keep warm.

7. To serve, reheat sauce. When all peppers are fried, arrange on heated plates; spoon a little sauce on top of each.

Note: You can substitute Anaheims for poblanos, if necessary.

GUACAMOLE FROM ROSA MEXICANO

Josefina Howard, who runs this fine Mexican restaurant (Rosa refers to a bright pink color, not a flower or woman) in New York City, suggests that you try this guacamole with serranos one time, jalapeño the next to find your favorite. The two-step technique she recommends is a revelation.

4 servings as an appetizer

SEASONING PASTE
1–2 teaspoons minced serrano or
    jalapeño (do not remove seeds or ribs)
1 tablespoon minced white onion
1 tablespoon chopped coriander leaves
¼ teaspoon salt
½ large Hass avocado, peeled and diced

GUACAMOLE
¼ cup medium to hard ripe tomato cut in
    ½-inch cubes
2 tablespoons white onion, cut in ¼-inch
    dice
1 tablespoon chopped coriander leaves
¼ teaspoon salt
Remaining ½ large avocado (see
    seasoning paste, above)
½–1 teaspoon minced serrano or
    jalapeño, to taste

1. Combine seasoning ingredients—chili-pepper, onion, coriander, and salt in mortar or heavy bowl (see Note). With pestle or back of spoon smash mixture to a paste. Add ½ avocado; crush to a rough texture.

2. Add tomato, onion, coriander, salt; mix lightly. Score avocado flesh in ½-inch squares, cutting down to skin. Run knife around flesh as close to skin as possible to release these cubes (into the bowl). Add remaining chili-pepper. Mix to blend. Serve at once.

Note: At Rosa Mexicano they use a heavy, black volcanic stone Mexican mortar *(molcajete)*, which performs this job perfectly.

JOSEFINA'S JALAPEÑOS STUFFED WITH SARDINES

For confirmed chili lovers, this nippy appetizer comes from New York City's Rosa Mexicano restaurant. The assertive sardine and jalapeño flavors balance each other neatly—but don't hesitate to experiment with other stuffings for chilics, which are mellowed a bit by the vinaigrette.

4 servings as a first course

8 full, fat jalapeños
½ cup olive oil
½ cup sherry vinegar
Pepper to taste
¼ teaspoon thyme
3 small garlic cloves, peeled
Salt to taste
2 tins sardines packed in olive oil, each 3¾ ounces
Garnish: Shredded iceberg or Boston lettuce, small onion rings

1. Keeping stems intact and charring just enough to blister the skin, roast and peel jalapeños as directed in Preparation. Slit each along its length from stem to tip. With a small knife or your finger (if you're an old hand at chili cleaning) gently remove seeds and veins. Rinse under a gentle stream of water.

2. Combine olive oil, vinegar, pepper, and thyme in a shallow dish. Crush garlic and salt to taste until puréed. Add to dish and blend. Taste for seasoning. Add jalapeños and turn to coat. Cover; let stand at least 1 hour, lightly covered.

3. Lift sardines from tins onto a plate; drizzle with a little packing oil. Shred and crush slightly, but do not mash to a paste. Divide among peppers, stuffing snugly. Tidy up and shine by dabbing with vinaigrette.

4. Place on lettuce, slit sides up. Garnish with onion rings.

—

MOUSSE DE CHILE POBLANO

This is the only nontraditional dish served at the Rosa Mexicano restaurant in New York City. It is a rich but light cross-cultural appetizer, based on Paula Wolfert's Red Pepper Mousse from her extraordinary book *The Cooking of South-West France.* The velvety poblano, with its depth and heat, works wonderfully in translation. Although delicious alone, the mousse makes a memorable sauce for chilled shrimp, lobster, or salmon.

4 servings

1 tablespoon vegetable oil
1 clove garlic, mashed or minced
1 medium white onion, thinly sliced
4 medium-large poblanos, roasted, peeled, veins and seeds removed (see Preparation), cut in thin strips
⅔ cup heavy (or whipping) cream
Salt and pepper to taste
Cilantro sprigs for garnish

1. Heat oil in medium skillet over moderately low heat. Add garlic; stir for a moment. Add onion; stir a few minutes to barely soften. Add poblanos (reserve a couple of pieces for garnish); cover and cook until softened, about 5–10 minutes, stirring occasionally.

2. Purée in blender or processor. Place purée in sieve over small bowl. Re-frigerate for at least an hour to chill and drain.

3. Shortly before serving, whip cream to form soft peaks. Add salt and pepper to poblano purée. Fold in whipped cream gradually, adding enough to make a softly moundable but not soupy mixture; amount will vary with moisture content of peppers.

4. With 2 large spoons, shape oval poufs of mousse, arranging several on each of 4 serving plates. Decorate with narrow strips of poblano and sprigs of coriander.

Note: I find the creamy mixture works well if prepared hours ahead. The flavors develop and the consistency becomes a bit firmer.

—

CEVICHE OF RED SNAPPER FROM ROSA MEXICANO

This traditional marinated raw fish dish, tart and hot, clean and light, is among the most popular at the New York restaurant.

6 servings

1½ pounds fillet of red snapper
⅔ cup lime juice
⅔ cup lemon juice
½ cup light, fruity olive oil
Salt to taste
Pepper to taste

2 tablespoons chopped cilantro leaves
1 medium white onion, finely chopped
2 large ripe tomatoes
4 fresh serranos, finely minced, seeds and all (see Note)

1. Cut fish in 1¼-inch squares (see Note). Combine with lime and lemon juice in dish; refrigerate for about 5 hours. By that time interior should be opaque, no longer raw-looking; check to be sure.

2. Drain, then rinse very delicately. Combine in a serving bowl with the oil, salt, pepper, cilantro, and onion. Without peeling, cut shell of tomatoes in ½-inch pieces (reserve interior pulp for another use). Add to fish with serranos.

3. Cover and refrigerate about an hour. Season with salt and lemon when you serve; it should not be ice cold.

Note: If you prefer less piquancy, remove seeds and veins before chopping peppers, and cut down to 2 serranos. If you have a can of jalapeños en escabeche, add 2 teaspoons of its liquid, as Josefina does. Fish in smaller cubes, which I prefer, takes less time to marinate. I cut ½-inch dice, which take about an hour to "cook."

CEVICHE WITH CHERRY TOMATOES AND AVOCADO

I like to add 1 pint sliced cherry tomatoes and ¼ cup minced parsley to the marinating fish. When serving, I fold in 1 large avocado, cut in ½-inch dice. This will be plenty for 8 diners.

Note: Only a few chili-pepper recipes are given in this section, to exemplify several varieties and techniques. Hot peppers are included throughout the book as a seasoning; see the following recipes:

CHINESE CABBAGE
(*Brassica rapa* subspecies *pekinensis*)
also Chinese Celery Cabbage, Napa, Nappa, Pe-Tsai, Wong Bok, Peking Cabbage, Shantung Cabbage, Hakusai, Chihli Cabbage, Michihli, Chinese Leaf, Chou de Chine

*Y*es, all the above are commonly used names for this worldly vegetable—and there are a half-dozen other less common ones. To further confuse the unwary, the cabbage that wears them has two distinct forms—one long and narrow with leaf tips branching outward; the other shorter and stouter, with leaves curving inward. When

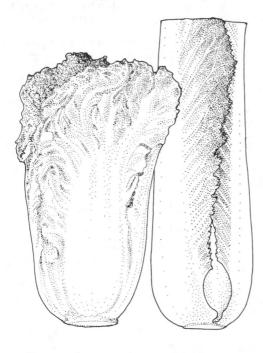

Liberty Hyde Bailey, probably the greatest horticulturist of modern times, attempted to make order of the Brassicas in the early part of the century, he had 2,400 pages of family trees to sort out and they're still being organized by contemporary taxonomists this minute. When it is your turn to choose between a mere two similar cabbage forms, just point, for the impossibly general rubric "Chinese Cabbage" might land you a bagful of different green things, all of which go by this name (most commonly, bok choy, see page 36).

Chinese cabbage proper is thinner-leafed than our common round cabbages; it is also much more tender, crisp, juicy, and mild. The pearly, wide, pale ribs fan out into crinkled, veined leaves with crimped, undulating borders of apple green. The ribs of the upright, narrow kind are a bit darker, crunchier, and firmer, and the leaf tips (sometimes trimmed off at the top of the rib shafts) are coarser. Both are considerably more delicate in flavor than round cabbages, with a fresh, radishy edge. In *Jane Grigson's Vegetable Book* (a plain title for an extraordinary work) she writes of Chinese cabbage that "raw in salad, cooked in Chinese or Western style, it will delight the cabbage-hater," which, in fact, it seems to do.

SELECTION AND STORAGE: You should be able to find Chinese cabbage year round in most markets, with one of the two types generally predominant in an area. Look for tightly packed, firm heads, with no signs of browning. Although the leaves should be quite crisp, I find that when limp they have a flavor that is appealing for lightly cooked dishes. Of the twenty or so books consulted on the matter I found the majority of authors stating that one variety or another is clearly superior—with a tie the result.

Taste for yourself and let function follow form and flavor; select by familiarizing yourself with the two kinds, then choosing what fits the recipe.

If the cabbage is in good shape, it should keep, tightly wrapped in plastic in the vegetable drawer of the refrigerator, for about 2 weeks. If you'll be using it in salads, store only 3–4 days.

USE: Use Chinese cabbage as you would round head cabbage—with these differences: separate central ribs and puffy leaf parts for most cooked dishes; cook it for less time; season with a light hand, for it is a delicate vegetable. It is delicious through the textural gamut, from crisp-raw, to tender-crunchy, to a silky-soft "overcooked."

Raw, the succulent white central ribs can be sliced or coarsely shredded for salads or slaws (they mix enthusiastically with many vegetables and firm fruits) or cut in strips for raw-vegetable platters. I prefer the somewhat dry, slightly bitter leafy parts cooked. For a different kind of tender salad, blanch and marinate the leaves and stems to soften and mellow. Or shape blanched whole leaves into stuffing packets for picnics or hors d'oeuvres.

In Japan, China, and Korea, Chinese cabbage is a standard part of meals in the form of simple salted and spiced pickles—whether vinegary-sweet and fresh, or hot-peppery and long-fermented.

Add ribbons of Chinese cabbage to delicate broths during the last few minutes of cooking; or simmer for a longer period of time in thick, stewy soups. Dice the crisper narrow stalks for a celery-like contribution.

That celery-ish quality of the narrow cabbage is welcome in fried-rice combinations or in savory stir-fries. For the latter, toss ribs with fat about 2 minutes, add a few spoons of broth to soften the cabbage, then add the leaves and toss another minute or so. Boil off excess liquid, if necessary. Additional meat fat or oil stirred in at the last minute adds succulence and blends flavors (chicken fat is particularly suited to Chinese cabbage).

The vegetable also takes beautifully to long, slow braising, becoming tender and flavorful as it absorbs cooking liquid. Slice the cabbage in wide chunks, or quarter it lengthwise. Or use only the hearts (there are numerous baby leaves sprouting from the central stalk) of the cabbage, reserving the outer leaves for another dish. Cook slowly in a rich, meaty seasoning liquid—particularly one with ham or duck.

PREPARATION: For most dishes, you'll separate the leaves from the central core (which is delicious, and should be sliced and enjoyed, not discarded). Wash Chinese cabbage fairly casually, checking for smudges of soil. For stir-frying, salads, or soups, cut the separated leaves in julienne strips, wide ribbons, or squares. For dishes in which you'll be cutting the cabbage lengthwise, don't separate the leaves but simply rinse the outside. How you cut it depends completely on what guise it will take. Trim the base, then halve or quarter or cut in sixths lengthwise for braising.

NUTRITIONAL HIGHLIGHTS: Chinese cabbage is extremely low in calories—about 16 per cup, cooked. It is an excellent source of folic acid and vitamin A, a good source of potassium and vitamin C, and is very low in sodium.

RICHARD SAX'S HOT AND SOUR SOUP-STEW

Colorful peppers, carrots, ham, and cellophane noodles (clear strands that are also called mung-bean threads), enliven friend and colleague Richard Sax's version of a familiar Chinese soup. This one, thick with slivered vegetables and meat, and only lightly hot and sour, makes a well-balanced main dish that can be prepared ahead.

4 servings as a main course

1 small packet (about 3 ounces) cellophane noodles

1 pound Chinese cabbage

2 tablespoons vegetable oil

1 medium onion, sliced thin

2 thin carrots, sliced thin on a diagonal

1 large garlic clove, minced

1 teaspoon grated fresh ginger

1 medium red bell pepper, slivered

Big pinch hot pepper flakes, or to taste

3 cups chicken broth, preferably homemade

2 cups water

1 tablespoon soy sauce

1 cup Smithfield ham (4–5 ounces), cut in fine julienne; or substitute another firm ham, such as prosciutto

½ cup thin-sliced mushrooms

About 1 teaspoon Oriental sesame oil

1 tablespoon rice vinegar, or to taste

Optional: Salt and hot pepper sauce

2 tablespoons thin diagonal slices scallion greens

1. Place noodles in bowl and pour over boiling water to cover. Let stand about 10 minutes, then drain. With scissors cut into convenient lengths.

2. Meanwhile, separate leaf and stalk parts of cabbage leaves. Cut leaves on diagonal in ½-inch slices, crisp center stalks in ¼-inch-wide diagonals.

3. Heat oil in flameproof casserole; stir in onion and carrots and sauté 2 minutes. Add garlic, ginger, bell pepper, and pepper flakes; stir 30 seconds, until fragrant.

4. Add cabbage stems and toss 1 minute: add leaves and stir 30 seconds, or until wilted. Add broth, water, and soy sauce. Bring to a boil; cover, then boil gently for about 2 minutes, until cabbage is crisp-tender.

5. Add ham, mushrooms, and drained noodles. Return to a boil, cover, then remove from heat. Let steep 5 minutes.

6. Stir in sesame oil and vinegar to taste. Season with salt and hot pepper sauce, as desired. Ladle into deep bowls and sprinkle with scallions.

Note: You can substitute bok choy for the Chinese cabbage—separating stems and leaves the same way, but cooking a minute longer—for a crisper, more colorful effect.

MARINATED CHINESE CABBAGE SALAD

A fresh salad of partly cooked, soft, chewy leaves (the curly rounder kind of Chinese cabbage is nice for this) and crunchy stems, seasoned with vinegar, hot pepper, fennel, soy sauce, and garlic—a pleasing blend of East and West. Enjoy with grilled meat or fish, or tossed in a salad with cold poultry or pasta.

4 servings

½ cup rice vinegar
2 tablespoons soy sauce
2 teaspoons sugar
½ teaspoon kosher salt
1 or 2 tiny dried hot peppers
2 medium garlic cloves, sliced
1 teaspoon fennel seeds
2 pounds Chinese cabbage
3 tablespoons peanut or corn oil

1. In nonaluminum pan combine vinegar, soy sauce, sugar, salt, peppers, garlic, and fennel seeds. Simmer, covered, 10 minutes. Let stand, covered, while you prepare the cabbage.

2. Remove leaves from core and rinse them. Slice exposed core thin as you remove leaves. Slice leaves apart from each central rib. Stack leaves in colander and pour a kettle of boiling water over them.

3. Slice ribs diagonally to make strips about ¼ inch wide and 2 inches long. Drop into large kettle of boiling salted water with sliced core pieces. Over highest heat return to boil. Drain at once, then cool in ice water. Drain well, then dry.

4. Dry leaves somewhat and slice ½ inch wide. Combine in serving bowl with ribs and cores. Strain warm dressing over cabbage; toss well. Add oil and toss again. Remove peppers, if hot enough. Chill for at least an hour, or up to several days.

BRAISED CHINESE CABBAGE

Two unusual ingredients have been added to this classic braise—Chinese cabbage and ginger; otherwise the components and techniques are similar to those you would use in a slow-cooked French vegetable dish. Although the prosciutto is not strictly orthodox, ham is (at least in French chopped-vegetable seasoning mixtures—mirepoix), and the savor that it lends is delicious and distinctive.

4 servings

2 pounds firm Chinese cabbage (the long, narrow kind works best)
2½ tablespoons butter
2 ounces prosciutto (or another firm, flavorful ham), cut in 2 slices, then diced
1 medium onion, minced
1 medium carrot, minced
1½-inch ginger chunk, peeled and minced
1½ cups chicken broth
½ cup dry vermouth
White pepper to taste

1. Rinse cabbage and cut carefully into quarters lengthwise, keeping leaves attached to core.

2. Heat 1½ tablespoons butter in a skillet; stir in prosciutto, onion, and carrot. Stir over moderately low heat until softened—about 10 minutes.

3. Spread half the minced vegetables and prosciutto in a baking dish (or, better, a baking-serving dish, if you have one the right size) that will hold the cabbage in one tight layer. Pack the cabbage in the dish; sprinkle the remaining vegetables on top. Bring broth and vermouth to a boil in skillet in which you cooked the vegetables; pour over cabbage. Cover with buttered waxed paper and a close-fitting lid or foil.

4. Bake in preheated 350-degree oven until soft, about 1½ hours. Drain juice from dish into a saucepan. Boil over high heat until reduced to a few tablespoons. Off heat stir in remaining butter and pour over cabbage.

Note: This can be prepared ahead, if you wish. Complete all steps except reduction of the stock. At serving time, reheat cabbage in oven uncovered. Meanwhile, reduce stock in a small pot over high heat; pour over heated cabbage, and serve.

HOT-SWEET CHINESE CABBAGE WITH GINGER AND TOMATOES

For a quick and easy change-of-pace vegetable, toss together these ingredients in a pan and let them bubble until the cabbage loses its crunch. The flavor develops with cooking, so do not simply stir-fry. The sweetness and heat make an appealing accompaniment to simple broiled or pan-fried meat or seafood.

4 servings

1½ pounds Chinese cabbage
½ pound ripe tomatoes, roughly chopped (peel if you like)
1½ tablespoons minced fresh ginger
¼ cup golden raisins
2 tablespoons brown sugar
2 tablespoons corn oil
2 tablespoons cider vinegar
½ teaspoon salt, or to taste
⅛ teaspoon crushed hot pepper flakes, or to taste

1. Trim base and tip of cabbage, if necessary. Separate leaves and rinse well, especially bases. Stack leaves and cut lengthwise into long strips about ½ inch wide. Cut strips diagonally into 2-inch lengths. There should be about 10 cups.

2. Combine all ingredients in deep, wide, heavy nonaluminum skillet or Dutch oven. Stir on high heat until most liquid exudes. Adjust heat and stir often until cabbage is quite tender and juices have reduced to a shiny slick—about 15 minutes.

🍂 *ADDITIONAL RECIPE*
Stir-Fried Beef, Taro, and Cabbage, page 460

CHINESE CELERY CABBAGE
See Chinese Cabbage

CHINESE PEAR
See Asian Pear

CHINESE WATER CHESTNUT
See Water Chestnut

CHRISTOPHINE
See Chayote

CILANTRO
(Coriandrum sativum)
also Coriander, Chinese Parsley, Mexican Parsley

W as there culinary life in the United States before cilantro? It hardly seems possible that five years ago the fresh herb was difficult to find, and required an explanation each time it appeared in a recipe. Today, with the country's growing Asian and Latin population (it is a staple in the cuisine of both groups), cilantro is available nationwide.

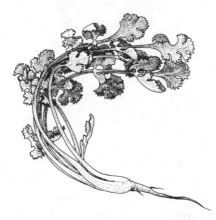

The dried seeds of the cilantro plant, usually called coriander, have played a role in good food since ancient Egyptian times or perhaps even earlier (the first documented appearance of the seeds is in a twenty-first dynasty tomb). Throughout recorded history the seeds' unusual fragrance—at once sweet, musky, herbaceous—has been part of liqueurs, confections, pickled fruits and vegetables, soups, and stews. It is probably most familiar to modern cooks in Indian mixed spices (such as curry powder and garam masala) and in the standard blend called "pickling spice," which originated in India but is a mainstay in American "put-ups."

The plant that grows from these grains has been less widely accepted or simply ignored in favor of the seeds. Its curious aroma elicits adoration or alarm in much the same way that hot peppers do. In the classic text *The Vegetable Garden* by Vilmorin-Andrieux (first published in English in 1885, now available in a facsimile edition from Ten Speed Press), the authors relate: "Some writers say the leaves are used for seasoning, but this statement seems odd, as all the green parts of the plant exhale a very strong odour of the wood-bug, whence the Greek name of the plant." Maybe if I knew what the bug (*koros* or *koris* in Greek) was like I could describe the smell, but I have never met the namesake wood-bug. Cilantro's name in Chinese, ironically enough, means fragrant plant. *Chacun à son gout!* I would probably love the taste of wood-bugs!

For the most part, French and English still shy away from this strange herb, with its wild, uncharacterizable savor. But all of Asia and South and Central America (*cilantro* itself is the Spanish name for the plant) make use of its heavily aromatic, lacy green leaves (and often stem and roots). Although it is primarily through Mexican cooking that Americans have become familiar with cilantro, the plant is not native to that area, but to the Mediterranean.

Because contemporary cooks in Spain eschew the green (in neighboring Portugal, however, it is as common as parsley), it has never been clear who transported it to

South America. Elizabeth David, doyenne of British culinary historians, has recently demonstrated the likelihood of a Spanish connection by unearthing recipes that include cilantro in a sixteenth-century book from Spain. She offers recipes for most-appetizing pottages, probably derived from earlier Arabic dishes, that make use of green coriander, pounded together with the dried seed, toasted almonds, and a generous array of spices.

SELECTION AND STORAGE: Buy cilantro year round, choosing only the very freshest, brightest, liveliest bunches, as it perishes very quickly and becomes flat and even unpleasant. Look for very leafy plants with small stems and plenty of roots, if possible. Not only are the roots delicious in cooking but the plant keeps much longer with them attached. Set the cilantro in a bottle of water, as you would a bouquet of flowers, then enclose the leaves tightly in a puffed-out plastic bag. Refrigerated, fresh coriander will keep for a week or two this way. If the roots have been cut off, wrap the stems in damp toweling and enclose the whole in plastic (and get after your produce man to keep the roots in future). It will keep in your crisper for two or three days.

Although freezing puréed cilantro is often recommended, I find it tasteless or bitter. Dried cilantro is dead. Cilantro roots, however, freeze with little loss of their heavenly flavor or texture; you can simply rinse, then add to your frozen cache whenever you have a new bunch.

USE: Cilantro, unlike most herbs (except perhaps basil and sometimes parsley), is used in quantities and preparations that make it qualify as vegetable as well as herb. Chopped in generous amounts with tomatoes or tomatillos and chili-peppers, it makes an unforgettably pungent sauce. Simmered with thickening agents, such as nuts and bread, it becomes a completely different kind of delicacy (see Cornish Hens with Aromatic Green Sauce, page 470).

Use it as a garnish, a fresh herbal flavoring to be chopped or left in whole leaf form. In India cilantro is used in enormous volume in fresh relishes, chutneys, and salads. The Chinese steam fish with it. The flavor of cilantro blossoms eloquently when it is combined with warm liquids, as in soups—where it figures extensively in all Asian cuisine. Thais use the roots for dishes to be long-cooked, then stir in the leaves at the last minute, or lavish them over the completed assembly.

PREPARATION: Do not wash cilantro until you are ready to use it, as its perfume is most volatile. Rinse gently and blot dry, or whirl in a salad spinner and use at once.

NUTRITIONAL HIGHLIGHTS: Cilantro is just about without calories (5 per cup). It is a fairly good source of vitamin A.

❧ *Recipes that include a large proportion of cilantro follow. However, the herb figures prominently with other uncommon ingredients (notably chili-peppers and tomatillos) in recipes throughout the book. See also:*
Robbie's Salsa (page 126)
Mardee Regan's Chunky Poblano-Tomato Salsa (page 127)
Guacamole from Rosa Mexicano (page 130)
Lemon Grass Seasoning Paste (page 277)
Mardee Regan's Green Sauce (Salsa Verde) (page 469)
Cornish Hens with Aromatic Green Sauce (page 470)
Tomatillo, Dried Chili, and Cilantro Sauce (page 471)

CITRUS AND AVOCADO SALAD WITH
INDIA JOZE CILANTRO DRESSING

An idea from the king of cilantro, Joseph Schultz, who says this dressing (slightly adapted) is a favorite at his restaurant, India Joze, in Santa Cruz. Try it on fruit or chicken salad, vegetables or grains—but don't prepare the fresh, light herbal dressing ahead.

4–6 servings

½ pound escarole, Belgian endive, or chicory

1 large grapefruit

2 medium navel oranges

1 medium-large, very ripe avocado, pitted, peeled, into ½-inch dice

DRESSING

⅓–½ cup coarsely chopped cilantro leaves, not packed

3 tablespoons lemon juice

3 tablespoons corn oil

2 tablespoons peanut oil

1 tablespoon honey

¼–½ teaspoon salt, to taste

1 very small ice cube

Tiny chili-pepper, such as serrano, seeded and minced

1. Rinse escarole and dry thoroughly. Cut in bite-sized pieces; wrap and chill. Slice rind and all pith from grapefruit, then cut out pulp from between membranes. Peel and remove pith from oranges, then cut fruit in half lengthwise. Slice across in thin half-rounds. Chill.

2. To serve, arrange escarole on serving dish or platter. Arrange grapefruit and orange over this. Top with avocado dice.

3. Combine cilantro, lemon juice, corn and peanut oils, honey, salt, and ice in processor; whirl to purée. Add minced hot pepper, adjusting to piquancy you prefer. Pour over salad. Serve at once.

RICE WITH COCONUT, CILANTRO, DATES, AND LEMON

The light, fluffy, dry texture of this aromatic dish makes it the perfect partner for spicy, soupy curries or creamy stews. Cilantro adds color and an inimitable flavor—as always.

6 servings

1 fresh coconut (shake to be sure there is plenty of juice)

1¾ cups long-grain white rice

About ½ teaspoon salt

¾ cup thinly sliced, pitted dates

1½ teaspoons grated lemon zest

¼ teaspoon fennel seeds, crushed in a mortar

About 3 tablespoons lemon juice

¾ cup chopped cilantro leaves

1. Puncture 2 coconut "eyes," using a clean nail and a hammer. Drain; strain and reserve juice. Set coconut in preheated 375-degree oven and bake 10 minutes. Crack shell with hard taps from hammer, hitting around the equator. Pry meat from shell in chunks; drop in ice water. Using thin slicing blade of processor (or a vegetable peeler), make 1 cup slices; reserve. Wrap and freeze remaining coconut if you won't use within a few days.

2. Add water to drained coconut liquid to equal 2¾ cups. Combine with rice in 2-quart heavy saucepan; bring to a rolling boil, stirring now and then. Add salt; turn heat to lowest point. Cover pot and cook 20 minutes. Remove from heat; let stand, covered, for 15–25 minutes.

3. Fluff rice gently into a warm serving dish. Add coconut, dates, lemon zest, fennel, and lemon juice to taste; toss to mix. Add cilantro, toss lightly, and serve.

SPAGHETTI WITH CILANTRO, CORN, AND TOMATOES

Fragrant cilantro, sweet corn, and summer tomatoes have so much color and flavor that you may be surprised to find this a low-calorie meal.

2 servings

2 very ripe medium tomatoes, stem ends removed
1 medium ear fresh corn, husked
½ pound spaghettini
1 egg
1 tablespoon red wine vinegar
½ teaspoon sugar
Salt and pepper to taste
1–2 tablespoons full-flavored oil, to taste
⅓ cup finely minced cilantro
¼ cup chopped red onion

1. Drop tomatoes and corn into a large pot of boiling, salted water; return to a boil on highest heat. Boil 15 seconds. Remove tomatoes; let corn boil 1 minute, then remove. Cover pot and lower heat.

2. Peel tomatoes, halve, and squeeze out seeds. Cut one tomato into ½-inch dice. Cut kernels from cob.

3. Boil spaghettini until just barely tender. Meanwhile, whirl egg in processor until pale and fluffy; cut up remaining tomato and add with vinegar, sugar, and salt and pepper to taste. Whirl to blend well.

4. Toss drained pasta in warm serving dish with oil. Add sauce and toss to coat. Add corn, cilantro, onion, and remaining tomato; toss gently and serve at once.

INDIA JOZE CHICKEN STIR-FRIED WITH CILANTRO

I could eat this once a week and still crave it in between. It is a rare treat to find a dish that takes 5 minutes to prepare that has such subtlety, balance, and finish. From chef Joseph Schultz, alias India Joe of Santa Cruz. Try it with rice cooked with lemon grass.

2 servings

2 tablespoons peanut oil

¾ pound boned and skinned chicken breast, cut in bite-size rectangles about ½ inch thick

2 thin scallions, cut into 1½-inch diagonals

2 teaspoons minced cilantro roots (see Selection and Storage, above)

¼ teaspoon ground pepper

1 teaspoon minced garlic

1 tablespoon fish sauce (see Note)

½ cup chicken stock

1 tablespoon white vinegar, either distilled or rice vinegar

½ teaspoon sugar

About 2 tablespoons minced cilantro leaves

1. Heat wok on moderately high heat; pour oil around rim, then tip wok to distribute. Immediately add chicken and scallions and stir-fry until chicken is slightly whitened, about 30 seconds.

2. Add cilantro roots, pepper, garlic, and fish sauce; toss until chicken is cooked through, about 2 minutes. Scoop into warmed dish.

3. Add stock, vinegar, and sugar to wok. Boil briefly to reduce to a slightly syrupy consistency. Add chicken and toss. Return to dish and toss with cilantro leaves. Serve at once.

Note: Fish sauce, *nam pla* or *nuoc mam*, is available in all Oriental stores and some supermarkets. It lasts forever and is worth having.

CLEMENTINE
(Citrus reticulata)

*T*his appealing, diminutive fruit is, according to most citrus specialists, a variety of the common mandarin, a name applied to a number of citrus fruits that have, among their distinguishing characteristics, a peel that is easily pulled from the flesh. Sometimes called zipper-skinned, such fruits were once referred to as kid-glove oranges, as

it was said a lady could eat the fruit without soiling her hands. Confusingly, what the rest of the world has long known as *mandarin* is dubbed by many Americans *tangerine*. (The word, originally spelled Tangierine, means a native of Tangier; it has been used in English since the mid-nineteenth century to describe a mandarin originally from Morocco, but now refers to any number of mandarins.)

At any rate, the tender, silken-fleshed, sweet clementine is a mandarin—as are the Honey and Dancy varieties that we grow and know as tangerines. But the bright orange clementine is more deeply flavored than American-grown varieties, with thinner membranes, more bountiful juice, and a refreshing bittersweet zip. And what's more, the fruit that comes into our markets is virtually seedless—an instant hit with children.

The clementine, write many authorities, was an accidental hybrid planted by Father Clément Rodier around 1900 in the garden of his orphanage in Misserghin, near Oran, Algeria. Other authorities believe it to be identical to a Canton mandarin that already existed. It is still cultivated primarily in North Africa, and in Spain. Although the clementine was introduced into the United States Citrus Research Center at Riverside, California, as early as 1909, it is still struggling to take root beyond small groves in that area.

SELECTION AND STORAGE: Look for this glossy, tightly packed, petite fruit (smaller than any of the U.S. mandarins or tangerines) from late November to April—but expect the largest quantity during December and January. Select it as you would other citrus fruits, by hefting it for weight. Press gently: it should be firmish, but have some give to the skin, indicating juiciness. Generally speaking, the smaller the fruit, the more intense its savor. In my experience it is the clementines from Morocco (each so marked, *Maroc,* with little stickers) that seem to be particularly fine-textured and pungently flavored. The ones from Spain that I have sampled, although undeniably delicious, are a bit more like our more common American tangerine/mandarin varieties in their slightly puffy skin, firmer membranes, and blander taste. Buy many more clementines than you think you'll need, because the fruit will be devoured, like peanuts. You can store them in the refrigerator for about a week.

Use: Enjoy these bright-tasting fruits as you would the finest tangerines—simply. Keep a bowl of them for anyone who might drop in, or serve them after dinner, along with toasted pecans and aged rum or Armagnac. Offer a dish of gleaming clementines along with sweetened mint tea and pastry as an afternoon (or any time) pick-me-up, as they do in Morocco. Garnish poultry and seafood dishes with clementines. Include them in gelatine desserts, puddings, custards, and fruit cups. Set clementine sections in tarts filled with pastry cream (or replace the oranges in the Tart of Blood Oranges on page 34).

NUTRITIONAL HIGHLIGHTS: Clementines are a good source of vitamin C and contribute a fair amount of fiber.

CLEMENTINE GELATINE

I love fresh fruit gelatine, particularly when made with clementine. Petite segments are captured in cool wine jelly flavored with the rind and juice. A refreshing, light dessert with real fruit flavor.

4 servings

¾ cup water
1 envelope gelatine
⅓ cup sugar
4 very small clementines, scrubbed
1 lemon
1 cup dry white wine

1. Pour water into small nonaluminum saucepan; sprinkle in gelatine, then sugar. With a swivel peeler, remove colored rind from 3 clementines, avoiding white pith. Do same to ½ lemon. Add rinds to pot.

2. Squeeze juice from remaining clementine; measure. Squeeze and add enough lemon juice to total ¼ cup. Add to pot; add wine. Cook over moderately low heat, stirring often, until clear—about 5 minutes. Strain through a fine sieve into a pitcher.

3. Pour ¼ cup gelatine mixture into each of 4 dessert dishes or wide-bowled wine glasses. Reserve unused gelatine mixture at room temperature. Refrigerate dishes until firm, about 1 hour.

4. Meanwhile, remove white pith from the 3 rindless clementines. Scrape off any fibers that remain. When gelatine in dishes is firm, divide clementine sections over it. Reserve ¼ cup liquid gelatine; distribute remainder evenly over sections.

5. Chill until set, about ½ hour. Spoon remaining gelatine over each dessert; tip to distribute evenly. Chill until serving time.

BAKED CLEMENTINE CUSTARD

Light and delicate, this simple dessert is low in calories. The sweet little segments of clementine fit into custard cups where they nestle neatly beneath their milk-and-egg topping.

4 servings

2 eggs
1¼ cups milk
2 tablespoons brown sugar
Pinch salt
2 small clementines
¼ teaspoon ground cinnamon

1. Beat eggs to just blend; stir in milk, sugar, and salt. Mix well, but do not beat until foamy. Strain.

2. Rinse clementines and grate enough rind to make ½ teaspoon. Add to custard mixture. Peel and section fruit; cut each piece in half, then arrange in four 6-ounce (approximately) custard cups. Gently pour custard mixture over clementines. Rub cinnamon through a fine sieve to dust desserts evenly.

3. Set custard cups on a towel in a baking pan; pour boiling water into pan to come halfway up dishes. Bake in preheated 350-degree oven until just set—about 25 minutes.

4. Remove from the water and cool on a rack. Chill before serving.

≈ *Clementines can be substituted for blood oranges in the Tart of Blood Oranges on page 34 or for kumquats in Barbara Spiegel's Candied Kumquat Tart on page 272.*

CLOVER - RADISH
See Radish Sprouts

COLLARDS
(Brassica oleracea acephala)
also Collard, Collard Greens

*T*he flavor of collards, which is between cabbage and kale, also describes its position in the large Crucifer family. *Acephala*, meaning without a head, refers to its loose-leafed (nonheading) shape. Its English name derives from the Anglo-Saxon *cole-wort:* cabbage plant. The deep-green leaves, each on a fairly long, heavy stalk (too

tough to eat) resemble cabbage, but are oval and fairly flat and paddlelike, not round and curved. Collards look sturdy and primitive, which they are, having kept their present form for at least two thousand years.

Oddly, despite their age, they appear in the culinary literature of only a few countries. Most commonly associated with "soul food" in the United States, collard greens arrived with the African slaves and have been raised almost exclusively in the South ever since. There is really only one traditional way to cook them—boiled until very soft with a piece of salt pork or smoked hock—and perhaps there is no better method of preparing greens that will share equal table space with black-eyed peas and/ or sweet potatoes and crunchy cornbread. The assertively earthy, fleshy leaves are substantial enough to replace meat, and the meal as a whole is an inspired and nutritious blend of coarse and smooth, strong and bland, granular and chewy.

In Brazil, collards, called *couve*, are paired with a much heftier quantity of pork as part of the celebrated *feijoada completa*. In parts of Africa and India dark, intense greens, collards among them, are often treated to an intriguing range of spicy-hot and aromatic flavorings. These are very different indeed from the salty, smoky tastes favored in the American South and Brazil and worth investigation if you are a fan of the hearty green leaf.

SELECTION AND STORAGE: Look for collards year round in supermarkets, produce stands, or stores that carry "soul food" with largest supplies available from December through April. Choose relatively small, firm, springy leaves that show no yellowing or insect holes.

Store collards in the refrigerator, wrapped in damp toweling, then plastic. They should keep for a few days to a week if they were in prime condition when purchased. Although they will not spoil, they keep less well than head cabbage, becoming dried and limp fairly quickly.

Collards freeze successfully: boil cleaned, sliced leaves for a few minutes, until barely limp; drop in ice water, then drain. Pack closely in airtight containers and freeze for several months.

USE: Collards can be cooked long and slowly (the more hours the better) to yield a soft, mellow mass of leaves. Or the leaves can be simmered in seasoned broth for 15–30 minutes for a texture that is medium-firm, like sautéed cabbage. Serve collards alone, or combine with potatoes, brown rice, cracked wheat, beans, or kasha; layer or top with a light cheese, curry, or cream sauce or poached eggs.

Blanch and chop collards to use for stuffing ham, pork, or lamb. Or combine with ground meat or cheese in calzone or a deep-dish rustic pizza.

For a complex effect, mix blanched collards with other greens, such as escarole or Swiss chard or spinach in a soup, sauté, or braise. Add raisins and currants and toasted pine nuts for a pleasantly sweet note. Season delicately or forcefully; while collards have plenty of taste of their own, they can support a wide range of pungent additions: garlic or onions, hot peppers, fresh ginger, anchovies, or curry spices. Collards take kindly to crispy garnishes such as fried croutons or crumbled bacon.

PREPARATION: Collards, like many greens, need very thorough washing. Dunk into a sink filled with tepid water and swish around. Lift the leaves out gently, so debris sinks to the bottom. Repeat as many times as necessary.

Strip or cut the stems from the leaves and discard them. Stack or bunch the leaves and cut into strips that best suit the dish.

NUTRITIONAL HIGHLIGHTS: Collards are very low in calories—about 30 per cup, cooked. They are an excellent source of folic acid and vitamin A, and contain quantities of potassium, calcium, iron, and zinc.

BRAISED COLLARDS WITH GINGER AND CHILI-PEPPER

Collards treated this way become chewy-soft, with an earthy freshness and pleasingly nippy bite.

3–4 servings

1 pound collards, cleaned (see Preparation), cut into thin strips

2 cups chicken broth (or any poultry or meat stock)

3 tablespoons butter

¾ cup chopped onion (1 medium onion)

1 teaspoon minced garlic

1 tablespoon grated fresh ginger (no need to peel, just rinse)

1 jalapeño, stem and seeds removed, minced (or use Fresno)

Black pepper to taste

1. Combine collards with broth in nonaluminum pot. Simmer, covered, until tender but not mushy. Timing will vary, but 35 minutes is average.

2. Heat 2 tablespoons butter in large skillet; stir in onion and garlic. Soften slightly over moderate heat. Add ginger and jalapeño and stir for a moment.

3. Add collards and stir over moderate heat until liquid has almost evaporated. Remove from the heat, stir in the remaining tablespoon butter and black pepper.

Note: You can substitute turnip greens in this dish, or combine a variety of greens for a particularly interesting effect: kale, collards, Swiss chard, mustard greens—any and all.

COLLARD GREENS WITH CORNMEAL DUMPLINGS AND BACON

Collards are long-cooked with smoky bacon until they are soft and succulent, then topped with light, fluffy dumplings in this adaptation of a Southern classic.

4 servings

2 pounds collard greens, cleaned (see Preparation), cut in thin strips

½ pound slab bacon, in one piece

1 tablespoon sugar

DUMPLINGS

½ cup flour

¾ cup yellow cornmeal, preferably coarse, stone-ground

1 teaspoon sugar

1½ teaspoons baking powder

¼ teaspoon salt

¼ teaspoon crushed hot pepper flakes

¼ cup sliced scallion greens

1 egg

1 tablespoon bacon fat, reserved from step 2 of recipe

To serve: Pepper vinegar or hot pepper sauce

1. Combine collards in nonaluminum pot with water to just about cover (8–10 cups). Add bacon and sugar and boil gently, partly covered, until greens are very, very soft—at least 2 hours, preferably more. Add water as needed to maintain the same level throughout cooking. When cooked, taste cooking liquid; if it seems flat, boil briefly to concentrate it. Set aside ½ cup liquid.

2. Remove bacon from pot and cut off and discard rind, if any. Cut into strips about 1 inch long and ¼ inch wide. Brown in a covered skillet—about 10 minutes. Drain bacon and reserve fat.

3. For dumplings: Whisk together flour, cornmeal, sugar, baking powder, salt, and hot pepper in a mixing bowl. In a small bowl combine scallions, egg, and 1 tablespoon reserved bacon fat; stir in reserved ½ cup cooking liquid ("pot likker," in the South). Pour this wet mixture into the dry one, mixing only enough to barely blend ingredients.

4. Bring greens to a boil. Drop dumpling batter by tablespoons over greens, leaving small spaces between batter lumps. Make about 10 dumplings. Cover pot and boil gently for 10 minutes. Uncover and boil a few minutes longer, until dumpling tops have dried a bit.

5. Sprinkle bacon over dumplings and serve immediately, with hot sauce.

SOUP OF COLLARDS AND SAUSAGE

This warming winter soup can be made with a number of alternative roots or tubers that nicely complement the strong collard greens. For the most traditional flavor, potatoes fill the bill—as they do regularly at tables all over the Iberian peninsula. I find the light sweetness of pumpkin, calabaza, or butternut squash pleasant and mellow: or you might enjoy sweet potatoes—either orange or the Latin American white boniato—for a new taste combination.

6 servings

2 tablespoons lard, bacon fat, or goose fat
1 pound cooked or partly cooked garlic sausage, such as linguiça or kielbasa
1 large onion, diced coarse (1 cup)
1 large carrot, chopped coarse (¾ cup)
1½ pounds collards, cleaned (see Preparation), cut in thin strips
2 quarts water
About 2 pounds winter squash, or all-purpose or sweet potatoes
Salt and pepper to taste

1. Heat fat in a large pot; chop ¼ pound of the sausage and stir in with onion and carrot. Stir over moderate heat until vegetables are slightly softened. Add collards and stir over high heat until softened and reduced in volume.

2. Add water and simmer, partly covered, for 15 minutes. Meanwhile, peel squash or potato; cut into slices about ¼ inch thick and 2 inches long. Add to soup and simmer, partly covered, until very tender—about 25 minutes. During the last 10 minutes, add remaining sausage, sliced. Season with salt and pepper.

3. Remove soup from heat and cool completely, uncovered. Re-cover pot and refrigerate for about a day to blend and intensify the flavors.

SPICY COLLARDS

Based on a dish that is part of a complex Ethiopian assembly, this relatively uncomplicated treatment demonstrates another useful approach to a favored Southern green. Serve the soft, aromatic leaves—which become more like spinach than cabbage when cooked this way—with a complementary grain, vegetable, or egg dish for an unusual vegetarian meal.

2 or 3 servings as a side dish

1¼ pounds small-stemmed collard greens, cleaned and stripped (see Preparation)
2 tablespoons butter
2 tablespoons minced shallots
½ teaspoon grated fresh ginger
¼ teaspoon cardamom
¼ teaspoon cinnamon
⅛ teaspoon nutmeg
¼ teaspoon salt, or to taste

1. Drop collards into a large pot of boiling, salted water. Boil until tender; timing varies, but about 15 minutes is average. Test often. Drain leaves well, then chop fine.

2. Heat 1 tablespoon butter in pan; stir in shallots and cook on moderately low heat about 3 minutes, until soft. Add ginger, cardamom, cinnamon, nutmeg, and salt. Toss for a minute.

3. Add collards and stir 3 minutes, to season and warm thoroughly. Off heat stir in remaining butter, cut in small pieces. Season to taste. Serve warm or at room temperature.

Note: You can use any combination of greens for this—mustard, Swiss chard, kale, turnip greens, but shorten the cooking time.

BEEF BRAISED WITH COLLARDS IN BEER

Collards are ideal for stewing or braising: impossible to overcook, they soften and absorb meat juices, but do not lose their own distinctive tang. Here the flavor is accentuated by beer, enriched by beef and bacon, and sharpened with hot pepper for a strong, warming, well-balanced dish. Lamb and pork make equally delicious partners for the collards, but require a bit less cooking time.

5 or 6 servings

5–6 ounces slab bacon, cut in ¼-inch bits
2 pounds beef chuck, cut in 1-inch pieces
2 tablespoons flour
3 pounds collard greens, cleaned and
    stripped (see Preparation)
2 medium garlic cloves, chopped
18 ounces (2¼ cups) beer
1 heaping tablespoon brown sugar
¼–½ teaspoon hot pepper flakes
1 teaspoon salt
Black pepper to taste
2 tablespoons cider vinegar

1. Cook bacon slowly in a wide, heavy skillet or Dutch oven, stirring often until well browned—about 10 minutes. With slotted spoon transfer pieces to casserole of about 3½–4-quart capacity. Set aside 2 tablespoons fat.

2. Flour meat evenly. Brown in fat remaining in skillet over moderate heat, turning until deeply colored. Add to bacon in casserole.

3. Cut leaves in 4-inch strips. Heat reserved fat in skillet. Add collards and garlic, and stir over moderate heat for a few minutes until wilted and softened.

4. Add to casserole. In a small pot combine beer, sugar, hot pepper, salt, black pepper, and vinegar; bring to a boil. Pour over meat and collards, then stir. Cover and bake in preheated 350-degree oven until very tender, about 1½–2 hours, stirring halfway through cooking time. (Can be prepared ahead.)

CORIANDER (OR FRESH CORIANDER)
See Cilantro

CORN SALAD
See Mâche

CURRANT, RED
(Ribes rubrum)

With the current (unavoidable) interest in "specialty produce" in America and the wealth of adventurous chefs and home cooks, a currant revival seems like a natural. The tiny scarlet berry, its taut, translucent skin as shiny as blown glass, has an acid punch that belies its fragile appearance. As a garnish, casually in tune with the

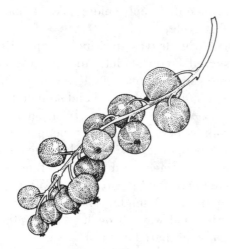

Oriental and California-type restaurant presentations, it can't be beat for a simple and immediate burst of flavor and color.

The beauty of the red currant has inspired painters since the Dutch and Flemish masters, but comparatively few cuisines have adopted it. Although it grows wild in almost all temperate and subarctic regions, only in Great Britain, Scandinavia, Germany, and Russia is it more or less commonplace. In America both jelly and wine made from the berries used to be found in every good cook's pantry but have fallen out of use in recent years.

This may be due to the gradual distrust with which farmers have come to look upon the pretty garden shrub, for it is one of the hosts for a deadly fungus that kills white pines (the currant itself is unaffected). But horticultural studies are beginning to suggest that gooseberries (close relatives) and black currants may actually be the main culprits. The black currant, which is difficult to obtain (for the reason just cited), is starting to be imported from New Zealand. It is another species *(Ribes nigrum),* unlike the less common white currant, which is a colorless offshoot of the red currant.

The supposed origin of the word *currant* shows the difficulty of trying to make logic of historical bramble bushes. *Currant* is presumably a distortion of the name Corinth, the Greek city from which were shipped the minute raisin grapes that we know as dried currants. It is accepted that the red, black, and white currants, none of which arc related to this grape, acquired their common name because of a resemblance to it, and became "English currants" (in the sixteenth century) to distinguish themselves from the Corinthian ones.

SELECTION AND STORAGE: Currants are fruits of summer in the United States, appearing from June into August. But we now have an occasional supply coming from New Zealand between December and February. Look for the ripest, which is to say the richest red berries, for most flavor and a good acid balance. For jellies and other preparations for which you want a very sour base, seek paler berries. Check to see that the fruit is quite firm and translucent, not mushy or opaque. You're bound to have a few smashed berries, but look out for too many. Estimate a net yield of about 2–2½ cups stemmed berries for each quart (or each pound) of currants.

Try not to keep the currants for more than a few days, but if you do (or if the fruit is in less than peak condition), gently lift from the box and remove crushed or moldy berries. Spread the clusters on paper towels in a single layer in a basket or dish and refrigerate as long as they seem firm and shiny, usually 3–4 days.

Or freeze the currants: Rinse, stem, and place in small freezer containers; seal and freeze up to a year. Or toss with sugar, 2 tablespoons per cup of fruit; let sugar dissolve, then cover and freeze. Either way the fruit remains round, distinct. Like cranberries, currants ought not to be defrosted before being used in a recipe; allow to warm only a few minutes, if necessary, or until you can scoop the berries from the containers.

USE: To eat uncooked, look for the deepest red currants you can find and sugar them heavily; then pour on cream. For a perfect garnish, simply toss the cleaned berries over vegetables, meats, salads, desserts—anything. Or toss currants with salad components and dressing (a mild one) for spurts of pleasantly sour juice. Purée raw berries with the dressing in place of vinegar.

Use currants in sweet or savory sauces, to point up and heighten the flavor, as lemon or vinegar does. Make lightly thickened sweet-and-sour sauces for game, fowl, lamb, or pork, or a sweet sauce for puddings, light cakes, and creams.

Use heavy currant syrup (see recipe) to sweeten, color, and flavor fresh and cooked fruit compotes. Combine with puréed red berries and cornstarch, arrowroot, or potato starch for a Russian- or Danish-style pudding or in the famous layered summer pudding of England, to be sloshed with cream.

Add the syrup to fruit punches or alcoholic beverages for a colorful, brightly acid drink.

PREPARATION: Wash currants when you will be using them, not before. Gently swish them about in a bowl of water, then lift out tenderly onto a soft towel. Although the task looks endless, currants are speedily detached from their skinny stems (you can use a fork to comb off the berries, if this is easier). Berries plink and hurtle into a waiting bowl at the smallest provocation—and they're fun to watch and chat over.

NUTRITIONAL HIGHLIGHTS: Currants are very low in calories and sodium, and a fairly good source of vitamin C, potassium, and fiber.

SALAD OF SMOKED CHICKEN, ENDIVE, AND RED CURRANTS

The bright borschty-pink dressing for this salad thickens considerably and develops a rich, sour cream flavor, thanks to the interaction of the fruit acid and heavy cream. As a variation for fruit-based salads, follow the directions below, substituting a scant tablespoon grated ginger for the horseradish and adding a little more sugar.

When you want to whip up a fast, elegant little luncheon, add toasted almonds, breadsticks, poached peaches, and lemon sugar cookies to your menu, and serve a relatively dry iced Riesling—from Germany, Alsace, or California—throughout.

4 servings

2⅔ cups stemmed red currants (about 1–1¼ pounds unstemmed), rinsed and dried

1 cup heavy (or whipping) cream

1 teaspoon coarse kosher salt, approximately

1 tablespoon sugar, approximately

1 heaping tablespoon prepared horseradish (not drained)

1 pound Belgian endive, rinsed, dried, and cut into thin julienne strips about 2–3 inches long

1 pound lightly smoked chicken (or turkey), cut into julienne strips about ⅛ inch thick and 2 inches long

1. Combine 1 cup currants, cream, salt, sugar, and horseradish in blender or processor; whirl to a fine purée. Press through a fine sieve and refrigerate.

2. Arrange endive and chicken on chilled salad plates. Pour the dressing over each, then strew remaining currants over all.

MY MOTHER'S CURRANT JELLY

My mother, Nina Schneider, is an unstoppable gardener who changes the tilt of trees, the lay of the land, and the number of fruits a shrub should produce to suit her vision of the world. So, despite her reluctance to stop gardening long enough to make jelly, when her currant bushes on Martha's Vineyard overflowed, as does everything she plants, she was forced to reconsider. The tender, glowing, tart jelly that resulted deserves to be recorded. Although, in fact, jelly must follow a pretty standard route to avoid ending up as syrup for ice cream, my mother's recipe makes better reading than most (she is also a novelist).

There I was and there were currants. . . . Have you seen currants grow? It is as if nature intended them to remain hidden. . . . Exquisite clear red jewels dangling like Oriental ornaments from fine green threads, tucked deep inside the

strong dark green shrubbery that must be parted. . . . So I gathered a spaghetti strainer full (1½ quarts), using a combination of greenish, pale pink, and red berries. To stem or not to stem? Compromise is the better part of valor. I stemmed about two-thirds and left the rest unstemmed.

I had a large copper pot, fairly wide. From earlier times I remembered how boiling jelly has a tendency to roil and expand unbelievably, and unless the pot is really ample the concoction will boil over and make a cursed mess on the stove. A hurried analysis of a dozen cookbooks gave no precise word on whether to add water or not, so I mashed a couple of layers and added ¼ cup water. Cook the fruit over low heat, at under a simmer, until the color is almost entirely drawn out of the berries. (This took 20 minutes on an electric range.)

Now the jelly bag part. I had none. So I improvised with a large strainer and a hopelessly discolored damask napkin. To save juice, wet the napkin or whatever (cookbooks recommend sewing a bag, etc.) and wring out water. Allow the juice to drip through the strainer and the damask napkin until no more juice comes clear. I confess I gave a few squeezes here and there, with a spoon, to encourage the dripping. I had about four cups of clear juice.

Put back into the kettle. Boil the juice rapidly and skim off white scum for 4– 5 minutes. Add 3¼ cups sugar and stir until dissolved. Then boil without stirring for 5 minutes, after which you begin testing for jelling.

A cold spoon.

A small amount of jelly, let cool a bit, and let it drip from the side of the spoon (not over the pan). Keep testing until syrup thickens to the point where two drops join and fall as a single larger drop. If you are the sort who has a jelly thermometer, this is between 220–222 degrees. [Author's aside: I am the sort who has four jelly thermometers, all of which disagree when it comes to the jelling point; always test as suggested.] This stage should be reached before 20 minutes. Possibly less if the fruit is tart.

Pour into sterilized glasses. (I got five half-pints.) Since I make the jelly for oncoming children I don't bother with wax and the rest of the careful processing, but keep in refrigerator. The jelly came out clear, tart, and firmed up immediately.

Note: If your children are not oncoming, you may prefer to seal the jelly as described on page 376.

—

RED CURRANT SYRUP

Easily prepared, this very sweet, thick syrup will last for months in the refrigerator. Add ruby coloring and a bright flavor to fresh or poached fruits when you sweeten them with this; if you have more fresh red currants at the time, toss a few into the mélange for a sharp, pleasant touch. Or blend the syrup with sparkling water or add a touch to white wine as you would cassis (black-currant syrup) for a different kind of kir. Or, for a stronger brew, blend into iced vodka or gin.

Makes 2 cups syrup

1 pound red currants
1½ cups sugar

1. Dip the currants into a bowl of water to wash them; lift out gently. Pull currants from stems and measure. There should be 2–2¼ cups; if you have less, either add more currants or add raspberries or strawberries to equal that amount.

2. Combine the berries in a nonaluminum saucepan with the sugar; crush roughly until syrupy. Cover with a clean cloth and let stand 12–24 hours.

3. Wash down the sides of the pan with a wet brush; then bring to a boil over moderate heat, stirring. Cover the pan and boil gently for 2 minutes.

4. Strain through a very fine sieve. Pour into a scalded 2-cup canning jar; cap loosely and let cool. Tighten the cap and refrigerate up to 6 months.

—

RED CURRANTS IN SYRUP

Sweet Red Currant Syrup (above) and stemmed scarlet berries enliven all summer fruits. Peaches, nectarines, plums, strawberries, raspberries—all will be enhanced by the addition of this brilliant compote. The sugary currants will last for weeks in the refrigerator, so keep them handy for quick and special desserts. The following should be enough to add tart-sweet flavor and color to about 8 servings of fresh fruit.

½ cup Red Currant Syrup (see preceding recipe)
½ pound red currants, rinsed and stemmed (about 1 cup)

Combine the Red Currant Syrup and currants and bring to a boil, stirring gently all the while. Remove from the heat without cooking any longer, or the berries will burst. Pour into a storage container; cool and chill.

GLACÉED WHOLE RED CURRANTS

This is undoubtedly one of the most stunning desserts ever devised. Bunchlets of currants are dipped into sugar syrup (cooked to the hardcrack stage) that forms a transparent shell over each glassy berry. When you bite the crackling-hard coating, the tart juices gush out and mingle with the sugar. With sparkling wine, this makes an exquisite finale to an elegant meal.

Working with sugar coating is tricky, and even more so when you dip breakable, juice-laden berries. Do not prepare this recipe on wet days or more than an hour before you plan to serve the currants—or you may wind up with pools of pink syrup and naked berries. Although some may prefer to glaze a larger amount of currants, I find that without another pair of hands, this is all I can handle.

2 cups whole, firm red currants with
    stems
1 cup sugar
½ cup water
1/16 teaspoon cream of tartar

1. Dip currants into a bowl of water; set gently on an absorbent towel to dry. Be careful not to break any berries. Lightly oil a sheet of aluminum foil.

2. Combine sugar, water, and cream of tartar in a small saucepan; bring to a boil, stirring gently. Cover pot and boil 2 minutes. Uncover and boil over moderately low heat until temperature reaches 290–300 degrees; the syrup will thicken and yellow slightly. Set immediately over a pan of simmering water.

3. The moment that the syrup stops bubbling, dip in a bunch of thoroughly dried currants, holding it by the stem; dip quickly in and out to coat lightly but thoroughly. Do not let berries remain in syrup for more than a second or they will heat through and burst. Let excess drip off into the pot. Set bunch gently on foil to cool and harden.

4. Repeat until all berries are coated. Reheat syrup when necessary to keep it thin enough to coat each bunch with no more than the thinnest sugar shell. If syrup thickens, the coating will be dense.

RED CURRANT VINEGAR

Decant this brilliant red vinegar into pretty pint bottles for a beautiful gift. Its light, slightly fruity flavor works well with composed meat or fruit salads; or try a tiny dash in stewed or poached fruits—as you would use a few drops of lemon juice—to point up the flavor.

Makes 2 pints

1 pound red currants, rinsed and
    stemmed (see Preparation), about 2½
    cups
1 quart distilled white vinegar or rice
    vinegar
¼ cup sugar

1. Scald two 3–4-cup canning jars with boiling water; pour boiling water over the lids as well, and let stand in a bowl. Divide currants between jars.

2. Combine vinegar and sugar in non-aluminum pot; bring to a boil. Pour over the currants. Place a piece of parchment on top of each jar, then screw on lids.

3. Let jars of vinegar stand in a dark place for a week or more, giving them a shake whenever you think of it.

4. Strain currant vinegar through a sieve to extract all liquid; press down very gently on berries to do this, so that no solids pass through mesh. Strain through a single layer of fine-meshed cheesecloth or muslin; then double the cloth and strain again.

5. Funnel vinegar into clean bottles and store in a dark place for a few weeks to mellow.

BERRY BREAD PUDDING

Summer pudding, which is what this really is, is a standard in England and a dessert we would do well to add to the American table. Since the ingredients are now available to us at other times of the year, the estival appellation no longer holds.

To make this old-fashioned sweet, tart berries are heated briefly to release their rich juices, then layered with soft bread that soaks up the goodness. After being weighted and refrigerated, the gala pink-red affair is unmolded onto a serving dish, its deep-hued syrup forming a syrupy moat. The currants are a must, but the other berries are variable: blackberries, strawberries, boysenberries and dewberries are all fine complements—singly or severally.

8 servings

1 quart red currants, rinsed and
    stemmed
3 tablespoons water
1 quart raspberries (or see above), rinsed
½–¾ cup sugar
1 large loaf firm, close-grained white
    bread (slightly sweet breads, such as
    the Jewish challah, are particularly
    delicious)
Crème fraîche or whipped heavy cream
Fresh or candied flowers for decoration
    (violets or roses are lovely)

1. Combine currants and water in nonaluminum saucepan; bring to a boil, covered. Turn heat to low and simmer 2 minutes. Uncover and cook briefly, just until soft.

2. Press contents of saucepan through fine disk of nonaluminum food mill, discarding seeds. Return currant purée to saucepan; add raspberries and ½ cup sugar and boil, stirring, just until crystals dissolve. Taste and add more sugar, as needed. If necessary, cook briefly until raspberries have softened somewhat.

3. Slice bread ¼ inch thick and trim off crusts. Line bottom and sides of 6-cup bowl, mold, or soufflé dish with slices, cutting as needed to fit together tightly.

4. Pour berry mixture into mold; cover with bread slices cut to fit. Cover loosely with plastic wrap. On top of this set a bowl, pot top, dish, or pan with diameter about an inch less than the mold's. Place a 3–4-pound weight on this. Refrigerate about a day.

5. Run a knife around edge of pudding. Invert on platter with rim (to hold juices). Cut dessert in slices; top each with cream and flowers.

Note: This recipe has been slightly adapted from the one for Summer Pudding in *Ready When You Are: Made-Ahead Meals for Entertaining.*

D

DAIKON
See Radish, Oriental

DANDELION
(*Taraxacum officinale*)
also Dandelion Greens

*H*ere is another example of an old-time vegetable made new-fangled, brought back to life by sophisticated consumers and restaurateurs. The infamous weed has long been stewed with a bit of pork on the back of stoves in the American South, or used for numerous home remedies, or had its root dried and ground to make a chicory-like brew, or had its buds and deep taproot cooked by appreciative foragers, or had comforting wine made from its flowers—but it is only recently that the plant has gained culinary respect.

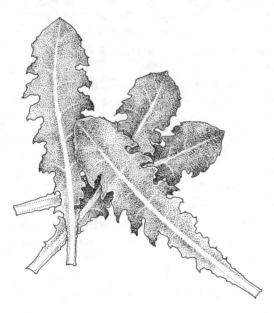

Longer-leafed than its wild forebear, the cultivated dandelion (which is what we see primarily in markets), with its saw-toothed, barb-shaped leaves, is also less bitter. Its paler stalks are similar in color, texture, and flavor to curly chicory, although the leaf is drier. Apparently cultivated dandelions did have a small place for those in the know before the current resurgence of American cooking. Fannie Farmer noted in the original version of her classic cookbook (1896): "Hothouse . . . dandelions appear in the market the first of March, when they command a high price." *The Picayune's Creole Cookbook* of 1901 offers several delicious recipes for "the deeply-notched leaves [that] closely resemble Chicoree," which "through cultivation . . . is now numbered among the best of the early spring salads." But the recipes are Creole French—and the French like bitterness.

It is probable that today's well-traveled diners tasted an unforgettable salad in France, one with warm bacon cubes and thick toasted croutons; or that they enjoyed the subtle bitterness of dandelions braised with olive oil, garlic, and a touch of hot peppers in a trattoria in Italy. However the changes have come round, we now have a constant supply of the tangy, chewy leaves (cultivated from French seed, naturally) that have long contributed to the European repertoire of glorious greens.

SELECTION AND STORAGE: Although dandelions are most abundant and tender during April and May, they can be enjoyed year round, in varying stages of delicacy or durability. When small and crisp and pale, use alone, for a salad; when larger and firmer, mix with other salad greens or cook them. Generally speaking, the paler the leaves, the more tender. Choose lively-looking dandelions with thin stems, preferably attached at the base. Avoid flabby leaves that are yellowing or brown-tinged.

Wrapped tightly in plastic, dandelions will stay crisp for a few days in the refrigerator. Although they do not alter much in appearance, they dry out and lose their springiness and fresh flavor.

USE: Dandelion greens are most often served in salad, where their unique texture, shape, and strong flavor excel. I like them best with heated dressings, either creamy and sweet-sour (in the Pennsylvania Dutch style) or smoky, hot-peppered, and garlicky. The heat softens the slightly fibrous texture of the leaves and mellows the bitter edge. This pleasant bitterness is enhanced by assertive tastes, to which dandelions stand up with enthusiasm: the rich "new" nut oils (hazelnut and walnut, particularly —as well as the nuts themselves), fruit-flavored vinegars, sherry and balsamic vinegars, and cheese with bite—such as blues and goats. If softer flavors are in order, dandelions are delicious with a simple olive oil and light vinegar dressing, especially together with a sweet vegetable—beets being the all-time best match.

The traditional smoked-pork flavoring for cooked dandelions is still wonderful, whether you use bacon, pork hocks, or a bit of diced end of prosciutto or country ham. Unlike many other bitter greens, dandelions do not improve with long cooking. I think a few minutes of tossing in a skillet over medium heat (or covered cooking, then tossing if the leaves are chewy) is all the vegetable needs—up to about 15 minutes, if they're on the tough side.

For dishes in which you wish to keep some of the green flavor but dispel the bitterness, drop the dandelion into boiling water and boil until tender. Drain, refresh in ice water, then drain again. Chop and set aside until serving time, when you can use the vegetable as you would chopped blanched spinach—in cream or cheese sauces, soups, gratins, casseroles, and layered pasta dishes.

PREPARATION: Dandelions require thorough cleaning. Cut apart their joined stems (if this has not already been done). Dunk them into a sink filled with water, swishing them about. Lift out gently so soil sinks to the bottom. Repeat, if necessary, until you are sure the greens are cleaned. For cooking, cut into manageable pieces and proceed (there is no need to dry). For salads, spin-dry or wrap in soft toweling to absorb all moisture.

NUTRITIONAL HIGHLIGHTS: Dandelions are very low in calories, at about 35 per cup cooked. They are an exceptional source of vitamin A, a fair source of calcium and iron, and supply a fairly decent amount of potassium and vitamin C.

SALAD OF DANDELION AND FRESH GOAT CHEESE

This is a light, simplified version of a salad that has become synonymous with the California school of cooking. Although the fried goat cheese often served in this combination is delicious, this plainer style is easier and fresh-tasting. Look for the mildest American or French goat cheese; it should be fairly tender but not mushy-creamy. If you don't have sherry vinegar, substitute red wine vinegar; if walnut oil is lacking, replace it with peanut oil.

4 servings as a light first course

¾–1 pound tender dandelion greens, washed and dried (see Preparation)

About ¼ pound soft, fresh white goat cheese (not aged), cut in ½-inch cubes

⅓–½ cup diced red onion

2 tablespoons sherry vinegar

2 tablespoons walnut oil

½ teaspoon sugar

3–4 tablespoons coarsely chopped walnuts

1. Cut off and discard stem bases. Cut each stalk into 2-inch pieces. Pile on a serving dish; intersperse with cheese. Sprinkle with onion to taste.

2. In small nonaluminum pan combine vinegar, oil, and sugar; bring to a boil, stirring. Pour over salad and toss lightly. Sprinkle with nuts and serve at once.

DANDELION GREENS WITH GARLIC

Treated this way, dandelions become an all-purpose side dish. Rich in flavor, texture, and vitamins and minerals, cooked dandelion greens team up nicely with roasted or grilled lamb, pork, duck, turkey, chicken, beef, or liver.

4 servings

3 tablespoons pork, chicken, duck, goose, or bacon fat

1 teaspoon minced garlic

1½ pounds tender dandelion greens, cleaned and trimmed (see Preparation), in bite-sized pieces

About ½ cup stock such as chicken, beef, turkey, ham, pork, duck

Salt and pepper to taste

Optional: Hot pepper sauce or pepper vinegar

1. Heat fat in a large skillet; add garlic and stir. Add greens and stock and cook over moderate heat, partly covered, for 2 minutes.

2. Uncover and continue cooking until greens are tender and liquid has almost evaporated. (Timing can vary considerably—from 3–4 minutes to 15, depending upon the age and size of the leaves.) If liquid evaporates before leaves are sufficiently tender, add stock.

3. Season to taste with salt, pepper, and hot sauce or pepper vinegar.

FELIPE ROJAS-LOMBARDI'S DANDELIONS
WITH PENN DUTCH DRESSING

Felipe Rojas-Lombardi, the executive chef of the Ballroom Restaurant and Tapas Bar in New York City, draws from a vast culinary vocabulary based on familiarity with the cuisines of many countries. In the simple first-course salad that follows, the influence is from the Pennsylvania Dutch, but I think you'll find the dressing more subtle and less sweet than others of that origin.

6 servings

1¼–1½ pounds dandelion greens, as small and thin as possible, cleaned and trimmed (see Preparation)

½ pound bacon, diced

3 tablespoons flour

1 cup milk, approximately

Approximately ⅓ cup sherry vinegar

About 1½ teaspoons sugar

Salt to taste

About ¼ teaspoon white pepper

1. Dry dandelions thoroughly. Wrap in a towel and chill thoroughly.

2. Fry bacon in skillet until crisp and browned; transfer to paper towels to drain. Discard all but 3 tablespoons bacon fat; strain this to remove all solid bits.

3. Heat fat in small saucepan; add flour, stirring over low heat for several minutes. Add milk and continue stirring over low heat for a few minutes longer. Add ¼ cup vinegar and 1½ teaspoons sugar and stir for a moment; adjust to desired pouring consistency by adding vinegar to taste. Taste for sugar, salt, and pepper. Set aside.

4. Arrange chilled greens on 6 plates. Heat dressing, thinning, if necessary. Pour over greens; sprinkle with bacon, and serve immediately.

PLAIN-COOKED MILD DANDELION GREENS

If you like the flavor of dandelions, but do not enjoy the depth of bitterness, you can blanch the leaves to mellow the taste, as you would in French-style green preparations. Although the initial boiling and draining will eliminate some of the valuable nutrients, blanching is a time-honored way of retaining the color and texture of green vegetables.

4 servings

1½ pounds dandelion greens, cleaned (see Preparation)
2 tablespoons butter, or ½ cup heavy (or whipping) cream
Salt and pepper to taste

1. Drop greens into a large pot of boiling water. Boil until tender—about 5 minutes. Drain, drop into a bowl of ice water, then drain again. Chop and reserve.

2. Shortly before serving, sauté dandelions in a skillet in butter until heated through. Or boil cream for a few minutes to reduce it slightly, then add greens and simmer until almost no liquid remains. Season with salt and pepper and serve.

RICE WITH DANDELIONS

Chopped dandelion greens give rice a pleasing bitterness and aroma. Not for every taste, perhaps, but bitter greens just aren't.

4 servings

10–12 ounces tender dandelion greens, washed and trimmed (see Preparation)
2 tablespoons butter
½ teaspoon minced garlic
1⅔ cups chicken stock or broth
1 cup water
1½ cups long-grain white rice
Salt to taste

1. Chop dandelions in small bits. Heat butter in heavy 2-quart saucepan and add garlic and greens. Stir over moderate heat to wilt. Lower heat and cook until tender, stirring often, about 5 minutes.

2. Add stock, water, and rice, and bring to a full boil, stirring now and then. Add salt, if needed. Turn heat to lowest point and cover pot. Cook 20 minutes.

3. Remove from heat and let stand 20–45 minutes. Fluff gently into a warm serving dish. (Can be kept in very low oven, covered, for half an hour, or can be reheated.)

DASHEEN
See Taro

DELICATA SQUASH
(Cucurbita pepo)
also Sweet Potato Squash

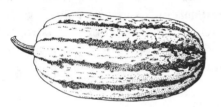

*T*he delicata is a reentry in the squash competition, having first arrived on the scene as early as 1894, introduced by the now-defunct Peter Henderson Company of New York City. Lightly ridged, oblong, 6–9 inches in length and 2–3 in diameter, the delicata may weigh as little as 6 ounces (virtually unheard-of among hard-skinned squash) or up to 3 pounds. The skin is a rich ivory, mottled and striped with spruce green (and occasionally orange). With only a very small cavity, the delicata contains a generous amount of pulp. A pretty corn yellow, the flesh does, in fact, taste and smell like a blend of corn, butternut squash, and sweet potato. Fine, moist, and creamy, the meat is generally of superb quality, and the skin, properly cooked, can be tender enough to eat.

SELECTION AND STORAGE: Look for delicata from midsummer through late fall, selecting specimens with well-defined stripes. The background color should be warm yellow-cream (any green tinge indicates immaturity). Avoid squash that shows pitting, soft spots, or blackening at the stem—which should always be intact. Store 2–3 weeks at room temperature, preferably on the cool side. Do not refrigerate.

USE: I have cooked only relatively small samples of this squash, so I cannot judge the larger ones. In general, the squash needs no more than to be cleaned, cut in two, moistened inside with butter, cream, or oil; seasoned lightly; then baked. Steamed, it is light and lovely, but less flavorful than when baked. Serve hot, warm, or at room temperature, with very little embellishment.

PREPARATION: For tiny squash, keep part of the pretty skin intact, removing whatever quantity you don't want with a vegetable peeler. Cut out the stem end (make a neat plug to replace during cooking), then scoop out the seeds with a melon-ball cutter or teaspoon. Or make little boats by halving the squash lengthwise (first knocking off its tough stem) then cleaning out seeds and fiber. To prevent halves from tipping, shave away a bit of the underside. Or peel delicata, leaving the green ribs; then cut across into scalloped circles for steaming or braising.

NUTRITIONAL HIGHLIGHTS: Delicata is an excellent source of vitamin A and has substantial amounts of vitamin C, iron, and potassium. It is modest in calories and low in sodium.

DELICATA SQUASH HALVES BAKED WITH CREAM AND BASIL

No time or trouble is required to prepare this. The very small amount of cream flavors, moistens, and lightly glazes the smooth squash while adding very few calories. Set the halves in the oven to bake during the last 45 minutes of roasting time when you prepare turkey, ham, or chicken.

2 servings

1 delicata squash, about 1 pound, rinsed
Salt and sugar to taste
2 big pinches dried basil, crumbled
2 tablespoons heavy (or whipping) cream

1. Cut or knock off squash stem. Hold squash upright on this relatively flat end and very carefully slice down with a heavy knife to make 2 long halves. With melon-ball cutter scoop out all seeds and fibers. Shave a thin sliver from each curved underside so halves do not tip.

2. Sprinkle interior of squash with salt, sugar, and a big pinch of basil. Place a tablespoon of cream in each. Crimp foil to cover each half and set in pan.

3. Bake in 350-degree oven about 40–50 minutes, until very tender. Remove foil; carefully spoon up a little cream from cavity to moisten cut rim. Return to oven and bake, uncovered, for 5 minutes, or until lightly browned and bubbling.

STEAMED DELICATA RINGS WITH WALNUT DRESSING

This squash looks delightful cut in rings, the scalloped form of each decorated with bits of striped skin. You can also serve the steamed squash hot with lemon butter or Nutmeg Cream (page 206) for an equally delicious side dish.

2 servings

1 delicata squash, about 1 pound
1 tablespoon lemon juice
½ teaspoon sugar
Salt to taste
2 tablespoons imported walnut oil
1 tablespoon corn oil
3 tablespoons finely chopped walnuts

1. With vegetable peeler remove skin from squash, leaving what remains naturally in the indentations. Cut out stem end. With melon-ball cutter scoop out all seeds and fibers. Slice squash crosswise into rounds about ¾ inch thick.

2. Set squash in single layer (or overlapping somewhat) on rack of steamer. Cover and steam until tender, about 8–10 minutes. Gently transfer slices to a platter to cool somewhat.

3. Combine lemon juice, sugar, and salt; stir to dissolve. Add walnut and corn oils and blend. Spoon over squash rings; turn to coat. Let stand at room temperature until serving time (or chill, if you prefer).

4. Sprinkle slowly with nuts (or they fall off) and serve.

E

EGGPLANT
(Solanum melongena)
"new" varieties marketed as White Eggplant, Oriental or Japanese Eggplant, Chinese Eggplant, and Baby or Italian Eggplant

*P*etite as a plum to honeydew-sized; antique ivory to striped violet and cream to glossy raven-purple; narrow and sleek to full and bosomy—a whole gorgeous gamut of varieties is the happy consequence of a recent influx of Asian and Middle Eastern immigrants who brought with them wondrous eggplant forms and a wealth of recipes

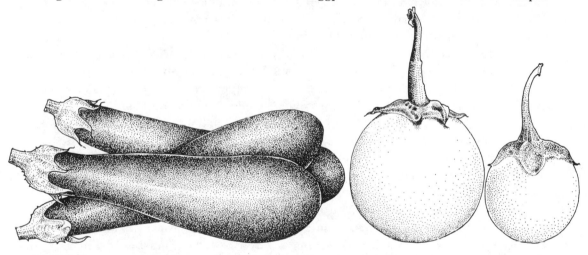

to contribute to the melting pot. In countries where meat is less emphasized, eggplant is a star performer, adding bulk and a fleshy texture to dishes that contain little or no animal fat. In addition, its subtle savor and melting consistency provide a bare minimum of calories, a boon for today's health-conscious American cooks, who have begun to explore vegetarian cuisines that much of the world enjoys.

How do new varieties differ from our "old" eggplant? Broadly speaking, they offer more nuances of texture, taste, and color, as well as sizes that can be exploited for a different range of cooking techniques (further discussed in the Use section):

☐ White eggplants (if you've seen the egg-shaped kind, you'll understand at once how this vegetable got its name), whatever shape or size, are firmer, less moist, and hold

169

their shape better than purple ones. They are also closer-grained, creamier, and less bitter. The flesh can be more heavily seeded (although seeds are often less acrid) and skins are usually considerably tougher and thicker.

☐ Small, deep-colored eggplants (sometimes called Italian or baby) that are either round or the shape of "conventional" market varieties are similar to the large but tend to have more delicate skin and finer flesh.

☐ Purple and striated small eggplants that are narrow and rather straight will all give you more skin per fruit (botanically, the eggplant is actually a berry)—which some of us happen to think is delicious, particularly on the thin-skinned kinds. These skinny eggplants, usually referred to as Oriental or Japanese, are just about always sweeter and smoother than the large.

☐ Pale violet or amethyst eggplants, slim, sleek, and comparatively lightweight, are usually called Chinese eggplants. They are even sweeter and more tender than the darker varieties, and contain fewer seeds.

☐ Rock-hard, round green, or green and white eggplants, some the size of cherries, appear in some Southeast Asian groceries. These are used mainly for pickling.

SELECTION AND STORAGE: It is important to select eggplants that are relatively heavy for their size. High solid content indicates fruit that has been cultivated in an even, stress-free environment, that has been exposed to appropriate quantities of heat and moisture. Heft a few of the same size to determine the best candidates.

Be vocal about demanding absolutely smooth, taut-skinned, shiny eggplants. They are *highly* perishable, and once they show flabby, bronzed, dented, or pitted areas, you can be pretty sure they're bitter. When you press an eggplant, it should feel firm; the flesh should dent but bounce back (although the long, narrow Oriental varieties are more tender). If the indentation remains, you have an overmature specimen. Finally, check the fuzzy green caps and stems, which should be intact and mold-free.

As for storing eggplants—don't. They deteriorate in both cold and heat. Try not to purchase more than a day in advance. Keep in a cool, not cold, place in a plastic bag.

USE: Of course you can use miniature and Oriental and white eggplants for everything that you would the "normal" ones, but it makes sense to develop an idea of which recipes will best exploit the virtues of each.

Use white eggplant when you need a particularly close-grained, firm-textured quality (such as when rolling slices, as in the Sicilian Eggplant Rolls). It holds its shape well whether baked or fried, even steamed, rarely becoming mushy. Use it, as well, when you want a dish to have a paler color than the khaki-ish one that results from the purple. For the most part, you will not want to include white eggplant in recipes in which the skin is kept on, as it tends to be thick and tough.

Use long Japanese or Oriental eggplants when you want the thinnest skin, whether whole (they are delightfully dainty), halved and fried, in diminutive slices, or partly sliced (as the Dragon Tails, page 176).

Use the oblong, pear-shaped, or round dwarf varieties for making lovely individual stuffed portions, for neat skin-on slices to top a pizza or galette, or to partly slice and fan (Grilled and Fried Eggplants, page 171).

However you decide to cook an eggplant, cook it thoroughly. It is both unpleasant and possibly harmful when undercooked—and difficult to overcook; it just becomes creamier.

PREPARATION: Most small eggplants that are purple or purplish require only a rinse and trim—unless they have been waxed (don't buy these), which you can tell by scratching with a fingernail (and about which you should complain to your grocer). In most cases the color, texture, and flavor of the skin will enhance the dish. M. F. K. Fisher, most-eloquent culinary philosopher, has addressed herself to the question of peeling of vegetables and has stated empathically: "All of them whether tender or hard, thick-skinned or thin, die when they are peeled . . . even as you and I" (*The Art of Eating,* Vintage Books, 1976). White eggplants, unfortunately, may have to be thus slaughtered to be eaten. Examine each individual before execution.

Eggplant is traditionally salted to rid it of bitterness. Although it does draw out moisture, which is helpful in some dishes, I have not found this step predictably useful in eliminating acridness; it usually just adds unnecessary salt and preparation time to the recipe.

NUTRITIONAL HIGHLIGHTS: Eggplant is very low in calories at about 30 per cup, cooked. It is an excellent source of fiber and fairly good source of potassium and folic acid.

GRILLED AND FRIED EGGPLANTS

The texture of these small eggplants remains velvety-firm even after broiling and peeling. Dipped into a light batter and quickly fried, the eggplants make crisp and attractive individual portions.

8 servings

8 small, dark, rounded eggplants, each about 4–5 inches long and weighing about 4 ounces
1 cup water
½ teaspoon salt
1 cup flour
Vegetable oil
Lime wedges

1. Rinse eggplants but do not trim off caps. Cut a tiny slit in each to prevent bursting. Set on preheated broiler rack as close as possible to heat source. Broil, turning once, until the skins have blackened and become puffy, about 5 minutes. Do not let eggplants become soft.

2. Holding stem of each eggplant, carefully pull off its skin. Gently press each to flatten it. At this point you can leave the eggplants for several hours, lightly covered, or go to the next step.

3. Prepare batter: Mix water and salt in a bowl. Sift in flour, beating with a fork. Cover and let stand for at least an hour.

4. When ready to serve, heat ¼–½ inch vegetable oil to 350 degrees in a wide skillet, preferably electric. Dip each eggplant in batter. Fry in one very large skillet or two smaller ones until richly browned on both sides—about 5 minutes total. Drain on paper towels and serve at once with lime wedges.

BABY EGGPLANTS WITH AROMATIC YOGURT SAUCE

Baby eggplants have smoother, more compact flesh than larger ones, and therefore work particularly well when baked whole; they keep their shape and cook evenly within. For this recipe, eggplants are simply baked, then dressed with a sauce made of grilled eggplant, yogurt, and fragrant seasonings. The thick purée tastes smoky, spicy, and rich—like a mixture of sour cream, tahini, and mayonnaise.

6 servings

8 very small, dark, round eggplants,
    about 4 ounces each
Olive oil
2 teaspoons whole coriander seed
2 teaspoons whole cumin seed
About ¾ teaspoon kosher salt, or to taste
1 cup yogurt
Cayenne pepper to taste
About ⅓ cup slivered fresh mint leaves

1. Rinse and dry 6 eggplants. Brush them all over with olive oil and set in a baking pan. Cover with foil and bake in a preheated 425-degree oven until very tender, but not disintegrating—from 30 to 45 minutes. Arrange on a serving dish and set aside.

2. Without trimming the 2 remaining eggplants, set them directly in a gas (or charcoal) flame, turning until very soft and charred on all sides, top and bottom —about 5 minutes. (Alternatively, set eggplants as close as possible to broiling element; turn until done.)

3. Let the 2 eggplants cool somewhat, then peel thoroughly; cut off stems. Crush lightly with a fork and set in a sieve to drain for at least 10 minutes. Meanwhile, stir coriander and cumin in a small, heavy pan over moderately low heat until the aroma changes from a delicate perfume of spice to a lightly toasty one, about 2 minutes; do not burn or sauce will be bitter. At slightest sign of smoke, immediately scrape the spices into a dish to cool. Grind fine in a spice mill.

4. Sprinkle spices and salt over drained eggplant in a bowl; mash well with a fork. Add yogurt. Adjust seasoning to taste, adding cayenne at this time. Chill well. At serving time sprinkle dressing heavily with mint, then spoon alongside or over the eggplants.

WHITE EGGPLANT IN COCONUT SAUCE

White eggplant is well suited to this recipe, as the flesh does not turn the dingy color of the darker vegetable, but remains a pale green (admittedly with a touch of gray). Do not reserve this subtle, rich dish for Eastern meals, which you might consider doing, at first glance. Its mysterious but mild flavor can accompany many simple foods —whether homey broiled chicken or fancy giant shrimp.

4 servings

1 tablespoon butter
½ teaspoon minced garlic
1 small hot chili-pepper (preferably a yellow or orange variety), seeded, minced
1¼ cups coconut milk (see Note)
Grated rind of 1 lemon, about 1 teaspoon
½ teaspoon salt, or to taste
½ teaspoon sugar
Medium-large white eggplant (1¼–1½ pounds), peeled and cut into ¾-inch cubes

1. Heat butter in a heavy flameproof casserole and stir in the garlic and chili; stir over low heat until lightly colored. Add coconut milk, lemon, salt, and sugar, and bring to a simmer, stirring.

2. Add eggplant cubes and simmer, stirring often with a rubber spatula, until tender throughout—about 15 minutes. Adjust seasoning and serve; or cool and reheat for maximum flavor.

Note: If you prefer to control the heat, sliver off the ribs before mincing; or add the whole pepper (with slits cut in it) with the coconut milk. Remove when bite is right.

You can use unsweetened canned or bottled coconut milk or prepare your own fresh coconut milk, following directions on page 55.

SICILIAN EGGPLANT ROLLS

Eggplant is *the* Sicilian vegetable par excellence, often appearing several times in a single meal in different guises. Here fine-textured white eggplant slices are rolled around prosciutto and mozzarella, then sauced with a light sweet-sour purée of tomato. If no white eggplant is available, make this with the dark, as they do in the dish's land of origin.

Makes 10 rolls

2 smooth, rather slender white eggplants about 8 inches long, each about 1¼ pounds

2 teaspoons coarse kosher salt

1¼ pounds (8 medium) ripe plum tomatoes

Olive oil as needed

½ cup sliced white part of scallions

1 teaspoon dried basil　.

About 1 teaspoon sugar

Salt as needed

About 2 teaspoons lemon juice

10 slices prosciutto, not too thin, to weigh about 6 ounces

½ pound mozzarella cheese, cut in 10 thin slices

Fresh basil leaves

1. Peel eggplants and cut lengthwise in even slices ⅜ inch thick (you need 10 even, non-end cuts). Place slices in enameled, stainless, or plastic colander, sprinkling salt between layers. Set waxed paper on top. Weight and drain 30 minutes or more.

2. Purée tomatoes. Strain to remove seeds and skin; reserve.

3. Heat 1 tablespoon oil in skillet and add scallions; stir briefly to soften. Add tomatoes and dried basil and simmer, covered, 15 minutes. If watery, simmer a bit uncovered; but do not cook to thick consistency. Strain through coarse sieve to remove basil and scallions. Taste and season with sugar, salt, and lemon juice; sauce should be tart-sweet, not salty (ham and cheese will be).

4. Rinse and dry eggplant. Spread slices on heavily oiled roasting pan or baking sheet. Brush each slice with oil. Bake about 8 minutes per side, turning once, or until slices are tender throughout, not mushy; check frequently (timing changes with varieties). Transfer to waxed paper to cool.

5. Cut off wide edge of fat from each prosciutto slice (save for cooking another dish). Place slice on each slice of eggplant; set cheese slice in center of each.

6. Pour thin layer of tomato sauce in serving dish large enough to just fit all rolls. Working from narrow end, roll up each of the slices of eggplant with ham and cheese and set, seam side down, in sauce. Pour remaining sauce in a band down the center of the rolls. Set a large basil leaf or two on top of each roll. Serve at room temperature.

BARBARA SPIEGEL'S WHITE EGGPLANT
STEAMED WITH SESAME OIL

My pal regularly invents tasteful low-calorie recipes, which she shares with me. This simple, speedy dish plays up the best qualities of small, white eggplants—their sweetness, creaminess, and smooth texture—which make them likely candidates for steaming, unlike the common large purple eggplants.

2 servings

2 long, narrow white eggplants, about 5 ounces each

1 jalapeño chili-pepper, seeded, deveined, and cut into tiny slivers

1 teaspoon Oriental sesame oil

2 teaspoons corn oil

¼ teaspoon salt

1½ teaspoons vinegar

2 teaspoons finely minced scallion green

1. Slice eggplants diagonally ½ inch thick. Place on steamer rack (bamboo steamer is preferable, but not required). Divide jalapeño evenly over slices. Combine sesame and corn oils and drizzle evenly over eggplant. Sprinkle with salt.

2. Set rack over boiling water. Cover and steam until creamy-tender, about 10 minutes. carefully transfer to serving platter. Sprinkle with vinegar, then scallions.

3. Serve warm, or at room temperature.

EGGPLANT-TOMATO-ONION DRAGON TAILS

With slices of tiny onions and cherry tomatoes tucked into slits made in their sleek skin, these narrow eggplants resemble curved, scaled dragon tails. The somewhat fanciful presentation and the fact that they taste best at room temperature make these lush-textured beauties fine choices for buffet parties.

6–8 servings

8 long, very narrow Oriental eggplants, about 4 ounces each

8 small onions (smaller in diameter than the eggplants), sliced thin

1 pint cherry tomatoes, sliced

1 teaspoon thyme

1 teaspoon fennel seeds

1 teaspoon rosemary

¼ teaspoon sugar

2 medium garlic cloves, sliced

1 teaspoon coarse kosher salt, or to taste

Black pepper to taste

4 tablespoons full-flavored olive oil

1 tablespoon vinegar

1. Make about 6 long, shallow, diagonal cuts (almost parallel to the surface) in each eggplant. Set in an oiled baking pan to fit with a little extra space.

2. Press both a slice of tomato and one of onion firmly into each slit. Chop leftover onions and tomatoes; scatter around eggplants. Sprinkle thyme, fennel, rosemary, sugar, garlic, salt, and pepper over all. Drizzle oil slowly and evenly over the top. Sprinkle with vinegar.

3. Cover tightly with foil and bake in center of preheated 425-degree oven until very tender. Timing can vary considerably, from 30 to 50 minutes; check often. Remove foil; baste eggplants thoroughly with pan juices, painting gently with a soft brush. Set on upper shelf of oven and bake (uncovered) until browned and soft —about 15 minutes; baste several times.

4. Cool eggplants slightly. Transfer carefully with a large spatula to a serving dish. Serve warm or at room temperature.

EGGPLANT, PASTA, AND GRILLED PEPPER SALAD

This cheery salad for all occasions displays a rainbow of summer's vegetables in simple garb—little more than oil, garlic, and plenty of verdant basil.

6–8 servings

5 small purple eggplants, each 4 ounces

About ½ cup olive oil, or more to taste

3 large, thick red and/or yellow bell peppers

About 1½ teaspoons salt

1 pound curly pasta, such as rotini or fusilli

2 large tomatoes, peeled preferably by flame method (page 23)

1 large garlic clove, minced

About 24 Calamata olives, or other pungent black olives, halved and pitted

About ½ cup coarsely slivered basil

Dash vinegar

Black pepper to taste

1. Trim off eggplant caps. Slice eggplants in half lengthwise, then in crosswise slices about ¼ inch thick. In a very large skillet sauté eggplant (in batches) over moderate heat until browned and tender, using as much oil as needed to prevent sticking. Reserve.

2. Set peppers on preheated broiler pan as close to heat source as possible. Turn until blackened and blistered all over, but not charred deeply. (Or do the same directly in a gas flame.) Let stand a minute or two, then wrap in damp towels or enclose in plastic bag 5–10 minutes to steam off skins.

3. Cut off stems and scrape off skins. Cut open peppers and remove seeds and membranes. Rinse peppers; cut into ½-inch squares. Toss with salt to taste and about 1 tablespoon olive oil. Set aside.

4. Dump pasta into boiling salted water and cook until just barely tender; be careful not to overcook, as the pasta softens when dressed. Drain well; toss with 2 tablespoons olive oil. Cool, tossing occasionally.

5. Cut tomatoes in coarse dice. Combine with garlic, 2 tablespoons oil, and salt to taste. Combine pasta, eggplant, peppers, tomatoes, and olives. Season assertively and let stand, lightly covered, for several hours or more before serving.

6. At serving time, toss gently with the basil and adjust vinegar, salt and pepper to taste.

ENOKIDAKE
(Flammulina velutipes, formerly Collybia velutipes)
also Enokitake, Enoki, Enok Mushroom, Golden Mushroom, Velvet Stem

A delicacy well-known in Japan, where its diminutive size is particularly appreciated for garnishing clear soups, enokidake (en-oh-kee-DAH-kay) have a flavor that is most uncharacteristic for a fungus: not earthy, but slightly acid and fruity, more like a grape than a mushroom. Long-legged, tiny-capped, bright white, and slightly crunchy,

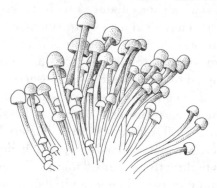

enokidake flourish in North American forests, but only the cultivated form (which looks very different from the wild) is presently marketed.

Cultivation, which originated in the Orient and has been practiced for about twenty years, takes place as follows: A mixture of rice bran, water, and sawdust is sterilized in a heat-resistant container into which the spawn is introduced. The mushrooms develop for about 2 months in darkened, temperature-controlled rooms; at the end of that time the fungus, white as a result of the sunless environment, is sufficiently mature to harvest. The spaghetti-like strands of stem, clumped together at the base and topped with gumdrop-like caps, are packed into plastic packages of about 3.5 ounces each and sent to market.

SELECTION AND STORAGE: Enokidake are available year round, erratically, in many Oriental groceries and some supermarkets, primarily on the East and West coasts. At this writing, they are sold in small plastic packets, so there is little selection possible. Press the plastic gently to feel that the mushrooms are firm, not flabby, and try to check out the base; the heavy stem-joined end should not be watery or browned, although creamy-beige is acceptable. While enokidake will always be more moist than other mushrooms, they should not be slimy or slippery-looking, nor should the caps be anything but clean white.

Store in the refrigerator in the original wrapping for 4–5 days.

USE: Enokidake are delightful eaten raw, so that their crisp texture and fleeting aroma can be enjoyed. Once trimmed, they can be popped into salads and sandwiches, used rather as you would delicate sprouts. When added to clear broths or sukiyaki, they are tossed in at the last moment, or they become tough and fibrous. The one exception I have tasted was a dish in which the entire contents of a package, trimmed but not separated, were sautéed over high heat until the mushrooms were browned, even a little burned. This released another dimension of taste.

PREPARATION: Trim the heavy, spongy base mass from the mushrooms, as well as an inch or two of the stringy stems. Separate the stems, and that's it.

NUTRITIONAL HIGHLIGHTS: Enokidake are low in calories. They also provide small amounts of thiamine, riboflavin, and niacin, and are high in fiber.

—

JIM FOBEL'S ENOKIDAKE SALAD

Jim Fobel, friend and author *(Beautiful Food)*, always devises pretty dishes. This warmish tangle of white, celery-green, pink, and scarlet strands highlights the flavor and texture of each component.

4 servings

1 medium-sized, thick, smooth-sided red bell pepper
2 medium Belgian endive (6 ounces), or 1 endive and 1 radicchio di Treviso (the narrow spears)
2 packages (each 3.5 ounces) enokidake
3 tablespoons olive oil
2 ounces firm ham (Smithfield, Westphalian, prosciutto, or Black Forest), cut in extremely fine julienne strips (⅓–½ cup)
1½–2 tablespoons lemon juice
Salt and pepper to taste

1. Place pepper directly in gas flame (alternatively set in broiler pan as close to heat as possible); turn until blackened all over. Let stand for a minute, then enclose in damp toweling or a plastic bag and leave for 10 minutes. Halve, remove stem, seeds, and ribs; scrape off all skin; rinse and dry. Cut in fine julienne strips. Cover; refrigerate.

2. Rinse and dry endive (and radicchio); cut out core at base. Slice into thin julienne strips. Cut off heavy base of enokidake and as much stem as necessary; rinse for a second, then roll gently in toweling. Cover and refrigerate endive and enokidake.

3. At serving time combine red pepper, endive, and radicchio in a large bowl. Heat 1 tablespoon oil in a skillet; add ham and toss over high heat to heat through. Add to bowl. Heat remaining 2 tablespoons oil and toss enokidake for 15 seconds over high heat, to just begin to wilt. Add mushrooms and oil to bowl; toss with lemon juice and salt and pepper to taste. Divide among 4 serving plates and serve at once.

SALAD OF ENOKIDAKE AND CUCUMBER

Fresh and clean, this pale, crunchy salad goes well with rather light foods that are simply seasoned.

6 servings

2 packages of enokidake (each 3.5 ounces, approximately)

3 large Kirby cucumbers, or another kind that is not waxed

3 tablespoons lemon juice

1½ teaspoons sugar

¼ teaspoon salt, or to taste

½ cup sour cream

1 scallion green, very thinly sliced

1. Rinse enokidake, then pat dry. Trim off 1–2 inches of the heavy base; halve stems crosswise.

2. Scrub cucumbers well; do not peel. Seed if necessary; slice into fine julienne slivers about the size of the mushrooms. Toss both in a serving dish.

3. Stir together lemon juice, sugar, and salt in a bowl. Blend in sour cream. Drizzle over the vegetables, then sprinkle with scallion.

Note: Hothouse or "burpless" or English cucumbers (all the same thing) are as good as Kirby and look even prettier with their dark peel. Use 1 instead of 3.

SOUP OF SHRIMP AND ENOKIDAKE

Fragile white enoki mushrooms and pink shrimp float in a tart, hot fish broth that makes a light and warming first course.

6 servings

6 ounces shrimp in the shell

About 1½ pounds meaty bones from lean fish, cut up

6 cups water

About 5 tablespoons dry sherry

1 celery stalk with leaves, sliced

Knob of ginger, about 3 inches long and 1 inch wide, sliced

Optional: Few thin leaves lemon grass, cut up

½ teaspoon grated lemon rind

Big pinch cayenne pepper

1 package enokidake (about 3.5 ounces)

1 scallion green, sliced very thin

Salt

1. Peel off shrimp shells and place them in a large saucepan with the fish bones and water. Simmer for 1 minute, skimming thoroughly. Add ¼ cup sherry, celery, ginger, and optional lemon grass; simmer, partly covered, for 25 minutes. Meanwhile, devein shrimp and cut them in thin diagonal slices; sprinkle with the lemon rind and cayenne.

2. Strain broth through a sieve lined with several layers of dampened cheesecloth; discard solids. Return broth to rinsed-out saucepan and add sherry and salt to taste.

3. Rinse enokidake, then trim off most of the base, leaving 2–3 inches of the stems; separate the stalks. Bring broth to a simmer. Add shrimp and return to a simmer, stirring. Off heat stir in mushrooms and scallion. Serve at once, in small bowls.

🦢 *ADDITIONAL RECIPE*
Salad of Radish Sprouts, Endive, Pepper, and Mushrooms, page 404

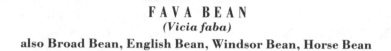

F

FAVA BEAN
(Vicia faba)
also Broad Bean, English Bean, Windsor Bean, Horse Bean

*H*ow can it be that fava beans, whose culture is so ancient that it has no known wild form, whose use is so widespread that it is considered common fare from China to England, Iran to Spain, Africa to South America, have *not* become part of American cuisine? In China fava beans have been included in the diet for close to 5,000 years.

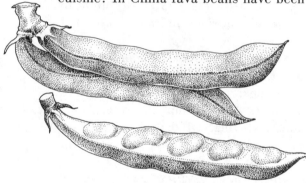

Romans consider favas their special province, as they have since ancient times (*faba*, which means bean, is named after the Fabii, a noble Roman family). In the south of France fava season is celebrated. Old English cookbooks refer to the broad bean (its usual name in most English-speaking countries) as "the common bean." On the Iberian peninsula broad beans appear dried, fresh, and fried and salted—as they do in China, where they are also sprouted. In a good part of the Middle East fava beans *are* the meal or meals of the day.

Although the venerable bean was introduced into this country in 1602 and hordes of people from the areas mentioned above have since made their homes here, the fava has not. Alice Waters grows it in her garden to make classy pasta dishes at her restaurants in Berkeley; Italian mothers and restaurateurs (not mutually exclusive, mind you) fill shopping bags with the dramatically large verdant pods when they pop in about April; curious cooks give them a whirl; but the unique vegetable remains a specialty item.

One reason may be that the time-consuming cleaning process is daunting for this nation in a hurry. To properly enjoy the fava, you must pick the tough skin off each bean, a distinctly labor-intensive job—though perfect for casual company chatting. The skinning yields beans of springtime-green (and occasionally reddish, brown, purplish hues) that resemble baby limas, pack plenty of subtle flavor, and are surprisingly melting in texture, not starchy. It also produces plenty of refuse (although tender pods can be eaten). The lack of enthusiasm for the fava may also be due to the fact that Americans have never developed a taste for bitterness. Here, bitter is bad, sweet is good. In many cuisines the two are considered equally desirable, not negative and positive. And favas often do have a bitter aftertaste, as fresh as grass.

SELECTION AND STORAGE: Fava beans are harbingers of spring, although they continue to appear into the summer. Look for the smallest, crispest, most evenly green pods, with some discoloration to be expected. Because there is considerable waste when you shell and skin favas, buy a good deal more than you would of other beans. While it is generally recommended that you avoid the large, heavy pods (they may measure a foot or so) with slightly yellowing beans, I find them delicious, with a pronounced and appealing cheesy flavor that is different from the young beans, but worthwhile.

You can store the beans for a few days in the refrigerator, spread in a wide dish, but don't plan to keep the perishable vegetable longer than that. Once shelled, blanched, and skinned (see Preparation), the beans can be frozen in small plastic containers for longer storage.

USE: Most recipes that you'll see for fava beans apply to the large dried ones, which have little in common with the fresh other than being delicious. The following concerns the in-pod beans only.

If you have favas from a garden at your disposal, pick tiny beans (2–3 inches) and eat them whole, as they do in Europe, for an hors d'oeuvre. Or shell baby beans and eat them raw, with coarse salt, pepper, dry ham, crumbly cheese, and plenty of *vino*. I have never found such delicate specimens in the United States, but I have been told they exist.

Fresh fava beans are a luxury to be savored alone or with a few choice ingredients. Do not hide them or overcook them.

Gently stew fresh beans in a little butter, oil, or cream, lightly touched with savory, thyme, or sage.

Sautéed seafood, veal, and lightly smoked meats are elegantly embellished by the addition of favas during the last minutes of cooking. Or heat the beans briefly with the skimmed pan juices of roasted veal, chicken, or pork, then spoon over the meat.

Accent fresh pasta or rice with favas and wild mushrooms.

Cook large, heavy beans longer; then crush to make a purée, adding cream, butter, and a little lemon juice.

Cook pods alone trimmed of strings or with beans inside, for a sticky, messy, and savory dish. Or add trimmed pods to soups and vegetable stews.

PREPARATION: The way you prepare the beans will depend on their age and how you will cook them. Unless you are planning to stew the whole pod (see page 186), I find it is necessary to remove the skin from the beans, no matter how young. Many authorities consider peeling to be unnecessary, but I have yet to find favas that do not benefit from the removal of the bitter layer. See for yourself.

To shell favas, cut the tips from the pods, then press open the seams. Pull out the fat beans from the cushioned plush sleeping bag, where they are so neatly nestled, removing the little stems if necessary. Drop the beans into salted, boiling water. Boil 30 seconds (more than a minute and they mush when you try to skin them). Drain and drop in ice water. When they are cooled, slit each skin with your nail and pop out the bean, working carefully so they don't break.

If you are going to cook the pods (for this they must be quite small and tender; sample before cooking), with or without the beans inside, you'll want to pull off the strings on both sides. If resistant, zip them off with a vegetable peeler.

NUTRITIONAL HIGHLIGHTS: Fava beans are low in calories—about 80 per cup, cooked. They are relatively high in protein, iron, and fiber, are good sources of vitamins C and A and potassium, and contain modest amounts of the B vitamins.

Note: Eating raw or cooked fava beans, and even inhaling pollen from a plant, can be toxic to those who suffer from glucose-6-phosphate dehydrogenase deficiency. A very small number of individuals, primarily of Mediterranean origin (but some Africans, Arabs, and Asians have also been affected) inherit this imbalance which, when combined with other genetic factors (not yet isolated), causes severe hemolytic anemia in the presence of fava beans.

SHRIMP AND FAVAS WITH THYME

Pink shrimp with apple-green fava, briny-sweet and herbal-bitter, make an earthy yet sophisticated pair. If you cannot find fresh thyme, many other herbs will be equally delicious: savory, sage, oregano, or marjoram.

2 servings

1 tablespoon olive oil

1 tablespoon butter

About 2 ounces firm, salty ham (such as Smithfield or prosciutto), cut into tiny dice (about ⅓ cup)

¼ teaspoon minced garlic

¾ pound medium shrimp, shelled (or about 10 ounces shelled shrimp)

1 pound fava beans, pods and shells removed (see Preparation)

1 teaspoon minced fresh thyme

Pepper and salt

1. Heat oil and butter in skillet over moderate heat. Add ham and garlic and toss for a minute. Add shrimp, favas, and thyme, and toss just until shrimp become pink.

2. Sprinkle with pepper and salt. Cover pan and cook on lowest heat possible for 1–2 minutes, or until shrimp are just cooked through and juices exude slightly. Serve at once.

———— ▬ ————

FAVA RISOTTO WITH FRESH SAGE

The Italian custom of serving creamy risotto alone, as a course to be savored, is one I adore. Fava beans, with their very special color, texture, and subtle flavor deserve to star in a dish, not play in the chorus.

Good risotto depends upon perfect timing. This is one food where a minute's over- or undercooking makes a difference, so be sure the diners are understanding, and at the table as you finish the dish.

6 servings

3 ounces slab bacon, cut in narrow strips about 2 inches long

3 tablespoons finely minced shallots

1¾ cups arborio rice (see Note)

About 6 cups chicken stock

2 pounds medium-sized fava beans, pods and skins removed (see Preparation), to make roughly 1⅓ cups

2 tablespoons thinly slivered fresh sage leaves (see Note)

2 tablespoons butter

About 1½ cups grated Parmesan cheese

1. Stir bacon in heavy saucepan over moderate heat until well browned. With slotted spoon transfer to paper towel. Remove and reserve fat. Wipe out saucepan. Heat 2½ tablespoons bacon fat; stir in shallots and soften over low heat for a minute or two. Meanwhile, heat stock to simmering in another pan.

2. Add rice to shallots and stir 2 minutes. Ladle in ¾ cup hot stock. Adjust heat so that rice simmers but does not boil and stick; stir occasionally until liquid is almost absorbed. Continue adding hot stock in ¾ cup increments and stirring as needed until it is almost absorbed.

3. After 20 minutes, rice should be almost cooked; that is, it will be a bit too firm, but no longer hard in the center of each grain. At this point add bacon along with the portions of stock.

4. Within 5 minutes or so, rice should be properly firm-tender in texture. Add favas and sage and stir until hot through. Remove from heat and stir in butter and a few tablespoons or more hot stock to make a slightly soupy, creamy mixture. Stir in ¼ cup cheese. Spoon into heated bowls. Serve at once with cheese on the side.

Note: Arborio rice, a short-grain Italian rice, is required in order to achieve the special texture of this dish. It is available in many markets and all Italian specialty shops. If you cannot find fresh sage, substitute a small amount of fresh thyme or marjoram. Sage, however, is just what balances this subtle blend.

STEWED FAVA BEANS AND LEEKS WITH LEMON

Prepare this dish with small, young favas so that you can cook the pods, which add a slippery, interesting texture. Although the flavor is unique and appealing—a blend of okra and spinach—the look is less than classy. Save the messy mélange for a homey dinner for bean lovers; serve with bread to sop up the juices.

4 servings

3 small leeks (about ¾ pound)
1½ pounds small fava beans in the pod
About ⅓ cup olive oil
About ¼ cup lemon juice
About 1 teaspoon coarse kosher salt
1 cup water
Pepper

1. Trim off dark upper leaves of leeks for soup. Halve lower parts lengthwise; rinse carefully between layers. Slice ½ inch thick.

2. Carefully remove tails and strings from both sides of each fava pod with a paring knife; if they do not pull off, shave each off, as they are too tough to eat. Cut pods in sections between bean bumps.

3. Heat ¼ cup oil in a heavy saucepan. Stir in leeks and cook over moderate heat, covered, until softened slightly—about 5 minutes. Add beans, ¼ cup lemon juice, 1 teaspoon salt, and water; cover tightly and cook until very tender, almost mushy. This may take as little as ¾ hour, as much as 1½, depending upon maturity of beans. Stir now and then, adding water if mixture gets sticky.

4. When stew is sufficiently cooked, it will be soupy. If too liquid, uncover and simmer briefly, stirring gently. Cool to lukewarm or room temperature; add olive oil, lemon juice, salt, and pepper to taste.

FEIJOA
(Feijoa sellowiana)
also Pineapple Guava

*C*ommon usage has given this fruit the name of *pineapple guava* (and in some markets even worse: simply *guava*), which is mighty confusing, since it is not a guava *(Psidium)*. The mislabeling is particularly daunting for those who are not familiar with either genus, and would like to know what they are buying. But if you're acquainted

with guavas, you may have some idea what to expect inside a feijoa.

Both are members of the Myrtle family, which includes such aromatics as eucalyptus, bay-rum, clove, and allspice; and both are generously fragrant. Difficult to pin down, the scent and taste of the elongated-egg-shaped (and -sized) feijoa (fay-JO-a or fay-YO-a) suggest pineapple, quince, spruce, and Concord grapes—touched with lemon and menthol. (The fleshy flowers are said to make fine eating, as well.) The slightly bumpy, thin skin ranges from lime-green to olive. It encloses cream-to-tan granular, medium-soft flesh that surrounds a jellyish central cavity set with minute seeds. The taste is tart and perfumy, the texture gritty (but pleasantly, like pears) and dense.

Although it is native to South America (the fruit is named after a Señor Feijo, once a director of the national history museum in Spain; the *sellowiana* is for Herr Sello, a German explorer of South America), like a number of fruits that are part of today's marketplace the subtropical feijoa is exported primarily from New Zealand (a small crop is raised in California), where it has been cultivated since the beginning of the century. The success of today's two important varieties, modestly named Triumph and Mammoth, is due to a celebrated New Zealand nurseryman, Hayward Wright, whose name is attached to the best-known variety of kiwifruit grown today, which he also developed. Oddly, American horticulturists voiced considerable enthusiasm for the fruit when it was planted in California as early as 1900 and seemed to attract a good deal of attention. In Wilson Popenoe's remarkably contemporary-sounding 1920 textbook *Manual of Tropical and Subtropical Fruits* (now in facsimile edition, published by the Hafner Press), he writes that "in the dry climate of California [the feijoa] is eminently successful. Numerous small commercial plantings have been made in various parts of the state, and the fruit has begun to appear regularly in the markets." In the popular *Sunset All-Western Foods Cook Book*, published in 1947 by the Lane Publishing Company, feijoa is also part of the repertoire. (Yet an article published by the same *Sunset* magazine in 1984 introduced a "new fruit" that is "increasingly available in markets.")

Why was the attractive evergreen shrub with its brilliant red bottlebrush flowers relegated to the role of ornamental—its fruits ignored? Were Californians hoarding the entire production? After speaking with several dedicated nurserymen and farmers, the only likely reason I could assign for its temporary fall from grace was competition from the wildly successful avocado (so hard to remember that it is a relative newcomer), which was planted by almost every entrepreneur in the state. Feijoa growers today, who plant rootstock imported from New Zealand, are hoping it will be the next kiwi.

SELECTION AND STORAGE: Feijoas from New Zealand should be in the market during spring and early summer, while the California crop goes from fall to early winter. All should have a full, rich aroma when you buy them. If they are not as tender as a firmish plum or soft pear (they will not become creamy-soft), leave at room temperature for a few days (or speed up the process by enclosing in a paper bag with an apple) until they are. Before ripening, they will be very acid, sometimes bitter. As the reasonable Dr. Popenoe wrote: "To be appreciated, this fruit must be eaten at the proper degree of ripeness. M. Viviand-Morel says, 'everyone knows that the finest pears are only turnips if eaten a trifle too soon.' "

Once they are ripened, you can store feijoas in the refrigerator for a day or two. Or purée the raw fruit and freeze. Or prepare the cooked purée (see recipe below) and keep up to a week in the refrigerator or for months in the freezer.

USE: The feijoa is no shy violet; it holds its own in fresh or cooked form. When very ripe and succulent, the feijoa makes an intriguing, fresh addition to fruit salads and dessert combinations—used in moderation, as its pungency tends to dominate. You might consider it half flavoring, half fruit as you create new recipes. Sometimes the flesh is a bit tart and requires sugar, but taste before you sprinkle. Puréed, the uncooked fruit makes exceptional ices, ice creams, and mousses, particularly when blended with oranges, ginger, papaya, banana, strawberries, and lime.

Halved or sliced and gently poached in syrup, the feijoa can be served chilled with cream or combined with other cooked fruits. Or purée the fruit in syrup to use in soufflés, cream desserts, or as a sauce to accompany either roasted meat or plain cakes or puddings.

In Australia and New Zealand, where the feijoa is less pricy (and pronounced FEE-jo), it is used to make jelly and fruit butter, chutney, pie, relish, fritters—just about anything you might think of making with apples.

PREPARATION: Although the skin of the feijoa is delightfully scented, it is usually bitter, fresh or cooked. Taste for yourself, then pare, if necessary. When puréeing the feijoa, you need simply halve the fruit, scoop out all the pulp, and discard the rind; or, if it is not bitter, purée the whole fruit.

NUTRITIONAL HIGHLIGHT: Feijoas are a good source of vitamin C.

FEIJOAS IN SYRUP

Although the basic preparation below may not sound like much by way of quantity, it will transform a quart of mixed fruits into an unusual brunch opener or fragrant dessert. Or serve a small quantity of the fruit over ice cream or a pudding; the sweet syrup is as heady and aromatic as brandy or vanilla sauce.

Makes about 1¼ cups

½ pound (3 large) ripe feijoas
½ cup water
¼ cup sugar

1. Peel all dark green from fruits. Halve each lengthwise, then cut across in ½-inch slices.

2. Bring water and sugar to a boil in small nonaluminum saucepan. Add fruit. Reduce heat to lowest point. Cover and poach (no bubbling in the syrup) until fruits have softened slightly—about 4 minutes.

3. Gently pour into a dish and cool. Cover and chill.

FEIJOA FRUIT CUP

I have yet to meet the fruit combination that is not enlivened by the feijoa's powerful perfume and acid balance. Consider the following recipe as a model, not a group of specifics. The more tutti the frutti the better.

4 servings

1½ cups diced fresh pineapple
2 oranges, peeled, pith removed, segmented
1 banana, sliced
1 pint strawberries, rinsed, hulled, and sliced
1¼ cups Feijoas in Syrup (see preceding recipe)

Combine all ingredients and chill until serving time.

SAUTÉED SHRIMP AND FEIJOA WITH MINT AND GINGER

One of those rare pleasures of the table that take minutes to prepare and are delicious, unusual, and attractive. The half-moons of feijoa become soft and yellow-gold when sautéed, complementing the curled pink shrimp's color and texture. The few ingredients produce a complicated flavor that is at once lemony, briny, winy, minty, and fruity.

If you increase the recipe, the pan should be wide enough to hold the feijoa in a single layer.

2 servings

2 ripe medium-sized feijoas (about 6 ounces)
2 tablespoons butter
¾ teaspoon grated fresh ginger
½ teaspoon sugar
¾ pound medium shrimp, shelled (or 10 ounces shelled shrimp)
Salt and white pepper to taste
1 tablespoon minced fresh mint, or to taste (or substitute parsley)

1. Peel feijoas; cut off and discard both ends. Halve lengthwise, then cut crosswise slices ¼-inch thick (should equal about 1 cup).

2. Melt butter in heavy skillet; add feijoa slices and ginger; sprinkle with ¼ teaspoon sugar. Cook over moderate heat until slightly browned, about 1 minute. Turn slices over, sprinkle with remaining ¼ teaspoon sugar. Cook over slightly lowered heat, shaking pan to prevent sticking, until lightly browned and almost tender, about 2 minutes; timing depends on ripeness of fruit.

3. Gently scoop feijoas to the side of the pan. Add shrimp; sprinkle with salt and white pepper. Toss over moderate heat until slightly pinkish, but not cooked through—about 1 minute. Add mint. Toss all gently, then cover pan. Let stand off heat about 2–3 minutes; toss again and serve at once.

—

SALAD OF FEIJOA, ENDIVE, AND AVOCADO

There is no question that tart-sweet fruits have an affinity for avocado, and feijoa is no exception. Slivered into pieces of approximately the same size, the crisp, bittersweet endive; granular, quince-like feijoa; and creamy avocado produce a sum that is more than its parts.

4 servings

2 teaspoons sugar
½ teaspoon salt
2 tablespoons rice vinegar
2 tablespoons lime juice
¼ cup corn oil
2 medium-ripe large feijoas, about ½ pound
4 medium Belgian endive (about ½ pound), rinsed
1 medium avocado, peeled, pitted, cut into thin slivers about 1½ inches long

1. Mix together sugar, salt, and vinegar in a small bowl; stir to dissolve. Add lime juice and corn oil and blend. Peel feijoas thoroughly, then cut into thin julienne strips about 1½ inches long. Add to dressing and mix gently to blend. Refrigerate for ½ hour or longer.

2. Cut out base of endive, then halve lengthwise. Cut diagonal julienne shreds about 1½ inches long. Arrange these in a dish; cover with avocado. Pour feijoa and dressing over all.

3. Toss gently and serve at once.

—

FEIJOA SAUCE (OR PURÉE)

This useful luxury can be made when feijoas are in the market, then frozen in small containers for up to 6 months. The light, caramel-colored purée can be served as is, or to accompany vanilla or fruit ice cream, a light sponge cake, or gingerbread. The sweet, intense sauce goes a long way—so use sparingly. Or make the purée to serve as a base for ice cream, sorbet, tart filling, or soufflé.

Makes 2¼–2½ cups, approximately

1 cup sugar
1 cup water
2 pounds ripe feijoas

1. Combine sugar and water in non-aluminum saucepan large enough to hold the fruit; bring to a boil.

2. Halve feijoas crosswise and scoop out the pulp with a melon-ball cutter, avoiding any bright-green parts or skin, which are bitter.

3. Add to syrup and return to a boil, stirring. Remove from heat, set a light weight on the fruit to keep it submerged, and cool.

4. Purée thoroughly in a blender or food processor, in batches. Scrape the mixture through a fine sieve. Refrigerate or freeze.

FEIJOA ICE CREAM

Slightly tart and perfumy, this cream-beige dessert has a flavor that suggests a medley: coconut, banana, pineapple, grape, and pear—all seem to be part of the act. Don't expect a very smooth texture, as the consistency of the feijoa is slightly granular, like firm pears.

Makes about 1 quart

1 small, very ripe banana
About 2 tablespoons lime juice
1⅓ cups Feijoa Purée (preceding recipe), chilled
1 cup yogurt
1 cup heavy (or whipping) cream

1. Purée banana and 2 tablespoons lime juice in processor or blender until smooth. Add to feijoa purée. Stir in yogurt and heavy cream; add lime juice to taste.

2. Pour into the cream container of an ice-cream maker and freeze according to the manufacturer's directions. Pack tightly into a quart container and put in freezer to mellow for a day or so.

3. Allow to soften for about ½ hour in the refrigerator before serving. If you wish to accent the feijoa flavor, serve a spoonful of feijoa purée alongside each serving of the ice cream.

FEIJOA SOUFFLÉS

High-rising, light, with a bright fresh-fruit flavor, these petite individual soufflés can be assembled and baked very quickly, if you've made the fruit purée beforehand. The recipe can be doubled.

4 servings

⅔ cup Feijoa Purée (see page 191), at room temperature
1 tablespoon sugar, plus a little for the dishes
2 extra-large or jumbo egg whites
Big pinch cream of tartar
Big pinch salt
½ cup heavy (or whipping) cream, whipped to form very soft mounds

1. Preheat oven to 400 degrees. Lightly butter 4 soufflé dishes or custard cups of about ¾-cup capacity. Sprinkle interior of each sparingly with sugar to coat very lightly. Bring a kettle of water to a boil.

2. Beat egg whites, cream of tartar, and salt in a small bowl to form soft peaks; beat in the tablespoon of sugar gradually to form firm but not dry peaks.

Stir one-third whites thoroughly into feijoa purée. Pour this mixture over remaining whites; fold together gently with a rubber spatula.

3. Scoop into the dishes, smooth tops, then run a shallow groove in the surface of each (I use a chopstick) about ¼ inch from the rim. Set in a baking dish or pan, pour in boiling water to reach halfway up the dishes, and set in oven center. Lower heat to 375 degrees and bake 15 minutes, till lightly browned.

4. Bring to the table at once, delicately slice off each topknot pouf, and spoon cream into the cavity; replace the pouf and serve immediately.

FEIJOA-PLUM ICE

This delicate pink ice has a vivid perfume reminiscent of Concord grapes, ripe pears, and plum brandy. It is even more delightful when paired with Gingered Papaya Milk Sherbet (page 345). Should the plums available be less than lush, substitute 2 nectarines at their peak.

Makes about 1 quart

¾–1 pound (about 5) tender-soft, particularly pungent feijoas

About ¾ cup sugar

Pinch salt

2¼ cups water

3 large, juicy-ripe red plums, pitted and sliced

About ¼ cup lemon juice

1. Halve feijoas and scoop out pulp. You should have 1 cup.

2. Combine ¾ cup sugar, salt, and ¾ cup water in nonaluminum saucepan and bring to a boil; simmer 5 minutes. Add plums and simmer until soft—about 5 minutes.

3. Purée plums and liquid in a blender or processor. Add feijoa pulp to hot liquid; purée thoroughly. Pour into a bowl; add remaining 1½ cups water and ¼ cup lemon juice. Stir; adjust sugar and lemon juice, if needed. Chill.

4. Pour into the cream can of an ice-cream maker and process according to the manufacturer's directions. Pack into a quart container, then let ripen in the freezer a day or so. Before serving soften slightly in the refrigerator.

PEAR-FEIJOA BROWN BETTY

Crunchy, buttery bread cubes top a scented, syrupy mingling of pears and feijoas. Accompany with crème fraîche, heavy cream, sour cream, ice cream, or chilled lemon sauce. Try this for brunch, with café au lait.

4 servings

3 cups firm sandwich bread (white or whole-wheat) cut in ½-inch cubes

4 tablespoons unsalted butter, melted

4 ripe medium feijoas (½ pound)

About 1½ pounds ripe, tender pears, such as Anjou or Packham

½ cup light brown sugar, lightly packed

2 tablespoons lemon juice

Pinch salt

1. Spread cubes in single layer in pan; bake in preheated 350-degree oven until dried, about 15 minutes. Pour into a bowl and gradually add melted butter, tossing constantly to distribute evenly.

2. Peel feijoas and cut into ½-inch pieces, approximately. Core, peel, and cut pears into cubes of same size. (There should be about 4 cups fruit.) Set aside 2 rounded tablespoons sugar. Combine remainder in bowl with fruit, lemon juice, and salt; toss.

3. Spread ½ cup bread in buttered round 6-cup baking dish about 8 inches in diameter. Spread half fruit and juices over this; top with another generous ½ cup bread. Cover with remaining fruit and juice; press to even. Cover with bread cubes and press them into surface lightly.

4. Cover with foil and bake in preheated 375-degree oven until bubbling hot, about 30 minutes. Remove foil, sprinkle with remaining sugar, and bake until crisp, about 15–20 minutes longer. Serve hot.

 ADDITIONAL RECIPE
Note to Annabel Langbein's Apple and Cape Gooseberry Picnic Cake (page 81)

FENNEL
(Foeniculum vulgare, variety *Azoricum* or *dulce)*
also Finocchio, Florence Fennel; and Anise and Sweet Anise (both incorrect)

*D*escribing the uses of fennel is, for me, like explaining what to do with a tomato. It is a food that I have always loved and do not question. Perhaps it is because I was raised near Little Italy in Greenwich Village that I have always taken for granted this crisp, fragrant vegetable/herb, which I have just recently come to realize is relatively hard to find in much of the country.

In culinary terms, fennel means Italy, where it is served in dishes from hors d'oeuvres through dessert. The pale-green, feathery-topped vegetable, with its celery-like stems and swollen bulb-like base of overlapping broad layers, has been cultivated there forever. Ancient Romans used a number of fennel varieties to generously season pork, lamb, seafood, and beans. So do modern Italians, who still make a fennel-pork sausage as they did in the time of Apicius, and consume large quantities of both seeds and vegetable. The seeds, by the way, come from a nonbulbing variety of fennel currently grown and used throughout the temperate world, while the fleshy sweet vegetable is cultivated primarily in Italy, France, Greece, and the United States.

Fennel's taste, which is likened to licorice and anise, is lighter, less persistent than either; and it becomes even more delicate and elusive when cooked. Perhaps this licorice likeness explains why we see a comparatively small quantity in the United States. While for many Europeans these flavorings are as common in sweets and beverages as vanilla and lemon are for us, Americans seem to find both of them "strange." If this is so, it makes even more sense for produce handlers to stop calling it anise, as it is in so many markets. If you know someone who shies away from licorice or anise, gamble with fennel: chances are they'll be charmed by the fresh sweetness.

SELECTION AND STORAGE: Look for fennel from early fall through spring, with its peak season around holiday times. Choose fairly large, squat bulbs with a pearly sheen and no sign of splitting, drying, or browning; small bulbs are no less delicious but there is more waste in the trimming. The stalks should sport fluffy green fronds (if they have been removed, complain to your produce man).

Despite their celery-like appearance, fennel stalks do not store well—only 3–4 days—as they quickly dry out and lose their flavor. For optimum keeping, cut the stalks from the wide bases, wrap separately in plastic, and set in the coldest part of the refrigerator.

USE: I really can't think of how *not* to use fennel. It has body and texture like tender celery, for which many of the same cooking techniques apply, but it also functions as a seasoning herb.

Chilled raw fennel wedges, shards, or sticks, served with a crumbly-fresh Parmesan and chilled dry Marsala are one of the great taste combinations of all times. Or try fennel with mild, soft goat cheese and olives; or with a light cream cheese and figs for dessert—preferably with a light *vin santo*.

One of my favorite salads is very finely sliced fennel (the processor is best for this), dressed only with lemon juice, salt, and fine olive oil, then sprinkled lightly with chives. Slivered, sliced, or coarsely chopped fennel also combines well with sweet red or yellow bell pepper (grilled and peeled or crunchy raw), radish, apple, orange, lemon, or lush ripe tomatoes. Its aromatic crispness provides a delicious foil for the grainy and nutty flavors of wild or brown rice, cracked wheat, walnuts, or hazelnuts, as well as for salads of meat, fish, pasta, and/or cheese.

Blanched fennel slices absorb and flavor a vinaigrette; or cook slices in a seasoned court bouillon, à la grecque.

Parboiled fennel slices (about ½ inch thick) can be dipped in beaten egg, then fine crumbs, and fried in shallow fat for a memorable appetizer or separate vegetable course. Layer parboiled fennel slices with fennel sausage, top with crumbs and cheese, and bake about ½ hour; serve as a main or vegetable course.

Stir-fry or sauté fennel slivers to retain the vegetable's delicacy and freshness. Cook with shallots, garlic, leeks, mushrooms, red peppers, seeded strips of tomato, or julienned summer squash for a fast and interesting side dish.

Braise halved small fennel bulbs (for method see Braised Cardoons page 93) for a delicious accompaniment to roasts; it reheats admirably.

Use fennel in vegetable soups for a haunting flavor; or combine with leeks and potatoes for a vichyssoise-like purée, with or without cream. Adding fennel to fish chowders transforms them.

As a general tip, if you wish to sharpen or intensify the natural fennel flavor of a dish, add fennel seeds (in small quantities—they take over) and/or the licorice- and anise-flavored liquors Ricard or Pernod.

PREPARATION: Cut off and reserve the fennel stems and leaves, using the former for flavoring stews, soups, and braises; the latter for sprinkling over a dish as you would snipped dill. If slicing or chopping the fennel for a cooked dish, you can peel the stems and add them, as well. Cut out the knob-like core in the base of the bulb. For raw preparations you may want to remove the first heavy wrapping of layers, or at least de-string it, like celery. If the fennel seems a bit listless, soak it in ice water or in a bowl of water in the refrigerator for an hour or so.

How you cut the fennel will depend on what you are going to do with it. For neat raw strips, take off each layer (removing the hard central core), then slice it into strips of the desired size. For braising, halve or quarter the bulbs. For sautéing and stir-frying, slice thin across on the bias. To make slices, do not remove the core, which holds together the projections of stalk.

NUTRITIONAL HIGHLIGHTS: Fennel is very low in calories—about 30 per cup. It is a fair source of vitamin A and niacin.

FENNEL À LA GRECQUE

The time-honored method of poaching vegetables in a seasoned court bouillon—à la grecque—is modified in this recipe by browning the fennel slices slightly before poaching, which intensifies the flavor. Serve the richly aromatic chilled vegetable as an appetizer, side dish, or part of a buffet.

4 servings

1½ cups water
¼ cup dry vermouth
2 large garlic cloves, halved
½ teaspoon fennel seeds
½ teaspoon thyme
1 bay leaf, crumbled
1 tiny dried hot chili-pepper, or ¼
    teaspoon hot pepper flakes
1 teaspoon coarse kosher salt
½ teaspoon sugar
2 medium fennel bulbs, about 1¼ pounds
    (weighed with 2-inch top stalks)
3 tablespoons olive oil
3 tablespoons lemon juice
Lemon slices

1. Combine water, vermouth, garlic, fennel seeds, thyme, bay leaf, chili (crumbled), salt, and sugar in nonaluminum saucepan. Simmer, covered, 10 minutes. Let stand, covered, until ready to use.

2. Trim off and discard fennel stalks, saving feathery leaves. Trim base of bulb slightly without removing core. Cutting across as you would a loaf of bread, progressing from one short side to the other (the fennel is vaguely rectangular), make even slices ¼–½ inch wide (they'll have a tulip or artichoke-like shape). You should have about a dozen slices.

3. Heat oil in wide, nonaluminum skillet (12 inches or more). On moderately low heat brown slices lightly in single layer, turning once, about 10 minutes.

4. Remove garlic from court bouillon and discard; add liquid to fennel with lemon juice. Cover and simmer very gently 5 minutes. Uncover and simmer about 15 minutes, or until fennel is very tender.

5. Cool. Gently lift slices into serving dish. Pour liquid over. Cover and chill.

6. To serve, snip fennel leaves and sprinkle on top. Arrange lemon slices over all.

ADDITIONAL RECIPE
Sautéed Radicchio, Mushrooms, and Fennel,
    page 390
Salad of Ugli Fruit and Fennel, page 480

SAUTÉED FENNEL WITH LEMON

Once you've tossed together this utterly carefree dish you may wonder how you've managed without it. It is as basic, useful, and versatile as simply sautéed peppers, mushrooms, or snow peas—any or all of which will enhance it, as variations.

3 servings

2 medium fennel bulbs (with tiny top stalks, or very few), about 1½ pounds
2 tablespoons olive oil or butter
¼ teaspoon salt, or to taste
½–1 teaspoon finely grated lemon zest
Pepper to taste

1. Trim and reserve the fennel leaves (and cut off and reserve top stalks, if any). Quarter each bulb lengthwise; cut each quarter crosswise in very thin slivers. Mince 1 tablespoon of the fine leaves.

2. Heat oil in large, heavy skillet; toss fennel slices to coat. Add salt. Continue tossing frequently over moderate heat, until tender—about 10 minutes.

3. Toss with lemon zest and pepper to taste. Sprinkle with minced tops.

BAKED FENNEL

Fennel has so much flavor that it requires little to transform it into a delicious gratin to be served warm or at room temperature (as it is commonly served in Sicily, as part of the antipasto selection). Cooks think of fennel as a vegetable to be cooked with others; but when baked with little embellishment, it becomes a sweetly tender complement to roasted meats, grilled seafood, or pasta or grain salads.

4 servings

About 1½ pounds fennel (weighed without tops), or 2 medium bulbs
2 tablespoons olive oil
½ teaspoon coarse kosher salt
½ cup dry white wine
¼ cup water
½ cup finely grated Parmesan cheese

1. Quarter fennel bulbs and cut out tough bases and hard lower core parts. Slice bulbs thin and arrange in baking-serving dish to just barely fit (vegetable shrinks during cooking). Heat the oven to 375°.

2. Drizzle oil over fennel, then sprinkle with salt. Pour wine and water over. Place oiled sheet of waxed paper over fennel to fit inside rim of dish. Crimp a large sheet of foil over dish to seal.

3. Bake 35–45 minutes, until fennel is completely tender. Remove foil and paper and stir gently. Bake, uncovered, 30 minutes longer, until most liquid has evaporated.

4. Remove from oven and sprinkle cheese on top. Serve hot, warm, or at room temperature. Do not refrigerate or cover. Can remain all day at room temperature.

FENNEL WITH TOMATOES, MUSHROOMS AND HERBS

Like the delicious all-purpose ratatouille of Provence, this casual combination is flexible: add zucchini, sweet peppers, fresh herbs, wild mushrooms; garnish with olives. Serve hot, sprinkled with cheese, as a light main course, or cold, with hard-cooked eggs.

4 servings

2 medium fennel bulbs (about 1¼ pounds) weighed with 2-inch stalks

5 tablespoons full-flavored olive oil

1 large clove garlic, minced

1½ pounds tomatoes, peeled (see page 23), seeded, and cut in strips

¼ teaspoon summer savory

¼ teaspoon fennel seeds

1 teaspoon coarse kosher salt

¾ pound small mushrooms, trimmed and sliced

¼ cup dry red or white wine

Pepper to taste

About 2 tablespoons slivered fresh basil

1. Trim off fennel leaves; reserve. Cut off and peel stalks; slice into strips ¼ inch wide. Trim out cores from bases, separate layers, then cut these into ¼-inch-wide strips of convenient length.

2. Heat ¼ cup oil in wide skillet; add fennel and garlic. Toss over medium heat 5 minutes. Add tomatoes, savory, fennel seeds, and salt. Cover; simmer 5 minutes. Uncover and cook until liquid has almost evaporated.

3. Add mushrooms, wine, and pepper; stir. Simmer 10 minutes, until liquid is nearly evaporated and mushrooms tender. Transfer to serving dish. Cool.

4. Add remaining tablespoon oil and season to taste. Sprinkle with basil and minced fennel leaves to taste.

BAKED FISH WITH FENNEL AND GARLIC

For this savory dish, rich in the aromas of the Mediterranean, you can use fish fillets, steaks, or a whole fish. Select full-flavored, meaty fish, such as shad, king mackerel, or mackerel (a whole fish makes a beautiful presentation and you lose less juice).

2 servings

1 pound trimmed fennel (weighed with 2-inch stalks)
1¼–1½-pound whole fish or ¾–1 pound steaks or fillets
Salt and pepper
3 tablespoons olive oil
1 medium garlic clove, slivered
1 tablespoon lime juice
1 tablespoon butter
¼ cup water
Lime wedges or slices

1. Mince enough fennel leaves to equal 3 tablespoons. Cut 3 deep diagonal slashes in each side of whole fish if you are using it. Sprinkle both sides (and inside for whole fish) with salt and pepper. Heat oil on low heat in small pan with garlic; cook until garlic is golden, not browned. Remove from heat and stir in 2 tablespoons minced leaves and lime juice. Cool 10 minutes or longer.

2. Set fish in baking dish just large enough to hold it comfortably. Pour oil mixture over (and inside, if whole) fish. Let marinate about 15 minutes, turning occasionally.

3. Trim fennel base; cut off stalks and peel them. Cut bulb and stalks into strips about ½ inch wide and 1½ inches long. Melt butter in skillet and toss fennel to coat. Add water, salt and pepper to taste; cook over moderately low heat, covered, until tender, about 15 minutes; stir now and then. Remove cover and stir over moderate heat for a few minutes to evaporate liquid.

4. Meanwhile, bake fish in center of preheated 450-degree oven until opaque in center, gauging 10 minutes per inch at thickest part (or about 10 minutes for fillets and steaks, 15 minutes for whole fish).

5. Arrange fish and fennel together and sprinkle with remaining minced tops. Place lime on platter and serve at once.

FENNEL-STUFFED CHICKEN

With little effort you have both meat and vegetable dishes in one. The fennel perfumes the chicken, which lends its savor to the vegetable for a fine partnership.

2 or 3 servings

¾ pound fennel with leaves (weighed with 2-inch stalks)
3 tablespoons butter
2 tablespoons sliced shallots
¼ cup chicken broth or water
Salt and pepper
1 tablespoon Ricard or Pernod liquor
Small broiling chicken, about 2 pounds, giblets reserved and chopped (see Note)
¼ teaspoon fennel seeds

1. Trim off fennel stalks and leaves. Peel stalks and chop with leaves. Trim base of fennel bulb. Cut bulb into ½–1-inch dice, removing heavy bits of core, if necessary.

2. Heat 1½ tablespoons butter in medium-large skillet; add shallots and fennel. Stir over moderately low heat 5 minutes. Add broth, salt, pepper, and Ricard. Simmer, covered, until tender, but not soft, 5–10 minutes. Uncover, season if necessary, and stir over moderate heat to evaporate liquid. Scrape into a dish and cool.

3. Meanwhile, heat ½ tablespoon butter in same pan. Toss giblets about 15 seconds to brown slightly. Add to fennel.

4. Remove loose fat from chicken; sprinkle inside and out with salt and pepper. Stuff chicken tightly with fennel mixture. Sew closed. Truss. Set on rack in roasting pan.

5. Roast chicken in preheated 325-degree oven for 1 hour. Melt remaining tablespoon butter with fennel seeds in tiny pan. Baste chicken breast with this halfway through roasting time; then continue basting with pan juices throughout cooking. Raise heat to 400 degrees. Roast until chicken is browned to taste, about 15 minutes.

6. Let chicken rest 15 minutes before removing stuffing. Carve.

Note: Chicken browns much more evenly and deeply if allowed to dry out somewhat. If you have the time, pat dry and leave on a paper-towel-covered rack in the refrigerator, uncovered, for about a day, turning if it occurs to you. Let reach room temperature before roasting, or leave even longer to dry more.

SALAD OF SQUID, FENNEL, RED PEPPERS, AND CROUTONS

Fennel's affinity for seafood is well illustrated in this clean-tasting, low-calorie salad: a colorful, satisfying, and unexpected ensemble. You can substitute shrimp, scallops, and firm fresh fillets for the squid—or combine them all.

4 servings

1 bay leaf, crumbled
½ teaspoon fennel seeds
3 medium garlic cloves, peeled
¼ cup white wine or dry vermouth
5 tablespoons olive oil
1½ cups water
1½–1¾ pounds cleaned small squid
    (purchase 2–2¼ pounds if not
    cleaned; and see Note on how to
    clean squid, page 102)
4–5 tablespoons lemon juice
Salt and pepper to taste
3 thin slices close-textured white
    sandwich bread (or substitute 1½–2
    cups prepared croutons)
1 medium head fennel, stalks reserved
    for another use; a few tablespoons
    leaves minced for garnish
3 medium red peppers, in thin julienne
    strips about 1½ inches long
Greens of 3–4 scallions, thinly sliced
Large radicchio or red-leaf lettuce,
    rinsed, dried, torn in pieces

1. Combine bay leaf, fennel seeds, 2 garlic cloves, wine, 2 tablespoons olive oil, and water in medium saucepan. Boil gently, covered, for 10 minutes. Meanwhile, slice squid across in ¼-inch rings; halve or quarter tentacles to make neat mouthfuls.
2. Strain stock; return to saucepan.

Add squid and simmer, stirring, until opaque and curled at the edges; a minute or two should do. With slotted spoon transfer squid to small bowl and cool.
3. Boil stock gently to reduce to ½ cup, stirring occasionally. Pour over squid, add 2 tablespoons lemon juice; season with salt and pepper to taste. Cover and refrigerate.
4. Bake bread slices on sheet in 325-degree oven until firm but not crisp through. Rub each side with remaining garlic, cutting clove to expose a fresh surface for each bread slice. Cut bread in ¼–½-inch squares. Return to sheet and bake until crisp and brown, tossing now and then. The whole process will take about 20–25 minutes.
5. Trim any stringy, pithy outer layer from fennel, if necessary; coarsely chop remainder (there should be about 1½ cups). Toss in bowl with red peppers, scallions, remaining oil, 2 tablespoons lemon juice, and salt and pepper. Cover and refrigerate.
6. Arrange lettuce in wide serving bowl. Toss squid with vegetables and croutons. Season to taste, adding lemon juice if needed. Arrange on lettuce; sprinkle over minced fennel tops. Serve at once, or croutons soften.

SALAD OF PASTA, FENNEL, AND SARDINES

This free-form adaptation of the traditional Pasta con le Sarde makes use of the fennel tops so often discarded by cooks (and, worse, by produce marketers). When you next prepare a dish that calls for fennel bulbs, save the flavorful tops to replace the wild fennel (unless you can get it in your area) that is the basis for this unusual mixture. The thick pasta dressed with pine nuts, dried currants, saffron, tomatoes, puréed fennel, and sardines is a Sicilian dish that clearly shows the influence of its years of Arab domination.

4 servings

⅓ cup currants or raisins
½ teaspoon saffron threads
About ½–¾ pound fennel stalks and tops (enough to equal 4 cups, chopped), well washed
¼ teaspoon fennel seeds
1 cup water
1 can (3¾ ounces) sardines in olive oil
Olive oil, as needed
2 medium onions, coarsely diced
4 large, ripe tomatoes, peeled (page 23) seeded, and coarsely diced
Salt and pepper
1 pound imported Italian spaghetti, perciatelli, or linguine (preferably whole-wheat)
Lemon juice to taste
3 tablespoons pine nuts (pignolia)
Lemon slices for garnish

1. Combine currants with hot water to barely cover; cover and let soak. Combine saffron threads with 1 tablespoon hot water; set aside.

2. Chop thinnest stalks and feathery tops of fennel to make 4 cups, tightly packed. Combine in saucepan with fennel seeds and water. Boil gently, covered, 20–40 minutes, until very soft, stirring occasionally. Pour into processor; whirl to form coarse purée.

3. Meanwhile, drain oil from sardines; measure into nonaluminum skillet. Refrigerate sardines, covered. Add additional oil to skillet to equal 4 tablespoons. Stir in onions; cook until softened, about 5 minutes.

4. Add tomatoes, fennel, currants and liquid, saffron and liquid, and 1 teaspoon salt. Simmer, partly covered, for 10–20 minutes, until sauce is pudding-like and tomatoes soft; stir occasionally. Salt to taste.

5. Break pasta in thirds (I think this best suits a salad, but do what you prefer); drop into large pot of boiling salted water. Boil until not quite tender; it should be firmer than usual. Drain well.

6. Combine pasta in serving bowl with sauce. Adjust lemon juice, olive oil, salt, and pepper to taste. Let cool to room temperature.

7. While pasta cools, toast pine nuts in 300-degree oven (or toaster oven) until lightly golden, about 15 minutes, shaking a few times. Cool.

8. To serve, season cooled pasta and sauce as needed. Arrange sardines over pasta; top with nuts; decorate with lemon slices. The dish can remain at room temperature for 3–4 hours or so.

FIDDLEHEAD FERN
(Matteuccia struthiopteris)
also Ostrich Fern; Fiddlehead Greens
(Note: While Bracken Fern, *Pteridium aquilinum*, and Royal Fern, *Osmunda regalis*, are fern varieties traditionally consumed as fiddleheads, some authorities now advise against them.)

A fiddlehead is not a species of fern but a growth stage of any fern. When the tightly coiled new frond (or crosier) pokes up through the soil but has not yet begun to uncurl, it is called a fiddlehead. While Vermont and Maine are prime fiddlehead terrain in the United States, the bright, springy ferns emerge along rivers and streams as far

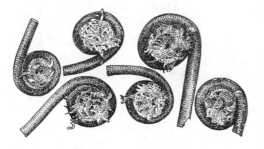

south as Virginia and as far north as Newfoundland, and extend west over almost half the country. In each locale the shoots sprout for about two weeks, then unfurl to inedible plumes. In parts of the South, fiddleheads may appear in early April; as the sun gets warmer, the season shifts northward, with final Canadian fern crops appearing as late as July.

Picked small, then cooked soon thereafter, fiddlehead ferns have a flavor that embraces asparagus, artichokes, and green beans (plus a hint of mushroom); the chewy texture is all their own. They look adorable on a plate, alone or as a garnish.

If you are plucking your own ferns from the moist forest floor, you should know that there is a great deal of disagreement about which species are edible and which are not. Although many types of fiddleheads have long been gathered for springtime delectation, there is considerable evidence that some (particularly the bracken fern, *Pteridium aquilinum*, consumed here and in Japan) may be extremely carcinogenic. While all the manuals I consulted found ferns in the small fiddlehead stage to be comfortably comestible, Dr. John Mickel, fern curator at the Bronx Botanical Garden in New York, was adamant that the ostrich fern, the fiddlehead commonly marketed, is the only one that is definitely non-carcinogenic.

SELECTION AND STORAGE: Look for fiddleheads from April through early July, usually in specialty markets. Choose jade-green ferns that are bouncy, firm, and bright, not flabby or yellowed. Select watchspring-coiled, small sprouts, no more than 1½ inches in diameter with no more than a few inches of tail (if any), or the fern will be fibrous and tough.

Fiddleheads do not store well. Although they do not spoil rapidly, they quickly lose their fresh flavor and elastic tone. If you must, wrap them tightly in plastic and refrigerate for as short a time as possible.

If you care passionately for year-round ferns, you can freeze them: Clean and trim the ferns, then drop into boiling water; return to a boil and cook 1 minute. Drain, drop in ice water, then drain again. Pack airtight and freeze. Although freezing is almost always recommended in guides to cooking wild plants, I find the process effective for retaining looks only; the ferns seem to become fibrous and fishy. I prefer to cherish them as vernal ephemera.

USE: While in theory you might use fiddlehead ferns in any way that you would green beans or Brussels sprouts, I find their special qualities underscored only in the simplest preparations. Think of them as you would artichoke hearts or asparagus. Serve the trimmed, boiled coils with melted butter and lemon, or a light cream, cheese, Hollandaise, or Maltaise sauce; or douse with a gentle vinaigrette. Use them as a first course, to garnish meats, as a side dish, or as a salad. In Japan they are served at room temperature with a sprinkling of soy sauce and sesame seeds, or as a garnish in thin miso soup.

PREPARATION: Trim the base of each fern to leave only a tiny tail beyond the circumference of each circular shape. Some fiddleheads will need to have the fuzzy or papery brown covering or scales removed by being rubbed between your palms. All should be well rinsed.

NUTRITIONAL HIGHLIGHTS: Fiddlehead ferns are an excellent source of vitamin A and a fairly good source of vitamin C and fiber.

BASIC FIDDLEHEAD FERNS

One basic preparation will yield pretty, pliant ferns ready to be sauced, sautéed, or dressed for salad. Having experimented with steaming, poaching, braising, and boiling, I find that the last works far better than other methods, retaining texture and color while eliminating the bitterness that is sometimes present in these furled sprouts.

4–6 servings

1 pound fiddlehead ferns, each about 1–1½ inches in diameter

1. Trim base of each fern, if necessary, to leave only a tiny tail beyond circumference of each circular form. If furry brown covering remains on ferns, rub it off. Rinse briskly under running water.

2. Drop ferns into a large pot of boiling, lightly salted water. Boil until tender throughout—about 5 minutes—testing often; undercooked, the full flavor will not develop. Drain well and serve at once, with melted butter. Or try one of the following alternatives.

FIDDLEHEADS WITH SAUCE

Serve the hot, drained ferns with about 1 cup Hollandaise, Maltaise, cream, or cheese sauce.

FIDDLEHEAD FERNS SAUTÉED IN BUTTER

Drop cooked ferns into ice water to cool. Drain and refrigerate until serving time, covered. At serving time heat 3 tablespoons butter in a large skillet; sauté ferns until heated through.

FIDDLEHEAD FERNS VINAIGRETTE

Drop the drained ferns into ice water to cool. Drain and dry well. Combine with ¾ cup light mustard vinaigrette.

Nutmeg Cream

Prepare ferns as in basic recipe. Serve hot with this intriguing alternative to Hollandaise or cream sauce:

4–6 servings

1 cup heavy (or whipping) cream (not ultrapasteurized, if possible)
¼ teaspoon salt, approximately
About 1½ teaspoons freshly grated nutmeg
Few drops lemon juice

Whip cream and salt until slightly thickened. Add nutmeg gradually (nutmeg can vary dramatically from one seed to the next, so taste as you add). Add lemon juice and beat until quite firm. Scoop into a cheesecloth-lined sieve, cover with plastic, and refrigerate 1–2 hours before serving.

FRESNO (PEPPER)
See Chili-Pepper, Fresno

G

GLASSWORT
(Salicornia europea and *Salicornia herbacea)*
also Samphire, Marsh Samphire, Sea Pickle, Sea Bean, Pousse-pied

*T*here are two edible plants, both called samphire, both venerable, both known in England and France, where they grow wild along the seacoast, marshes, and in cliff crevices. One is *Salicornia*, of the Goosefoot family, the other is *Crithmum maritimum* (sometimes called rock samphire), a fragrant fleshy plant of the umbelliferous clan.

The names for both developed along similar lines: the French called the plant *perce-pierre* (rock-piercer) and *Saint-Pierre* (from Saint Peter, the rock upon which [whom] Christ built his church); along the way the names were corrupted, both in English and French, into *sampier, sampyre, passe-pierre, pousse-pierre,* and *samphire*. Both plants wound up in old cookbooks as *samphire*, both often pickled. (To further confuse, it is probably *Salicornia stricta*, which was used in glass manufacture, not *europea* or *herbacea*, above, that gave us the common name "glasswort.")

What we have in the United States is *Salicornia*, a green succulent that grows near salt marshes, a small plant that resembles baby aloe, jointed together cactus-style; or it may look like birds' feet. It seems more like a plant that should grow in the ocean than one that gets wet only at high tide. It is very crunchy and salty, like brined baby string beans. When young, it is crisp, pleasantly deep-sea tasting, an unusual summer pleasure that grows in abundance along the Atlantic and Pacific coasts, and, I have heard, in the alkaline marshes of deserts in the Southwest. It is easy to recognize and there for the picking, whereas— incomprehensibly—what is marketed in the chic shoppes on the East Coast is flown in from France, for a small fortune, of course.

SELECTION AND STORAGE: Glasswort is a summer treat; by fall, although it still flourishes, it develops a fibrous center filament that makes chewing hard going. When you choose the plants, select ones that are firm and bright, not flabby or slimy. No soft or discolored spots should be evident. Inevitably, some will be in less-perfect condition; pick through delicately.

Although long storage is acceptable (in good condition, it takes weeks to show signs of spoilage—a fact you might take into account when you're buying), I think it becomes tougher and loses much charm if kept more than a few days. Spread in a shallow layer in a basket or on a plate, then refrigerate.

USE: I've not done much experimenting with this fleeting delicacy, but I can generalize about the uses as far as I've gone. Glasswort makes the cutest little garnish you ever did see, just as is. Toss it into salads, fresh, for a saline crunch. Or blanch, refresh, and chill, then combine with vegetables, seafood, poultry, or meat in a composed salad.

Chef Felipe Rojas-Lombardi stuffs a whole fish with glasswort, places it in a close-fitting container tightly surrounded with more of the same, leaving no spaces. He then bakes the fish until just done, delicately removes (and discards) all the glasswort and serves the sea-fresh creature at once. Glasswort must make good pickles, judging from the history books. Plain-cooked glasswort—sautéed, steamed, or boiled—loses its appealing texture and is too salty and fishy for my taste.

PREPARATION: Trim the wiry little roots from each plantlet. If bases are heavy, trim as necessary. Depending upon the size, you may want to cut the plants into 1½–2-inch twiglets for bitability.

NUTRITIONAL HIGHLIGHTS: Although I have found no information on this plant, it must be high in sodium.

SALAD OF GLASSWORT, ORIENTAL RADISH, AND CUCUMBER

Crisp, sea-tangy, salty, and sweet, this unusual salad, Oriental in feeling, briskly complements fried seafood or grilled poultry.

Do not refrigerate for more than a few hours before serving, or the glasswort may begin to exude moisture and shrivel.

4 servings

⅓ cup distilled vinegar or rice-wine vinegar
2 tablespoons sugar
¼ pound Oriental radish (daikon), or another long, white radish
1 medium-large cucumber, peeled
½ teaspoon coarse kosher salt
¼ pound glasswort, trimmed (see Preparation)
1 tablespoon hulled white sesame seeds

1. Combine vinegar and sugar in a small nonaluminum pan; bring to a boil, stirring. Let cool completely.

2. Cut radish in thin julienne strips about 2 inches long. Halve cucumber lengthwise, scoop out seeds, then cut strips the same size. Combine radish and cucumber in a sieve set over a bowl. Toss with salt. Allow to drain 15 minutes or more. Squeeze out as much moisture as possible.

3. Combine radish, cucumber, and glasswort in serving dish with dressing; toss to coat. Chill for about an hour.

4. Meanwhile, toast sesame seeds in a small pan, stirring over low heat until they are just golden; cool. To serve, sprinkle the seeds over the chilled salad.

SALAD OF SCALLOPS, SHRIMP, GLASSWORT, MUSHROOMS, AND TOMATO

Enjoy this light salad on a hot evening; it's cool as a sea breeze.

4 servings

½ pound glasswort, trimmed (see Preparation)

2 large tomatoes, about 1 pound

1 pound sea scallops

5–6 ounces shrimp in the shell

Salt

¼ cup lime juice

2 tablespoons minced chives

⅓–½ cup light vegetable oil, to taste

⅓ pound small, firm mushrooms, thin-sliced

White pepper

Leaves of soft lettuce, such as oak leaf or Boston

1. Drop glasswort into boiling water; return to a boil over highest heat, then skim out with a sieve. Cool on wide plate; refrigerate.

2. Drop tomatoes into the boiling water and count to 10; remove and run under cold water. Peel, halve horizontally, squeeze out seeds. Halve each piece, then cut into thin slices.

3. Pour a few inches of water into a small pot and bring to a boil; add scallops and shrimp and bring to a simmer. Remove from the heat, cover, and let stand for 5 minutes. Peel shrimp; halve lengthwise, deveining. Halve scallops, then cut into thin semicircles.

4. Combine seafood and tomato; salt lightly. Blend lime juice and chives; add oil gradually, adjusting to taste. Pour two-thirds over seafood salad. Toss, cover, and chill.

5. To serve, toss glasswort and mushrooms with remaining dressing and plenty of pepper; add chilled seafood and toss. Arrange on lettuce.

GOA BEAN
See Winged Bean

GOBO
See Burdock

GOLDEN NUGGET, GOLD NUGGET
(Cucurbita maxima)

A fairytale miniature pumpkin, this salmon-colored, finely-ridged, hard-shelled squash ranges from orange- to grapefruit-sized. Developed in North Dakota (in 1966) at the State University, where a great deal of research has been done with winter squash, the golden nugget has rather a spare quantity of flesh (the cavity is large),

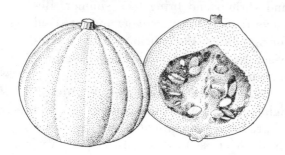

which is as brightly orange as the skin, moist, fairly firm, and very smooth. The flavor is mild and squashy, and can range from delightfully sweet and buttery to not-so-sweet and dull-bland. This is a squash in which full maturity is absolutely essential or it will have no taste. Be sure you follow selection guidelines.

SELECTION AND STORAGE: Golden nugget is usually available summer, fall, and winter. Select as you would other winter squash—by looking for the hardest rind, then checking for soft spots and pitting. The stem, which should always be intact, should look rounded and corky, not blackened or green. It is important that the rind have a dull, matte look; a shiny finish indicates that the squash was picked when immature and that it is probably virtually tasteless. You can store golden nugget longer than most other small squash—as long as two months at room temperature, preferably cool. Do not refrigerate.

USE: Unless you have a guillotine or scimitar, you may find the uses of this squash to be as limited as I do. Too dangerously hard and slippery-round to halve, it must be cooked whole, either baked or steamed.

NUTRITIONAL HIGHLIGHTS: All winter-type squashes are excellent sources of vitamin A and have substantial amounts of vitamin C, iron, and potassium. They are modest in calories and low in sodium.

BASIC GOLDEN NUGGET SQUASH PREPARATION

Golden nugget, however diminutive, resists cleaving before cooking. Thus, there is not much choice but to cook it whole. If large, halve the squash after cooking and serve ½ per person.

Allow 1 squash per person

Bake at 350 degrees for about ¾–1 hour, being sure that the pulp is really soft when you poke a toothpick in. (The hard carapace gets crisp-hard, resembling a gleaming lacquerware basket, and makes a handsome presentation.) Cut off the top, then scoop out the abundance of seeds and any fiber that clings to them. You can then add seasoning, butter, and salt, as you like. (Or spoon a precooked stuffing into the cavity, such as bread cubes, grains, nuts, dried fruit.) Return the squash to the oven to heat through, as necessary.

Or place the whole squash on a steamer rack over boiling water. Steam about 15–20 minutes, or until very tender when pierced. Gently slice off the cap, clean out seeds and fibers, and serve as is, or stuffed with small vegetables (such as pearl onions, chestnuts, peas) or vegetable dice. Or halve or quarter, if preferred.

GOOSEBERRY
(Ribes uva-crispa or Ribes grossularia, and Ribes hirtellum)

Gooseberry varieties differ enormously. The berries run from fuzzy-prickly to satin-smooth, from translucent to opaque, from white through shades of green to deep purple, from the size of a blueberry to that of a cherry tomato, from mouth-puckering to lightly sweet. Most common in American markets are the small- to medium-sized celery-green summer berry and the very large, striated yellow-green to purplish winter berry. All are taut-skinned, tendril-tipped—and exceptionally beautiful.

Given the English passion for these crisp, highly acid berries, it is curious that they have become so rare. A staple in the American larder from colonial days, when gooseberry wine, vinegar, pie, pudding, fools, and preserves were standard fare, the berry had virtually disappeared from cookbooks by the nineteenth century.

Judging from horticultural journals of the last few years, it seems the fruit is moving toward a revival of sorts. In some locations the bush is host to a disease that kills white pine, which is probably one of the reasons it has lost popularity, but there are fewer and fewer restricted areas. At the same time, less prickly, more pickable, larger berries are being developed. The small-fruited American species *(Ribes hirtellum)* and large-fruited but mildew-prone English variety have parented a number of varieties now available from nurseries around the country. Small-scale farmers are selling their crops at roadsides or trucking them to the newly flourishing greenmarkets. While gooseberries are cultivated on a commercial scale in Oregon, they are almost all canned, not sold in fresh markets. As usual in the specialty produce business, our fresh berries usually come from as far away as you can get—New Zealand.

Few etymologists agree on the origin of the (thoroughly unsuitable) name *gooseberry*. Suggestions that it derives from the Frankish *krusil* (meaning crisp) or a variation of *gorse* (a prickly shrub) or the once common English dish that combined the berries with goose do not impress the Oxford English Dictionary—which offers no alternatives. One explanation offered is that gooseberry is a corruption of the German *Jansbeere* (John's berry, named because it ripens during the time of the Feast of St. John). Another possible source is *groseille*, the French word for currant—and, as a matter of fact, the word for gooseberry too, since the French don't bother to give the berry an identity of its own. It is *groseille à maquereau*, or currant for mackerel, because the gooseberry was apparently used almost exclusively as a sauce for that oily fish.

SELECTION AND STORAGE: Look for the very large berries from New Zealand from November to January, and the smaller American fruit during the summer. Choose hard, dry berries, with a rich sheen. If you are looking for less tartness, head for the pinkish or purplish ones.

Gooseberries store miraculously well. They will stay firm and bright for about 2 weeks in the refrigerator, turning gradually pinker and softer. Once they have become purply, they'll still be good for purées for another week. Or you can stock up on gooseberries by canning them in syrup (see page 214) or freezing in the same syrup.

USE: Gooseberries are sensationally versatile, suiting every part of the meal, but their extreme sourness needs careful balancing. Do not overdo the sugar, or the whole point is lost. Some enjoy gooseberries whole, uncooked, with a snowfall of sugar, splashed with cream. Many varieties are too sour for this treatment, so taste a few before you heap up a bowlful. To retain the shape of the berries, poach very slowly, lest the seeds shoot out and skins collapse.

In Scandinavia, Hungary, and Russia a chilled or hot soup of gooseberries and chicken stock or wine, thickened with potato or cornstarch, then topped with whipped or sour cream, is a favorite first course. In the latter countries and England, cooks devise tart sauces of berries and poultry stock, thickened with eggs and a bit of flour, to serve with fowl (see Roasted Pork Loin with Gooseberry Sauce page 215, which adapts well to chicken). I find no thickening necessary, as the tiny seeds and juicy pulp, when mixed with cream or meat juices, thicken up surprisingly—thanks to the enormous amount of pectin. Include gooseberries in a stuffing for poultry or pork.

A sweet dessert purée thickened to pudding consistency, chilled, then doused with the sharp berry's perfect partner, heavy cream, is also at home in Scandinavia, Hungary, and Russia. The most famous use of the berry with cream is gooseberry fool, with which the word "gooseberry" has become almost synonymous.

Whole gooseberries, gently poached in heavy sugar syrup, can be served as a dessert or meat accompaniment (see Gooseberries in Simple Syrup for suggestions). In England, the syrup in which the berries bathe is often flavored with elderflowers, muscat wine, or orange-flower water, all of which suit them mysteriously well.

PREPARATION: Unless you sieve the berries, you'll want to nip off the little stems and tops—called tops and tails in England—which is most easily done with scissors.

NUTRITIONAL HIGHLIGHTS: Gooseberries are low in calories, about 70 per cup, and low in sodium. They are high in vitamin C and fiber and a good source of potassium.

GOOSEBERRIES IN SIMPLE SYRUP

The easiest way to prepare gooseberries for use in any dessert is to cook them for a few minutes in sugar syrup. Once chilled, they firm and plump, ready to be incorporated into fruit compotes, drained and placed on a pastry-cream-coated tart shell, spooned over shortcake biscuits, or gingerbread and cream, used as garnish with smoked meats, or served in a small amount of syrup with vanilla ice cream or heavy cream.

For each pint of gooseberries you should figure 1 cup water and ½ cup sugar. I prefer to use riper, purply-pink gooseberries for this, as they become a lovely rose hue once poached. If you can find only light-green berries, try letting them ripen a few days at room temperature (or for a week or so in the refrigerator); they usually change color.

Makes 1 pint

1 cup water
½ cup sugar
1 pint gooseberries, topped, tailed, and
    rinsed (see Preparation)

Boil water and sugar in a nonaluminum saucepan. Add berries and cook over very low heat (the syrup should not bubble) until they are barely tender and almost opaque—about 4 minutes. Gently pour into a dish and cool, then chill until serving time.

GOOSEBERRIES IN HONEY SYRUP FOR STORAGE

When you can get your hands on a goodly quantity of berries, this is a useful and delicious way to preserve them for later use—to eat as they come from the jar, in fruit compotes, with shortcake, on tarts or tartlets. Purée for a brisk sauce, or thin and chill for fruit soup, topping with whipped cream. You may have some berries and syrup left over when you have filled your canning jars, especially if the berries are very large, but you should figure on the following quantities *for each quart* of gooseberries that you put up.

2 pint jars

2 cups water
¾ cup sugar
½ cup fragrant, light-colored honey
1 quart gooseberries, topped, tailed, and
    rinsed (see Preparation)

1. Wash wide-mouthed pint-sized canning jars in hot, soapy water; rinse well. Pour boiling water over the jars and let stand.

2. Combine water, sugar, and honey; bring to a boil, stirring; skim. Pour about ½ cup syrup into each jar, then put in as many berries as will fit, leaving about ½ inch head space. Pour boiling syrup over the berries to cover. Place new canning lids on the jars; put on screw bands and tighten them.

3. Set jars on a rack in a large kettle tall enough to accommodate several inches of water above the jars. Pour boiling water over jars to cover by 1–2 inches. Bring to a boil, covered, then time exactly 10 minutes for processing.

4. With tongs, grasp jars (not lids) and remove from the water. Set on towels to cool completely. Depress lid centers; if flexible, refrigerate, as jars are not sealed. Store in a dark, preferably rather cool place up to a year.

ROASTED PORK LOIN WITH GOOSEBERRY SAUCE

I particularly like the acid bite of green gooseberries with rich pork; but this unusual sauce can be assembled with the degreased juices of any freshly roasted meat or poultry. The sauce will be a surprise to most; the combination of pan juices and berries produce a creamy-textured purée that feels and tastes as though fat and thickening have been added, but has none of the heaviness of either.

When you choose your pork loin, look for a long, narrow roast which will cook more rapidly and slice neatly. Ask the butcher for the bones (which should weigh about a pound) for the sauce. Plan to marinate the meat in the dry spice mixture for a day or more.

6 servings or more

3 pounds boneless pork loin, bones reserved (about 4 pounds total weight)
1 tablespoon coarse kosher salt
½ teaspoon peppercorns
1 bay leaf, crumbled
½ teaspoon allspice berries (whole allspice)
¼ teaspoon fennel seeds
1 small garlic clove, minced
1 tablespoon brown sugar
2 tablespoons peanut or corn oil

SAUCE
1 pint green gooseberries, rinsed, topped, and tailed
About 2 tablespoons brown sugar
Salt and pepper to taste
Watercress for serving

1. Stab meat here and there with a small skewer or knife. Set on a large sheet of parchment or waxed paper. Combine salt, peppercorns, bay leaf, allspice, and fennel in a spice grinder; grind to a powder. Pour into a dish and stir in garlic and brown sugar. Rub spice mixture evenly over pork. Enclose in the paper, then wrap in foil. Refrigerate 1–2 days.

2. In a flameproof casserole large enough to hold the meat and bones, heat peanut oil; brown bones on all sides, then transfer to a dish. Meanwhile tie meat to form a neat cylinder. Pat dry, then brown well on all sides. Pour out fat, then return the bones to the pan with the meat. Cover and set in center of preheated 300-degree oven. Roast until a thermometer measures 170 degrees in the center of the meat; test at about 1¼ hours. When meat is cooked through, transfer it to a cutting board, cover with foil, and set aside. Remove bones from pan.

3. Skim fat from pan juices, which will measure about ¾ cup. Add berries and 1½ tablespoons brown sugar to pan. Simmer, crushing and mashing as berries burst, until you have a thick, creamy purée—about 10 minutes. Add remaining sugar, salt and pepper to taste. Slice the meat, arrange on watercress, and serve the hot sauce alongside.

GOOSEBERRY AND APPLE PIE

This is my idea of what an old-fashioned pie should be: overflowing fruit—the juices only slightly thickened—packed between flaky butter-lard pastry layers, the upper crust crisped by a sugar glaze that browns and sparkles. If you like a quite acid pie, use the minimum sugar; for a sweet version, the larger amount should do.

Makes one 9-inch pie

CRUST

1¾ cups all-purpose flour

½ teaspoon salt

⅓ cup plus 1 tablespoon chilled lard

6 tablespoons (¾ stick) chilled unsalted butter

About 5 tablespoons ice water

FILLING

1½ pounds tart, firm apples—such as Granny Smith, Russet, Idared

1 pint gooseberries, topped and tailed

Generous ½ to ¾ cup sugar

1 tablespoon cornstarch

Pinch salt

GLAZE AND FINAL ASSEMBLY

1 egg white

1 tablespoon rum or brandy

1 tablespoon butter, cut into small bits

2 teaspoons sugar

Optional: Ice cream or hard sauce

1. Whisk together flour and salt in mixing bowl. Cut lard and butter into small bits and add to flour; with pastry blender work mixture into small flakes—more or less the size of oatmeal flakes. Add ice water, a tablespoon at a time, tossing flour mixture to incorporate evenly. Press dough together gently to form a ball; if pieces separate, sprinkle in a few more drops of water. Form dough into 2 disks, wrap in plastic, and refrigerate for at least 1 hour.

2. Quarter and peel apples; cut across in ¼-inch slices (there should be 3 cups). Combine in a bowl with gooseberries. Stir together sugar and cornstarch and toss with fruit. Let stand while you prepare pastry.

3. Place a roasting pan or baking sheet (not a good one, because it may warp) on lower level of oven; turn heat to 450 degrees. Roll one round of pastry on lightly floured board to form an 11-inch circle; trim with scissors. Fold dough in quarters, place center point in middle of a 9-inch pie pan, then unfold gently, easing into the pan. If necessary, trim edge of pastry to form ½-inch overhang.

4. Beat egg white and rum until foamy. Brush pastry sparingly with this. Roll remaining dough to form a circle ½ inch larger than pan; trim neatly. Heap fruit in pastry, distributing evenly and packing closely; top with butter bits. Brush exposed rim of pastry with glaze, and lay top crust on, pressing lightly. Fold over the overhanging pastry; press, then seal with tines of fork. Cut 6 small slits.

5. Cut pastry scraps into leaf and berry shapes, if desired. Lightly brush pie top with the glaze, set the designs on this, then brush with more glaze. Sprinkle sugar evenly over the pie.

6. Set pie on sheet in oven; bake 20 minutes. Lower heat to 375 degrees and bake about 35 minutes longer, until crust is well browned and juice bubbles up through slits. Cool on a rack.

7. Serve warm, with optional ice cream or hard sauce. Do not cover or refrigerate the pie or it will get soggy. Reheat briefly, before serving if it is no longer warm or tepid.

GOOSEBERRIES, APPLES, AND RAISINS IN WINE

Fruits poached in wine make a delicious tart-sweet finish for a fall meal. The monochromatic mixture is perfectly complemented by the mellowing effect of cream and by its whiteness. Try to find a real cream—not ultrapasteurized or thickened; it makes all the difference.

4 servings

1 cup plus 1 tablespoon sweet or semisweet white wine—the more aromatic the better

¼ cup golden raisins

About 4 tablespoons sugar (this will vary with sweetness of wine selected)

1 pint green gooseberries, topped and tailed

2 small Yellow Delicious apples, quartered, cored, peeled, and cut crosswise into ¼-inch slices

1 teaspoon cornstarch

Heavy (or whipping) cream

1. Combine 1 cup wine, raisins, and 3 tablespoons sugar in a nonaluminum saucepan. Bring to a boil, then cover and simmer gently for 5 minutes.

2. Taste: the syrup should be somewhat too sweet. Adjust accordingly. Add gooseberries. Poach until just barely tender, about 5–8 minutes. Do not let syrup bubble or berries may burst. With a slotted spoon gently transfer fruit to a serving dish.

3. Add apples to syrup and poach gently until just tender, 5–10 minutes; keep a close watch so they don't get mushy. With slotted spoon transfer apples to the serving dish. Stir remaining tablespoon wine into the cornstarch and add to syrup. Cook until syrup boils for 1 minute, stirring constantly. Pour over fruit and cool.

4. Chill fruits well. Serve with cream.

GOOSEBERRY-APPLE CRISP

Gooseberries and apples seem to have the most pleasant affinity, but you can substitute firm-ripe Bosc pears very nicely in this easy-to-assemble, old-timey sweet.
4–6 servings

5 tablespoons sugar

2 teaspoons cornstarch

Pinch salt

1 pint gooseberries (pinkish or green), topped and tailed

2 medium apples, such as Granny Smith or Yellow Delicious, peeled and cut into ½-inch cubes

⅔ cup quick-cooking oats

⅓ cup flour

¼ cup brown sugar

Big pinch allspice

3 tablespoons softened butter

Vanilla ice cream

1. Blend sugar, cornstarch, and salt in a mixing bowl; toss with gooseberries and apples until evenly coated. Scrape into well-buttered, shallow baking dish of 4–5-cup capacity, preferably about 9 inches in diameter.

2. Blend oats, flour, sugar, and allspice in the mixing bowl (wipe it out first). Add butter; pinch and squeeze to make coarse crumbs. Strew evenly over fruits.

3. Bake in upper middle of a preheated 350-degree oven until crisp and brown—about 45 minutes. Serve hot with ice cream.

GOOSEBERRY FOOL

You may do well to substitute crème fraîche, reduced and cooled cream (see page 261), or medium-thick egg custard for the rich cream (which we do not have) specified in this recipe, the best and most basic preparation for this quintessential dish. The recipe was written by E. S. Dallas in *Kettner's Book of the Table* (1877, Centaur Press, reprint, 1968)—so why tamper?

After topping and tailing—that is, taking off clean the two ends of the goose-berries—scald them sufficiently with a very little water till all the fruit breaks. Too much water will spoil them. The water must not be thrown away, being so rich with the finest part of the fruit, that if let to stand till cold it will turn to jelly. When the gooseberries are cold, mash them together. Passing them through a sieve or colander spoils them. [Note: Some berries—but very few—are tough enough to require sieving. Taste and decide for yourself.] The fine flavour which resides in the skin no art can replace. . . . Sweeten with fine powdered sugar [because of the cornstarch in our present-day equivalent, use extrafine sugar instead], but add not nutmeg or other spice. Mix in at the last moment some rich cream, and it is ready. The young folks of Northamptonshire, after eating as much as they possibly can of this gooseberry fool, are said frequently to roll down a hill and begin eating again.

GREEN TOMATO, MEXICAN
See Tomatillo

GROUND CHERRY
See Cape Gooseberry

GUAVA
(Psidium guayava or guyava or guajava)
also Guayaba, Goyave

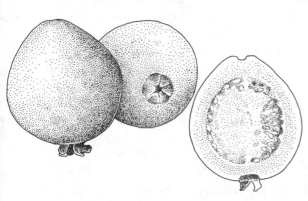

Although this fruit has come to be associated with Latin cuisine (probably because of the delicious and readily available Hispanic products canned guava nectar and guava paste), it flourishes around the globe. Native to Brazil, where they are still raised in considerable quantity, guavas are also commercially important in Hawaii, Australia, India, Colombia, Venezuela, Mexico, South Africa, and in lesser degree in areas of Southeast Asia, the Caribbean, and a few isolated groves in Florida and California.

However, since guava is extremely susceptible to fruit-fly infestation, we taste few of the myriad varieties produced outside the U.S., but must make do with the small quantity raised in Florida and occasional imports. Although guava also grows in southern California and Arizona, it is there primarily a dooryard fruit.

Guava may take many forms (but none are olive green and of an elongated egg shape; the fruit that fits this description is often called *pineapple-guava*, sometimes just *guava* by careless distributors or fruit sellers, but it is a feijoa *[Feijoa sellowiana]* for which see page 187). The true guava may be one of 140-odd species; either pear-shaped, somewhat ovoid, or rounded; from 1 to 4 inches in diameter; and with skin that is most often yellow-green or pale yellow (although there are exceptions). The flesh may be sweet to sour, may taste like strawberries or pineapple or banana, or all three, or none of the above, and may be colored white to yellow to salmon to red. It may be almost seedless, or packed with hard pips that "lie in obtrusive layers . . . like rows of buckshot" (*Cross Creek Cookery* by Marjorie Kinnan Rawlings, Scribner, 1981).

What all guava varieties have in common is an intense aroma—which may, depending on the fruit's ripeness, seem to emanate from either a locker room or the garden of Eden. As a member of the myrtle family, the guava's kin include a remarkable group of aromatics—clove, eucalyptus, the bay-rum tree (from which comes the heady oil used in colognes), allspice, and the above-mentioned feijoa. The somewhat acid flesh is unusually meaty, of a pleasantly gritty texture (the Aztec name for the fruit, *xalxocotl*, meaning sand plum, makes sensory sense). The perfume, full tutti-frutti flavor, and special consistency of the guava make it a rewarding subject for culinary investigation.

SELECTION AND STORAGE: You'll probably have little opportunity to choose, since this fruit is hard to come by. Keep an eye out—or, more exactly, a nose out—from late spring through early fall. Aroma is the key to most fruit, but to this one above all. Guavas should be very rich in fragrance: as they ripen, the odor changes from a rather musky, animal one (zoo-ish) to an extravagant floral bouquet. Obviously, fully ripe fruits are most desirable, but other stages will do. Select fruits that are as yellow and tender as possible, but don't hesitate to buy a slightly green specimen (as long as it has some aroma and tenderness), which will ripen at room temperature. As the yellow deepens, the fruit should become softer, rather like a ripe Bartlett (and equally bruisable). Because guavas may ripen at different rates—in one day or five—it is important to keep tabs on their ripening process. Expect the whole place to smell like guavas, and expect the fragrance to turn wild-sweet.

Once the fruit is ripe, use it within two days; or refrigerate for a day or two. If you keep it longer than that, the flesh may turn sandy and leathery, although the fruit does not spoil. Never refrigerate guavas before they are completely ripe.

You can purée and sieve guavas, freeze in individual ice-cube containers, then pop into a plastic bag and store in the freezer. Or make the cooked purée (see recipe) and freeze that.

USE: When tender-ripe, guavas can be enjoyed out-of-hand—peeling and seeding both depending upon which variety you've bagged. Peeled, seeded, and sliced, the sticky, dense pulp adds glorious color (the pink kind) and perfume to a fruit mixture, particularly one with shiny green triangles of kiwi or golden carambola star cuts. Or serve with warm biscuits and whipped cream, shortcake style.

Strained, and lightly sweetened, guavas yield a luscious, honeyed purée, sturdy enough to fold together with creams and custards without becoming liquid, or to use as a base for ice cream, ices, mousses, Bavarian cream.

Added to a braising liquid, then puréed, guavas produce a fruity-acid, thick sauce for duck, pork, or chicken. Simmered in a short-cooked stew or braise, they add unusual texture and aroma.

When poached in sugar syrup, the guavas can be chilled and served with cream, or combined with other cooked or fresh fruit. Puréed, they make a rich sauce to daub alongside a whole poached pear; or on ices, tapioca or rice pudding, or a delicate sponge cake.

Guava paste or candy is well-known, as is nectar; for both you'll need a windfall of guavas.

What guavas are less than perfect for is what every tropical cookbook I've seen suggests as their best use—jelly. Although loaded with pectin and acid, jelly's basic building blocks, guavas are entirely whimsical about "setting up." After a series of successes and failures with making jelly, I spoke with Janell Smith, who works with tropical fruits in Dade County, Florida, and was formerly the Extension Service home economist there. She said no question was asked more often than how to get guava jelly to set—and advised me to give up if I wanted a predictable recipe.

PREPARATION: This will depend upon what you're trying to accomplish, but a few basics may help. If you want fresh, cut-up guava, trim off the blossom end, then halve lengthwise. With a melon-ball cutter scoop out and reserve the seedy central pulp. Cut the shell that remains into small pieces to suit other ingredients. When you've cut up as many fruits as you'll need, purée the seedy pulp. Add sugar and lemon juice to taste; combine with guava pieces. Chill.

For a simple purée, cut up the rinsed fruit (no need to peel) and purée in processor or blender with sugar and liquor to taste. Press through a nonaluminum sieve. Adjust flavoring and chill. Alternatively, press the cut-up fruit through the fine disk of a nonaluminum food mill.

NUTRITIONAL HIGHLIGHTS: Guava is an extremely rich source of vitamin C. It is also a good source of vitamin A and potassium and is low in sodium and calories, with only 45 per ½-cup serving.

GUAVA FOOL

Those fetching English desserts, fools, are no more than puréed fruits swirled with cream. The goodness of the sweet depends upon obtaining a flavorful fruit with sufficient body and acid to complement the cream, one that will hold its own without being masked or becoming liquidy. Guava, with its distinct aroma and tart edge, makes a glossy, dense purée that perfectly pairs with cream—even if its origin is not the English countryside. A formula seems handy, rather than a recipe, since the dish is such a breeze to assemble.

For each serving

2 guavas, about 3 ounces each, fully ripe
4–6 teaspoons sugar
¼ cup heavy (or whipping) cream, not ultrapasteurized

Rinse guavas and trim off blossom ends. Cut in 1-inch pieces; place in container of processor or blender with 4 teaspoons sugar. Whiz to a purée. Taste and add sugar, as desired. Press through a fine nonaluminum sieve. Cover and chill. At serving time, whip cream to form soft peaks. Gently fold into the fruit purée, creating swirls and striations; do not blend, but keep the two flavors and textures somewhat separate.

Note: The delicious guava purée need not be limited to use in fools. It makes a beautiful sauce for rice or tapioca pudding and fresh or poached fruit; or spoon a dollop over angel-food, sponge, or pound cake; or serve as an accompaniment to roast duck, pork, or ham.

GUAVA CREAM

Shiny and moundable, this dessert has the unmistakable scent and granular texture of guava. Although it's so easy you might question its merit, the substantial body and rich aroma lift the dessert out of the ordinary.

2 servings

3 guavas, about 3 ounces each
About 3 tablespoons sugar
½ cup heavy (or whipping) cream, not ultrapasteurized
Optional: Additional cream, whipped

Rinse guavas and trim off blossom ends. Cut fruit in 1-inch pieces, reserving 2 small slivers for garnish. Combine in blender or processor with 3 tablespoons sugar and the cream. Whirl until puréed. Press through a nonaluminum fine sieve. Spoon into individual dessert dishes and chill, covered. To serve, garnish with fruit slice and additional cream, if desired.

JIM FOBEL'S GUAVA PURÉE

Delicious layered in the Guava and Passion Fruit Trifle following, this purée takes on a completely different personality when served as an accompaniment to roast duck, pork, turkey, or chicken. When served as such, 3 tablespoons per serving will suffice.

Makes about 1½ cups

8 medium guavas (1 pound)
½ cup sugar
½ cup dry sherry

1. Trim off slivers from ends of guavas; dice fruit (you should have about 3 cups). Combine in small saucepan with sugar and sherry. Bring to a boil over moderate heat.

2. Cook over low heat, stirring often, until guavas are tender—about 20 minutes.

3. Transfer mixture to food processor or blender; purée. Force mixture through nonaluminum sieve into bowl. Discard seeds. Serve hot or warm with roasted meats; cool to room temperature for trifle, or cover and refrigerate until needed.

GUAVA NUT TEA CAKE

Curlicues of guava set into a buttery nut batter make a thin, rich cake that is as pretty as it is unusual. The pink scrolls (and it really is worth finding the colored variety for this), as cheery as a Matisse découpage, become firm when baked—like fruit paste or dried fruit; be advised if you are not a fan of chewiness.

8 servings

½ cup plus 2 tablespoons sugar
½ cup pecans
5 ripe guavas, about 3 ounces each
3 tablespoons rum
1 stick unsalted butter (4 ounces)
1 egg
1 cup flour
1 teaspoon baking powder
¼ teaspoon salt
2 tablespoons pale jelly, preferably guava

1. Combine 2 tablespoons sugar and pecans in processor; whirl to a fine grind; scrape out and set aside. Clean container of processor.

2. Peel 3 guavas and halve lengthwise. With grapefruit spoon or melon-ball cutter scoop out and reserve central seedy area (leaving shell about ½ inch thick). Place seedy pulp in processor container.

3. Set shells on steamer rack over boiling water; cover and steam until tender, from 5 to 10 minutes, depending on guava variety. Set on plate, sprinkle with 1 tablespoon sugar; turn to coat; cool. Cut crosswise into ⅛-inch slices.

4. Cut up 2 remaining guavas; combine in processor with reserved pulp and 2 tablespoons rum. Purée, then press through a fine nonreactive sieve. (Or press guava pieces through fine disk of stainless-steel food mill.) Then stir in rum. Reserve. Butter 9-inch round pan. Fit a round of waxed paper in bottom; butter it. Lightly flour pan.

5. In small mixer bowl cream butter until light; gradually beat in remaining sugar. Add egg; beat on high speed until fluffy. Add guava purée. Sift together flour, baking powder, and salt. Add in 4 batches on lowest speed. Add nuts.

6. Spread batter evenly in pan. Arrange pattern of guava crescents on top. Press gently so fruit is flush with batter. Bake in lower half of preheated 375-degree oven until cake separates from sides and tests done in the middle—about 30 minutes. Cool 5 minutes. Carefully invert on a plate, then set right side up on a rack.

7. Stir together remaining tablespoon rum and jelly in tiny pan; heat to boiling. Paint over warm cake surface to coat thoroughly. Let cake cool completely.

JIM FOBEL'S GUAVA AND PASSION FRUIT TRIFLE

Luscious, soft, seductive are words that suit this exotic layered sweet. While the tropical extravaganza will be most delicious with all ingredients as listed, you can simplify by replacing the Passion Fruit Custard with orange: substitute orange juice sharpened with lime juice (2 parts orange to 1 lime) and add ¼ teaspoon grated orange rind. You might also buy the ladyfingers and baby macaroons at a bakery instead of making them.

8–10 servings

About 2 dozen Ladyfingers (recipe follows)
¼ cup fresh orange juice
1½ tablespoons fresh lime juice
1½ cups Guava Purée (see page 222)
About 5 dozen tiny Almond Macaroons (recipe follows)
Doubled recipe for Passion Fruit Custard (page 352) or orange custard (see head-note above)
1 cup heavy (or whipping) cream
3 tablespoons confectioners' sugar

1. Place 7 or 8 ladyfingers in bottom of 2-quart glass serving dish or soufflé dish. Combine orange and lime juices; sprinkle one-third over ladyfingers. Using ½ cup of the guava purée, drop dabs over the ladyfingers. Arrange about 18 of the macaroons over purée (reserve 12 pretty ones for top). Spread one-third custard over this.

2. Repeat step 1 two more times to make two more layers. Cover and chill at least 3 hours or overnight.

3. Several hours before serving, whip cream to form soft peaks. Add confectioners' sugar and whip until fairly stiff. Spread half smoothly over trifle. Scoop remainder into pastry bag fitted with ¼-inch star tip. Pipe 12 mounds around edge. Refrigerate until serving time.

4. To serve, garnish trifle with remaining macaroons, pushing them into the whipped-cream mounds.

Ladyfingers

Makes about 2 dozen

3 large eggs, separated, at room temperature
Pinch salt
⅛ teaspoon cream of tartar
½ cup sugar
1 teaspoon vanilla extract
½ cup less 1 tablespoon sifted flour
2 tablespoons cornstarch
½ cup confectioners' sugar

1. Beat whites in large bowl of electric mixer until foamy. Add salt and cream of tartar and beat to form soft peaks. Beat in ¼ cup sugar, a tablespoon at a time, beating 1 minute after each addition.

2. Beat yolks in smaller bowl until light; add vanilla and remaining ¼ cup sugar. Beat until light and thick. Scrape into whites and fold together delicately.

3. Combine flour and cornstarch in sieve and sprinkle gradually over eggs, folding with rubber spatula. Combine well without deflating.

4. Scoop half the batter into pastry bag fitted with ½-inch plain tube. Piping onto nonstick baking sheet (or parchment-covered sheet), form evenly spaced biscuits about 3½ inches long and 1¼ inches wide. Refill bag and pipe another sheet (or pipe all on one very large sheet). Sieve confectioners' sugar evenly over tops.

5. Bake in preheated 300-degree oven on middle and upper racks for 10 minutes; turn pans front to back and switch shelf positions. Bake 5–8 minutes longer, until pale gold. Turn off heat; let stand 5 minutes.

6. Set nonstick sheets on racks (or pull off parchment and cookies onto racks). Let cool until firmed up, then remove with spatula. Cool completely.

Almond Macaroons

Makes about 5 dozen

1 cup whole, unblanched almonds
¾ cup confectioners' sugar
2 large egg whites
Pinch salt
2 tablespoons plus 4 teaspoons sugar
½ teaspoon almond extract

1. Combine almonds and confectioners' sugar in processor and whirl to very fine texture. Scrape into a bowl.

2. Beat egg whites and salt in small mixer bowl to form soft peaks; beat in 2 tablespoons sugar, 1 at a time, whipping a minute after each addition. Add almond extract.

3. Fold almond powder gently but thoroughly into whites with rubber spatula. Scoop into a pastry bag fitted with ½-inch plain tube.

4. Press cookies about 1 inch in diameter onto nonstick baking sheet, or one covered with parchment, leaving ½–¾ inch between them. With wet fingertip smooth top of each. Sprinkle with remaining 4 teaspoons sugar.

5. Bake in center of preheated 325-degree oven for about 15 minutes, or until firm and very pale beige—not brown. Let stand 10 minutes to firm up, then remove from sheet and cool on rack.

Note: This recipe was adapted from Petite Almond Macaroons in *Ready When You Are: Made-Ahead Meals for Entertaining,* copyright by Elizabeth Schneider Colchie, Crown Publishers.

GUAVA, PINEAPPLE
See Feijoa

H

HAKUSAI
See Chinese Cabbage

HORSERADISH
(Armoracia rusticana)

*J*ars of grated horseradish in vinegar are a common sight at supermarkets all over America. But fresh horseradish roots (considerably more versatile and pungent than the prepared mixtures) are a fairly recent addition to the greengrocer's inventory—and *common* is hardly the word you're likely to think of upon seeing one for the first time.

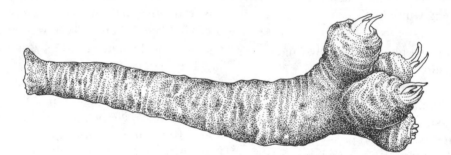

The root looks like something that may have belonged to a male mastodon and was fossilized for eons before arriving in the vegetable market. The taste, however, is not forbidding.

Horseradish, as is at once clear upon sampling, is a member of the Mustard family, with the same kind of cleansing bite, but an underlying sweetness; it seems more a potent flavoring (like garlic) than a hot spice. The root, which can be harvested into wintry weather and stores well, is beloved in cool climes, where it adds zest to a meat-and-potatoes diet. Its best-known and most-common use is as an accompaniment to roast beef, particularly in England. It can be served plain (Mrs. Beeton in her 1861 *Book of Household Management* recommends that shredded horseradish "be placed in tufts round the border of the dish, with 1 or 2 bunches on the meat") or mixed into a sauce for the meat. In the American South fresh horseradish is used in the same way (whether "neat" or stirred into sauce), as an accompaniment to beef.

Native to eastern Europe and western Asia, horseradish now grows wild in Britain, New Zealand, throughout Europe, and in North America. Its most dedicated users are German, Finnish, Norwegian, Danish, British, and Russian, with a smattering of Central Europeans making occasional use of the stinging seasoning. In America, the tenacious, long-lived plant is grown in considerable quantities in Illinois (primarily), New Jersey, Pennsylvania, Maryland, Wisconsin, and California. Its long, heavy taproot is peeled, grated, and processed with vinegar (and beets, for the sweeter red version), then bottled, or made into "cocktail sauce" or dried.

SELECTION AND STORAGE: Fresh horseradish root is most abundant in the late fall and early spring, but you should be able to find it all year. The crop is planted continuously and harvested during all but the most freezing and wettest weather. Each root has quite a different shape, but generally speaking they'll be from six inches to a foot long, and from one to three inches in diameter, with several rounded protuberances at one end. The skin is the color and texture of a scruffy, wrinkly, gnarled parsnip or parsley root (beauty is not this plant's strong point). It may have green tops, or not, depending upon the time of year.

Look for a root that is exceptionally hard and free of spongy or soft spots. Modern cultivation methods yield a vegetable relatively free of rootlets, but sometimes you'll have to pick through some rooty specimens. Avoid sprouting, greenish-tinged horseradish, which may have a bitter layer that requires deep paring.

To store horseradish, wrap it in a slightly dampened piece of toweling, then a dry one. Kept in the refrigerator, it should last for a few weeks if fresh when purchased. If softness or moldy spots develop, scrape them off, remove the dampened towel, and return to the refrigerator.

USE: Perhaps it is because we usually think of horseradish as a wet, vinegary preparation that it is used in such limited fashion. I suggest that you keep a root in the refrigerator and grate the firm, dry, fine seasoning over *everything* until you find what it best suits. Like good black pepper, this complex, aromatic flavoring enhances a wide assortment of foods. Like pepper, it should be grated directly on the food soon before eating, or its volatile flavor will dissipate (and the shreds will brown).

At its simplest, grate fresh horseradish on hot or cold vegetables, seafood (raw fish is delicious with the Japanese horseradish, wasabi, in the same way), or meat; sprinkle in sandwiches (scrumptious with beef, pork, or avocado), creamed soups and purées.

Stir grated horseradish into dressings for composed vegetable, meat, or seafood salads. Stir into hot puréed beans or beets, potatoes, parsnips, or celery root. Add to creamed vegetable dishes.

Add zip to mayonnaise or cream sauce with freshly grated horseradish. Swirl a bit into apple and/or cranberry sauce, or other fruit sauces to serve with meats. Combine with sour cream and a tad of lemon and sugar for a sauce to complement smoked fish.

Season roasting meats generously with the root; although the bite disappears, the sweetly turnip-like flavor remains. My inventive friend Joseph Schultz, proprietor of India Joze in Santa Cruz, includes chips of horseradish in lamb, potato, and onion stew, then accentuates with the freshly grated root at serving time, if a more pronounced flavor is desired.

PREPARATION: Pare and grate horseradish—but not in advance, unless it is being added to a sauce or preserved in vinegar. Peel the skin (and the growth layer beneath, if you have a greenish springtime root) from the amount you'll use. With a very sharp metal grater, grate the amount you need.

NUTRITIONAL HIGHLIGHTS: Horseradish is low in calories and sodium.

PREPARED HORSERADISH

The food processor has saved us from the weepy job of hand grating this pungent root. Home-prepared horseradish is firmer, more aromatic, and sharper than the bottled product. Do not stock up on it, though, as it loses its character with storage.

Remember that sprouting spring horseradish, usually greenish, requires deeper paring to rid it of a bitter taste. You'll see the layer that needs to be removed when you cut a cross-section. Pale beige horseradish needs only a shallow peeling.

Fresh horseradish, preferably not green-tinged

¼ cup vinegar (distilled white, rice, or white wine), plus additional for mixing

Salt and sugar, as desired

1. Peel the amount of horseradish you want to grate. Cut in ½-inch cubes. A handful at a time, process cubes with vinegar until texture is medium-fine, not puréed or pulpy.

2. Pour contents of container into strainer set over a bowl. Return liquid to container and process any additional batches of cubes, using the same vinegar.

3. Combine grated horseradish with enough vinegar to moisten well. Stir in salt and sugar (a big pinch of each for ½ cup prepared horseradish). Refrigerate in a glass jar, tightly covered. Although it will keep for weeks, the horseradish is at its zestiest when fresh.

RED HORSERADISH (HORSERADISH WITH BEETS)

Fresh horseradish mixed with cooked beets, vinegar, and seasonings, a favorite Eastern European condiment, is mellower and sweeter.

Makes about 1½ cups

¾ cup (about 3 ounces) Prepared Horseradish (see preceding recipe), made with red wine vinegar or cider vinegar

2 medium beets, cooked, peeled, finely grated (about 1 cup)

About 1 teaspoon salt

Sugar to taste

Vinegar to taste

Mix all ingredients, then taste and adjust seasoning. Chill several hours or more before using. Adjust seasoning again before serving. Keep refrigerated.

Note: The recipes above appear in a different form in *Better Than Store-Bought,* which I co-authored with Helen Witty.

HORSERADISH-ROASTED PORK

Don't be tempted to cut down what appears to be a staggering dose of horseradish. When roasted, the pungent root becomes almost sweet, retaining its flavor but little of its bite. You can follow this procedure with other fat-covered meats for a similarly brown-crusted roast: lots of savory goodness from one ingredient and little labor.

6 servings

3 pounds boneless center-cut pork loin, not trimmed or tied
Chunk of peeled horseradish about 2 by 2 inches, grated (about ¼–⅓ cup)
Salt and pepper to taste

1. Trim off the fat layer that covers the pork and any other easily removed fat parts. Set fat briefly in freezer until firm. Once cold, cut in 1-inch pieces. Combine in processor with 3 tablespoons horseradish and whirl to a purée.

2. Open out pork, cutting as needed to evenly distribute seasoning; sprinkle with salt, pepper, and remaining horse-radish. Tie roast into a neat, compact cylinder and place in roasting pan.

3. Sprinkle with salt and pepper, then spread puréed fat mixture evenly over meat. Set in preheated 450-degree oven and roast 20 minutes.

4. Lower heat to 325 degrees and roast meat until it registers 170 degrees on a meat thermometer. Timing will vary considerably, depending on the conformation of the meat; start testing after about an hour.

5. Let roast rest briefly before serving in thin slices.

HORSERADISH CREAM SAUCE

Although almost everyone knows how good any horseradish cream sauce is, we often need to be reminded about classics. Serve the mellow-pungent mixture with smoked fish—salmon, bluefish, trout, sable, chub, whitefish—or plain grilled salmon or bluefish. Spoon over smoked chicken or turkey, as well, or blanched hot vegetables.

The mustard and Tabasco, by the way, point up the horseradish savor, rather than adding new tastes. But if you want to add new tastes, try finely chopped or grated walnuts with a pinch of powdered sugar.

Makes ¾–1 cup

1 tablespoon lemon juice
1 tablespoon packed finely grated horseradish
½ cup heavy (or whipping) cream
¼ teaspoon salt
¼ teaspoon Dijon-type mustard
About 3 drops Tabasco or pepper sauce

Combine lemon juice and horse-radish. Whip cream to form soft peaks; season with salt and mustard. Fold together with horseradish mixture. Add pepper sauce to taste. (Can be made 30 minutes before serving.)

FISH FILLETS BAKED WITH HORSERADISH AND SOUR CREAM

This traditional Russian treatment for fish fillets provides a fast and fussless change of pace. The horseradish, mellowed by the sour-cream topping and the cooking (which takes away much of its bite), tastes remarkably like a combination of garlic, sweet pepper, and parsley rolled into one. I prefer to cook fillets of fish with a firm texture that do not become watery, such as catfish, sea bass, or mackerel.

2 servings

2 firm fish fillets, about ½ pound each
Salt and pepper
1 tablespoon lemon juice
1 teaspoon softened butter
About 2½ tablespoons finely grated fresh horseradish (not packed)
About 3 tablespoons sour cream

1. Place fillets in a buttered baking-serving dish in a single layer to just fit. Sprinkle with salt, pepper, and lemon juice. Rub with softened butter. Sprinkle horseradish evenly over each fillet. Dab with cream evenly, then spread to coat.

2. Bake in upper third of preheated 425-degree oven until fish just cooks through, about 15 minutes.

PURÉED BEANS WITH HORSERADISH

You can use any kind of large shell beans for this dish—limas, butter beans, cranberry beans, or the like. Generally speaking, you should get about 4 cups beans from 2 pounds of large-podded shell beans (such as the above), which will feed 4. Cooking times can vary, but since the beans should be soft for puréeing, it doesn't matter if they are a bit overcooked: I find 15–30 minutes is usual. If you haven't the time or inclination to shell beans, frozen limas work well here.

4 servings

4 cups shelled large beans
2 medium shallots, sliced
About 1 teaspoon coarse kosher salt
¼–½ cup heavy (or whipping) cream
2 tablespoons butter
About 1 tablespoon finely grated fresh horseradish, or to taste
Optional: Finely minced fresh dill

1. Combine beans, shallots, 1 teaspoon salt, and water to barely cover; simmer, covered, until very tender. Drain. Force beans and shallots through medium disk of a food mill.

2. Return to saucepan and stir a few minutes over moderate heat to evaporate excess moisture, if necessary. Add cream, adjusting to desired consistency. Add salt to taste. Stir in butter and horseradish to taste; amount will vary depending on its pungency.

3. Scoop into a heated dish; shape with rubber spatula; sprinkle with dill, if desired.

CHUNKY TOMATO HORSERADISH SALSA

A lightened version of "cocktail sauce" plus Mexican salsa, this is a thick but fresh-tasting tomato relish with a bright horseradish bite. Try the juicy sauce chilled, with breaded or fried seafood or chicken, grilled or barbecued foods, cold roast chicken or pork, and avocado.

Makes about 2½ cups

2 tablespoons corn oil

2 medium onions, in ¼–½-inch dice

1 large green pepper, in ¼–½-inch squares

1½ pounds tomatoes, peeled (see page 23), seeded, cut in ½–1 inch dice

About 2 teaspoons sugar

About 1 teaspoon kosher salt

Pepper to taste

2 tablespoons red wine vinegar

Tomato paste, as needed

About 2 ounces peeled horseradish, freshly grated (about ¼ cup)

1. Heat oil in medium nonaluminum saucepan or skillet. Add onions and pepper and sauté over high heat 2 minutes. Cover and cook on low heat 5 minutes.

2. Add tomatoes and cover. Simmer 5–6 minutes, until barely tender. Uncover; add 2 teaspoons sugar, 1 teaspoon salt, pepper to taste, vinegar, and tomato paste as needed for color and body. Boil, uncovered, stirring until mixture has thickened a bit and vegetables are tender but not soft, about 4 minutes.

3. Scoop into a dish and cool to lukewarm. Stir in horseradish to taste. Add vinegar, sugar, salt, and pepper to taste. Cool completely, then cover and chill.

HUNGARIAN WAX PEPPER
See Chili-Pepper, Hungarian Wax

J

JALAPEÑO PEPPER
See Chili-Pepper, Jalapeño

JAPANESE PUMPKIN
See Kabocha

JERUSALEM ARTICHOKE
(Helianthus tuberosus)
also Sunchoke, Topinambour, Racine de Tournesol, Girasole

*O*ne of the very few American natives from the northern part of the continent to be contributed to the Old World, the Jerusalem artichoke became part of the French larder at the beginning of the seventeenth century and was an overnight success.

Unfortunately, the route across the ocean and back has made succotash of the

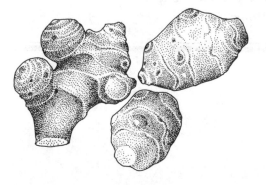

possibility of any single appellation. The scientific name is easy: *Helianthus* is from the Greek *helios* (sun) and *anthos* (flower); together they advise us that the plant is a member of the sunflower genus; and *tuberosus* applies to the roots, which are, of course, tubers. But that's about all that makes sense to any of the frustrated historians who have pursued the wild tangle of probable root words. In 1605 in Massachusetts Champlain sampled the vegetable, which was cultivated by Indians, and reported that it tasted like an artichoke (the heart, most probably, which it slightly resembles in texture and taste). Introduced to Europe shortly thereafter, the change to *girasol* or *girasole* (Spanish or Italian respectively, for sunflower), plus the word for artichoke does not seem completely impossible. But the move to "Jerusalem" requires quite a leap of the imagination. As written in an early botanical text: "Jerusalem Artichoke is considered to be a corruption of the Italian *Girasole Articiocco* . . . under which name it is said to have been distributed from the Farnese Garden at Rome," the custom having been to present newly discovered plants to the Pope, who then passed them along to his favorites, like Cardinal Farnese, who grew them in 1617. But some word-smiths claim that the word *girasole* was not used until the late nineteenth century. To make matters even less comprehensible, the moniker *topinambour* appeared on the scene, supposedly because a tribe of that name arrived in France around the same time as the vegetable. As a sales pitch the Jerusalem artichoke was hawked in the streets under the name of those Brazilian Indians.

What a shame that the North American Indian name *sunroot* was not packaged with the Jerusalem artichoke when it was sent to Europe via Champlain. But the story goes full circle, for a company in Iowa is selling the vegetable under the brand name Sun Roots. (And to further entice, Joan Nathan, culinary reporter par excellence, says that within the old city of Jerusalem there is an ancient field of Jerusalem artichokes —although all evidence suggests that there is no connection between the city and vegetable.)

In France and Italy the love affair with Jerusalem artichokes has run hot and cold, but mostly the latter, as it has in America. Although the plants with pretty yellow flowers will put down roots filled with delicious tubers just about anywhere you plant them, they do not seem to have taken a lasting foothold in the culinary repertoire in Europe or the United States. But, happily for our generation, this seems to be another upswing period, when the tuber is deemed a delicacy for man, as well as food for forage animals.

This is due, in part, to a reevaluation of our culinary roots and a fresh look at the best and simplest foods. A look, however, is not the point, for although the tubers can be smooth and pearly, like pale imitations of gingerroot, they are more often lumpy and bulbous, matte and sturdy. But the ivory flesh is extremely crisp, like water chestnuts, and the taste is sweetly fresh, in the same vein, with subtle undertones of artichoke heart and salsify.

SELECTION AND STORAGE: Although available year round, Jerusalem artichokes are at their sweetest best from fall through winter, waning in quality when spring arrives. Look for the smoothest, firmest tubers with the fewest hard-to-clean protrusions. Choose ones of equal size, if possible, so timing the cooking is easy. Normally colored tan-gold to cream, tubers may occasionally appear in reddish or purplish varieties. But tubers tinged with green or blotched should be avoided, as should sprouting ones.

Fresh Jerusalem artichokes in good condition can be stored for about a week in the refrigerator, wrapped in plastic. Check for softness, blotches, or excessive moisture. They darken and get mushy if canned or frozen, but will pickle fabulously (see recipe).

USE: Raw chokes have a clean, crisp texture that makes them a perfect crudité for creamy or oily dips and sauces, as well as a wonderful dieter's snack. They add crunch and flavor to salads of raw or cooked vegetables, meat, or fish combinations, whether grated, sliced, chopped, diced, or julienned. And they can be dressed well in advance of serving, as they do not become limp or discolor. If you do want a less crisp, more mellow taste, you can blanch Jerusalem artichokes (see Preparation).

As a simple hot vegetable side dish, steam or boil Jerusalem artichokes 8–15 minutes, depending on their size. Serve hot, with salt and pepper, brown butter sauce *(beurre noisette)*, melted butter and lemon, Hollandaise sauce, or Nutmeg Cream (page 206).

Whole tubers baked with a roast are a nutty-sweet alternative to potatoes. Sliced chokes make an appealing gratin, cream-sauced and cheese-topped. Purée broth-simmered chokes for a light, smooth soup.

Diced, sliced, or julienned Jerusalem artichokes can be stir-fried or sautéed for a few minutes, with or without other vegetables, meats, or seafood, for a crunchy dish. Combined with a bit of flour and egg, grated sunchokes make hearty pancakes.

Note: No matter how you cook this vegetable, it is important to check often as it cooks through. A few minutes can mean the difference between tender and collapsed.

PREPARATION: Jerusalem artichokes need merciless scrubbing with a brush, as they stubbornly hide sand and soil. You can peel them or not, depending upon your preference for mottled beige or white (and for waste or not). If you peel the tubers, it can be before or after cooking. If before, drop into a bowl of acidulated water after peeling. To retain the pallor while cooking, simmer in an *à blanc* liquid (see Cardoons, Basic Preparation 1, page 90). For dishes to be served cold, or reheated, you can drop the scrubbed, unpeeled tubers (trimmed to more or less the same size) into boiling, salted water; boil to the stage desired, then cool in ice water. Drain; remove the peel.

NUTRITIONAL HIGHLIGHTS: Jerusalem artichokes vary in calories depending on how long they have been stored, but their average is modest, at about 60 per ½ cup.

Caveat: Jerusalem artichokes cause extreme flatulence in some but have no effect on others; go easy the first time out.

ROASTED JERUSALEM ARTICHOKES

Once you've tried this simple recipe, it's bound to become a regular in your repertoire. Nothing could be easier to cook—but you must keep an eye on the chokes so that they do not overcook and become mushy.

The subtle flavor of the Jerusalem artichokes is enhanced by roasting in a film of oil. Leslie Revsin, a New York chef, uses walnut oil to underscore the nutty flavor. You can also use a combination of hazelnut and peanut oil, or oil and butter. Roast the chokes with any meat or fowl that you're cooking in an open pan. Scatter them around the meat during the last ½ hour of cooking, rolling to coat with fat, then let them finish roasting when you've removed the meat to let it rest before carving.

6 servings

2 pounds full, firm-fresh Jerusalem artichokes, very well scrubbed
2 tablespoons meat fat, oil, or butter and oil (see suggestions above)
Salt and pepper to taste

1. If chokes are very different in size, trim them to more or less the same dimensions, keeping as large as possible.

2. Roll the chokes in the fat or oil in a baking dish. Bake in a 350-degree oven until no longer crisp in the center, but not mushy—from 35–60 minutes; timing varies with how long chokes were stored. Sprinkle with salt and pepper to taste, and serve.

SALAD OF JERUSALEM ARTICHOKES IN MUSTARD DRESSING

Ivory, crunchy slices of Jerusalem artichoke are bathed in a mustard-spiked, creamy dressing and served with watercress for a salad that may become a regular in your home, as it has in mine.

4 servings

1 egg yolk
1½ teaspoons minced shallots
1 scant tablespoon coarse-grain mustard
1 tablespoon cider vinegar
Big pinch cayenne pepper
⅛ teaspoon salt, or to taste
5 tablespoons corn oil
1 pound Jerusalem artichokes, scrubbed ruthlessly
1 bunch watercress, trimmed, rinsed, and dried

1. Combine egg yolk, shallots, mustard, vinegar, cayenne, and salt in a small bowl; blend with a whisk. Gradually incorporate oil, whisking vigorously. Reserve.

2. Trim the chokes into fairly even-sized large pieces. Using slicing blade of a processor, a vegetable slicer, or a mandoline, cut chokes into very thin slices.

3. Combine artichokes in a bowl with dressing and chill for ½–1 hour. Serve on watercress.

CREAMY JERUSALEM ARTICHOKE SOUP

When we shared Thanksgiving with close pals and fellow food writers Bert Greene and Phillip Schulz, we took along this smooth, light purée, Small Asian Pears in Ginger-Vinegar Syrup (page 27), and Gooseberry and Apple Pie (page 216). Although some might consider it lily gilding, we topped each portion of soup with a lump of hazelnut butter (recipe follows). Post-soup came fennel-stuffed turkey, the best Thanksgiving bird I've ever had. For that you'll need *Greene on Greens* (Workman Publishing), page 178.

4 servings

2 tablespoons butter
2 medium stalks celery with leaves
   (strings removed), finely chopped
4 medium-large shallots, minced
1 pound Jerusalem artichokes, scrubbed
1 small sweet potato (6–7 ounces)
¾ teaspoon ground coriander
4 cups chicken broth
About ¾ teaspoon salt
White pepper to taste
¼ cup dry white wine
1 tablespoon cornstarch
About ½ cup heavy (or whipping) cream

1. Melt butter in a heavy pot; stir in celery and shallots. Stir over low heat for 5 minutes. Cut artichokes in ½-inch slices. Scrub and peel potato; cut in slices the same size.

2. Add artichokes and potato to the pot with coriander and broth. Simmer, partly covered, for 25 minutes, or until vegetables are soft. Cool briefly. Purée (in batches, if necessary) in processor.

3. Press soup through a fine sieve, then season with salt and white pepper. Stir wine into cornstarch; add to soup. Bring to a boil, stirring. Gradually add cream to taste. Serve as is, or with Hazelnut Butter.

Hazelnut Butter

Makes enough for 4 generous servings

¼ cup hazelnuts
3 tablespoons butter, chilled

Toast nuts in 350-degree oven (or toaster oven for this small amount) 15 minutes. Transfer to a coarse-meshed sieve and rub vigorously (protect your hand with a cloth) to remove husks. Rub stubborn nuts together or against the mesh to scrape off most skin. Cool completely. Combine cleaned nuts and butter in processor and whirl to desired texture, scraping down sides of container a few times. Form into a cylinder; wrap and chill until serving time.

JERUSALEM ARTICHOKES VINAIGRETTE

Simple and versatile, this can be served on a bed of radicchio or chicory for a first course, or combined with other julienned vegetables and meats for a main-course salad. Because the chokes do not become watery, the dish can be assembled well ahead of serving.

4–6 servings as a first course

2 tablespoons lemon juice
½ teaspoon salt
Black pepper
¼ cup light, fruity olive oil
1 scallion green, minced
1 pound Jerusalem artichokes, well scrubbed (or peeled, as you wish)
Minced fresh tarragon, dill, thyme, or basil to taste

1. Blend lemon juice, salt, and pepper; mix in oil gradually. Add scallion.

2. Cut artichokes into very fine julienne, preferably with a julienne blade on processor or vegetable slicer. Toss with dressing; add scallion and herbs to taste. Mix well. Cover and refrigerate for at least an hour, preferably more.

GRATED JERUSALEM ARTICHOKE PANCAKES

Both tender and crunchy, with an old-fashioned potato-pancake look, these savories go well with roast turkey or chicken. The hazelnut oil deliciously underscores the flavor of the chokes, but if you have none, substitute walnut oil or butter.

Makes 12 medium pancakes, 4–8 servings as a side dish

¾ pound Jerusalem artichokes, scrubbed and trimmed
1 large shallot, peeled
2 large eggs
½ teaspoon salt
Big pinch nutmeg
White pepper to taste
3 tablespoons flour
3 tablespoons corn oil
2 tablespoons hazelnut oil

1. Grate artichokes and shallot on shredding blade of food processor or vegetable mill. Blend eggs, salt, nutmeg, and white pepper in mixing bowl. Add artichokes and flour and mix well with hands.

2. Heat 1½ tablespoons corn oil and 1 of hazelnut oil in each of 2 very large skillets. Quickly place 6 heaping tablespoons of the mixture in each, spacing evenly. At once flatten hard with spatula.

3. Fry over moderate heat until nicely browned on each side, about 2 minutes per side. Serve immediately.

Note: I like to have all pancakes ready together, but if you prefer, you can do 6 at a time in one skillet, keeping the first batch warm on a towel-covered plate in a warm oven.

GRATIN OF JERUSALEM ARTICHOKES

Think of a combination of chestnuts, new potatoes, and cream with a hint of hazelnut, and you'll have a sense of this luscious gratin.

In addition to keeping the artichokes a pale beige, the initial cooking in milk seems to minimize the effects of a vegetable that "doth provoke wind," as the early cookbooks put it.

4 servings

1 pound Jerusalem artichokes, well scrubbed
1 cup milk
1 cup water
½ cup heavy (or whipping) cream
⅛ teaspoon nutmeg
White pepper to taste
¼ teaspoon salt, or to taste
1 garlic clove, halved
½ cup grated Gruyère, Emmenthaler, or Appenzeller cheese

1. Cut artichokes into even-sized pieces, as large as possible. Bring to a boil with the milk and water; simmer until not quite tender—about 8–10 minutes.

2. Drain, then cut into ¼-inch slices. Arrange in a shallow, buttered baking-serving dish.

3. Boil cream, nutmeg, pepper, salt, and garlic in a tiny pan; remove garlic. Pour cream over artichokes, then sprinkle with cheese. Bake in upper level of pre-heated 375-degree oven until bubbling and lightly browned—about 20 minutes.

PICKLED JERUSALEM ARTICHOKES

In this version of a Southern standard, the vegetables have a perky taste and crisp texture that make them far more endearing than the often syrupy or searing ones that show up in mail-order catalogues and specialty stores as "artichoke pickles." Adjust the pickling spices to your taste, but let the Jerusalem artichoke taste prevail.

Makes 4 pints

3 pounds Jerusalem artichokes, as regularly shaped as possible
Coarse kosher salt
1 medium onion, sliced
4 tiny dried hot peppers, or ½ teaspoon crushed red pepper flakes
2 teaspoons mustard seeds, slightly bruised
1 teaspoon celery seed
4 allspice berries
2 cups cider vinegar
1 cup water
1 cup distilled white vinegar
⅔ cup light-brown sugar
1 bay leaf, broken in 4 pieces

1. Scrape or pare thin skin from Jerusalem artichokes. Slice ¼ inch thick (if tiny, halve); you should have 2 quarts when finished. Place chokes in ceramic or glass bowl. Pour in enough water to cover generously. Holding chokes in bowl, pour water from it into measuring pitcher (or simply measure, once drained).

2. Add kosher salt to water, measuring ¼ cup to each quart. Stir to dissolve. Pour over chokes. Cover; let stand 1–1½ days at room temperature.

3. Rinse and drain chokes, then dry a bit with toweling. Divide evenly with onion rings among four clean, dry pint canning jars.

4. In nonaluminum pan combine hot peppers, mustard seeds, celery seed, allspice, cider vinegar, water, white vinegar, sugar, 4 teaspoons kosher salt, and bay leaf. Boil 5 minutes. Pour hot solution into jars, being sure each has its share of herbs and spices. Liquid should come to within ¼ inch of rims.

5. Wipe jar rims, cover with new two-piece canning lids, then screw on the bands. Place on rack in deep pot half filled with boiling water; add boiling water to cover jars by 2 inches. Bring to a boil. Cover pot and boil (process) 15 minutes.

6. Remove jars with tongs and set on towel. Cool for a day. Press centers of lids to be sure they remain depressed. (If they are flexible, refrigerate them, as they have not sealed.) Store several weeks or more before serving, refrigerated.

Note: The above recipe appears in slightly different form in *Better Than Store-Bought* (Harper & Row, 1979), which I co-authored (as Elizabeth Schneider Colchie) with Helen Witty.

JÍCAMA
(Pachyrhizus erosus, Pachyrhizus tuberosus)
also Yam Bean, Mexican Yam Bean, Ahipa, Saa Got

*T*he jícama (HEE-ka-mah) is the fleshy underground tuber of a leguminous plant (of which there are many similar species) that also produces pea pods on twining above-ground vines—hence some of its other common names. The vines, roots, beans, and mature pods are poisonous, but the immature pods are cooked up in

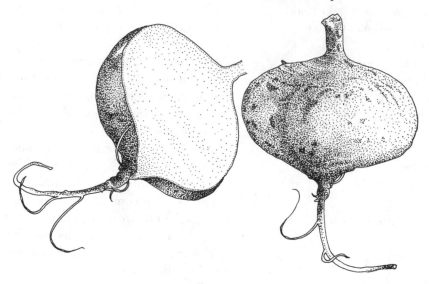

many countries. Although *Pachyrhizus erosus* started out life in Mexico and *Pachyrhizus tuberosus* in the headwater region of the Amazon in South America, the two species can for culinary purposes be treated as the same (some botanists believe they may even be the same species, with a varietal difference). The plant was carried by the Spanish from its sources to the Philippines during the seventeenth century. It then became a favorite crop of Chinese gardeners, and spread through Asia and the Pacific.

Despite its popularity there is surprisingly little culinary description of this extremely versatile vegetable outside Mexico. Why I cannot imagine. It has crunchy, juicy ivory flesh (the texture of water chestnuts) and a sweet, bland flavor that suits everything from fruit cup to stir-fried shrimp. It could not be easier to prepare, requiring only the peeling of its thinnish, sandy-tan, matte skin. Jícama is marketed in a useful range of sizes, from ½ pound to as much as 6 pounds. It can be eaten raw or cooked—and is very low in calories for so starchy-seeming a vegetable.

At present, jícama use is growing rapidly in the United States, where, thanks to a growing Latin and Oriental population, it now appears regularly in produce stands throughout the country, imported from Mexico. The only problem with the tuber is that occasionally you encounter one that is so bland (and sometimes so fibrous, too) that it is for all practical purposes worthless.

SELECTION AND STORAGE: The jícama is available year round, at Latin and Chinese markets and in many supermarkets. It may be turnip-shaped and rounded or lobed and blunt-tipped (four-leaf-clover-shaped in crosscut); it may be symmetrical or not. All forms and sizes are good for eating if fresh. Look for smooth, relatively unblemished roots (although patchy is normal) that look young when compared to their bin companions. Scratch the skin; it should be fairly thin and the creamy flesh should be very juicy. Heavy-skinned, dryish jícama may be fibrous and starchy instead of sweet —as dull as a raw potato. If you find you have a particularly starchy and/or fibrous jícama, use it in a cooked dish.

Store the jícama unwrapped in the refrigerator, free of moisture. Uncut, it will keep for 2–3 weeks, if in good condition. Once it has been cut, cover tightly with plastic and use within a week.

USE: Jícama can be used from appetizer through dessert, raw or cooked. You can cut it into slices, sticks, cubes, or rounds, or shred it. Use it to substitute for water chestnuts, if fresh are not available.

A standard Mexican jícama treatment is chilled slices sprinkled with chili powder, lime juice, and salt, to accompany drinks. Use jícama as a delicious, low-calorie alternative to crackers, for dips. Since it does not discolor, soften, or lose its crunch, it is particularly suited to garnishes or prepared-ahead hors d'oeuvres.

Salads—both fruit and vegetable—are jícama's forte, particularly those that are made ahead, as the bland vegetable benefits from a marinating or macerating time.

Jícama can be cooked in stir-fries and short-cooked braises. It is particularly receptive to full-flavored sauces, which it absorbs quickly without becoming soft. As a matter of fact, even paper-thin jícama seems to stay crunchy when cooked—or what one might have assumed would be overcooked. Although it is quickly dominated by strong seasoning, it keeps its characteristic freshness and crispness, as well as a lovely vegetable sweetness.

PREPARATION: Jícama must be peeled for use in any preparation. To do this, halve, quarter, or cut the tuber in as many lengthwise chunks as are conveniently handled for peeling. With a paring knife (a peeler is a waste of time and does the job poorly) pull off the skin from the sections, taking with it as much of the fibrous underlayer (the same color as the skin) as will come off easily. Finish by paring off additional parts of the fibrous underlayer as necessary.

NUTRITIONAL HIGHLIGHTS: Jícama is very low in sodium and low in calories, containing approximately 50 per cup (raw).

SALAD OF JÍCAMA, ORANGE, ONION, AND PEPPER

Bright and sweet, this easy salad can be served relish-style, along with grilled meat, or as a salad course.

3 servings

About 7 ounces jícama, peeled (see Preparation)

1 navel orange, peel and all pith removed

⅓–½ cup diced red onion

1 medium red bell pepper, cut in ½-inch squares

¾ teaspoon pure hot ground chilies (unseasoned chili powder)

¼ teaspoon salt, or to taste

2 tablespoons cider vinegar

2 tablespoons corn oil

1. Cut jícama into ¼-inch dice.

2. Cut orange in cubes about the same size; mix in bowl with jícama, onion to taste, and pepper.

3. Blend chilies, salt, vinegar; add oil and mix. Pour over salad; toss. Cover and refrigerate for an hour or longer.

SALAD OF JÍCAMA AND PAPAYA

Smoked and salted meats or fish go particularly well with this crunchy sweet salad. You can substitute mango, melon, or oranges for the papaya—but the papaya's seeds add a nice peppery bite.

6 servings as a first course or side dish

3 tablespoons fresh orange juice

Big pinch grated orange rind

1½ teaspoons sugar

½ teaspoon coarse kosher salt

2 tablespoons cider vinegar

3 tablespoons light vegetable oil, such as safflower or corn

½ pound jícama, peeled

1 ripe papaya, 1¼ pounds

About ¼ cup minced cilantro

2 Bibb lettuces, or 1 small Boston lettuce

1. Combine orange juice, rind, sugar, salt, and vinegar in a jar; shake to dissolve the crystals. Add oil.

2. Cut jícama in fine julienne strips, using a processor, vegetable cutter, mandoline, or knife.

3. Halve papaya; scoop out and reserve papaya seeds. Slice fruit in eighths and pare off skin. Cut pieces crosswise in thin slices. Combine with jícama; toss with dressing.

4. Add some papaya seeds and cilantro to taste; toss again gently. Taste for seasoning and additional papaya seeds. Arrange on the lettuce.

TOFU AND JÍCAMA IN AROMATIC SESAME CREAM

Both the jícama and tofu cubes absorb this rich, hot, and spicy sauce of Oriental and Middle Eastern parentage; the result is jícama that is less bland, and bean curd of unusual succulence and meatiness. Even those who profess indifference to tofu seem to be pleased with this treatment.

4 servings

1 pound jícama, peeled (see Preparation)
3½ tablespoons corn or peanut oil
1–2 jalapeño or serrano peppers, stemmed, seeded, and sliced
2 medium shallots, peeled and halved
1 large garlic clove
1 piece ginger, about 1 by 2 inches, peeled
2 tablespoons sliced cilantro stems and roots (roots are optional)
2 tablespoons soy sauce
1 tablespoon brown sugar
¼ cup tahini (sesame-seed paste)
¾ cup beef broth
1 pound firm-style tofu (bean curd)
Minced cilantro leaves to taste

1. Cut jícama into French-fry-sized pieces. Heat wok over moderate heat. Pour 1 tablespoon oil around rim, then rotate pan to distribute. Stir-fry jícama about 3 minutes, until it loses its raw flavor but not crunch. Transfer to large dish.

2. Combine chili, shallots, garlic, ginger, cilantro stems and optional roots in processor; whirl to a fine texture. Blend together soy sauce and sugar in a small bowl; stir in tahini, then beef broth.

3. Cut tofu in half crosswise, then into 1-inch dice. Heat wok; pour in 1½ tablespoons oil. Stir-fry tofu 1–2 minutes. Add to jícama.

4. Heat remaining tablespoon oil in wok. Add seasoning mixture from processor; stir-fry for a minute, tossing constantly. Stir broth mixture and add. Bring to a boil, stirring. Turn heat to low and add tofu and jícama; toss to coat with sauce. Cover and simmer on moderately low heat 2 minutes. Toss the pieces, recover and simmer about 2 minutes longer.

5. Scoop into heated serving dish and sprinkle with cilantro.

SALAD OF CHICKEN AND JÍCAMA IN PEANUT DRESSING

For this multinational salad, strips of cold poached chicken are combined with pickly-crisp strips of blanched jícama, then drizzled with a light, sweet peanut sauce.

4 servings

5 cups water
1-inch knob of ginger, sliced
1 celery stalk with leaves, cut up
5 scallions
¾ teaspoon salt
2½–3-pound chicken, quartered
1 pound jícama, peeled (see Preparation)
5 tablespoons cider vinegar
1 teaspoon sugar
About ¾ teaspoon hot chili oil (available in Oriental groceries)
2 tablespoons hot water
2 tablespoons smooth peanut butter
1 tablespoon soy sauce
1 tablespoon honey

1. In a heavy pot that will hold chicken in one layer, combine water, ginger, celery, 2 scallions (sliced), and ½ teaspoon salt. Boil 5 minutes covered. Add chicken pieces and return to a bare simmer.

2. Cover, turn off heat, and let stand 1 hour. Place chicken in a dish and let cool. Remove skin and bones, then cover and refrigerate. Strain, reserve, and refrigerate or freeze the light stock for another use.

3. Cut jícama in strips about ¼ inch thick and 2 inches long. Drop into a pot of boiling salted water. Return to a boil over highest heat and boil until the jícama just loses its raw starchiness—about 45 seconds. Drain; immerse in a bowl of ice water until just cooled, then drain again. Dry well.

4. Combine 4 tablespoons vinegar, ¼ teaspoon salt, sugar, and ¼ teaspoon chili oil in a bowl. Toss the jícama with this mixture, then cover and refrigerate until serving time.

5. Blend together hot water, peanut butter, soy sauce, honey, remaining tablespoon vinegar and ½ teaspoon chili oil in the order listed. Cover and let mellow until serving time.

6. Cut meat in strips. Arrange in the center of a platter. Drain jícama and arrange around the chicken. Drizzle peanut dressing over all. Slice remaining scallions (green part only) and sprinkle over the salad.

&❧ *ADDITIONAL RECIPE*
Michael Rose's Cactus Pear and Jícama Salad (page 68)

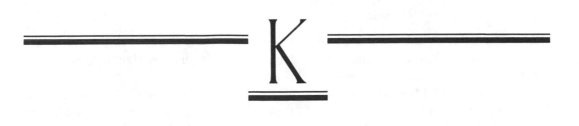

K

KABOCHA

*K*abocha (kah-BOW-cha) is a generic grouping (as well as a specific marketing name in this country) for many strains of Japanese pumpkin and winter squash of both *Cucurbita maxima* and *Cucurbita moschata* species. Home Delite, Ebisu, Delica, Hoka, Chirimen, Hyuga, Hoka, and Sweet Mama are all varieties that might be called

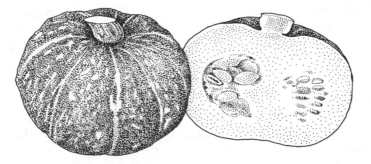

kabochas in a Japanese or American market. These Oriental squash, of flattened drum or turban shapes, deep green-skinned, superficially resemble the buttercup. What you cannot see is what they have in common with one another: exceptionally fine flavor, rich sweetness, and almost fiberless flesh.

How we happen to have the so-called kabochas is a curious story: According to the Sakata seed company, about fourteen years ago an enterprising grower in California planted Home Delite, Sakata's sturdy form of this squash, to supply Japan (which is conspicuously short of land) with a favored vegetable. He sold the entire crop to Japan, continued to plant, and soon expanded with acreage in Mexico. Japanese consumers like big squash (although this preference is changing), so some smaller ones have been left to be disposed of in Los Angeles, which is now making them available to American consumers (although only a mere 10–15 percent of the approximate 110 tons annual production is sold here).

Kabochas may range from 1 to 7 pounds, but average about 2 to 3. Their roughish, mottled rind is thick and deep green, with paler, uneven stripes and markings. The cooked yellow-orange flesh is softly fine-grained (more the texture of a baked pudding than a vegetable), tender and floury dry. The flavor is balanced between sweet potato and pumpkin. Japanese like squash to be delicately mealy (like a perfect baking potato, but more succulent) and *sweet*, which kabochas are.

SELECTION AND STORAGE: Look for kabochas most of the year, with some gaps in the spring. Select dull-skinned, full fruit that is heavy for its size. Avoid squash with signs of pitting, softness, or blackening of the stem (which should always be intact). You can keep the squash up to a month at room temperature, preferably cool. Do not refrigerate.

USE: A large kabocha can be used in all the ways that you would use winter-type squash and pumpkin. It can be baked, steamed, puréed, braised, chunked, or smoothed in soup, and baked in puddings, pies, and cakes. Use less sugar and more liquid in your recipe, however, as a kabocha is sweeter and drier than most winter squash. To enjoy a kabocha at its best and simplest, bake or steam it (see basic recipe) and serve with nothing but a slick of butter. I find the skin most edible, so prefer to serve the squash with most of it preserved, but take your choice. Or cut in chunks (incise the skin with decorations, as they do in Japan) and braise in seasoned liquid— juice, soy sauce with lemon and sugar, broth, or dashi, the Japanese cooking stock. Let cool. Serve at room temperature or chilled.

PREPARATION: If you want to cut up a kabocha, a heavy cleaver or giant knife usually does the job. However, some tough-rinded specimens need extra attention: Place your biggest, sharpest knife lengthwise on the squash (off center, to avoid the stem). With a wooden mallet or rolling pin gently hammer the part of the blade that joins the handle. Keep going until the squash is cut in two. Scoop out and discard the seeds and fibers.

NUTRITIONAL HIGHLIGHTS: All winter-type squashes are excellent sources of vitamin A and have substantial amounts of vitamin C, iron, and potassium. They are modest in calories and low in sodium.

BASIC KABOCHA SQUASH

Sweet, colorful kabochas can be baked or steamed. The result of either method will be rather dry and fine, like a perfect potato. The steamed has a somewhat more velvety finish.

TO BAKE A KABOCHA

Rinse the squash. Set in a pan and place in a 350-degree oven. Bake until easily pierced with a toothpick—about 1 hour for a 2-pound squash. Halve at once; scoop out seeds. Drizzle with butter and lemon. Cut into slices, as desired. Serve hot.

Alternatively, you can halve the squash (see Preparation), remove the seeds and fibers, then add seasoning and butter to taste. Cover with foil and bake in a pan in a preheated 350-degree oven until tender when pierced with a toothpick—about 45 minutes.

TO STEAM A KABOCHA

Halve (see Preparation) the rinsed kabocha. Scoop out the seeds and fibers. Peel or partly peel, as you like. Set cut side down on the rack of a steamer. Cover and steam 15–20 minutes, until tender when pierced with a toothpick.

You can also quarter the squash, if you prefer, or cut it into eighths. I like to cut lengthwise in eighths, then use a citrus stripper to remove about half the peel in a decorative pattern. Set on the steamer rack, cover the pot, and steam until just tender, 10–15 minutes, depending on the thickness. Serve with lemon and butter. Or cool to lukewarm, cut into smaller sections, pour Ginger Dressing (below) over all, then cool.

Ginger Dressing (for about 2 pounds kabocha)

4–6 servings

2 tablespoons sugar
⅓ cup lemon juice
2 tablespoons soy sauce
1 tablespoon finely grated fresh ginger
3 tablespoons dry or medium-dry sherry

Mix sugar and lemon until crystals dissolve, more or less. Add soy sauce, ginger, and sherry. Let stand as long as convenient, covered (or use right away). Spoon over lukewarm squash sections. Cool.

❧ *Kabocha can be substituted in calabaza recipes, pages 71–73, and buttercup recipes, page 64, but adjust by adding liquid when necessary, as kabocha is much drier.*

KAIWARE
See Radish Sprouts

KALE
(Brassica oleracea subspecies *acephala)*
also Curly Kale, Borecole, Kail

*P*robably the first of the cabbages to be cultivated, kale in all of today's principal forms was known two thousand years ago. The Latin *caulis*, meaning stem or cabbage stem, is the root of a family of cabbage names such as the Dutch *kool*, German *Kohl*, or the English *cole*. The distinctive part about kale's scientific name is the *acephala*,

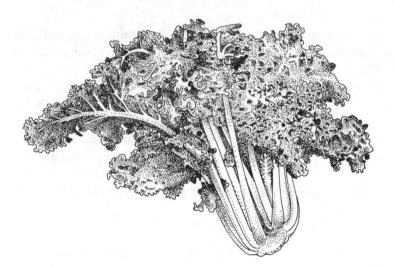

meaning headless, which separates it (and its brother collards, a non-curly sibling) from the rest of the brood.

Kale's ruffly leaves, each of which resembles a mammoth sprig of parsley, are unusual among the *Brassica* for their opened-out growing shape. It is also unusual for its gamut of beautiful varieties, some of which have been hybridized as ornamental plants. They show up in glamorous hues of variegated lavender and chartreuse, their leaves forming old-fashioned rosette forms on an upright stem. American market varieties are generally spruce green, with frilly leaves, or dusky bluish, with a less pronounced curl.

The flavor is cabbagy but mild. Cooked, kale has a delicate texture compared to other sturdy-seeming cabbages. It is particularly surprising that kale cooks so easily when you consider the unparalleled hardiness of the breed, which is able to withstand plenty of freezing weather (indeed, it improves with frost), but survives happily in the heat of the American South. Although it may have originated in the Mediterranean or

Asia (it has been around so long that no one is sure who brought and who took), it is in the colder climes that kale has earned its culinary devotees—in Scandinavia, Germany, Holland, and above all in Scotland. There, "to come to cail" with a family meant an invitation to dinner with or without kale. In typical Scottish preparations the unusually green wintry crop is puréed and served with oatcakes, layered with potatoes, stirred into barley soup, or cooked, then chopped and thickened with toasted oatmeal and cream to make a rich pottage. In England, however, kale is considered fodder—as it is, unfortunately, in many countries.

Perhaps because kale will grow on poor soil and has often been a survival crop, its connotations are bitter, and may recall hardship. Most immigrants who came to the United States from kale-growing countries have steered clear of the vegetable. In the South, the only area of the United States where it is a staple, kale is considered primarily a poor folks' crop.

But maybe the beauty and culinary value of kale have been discovered. Four times during the last winter I enjoyed kale in distinctly nonstraitened circumstances. The first and second times were in chic new French restaurants, where the vegetable du jour was steamed and buttered baby kale leaves. The next time was in a nouvelle American restaurant, where kale strips were punctuated with a confetti of Kentucky ham. The last was in a new-style Italian restaurant, where a light gratin of kale and Parmesan was offered.

SELECTION AND STORAGE: Although available all year, kale is at its most flavorful, tender, and abundant during the winter months. Select small deep-colored kale bunches with clean, slightly moist leaves. Avoid overly dry, browned, yellowed, or coarse-stemmed plants. Although kale should not be flabby, it is at its best when not too crisp. Look for kale that is marketed in a refrigerated or iced bin, or better, in an outdoor market in the winter; it wilts quickly once cut if kept in a warm area.

Since kale is happiest at about 32 degrees, unless you can leave it in the snow it is best to store it briefly, plastic-wrapped, in the coldest part of the refrigerator. Although it will not appear spoiled, kale should not be held more than a few days or it becomes flabby and bitter, losing its fresh green flavor and acquiring a more pronounced cabbagy one.

USE: Kale is as versatile as cabbage or spinach. Baby kale can be part of a salad (in moderation; it is a bit strong and chewy). Or serve it simply steamed for a few minutes, either whole leaves or strips. Or stir-fry it with pork, ginger, and garlic—or anything your creativity comes up with that day. Sauté it with oil, butter, or poultry or pork fat; add garlic, onion, ham, caraway or fennel seeds for flavoring. Either cook kale until very soft, in the traditional way, or crunchy-tender, in the new style.

For a stronger flavor, braise medium-sized kale in stock. Use it as the base for a creamed gratin, a layered pasta, or a thick purée. Add to main-dish soups based on beans, barley, or potatoes. Or make a puréed soup with the same ingredients, enriching it with cream. Blanch kale for a milder flavor.

Firm, colorful, and full-flavored, kale holds up well as a stuffing in country ham or pork leg. Combined with cheese, it is a zesty surprise in calzone, pizza, or thick rustic pies and turnovers.

PREPARATION: Unless they are minuscule, kale leaves should be stripped from their stems. Either hold a stem with one hand and run a knife along each side to free the leaves. Or fold the leaf halves together lengthwise, bend the stem, and pull the leaves free. Drop leaves into a sink filled with water and slosh about vigorously. Lift out gently, so debris sinks. Repeat until absolutely clean. Drain.

NUTRITIONAL HIGHLIGHTS: Kale is an excellent source of vitamin A, folic acid, and vitamin C. It is low in calories at 40 calories per cup, cooked.

BASIC KALE

When kale is to be served alone, as a side dish, I think it is best to blanch it. Although this diminishes some vitamins, it preserves the color, texture, and full flavor (unlike many vegetables, which lose character when precooked). It also means you can prepare the kale ahead, then finish to suit, as suggested below. Cooked this way, kale also loses less of its rather bouncy body, which means it goes a little further. I figure about 5 or 6 ounces per person when cooking tender, short- or thin-stemmed kale; buy more if the kale is heavier and leggier—and therefore has more waste.

Clean and strip kale (see Preparation). Drop into a large kettle of salted water. If you're cooking a hefty amount, add kale in batches, so that it will all wilt into the pot. (This takes a little longer than spinach, for example, which wilts immediately.) Boil vigorously, stirring down leaves now and then, until kale is just tender. Delicate kale may take about 4–5 minutes, heartier kale, longer. Drain, pressing down hard to express liquid; cool slightly. Chop with stainless-steel knife to size you wish. Reserve until serving time—as long as you like.

TO FINISH:
- ☐ Sauté kale in butter, goose fat, chicken fat, or bacon fat in a large skillet until heated through.
- ☐ Sauté kale in olive oil and minced garlic for a few minutes.
- ☐ Simmer kale in a skillet with heavy cream until it thickens to your taste; figure about ⅓ cup cream for two servings.

BASIC KALE, SOUTHERN STYLE

When you want a more cabbagy, smoky flavor and a more tender, soupy texture, cook kale the way greens are cooked in the South—with cured pork. Any cut or cure that is fatty and salty will do the trick; without these characteristics, the dish will be watery and insipid. Depending on how much meat you include, and how much you eat, this becomes a delicious meal-in-one if chunks of cornbread round it out. Figure on about 6–7 ounces kale per person as a side dish. About an ounce of meat per person will do for flavoring; use more for a meaty main course. If you're a hot-pepper fan figure on 1 tiny dried hot chili-pepper for 2 people.

Clean and strip kale leaves from stems (see Preparation). Combine in a nonaluminum pot with meat, optional hot pepper, and water to come about three-quarters of the way up. Boil gently, uncovered, until very tender, stirring often. Timing varies with toughness of kale; it can take from 40 minutes to 1½ hours. As kale is done, raise heat to boil away most of liquid.

SOUP OF BEANS, KALE, AND SQUASH

This is a hefty main-course soup, thick with vegetables and lightly spicy-herbal. You can use any one of a number of dried beans—chickpeas, black-eyed peas, Great Northern beans, navy beans, small lima beans, and pink beans are all good candidates. The palest varieties, though, will present the most appealing plateful of contrasting colors: orange squash, cream beans, and spruce-green kale. Like all hearty compound soups, this one improves with mellowing time.

6 servings

¾ pound dried beans
1 large bay leaf
1 teaspoon marjoram
2 tablespoons lard, bacon fat, or olive oil
3 medium leeks, thoroughly cleaned and sliced thin (4 cups)
1 teaspoon garam masala or curry powder
2–2½ pounds butternut squash or calabaza, peeled, cut in ¾-inch dice
6 cups meat broth or stock
Salt to taste
1¼ pounds small, tender kale; cleaned, stripped (see Preparation), cut in fine slivers
Grated Gruyère, Emmenthaler, or Parmesan cheese

1. Combine beans in a pot with water to cover by a few inches; boil for 2 minutes. Cover; let stand for 1 hour off heat.

2. Drain, then cover with fresh water; add bay leaf and marjoram. Cover and simmer until barely tender. (Timing varies considerably, from 15 minutes to about an hour, depending on which bean you've chosen and its state of dehydration, so test often.) Drain; reserve cooking liquid.

3. Melt lard in a large casserole; stir in leeks and cook 4–5 minutes, until softened. Add garam masala or curry and stir for a moment; add squash and broth and bring to a boil. Add beans and simmer gently, partly covered, until squash is tender—about 15 minutes. Add salt.

4. Add kale and enough reserved liquid to almost cover it. Simmer until kale is tender, pressing it gently into the soup as it wilts.

5. Serve at once, or, for maximum flavor, cool, cover, and chill the soup. Reheat and sprinkle with the cheese to serve.

&. *ADDITIONAL RECIPES*
Braised Collards with Ginger and Chili-Pepper (page 150)
Spicy Collards (page 152)

KALE TURNOVERS

Call these *pirogi*, *calzone*, *empanadas*, or simply *little pies*, depending on your background. Plump half-moons of whole-wheat dough packed with kale, smoked ham, rice, and cheese can be made large or small to suit. For a picnic, make the large size; to serve as an appetizer, or along with a soup course, make the smaller ones.

Makes 12 large turnovers or 24 small ones

DOUGH

1 cup milk

3 tablespoons butter

1½ teaspoons salt

1 package dry yeast

¼ cup warm water

1 teaspoon sugar

2 eggs, beaten

1 cup whole-wheat flour

About 2½ cups all-purpose flour

FILLING

1 pound small, tender kale, washed; no
    need to remove stems if tiny

3 tablespoons butter

1 teaspoon chopped garlic

2 cups cooked brown rice (preferably
    rather firm, medium-grain)

¼ pound prosciutto (or firm country
    ham), cut in thick slices, then diced
    (⅔) cup)

6 ounces mozzarella (plain or smoked) or
    Monterey Jack, diced

Pepper

GLAZE

1 egg

1 tablespoon water

1 teaspoon sugar

1 teaspoon caraway

1. Scald milk; combine in a large bowl with butter and salt. Let cool. Meanwhile, stir together yeast, warm water, and sugar; let stand until fluffy—about 5–10 minutes. If the mixture doesn't puff up, begin again with fresh ingredients.

2. Add the eggs, then the yeast mixture, to the milk. Stir in whole-wheat flour, then just enough white flour to make a soft mush. Spread remaining flour on board; scrape dough onto it. Knead well, adding flour as needed to make a smooth, soft dough.

3. Set in a buttered bowl and turn to coat all sides. Cover and let rise until at least doubled—about 1½–2 hours.

4. Meanwhile, boil kale in a large pot of salted water until barely tender—about 5 minutes. Drain; chill in ice water. Drain again, press out liquid, then chop fine (equals 2 cups).

5. Heat butter and garlic; stir for a minute. Add kale and cook over low heat 5 minutes. Cool completely. Add rice, prosciutto, cheese, and pepper to taste.

6. Quarter dough. Cut each part in 3 (or 6 if you're making small pies) and roll into balls. Cover all with a sheet of plastic wrap. Roll out a ball on a floured surface to form a circle about 6 inches in diameter (or about 3½ inches for small pies).

7. Take a heaping ¼ cup of the filling (or 1 tablespoon for small pies) and spread evenly on half the circle, leaving a margin. Paint edge of the circle with water; fold dough to make neat half moon. Press firmly with fingertip to close, then seal tightly with tines of fork. Brush off excess flour, then set on parchment-covered, nonstick, or lightly greased baking sheet.

8. Repeat step 7 until half the turnovers have been filled; then blend together egg, water, and sugar. Brush a thin layer on each pie. Sprinkle half the caraway over all. Bake in center of preheated 350-degree oven until well browned—about 35 minutes for large pies, about 15 minutes for small ones. Cool on a rack.

9. While the first batch bakes, make up the rest. Bake and cool.

Note: You can freeze these pies once they have cooled completely, if you wrap them tightly. To serve, allow to defrost in the wrapper, then remove and set on a baking sheet and heat through in a 350-degree oven.

KALE WITH POTATOES, ANCHOVIES, AND HOT PEPPER

Sturdy and flavorful, this is for lovers of simple, straightforward food. Although I would be satisfied with this dish and a tomato or pepper salad, the strong, earthy kale will complement a roast leg of lamb, pork, or smoked ham.

4 servings as a side dish

About 4 tablespoons olive oil
1 tablespoon minced garlic (2 large cloves)
1½ pounds small red potatoes, scrubbed, halved, then sliced ¼ inch thick
1½ pounds kale, stripped and washed (see Preparation), cut in ½-inch strips
½ cup water
½ teaspoon crumbled, dried hot chili-peppers or crushed hot pepper
6 anchovy fillets, drained and cut into ½-inch pieces
Lemon juice
Black pepper

1. Heat 2 tablespoons oil in a flameproof casserole; add garlic and stir over low heat until lightly colored. Add potatoes; toss. Add kale, water, and chilies.

2. Cover and cook over medium-low heat until potatoes are just barely tender, about 30 minutes, stirring now and then.

3. Add anchovies and lemon juice to taste. Toss with olive oil to taste. Serve, sprinkled with black pepper.

KALE, FLOWERING
(*Brassica oleracea* subspecies *acephala*)
also called Flowering Cole, Flowering Cabbage, Ornamental Kale, Salad Savoy

*T*his is a real show stopper. Walk into a market and try *not* to see if it's there. Rosettes of loose, ruffly-edged leaves of cream, violet, or spruce, each veined and etched with designs of one or all of the other colors, branch out (kale-fashion) from a central stalk. Like an old-fashioned wedding bouquet edged in lace, flowering kale is

the chic caterer's dream, its subtle hues and fluffy forms ideal for filling out table displays and formal cornucopias, holding container of dips, or standing in for fruit bowls.

You've seen this plant, usually called ornamental cabbage, in flower shops and malls. When I called the company that distributes the vegetable to ask how the ornamental and edible varieties differed, they responded that it was a "secret breeding process." I toted one from a greengrocer's to the florist and compared. There was no visible difference, although I have not dared cook the potted character for fear of sprays and the like.

And, if you ask me, the ornamental role is the one suited to flowering kale—unless you find the infant leaves, which add color and character to mixed salads. I have tried it raw, steamed, boiled, sautéed, braised, and salt-tenderized (in an attempt to preserve the color, which does not keep through cooking any more than red cabbage, although advertising states otherwise). Although it is not *bad* (just slightly leathery and nondescript), other members of the cabbage family cook far more successfully and cost considerably less (I paid 89 cents to $1.98 per pound). And "real" kale, its closest relative, is wonderful.

But, if taste is not your main consideration, serve flowering kale raw with a vinaigrette or cooked with vinegar to preserve the color.

NUTRITIONAL HIGHLIGHTS: One cup contains a spare 50 calories. Flowering kale, like "real" kale, is an excellent source of vitamin A, vitamin C, calcium, potassium, and iron. It is relatively high in sodium, with 140 milligrams per cup.

KIWIFRUIT, KIWI FRUIT, KIWI
(*Actinidia deliciosa*, formerly *actinidia chinensis*)
also Chinese Gooseberry

*U*nless you've been cruising about in a submarine for the last several years without surfacing, you will undoubtedly have met up with the kiwifruit, which has exploded in popularity during the last decade. The *enfant terrible* of the nouvelle cuisine, it burst onto the fashionable scene, and has gradually settled down to a more matronly existence as a household and supermarket staple.

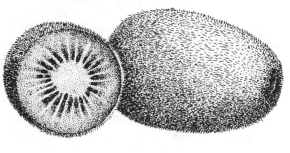

Many cooks, put off by its overuse and abuse in inappropriate restaurant guises, may not have fully explored it, however. This is a shame, for it can be a truly wonderful fruit, despite its odd exterior, ridiculous name, and some unfortunate press about being an "out" fruit in savvy culinary circles. The size and shape of a large egg, but more cylindrical, the unassuming kiwi looks and tastes like no other fruit. The tart-sweet flesh has a flavor utterly its own, but contains elements of citrus, strawberry, and melon. The soft cream-colored core, surrounded by a halo of poppyseed-like edible seeds, radiates as a sunburst into chartreuse to emerald pulp that is juicy and fine-textured. The very thin brown skin that holds together this plump package is covered with a light, bristly fuzz—hence the monicker that relates it to the hairy flightless bird from New Zealand, the fruit's main area of cultivation.

Curiously, although the fruit has been known in China (as *yang tao*) since ancient times, I can find only a single reference to it in Chinese cookbooks—and that a recipe from a contemporary restaurant. The Chinese gooseberry (no relation whatsoever to the gooseberry) is a climbing vine or shrub that is cultivated on trellises. It was introduced to New Zealand in 1906, then underwent considerable horticultural investigation. Hayward Wright, a nurseryman of great influence who has perfected strains of numerous exotic fruits, developed the Hayward variety: a firm, large, predictably delicious fruit that now accounts for almost 100 percent of the market. By 1953 the kiwi was being exported in small quantities (2,500 trays), still as the Chinese gooseberry. But, because Americans were afflicted with a virulent Communist phobia at the time, and were certainly not about to buy anything with a Chinese handle, the kiwifruit was born.

The unique fruit made speedy inroads, thanks to plenty of promotion and good distribution. By 1984, more than thirteen million trays were being shipped out of New Zealand, and by 1988, the United States was growing more than it imported, making the fruit a year-round, near-mainstream crop. Besides being simply delicious, kiwi is a fruit handler's dream. Thanks to its own furry protection and the fact that it is picked hard, it does not bruise or break as easily as most thin-skinned fruit. And kiwi has the ability to stay in a magical state of suspended animation for many months after it has been picked. If cooled directly upon harvesting, it will remain firm and on the verge of perfection until placed in a warmer area and exposed to ethylene gas, at which point it obediently begins to soften to peak form, reached within a week.

Kiwifruit had been grown in California on not much more than a backyard level since 1935, but by the sixties farmers there had picked up the torch and run—and have been running with it ever since. Thus, we have fruit year round, as the growing seasons in New Zealand and the United States are complementary. The fruit is also cultivated to some extent in Spain, Italy, Greece, Israel, South Africa, India, China, Bangladesh, Russia, Vietnam, and France (where one of its more fetching names is *souris végétale*—vegetable mouse).

SELECTION AND STORAGE: Buy kiwifruit all year, with the California product available from October through May, the New Zealand from June to October. Without wishing to be unpatriotic, I must admit that the imported fruit has tended to have a fresher acid-sugar balance, brighter color, smaller core section, and juicier flesh.

Choose *firm* fruit. Kiwis that are as soft as peaches or plums can be mushy or mealy, lacking flavor. It is difficult to find a poor fruit if you observe this simple rule. Ripe fruit will have the feel of a not-quite-tender nectarine. Fruit that is small, unevenly shaped, or formed into a cluster or fan (like some giant strawberries) is just as delicious as perfectly symmetrical large fruit—and cheaper.

To ripen kiwis, set in a fruit bowl for a few days, or enclose in a paper bag with a banana to speed up the process. Enjoy the fruit, chilled, when it has softened slightly. Refrigerate, once ripened, as long as the fruit keeps its plump tautness.

USE: Peeled kiwi, cut in slices, half circles, or quarter circles (wedges) is the best edible garnish since orange. It is bright and acid, and it won't discolor, no matter how far ahead you prepare it.

Halve chilled kiwis crosswise, dip in with a grapefruit spoon (my preference, but not at all necessary), and spoon out your morning ambrosia and vitamin C. Have two.

Place slices of kiwi on canapés, with cream cheese or ham. Add to raw and fresh fruit compotes and salads. Combine with vegetables such as avocado, radicchio, endive—as you would oranges. Toss with light seafoods, chicken, ham, or duck in a gingery dressing.

Like papaya, kiwi contains an enzyme that tenderizes meat. To exploit this and add flavor, purée the flesh, then spread on meat that has been pricked here and there with a knife tip; let rest 30 minutes before grilling. Or, more economically, apply the scooped-out, opened-up skins to the surface of the meat. The same enzyme, by the way, prevents gelatine from setting (as does raw pineapple), so poach the fruit lightly if you want to include it in a mold (knowing it will lose a little color and flavor).

Purée kiwi only until liquefied; long processing crushes the slightly bitter seeds. Sweeten with maple syrup, honey, delicate liqueurs, or sugar syrup; add a dash of orange, lemon, or lime. Pour alongside sliced fresh or poached fruit. Or serve with angel-food or sponge cake, then decorate with raspberries or strawberries.

Make brisk and delicious ices and sorbets. Arrange the beautiful slices on fresh fruit tarts, cheesecakes, and tortes; finish with a clear glaze.

PREPARATION: Although the skin is edible, and many people do eat it after rubbing off some of the fuzz, I find it unpleasant. The simplest way to peel the kiwi is to slice off both tips, then simply zip off the skin with a vegetable peeler. Cut with a stainless-steel knife.

NUTRITIONAL HIGHLIGHTS: Kiwifruit is an excellent source of vitamin C and a good source of potassium. It is low in sodium and calories—at about 55 per fruit.

SALAD OF KIWI, ORANGE, GRAPEFRUIT, AND WATERCRESS

Colorful, and pleasantly bittersweet, this salad works particularly well with roasted pork or smoked meats. For a deliciously garish change, substitute thin ribbons of radicchio rosso for watercress.

4 servings

1 large navel orange, peel and pith removed

1 large pink or red grapefruit, peel and pith removed

2 tablespoons lemon juice

1 tablespoon rice vinegar

¼ teaspoon salt

Big pinch cayenne pepper, or to taste

2 teaspoons fragrant honey

3 tablespoons corn oil

3 large kiwifruit, peeled (see Preparation)

1 bunch watercress, trimmed, rinsed, dried

1. Halve orange lengthwise, then cut across into very thin half-rounds. Do the same with the grapefruit. Place both in a dish.

2. Combine lemon juice, vinegar, salt, cayenne, and honey; mix to blend. Add oil. Drain juice from cut fruits into this.

3. Arrange watercress around a serving dish. Arrange grapefruit and orange, overlapping, within this. Cut kiwifruit in thin rounds and arrange in center of salad. Cover and chill until serving time.

4. To serve, pour dressing over all.

BARBARA SPIEGEL'S KIWI-FISH KEBABS

From her summer spot on Cape Cod, where she must feed more people in a summer than I do in ten years, Barbara Spiegel writes: "Tuna and kiwi are an unlikely couple, but the marriage is a happy one. A covered charcoal grill is ideal for this recipe. Cook the kebabs on a well-oiled grill over coals that have a good coating of white ash—the stage reached about 45 minutes after fire is started." Do not be surprised that the kiwi fades to a washed-out vegetably color.

2 or 3 servings

1-inch chunk ginger, approximately
1 medium garlic clove, minced
3 tablespoons fresh lime juice
1 tablespoon minced medium hot chili-
    pepper (Anaheim or New Mexico)
¼ teaspoon coarse kosher salt
Pepper to taste
¼ cup olive oil
1 pound fresh tuna or swordfish steak,
    cut 1 inch thick
3 firm-ripe kiwis, peeled (see
    Preparation)

1. Grate ginger; press in sieve to extract 1½ teaspoons juice. Combine with garlic, lime juice, chili, salt, and pepper in dish that will hold fish; stir, then blend in oil.

2. Cut fish in 1-inch cubes. Mix with marinade. Cover and refrigerate about 2 hours.

3. Quarter kiwis lengthwise (do not cut smaller). Brush with marinade. Thread fish and kiwis on skewers, beginning and ending with fish; use 4 kiwi wedges on each.

4. Broil 5–6 minutes, turning once halfway through cooking.

LAYERED FRESH KIWIS, ORANGES, AND POMEGRANATE

Although this is too easy to be called a recipe, strictly speaking, I find it helpful to suggest amounts, even when there is no "real" preparation involved. Glittering, refreshing sliced fruits brighten breakfast or brunch, or provide a clarifying final note to a rich dinner. If you are not in pomegranate season, substitute strawberries cut in narrow strips or a combination of red currants and strawberries.

4–6 servings

3 large navel oranges, all rind and pith
    removed
1–2 tablespoons sugar
About ½ teaspoon orange-flower water
3 large kiwis, peeled (see Preparation)
1 large pomegranate

1. Halve oranges lengthwise; cut across into very thin half-rounds. Arrange in a 1-quart glass bowl, preferably a straight-sided soufflé dish. Sprinkle with half the sugar and half the orange-flower water.

2. Halve kiwis lengthwise, then cut across into thin semicircles; arrange over the oranges. Sprinkle with remaining sugar and orange-flower water. Tip the dish and baste fruit with accumulated juices. Chill.

3. Cut out blossom end of pomegranate, removing with it some of the white pith and taking care not to pierce the red kernels within. Lightly score skin in quarters, then gently break fruit in half, then in half again, following the score lines. Bend back rind and pull out seeds. Sprinkle over chilled fruit.

CHICKEN, KIWI, AND RED ONION SAUTÉ

Kiwi's lemony edge and clarity add freshness to savory dishes. This combination of sweet, long-cooked onions, salty ham bits, and tender chicken gets its tart finish from the light fruit.

2 or 3 servings

2 tablespoons light olive oil
2 cups thinly sliced red onions (2 medium onions)
½ teaspoon coarse kosher salt
Pepper to taste
2 medium chicken breasts, boned and skinned, well trimmed (about 1 pound)
1–2 tablespoons corn oil
2 kiwis, peeled (see Preparation)
¼ pound firm ham (2 thick slices), cut in ½-inch squares
¼ cup chicken stock
¼ cup dry white wine
2 teaspoons chopped fresh thyme or 1 teaspoon dried thyme

1. Heat olive oil in heavy, wide skillet over high heat. Add onions; cook on high heat for 5 minutes, stirring occasionally. Season with ¼ teaspoon salt and pepper. Turn heat to medium-low; cover and cook until onions are slightly caramelized, about 15–20 minutes. With slotted spoon transfer to plate.

2. Cut chicken in quarters lengthwise, then across in strips ½ inch wide. Add corn oil to pan as needed and heat. Over moderate heat cook chicken 4–5 minutes, turning once halfway through. Quarter kiwis lengthwise; cut crosswise slices ⅛ inch thick. Sprinkle cooked chicken with remaining salt and pepper. Transfer to plate with onion.

3. Scatter ham in pan and cook, stirring, for 1–2 minutes. Add kiwis and sauté gently for barely 2 minutes. With slotted spoon transfer to plate. Add stock, wine, and half of the thyme. Boil, stirring, to reduce to ¼ cup. Add onion, chicken, ham, and kiwis. Mix into sauce to barely warm through. Sprinkle with remaining thyme and serve at once.

KIWI SORBET

Frosty, tart, and refreshing, this simple ice suggests the flavors of citrus and strawberry, as well as kiwi. Wonderful after a light summer lunch or to wind up a complex cool-season dinner.

Makes 1¼–1½ quarts

⅔ cup sugar
1½ cups water
5–7 kiwis (2 cups purée)
¼ cup fresh lime juice
1 cup fresh orange juice
Optional: 1–2 drops green food coloring

1. Combine sugar and water and bring to a boil, stirring. Simmer for 5 minutes, then cool and chill.

2. Halve 5 kiwis and scoop flesh into container of a food processor (a melon-ball cutter works well). Add the lime juice and purée the mixture (do not overprocess); you should have 2 cups. Add kiwis, as necessary, to equal this amount. Scrape into a bowl; chill.

3. Combine chilled syrup, kiwi purée, orange juice, and optional food coloring in the can of an ice-cream maker. Freeze according to the manufacturer's directions.

4. Pack into a container and ripen in the freezer for about a day. Allow to soften briefly in the refrigerator before serving.

KIWI BUTTERMILK CUSTARD

Five minutes' assembly time produces a delicate, low-calorie dessert somewhere between Chinese almond float and old-fashioned blancmange. The white molded custard/pudding is lifted from the ordinary by an astringent purée of kiwi and a vivid garnish of ruby pomegranate seeds.

2 servings

1 rounded teaspoon gelatine
3 tablespoons water
4 teaspoons sugar
1 cup buttermilk
¼ teaspoon almond extract
½ teaspoon vanilla extract
1 large kiwi
About 2 teaspoons fragrant honey
Pomegranate seeds, in season (or sliced
    strawberries or raspberries)

1. Sprinkle gelatine over water in tiny saucepan; let stand until soft, about 3 minutes. Stir over low heat to dissolve granules completely. Stir in sugar (and pinch of salt, if you have unsalted buttermilk).

2. Off heat add buttermilk and extracts. Pour into two rinsed-out custard cups of ¾-cup capacity. Refrigerate, loosely covered, until set—about 2 hours or more.

3. To serve, halve kiwi and scoop

flesh into processor or blender (a melon-ball cutter is handy). Add 2 teaspoons honey and purée until smooth; do not overprocess. Taste and add honey as needed. Run a knife gently around edge of custard and invert on serving dish. Spoon sauce around custard; sprinkle pomegranate over. Serve at once.

—

KIWI FOOL

When I first encountered the frivolously dubbed English fool, it was made of the most traditional of fool-ish fruits, gooseberries (see Gooseberry Fool, page 218). At the time, however, no gooseberries were to be found in New York, where I live. The kiwi, similarly tart and green, made a delicious substitute that has become a worthwhile dessert in its own right.

6 servings

12 medium kiwis
About ⅓ cup sugar
2 tablespoons water
4 teaspoons cornstarch
1 cup Reduced Cream (recipe follows) or crème fraîche
Garnish: Tiny strawberry, kiwi, or orange wedges

1. Halve kiwis; scoop pulp into a bowl (a melon-ball cutter is handy). With whisk or masher form a coarse purée.

2. Combine 1 cup purée in small non-aluminum pan with ⅓ cup sugar. Stir together water and cornstarch and add to pan. Bring to a simmer, stirring. Simmer 2 minutes, until thick and clear. Taste for additional sugar, oversweetening slightly. Scrape into a bowl; let cool.

3. When purée has cooled somewhat, stir in remaining kiwi. Blend well, cover, and chill thoroughly.

4. Whip Reduced Cream to form soft peaks. Partly fold together with chilled purée, so there are distinct bands of color and white; do not blend. Garnish and serve; or chill several hours, if you prefer.

Reduced Cream

Makes 1½ cups, approximately

Simmer 2 cups heavy cream in heavy saucepan, stirring often, until reduced to 1½ cups, or slightly more. Pour into a bowl; set in a bowl of ice and water and cool, stirring often. Cover and chill. Whisk before using. Lasts for at least 1 week, refrigerated and covered.

🍃 *ADDITIONAL RECIPES*
Kiwi, Banana, Orange, and Cactus Pear Fruit Cup (page 67)
Lychees, Berries, and Kiwis with Honey and Lime (page 285)
Pineapple and Kiwi with Mango Purée (page 300)
Salad of Pomegranates, Persimmons, and Kiwis (page 372)
White Sapote, Kiwi, and Strawberry Salad (page 414)

KNOB CELERY
See Celeriac

KOHLRABI
(*Brassica oleracea* subspecies *gongylodes*)

*K*ohlrabi is certainly not new on the scene, but to see shoppers in a produce section poke at it in wonder (particularly the violet variety), you'd think it had just landed on earth. Although the exact origins of early *Brassica* species are lost in historical root cellars, kohlrabi as well as a dozen other oleraceae—such as broccoli, kale,

Brussels sprouts, cauliflower, cabbage—are no evolutionary adolescents. Maybe cooks have stayed shy of it because of encouragement from a very dangerous crew: food writers.

Mrs. Beeton, in her *Book of Household Management*, offers no recipes for the vegetable, but this description: "This variety presents a singular development, inasmuch as the stem swells out like a large turnip on the surface of the ground, the leaves shooting from it all round. . . . Although not generally grown as a garden vegetable, if used when young and tender, it is wholesome, nutritious, and very palatable." Damning with faint praise, if you ask me. The opening paragraph on the subject in *Jane Grigson's Vegetable Book* (a valuable and delicious work) begins: "There are better vegetables than kohlrabi. And worse."

In *The New James Beard* the usually generous gentleman wrote: "Kohlrabi. A small pale-green, slightly knobby, turnip-shaped vegetable. Sometimes called cabbage turnip but with the virtues of neither. Not one of my favorites." And Bert Greene, who loves *everything*, headed his childhood list of enemy vegetables with kohlrabi (but has since converted, passionately, as you can see by the recipe that follows).

It is the enlarged stem of the kohlrabi (from which spring collard-like leaves) that gives the "turnip" name to the crispy green vegetable; but it does not taste like a turnip, nor is it a root. It is sweeter, juicier, crisper, and more delicate than any turnip. Nor does it taste cabbage-like, although the cooked leaves do have a kale-collard flavor.

The vegetable, which needs no sales pitch in Hungary, Germany, Russia, northern France, Italy, Austria, Israel, and China (and in American communities made up of people who originated in those places), tastes to me like the freshest, crunchiest broccoli stems, touched with a hint of radish and cucumber—and is certainly worth a try or two.

SELECTION AND STORAGE: Kohlrabi is erratically available all year, with an abundance during early summer. It can be found in supermarkets and produce shops. Choose small or medium-sized kohlrabi with the smallest, smoothest bulb-stems you can find, free of cracks or visible fibers. Leaves, if they have not been cut off by thoughtless distributors or shopkeepers, should be firm and green, with no yellowing. Although the larger kohlrabi (about the size of tennis balls) are useful for some dishes, particularly stuffed preparations, they are less sweet and tender than small ones.

Wrap and refrigerate kohlrabi, separating leaves from stems. The leaves will last only a few days; the rounded stems up to a week.

USE: A kohlrabi bulb is light, refreshing, and versatile in its raw state. Use it peeled and sliced with crudités or cut in dice or julienne for vegetable or meat salads. Grate or shred kohlrabi to add to slaws or toss with remoulade sauce. If you blanch the kohlrabi, refresh, and chill, the flavor and texture are better developed and the vegetable will not become watery when dressed. Bathe slices in warm or cold dressings—sweet or sour, herbal or spicy-hot, creamy or not.

While most traditional kohlrabi dishes are quite elaborate—stuffed, creamed, and crumbed—I find the sweet delicacy is most rewarding when it stands almost alone, or is sparingly seasoned and sauced. At its simple best, kohlrabi is peeled and steamed (my preference) or boiled until crisp-tender. Although it is often written that kohlrabi's flavor is best retained by cooking with the skin, I find it more of a nuisance to clean and less tasty when treated this way. Either operation will take about 15 minutes if bulbs are whole. Coat the steamed vegetable with a light lemon-egg sauce (avgolemono) or cream or cheese sauce, or toss with lemon and butter. Slice raw kohlrabi or cut in strips and sauté or stir-fry, seasoning lightly with such aromatics as marjoram, basil, chives, nutmeg, shallot, ginger.

Cook both leaves and bulb in soups. Add whole peeled kohlrabi to braised dishes and stews and cook about 20 minutes; halfway through the cooking time, add the trimmed leaves. If you want to cook the leaves alone, trim, then boil until tender—about 2–3 minutes. Drain, then set aside until ready to serve. Chop or slice, if desired, then sauté in oil or butter.

Kohlrabi can be peeled, parboiled, hollowed, and stuffed, then braised; the braising liquid is then thickened and served as a sauce with the stuffed vegetable. This is particularly useful with larger bulbs.

PREPARATION: Cut the stem-leaf parts from the stem-bulb section. Wash the leaves in a sink filled with warm water. Strip the stems by folding together the two sides of each leaf and pulling off each stem with the other hand (discard stems). The bulbous part must be pared and trimmed thoroughly to remove all traces of the fibrous underlayer just beneath the skin. (Try not to be disappointed when the stunning lavender to violet kohlrabi turns khaki when cooked, or loses its skin-deep regal hue when peeled.)

NUTRITIONAL HIGHLIGHTS: Kohlrabi is an excellent source of vitamin C and potassium. It is high in fiber and very low in calories, with about 40 per cup (raw).

SAUTÉED SHREDDED KOHLRABI

This is one of those obvious, delicious everyday dishes that you may have missed. The basic treatment of this sweetly crisp vegetable is now standard in my house, with variations that include shallots or onions, caraway or fennel seed and a soupçon of mustard, a snippet of jalapeño, or a sprinkling of freshly snipped dill or marjoram.

For each person allow 2 medium kohlrabi bulbs (weighed with leaves, about ½ pound). Peel the bulbs, then halve. Shred coarse (a processor blade is ideal). Sauté for a few minutes in olive oil or butter in a wide skillet, until tender to taste. Season with salt and pepper and serve. (Note: If you want to add the leaves, sliver them, boil until tender, then add to the sauté at the end.)

KOHLRABI LEAVES

When kohlrabi leaves are cooked alone, as a side dish, you'll need about 6 ounces of them per serving (about 1 small bunch). Blanched and sautéed, the leaves have a smooth, fleshy texture and deep-green spinach color; the flavor is much like Swiss chard or spinach with a dose of kale.

Drop the trimmed leaves into a large pot of salted, boiling water. When water returns to a full boil, stir, then boil until barely tender, 2–3 minutes. Drain well, pressing the leaves. You can leave the soft, thickish leaves whole, or slice or chop to suit. The kohlrabi can be left for hours, at room temperature or refrigerated until needed.

To reheat, warm butter, bacon fat, goose fat, or olive oil in a skillet and sauté the leaves until hot through. Season with salt and pepper, or pepper vinegar. You might add garlic, shallots, or onions before tossing the leaves; or combine the cooked vegetable with sautéed mushrooms for a lovely earthy flavor. Or garnish with anchovies or olives or lemon or all of them.

KOHLRABI CHIPS WITH TWO DIPS

Although you might include kohlrabi slices in just about any hors d'oeuvre platter or crudité presentation, the crisp-sweet bulb is particularly suited to the two distinctive (and easy to prepare) dips offered here—which also go nicely with each other.

4 servings

ANCHOVY DIP

1 jalapeño, preferably red; roasted, peeled, seeds removed (see page 125, to peel chili-peppers), minced

1 tablespoon finely chopped anchovies packed in olive oil (3 fillets)

½ teaspoon minced garlic

2 teaspoons red wine vinegar

About ¼ cup full-flavored olive oil

2 tablespoons finely minced parsley

TOMATO-CHEESE DIP

3 ounces fresh, soft, light goat cheese or Italian cream cheese

1½–2 tablespoons finely chopped sun-dried tomatoes packed in oil

1½–2 tablespoons minced fresh basil (or substitute a small amount of fresh marjoram or thyme to taste)

About 3 tablespoons heavy (or whipping) cream

4 medium kohlrabi bulbs (leaves reserved for another use), chilled

1. Combine jalapeño in a bowl with anchovies, garlic, and vinegar; crush with the back of a spoon to make a coarse purée. Gradually add oil, to taste. Add parsley. Cover and let mellow at least an hour before serving.

2. Combine cheese and 1½ tablespoons each chopped tomatoes and basil in a bowl; blend. Gradually stir in enough cream to make a fairly soft, scoopable texture. Add more tomatoes and basil, to taste. Cover and chill for at least an hour before serving.

3. Peel kohlrabi thoroughly. Halve lengthwise, then cut each half across into fairly thin slices. Arrange slices in a bowl and serve with the dips.

SALAD OF KOHLRABI AND GRILLED RED PEPPER

Crispy kohlrabi slices—like a cross between fresh water chestnuts and broccoli stems—combine prettily and tastily with smoky-soft red pepper bits and dill.
4 servings

1 thick-skinned, smooth-sided medium red bell pepper
4 medium-small kohlrabi (about 1½ pounds weighed with leaves)
2 tablespoons lemon juice
Salt to taste
3 tablespoons light olive oil
About 2 tablespoons minced fresh dill
Pepper

1. Grill pepper directly in a gas flame until blackened all over. (Alternatively, you can broil it as close as possible to heating element of a broiler.) Wrap in damp toweling and let stand 5–10 minutes. Scrape off all skin. Remove ribs and seeds; cut flesh in ¼-inch dice.

2. Cut off kohlrabi leaves and reserve for another dish. Peel bulbs and cut in ¹⁄₁₆-inch slices, then into julienne strips the same width. Combine in a serving dish with pepper dice.

3. Blend together lemon juice and salt; add oil and mix. Toss with the kohlrabi, red pepper, dill, and pepper to taste.

KOHLRABI WITH AVGOLEMONO SAUCE

A lightened version of the silky Greek lemon and egg sauce coats crisp kohlrabi for a side dish or separate vegetable course.
4 servings

8 small kohlrabi, tops removed and reserved for another dish
2 cups chicken broth
Big pinch ground fennel
Pinch finely crumbled thyme
1½ teaspoons arrowroot
1 egg
1 egg yolk
About 2 tablespoons lemon juice
White pepper and salt
Few fine snippets of chives

1. Trim and peel kohlrabi; quarter. Combine broth, fennel, and thyme in a saucepan; bring to a boil. Add kohlrabi, lower heat, and simmer, partly covered, until tender, about 15 minutes.

2. Drain and reserve broth. Arrange kohlrabi in serving dish and set in warm oven.

3. In a small heavy saucepan, blend together arrowroot with a tablespoon of broth. Add egg and yolk and beat to blend. Add 2 tablespoons lemon juice and 1¼ cups broth. Cook over low heat, stirring constantly, until thickened. Do not allow to simmer; arrowroot thickens before bubbling. Adjust flavor with additional lemon juice, white pepper, salt. Add broth, if you prefer a thinner sauce. Pour over vegetable. Sprinkle with chives and serve.

KOHLRABI WITH ANCHOVY AND OLIVE DRESSING

At the Ballroom Restaurant in New York City, Felipe Rojas-Lombardi serves an assortment of *tapas*, the irresistible Spanish nibbles. Included in the selection are these crisp slices of kohlrabi, lightly dressed with a piquant sauce of salty olives and anchovies, fresh herbs, and minced serrano pepper.

6 servings

12 very small kohlrabi (about 2 inches in diameter), tops trimmed
¼ cup full-flavored olive oil, preferably Spanish
1 large garlic clove, crushed or minced
1 serrano chili-pepper, seeded and minced (or use ½ jalapeño)
1 teaspoon chopped fresh thyme, lemon thyme, marjoram, or oregano
¼ cup red wine vinegar
8 anchovies packed in olive oil
12 black olives, preferably Calamata, pitted and chopped coarse
1 tablespoon minced parsley
Coarse kosher salt to taste

1. Pare kohlrabi, removing all heavy fibers. Drop into boiling salted water; boil 3 minutes. Drain, then cool in ice water. Drain.

2. Heat olive oil, garlic, and a pinch each serrano and thyme in small nonaluminum pan. Add vinegar and simmer to reduce slightly. Let cool somewhat.

3. Chop 2 anchovies and 4 olives and add to warm dressing with remaining thyme, parsley, and salt to taste. Let stand at least 30 minutes, or as long as you like.

4. Dry kohlrabi; slice thin. Divide slices evenly among 6 serving plates. Spoon dressing evenly over all. Coarsely chop remaining olives and sprinkle over. Place an anchovy on each serving.

—

BERT GREENE'S HUNGARIAN KOHLRABI SOUP

Food writer and *copain* Bert Greene is an incomparable storyteller and creator of delicious recipes that *work*. You can verify the first by reading *Greene on Greens* (Workman Publishing, 1984). For the second you can cook from the same, or try out the following generous soup-stew, a sample from that wonderful work.

6 servings

2 strips bacon, chopped
2½ tablespoons unsalted butter
1 large onion, halved, sliced
1 clove garlic, chopped
2 large ribs celery, chopped
1 large carrot, chopped
1 tablespoon chopped fresh parsley
3½ cups chicken broth
3½-pound chicken, cut in serving pieces
1 cup water
1 pound kohlrabi with leaves
1 tablespoon flour
1½ tablespoons lemon juice
Salt and pepper

1. Sauté bacon in medium saucepan over moderate heat until crisp. Add 1 tablespoon butter and onion; cook 1 minute. Add garlic, celery, carrot, and parsley. Cook, covered, 5 minutes. Add 1 cup broth and cook, covered, until vegetables are tender, about 10 minutes.

2. Transfer mixture to blender or processor. Blend until smooth. Strain into large saucepan. Heat to boiling. Add remaining broth, chicken, and water. Simmer, covered, skimming surface occasionally to remove fat, until chicken is very tender, about 30 minutes.

3. Meanwhile, trim, peel, and dice kohlrabi bulbs. Wash leaves and cook 1 minute in boiling water; then rinse, drain, and set aside.

4. Remove chicken from soup. Add diced kohlrabi; cook, uncovered, until tender, about 15 minutes.

5. Meanwhile, remove bones (and skin, if desired) from chicken and cut meat in chunks.

6. Melt remaining 1½ tablespoons butter in small saucepan. Stir in flour. Cook, stirring, for 2 minutes over low heat. Whisk in 1 cup soup; pour this mixture into the large saucepan. Cook until slightly thickened, about 10 minutes. Add chicken and kohlrabi leaves; cook 5 minutes. Add lemon juice and salt and pepper to taste.

KUMQUAT
(Fortunella)

*T*he name *kumquat* comes from the Cantonese for golden orange, a likely description of this brilliant fruit. Introduced into the United States about 1850, the kumquat has been cultivated ever since in small quantities in Florida and California. The two varieties that have been most successful are the oblong Nagami and the round Meiwa,

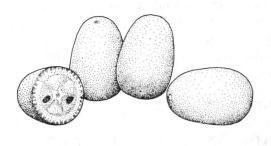

both about 1½ inches long, both of Japanese origin. Although similar, the Meiwa is usually sweeter and more tender.

The kumquat was considered a *Citrus* until 1915, when scientists found cellular differences sufficient to warrant moving it into its own genus, *Fortunella* (named after Robert Fortune, an English traveler who introduced the kumquat into Europe in 1846). I think a better reason to have moved its grouping might be that it is the only fruit with a rind that is deliously sweet and pulp that is puckery-sour!

SELECTION AND STORAGE: Kumquats can appear in the market as early as October and last as late as May, but for the most part, they offer their golden glow in the dead of winter. Whether loose, in baskets, or plastic-filmed, the fruits should be pressed to determine that they are firm, like baby mandarins, not soft-wet. Because of their thin skin, they spoil more rapidly than oranges.

If you'll be using kumquats within a few days they can remain at room temperature; otherwise, keep them refrigerated, for about two weeks. If you've found the pretty ones picked with attached leaves and twigs, do not plan to keep them as long, as the leaves dry quickly.

USE: Serve kumquats as you would grapes, as part of a formal fruit bowl (they look most decorative with their sharply neat, deep green leaves attached). Or offer them alone on a dish as a palate refresher. (I have read that in China it was once customary to set a small, well-fruited potted plant on the table so the fruit could be nibbled by diners between courses.) One simply consumes the entire kumquat in a mouthful. This powerful, orangelike flavor punch is a treat or not, depending on your tastesbuds. I think they're wonderful.

Thick rounds of the diminutive fruit make the perfect garnish for cocktails, both in size and flavor. Substitute kumquats in duck à l'orange and other orange-based dishes. A third-generation Florida citrus grower tells me that nothing beats a crown roast of pork, each exposed bone tip topped with a kumquat to flavor and beautify the meat.

For a sweet-sharp, colorful addition that will change your approach to salads, try this: Plump and tenderize the fruits by blanching in boiling water for 20 seconds, refresh in ice water, dry, then thin-slice. Meat, fish, fruit, and vegetable salads benefit from the inclusion of this special tidbit.

Blanch, slice, and seed kumquats to add to stuffings, cakes, and muffins. Or halve, seed, then purée the kumquats to use as both flavoring and thickening agent in sauces, dressings, cakes, creams, and frostings. Transform the glowing orange fruits into marmalade or poach them in a thick sugar syrup, both time-honored treatments for a bittersweet delicacy.

PREPARATION: Kumquats should be washed to remove fungicides, then dried. If they're to be left whole, that's the extent of preparation. For other presentations, most varieties will need to be seeded, one way or another. Depending upon what form the fruits will take in the dish being prepared, they can be sliced, or halved, or quartered lengthwise, then seeded, by simply plucking out the pits with a knife tip.

NUTRITIONAL HIGHLIGHTS: Kumquat is a fair source of vitamin C, and very low in sodium. It has a moderate amount of calories.

SALAD OF KUMQUATS, AVOCADO, AND BOSTON LETTUCE

Blanching kumquats softens the skin, swells the pulp to its juiciest, and modifies the peel's bittersweet boldness.

4 servings

1½ tablespoons golden raisins
1 tablespoon balsamic vinegar (see Note)
3 tablespoons light vegetable oil
1 tablespoon water
⅛ teaspoon salt, or to taste
12 kumquats (about ¼ pound, or ¾ cup)
1 medium head Boston lettuce, rinsed and dried
1 large avocado, preferably Hass variety, peeled and pitted

1. Combine raisins, vinegar, oil, water, and salt in a tiny nonaluminum saucepan; simmer 1 minute. Cover and let stand until serving time.

2. Drop kumquats into a pot of boiling water; return to a boil over highest heat, then boil 30 seconds. Drain at once and drop into a bowl of ice water. When cold, dry and refrigerate.

3. Arrange lettuce on 4 salad plates. Thin-slice avocado halves on a slant. Pick up a quarter of the slices on the knife blade, then set down on the lettuce and spread out in a fan shape. Slice kumquats paper thin; pick out seeds. Divide evenly over avocado and lettuce.

4. Heat dressing, stirring. Drizzle over salads. Serve at once.

Note: Or substitute sherry, malt, or cider vinegar, plus a pinch of sugar.

BROCCOLI AND KUMQUAT SALAD WITH OLIVES

Miniature orange rounds, forest-green broccoli, shiny black olive shards, and a garlicky-citrus dressing make this bright salad a lively complement to game, pork, lamb, turkey, or ham. Try it on kumquat doubters.

3 servings

1 bunch broccoli, about 1 pound
10 medium kumquats (about ¼ pound)
3 tablespoons full-flavored olive oil
¾ teaspoon minced garlic
2–3 tablespoons lemon juice
½ teaspoon sugar
¼ teaspoon salt, or to taste
Black pepper to taste
8–10 oil-cured black olives, pitted and quartered lengthwise

1. Peel broccoli stems. Cut stems and flowerets in large bite-sized pieces. Place on steaming rack over boiling water. Cook on high heat, covered, until not quite tender—about 4 minutes; broccoli continues to cook off heat, so take care. Lift out rack with broccoli and cool, then chill.

2. Return water to a boil; drop in kumquats. Return to a boil over highest heat; boil 15 seconds. Drain. Drop in cold water to cool. Quarter 4 kumquats; pick out seeds. Slice remainder thin.

3. Heat oil and garlic in small skillet over very low heat until garlic colors lightly—about 5 minutes. Combine in processor or blender with 2 tablespoons lemon juice, sugar, salt, pepper, and quartered kumquats. Purée to fairly rough consistency.

4. Toss dressing with sliced kumquats. Cover and chill. To serve, add olives; toss with broccoli. Add lemon juice, salt and pepper to taste.

BARBARA SPIEGEL'S CANDIED KUMQUAT TART

This rich, very sweet confection has been slightly adapted from a recipe prepared by Barbara Spiegel. Rounds of glistening kumquat (they look like baby apricot halves) top an almond-butter filling in a cooky crust. Serve thin slices with espresso or strong, black tea. Unlike most fruit pastries, this one can be kept for about a day, *uncovered*, at room temperature, before it begins to soften.

8 servings

PASTRY

1¼ cups flour

4 teaspoons sugar

¼ teaspoon salt

8 tablespoons chilled, unsalted butter,
    cut into tiny pieces

1 egg yolk

2 tablespoons orange juice

TOPPING

1 cup orange juice

½ cup fresh lemon juice

1¼ cups sugar

¾ pound (about 25) kumquats

FILLING

2 egg yolks plus 1 egg

½ cup sugar

6 tablespoons butter, softened

⅞ cup blanched almonds, finely ground

¼ teaspoon almond extract

1 tablespoon Armagnac, Cognac, or other
    brandy

1. Make pastry: Combine flour, sugar, and salt in processor; whirl to mix. Add chilled butter pieces and pulse machine on and off until pieces resemble oatmeal. Scrape into a bowl and squeeze any obvious butter bits to break up. Blend together egg yolk and juice. Sprinkle into flour mixture, tossing with fork to incorporate evenly. Mass together into a ball. If dough does not hold together, add a few drops of water. Form a thick disk, dust with flour, and refrigerate for an hour, or up to 2 days.

2. Roll pastry on lightly floured surface to form 13-inch circle. Set loosely in 9½-inch fluted tart ring with removable bottom. Trim dough to make a 1-inch overhang. Turn this inward and press against side to make an even wall. Freeze 15 minutes or more.

3. Line shell with foil, covering rim. Fill with dried beans or other weights. Place in center of preheated 375-degree oven for 15 minutes. Lift out foil and weights. Prick bottom and sides with skewer in several places. Bake 10 minutes longer. Set on rack.

4. Combine orange and lemon juices with sugar in a small, heavy nonaluminum saucepan. Bring to a boil; skim. Simmer gently to form a fairly thick syrup—about 20–25 minutes (do not caramelize).

5. Meanwhile, combine kumquats in a pot with water to cover; set over highest heat. As soon as water comes to a boil, drain. Refresh in ice water; drain again. Trim off a sliver from both ends of each kumquat, then cut fruit in 4–6 slices, removing seeds. Add to syrup; simmer very gently until shiny and transparent, 10–15 minutes. With slotted spoon remove to waxed paper; arrange in single layer. Reserve jellyish syrup.

6. Whirl egg and yolks in processor; with motor running add sugar. Process

until very pale and fluffy. Beat in butter; add almonds, extract, and Armagnac. Scrape into prepared shell.

7. Bake in oven center (still at 375 degrees) until evenly browned—20 minutes. Let cool completely on rack.

8. When tart has cooled entirely, choose prettiest kumquat slices (you'll have extras), turn them over, then arrange, side by side, touching, in concentric circles. Heat jellied syrup and spoon over enough to coat the surface thoroughly. (Save leftover for toast, or another tart.) When cooled, remove tart from pan and set on plate.

Note: Clementines can be substituted for kumquats in this tart. Blanch them twice. Before placing the slices on the tart, halve and quarter them, as suitable for the design. The tart will be difficult to cut if they are left whole.

BAKED FISH WITH KUMQUATS AND GINGER

Because shad is oily and flavorful, it takes kindly to strong, tart seasoning without losing its identity (other oily fish, such as mackerel and sablefish, would do well also). Preparation is minimal, presentation is attractive.

If you're cooking for company, assemble the dish ahead of time. Increase recipe for as many as you wish, keeping the fish in a single layer; cover, then refrigerate. Let stand at room temperature for ½–1 hour before baking and add a few minutes to the cooking time.

2 servings

1 tablespoon butter, softened
About ¾ pound shad fillet (not skinned)
Salt and pepper
6 medium kumquats (about 3 ounces)
1 small piece ginger, about 1½ inches, peeled
2 teaspoons small capers, drained
1 tablespoon lemon juice

1. Smear ½ tablespoon butter in a baking-serving dish to hold the fish closely in one layer. Cut fish across into 2 or 4 pieces and arrange in the dish. Salt and pepper very lightly.

2. Drop kumquats into boiling water. Return to a boil and boil for 30 seconds, timing carefully. Drain, rinse in cold water. Cut across into thin slices, removing seeds as you go.

3. With vegetable peeler, shave ginger into translucent slices. Place on shad (they should just about cover surface). Top with kumquats and capers; sprinkle with lemon juice; dot with remaining butter.

4. Bake in upper third of preheated 450-degree oven until opaque throughout —about 15 minutes.

LEMON GRASS
(Cymbopogon citratus)
also Takrai, Sereh

My vote for the next great seasoning power after ginger and cilantro is this remarkably potent, yet soft-spoken newcomer to American kitchens. Like the afore-mentioned two, lemon grass can be used raw or cooked, as background coloring or for brilliant foreground dazzle, and as an intensifier or disperser of flavors. And it is versatile enough to be a part of every phase of a meal, from soup through after-dinner tea.

Its membership in the grass family, Graminae, is immediately apparent when you see the long (about 2 feet) gray-green stalks, which are as stiff as beach grass. Inside the fibrous stem layers (the very long leaves are cut off before the lemon grass gets to market) is a paler tubular core that resembles a firm scallion bulb. This more tender part is slivered into dishes, adding its inimitable lemony pungency. The straw-like upper stalks can lend their flavor to liquids or be used for steaming, but are too harsh-textured to be eaten.

Lemon grass's airy, floral aroma—a combination of lemon and lime peel and fresh-cut hay—will be vaguely familiar to those who are familiar with the comparatively coarse sister of this elegant grass, *Cymbopogon nardus* or citronella, a component in many insect repellents. Both grasses, probably native to Malaysia, have long been cultivated for their aromatic oils, which are used in cosmetics and fragrances, and for their tenacious roots, which have proved extremely effective in preventing soil erosion. In Southeast Asia and Western Africa lemon grass is used to combat malaria, hence another of its names, fever grass. In Vietnam it is combined with rose hips and rose petals to make a restorative bath for women after childbirth. It is also cultivated in India, Australia (mainly to use in dishwashing liquids), throughout Central America (where it is used only as a tea, often with brandy), and in Florida and California.

It is in Asia that the full flavor range of lemon grass is explored in cooking. Elsewhere, it is generally dried and infused as a beverage. Although the tea brewed from the stalks is delicious, as is the dried seasoning, the taste that results is but a pale shadow of the fresh herb.

SELECTION AND STORAGE: You can find lemon grass year round in Oriental markets (particularly Thai, Vietnamese, Cambodian, Laotian) and some supermarkets. Look for the fullest, greenest stalks.

Separate the bulb and leafy upper stem, wrap each in foil, then store lemon grass in the refrigerator, for up to two weeks. I have tried storing the root in water, as suggested in several books, but found it dried out quickly (and is much too tall, in any case, unless you happen to have a meat locker or walk-in refrigerator).

Lemon grass freezes fabulously well. Separate the drier top stalks from the bulbous base and wrap both parts tightly in foil. Freeze as long as you like, either breaking or cutting off pieces as you need them. Although lemon grass loses a tiny bit of its freshness this way, it does not dry out and is easier to cut than the fresh, as the freezing softens the tough fibers. You can also snip the stalks into small pieces and let them dry in a dark place. Store airtight in a dark place either as is, or ground to a powder.

USE: The fibrous upper stems and outer leaves, too tough to chew, impart their rich aroma to soups (one stalk will season a quart of stock or so). Or brew a strong, pale green tisane as follows: bruise the tops of two stalks, combine with 1 quart cold water, bring to a simmer, remove from heat, and cover for 15 minutes; strain and reheat or chill. Or place the stalks inside the cavity (or underneath) a fish or chicken, then steam for a subtle effect. Add to rice when cooking or to the poaching liquid for fruits and vegetables. However you use the leaves, they will not become bitter with long cooking, so they can remain in the dish until serving time.

The pale inner stalks are edible if finely slivered. You'll have to discover your own seasoning levels for the herb, but as a rule of thumb, use rather as you would fresh ginger, either raw or cooked, as the dish dictates. Try in soups, braises, steamed dishes, stir-fries (which require a much more substantial amount of the grass than any other cooking method will), or in marinades (especially for seafood and chicken). Include in salads, particularly cold meat and fish salads sharpened with hot pepper— for which the grass has a distinct affinity. Season cooked or raw vegetables.

Prepare a seasoning paste by puréeing lemon grass with other aromatics (see one such possibility on page 277) for use with poultry, meat, and seafood. Experiment freely with taste combinations, as lemon grass, like lemon rind, suits an exceptionally wide range of other seasonings, but is much less strident.

PREPARATION: To use the inner stalks of lemon grass for cooking, first remove, wrap, and freeze (or dry) the tough outer leaves for later use. Either slice the lemon grass very fine crosswise, like a scallion (although it is much tougher), or slice and chop. However incorporated, it should be in tiny particles, as it can be fibrous. Just before adding to your dish, pound the leaves or stems lightly with a heavy object to help release the volatile oils.

CHILLED AROMATIC SHRIMP WITH LEMON GRASS DIP

For a very special first course or hors d'oeuvre, serve this fresh and fragrant combination. Or sauté the marinated shrimp in olive oil for a few minutes and serve it hot, as a main course. Or steam shrimp as indicated and serve plain, without sauce, which is also delicious. I am partial to the kick that the jalapeño adds, but the dish works without it, if you are not a chili-pepper fancier.

6 servings as an appetizer

MARINADE
1 large stalk lemon grass, upper leaves and outer layers removed (see Preparation)
2 medium scallions, sliced
1 jalapeño chili-pepper (or Fresno or serrano) seeded and sliced
3 tablespoons coarsely cut mint leaves
¼ teaspoon minced garlic
1 teaspoon coarse kosher salt
½ teaspoon sugar
3 tablespoons corn oil
3 tablespoons lime juice
1½ pounds medium shrimp in the shell
½ cup heavy (or whipping) cream
Mint sprigs and lime wedges for garnish

1. Slice lemon grass thin (you'll have about 3 tablespoons). Chop coarse in processor. Add scallions, jalapeño, mint, garlic, salt, sugar, oil, and lime juice. Whirl to fine purée.

2. Strip shells from shrimp, leaving shell on tail intact. Slit along both sides, then clean as necessary. Combine shrimp and marinade in a bowl; toss to coat well. Let stand, covered, for about 1 hour at room temperature, tossing now and then.

3. Place shrimp in overlapping single layer in heatproof dish on steamer rack over boiling water. Cover and steam until not quite cooked through—about 2 minutes. (Depending on size of steamer, you may have to steam shrimp in batches.) Do *not* discard cooking liquid.

4. Arrange shrimp around serving plate, leaving center empty. Pour cooking liquid into heavy skillet. Boil, stirring, until only thick purée remains. Add cream and boil, stirring constantly, until thickened to a rich pouring consistency. (Do not reduce too much, as sauce thickens considerably when chilled.) Cool in skillet, stirring often to prevent the formation of a skin.

5. Scoop sauce into a small dish and set in the center of shrimp plate. Decorate with mint sprigs and lime wedges, if desired. Cover tightly and refrigerate. Serve chilled.

—

LEMON GRASS SEASONING PASTE

This fragrant, mild-hot, lemony paste is easy to make and stores for weeks in the refrigerator. Spoon out spontaneously to season lamb, beef, pork, chicken, duck, fish, shellfish—and just about anything but dessert. When marinating meat or fish, spread generously and let rest for an hour or so at room temperature before cooking for maximum effect. For vegetables and soups, stir in a little of the paste at the end of cooking time. The mixture adds an apple-green tinge, so plan accompaniments to match.

Makes ¾ cup (or enough for about 3 medium chickens, 3 flank steaks, 1 lamb leg, 2 large fish, 4 pounds shrimp)

1 large stalk lemon grass (about 1½–2 feet long), edible parts only (see Preparation)

Piece of fresh ginger, about 2 by 1 inch, peeled and cut up

3 medium garlic cloves, sliced

2 medium shallots, sliced

3 jalapeño chili-peppers, stems and seeds removed

1 large medium hot chili-pepper, such as Anaheim or poblano, seeded, cut up

3 tablespoons coarsely chopped cilantro stems

1 tablespoon coarse kosher salt (or to taste)

5 tablespoons corn oil, approximately

1. Cut lemon grass bulb and stem in 1-inch pieces. Combine with ginger, garlic, shallots, chili-peppers, cilantro, and salt in container of processor or blender.

2. Chop fine. Add 2 tablespoons oil; purée as fine as possible. Pour into a container. Seal by covering with remaining oil, or as needed. Refrigerate, covered. Lasts for weeks.

AROMATIC BROTH WITH VEGETABLE SLIVERS

Colorful, crisp vegetables decorate this citrusy clear soup. The unmistakable perfumes of lemon grass and coriander with a nip of chili reveal the Southeast Asian origins of this Americanized dish.

4 servings

Upper stems and heavy outer leaves from 1 large stalk lemon grass
4 cups light meat, fish, or poultry stock
½ cup sliced cilantro stems
1 serrano or jalapéno chili-pepper (no need to slice or seed)
½ teaspoon grated lime zest
Lime juice to taste, about 1–2 tablespoons
Salt and pepper to taste
3 ounces snow peas, strings removed
1 medium carrot, peeled
4 medium red radishes
Green part of 1 medium scallion
2 tablespoons whole cilantro leaves (separated from stalks), packed

1. Cut lemon grass in 2-inch pieces; bruise lightly. Combine with stock, cilantro stems, chili, and lime zest in saucepan. Simmer, covered, 15 minutes (halfway through, taste and remove hot pepper, if desired; or leave in longer for more heat).

2. Strain. (Solids can be reused with more cilantro to flavor another batch of broth.) Add lime juice, salt and pepper.

3. Cut snow peas in thin diagonal strips. With vegetable peeler shave 2-inch ribbons of carrot. Thinly slice radishes and scallion.

4. Bring soup to a boil: stir in snow peas and carrots and boil until just tender —about 1½ minutes. Stir in radishes, scallion, and cilantro; bring to a boil. Serve at once.

—

THAI CALAMARI SALAD WITH LEMON GRASS

The tart-hot taste play of this lemony squid dish is refreshing, bright, but plenty piquant—so beware. Adapted from a recipe from my globe-trotting friend Joseph Schultz, author of *The Calamari Cookbook* and founder of India Joze Restaurant in-Santa Cruz, California. I like this as part of a cool meal, along with rice or noodle salad and a crisp vegetable dish.

4 servings as a first course, 2 servings as a main course

¾ pound cleaned small squid (or 1 pound if not cleaned; see Note on page 102, to clean squid), thin-sliced in rings, tentacles divided

About ⅓ cup thin slivers of red onion

½ teaspoon crushed hot pepper flakes

2–3 teaspoons fish sauce, or to taste (see Note)

3 tablespoons lemon juice

2-inch piece tender inner part of lemon grass stalk base (see Preparation), very finely slivered (to make 1 tablespoon)

1½–2 teaspoons brown sugar

Fine-slivered fresh hot red chili-pepper or Tabasco sauce to taste

Bibb or iceberg lettuce, slivered

Cilantro leaves, minced

1. Combine squid in skillet with lightly salted boiling water to barely cover. Simmer 1 minute, or until opaque throughout. Drain. Combine in dish with onion to taste.

2. In tiny pan stir pepper flakes over low heat until aromatic and toasty; be careful not to burn—about 30 seconds. Transfer to small dish; add 2 teaspoons fish sauce, lemon juice, lemon grass, 1½ teaspoons brown sugar, and hot pepper or pepper sauce to taste. Toss with squid and onions. Let stand 5 minutes. Adjust seasoning, which should be quite fierce.

3. Cover and chill. Serve on lettuce, sprinkled with cilantro.

Note: Fermented fish sauce (also called fish gravy or *nuoc mam* or *nam pla*), a salty concoction similar to soy sauce, is available in all Oriental groceries. It lasts virtually forever, is inexpensive, and is worth having around even if you don't use if very often.

LITCHI
See Lychee

LONGAN
(Euphoria longana)
also Long An, Lungan, Dragon's Eye

*L*ongan fruits, which range from olive to baby plum sized, from spherical to ovoid, are covered with a thin, rough-to-prickly brown shell (pericarp). When this is removed (like an easily peeled shell from a hard-cooked egg), the juicy, translucent gray-white pulp is revealed. This aril clings to a large, smooth, ebonylike seed that

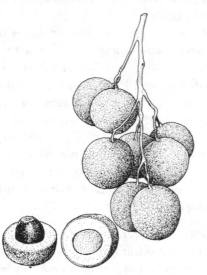

makes any kind of consumption other than pulling with your teeth rather tricky. (Growers tell me that new varieties will have a better ratio of pulp to pit, and that many will be "freestone.") But the job is rewarding. The soft meat feels like a peeled grape to the tongue, and has a sweeter taste—haunting, with hints of gardenia, spruce, and musk. And like pistachios, the extricating is entertaining.

Native to Southeast Asia, the longan is still cultivated there on a large scale, as it is in parts of China and India—like its closest relative, the lychee. Both fruits were introduced into the United States through the efforts of W. N. Brewster, a missionary in Fukien Province, China. Like the lychee, the longan is a majestic shade tree, thickly hung with dark evergreen leaves, and has enjoyed some success in this country, but primarily as an ornamental.

Unlike the lychee, however, the longan is less picky about its soil requirements, produces a heavier crop, and, most important, can withstand much colder temperatures. Growers in Florida, who distribute a tiny crop on the East Coast, think the fruit has good commercial potential, now that the market for specialties has opened up so dramatically.

SELECTION AND STORAGE: Look for heavy, uncracked longans during July and August, generally in Oriental markets. (In fact, the Oriental demand is so great that these fruits may not show up anywhere else.) They last very well—for several weeks—if refrigerated. Or store them for months in an airtight container in the freezer. Defrost just before using, leaving the fruit slightly frozen, or it becomes flabby. Or peel and freeze in sugar syrup, having first pitted the fruit—time-consuming as it may be.

USE: Although it is possible to pull the pulp from the longan stone it is tiresome and often tears up the fruit. But, if you have the patience to peel and seed longans, the soft fruit mixes beautifully with other tender exotics for a memorable dessert. Or poach the longan gently in light sugar syrup for a sweet-scented close to a meal.

NUTRITIONAL HIGHLIGHTS: Longan is an excellent source of vitamin C and a good source of potassium. It is low in calories, with about 60 calories in ½ cup. Very, very low in sodium.

&. *Longan can be substituted for lychees in recipes on pages 285–286, if the ones you find are less clingstone than most.*

LONG-BEAN
See Yard-Long Bean

LOQUAT
(*Eriobotrya japonica*)
also Japanese Plum, Japanese Medlar
(not to be confused with the Medlar, *Mespilus germanica*)

*U*nless you live in California or Florida you will probably suffer from the same loquat-lack that I do. To make a long story short, loquats bruise. If loquats were to be marketed blemish-free, they would have to be harvested rock-hard and inedible (as much of our fruit is at present). When I spent some time in Portugal, I watched with

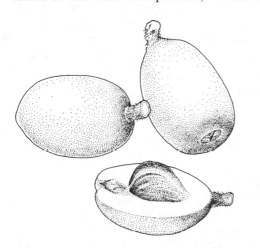

fascination as women in the market picked through sunny heaps of fruit, avoiding the perfect-looking firm specimens and selecting the bruised and tender. In China (where loquats originated), Japan, India, throughout the Mediterranean, Central America, and part of South America the small golden loquat's delicacy is a fact of life—and the fruit is eagerly consumed in abundance, even with imperfections.

Although there have been many attempts to market the lovely loquat, there has been little success. In a June 1985 newsletter from the Rare Fruit Council International of Miami, Robert J. Knight, Jr., research scientist at the United States Department of Agriculture, wrote that "to date no Western country has followed the admirably successful Israeli effort to commercialize loquat culture . . . and the time for such an effort is overdue." He points out that the fruit has, in addition to its other virtues, the earliest harvest time of any spring fruit, appearing before apricots, plums, cherries, and nectarines. And, because it is not confined to a tropical climate, large areas in Florida, California, and other warm parts of the country afford the opportunity for culture.

The loquat, of the extraordinarily far-reaching Rosaceae (which, in addition to roses, includes just about all the tree fruits and berries that we know), most resembles the apricot in size and color, but has one or more very large seeds and is a bit pear-shaped. The flesh, which can be creamy to orange, has an unusual consistency, juicy and tender, yet crisp-firm. Both taste (a delightful balance of sweet and acid) and texture suggest plum, lychee, grape, and cherry. Depending upon the variety, the flavor can vary from very light to honey-rich.

SELECTION AND STORAGE: Loquats have a very brief season: from March through May in Florida; through June in California. Select big fruits (or there is much waste because of the large seeds) that are tender and sweet-scented. If there is a choice, pick fruits without stems.

Refrigerate the loquats only if they are on the verge of spoiling. However, it is better to put them up in syrup, as they lose none of their delicate perfume that way. Once cooked, they freeze well in small plastic containers.

USE: Loquats are a light and juicy nibble. Although the ones I have tasted required peeling (a cinch, by the way), connoisseurs tell me that most varieties do not. Peeled and quartered loquats blend prettily with fresh berries and kiwis or other light fruits.

Poaching in sugar syrup brings out the natural flavors. Serve loquats in syrup for breakfast, brunch, or dessert; combine with other delicate, soft cooked fruits, taking care not to overpower. (Frozen poached loquats taste heavenly with fresh lychees.) Set drained halves on tart shells coated with pastry cream; or fill a white cake with the slivered fruit and whipped cream. Nestle in meringue shells.

Chicken and shrimp are respected loquat escorts, but I have not had the opportunity to enjoy them together. Nor have I had the chance to test nearly as many recipes as I would like—for the reasons cited in the opening tirade!

PREPARATION: Loquats must be stemmed, seeded, and often peeled. The job is faster and easier than it may sound. Rinse the fruit and remove stems. Slice off the blossom end, then halve. Pop out the large, closely fitted seeds; pull off the peel. Or you can simply slice off the blossom and peel the fruit, keeping it whole, if that is more suitable.

NUTRITIONAL HIGHLIGHTS: Loquats are an excellent source of vitamin A and are low in calories.

LOQUATS IN SYRUP

Loquats poached in syrup are delicious golden-orange mouthfuls, the texture of apricots crossed with lychees, and faintly fruity-floral in flavor. Although beautiful alone, they look and taste especially delightful with lemon ice or Gingered Papaya Milk Sherbet (page 345). Mix them with strawberries or halved cherries for a compote, or serve with plain cake or meringue shells and cream.

4 servings

1 cup water
½ cup sugar
1 long strip lemon peel
2 tablespoons lemon juice
1 pound ripe loquats (weighed without stems)

1. Combine water, sugar, and lemon peel in saucepan. Simmer, covered, 3–4 minutes. Turn off heat and let stand while you prepare loquats.

2. Rinse stemmed loquats, trim off blossom ends, then halve and pit them. Pull off skins (or do this first, as you prefer). If loquats are relatively large, cut into quarters. (*Note:* If you do not object to cooked fruit with pits, poach the fruits whole for more flavor.)

3. Add fruit to syrup and bring to simmer. Cover and poach gently, on lowest heat, until fruit is tender to taste—about 5 minutes.

4. Uncover and cool in syrup. Pour into dish and chill thoroughly.

Note: After loquats have cooled in syrup, they can be packed into freezer containers and frozen for months.

LYCHEE
(Litchi chinensis)
also Litchi, Lichee, Leechee, Lichi, Laichee

One of the most revered of Chinese fruits, the lychee has been enjoyed for over two thousand years in the Orient. The majestic trees (which grow to forty feet), are densely covered with coppery evergreen leaves through which emerge clusters of brilliant-colored fruits that hang like bunches of strawberries. While the beauty of the

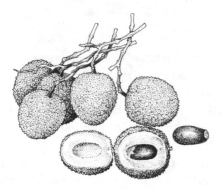

tree has made it a favorite ornamental, fruit production is erratic. Because it bears unpredictably and slowly and is extremely vulnerable to cold, the lychee has never become a major commercial crop in the United States. China remains the largest producer today, with smaller amounts raised in Thailand, the Philippines, Taiwan, India, South Africa, Australia, Hawaii, Mexico, and Florida.

Few who taste lychees are indifferent to their juicy softness and lyrical perfume. The size of smallish Ping-Pong balls, slightly ovoid, the fruits have a thin, crisp shell (pericarp) that resembles a bur without stickers; this can be a glorious russeted rose color or barky brown. When the shell is cracked open at the stem end with a fingernail, a translucent, gray-white pulp (the aril) is revealed; embedded in the center is a large, mahogany-like seed. The taut, membranous flesh (which looks more like a sea creature than a fruit) slips from the shell like a hard-cooked egg. The consistency is similar to a peeled grape but more close-textured; the taste and aroma are reminiscent of muscat grapes and roses, but sweeter.

Although a vast number of lychee varieties exist, only the Brewster (named after the missionary who introduced this fruit and the longan from China) and Mauritius are available with any regularity in the United States—and this in extremely limited quantities. If fresh lychees are absent, canned ones are remarkably luscious.

Dried lychees, chewy and smoky, have nothing in common with the fresh or canned fruits. Although they are sometimes called lychee nuts, the "nut" (central seed) itself should not be consumed, only the raisiny pulp that clings to it.

SELECTION AND STORAGE: Look for lychees in Oriental markets in the summer. Pick the heaviest and fullest ones, with stems. The rosier the color, the fresher. Shells may be mottled with brown, which occurs very soon after picking; but as long as the fruits are full and heavy, not shriveled or cracked, they'll be heavenly.

Surprisingly for such a delicate creature, the lychee will keep without spoiling for several weeks in the refrigerator—although some perfume will be lost. The flavor remains amazingly true if the fruit is frozen in the shell in an airtight container, although the pulp softens and loses its delightful tautness. Once frozen, lychee is best used in fruit cup or cooked dishes, where the taste comes through, but peak texture won't be missed.

USE: Feast on lychees, straight from the shell, with a bottle of light Asti Spumante or another fruity, sparkling dessert wine. Personally, I find the sensuous act of withdrawing a lychee from its lair to be so pleasant a part of the "lychee experience" that I am reluctant to eat the fruit any other way but "straight." Or peel, halve, and seed, then combine with bits of soft fresh fruit, such as raspberries, kiwi, strawberries, mango, apricot.

Add lychees to a hot sweet or savory sauce during the last minute of cooking, or when you reheat it. They offer an inimitable sweetness, fruitiness, and perfume to dessert sauces or reductions of chicken, duck, or veal stock (see Chicken Suprêmes with Lychees, page 286).

PREPARATION: Peeling lychees is pleasantly sticky, not messy. If you are preparing a fruit cup, you need to crack the shells at the stem end (a fingernail does the job), pull them off, then extract the glossy seed—which is best done by first loosening it from the stem end, then halving the fruit to remove it completely.

NUTRITIONAL HIGHLIGHTS: Lychees are low in calories. They are an excellent source of vitamin C and a very good source of potassium.

LYCHEES, BERRIES, AND KIWIS WITH HONEY AND LIME

The simple recipe that follows—more of a suggestion than a recipe—is merely a felicitous mélange of complementary hues and aromas that I have found appealing. I imagine that raspberries, apricots, juicy-soft plums, or sweet-ripe melons would suit the lychee perfume as well as the fruits recommended below. If you are a less fanatic fruit purist than I, you might enjoy a whisper of cherry or raspberry eau-de-vie sprinkled in at the last minute.

6 servings

2 dozen large, heavy lychees in the shell (about 1½ pounds)

1 pint small, fragrant strawberries, stemmed and halved

4 kiwis

2 tablespoons delicate, pale honey, approximately

Lime juice to taste

1. Remove shells from lychees. Gently pull fruit from large central stone; it usually comes off in 2–3 pieces. Place in a bowl. Add strawberries.

2. Cut ends from the kiwis; remove skin with swivel peeler. Halve lengthwise, then cut across into thin slices; add to other fruits in bowl. Toss gently with honey and lime juice to taste.

3. Refrigerate for at least 2 hours before serving.

CHICKEN SUPRÊMES WITH LYCHEES

Halved boned chicken breasts, called *suprêmes* in French, are a delicate, elegant *raison d'être* for sweetly perfumed lychees. Floured, browned, and briefly cooked, the *suprêmes* retain all their juice and flavor—and help to produce a rich, golden sauce/glaze.

The dish is also delicious made with veal steaks about ¾ inch thick, browned and cooked slightly longer.

2 servings

⅔ cup homemade chicken or veal stock
8 lychees
1 large chicken breast, boned and
    skinned (to equal ¾-1 pound)
Flour for dredging
2 tablespoons butter
1 tablespoon corn oil
¼ cup light, medium-sweet (or medium-
    dry) white wine
Salt and white pepper

1. In small pot boil stock to reduce to about ⅓ cup; reserve. Break stem end of lychee shells with fingernail; remove shell entirely. Halve each fruit, loosening seed from stem end to remove it. Halve chicken breast neatly.

2. Flour breast and pat off excess. Heat 1 tablespoon butter and the oil in heavy skillet (with close-fitting cover) to hold meat with little extra space. Brown chicken lightly over moderately low heat, about 2 minutes per side. Transfer to a plate; pour most fat from pan.

3. Without rinsing pan, add stock and wine. Simmer, stirring, until color deepens and liquid reduces to 4–5 tablespoons. Add salt and pepper to taste. Return chicken and accumulated juices to pan. Cover and cook on low heat 2 minutes. Turn and stew gently about 2 minutes longer, until just cooked. Set chicken on cutting board to rest.

4. Add lychees to pan and simmer gently, covered, for a minute or less to plump and heat fruit. Remove from heat and season. Add remaining tablespoon butter and swirl pan to incorporate. Quickly cut *suprêmes* in thick diagonal slices and set on 2 warmed plates. Spoon sauce and lychees over meat and serve at once.

M

MÂCHE, CORN SALAD
(*Valerianella locusta*)
also Lamb's Lettuce, Lamb's Tongue, Field Salad

*D*ear as a bunch of violets, these greens arrive in the market in soft clusters, rosettes of downy leaves that perk up the spirit like spring rain. Of the tumble of fetching names that belong to this ancient salad, I find the French *doucette* (little sweet or tender one) the most charming and most suitable. What is currently touted here in

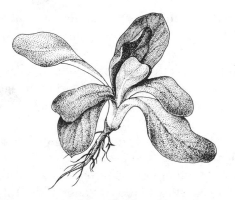

our fanciest markets is the imported mâche, which is more chic than corn salad to the ear (and pricier to the purse), but is the same plant. However, we should be grateful that an awareness of sophisticated European food, particularly French, has returned this once common leaf to the American table.

In *Mrs. Rorer's New Cookbook* written in 1902 there is an entry under "Corn Salad" which states simply: "This plant grows wild in Southern Europe and is cultivated in the eastern part of the United States for early spring salads. It comes just between the winter and spring lettuce. The size and flavor of the leaves are greatly improved by cultivation." Most cultivation takes place in Europe at present. The majority of our supply of mâche is imported, at great expense, from countries that have not tired of it. Although many small farms in America are now beginning to plant the crop, it is not yet competition for the superior French and Belgian greens. One produce manager explained that Americans (with the possible exception of Californians) do not understand the growing, packing, and storage requirements of such a delicate creature, nor are they willing to go through the hard work necessary to produce it.

This is not the case in France, Italy, Holland, Belgium, Germany, Austria, and Britain, where the mild leaf has always been considered a beloved harbinger of spring and salad extraordinaire. Cultivated since neolithic times, corn salad's place of origin has been obscured by the ages, but temperate Europe is the general area of its earliest growth and remains the primary area of popularity for the vegetable. The name *lamb's lettuce*, a translation of the ancient Roman *lactuca agnina*, suggests the same pastoral environs as *corn salad*. *Corn* here refers not to our maize but to the British word *corn*, meaning grains in general, with which corn salad grows in pleasant proximity, whether wild or cultivated. (Lamb's lettuce is *not* related to lamb's-quarters, of the Goosefoot family [Chenopodium], a different character altogether.)

Variable in nature, the leaves may be broad or narrow, dark or medium green, round or spoon-shaped, and sweetly nutty or simply green-flavored, like Bibb or butter lettuce. What I have enjoyed in the United States offered freshness, a velvety texture, and mild flavor. Europeans who have the greens regularly available tell me that wild mâche is considerably tastier than cultivated, and, barring that, mâche grown outdoors is tastier than that raised in a greenhouse. Since it is a favorite garden plant, it seems worth a try if you have a plot.

SELECTION AND STORAGE: Mâche is available in fancy markets year round. It is generally sold in bunchlets, its roots attached, held together in a twist or cone of clear plastic, like a bouquet. It should be spankingly clean-leaved and clear green, with no evidence of softening or wetness in the leaves. It is always expensive and should be in dandy shape.

Mâche is very perishable; do not store it. Its fleeting flavor and dewy freshness demand immediate attention.

USE: Simplicity is imperative here, or you will lose the very special qualities of the leaf. It makes a beautiful and flavorful garnish for cream soup or delicate vegetable purées. Or surround roasted veal or chicken with the leaves for a graceful and tasty wreath to soak up the juices. Tuck beneath the edge of a wild-mushroom omelet or around a potato or rice salad dressed with light oil and a bare hint of wine vinegar. Although it may be heretical, I love mâche in a sandwich of delicate, soft cheese and toasted, close-grained white bread.

As a salad, nothing compares with the delicacy of a toss of soft mâche and fragrant oil, cream, or melted butter with a touch of lemon juice or vinegar. The nuttiness of the leaf is deliciously enhanced by a soupçon of hazelnut or walnut oil and a sprinkle of nuts to match. When combining with other leaves, stick to the soft and mild—Bibb, Boston, oak leaf. The traditional accompaniment of julienned beets, baked or boiled, brings out the earthiness and sweetness in an unforgettable way. A mimosa garnish—sieved hard-cooked egg whites and yolks—is also standard. Do not dress the leaves until the moment you eat them, or they absorb the dressing and lose their texture.

It is often suggested that field salad be cooked "as spinach," but the hothouse variety we now have does not respond well to this treatment.

PREPARATION: Mâche, which hides sand in its smooth, pretty leaves, requires gentle but serious washing. Trim off the rootlets, then dunk the leaves up and down in a bowl of water; lift out. Repeat. Either pat dry on a very soft, thick towel or spin dry, then blot delicately with a towel. Chill until serving time.

NUTRITIONAL HIGHLIGHTS: There is no data available, beyond the fact that mâche is very low in calories, but similar greens (from which it would be reasonable to impute equivalencies) are generally a good source of vitamin A and a fairly good source of vitamin C, as well as being very low in sodium.

SALAD OF MÂCHE AND BEETS

In France one of the traditional accompaniments to mâche is beets. The earthy sweetness and glowing color provide a delicious and beautiful complement.

6 servings

1 pound (8 or 9) smallish beets (weighed with 2 inches of tops)
½ teaspoon salt
1 tablespoon balsamic vinegar
1 tablespoon red wine vinegar
Optional: Few drops hot pepper sauce or pepper sherry
3 tablespoons olive oil
3 tablespoons corn oil
3 small bunches mâche (about 8 ounces), cleaned (see Preparation) and thoroughly dried
1–2 tablespoons finely slivered scallions

1. Do not trim little bits of stem from beets. Boil the beets until tender, about 20 minutes or more. Drain and let cool until you can slip off the skins; slice off the stems. Cut fairly thin slices; cut these into strips ¼–½ inch wide.

2. Combine salt, vinegars, pepper sauce, and blend; add olive and corn oils and mix well. Toss beets with about two-thirds of the dressing.

3. To serve, toss mâche gently with remaining dressing and arrange around a platter. Scoop beets into center, sprinkle with scallions, and serve.

MÂCHE, BIBB LETTUCE, AND MUSHROOMS WITH CREAM DRESSING

Velvety, beautiful mâche needs light partnering if it is to be appreciated. Here, a gentle topping of lemony cream enriches the baby leaves, but does not hide them.

2 servings as a first course or salad

1 bunch mâche (about 1¼ cups leaves)
1 good-sized Bibb lettuce
2 teaspoons lemon juice
½ teaspoon sharp mustard
¼ teaspoon sugar
⅛ teaspoon salt
White pepper to taste
2½ tablespoons heavy (or whipping) cream
1½ tablespoons corn oil
¼ pound firm, small mushrooms

1. Gently separate mâche leaves at base. Separate Bibb leaves; break into small pieces. Delicately rinse both in bowl of water. Spin dry; roll in toweling; chill .

2. In a small bowl whisk together lemon juice, mustard, sugar, salt, and pepper. Beat in heavy cream; gradually beat in oil. Chill at least ½ hour.

3. Peel mushrooms (not necessary, but nice for salads). Cut in very thin slices. Arrange lettuce and mâche in bowl; set mushrooms in the middle.

4. Pour on dressing at the table, then toss lightly. Serve at once.

MALANGA, YAUTIA
(Xanthosoma species)
also Tannia, Tannier, Malanga Amarilla,
Yautia Amarilla, Yautia Blanca, Cocoyam

*T*here may be more confusion about this vegetable than any other in the global vege-table bin. The forty or so species, all native to the American tropics, include some of the oldest root crops in the world. Their close resemblance to a related tuber, *Coloca-sia esculenta* (most commonly known as *taro*), has produced a score of common

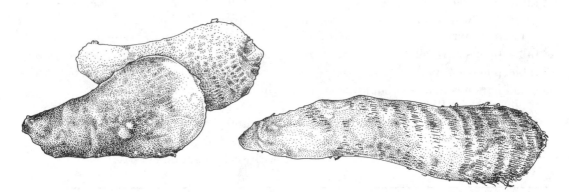

names that overlap the two, blurring the distinguishing characteristics. To further tangle, some species of each produce tubers in shapes and colors almost exactly like the other genus, distinguishable only by the leaves—which most American cooks are not likely to have on hand.

The malanga and taro that do appear in the United States, however, are a bit easier to identify. Malanga or yautia (the Cuban and Puerto Rican names, respectively, and the ones you are most likely to encounter) is shaggy and brown, with patchy, thin skin through which is visible beige, yellowish, or reddish flesh. It may be shaped like a long Louisiana yam, or may be curved, or look like a cartoon caveman's club. It generally ranges from about ½ to 2 pounds—although it can be heavier. The interior may be cream, yellow, or pinkish and has an extremely crisp, slippery texture.

Cooked malanga has a unique texture and flavor—one of those love-it-or-hate-it foods. Its taste is far more pronounced than that of most starchy tropical tubers, tending more toward nuts than potatoes. (Stephen K. O'Hair of the Agricultural Re-search Station at the University of Florida, a specialist in such vegetables, describes the flavor as similar to that of black walnuts.) It is also vaguely musty and earthy. The smooth, melting quality that the crisp tuber develops when boiled is most surprising—somewhere between that of cooked dried pinto beans and a waxy new potato.

Note: In Cuban or Puerto Rican markets, where most malanga is sold, there is an additional identification problem: malanga isleña, so called in Cuban markets, is actually taro (see page 458), not malanga. Malanga amarilla (yellow malanga), which has the characteristic barrel shape of taro, is, in fact, malanga. Experts have assured me that this yellow- to apricot-fleshed variety is the only malanga in which the rounded central corm is eaten rather than the smaller, irregularly club-shaped surrounding cormels.

SELECTION AND STORAGE: Malanga is available year round in Hispanic markets and many supermarkets. It should be relatively light-colored, very hard, with no soft, shriveled, or moldy areas. Prick the malanga with your nail; it should be juicy and crisp—like a water chestnut—not dry or soft. The best produce markets will display sliced tubers to show you just how fresh they are.

Malanga can be stored at room temperature for a few days, no longer; it dries out or becomes soft surprisingly quickly. Some cooks tell me that malanga will keep longer in the refrigerator, but in my experience this has not been true.

USE: In most countries that cook malanga, it is peeled and boiled—that's it—to be served with spicy sausages, salty dried meat and fish dishes, or rich stews. Or a chili-pepper or garlic sauce (such as the ones on page 509 and page 522) is poured over the hot vegetable, which acts as a soft blotter for strong seasonings. To prepare this way, simply boil the peeled vegetable in rather large (medium-potato-sized) pieces in salted water until just tender, about 20–25 minutes.

Boiled malanga can be pressed through the medium disk of a food mill, thinned with hot milk and cream, then seasoned with nutmeg, salt, pepper, and a dash of sugar for an unusual purée.

Malanga makes crisp, flavorful chips and crunchy, savory fritters. Grated malanga produces a chewy, tasty pancake.

Once cooked through in liquid, malanga begins to soften and dissolve, creamily, making it an ideal soup medium. Slightly mucilaginous and earthy, it blends with both herbs and spices, smoky meats, and other root vegetables.

Malanga makes an interesting contribution to stews, adding flavor, thickness, and creaminess; be careful not to overcook, however, or it disintegrates. When using this way, go lightly, as the flavor can overpower; use one or several Latin starches—taro, boniato, yam, plantain—rather than malanga alone.

If you wish to experiment, you should know that when baked malanga's texture becomes denser and waxier, its flavor somewhat cheesy and sourish. Although many starchy roots are recommended for inclusion in desserts, I find this one too aggressive.

PREPARATION: Scrub the malanga with a brush under running water. Trim off ends. Pare with a knife to remove skin and imperfections. Rinse each piece as you finish peeling and place in cold water to cover; refrigerate for up to a day before cooking, if you like.

NUTRITIONAL HIGHLIGHTS: Malanga is high in calories, at 135 per ½ cup, cooked.

MALANGA CHIPS

For this recipe, you'll need a food processor to make thin, long slices of the malanga—which is an ideal vegetable for deep-frying. Its big flavor holds up to the process while the high starch content makes for a crispy-dry chip of even consistency. Serve as a cocktail companion (sprinkle with a little chili powder, if you like), hot from the pan. Or keep warm up to ½ hour in a low oven.

Makes about 6 servings

1 pound small malanga of any variety
Corn oil for deep frying
Salt to taste

1. Scrub malanga. Pare thoroughly. Place in cold water until ready to cook. Heat oil about an inch deep to 350 degrees, preferably in a wide electric frying pan.

2. With 2-millimeter slicing blade in place, cut paper-thin lengthwise chips from malanga—enough to cover oil surface. (This can be done with wide feed tube; if yours is small, halve malanga.)

3. Place slices gently in oil. Fry until golden on both sides, about 2 minutes. Drain on paper toweling; sprinkle with salt. Serve at once, or keep warm briefly in 200-degree oven.

MALANGA FRITTERS FROM THE BALLROOM

Michael Rose makes these garlicky nibbles for the Tapas Bar at the Ballroom Restaurant in New York City. Golden and crunchy, with sharp little tendrils of shredded malanga, they are right at home with margaritas or rum drinks.

Approximately 6 appetizer servings

2 medium-large malangas, about 1¼ pounds
2 large garlic cloves, minced
1½ teaspoons coarse kosher salt
1 serrano chili-pepper, seeded and minced (or substitute jalapeño)

1 egg, beaten slightly
2 tablespoons minced parsley
Peanut or soy or safflower oil for deep-frying
Minced parsley for garnish
Lemon wedges

1. Peel malanga and place in cold water. Using a standing hand grater, shred coarse; there should be about 3 cups. Add garlic, salt, serrano, egg, and parsley; blend.

2. Heat oil for deep-frying to 350–375 degrees, preferably in wide electric skillet or deep-fryer. Form malanga mixture into loosely packed balls in the palm of your hand, using about 1½ tablespoons of the mixture for each. Drop into hot oil (do not crowd); brown well.

3. Set on heated plates. Sprinkle with parsley; serve with lemon.

Note: This can be made with any kind of malanga, or with taro.

MALANGA FRITTERS FROM SABOR

This version of fritters comes from Gail Lewis, who runs the cozy Sabor Restaurant in New York City's Greenwich Village. The irresistibly crunchy tidbits have a chewy interior that bursts with garlic flavor.

8 appetizer servings

4 good-sized garlic cloves, peeled
½ cup flat-leaf (Italian) parsley
About 1½ teaspoons coarse kosher salt
¼ teaspoon ground pepper
2 pounds firm, crisp malanga
2 tablespoons flour
Vegetable oil for frying
Lemon wedges

1. With motor running, drop garlic and parsley into food processor; chop to fine texture, scraping down sides of container. Add 1½ teaspoons salt and the pepper.

2. Peel malanga; cut into 1-inch chunks. Add to garlic mixture, turning machine on and off to make tiny but distinct pieces; do not purée or fritters will be gummy. Taste for salt, oversalting slightly. Add flour and turn processor on and off to barely blend. Let the mixture stand for about an hour.

3. In a wide, deep skillet (preferably electric) heat about an inch of oil until it reaches 375 degrees. Scoop up heaping teaspoons of malanga mixture to form 1½-inch lumps; dislodge into the oil with another spoon, shaping as regularly as possible. Maintaining heat at about 350 degrees, fry malanga until golden and well cooked inside—about 3 minutes. Serve as you go, or place on a paper-covered plate in a low oven. Accompany with lemon wedges.

Note: You can substitute taro for malanga, or use a combination of the two.

___

MALANGA-YAM PANCAKES

Maricel Presilla, whose knowledge of cooking tropical roots and tubers is considerable, shared a version of this traditional recipe with me. Untraditional is the way her husband, Alejandro, likes the cakes—for breakfast with maple syrup. They are chewy-crisp and as versatile as potato pancakes, which they resemble. For variety, add onion, garlic, caraway, poppy seeds, chilies, or curry to the mixture.

Makes 8 large pancakes

½ pound malanga (see Note)
½ pound yam (see page 506) or baking
    potato (see Note)
1 extra-large or jumbo egg
2–3 tablespoons finely chopped cilantro
    or parsley
1 teaspoon lemon juice
1 teaspoon coarse kosher salt
2 tablespoons butter
2 tablespoons corn oil

1. Peel malanga and yam. Set in cold water to cover (can be done ahead). Beat egg in mixing bowl; blend in cilantro, lemon, and salt.

2. Grate malanga and yam on large holes of standing hand grater; there should be 2 cups loosely packed shreds. Combine with egg mixture and let stand about 10 minutes.

3. Heat 1 tablespoon each butter and oil in each of 2 large skillets (preferably nonstick). Stir malanga mixture. Divide evenly into the pans to make 8 mounds, pressing each to form a large, even round. Fry on moderately low heat until golden brown on both sides, about 5 minutes.

4. Place on heated plate and serve at once.

Note: You can use taro, malanga, yam, yuca, boniato, or any tropical tuber for this, as well as "regular" potato or a combination of any of these.

MALANGA AND SPINACH SOUP

Nothing timid about this sultry soup. Malanga's curious characteristics are well illustrated here; it tastes musky and meaty, qualities that are underscored by the soft spinach and earthy dried mushrooms. It has a unique texture, at once slippery and creamy: the malanga dice do not break up and disintegrate, but melt, become smaller and smoother as they cook, as tender as puréed beans, thickening the soup and, at the same time, remaining distinct pieces.

4 servings

Enough dried mushrooms, preferably wild, to equal 3 tablespoons broken pieces
½ cup warm water
2 tablespoons strong olive oil
2 teaspoons chopped garlic
1½ pounds malanga, scrubbed, peeled, and cut in ½-inch dice
¼ teaspoon hot pepper flakes
6 cups chicken or beef broth
1¼ pounds tender spinach, well washed
Salt to taste

1. Combine mushrooms and warm water; soak about ½ hour, stirring occasionally. Drain, reserving liquid. Strain liquid through cheesecloth, if necessary, to remove soil. Quickly rinse mushrooms.

2. Heat oil and garlic in large pot until slightly colored and softened. Add malanga, pepper flakes, mushrooms, and mushroom liquid, stirring. Add broth and bring to a boil.

3. Simmer, partly covered, until malanga is tender—about 20–25 minutes.

4. Meanwhile, strip stems from spinach; slice leaves coarse. When malanga is tender, add spinach. Bring to a boil, stirring. Boil gently until spinach is very tender and malanga has thickened soup a bit more—about 5 minutes.

&. *ADDITIONAL RECIPES*
Puréed Taro Soup (page 462)
Sandra Allen's Chunky Taro-Sausage Soup (page 463)
Maricel Presilla's Yams in Garlic-Citrus Sauce (page 509)
Smoky Yam-Celery Soup (page 510)
Maricel Presilla's Escabeche de Ñame (page 511)
Michael Rose's Yuca con Mojo (page 522)

MANGO
(Mangifera indica)

*I*magine that you had tasted just one apple in your life—a Red Delicious stored beyond its time. You would have little appreciation for the mealy fruit's truly delicious siblings, and little wish to purchase other varieties in future. If you have tasted only a bland, immature, fibrous mango and assumed it to be representative of the species,

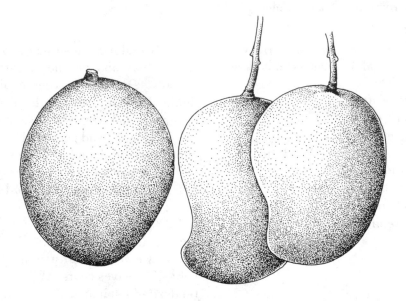

keep tasting. There are more differences between good- and poor-quality mangos than between some mangos and apples!

Mangos are considerably better known than apples in more than half the world, where they are a staple, second only to the banana and coconut. The fragrant fruit, a native of Southeast Asia, has been cultivated for as long as 6,000 years, according to some estimates. Asia still accounts for more than three-quarters of the world's mangos, with India the main producer. About 15 percent of the mangos in our markets are grown in Florida, with the rest imported, primarily from Haiti and Mexico (new markets are opening up in Central and South America as this is being written). The towering evergreen mango tree, thick with shining, leathery leaves, offers both shade and sustenance. From its branches long stems hold clusters of fruits, cherry-like, that may be green-yellow-red (and shades in between) and range from a few ounces to a few pounds. The skin, smooth as thick glove leather, encloses yellow to red flesh that is softly moist and richly flavored, silky as custard or fiendishly fibrous, perfumed with pine and peach, or simply turpentine.

Where mangos grow, you can pluck a juicy "sucking mango" from the omnipresent mammoth trees, poke a hole in it, and slurp away at the refreshing nectar to quench your thirst on the spot. "Slicing mangos," whether green (eaten cooked), ripe, or dried, are a constant snack, part of every meal, and often the meal itself.

MANGO VARIETIES: In the French West Indies, mangos are marketed in three sizes: *mangues* (the largest), *mangots*, and *mangotines*. The names that accompany these charming sizes are similarly sweet and girlish: varieties such as Julie, Amelie, and Zephirine. No such romantic nonsense in our country, where mangos are named primarily after growers—virtually all of whom hail from Florida (the only place warm enough for a predictable crop). Most of the contemporary commercial varieties, whether they grow in Florida or South or Central America, have actually been refined and developed by American breeders. That does not make the American mango growers too happy, as they now must compete with foreign growers who offer the same kinds of mangos but are able to produce them less expensively, in better growing conditions, with fewer regulations.

While many different mango varieties may show up in American markets (if you can get your hands on the little Asian ones, hoard them), the fruits that are regularly available here are described below, with Keitt and Tommy Atkins leading the pack in volume. Unfortunately, mangos are not generally sold by varietal names, as apples are, so it is difficult to learn to appreciate the differences.

Haden averages a little less than a pound, and is quite round for a mango, with only a slightly oval shape or suggestion of kidney form. Its skin turns from green to yellow-orange when ripe, with a pretty crimson blush. Although less fibrous than Tommy Atkins, the flesh is almost as firm, with quite a rich mango flavor and beautiful light pumpkin color.

Keitt is the heftiest, plumpest, largest mango variety available, averaging 1¾ but reaching 3 pounds. Unlike most of the popular market types, it is yellow-to-green when ripe, with only a very faint yellow or rose blush. Fat and comparatively rounded, it is definitely not a one-person fruit. The yellow-gold flesh is juicy, fiberless except close to the seed, and close-grained. Light in aroma, it has a full flavor, with pronounced lemony tang and medium sweetness.

Kent is a large, particularly plump fruit (most mangos are flattened; this one is fat), irregularly oval, with an average weight of 1¼ pounds. Its skin when ripe is orange-yellow, green-speckled, and blushed slightly with deep red. It has a remarkable quantity of buttery, yellow-gold, juicy, fiberless flesh. The sweet, richly tropical flavor has a lovely acid-lime finish, with piny overtones.

Palmer is full-plump, a blunted, elongated oval. Quite hefty, it averages 1¼ pounds. Its rosy speckled skin has a yellowy flush when ripe, and its apricot flesh is smooth and quite free of fiber, except around the seed. The very sweet, flavorful pulp is deliciously fruity but less aromatic than some. The flavor seems more that of a temperate-climate fruit—a peach, for example—than a tropical one.

Tommy Atkins, our most common mango, is medium-large, averages 1 pound, and is neatly oval, with a rounded apex. The skin is quite thick, orangy or rosy yellow, speckled or blushed. The flesh is yellow, mild, and less flavorful and sweet than the aroma suggests; it is comparatively firm and contains numerous fine-textured fibers. This mango seems sturdily all-purpose and bland; more a delicious apple than a tropical creature, more appealing to the eye than anything else.

Van Dyke is smaller than any above, averaging 10 ounces—and therefore better for a single serving. The ripened skin can be yellow, red orange, or yellowish red when ripe. Oval-shaped, the fruit generally has a slight nipple-like protuberance called a *nak* at its apex. The aroma is piny and pleasantly sharp, the flesh brilliant orange with a moderate amount of fiber and distinct, full pineapply flavor.

SELECTION AND STORAGE: Florida mangos are in season during the summer. The imports have a much longer season, beginning in January (usually with flat, elongated, yellow Haitian mangos) and continuing through the fall. Select full, firmish part-ripe fruit that shows some yellow or red (except for the Keitt, which may remain green when ripe). Full-ripe fruit will be almost as tender as avocado. Whether partly or fully ripe, the skin should be taut. Stay away from mangos that have soft spots or that look flabby, with skin appearing too large for the pulp. But brown-speckled or splotched fruit is fine for eating.

Most important in determining ripeness or potential quality is the aroma. Sniff the stem end: there should be a pleasant scent, no matter how light. No perfume usually means no flavor. If the smell is slightly alcoholic or sour, reject the fruit, which has begun fermenting.

To ripen greenish fruit, keep at room temperature until tender and aromatic. Chill briefly before serving, or up to a few days if you must hold the fruit. Mangos do not do well in the cold.

To freeze, cube the flesh (see Preparation), purée in a processor, then press through a sieve. Add lime juice and sugar, if desired. Pack in small containers and freeze for months. Figure that the cup yield will be roughly the same as poundage.

USE: Green mangos, tart and crispish, are cooked up into relishes, salads, vegetable side dishes, and even main courses in the tropics. It seems unlikely that those of us who do not have fruit in abundance will use it that way.

Like all fine fruits, mango at its best needs no embellishment. But the dense, honeyed pulp takes most comfortably to cooking and combining without losing its special qualities.

Mango's color, perfume, and texture work wonders for fruit and vegetable salads, or for combined salads of chicken, pork, or smoked meats, hot or cold.

In Asia, chilled slices of mango are paired with sweet, sticky glutinous rice and coconut milk for dessert or breakfast; less traditionally, rice or tapioca puddings are transformed. Arranged in a tart shell over pastry cream (coconut, rum, lemon, or vanilla flavored) mango shines. Sauté mango slices as you would bananas—in sugar, butter, and liquor. Top with ice cream.

Purée mango, adding fruit liquor, rum, or gin and lime juice to taste; pour over sliced fruits, ice cream, sponge cake, or angel cake. The golden purée has a smoothness usually associated with cooked, sweetened, and thickened sauces, but it is lighter on the tongue. Puréed mango (freezable) makes a luscious base for parfaits, ices, ice creams, sherbets, mousses, or frozen soufflés.

PREPARATION: Do not try to halve a mango then twist apart the two parts like an avocado, as a number of recipe books direct: You'll wind up with mango purée and skin. For this most clingstone and clingpeel of fruits, the following method for isolating the flesh is most reliable.

TO PEEL AND CUBE MANGO:

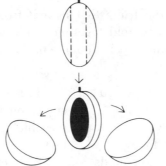

Set mango stem end up with narrow side facing you. Make vertical slice about ½ inch to right of stem so it barely clears the long, flat, narrow stone that runs almost the length of the fruit. Do same on the other side. Pare skin from seed section, then cut off flesh from seed.

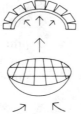

With butter knife, score flesh of each half in squares of desired size, cutting to but not through the skin. Press skin so cut side pops outward, hand grenade-like (also called hedgehog fashion). Slice cubes from skin.

TO SLICE: Divide fruit in seedless halves, as above. Slip paring knife under skin of cut half. Slowly carve out flesh in a single piece, cutting as close to skin as possible. Slice these hemispheres (more or less) to suit.

For large, plump mangos this slicing method works best: Holding the whole mango cradled in your palm, with a very sharp knife score the skin of the upturned half in lengthwise quarters. Gently pull the skin off. Cut the exposed flesh in slices, cutting each from the seed as closely as possible (still resting the mango in your hand). Do the same to the other side, which is going to be a bit trickier, but it does work.

Note: Mangos belong to the Anacardiaceae or cashew family, which includes such irritants as poison ivy and poison oak. Touching the juice may seriously swell and blister the skin of some allergic people, although eating the ripe fruit (the green can be harmful) may not bother these same individuals.

NUTRITIONAL HIGHLIGHTS: Mango is a superior source of vitamins A and C and a very good source of potassium. It is low in sodium and high in fiber. One medium fruit contains about 135 calories, which is moderately high.

PINEAPPLE AND KIWI WITH MANGO PURÉE

There are no limits to the fruits that benefit from proximity to a thick, golden mango purée. To meld flavors, fold together purée and fruits. For distinct flavors, arrange the fruits on plates and spoon a puddle of the sauce next to each arrangement.
4 servings

1 meaty mango, about 1 pound, peeled and cubed (see Preparation)
About 2 tablespoons lime juice
About 1 tablespoon fragrant honey
½ medium pineapple, about 1½ pounds
4 kiwis, chilled

1. Press cubed mango through a sieve, pushing through as much pulp as possible. Add lime juice and honey to taste.

2. Peel the pineapple; halve lengthwise. Cut in narrow crosswise wedges. Cut both ends off kiwis, then peel (I find a swivel vegetable peeler does this best). Quarter each lengthwise, then cut across in thin slices.

3. Either alternate layers of purée, pineapple, and kiwi in dessert glasses or fan the fruits on 4 dessert plates, then pour the sauce alongside.

Note: If you are preparing the fruits for dessert, rather than a breakfast or brunch, you might want to add bourbon, eau-de-vie, or rum in place of the lime juice.

MARY BETH CLARK'S MANGO AND SMOKED CHICKEN SALAD

New York cooking teacher Mary Beth Clark recommends this tropical pleasure for sultry evenings, when you want to stay clear of the stove. It makes for easy entertaining, as the chicken in curry mayonnaise (which should mellow for a day) improves if prepared ahead. Don't balk at the long ingredient list, which is mainly spices.

4 servings

CURRY MAYONNAISE
1 large egg yolk
¼ teaspoon dry mustard
⅛ teaspoon coarse kosher salt
1 tablespoon lemon juice
⅓ cup light vegetable oil (sunflower, safflower, or soybean)
⅓ cup light olive oil
½ teaspoon ground turmeric
½ teaspoon ground coriander
¼ teaspoon ground cumin
1/16 teaspoon ground cardamom
1/16 teaspoon dried dill
1½ teaspoons white wine vinegar

SALAD ASSEMBLY
1½ pounds smoked chicken or turkey breast
2 small, tender celery stalks, cut in ¼-inch dice (⅔ cup)
3 tablespoons minced onion
White pepper and ground allspice to taste
2 mangos, ¾–1 pound each, ripe but not soft, peeled and halved (see Preparation)
Optional: 4 teaspoons snipped chives
½ cup chopped toasted macadamia nuts

1. Make mayonnaise (ingredients should be at room temperature): Combine egg yolk, mustard, and salt in processor, blender, or bowl; beat lightly. Add lemon juice and beat until slightly foamy. Gradually add oils, blending constantly. When oil has been added, blend in remaining ingredients. Cover tightly and refrigerate 1–5 days.

2. Remove skin (and bone, if necessary) from chicken. Cut flesh in 1-inch pieces. Combine with celery, onion, and mayonnaise (add gradually; you may not want to use it all). Season with white pepper and allspice to taste. Cover and chill for 2–24 hours before serving.

3. Cut mangos vertically in ½-inch slices. Arrange in a fan shape on each of four plates. Place salad on the base of the fan. Sprinkle 1 teaspoon chives (if desired) and 2 tablespoons nuts over each.

RED CABBAGE AND MANGO SALAD WITH GINGER

Do not be put off by the odd sound of this brilliantly colorful, sprightly salad, with its pleasing contrast of textures and flavors. The crunchy fuchsia cabbage, vinegar-sautéed to retain its brightness, is set off by the tender, sweet mango chunks. Serve with barbecued chicken or ribs, grilled lamb, curries, or fried foods.

4 servings

1½ pounds red cabbage (1 very small cabbage)

2 tablespoons corn oil

1 tablespoon grated fresh ginger (no need to peel; just rinse)

3 tablespoons cider vinegar

3 tablespoons water

1½ teaspoons sugar

1 tablespoon soy sauce

Optional: Finely slivered fresh hot red chili-pepper to taste

Ripe mango, about 1 pound, in ½–¾-inch chunks (see Preparation)

1–2 tablespoons lime juice

1. Quarter cabbage and rinse. With curved side on cutting surface, diagonally cut core from each piece. Holding knife at same angle, continue cutting very thin slices. You should have 5–6 cups shreds.

2. Heat oil in wide skillet (not aluminum or iron). Add ginger and cabbage; toss to coat. Add vinegar and water. Toss over medium heat until crisp-tender—about 5–7 minutes (do not hurry by cooking on high heat: liquid cooks off too quickly). Add sugar, soy sauce, and optional chili; toss.

3. Transfer to wide serving dish. Cool; chill completely.

4. Sprinkle mango with lime juice to taste. Toss with chilled cabbage. Adjust seasoning by adding vinegar, lime juice, sugar (dissolve in either acid), soy sauce, and ginger, as needed.

JIM FOBEL'S FAST AND FRESH MANGO CHUTNEY

Unless you have a mango tree or a friend in the islands, it does not make sense to put up big batches of mango chutney—which is why sensible Jim Fobel devised this recipe. The quickly prepared, bright, spicy condiment can be used at once or stored in the refrigerator up to a week. It suits curried Indian foods, Chinese dishes (use as you would plum sauce), roast pork, beef, duck, turkey, and shrimp. It is also lovely, says Jim, dabbed on cream cheese-topped warm biscuits.

Makes about 2 cups

¼ cup packed brown sugar, light or dark

¼ cup sherry

¼ cup distilled white vinegar

¼ cup raisins, golden or dark

5 whole cloves

½ teaspoon freshly grated nutmeg

¼ teaspoon cinnamon

¼ teaspoon salt

½ cup (1 small) finely chopped onion

1 large or 2 medium (1½ pounds) firm-ripe mangos, cut in small cubes or coarsely chopped (see Preparation) to equal about 2 cups

2 tablespoons lime or lemon juice

1. In heavy, medium-sized nonaluminum saucepan combine sugar, sherry, vinegar, raisins, cloves, nutmeg, cinnamon, salt, and onion. Bring to a boil, then reduce heat and simmer 5 minutes.

2. Add mango and simmer, stirring, until thick—about 5 minutes. Remove from heat and stir in lime juice. Cool. Spoon into serving dish, then cover. Chill 2 hours or more.

MANGO-STRAWBERRY PARFAIT

Select particularly sweet-scented fruit for this low-calorie layered pink-and-peach dessert, or the taste will be bland.

4 servings

1¼ teaspoons gelatine

¼ cup water

1 large, ripe mango (1–1½ pounds), chilled

2 tablespoons rum

1 tablespoon lemon juice

1 egg white

Pinch salt

2½–3 tablespoons sugar

1 pint strawberries, rinsed and hulled

¼ teaspoon vanilla

½ cup yogurt

1. Sprinkle gelatine over water in a small saucepan; let stand 3–4 minutes to soften. Heat gently until granules dissolve.

2. Scrape mango flesh into processor container; add rum and lemon juice and whirl to purée; add gelatine and blend.

3. Beat egg white to form soft peaks; add salt. Gradually beat in 1 tablespoon sugar, forming moderately soft peaks. Fold together with mango purée and chill 2 hours or more.

4. Slice berries (reserve 4 for garnish). Mash roughly with remaining sugar to taste and vanilla; add yogurt. Chill until serving time.

5. To serve, layer mango and strawberry mixtures in stemmed glasses and top with the whole berries. Serve at once.

CARAMELIZED MANGO SLICES WITH ICE CREAM

Fast, easy, luscious: the same technique and flavoring as flamed bananas with the added beauty and perfume of mango slices. Vary the liquors to suit your taste and what you have on hand, substituting apricot, peach, or coconut liqueur for the orange, and bourbon or brandy for the rum.

2 servings

Ripe mango, about 1 pound
1 tablespoon butter
1 tablespoon brown sugar
1 tablespoon lime or lemon juice
2 tablespoons orange liqueur
2 tablespoons rum
2 large scoops vanilla, strawberry, or
    lemon ice cream
Slice of lime or lemon

1. Halve and peel the mango (see Preparation). Cut each half in 4 or 5 long slices.

2. Heat butter in heavy 9-inch skillet over moderately low heat. Add brown sugar and lime juice; stir. Add mango slices. Shake pan gently until fruit has softened and plumped a bit, 2–4 minutes, depending on ripeness.

3. Add liqueur and rum and tilt pan to flame. Shake for a moment until flame dies. Immediately divide between 2 dessert plates. Put a scoop of ice cream on each and serve at once, garnished with lime.

MANGO-BANANA SHERBET

Creamy, smooth, and full-flavored, this beautiful peachy-golden dessert tastes more like light ice cream or ice milk than sherbet.

Makes about 1 quart

1¾ cups water
About ½ cup sugar
2 medium mangos (about 1¾ pounds),
    chilled
1 medium-large very ripe banana
About ¼ cup lemon juice
About ¼ cup light rum

1. Combine water and ½ cup sugar and bring to a boil, stirring; simmer 5 minutes. Cool, then chill.

2. Peel and cube mangos (see Preparation). Purée in processor. Strain through a sieve into a bowl.

3. Purée banana, ¼ cup lemon juice, and ¼ cup rum. Add to mango mixture with chilled syrup. Taste and adjust sugar, lemon juice, and rum.

4. Pour into cream can of ice-cream machine and freeze according to the manufacturer's directions.

5. Scoop into a container and put in freezer for at least ½ day. Soften slightly in the refrigerator before serving.

MANIOC
See Yuca

MAUI ONION
See Onions, Sweet

MIRLITON
See Chayote

MONSTERA, CERIMAN
(Monstera deliciosa)

*C*hances that you will come across this amazing fruit are small unless you live in a big city on the East Coast, where the fruit is sometimes sent, or in California or Florida, where it flourishes. But monstera (Mon-STAIR-a)—the name it is known best by in Florida, although horticultural literature and the rest of the English-speaking world use *ceriman*—is so tasty and such a novelty that it is included here.

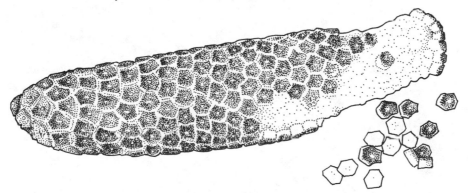

Familiar to many as the split-leaf philodendron, this native of tropical American forests, a member of the Arum family (to which belong more than 1,500 tropical species), is unlike any other fruit bearer you may have met heretofore. Its tremendous leaves (as wide as 3 feet) are perforated with decorative découpage (fenestration) that make it a well-represented ornamental in greenhouses, homes, and warm gardening areas around the country. Its flower consists of a central spadix surrounded by a hoodlike spathe—like others in the family, such as the jack-in-the-pulpit, calla lily, and anthurium. Twelve to fourteen months after the flowers appear the nearly foot-long spadix, the reptilian fruit, begins to ripen (one year's crop ripens as the next year's forms alongside it). The hexagonal puzzle pieces of this plantain-in-armor-plate soon begin to split from each other and from the creamy, banana-ish pulp within.

Only then is the fruit edible, for before that, sharp calcium oxalate crystals will irritate the tender membranes of the mouth, tongue, and throat (though they are not actually toxic, I am assured by plant pathologists who specialize in tropical fruits). Nor would you be inclined to eat the fruit prematurely in any case, because it tastes terrible. When ripe or softly overripe, however, it is scrumptious. The grayish-white pulp forms closely packed "kernels," whose tesselated pattern matches the design of the thick crocodile-pineapple scales. Pluck out this luscious, highly aromatic flesh (a fork does the job best) and savor a memorable blend of pineapple, mango, and banana. As you detach the fleshy plugs, you'll see a central core or stalk that is streaked with black and gray, which is normal.

SELECTION, STORAGE, AND PREPARATION: When you get your monster home, let it remain at room temperature; do not refrigerate. As the scales loosen or pop off, fork out the delicious pulp beneath. The fruit dictates when it is edible (it ripens rapidly if unevenly). Wrapping the fruit in plastic encourages it to ripen quickly and more or less all at once.

Although the Dade County Extension Service recommends combining it with cold water and condensed milk, I'd refrain. Enjoy the marvelous full flavor of this scarce and unusual fruit all by itself.

MOREL
**Black Morel *(Morchella angusticeps* or *Morchella elata)*
Yellow Morel or Golden Morel *(Morchella esculenta)*,
White Morel *(Morchella deliciosa)*; also called Morille**

*M*orels bring out spring madness: mycophiles mislead old friends to guard a secret woodland cache of the precious fungus, or pay wild prices in the marketplace to take them home; or spend hours waiting in line at restaurants that offer this fleeting delight. Like chanterelles, these celebrated mushrooms defy all efforts at cultivation

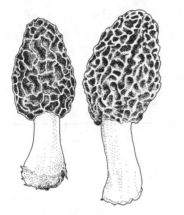

in captivity. Thin-fleshed, spongy, colored dark brown, yellow, or off-white, shaped like a rounded hollow Christmas tree, the pitted cap can be as small as a wild strawberry or as large as a lamb chop. The flavor of morels varies; it may suggest warm autumn leaves, hazelnuts, or even nutmeg. As with truffles and caviar, tasting is believing. Until recently, morels were obtainable only if you had a mushroom hunter for a pal. Now they are gathered in the wilds of the Pacific Northwest, Wisconsin, Michigan, and some areas of the East Coast.

SELECTION AND STORAGE: Beware of false morels or Gyromitras; in the West they are generally safe, if cooked thoroughly in an open pan, but in the East and Midwest the species isn't always edible. False morels, unlike morels, have caps that look like convoluted brains, and are not cone-shaped; in addition, the stems are thick and chambered, while true morels have straight, hollow stems.

Look for morels from early spring into July. Choose ones that smell sweetly earthy and nutty, with no sour tinge or slightly animal aroma. The pitted and whorled surfaces should not be wet or slippery, but rather spongy and quite dry to the touch. If they are too dry, almost crumbly, they are difficult to handle, but the flavor is not affected. Choose caps that are as clean as possible—although you may have no choice. Depending on the weather and where the fungi grew, they may be soil-speckled and slightly damp or dry and clean. Store accordingly, spreading in a single layer in a basket or dish in the refrigerator: If damp, cover with a sheet of paper towel; if dry, cover with a piece of barely moistened cheesecloth. Use within two or three days.

USE: Morels, with their maze of honeycomb-like ridges, are the perfect partners for sauces, which they flavor and absorb at the same time. The simpler the sauce, the better, as the mushroom fragrance is lost among overpowering flavors. Stick to light meats—chicken, Cornish hen, veal, rabbit, quail, turkey, pheasant—or starches and grains, such as pasta, rice, cornmeal, and potatoes, when combining morels with other foods. I find that a slow simmer in a light poultry or veal stock or in cream better develops the morel taste and texture than a sauté. Once cooked, liquid can be evaporated over moderate heat and the mushrooms browned lightly.

PREPARATION: Clean morels just before you cook them, not ahead of time. Trim off and discard the heavy tip of the base. Depending on the size of each mushroom, it can be left whole, halved lengthwise (if small), or cut across into ¼–½-inch rings, which resemble miniature wreaths. Slice off and chop any tough stems so that they will cook more quickly. It is always best to avoid subjecting mushrooms to water, but often morels are so dirty that you will have no choice. If that is the case, rinse them quickly in a colander under running water, tossing vigorously to dislodge any soil. Immediately blot dry on soft, absorbent towels. Cook at once.

NUTRITIONAL HIGHLIGHTS: Morels are very low in calories and a good source of vitamin D. They are high in fiber and contribute a fair amount of thiamine, riboflavin, and niacin.

Note: Do not eat raw morels, as they cause illness in many.

MORELS IN CREAM

Fresh morels are better served with a hot bath in thin cream than a searing experience in a buttery pan. The gentle cooking seems to enhance the flavors, while a sauté diminishes the subtleties.

3 or 4 servings as a side dish or first course

¾ cup light cream (see Note)
2 tablespoons minced shallots
⅛ teaspoon salt, or more
½ pound small fresh morels, trimmed, sliced, and cleaned (see Preparation)
Pepper
Minced fresh tarragon, chervil, or basil to taste

1. Combine cream, shallots, and ⅛ teaspoon salt in a small saucepan and simmer, covered, until shallots are soft—about 5 minutes.

2. Add morels to cream and simmer, covered, for 10–15 minutes, until tender; stir occasionally. Bring to a gentle boil and reduce cream to desired consistency. Add salt and pepper to taste and sprinkle with the herb.

Note: If you cannot get light cream in your neighborhood, complain to the grocer. Then, use heavy (or whipping) cream instead (half-and-half doesn't hold up to the job). Do not reduce too much or the rich cream will overpower the fragile fungus.

ROAST CHICKEN WITH MOREL STUFFING

Perfect for a springtime Sunday supper, or an elegant dinner party, this classic combination of butter-roasted chicken and tender morels is at once subtle and down-to-earth.

6 servings

4 tablespoons butter
¾ pound fresh morels, trimmed, sliced, and cleaned (see Preparation)
Chicken liver and heart, reserved from roasting chicken (below)
1 teaspoon salt
¹⁄₁₆ teaspoon cinnamon
⅛ teaspoon pepper
3½-pound chicken, approximately (see Note)
1 cup veal or beef stock
Watercress

1. Melt 2 tablespoons butter in a large skillet. Stir in morels; sauté over high heat until liquid evaporates. Chop liver and heart; add to skillet and sauté 30 seconds. Transfer to dish and toss with ¼ teaspoon salt, cinnamon, and pepper. Cool.

2. Remove loose fat from chicken. Dry bird and set on a rack until stuffing is cooled.

3. Distribute 1 tablespoon softened butter under breast skin. Fill cavity with morels, then sew closed; truss as usual, or as follows: Tie a length of string a yard long around the chicken's tail part so that you have an equal amount on each side; cross the drumsticks and tie together with this. Fold wings under the breast, tucking under neck skin to be held by them. Extend string on each side along breast into hole made by tucked wing. Turn bird over and tie ends of string together over the back.

4. Rub remaining tablespoon butter over chicken. Set bird, breast side down, on a rack in a pan. Roast 45 minutes in 325-degree oven.

5. Baste; sprinkle with ¼ teaspoon salt. Gently turn breast side up. Sprinkle with remaining ½ teaspoon salt and return to oven for 45 minutes, basting occasionally. Raise heat to 400 degrees and roast chicken until golden, about 15 minutes longer.

6. While chicken rests before carving, add stock to roasting pan (first skimming a little fat from juices if there is an overabundance). Simmer, stirring, until reduced by half. Carve chicken and arrange on a platter with watercress. Remove thread and pour morels and accumulated juices into reduced stock; bring to a simmer. Pour into a bowl and serve, spooned over the chicken.

Note: I find poultry browns better if allowed to dry somewhat before roasting. If you have the time, set the bird on a towel-covered rack in the refrigerator for a day, turning if you think of it. Let reach room temperature before roasting.

MORELS WITH PASTA IN LIGHT HERBAL CREAM

Soft noodles studded with succulent rounds of lacy-edged fresh morels are a delight to be savored at leisure, *à deux*.

2 generous main course servings, or 4 as an appetizer

½ cup light cream (see Note)
⅛ teaspoon dried tarragon
⅛ teaspoon dried thyme
1 tablespoon finely minced shallot
⅛ teaspoon salt, or more
¼ pound fresh morels, preferably small, trimmed, sliced, and cleaned (see Preparation)
½ pound fresh linguine, tagliatelle, or fettuccine
Pepper

1. Combine cream, tarragon, thyme, shallot, and ⅛ teaspoon salt in heavy 1-quart pot. Simmer, covered, until shallot is soft—about 5 minutes.

2. Add morels to cream; cover and simmer gently until tender—about 10–15 minutes.

3. Boil noodles in large pot of salted water until just tender. As they are finishing, uncover morels and boil for a few minutes, if necessary, to thicken slightly (sauce should not be too thick, however, but liquidy).

4. Drain noodles and combine at once with sauce. Season with salt and pepper and serve at once.

Note: If they don't carry light cream in your store, tell them they should. Then substitute heavy (or whipping) cream, being careful not to let it reduce and overpower the morels with its richness.

MUSHROOMS
See Bolete, Chanterelle, Enokidake, Morel, Oyster Mushroom, Shiitake, Wood Ear

MUSTARD GREENS
(*Brassica juncea* subspecies *rugosa*)
also Curled Mustard, Southern Curled Mustard

"*M*ustard greens" means different things to different people because the varieties can be dark, light, short, fat, smooth, curly, and so on. The kind most common in our markets in the United States has oval leaves of brilliant parrot or emerald green, frilled or scalloped around the edge, attached to fairly long stems. Rather soft and

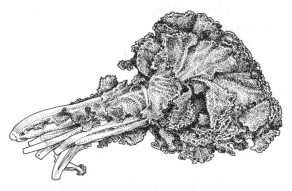

thin, with a slightly fuzzy finish and crinkly texture, they are cultivated and cooked in the largest volume. (The thick, smooth, swirling leaves of crispy, ultra-strong Chinese mustard greens appear exclusively in Oriental markets.) Sharp and pungent, mustard greens are the most powerful of the so-called bitter greens—with a taste very like that of prepared mustard, a hint of radish, and pleasant perfumy edge.

Why the leaves of the plant are so rarely used in cooking is a mystery to me. Although the seeds of mustard varieties are part of the larder in many parts of the world, both as a whole or ground spice and a prepared spread, I can locate very few cuisines that make use of the green. Despite the fact that the British devour tons of prepared mustard with their beef and chomp on the infant sprouts of closely related species in tea sandwiches, they do not go near the adult leaves. Only in some areas of India, China, Africa, and the American South does the green seem to have met up with the saucepan or stewpot. And very, very few recipes exist even among those who take the green for granted. Either no one really likes mustard greens or everyone knows how to cook them.

From all indications the plant has been cultivated in considerable quantity since prehistoric times and has only recently lost favor. Giuliano Bugialli wrote in his *Classic Techniques of Italian Cooking:* "Mustard greens were widely used in Italy in the Middle Ages, but have gradually declined in popularity. It is strange to think that one fourteenth-century cookbook has as many recipes for mustard greens as for any other vegetable, and yet that cooked green is unknown in Italy today."

SELECTION AND STORAGE: You can find mustard greens year round in markets that carry them, with the most bountiful supply from December through April. While some varieties are naturally chartreuse, avoid yellowed or brown leaves, or ones that are very dry. Stay clear of coarse, fibrous stems. Pick the smallest leaves for salads; for cooking, small, medium, or large leaves will do—tenderness does not seem to depend upon size.

Mustard greens fade quickly, becoming dry and yellowed within a few days. Wrap them tightly in plastic and keep in the refrigerator for as short a time as possible.

USE: Mustard leaves add a hot, radishy bite to salads, as well as a beautiful color and unusual texture. Their sharpness is best balanced by heated and/or sweet dressings, which temper the pungency.

Slivered mustard greens lend depth and brilliance to soups, a role they assume often in Chinese cooking in clear broths—although they suit creamy purées, as well.

In India mustard greens get a very long, slow cooking, with loads of butter for a velvety, mellow flavor. Ethiopians blend them with sweet spices and butter or intensify the heat with powerful chili-peppers and stew them with beef. They are then dipped up with soft, thin bread.

If you do not fancy much bite, combine the sharp greens with mellow ones, such as spinach or Swiss chard; or purée and thicken with bland vegetables such as beans and potatoes. If you want no bite at all, but a light flavor and brilliant color, blanch the greens in boiling water for a minute before cooking. This eliminates just about all the bitterness (but a good deal of the flavor, as well). The greens can then be sautéed, like spinach, or puréed.

Do not cook in aluminum or iron pans.

PREPARATION: Clean mustard greens by removing any wilted or yellow leaves, then dropping into a sink filled with tepid water. Dunk up and down, then lift out gently so sand falls to the bottom. Drain sink, then repeat until you are sure leaves are thoroughly cleaned. For salads, drain and spin dry, then wrap in toweling and refrigerate. Strip the leaves from the stems at serving time. For cooking you need not dry the leaves; just remove and discard the stems.

NUTRITIONAL HIGHLIGHTS: Mustard greens are very low in calories, with only 20 calories per cup (cooked). They are a splendid source of vitamin A and a fairly good source of vitamin C, calcium, and potassium.

SAUSAGES AND MUSTARD GREENS WITH SPAGHETTI

For those fond of the distinctive bitterness of mustard greens, this rustic dish will be a satisfying meal-in-one. The sweet sausages, bland pasta, and intense greens balance naturally.

2 servings

¾–1 pound sweet Italian sausages
About 1 pound small mustard greens (or
    1½ pounds large, leggy ones),
    washed and stripped (see
    Preparation)
½ cup water
¼ teaspoon salt, or to taste
½ pound spaghetti
1 tablespoon olive oil
Vinegar to taste
Pepper

1. Prick sausages; cook, covered, in a large flameproof casserole with a thin layer of water for about 5 minutes, until no longer pink. Uncover, evaporate liquid, and cook over moderate heat, turning often, until browned on all sides. Transfer to a board.

2. Chop mustard leaves; put into casserole and cook over high heat until wilted. Add water and salt and simmer, partly covered, for about 15 minutes, or until tender.

3. Slice sausages and add. Stir over moderate heat, uncovered, until liquid evaporates.

4. Meanwhile boil spaghetti until tender; drain. Toss in a heated bowl with oil. Add the mustard greens and sausages. Season with vinegar and pepper and serve.

SALAD OF MUSTARD GREENS AND AVOCADO WITH SWEET-HOT DRESSING

When boiling hot, sweet dressing is poured over mustard greens, it softens the texture and modifies the bitterness. (If they still remain too strong for your taste, however, try combining them with lettuce and other milder greens.) Although both Southerners and Pennsylvania Dutch include such dressings in their repertoire, this recipe is taken from neither—being lighter and less sweet.

4 servings

1 pound small, short-stemmed mustard greens, washed (see Preparation)
4 scallion greens, thinly sliced
⅓ cup cider vinegar
2 tablespoons brown sugar
1 tablespoon corn oil
About ½ teaspoon Worcestershire sauce
About ¼ teaspoon Tabasco or other hot pepper sauce
1 large avocado, diced

1. Spin-dry mustard greens or dry thoroughly on soft towels. Strip leaves from stems and cut into thin slivers. Place in a bowl with scallions.

2. Combine vinegar, sugar, oil, Worcestershire, and Tabasco in a small non-aluminum pot; bring to a boil, stirring. Pour onto greens and toss quickly; add avocado, toss gently, and serve at once.

SCALLOPS AND SHRIMP WITH MUSTARD GREEN SAUCE

A beautiful and elegant first course or main dish, rich in complex taste. The shrimp and sea scallops are succulent and pale, with a sweetness that is as complementary to the sauce as the coloring.

4 servings as a main course, 6–8 as a first course

1 pound medium shrimp
½ pound or more meaty fish trimmings or meaty fish bones
2 tablespoons vegetable oil
1 large shallot, chopped
¼ cup dry vermouth
2½ cups water
10 ounces small mustard greens, well washed (see Preparation)
1 tablespoon coarse kosher salt
⅔ cup heavy (or whipping) cream
1 tablespoon butter
½ pound sea scallops, halved horizontally, if small, horizontally and crosswise, if large
Pepper

1. Shell and devein the shrimp, reserving shells. Rinse fish bones thoroughly, removing gills and sacs, if any. Heat 1 tablespoon oil in medium saucepan. Add shells, fish bones and trimmings, and shallot; stir for a few minutes. Add vermouth and water; bring to a simmer, skimming. Simmer 20 minutes, partly covered.

2. Strip mustard green leaves from stems. Boil 2 quarts water; add salt. Drop in leaves. Boil 2 minutes. Drain, drop into ice water; drain again (do not squeeze dry). Purée in blender or processor. Press through sieve, leaving as little solids as possible.

3. Strain fish stock through sieve lined with damp cheesecloth. Boil to reduce to ⅔ cup. Add cream and boil to reduce to ¾ cup. Add mustard greens and simmer until desired consistency and flavor are achieved, stirring often.

4. At the same time, heat remaining tablespoon oil and the butter in large skillet. Sprinkle shrimp and scallops with salt and pepper. Sauté until barely cooked through—about 2 minutes. Cover and let stand 2 minutes. Pour accumulated juice into sauce and boil a moment; season.

5. Divide sauce among 4 heated plates. Set scallops and shrimp on the sauce and serve.

Note: Sauce can be prepared ahead, if you wish. When cream mixture has reduced sufficiently, pour into dish in bowl of ice water to cool, stirring occasionally. Cover and refrigerate until about 10 minutes before serving time. Heat on low, add mustard greens, and proceed with step 4.

≥ᴥ *Mustard greens can be substituted for collards in Braised Collards with Ginger and Chili-Pepper (page 150) and Spicy Collards (page 152).*

ÑAME
See Yam

NAPA (OR NAPPA)
See Chinese Cabbage

NOPALES, CACTUS PADS
(*Opuntia ficus-indica* and other Opuntia species)
also Nopalitos, and, incorrectly, Cactus Leaves

*F*ive years ago if you had not been brought up in a Mexican community or read cookbooks with a fine-toothed comb, you would probably never have encountered a *nopalito*, or been able to find out what it was. Now, with the Mexican population growing and restaurants popping up overnight, it is possible to pick up fresh cactus

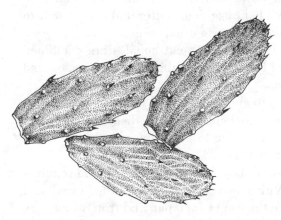

pads in supermarkets throughout a good part of the country. What is mysterious is why Mexico and a few parts of Central America are the only countries that have incorporated the (admittedly unlikely) vegetable into their meals and cookbooks, since many people in southern Europe, North Africa, South Africa, Southwest Asia, Australia, and Central and South America choose to consume quantities of the cactus pear, colorful offspring of several Opuntia varieties that supply the pads.

The above might lead one to the conclusion that nopales (no-PAH-les), to use their most common Mexican name, are good only if you're starving, which is far from the case—although you might certainly call them an acquired taste, or more exactly, texture. If okra doesn't appeal to you, pass over the next pages, but if you like the idea of a vegetable that is soft but crunchy, with the flavor of green pepper, string beans, and asparagus (all touched with a sorely citric edge) and the slipperiness of okra, read on.

SELECTION AND STORAGE: Most markets stock the tender new growth of the cactus, which is what you want—not the larger plate- to platter-sized pads. These are at their peak in midspring, but can be found erratically from early spring through late fall. Select medium-green, crisp-firm, smallish paddles (very small ones have a relatively higher proportion of prickers and eyes, which will require longer cleaning time). Cultivated nopales (most are wild) have a thinner, prickerless pad. They should show no dryness, limpness, sogginess, or fibrous joints.

If the nopales are bright and firm, they should last for weeks in the refrigerator, wrapped in plastic.

USE: I prefer the flavor of cooked nopales, although they can be eaten raw. Steam them quickly over boiling water for a few minutes (do not cook away the pleasing crunch), then slice to suit; or sauté cut-to-size pieces in butter or oil for a few minutes; or follow the long-cooking method described in Nopales with Tomatoes and Herbs (page 318), if you wish to cook off the sticky substance and don't mind a softer, grayish vegetable.

Cooked nopales combine particularly well with scrambled eggs and omelets—with or without cheese, onions, cilantro, scallions, or oregano and salsa. Mingle diced, sautéed bits with chili-pepper and sausage or grated cheese in tortillas. Cool steamed pads, cut into strips, and combine in the traditional Mexican salad of skinned, cubed tomatoes, onion, oregano, cilantro, chilies, and oil and vinegar; add crumbled feta and olives for a delicious variation. Or use in any salad, as you would a cooked green vegetable.

Stir squares of raw cactus into soups about ten minutes before cooking is completed to add texture and a slight tartness, and to thicken slightly, as okra or filé powder would. Stir dice into chili or beans during the last quarter hour of cooking.

In Mexico cooked small cactus pads or strips of large pads are sandwiched to enclose a piece of cheese, then dipped into a light egg-flour batter and deep-fried, to be served as is or briefly heated in a rich sauce of puréed dried chilies.

At a restaurant in New York City, barely cooked thin-cut nopales are combined with diced onions and tomatoes, then heated briefly in a combination of vinegars and oil to be served with nut-crusted meat or fish.

While boiling at length is generally the method recommended for cooking nopales, I find all others superior. And, although service alone, as a side dish, is a frequent suggestion, nopales seem to be much more enjoyable to most diners in combination with a variety of contrasting textures and seasonings.

PREPARATION: Cactus sold in American stores is quite free of stickers, and requires only a minor amount of care and cleaning. With a swivel peeler, zip off the "eyes" and any stickers, a fast and easy job. Then shave the rim of each pad and trim off any dry or fibrous areas. All of this is as fast as peeling a cucumber, or faster. Rinse thoroughly to remove any stray prickers and some of the sticky fluid that will be exuded.

NUTRITIONAL HIGHLIGHTS: Nopales are an excellent source of vitamin A and vitamin C. They also contain a fair amount of the B vitamins and iron.

SCRAMBLED EGGS WITH NOPALES

For a change from unadorned Sunday brunch eggs, try this quick-to-prepare, pleasantly different variation along with a little ham and ripe tomatoes.

3 servings

2 tablespoons pine nuts (pignolia)
2 tablespoons butter
¼ pound nopales, de-prickered, rinsed, cut in ¼-inch squares (see Preparation)
2 tablespoons peeled and diced medium-hot green chili-pepper (see page 125, to peel chili-peppers)
7 eggs
Salt and pepper

1. Toast nuts in a skillet over low heat until lightly browned, stirring often; reserve.

2. Melt 1 tablespoon butter in the skillet and stir in cactus; toss gently over moderate heat until crisp-tender—about 4–5 minutes. Stir in chili-pepper.

3. Blend eggs, adding salt to taste. Stir remaining butter into cactus and chilies; add eggs and stir often until set to taste.

4. Sprinkle with pepper and pine nuts and serve at once.

SAUTÉED NOPALES, PEPPERS, AND CORN

This simple and quick side dish is unusual—but likable. The sorrel-sour taste of the crisp cactus is sweetly complemented by the accommodating corn.

4 servings

2 large red bell peppers
1 medium-large onion
2 tablespoons butter
3 or 4 ears of small summer corn
½ pound fresh, firm nopales, deprickered, cut in ¼–½-inch dice (see Preparation)
Finely minced cilantro or parsley

1. Halve peppers, then remove seeds and stems. Cut into ¼–½-inch squares. Cut onions the same size. Cook both vegetables in butter in a heavy pan over moderate heat until just softened.

2. Shuck corn, then cut from cob (there should be about 1½ cups).

3. Add nopales and corn to peppers and onion; stir over high heat until vegetables are cooked through, but firm-tender, about 5 minutes. Sprinkle with herbs and serve at once.

NOPALES WITH TOMATOES AND HERBS

This unusual long-cooking technique, recommended by Diana Kennedy in *Recipes from the Regional Cooks of Mexico*, produces nopales that are free of the sticky coating that some dislike. The cactus acquires a grayer tinge and slightly more tart flavor cooked this way.

4 servings

1 pound nopales, small and thin, prickers removed (see Preparation)

About 2 tablespoons full-flavored olive oil

2 medium garlic cloves, minced

About ¼ teaspoon salt

¼ cup chopped sweet onion, such as Vidalia, Walla Walla, Maui, or Spanish

1 tablespoon red wine vinegar

About 1 pint small, full-ripe cherry tomatoes, halved

Fresh minced herbs to taste: oregano, thyme, basil, savory

Pepper to taste

1. Cut nopales into strips about ¼ by 2 inches.

2. Heat 2 tablespoons oil in large skillet; add garlic and toss. Add cactus and ¼ teaspoon salt; toss to coat. Cover and cook over moderately low heat until sticky juices are thoroughly exuded and cactus is not quite tender—about 5–8 minutes; stir fairly often. Mixture will be quite soupy.

3. Uncover and stir often over moderate heat, until tender and no longer sticky, about 10 minutes.

4. Off heat toss with onion and vinegar; add tomatoes and herb and toss gently. Add salt, pepper, and additional olive oil to taste, if desired. Serve warm, or at room temperature.

NOPALITO-CHEESE CRISPS ON TOMATO PURÉE

Although they take a bit of time to assemble, cornmeal-coated packets of cheese-stuffed cactus are a colorful and unusual first course for a new-style Mexican or Southwestern dinner.

4 generous first-course servings

SAUCE

2 medium garlic cloves

1½ pounds very ripe tomatoes, peeled (see page 23) and seeded

1–3 teaspoons tomato paste

Salt to taste

STUFFED NOPALES

1 pound tender, thin nopales, prickers removed (see Preparation)

Corn oil for frying

About ½ pound fairly firm cheese, such as Monterey jack or Cheddar

3 eggs

½ teaspoon salt

1½ cups stone-ground cornmeal

Optional: Thin strips of peeled medium-hot chili, such as poblano or chile verde (see page 125 to peel chili)

About 2 tablespoons minced cilantro

1. With motor running, drop garlic in processor; mince. Add tomatoes and 1 teaspoon paste; purée. Strain through sieve into saucepan.

2. Simmer until lightly thickened, stirring often. You should end up with about 1 cup. Add salt and more tomato paste to taste. Reserve.

3. Drop nopales in boiling water and cook until tender—about 5 minutes. Drain. Set on towels to dry. Cut in neat rectangles about 1½ by 2½ inches.

4. Heat 1 inch oil in a skillet, preferably an electric one or similar thermostatically controlled frying unit. Cut ⅛-inch-thick rectangles of cheese a little smaller than cactus pieces. Beat eggs and salt in bowl. Spread cornmeal on a plate.

5. Sandwich a slice of cheese (and optional chili strip) between 2 cactus pieces. Holding carefully, dip thoroughly in egg mixture, then coat completely with cornmeal. Drop into heated oil and continue assembling and frying "sandwiches." Set tomato purée over low heat.

6. Fry each package until well crisped and golden, about 5 minutes, turning once. Drain on paper toweling. Pour about ¼ cup tomato purée on each of 4 heated serving plates. Divide crisps among plates and serve at once, sprinkled with cilantro.

SALAD OF NOPALES AND CRACKED WHEAT

A Middle Eastern tabbouleh salad with a Southwestern touch—tender-crisp, slightly slippery strips of cactus. This dish is particularly suited to those not yet familiar with the unusual vegetable, its eccentric texture barely evident in an otherwise familiar culinary alliance.

6–8 servings

1½ cups cracked wheat or bulgur wheat, coarse cut

5 cups boiling water

¾ pound small nopales, prickers removed (see Preparation)

⅓ cup lemon juice

1½ teaspoons coarse kosher salt, or to taste

¼ cup full-flavored olive oil

1 small red onion, coarsely diced (¾ cup)

1 fresh medium-hot chili-pepper (such as poblano or New Mexico)

1 cup coarsely minced cilantro

1. Combine cracked wheat and boiling water in a bowl; let stand until wheat is no longer crunchy in the center, about ½ hour. Drain in colander lined with cheesecloth, then twist the corners of cloth together to squeeze out as much liquid as possible. Dry wheat on a towel, tossing.

2. Place nopales on a steamer rack over boiling water; cover and cook until barely tender throughout—about 4 minutes. Let cool entirely. Cut in strips ¼ inch wide.

3. Combine lemon juice, salt, and olive oil; blend. Toss with nopales and onion. Remove stem and seeds from chili, then cut into small dice. Add to nopales and toss. Combine with cracked wheat and cilantro and mix well. Cover and chill until serving time.

O K R A
(Abelmoschus esculentus and *Hibiscus esculentus)*
also Lady's Fingers, Gombo, Quingombo, Okro, Ochro, Bamia, Quiabo

*O*kay, let's get this straight: okra is a lovely, tender, sweet-tasting vegetable—that is slippery, slimy, mucilaginous. If the mere idea of such a texture repels you, you shouldn't bother with it. Just about every cookbook that addresses the subject implies, in some fashion, that this slipperiness can be avoided if you will just cook the poor pod

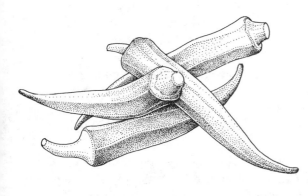

properly. I disagree: the deliciously smooth, light, clean slick that okra exudes is supposed to be there.

As a nation we seem to have a horror of slipperiness in food (noodles are the exception). In Japan, the slithery slurp of soft seaweed is desirable, as is okra's texture: in China a slippery sensation balances a crisp one in a meal, as bitter does sweet. In the Balkans, the Caribbean, the Middle East, South America, Africa, India, recipes for okra do not begin with apologies, and cooks do not hide its stickiness: they *like* it. At any rate, it may be that an aversion to such a texture is often the result of habit, not genuine distaste. Not long ago vegetables were cooked to a pulp and everyone salted food at the table without tasting. Culinary and nutritional awareness has changed those habits. There's a lot of good slippery stuff out there to try. End of sermon.

On the subject of okra, Waverley Root wrote: "A vegetable is not without honor, save in its own country" (*Food*, Simon and Schuster, 1980)—in this case, our country, not its, since okra probably began its wanderings somewhere around Ethiopia. The unusual vegetable, a member of the Mallow family (like cotton) was a well-liked food and pleasing to the eye (as its scientific name reveals, it is a hibiscus) with "attractive dark-eyed sulfur-yellow flowers" (U.S. Department of Agriculture Handbook 323). It spread to North Africa and the Middle East and reached Brazil about halfway through the seventeenth century. But neither explorers nor conquerors brought it to the southern United States; slaves did. The gumbo of Louisiana took its name from the same vegetable that was called *ngombo* in Angola. The word okra itself comes from *nkruma* (one of many transliterations) from a Ghanaian language.

Like other soul foods, okra's transition from "ethnic food" to chic vegetable has been recent, a result of the American restaurant boom and increased interest in regional "real" food. Although okra had made its way into American kitchens by the late 1800s, recipes for it were much the same until the turn of the century: "Boil until dissolved, then strain," was the most common advice, as it was used almost exclusively as a thickener, with soups its raison d'être. Gradually the vegetable itself began to be acknowledged as well: a pretty, bright, tender pod with a fresh taste between that of asparagus and eggplant. Although still cooked excessively by contemporary standards, the amount of time that Mrs. Rorer suggested in her 1902 cookbook—30–45 minutes —was considerably less than the two hours in some earlier books. That same year Escoffier recommended okra as a creamed vegetable or garnish in his *Guide Culinaire* and simply indicated cooking "until tender," leaving room for plenty of interpretation. A glance through cookbooks published during the last ten years suggests a range of thirty seconds to fifteen minutes: a whole new way of thinking.

SELECTION AND STORAGE: Okra can be found year round, but is most abundant during the summer months. There will be differences in size, shape, and color (a burgundy baby is newly available) from one variety to another, but okra is always picked in an infant stage, or it will be better suited to rope making, a common use for the mature vegetable. The torpedo-shaped pods may vary from 2 to 7 inches long, or thereabouts, but all should be bright-colored, with no signs of spotting or molding. Check carefully for dryness and flabbiness, which indicate the cooked vegetable will be woody and fibrous.

Okra keeps very poorly, a day or two at most. Store in a paper bag in the warmer part (usually the upper shelf) of your refrigerator, as it becomes damaged by cold below 45 degrees.

USE: Just about all that you can't do with okra is make dessert from it and, to my taste, purée it. It can be steamed, boiled, pickled, sautéed, deep-fried (dip in salted beaten egg, then fine cornmeal), braised, or made into salad and soup. It can even be cut, dried in the sun, and hung in a necklace to wait for the next crop, if you're old-fashioned.

Tiny fresh okra, untrimmed, merely blanched or steamed, cooperate with the same kind of hot and cold sauces that asparagus do. Marjorie Kinnan Rawlings describes such a feast in her *Cross Creek Cookery* (Scribner, 1981): "Arrange like the spokes of a wheel on hot individual serving dishes. Place individual bowls of Hollandaise in the centres of the dishes. The okra is eaten as one eats unhulled strawberries, lifting with the fingers by stem ends and dipping into the Hollandaise. I recommend this to those who think they don't like okra."

Okra works well with acids—such as tomato, lemon juice, and vinegar; with spices and herbs; and in vegetable combinations, such as ratatouille or other medleys, Mediterranean or Asian. In fact, any recipe for eggplant seems to suit it, provided you cut the cooking time considerably.

Sliced and added to soups during the last ten minutes of cooking, okra thickens with remarkable power, rather like cornstarch. For clear soups, the flowerlike rounds of bright green and quickly achieved clean viscosity make for a delightfully simple and attractive finish. Figure on about 1 cup sliced pods for each 3 cups liquid.

However you cook, stay clear of aluminum or iron pans.

PREPARATION: For tiny okra, you need only rinse it, dry well, then cut off the stem and very top of the caps. For slightly larger okra, you will need to shave off the cap, but do not open the capsule to expose the seeds. For dishes in which the okra will be sliced, cut off the caps from the well-washed and dried okra, then slice. Some fuzzy varieties may also need rubbing with a towel prior to washing and trimming.

Even though I like the okra slipperiness, out of curiosity I have tested some of the techniques offered in cookbooks to supposedly rid it of this quality. So that you do not waste your time on the same, let me tell you that there is no difference whatsoever (except a tad less flavor) when okra has been soaked in water acidulated with vinegar, whether for ten minutes or two hours. Nor does a preliminary blanching affect this trait.

NUTRITIONAL HIGHLIGHTS: Okra is a good source of vitamin A and vitamin C. It also provides a modest amount of folic acid and calcium.

STEAMED OKRA

Sweet, tender, brightly verdant—okra prepared this way is one of the two best dishes for beginners (the other is deep-fried). It keeps its full flavor and becomes less mucilaginous than when cooked by other methods. This has become more common than string beans in my home.

A caveat: there is no hiding poor quality in this naked presentation. Use only crisp, small, unblemished, green-green pods.

4 servings

1 pound fresh, small okra pods
Butter to taste
Salt and pepper

1. Rinse okra. Shave off stems and top of caps without cutting into the pods.

2. Place on a steamer rack over boiling water. Cover and steam until just barely tender, 3–5 minutes, depending on size of pods.

3. Turn immediately into a hot dish, toss with butter, salt, and pepper. Serve at once.

MARINATED OKRA FROM MR. B'S

In New Orleans the Brennan family rules the restaurant roost, from Commander's Palace to Mr. B's, the most "now" of the places run by the legendary dynasty. Ralph Brennan features dishes with (as he puts it) a "creole/cajun touch" and a "contemporary flair." This plain and simple first course is lighter and fresher than most okra dishes you'll meet up with in Cajun country.

4 servings

1 pound very small okra pods
¼ cup red wine vinegar
About ¼ teaspoon salt
⅓ cup olive oil
1 small red onion, sliced and separated into rings
Lettuce
1 pint cherry tomatoes

1. Trim okra stems without cutting into the pods. Drop into boiling salted water and cook until just tender, but not soft—about 3–4 minutes. Drain, then drop into ice water. Drain and dry.

2. Combine vinegar and salt to taste. Add olive oil and onion. Cover and chill in nonaluminum container for 2 hours or more. Drain and serve on lettuce, garnished with cherry tomatoes.

Note: If you like, steam okra, as I do, instead of boiling.

OKRA, TOMATOES, AND ONIONS WITH BACON

While the combination of okra and tomatoes may be familiar, it is such a delicious pairing that it warrants frequent repetition. Here, a smoky underpinning of slab bacon adds its distinctive savor to the speedily cooked sliced okra, diced onion, and sweet strips of plum tomato. I cook the okra just until it loses its crunch, but some may prefer a meltingly soft vegetable. Both are delicious: it's simply a matter of taste.

4 servings

5 ounces fatty slab bacon, cut into ¼-inch dice
1 large onion, cut into ½-inch dice (about 1¼ cups)
1 pound tender okra, rinsed and well dried

1 pound plum tomatoes, peeled (page 23), seeded, cut into ½-inch pieces
½ cup water
Pepper to taste
Minced parsley

1. Gently cook bacon in a heavy skillet or flameproof casserole until it is well browned and has rendered a good bit of fat. Skim out pieces with a slotted spoon and reserve them. (Drain off some fat, if you like.) Add onion to fat in pan and cook, covered, until soft, 7–8 minutes.

2. Trim off caps from okra; cut okra into ½-inch slices. Add to onions with tomatoes and water; bring to a simmer. Cook, partly covered, over moderate heat until okra is just tender—about 10 minutes. Toss with the bacon and pepper to taste. Sprinkle with parsley and serve hot.

PICKLED OKRA

Okra makes a particularly good tart-hot pickle, as the vegetable retains its flavor and tender-crisp texture. Serve alongside rich smoked pork, with braised bean dishes, or as a condiment to accompany sweet Oriental pork, shrimp, and chicken dishes.

Makes about 6 pints

2½ pounds very small, bright fresh okra pods
6 tiny dried hot chili-peppers or ¾ teaspoon crushed hot pepper flakes
6 medium garlic cloves
3 teaspoons mustard seeds, lightly bruised
1½ teaspoons dill seeds
1½ teaspoons coriander seeds
2 cups cider vinegar
2 cups rice vinegar
2 cups water
4 tablespoons coarse kosher salt

1. Rinse okra, then dry on a soft towel. Trim stems, but leave a little nub; do not cut into caps or pods.

2. In each of 6 clean pint canning jars place a dried pepper, a garlic clove, ½ teaspoon mustard seeds, ¼ teaspoon dill seeds, and ¼ teaspoon coriander seeds. Pack okra pods in jars, with tips and stems alternating. Pack just firmly enough to keep upright.

3. In nonaluminum saucepan combine cider and rice vinegar, water, and salt. Bring to a boil. Fill jars to within ½ inch of rims. Wipe rims, place a new 2-piece lid on each, then fasten screwbands.

4. Place jars on rack in deep kettle half filled with boiling water. Add boiling water to cover lids by 2 inches. Bring to a boil; cover, and boil (process) 10 minutes.

5. Transfer jars to a towel. Cool completely. Store for about a month before serving.

BARBARA SPIEGEL'S CAPE COD GUMBO

Barbara Spiegel summers in Falmouth, on the Cape. One big dinner party she gave there featured this Louisiana-style soup-stew—transformed to a different kettle of fish by its Massachusetts ingredients. What both gumbos have in common is okra, used as a thickening agent.

10–12 servings

½ cup corn oil

1½ cups finely chopped onion

1½ cups finely chopped celery

1 cup finely chopped carrot

3 large garlic cloves, finely chopped

2 medium red bell peppers, finely chopped

2 medium yellow bell peppers (or substitute green), finely chopped

¾ pound Canadian bacon, finely chopped

2½ pounds okra, trimmed and sliced

1–2 teaspoons cayenne pepper

28-ounce can peeled tomatoes, crushed (or pressed through food mill)

15 cups broth (see Note)

5 pounds littleneck clams, well scrubbed

2½ pounds sea scallops

9 cups freshly cooked long-grain white rice (2½ cups raw)

1. Heat ¼ cup oil in large, heavy skillet; add onion, celery, and carrot. Cook over medium heat, stirring occasionally, for 10 minutes. Add garlic and peppers; cook, stirring occasionally, until peppers soften, about 10 minutes. Transfer to large soup pot.

2. Heat remaining ¼ cup oil in frying pan over moderately high heat; add Canadian bacon, half the sliced okra, and cayenne pepper to taste. Stir and scrape until very sticky, about 10 minutes.

3. Pour in tomatoes; scrape and stir to deglaze the sticky pan. Transfer mixture to soup pot.

4. Add broth; cook at a gentle simmer, partly covered, for 2 hours or longer, as convenient (up to about 3 hours is fine). Season to taste (taking note of the fact that the salty seafood is yet to come).

5. Fifteen minutes before serving, add remaining 1¼ pounds okra to simmering soup. Five minutes before serving, turn heat to high and add clams and scallops. Cover pot and cook only until clams open, 2–3 minutes.

6. Ladle into bowls and top with hot rice, southern-style (or pour the soup over the rice, northern-style).

Note: For this large quantity of liquid, use what is convenient, combining chicken broth, fish stock, clam broth, and water. If using bottled clam broth, include no more than 5 cups, or you risk oversalting.

MARTHA WASHINGTON'S SHRIMP AND OKRA IN PEANUT SAUCE
(Caruru)

This intriguing and luscious recipe comes from a lively Brazilian caterer, Martha Washington (yes, her real name), who got it from her sister Ruth. She serves it with white rice that has been lightly browned in butter with onions, then cooked in coconut milk—exactly the right accompaniment. In Brazil the dish is served on September 27, to celebrate the feast day of Cosme and Damião, patron saints of twins.

4–6 servings

1 pound firm, small okra
3 limes
Salt
1 pound medium shrimp in the shell, rinsed
2 tablespoons water
3 tablespoons olive oil
1½ tablespoons minced garlic
1 medium onion, chopped
¼ cup coarsely chopped parsley
1 tablespoon palm oil (dendê; see Note)
½ cup very finely ground roasted, unsalted peanuts
½ ounce ground dried shrimp (see Note)
Hot pepper oil (see Note)

1. Rinse okra pods and dry each thoroughly. Trim off caps, then cut across in ¾-inch slices. Combine in a bowl with juice of 2 limes and big pinch salt; let stand 15 minutes or longer.

2. Combine shrimp in pan with juice of remaining lime and 2 tablespoons water; cover and simmer 2 minutes. Uncover and cool.

3. Combine okra in nonaluminum saucepan with salted water to cover; simmer, covered, for 5–10 minutes, or until tender to taste (in Brazil, they like it cooked soft). Meanwhile, peel shrimp (reserve cooking liquid). Drain okra.

4. Heat olive oil in large skillet over moderately low; add garlic and stir until golden. Add onion and stir until softened. Add shrimp, parsley, and 2 tablespoons reserved cooking liquid; salt to taste. Remove from heat and stir in palm oil.

5. Add okra. Blend peanuts and dried shrimp thoroughly; stir into the okra-shrimp. Add hot oil and salt to taste. Reheat, if necessary.

Note: Palm oil is available in some South American shops; although it adds an inimitable flavor, it can be left out, since there is no substitute. Dried shrimp and hot oil (chili oil) can be found in Chinese and Asian groceries.

ONIONS, SWEET
MAUI, VIDALIA, WALLA WALLA
(Allium cepa)

While the onions listed above are rather different from most other large onion varieties, they are similar to one another (growers of each will probably come after me with pitchforks for saying such a thing). Although planted in different places (each name indicates the growing area) and harvested at different times, the onions are all relatively large, pale, and exceptionally sweet, mild, and juicy.

Maui onions are grown, not surprisingly, in Maui, Hawaii. Like the Vidalias, they are a Yellow Granex type hybrid. When cultivated in Hawaii, the soil and weather conditions on the island produce an onion that is low in bite, high in sugar and moisture; when planted elsewhere, the results are more like common yellow onions. The earliest sweet onion marketed, it may appear in markets, primarily on the West Coast, from April or May through June. The Maui is usually pearly-pale and flattened; but it may also be yellowish and globose or teardrop-shaped.

Vidalia onions (named for a town in Georgia, pronounced with a long "i") have become chic fare during the past few years. Like the Maui, they are a hybrid of the Yellow Granex type, which when planted in other parts of the country (usually Texas, Arizona, and California), can be as biting as other yellow onions. But growing conditions in the South permit farmers to harvest the onion early, when slightly green, before it has developed the strong taste and "heat" that come with the usual two to three weeks of field drying that most onions require. The quite large, flattened, pale onions are briefly available during May and June in specialty shops and through mail-order sources (in season only; do not try to keep them or order them beyond late spring). The juicy, sweet allium is usually marketed with a decal that declares its place of origin or in a sack that does the same.

Walla Walla Onions or *Walla Walla Sweets*, grown in the state of Washington in and around the city whose name they bear, are available, mostly by mail order, during July and August. The name Walla Walla is applied to a distinct variety that has been raised for about seventy-five years, primarily from strains developed from Italian seeds. These onions are generally very large, but can range from a mere 3 ounces to nearly 1½ pounds. For the most part they are light gold-beige, quite round—close to the shape of a Spanish onion—and creamy, with very thick layers that make perfect onion rings. They are at their best raw, or only lightly cooked, as they quickly become mushy when subjected to heat.

SELECTION AND STORAGE: Look for Maui onions from April through June, Vidalia onions during May and June, and Walla Wallas during July and August. They are all extremely perishable because of their high moisture content, deteriorating much more rapidly than stored onions. Choose ones that are absolutely dry, firm-crisp, and shiny-smooth. Buy them as close to harvest time as possible, as they quickly lose mildness and crispness. To my taste, all of these sweet onions lose their distinctive charm soon after purchase, but they can be kept for a bit if you use them for cooking.

Store them in one of several ways, but remember that the sooner used, the better they'll be. The traditional (if unusual) method is to hang them in stockings or panty hose, tying knots between the onions, and store in a cool cellar or garage. Cut off the bottom onions as you want them. Or place the onions on wire racks, not touching, in a cool place with good ventilation. Lacking a cellar or garage, wrap the onions separately and store in the refrigerator. Although freezing is recommended, I disagree heartily.

USE: While sweet onions have been developed primarily for use on burgers—where they are unquestionably superior to others—they taste pleasant in a number of other combinations in their pristine state. Try them on slices of close-grained bread, well-coated with sweet butter, then sprinkle with salt and pepper for a first-rate sandwich; or combine with rare roast beef or thinly sliced Cheddar on dark pumpernickel.

Try all fresh sweet onions in salads and salad dressings; even if you do not normally enjoy onions this way, you will probably find these appealing. The mild, crunchy, pale flesh is crisp, brimming with juice—not overwhelming. (But go easy: They *are* onions.)

Blend and cook sweet onions in ways that will not hide their delicate taste. Dip in a beer batter or tempura batter and fry for delectable rings. Chop in dressings, un-cooked sauces, relishes, and composed salads. If they are roasted in the oven or on the grill, sweet onions remain crisp and juicy. For the latter, wrap the onion tightly in foil and grill over moderately high heat, gauging about an hour for a medium-sized sweet onion. Serve in the foil and let diners peel, butter, salt, and pepper their own. Do not use sweet onions to replace stored onions as seasoning; they lack authority.

Although promoters claim that these onions are best enjoyed eaten out of hand, like apples, I suggest you refrain from such snacking.

NUTRITIONAL HIGHLIGHTS: All onions are relatively low in calories, at about 30 per ½ cup; they are also low in sodium. They provide an especially generous amount of fiber.

APPLE AND SWEET ONION SALAD WITH
BUTTERMILK DRESSING

Sprightly and simple, a natural for picnics and barbecues, this crisp salad is as much a relish as a side dish.

4 servings

2 small sweet onions, about 4 ounces each, chilled

2 small, tart, firm apples, chilled (about ¾ pound)

2 tablespoons cider vinegar

1 teaspoon sugar

⅛ teaspoon salt

About ¼ teaspoon celery seeds

Big pinch cayenne pepper

¼ cup buttermilk

2 tablespoons corn oil

¼–½ teaspoon Worcestershire sauce

1. Peel onions; halve lengthwise, through stem. Cut halves crosswise in thin slices. Separate layers and place in bowl. Quarter apples and core them. Cut quarters crosswise into paper-thin slices and toss with onions.

2. Combine vinegar, sugar, salt, celery seeds, and cayenne, and stir to dissolve. Add buttermilk and stir; add oil gradually, beating with whisk to blend. Add Worcestershire to taste. Toss with apples. Chill until serving time.

BARBARA SPIEGEL'S SWEET-ONION-SESAME DRESSING

This zesty caramel-colored sauce—the body of which is provided by puréed onion —contains an unusually hefty amount of sesame oil, the intensity of which is surprisingly modified. This quantity of sauce should dress 1½ pounds freshly cooked small asparagus, or string beans, or broccoli. Or pour it over sliced Oriental or red radishes and serve at once.

Makes about 4 servings

2 tablespoons corn oil

2 tablespoons dark (Oriental) sesame oil

1 tablespoon soy sauce

1 tablespoon dark Chinese vinegar or balsamic vinegar

1 small sweet onion, coarsely chunked

Optional: Water in which vegetable cooked

1. Combine corn and sesame oils, soy sauce, and vinegar in processor; whirl to blend. Add onion and purée roughly, adding a few tablespoons of the cooking water, if desired, for fluidity. Adjust flavors to taste.

2. Pour dressing over hot vegetables. Let stand for an hour or more to season; or serve at once, if you prefer a hot dish.

ROASTED SWEET ONIONS WITH HERBS

When you're roasting ham, chicken, turkey, lamb, pork, or game, cook up whole onions, tender but crisp, to serve with the meat. For each person, select a medium-large, regular-shaped onion weighing about ½ pound. Rinse the unpeeled onions, dry them, and set root end down in a baking pan. Bake at 325–375 degrees (at whatever temperature you're roasting the meat) until tender when pierced with a knife, but not soft; the onion should be slightly al dente. Timing varies, but hovers around an hour. Cool a few minutes while the roast rests, then peel each onion and cut off its root end. Pull out a small central plug from the top and insert a teaspoon of duck, bacon, pork, chicken, or goose fat or butter and a sprinkle of herbs, salt, and pepper. Raise heat to 425 degrees and bake onions about 10 minutes longer, until lightly colored. Serve hot.

ROASTED-SWEET-ONION RELISH WITH BALSAMIC VINEGAR

This relish for grilled and barbecued foods lies somewhere between a salad and a sauce. Roasting the onions before combining with seasonings intensifies the flavor and sugar mellows any harshness.

Makes about 1 quart

6 medium sweet onions, about 2 pounds
About ½ teaspoon salt
3 tablespoons balsamic vinegar
1 teaspoon paprika
Pepper to taste
3 tablespoons olive oil

1. Set onions in pan in preheated 375-degree oven and roast until not quite tender throughout—about 35 minutes; they should still be slightly crisp-firm in the center.

2. Let stand until cool enough to handle. Peel, then cut into even ¼–½-inch dice. Combine well with salt, vinegar, paprika, and pepper to taste; toss to mix. Add oil and toss to coat. Let cool.

3. Chill for at least 24 hours, preferably more, before serving.

DEEP-DISH SWEET-ONION PIE

If you were to cross an Alsatian onion tart and a Sicilian pizza you might come up with this plump, chewy pie. Served with a ripe tomato salad and crisp Italian white wine, it makes a lovely lunch or light supper; cut into small rectangles and offered with an icy Riesling or Gewürztraminer, it makes a luscious appetizer.

6 servings as a main course

CRUST
1 packet dry yeast
¼ cup warm water
¼ teaspoon sugar
2 tablespoons butter, cut small
⅓ cup milk
1 teaspoon salt
½ teaspoon caraway seeds
About 2¼ cups all-purpose flour

FILLING
2 tablespoons butter
4 medium-large sweet onions cut into ½-inch dice (3 cups)
1½ tablespoons flour
¾ cup milk
¼ teaspoon salt
½ pound cottage cheese
3 eggs

1. Dissolve yeast in warm water with sugar. Proof until fluffy; if mixture does not bubble up, begin again with fresh ingredients.

2. In small saucepan heat butter, milk, salt, and caraway seeds, stirring until butter almost melts; do not heat more than this. Pour into large bowl. Add ¾ cup flour and stir; add yeast mixture, then another cupful of flour. Gradually knead in however much flour is easily absorbed, not more; dough should not be stiff.

3. Turn dough onto floured surface and knead until medium-soft, smooth, and no longer sticky, adding flour as needed. Place in buttered bowl, turn to coat. Cover bowl with plastic and let rise until at least doubled in bulk—about 1 hour.

4. Meanwhile, prepare filling: melt butter in heavy skillet over moderately low heat. Stir in onions; continue stirring often until onions are pale golden and soft, about 30 minutes (lower heat if onions begin to brown).

5. Add flour and stir 2 minutes. Add milk and salt and stir over moderate heat a few minutes, until mixture is thick, almost pasty. Blend together cottage cheese and eggs in a bowl; stir onion mixture into this. Season to taste.

6. Roll dough on lightly floured surface to form rectangle slightly larger than baking dish or pan you'll be using, which should be about 12 by 8 by 2 inches. Butter dish and press in dough to extend about three-quarters up sides of dish. Press dough well into dish to cover evenly. Pour in filling.

7. Bake in center of preheated 375-degree oven until crust is nicely browned and filling is golden—about 45 minutes. Cool 15 minutes, then gently lift out pie with large spatulas. Let cool slightly on a rack before cutting into serving pieces. (Can be reheated.)

ORIENTAL PEAR
See Asian Pear

OYSTER MUSHROOM
(Pleurotus ostreatus group)
also Tree Oyster, Pleurotte, Shimeji

*O*ne of the more popular "exotics" offered in elegant American restaurants of late, the oyster mushroom has an elusive flavor and exceptionally melting texture.

It is the cultivated variety that we find in markets today, although clusters of silvery-taupe and purplish-brown wild oyster mushrooms, overlapped like curving wavelets, cling to stumps of poplars, willows, aspens, and oaks throughout North America

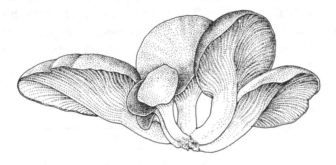

(and Europe and the Orient). Beige-cream, usually fan-shaped, the cultivated fungi are primarily smooth, deep-gilled caps that narrow at the bases to short stems, which attach them to a cluster of kin. They can be as tiny as peas or as broad as fried eggs, depending on the strain and its provenance. Raised in California, Canada, and several southeastern states, oyster mushrooms now appear regularly in many markets, thanks to the ingenuity of Hungarian and Oriental mycologists and entrepreneurs who developed relatively foolproof methods for their commercial cultivation.

To grow *Pleurotus*, spawn (the threadlike root filaments produced by germinating spores) is mixed with straw and placed in a controlled environment. Within 4 to 5 weeks the first crop is harvested. Or the spawn may be "planted" in poplar disks and allowed to mature outdoors in amenable climates. Several other cultivated *Pleurotus* types are imported from Spain and France, as well. While the different kinds do vary considerably with respect to size and color, what they all have in common is extreme tenderness and delicacy of flavor.

SELECTION AND STORAGE: Happily, oyster mushrooms are now available more or less year round; but keep an eye out for price fluctuations. Look for silky-downy caps (like chamois), evenly colored buff-to-dun or pearly gray; there should be no darkening areas. The mushrooms should be dry to the touch, but not powdery—and never wet, which indicates spoilage, a common occurrence. They are extremely perishable, so buy carefully.

Store them as short a time as possible, as they pick up flavors from other foods and lose their own. Spread the untrimmed clumps in a shallow basket or dish, cover with barely dampened cheesecloth, then refrigerate. If the mushrooms seem damp while stored, remove the cloth.

USE: Cultivated oyster mushrooms, lighter in flavor than their wild forebears, can be cooked as you would common button mushrooms *(Agaricus bisporus)*, but more rapidly. Their subtle taste is best suited to dishes with few ingredients that are simply prepared. Maintain the fleeting flavor by adding a modicum of butter, cream, and stock, rather than generous quantities of fats or oils. Serve in soup, creamed, lightly sautéed as an accompaniment to white meats or seafood, or made into a sauce. Combine with pasta or grains, eggs, rice, polenta or other cornmeal preparations.

PREPARATION: Washing or cleaning is usually not necessary for these cultivated caps. If bits of the sterilized growing compound cling to the fungi, simply brush them off. Cut off and discard the very tips of the stems, then break large caps into oversized mouthfuls (they shrink). If they are small, trim the heavy part of the bases, leaving caps and small stems whole. If you occasionally find stems that are heavy, thin-slice them; for the most part, though, they will be virtually nonexistent or have almost the same texture as the cap.

NUTRITIONAL HIGHLIGHTS: Oyster mushrooms are a good source of B vitamins riboflavin and niacin, as well as fiber.

OYSTER MUSHROOMS "SAUTÉED" WITH BUTTER AND BROTH

I find that fragile oyster mushrooms—particularly the small, downy ones from France—tend to develop a bitter, seared taste when subjected to straight sauté methods. Instead, cook in broth until it evaporates. They quickly soften, retaining their delicacy and the benefits of butter as an enrichment rather than a browning medium.

2 servings

About ½ pound fairly small, even-sized oyster mushrooms
½ cup chicken or veal stock
1½ tablespoons butter
Salt and pepper to taste

Break mushrooms into even-sized mouthfuls. Boil stock and butter in a skillet. Add mushrooms and toss gently over high heat until most liquid has evaporated—about 5 minutes. Serve up, hot.

CREAMY OYSTER MUSHROOMS

Accompany simple grilled or roasted meat or fish with gently cooked, velvety oyster mushrooms enriched with butter and cream.

4 servings

1 pound oyster mushrooms
4 tablespoons butter
2 tablespoons minced shallots
1 cup rich poultry stock
½ cup dry white wine
½ cup heavy (or whipping) cream
Salt and white pepper to taste
Optional: Minced parsley, chervil, or
    another very mild herb

1. Trim tips from mushroom stems. Separate caps; if large, break into generous bite-sized pieces.

2. Heat butter in a large skillet; stir in shallots and cook over medium heat until slightly softened. Add mushrooms and toss. Add stock and toss over moderately high heat until liquid evaporates. Add wine and toss until nearly evaporated. Add cream; stir until thickened to taste.

3. Season and sprinkle with herb. Serve at once.

PUFFY MUSHROOM OVEN PANCAKE

Any fresh mushrooms (chanterelles or morels, particularly) would do for this brunch or Sunday-supper dish. It takes only minutes to assemble, then rises in the oven to a golden pancake that resembles both popovers and Yorkshire pudding.

2 servings

½ pound oyster mushrooms
1 tablespoon minced chives
¼ cup yogurt
2 tablespoons sour cream
2½ tablespoons butter
¼ teaspoon salt
Pepper to taste
¾ cup milk
⅓ cup all-purpose flour
2 large eggs, beaten to just blend

1. Remove mushroom stems; reserve for another use. Slice caps thin. Blend together chives, yogurt, and sour cream; reserve for sauce.

2. Melt 1½ tablespoons butter in a heavy skillet over moderate heat. When sizzling, stir in mushrooms and toss 1 minute. Add ⅛ teaspoon salt and toss until liquid evaporates; reserve.

3. Whirl together remaining salt, pepper, milk, and flour in processor. Add eggs and barely blend; do not overmix.

4. Heat remaining butter in preheated 400-degree oven in skillet until browned and sizzling; at same time, reheat mushrooms. Pour into prepared skillet; immediately pour batter over them.

5. Bake in oven center until puffed and lightly brown—25 minutes. Serve at once, with sauce.

BRAISED VEAL AND OYSTER MUSHROOMS

Although this is definitely a simple stew in appearance, the intense flavors of its few luxurious ingredients make it a dish to reserve for friends who appreciate unshowy food. The extravagant quantity of mushrooms provides both the lush texture and necessary moisture. Long cooking develops the pleasures of the oyster mushrooms, deepening the flavor and increasing their succulence.

6 servings

2 pounds lean stewing veal, cut in 2-inch
    pieces
2 tablespoons flour
2 tablespoons olive oil
2 tablespoons butter
4 small shallots, minced
2 small celery stalks, minced
¼ cup white wine or dry vermouth
2 pounds medium-size oyster mushrooms
¾ teaspoon salt
Pepper
¼ teaspoon nutmeg
⅛ teaspoon summer savory

1. Toss veal to coat thoroughly with flour. Heat oil and butter over moderate heat in a large skillet; add veal and brown lightly on all sides. With slotted spoon transfer meat to a flameproof casserole just barely large enough to hold both veal and mushrooms.

2. Stir shallots, celery, and wine into fat that remains in pan. Cover and cook until softened, stirring a few times— about 5 minutes. Scoop the mixture over the veal.

3. Trim stems from mushrooms and save for making stock (they can be frozen). Press mushrooms into casserole to fit tightly; add salt, pepper, nutmeg, and savory. Heat until sizzling.

4. Place in center of 300-degree oven and bake until very tender—about 2 hours, stirring after about 45 minutes.

🖎 *ADDITIONAL RECIPES*
Richard Sax's Chicken with Celeriac and
    Mushrooms (page 100)
Warm Salad of Two Mushrooms, Celery, and
    Parmesan (page 105)

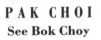

PAK CHOI
See Bok Choy

PAPAYA
(Carica papaya)
also Papaw, Pawpaw, Lechosa, Fruta Bomba

*A*n extraordinarily generous bearer, developing its mammary-like burdens within a year of planting, the papaya looks more like an Indian fertility goddess than a tree—which it isn't, anyway. It is a shrub or herb or plant or whatever botanists want to call it, the branchless trunk of which grows to about 20 feet but does not harden to bark.

Atop this shaft rests a radiating crest of giant leaves under which cluster the ponderous fruits, giving the whole the look of a coconut palm. Papaya is a member of a very small family—only two genera, about thirty species—that is very closely related to passion fruit, but in no way related to the American wild fruit called pawpaw (a member of the Annonaceous family).

Green, orange, rose, or yellow-skinned; weighing from ½ pound to 20; shaped like avocados, or bananas, or pears, or giant pecans, papayas have naturalized in many forms world-wide. (Pear-shaped fruit come from hermaphroditic trees; round papayas are produced by cross-pollination of single-sexed trees.) The yellow-to-sunset, smooth flesh is superficially similar to that of a melon, which gives the fruit one of its other names, tree-melon (*papaya* comes from the Carib *abadai* or *ababai*). This sweet pulp, light and refreshing when cooked or raw, spoonable as banana or fiberless mango when ripe, can be very delicately floral or somewhat musky or sour. The centered cavity is filled to bursting with wrinkly, black-gray seeds (looking like capers crossed with beluga caviar), encased in a glistening, gelatinous coating. These softish, edible seeds (which are white or light gray if the fruit is immature) taste something like nasturtium, watercress, and pepper.

Starting a bit above the Tropic of Cancer and moving south, papayas of one kind or another are as common as apples are to us. Unfortunately, in the United States, only Hawaii and Florida squeak into that geographical boundary—which makes available a limited quantity in varying degrees of ripeness, unless you are close by either state. Because the papaya's thin skin does not protect it sufficiently from bruising if shipped when ripe (and because the present method for preventing insect infestation necessitates picking while still quite hard), the fruit must be harvested when still green—too green to develop a full flavor. Fortunately, like the avocado, the fruit will ripen at room temperature, but it will never have the very rich taste of tree-ripened fruit. It can be absolutely lovely, however, if harvested when partly ripe, rather than dead-hard-green. However, the business of growing, harvesting, and shipping papayas is presently in a state of flux. Most signs indicate that we should soon have better, riper fruit.

The majority of our papayas come from Hawaii and are primarily the yellow, pear-shaped Kapoho Solo variety, with a minor percentage of the rose-fleshed Sunrise available (for the most part on the West Coast). The diminutive and attractive Solo was developed in the mid-1970s in Hawaii, where papayas have been flourishing fabulously since about 1919. Its success is due in part to what its name suggests: it can be consumed by a single fruit lover, not the large family required for most varieties. Some eastern markets receive larger papayas, which are more pungent and musky.

SELECTION AND STORAGE: Papayas are available pretty much year round, because the prolific plant continues to fruit and flower simultaneously. Peak supply is in the spring and fall. The Hawaiian Solo, usually weighing between ¾ and 1½ pounds, is the main papaya you'll see in most markets, but fruit from Florida, Mexico, the Philippines, Haiti, the Dominican Republic, Costa Rica, Belize, Puerto Rico, Venezuela, the Bahamas—and more—is becoming more widely available.

Look for small Hawaiian fruit that is partly or completely yellow, depending on when you want to use it. Gauge its ripeness more by feel than look. It should have the same kind of give as a ripe avocado. Don't go for the cosmetically perfect: a spotty look, with good coloring, will usually have more flavor. If partly ripe, leave in a dark place at room temperature for a few days; speed up the process by enclosing the papaya in a paper bag with a banana. The larger varieties should be selected as above, but few turn from green to yellow.

Chill a papaya once it is completely ripe, not before. Serve within a day or two or it loses its fragile flavor.

USE: In the many lands in which the papaya grows, it is used green and ripe, cooked and raw, every day. Because it is a rather costly item for us (and because all the green-papaya recipes tested were almost tasteless and would have been better served with chayote or a firm summer squash), my recommendations apply to ripe fruit only.

Like the apple, there is really no part of a meal in which a papaya does not fit, unless you overpower it. It is quite a gentle character and needs to be brought out.

Raw, the sliced, diced, or chopped flesh makes beautiful and subtly flavored fruit cups, benefiting from the addition of acid or rich fruits, such as pineapple, strawberry, orange, banana, coconut, or lime, its all-time best enhancer. Halved, the fruit forms its own dish, like cantaloupe or other small melons. Slivers of papaya and prosciutto meld marvelously. Salads of smoked meat, turkey, chicken, and seafood are sweetly complemented by papaya.

Purée papaya to make a golden dressing, adding ginger, cayenne, fresh hot peppers, or some of the peppery seeds for bite. Or make a similar marinade, spiced or not, to tenderize and season meat. Combine milk, buttermilk, or yogurt (or sweetened condensed milk, as is done in the Caribbean), honey, lime, and papaya; whiz in processor or blender for a breakfast shake that is special indeed. Or make a daiquiri with papaya, lime juice, rum, and sugar. Purée fresh papaya as a base for ice cream, ices, or milk sherbet.

Cooked papaya is a revelation, particularly in savory dishes, where it takes the roles of vegetable, fruit, sauce, and liaison—but you must have a flavorful specimen to start with, or season it sufficiently to make up for the blandness. Unlike other soft fruits, it does not turn mushy when cooked, but remains firm-pliant. Alternate cubes on skewers with marinated meat for satés or kebabs. Bake peeled halves with a roast, basting occasionally; or stuff unpeeled ones with minced and seasoned meat and serve as a main course. Simmer papaya to make a gorgeous, glossy purée or thinner sauce to serve with delicate meats or fish.

Sauté slices, sprinkling with a bit of sugar and lime, to accompany poultry, or serve for dessert. Or tuck sautéed slices, liqueur-enhanced, into crêpes. Papaya chutney, a traditional recipe in many countries, does not take advantage of the fleeting flowery flavor of the fruit, but underscores its rich texture. Poach slices in lemon or ginger-flavored syrup, or bake them with butter and brown sugar, crumbling an old-fashioned topping on them. Bake upside-down cakes, fresh fruit tarts, and puddings with papaya. In Tahiti, the simplest of desserts is made special with vanilla: Halve and seed papaya; sprinkle with sugar. Place a quarter of a vanilla pod in each, then drizzle with coconut milk (or cream), a little rum, and a sliver of butter. Bake about 25 minutes, then serve hot.

PREPARATION: If the fruit is not perfectly ripe, it may benefit from a curious ritual that was shown to me by a Brazilian cooking teacher, Sandra Allen, who explained that any bitterness would thereby be removed. She scored the fruit lengthwise in quarters, cutting delicately through the skin but not into the flesh, then turned the fruit onto its narrow stem end, set it in a glass so it wouldn't tip, and instructed me to leave it for a day. It was certainly the sweetest papaya I have tasted in this country. Since that time I have read about this scoring technique in Brazilian, French West Indian, New Caledonian, and Fijian cookbooks; consultation with numerous scientists has indicated that the slitting would help release the bitter papain enzyme present in green fruit, but that this should not affect ripe fruit, which has virtually none.

Papaya need only be halved and seeded, as you would cantaloupe. For cut-up fruit, the thin skin is easily removed with a vegetable peeler or a paring knife.

NUTRITIONAL HIGHLIGHTS: Papaya is a rich source of vitamin C and vitamin A, high in potassium, and a good source of fiber. It is low in calories, with about 55 per cup.

PAPAYA SLICES IN SYRUP

If you're not quite ready to enjoy a papaya that is ripening quickly, or you have one that just doesn't come up to par, poach it briefly in a flavorful syrup to keep for a few days in the refrigerator.

Serve alongside a meat course, as you might applesauce. Or mix with other fruit, or spoon the golden slices over rice pudding or vanilla pudding.

2–4 servings, depending on how used

1 firm-ripe papaya, about 1½ pounds
1 lime
Optional: 1 teaspoon cardamom pods (or
    ¼ teaspoon allspice berries)
¼ cup sugar
1½ cups water

1. Halve papaya crosswise; scoop out and discard seeds. Cut each half of the fruit into lengthwise quarters. Peel, then slice crosswise in ½-inch slices. Place in bowl.

2. Peel half the lime; place peel in a pot. Squeeze juice from lime over papaya. Bruise cardamom pods (if using) to crack open slightly; add to lime peel (or add allspice, if you wish). Add sugar and water and bring to a boil. Simmer, covered, for 10 minutes.

3. Uncover and add papaya. Keep just below a simmer until the fruit is tender throughout—about 5 minutes. Submerge and turn slices gently with a rubber spatula, if necessary. Turn into a serving dish, cool, and chill.

WARM PAPAYA BREAKFAST CAKE

A fluffy, nutty, springy-light cake topped with sour cream and a sunburst of papaya. The coffee-cake-style batter can be prepared in minutes with the help of a processor, then the cake is popped into the oven while you put together the rest of breakfast or brunch. Serve freshly baked, as the cake loses some of its charm when cooled.

4 generous servings

CAKE BATTER

¼ cup sugar

2 heaping tablespoons walnuts or pecans

1 cup all-purpose flour

1 teaspoon baking powder

¼ teaspoon salt

2½ tablespoons butter, chilled, cut in small pieces

⅓ cup milk

1 extra-large or jumbo egg

1 teaspoon vanilla extract

½ teaspoon lemon extract

TOPPING

1 tablespoon flour

3 tablespoons sugar

⅔ cup sour cream

1 small papaya (approximately ¾ pound), peeled, seeded, thin-sliced

1. Combine sugar and nuts in processor and whiz to medium-fine texture. Add flour, baking powder, and salt; whirl until thoroughly mixed. Add butter; turn machine on and off a few times to chop fine.

2. Blend together milk, egg, and extracts in measuring cup. With motor running, add to dry ingredients and process until just incorporated; do not overmix. Spread evenly in generously buttered 9-inch pie plate.

3. Blend flour, 2 tablespoons sugar, and sour cream for topping; pour over batter. Arrange papaya over this in an overlapping pattern. Cover with foil. Bake 15 minutes in upper third of preheated 375-degree oven. Remove foil; sprinkle with remaining tablespoon sugar. Bake 20 minutes longer, until side of cake is browned and topping rather firm. Serve warm.

WALNUT-STUFFED CHICKEN WITH PAPAYAS

Hidden beneath the browned skin of this roasted bird is a layer of nuts and sweet spices bound with butter. If you have never stuffed a chicken this way, don't hesitate; it takes no more time to accomplish than trussing a bird and is absolutely foolproof—as is the simplicity of carving that results. The chicken is roasted with papaya chunks, which absorb the cooking juices and, when puréed, form a creamy, pale sauce.

Plain-cooked white rice is just the right foil for the perfumed sauce and slices of sautéed, peachy-golden papaya that accompany the bird. Sip a fruity, spicy, full-bodied Gewürztraminer from California.

4 servings

3¼–3½-pound chicken (without giblets), *no holes* in the skin

½ cup walnuts

1 very thin slice white sandwich-type bread

2 large shallots, minced or grated

1 tablespoon grated fresh ginger

1 teaspoon paprika

¼ teaspoon nutmeg

¼ teaspoon cinnamon

15 cardamom pods (preferably) or ¾ teaspoon ground cardamom

Coarse kosher salt

3 tablespoons butter

2 medium papayas (about 2½ pounds total), peeled

Pepper

About ⅓ cup chicken broth

Lime juice to taste

About ¾ teaspoon sugar

1. Set chicken on its breast; with shears or sharp knife cut out backbone (freeze for stock) and remove loose fat. Turn bird over, open out, and press down with the palm of your hand to break ribs and flatten. Slip your hand under the breast skin. Move it slowly to loosen skin; continue under skin of second joint, then into the drumstick, freeing skin as you go. Carefully free skin from upper wings, as well.

2. In blender or processor grind walnuts and bread until coarsely chopped; add shallots, ginger, paprika, nutmeg, and cinnamon. Grind cardamom in a spice mill, sift it, and add (or substitute ground cardamom). Add 1 teaspoon salt and 2 tablespoons butter and whiz to a paste.

3. Using one hand to insert stuffing mixture under skin and the other to distribute by pushing it into place from the outside, evenly spread to cover bird. Arrange in a buttered pan (about 13 by 9 inches), skin side up. Smooth skin to make a neat shape and fold wing tips beneath breast. (Leave an hour to season, if desired.)

4. Peel one papaya and remove and discard most seeds; dice two-thirds of papaya and spread around chicken. Set pan in center of preheated 400-degree oven; roast 25 minutes, basting once. Sprinkle with salt and pepper; lower heat to 350 degrees and roast about 25 minutes longer, until nicely browned, basting often. Set on a platter and cover lightly with foil.

5. Pour contents of roasting pan into processor or blender; purée. Scrape into a small saucepan, add broth, and stir over low heat until bubbling. Season with lime juice and salt to taste.

6. Slice remaining 1⅓ papayas. Sauté in remaining butter in large skillet until slightly softened—about 2 minutes—sprinkling with the sugar to glaze slightly. Arrange with chicken. Serve sauce separately, placing a spoonful or two on each serving.

PAPAYA PURÉE

This unique papaya treatment is adapted from a recipe that my friend Joan Nathan (author of *The American Folklife Cookbook*) got from *her* friend the extraordinary chef, Jean-Louis Palladin of the restaurant Jean-Louis at the Watergate Hotel in Washington. Shiny golden-yellow, softly spoonable, this side dish will complement shrimp, chicken, veal, or pork. Although it has a delicate savor and *slight* sweetness, its buttery flavor is more vegetable than fruit-like.

4 servings

About 2½ pounds medium-ripe papaya (2 medium or 1 large)
3 tablespoons heavy (or whipping) cream
Salt
Generous amount white pepper

1. Peel papaya and halve; scoop out seeds. If using a large fruit, cut into eighths; if smaller, quarter. Drop into a pot of generously salted water. Boil 10 minutes.

2. Drain, then drop into a bowl of ice water to cool. Drain and purée in food processor, blender, or food mill. Scoop into a heavy saucepan.

3. Add cream, salt to taste, and pepper. Simmer, stirring, until mixture is smoothly thick, like rich applesauce—about 10 minutes. As with applesauce, you'll need to beware of volcanic splatters; stir with a pot top held shield-like between you and the active purée. Serve hot or warm (my preference).

PAPAYA-ROASTED PORK

This moist, pot-roasted pork derives its unusual flavor and richness, as well as its tenderness, from the puréed papaya in which it marinates. With the inclusion of the peppery black seeds, the lightly sweet brown gravy that results looks more like a meat sauce than one you would associate with fruit.

6 servings

About 3½ pounds firm, boneless center-cut pork loin
1 ripe papaya, about 1½ pounds
4 tablespoons bourbon or brandy
2 teaspoons ground coriander seeds
½ teaspoon ground allspice
2 teaspoons coarse kosher salt
1 tablespoon brown sugar
1 large garlic clove, minced
2 tablespoons vegetable oil

1. Open loin to trim off interior excess fat; leave a goodly outside covering. Stab meat here and there with a skewer or knife.

2. Halve papaya and scoop out seeds; rinse them and place in processor container with 2 tablespoons bourbon. Purée, scraping down sides often. Scoop out papaya flesh and add to container with coriander, allspice, salt, sugar, and garlic. Purée roughly.

3. Place meat and marinade in glass or ceramic dish to just fit. Turn to coat well. Cover with several layers of plastic and refrigerate for about 12 hours, turning occasionally.

4. Scrape off and reserve marinade. Dry meat, then tie with twine to form neat cylinder. Brown in oil in a heavy flame-proof casserole. Pour out fat. Add remaining 2 tablespoons bourbon to marinade; scrape into pan with meat.

5. Cover tightly and roast in preheated 325-degree oven until pork reaches an internal temperature of about 175 degrees (timing varies enormously with shape and size of roast; a narrow roast should be done in about 1¼ hours). Baste several times during roasting.

6. Let pork stand 15–30 minutes before carving. Meanwhile, spoon fat from sauce. Serve reheated sauce spooned over meat.

GINGERED PAPAYA MILK SHERBET

Exceptionally smooth, with a silky texture, this pastel-golden sherbet tastes like a clean fruit ice cream. Should you be in the mood for a dessert duo, serve with perfumy Feijoa-Plum Ice (page 193).

Makes a scant quart

1 fully ripe papaya, about 1¼ pounds

About 3 tablespoons white rum, or more to taste

2 tablespoons finely minced preserved ginger in syrup

About ½ cup sugar

2 cups milk, chilled

1. Seed, peel, and slice papaya. Toss together in a bowl with 3 tablespoons rum and ginger. Whirl sugar in processor until very fine-textured. Toss together with papaya. Let stand about an hour at room temperature, tossing occasionally.

2. Purée mixture thoroughly. When smooth, add milk gradually, with processor running. Add more rum and sugar, as needed. Pour into cream can of an ice-cream maker.

3. Freeze according to manufacturer's directions. Scrape into a container and let mellow in the freezer for about a day. Let soften in the refrigerator before serving.

 ADDITIONAL RECIPES
Salad of Jícama and Papaya (page 242)
Ugli Fruit, Papaya, and Strawberries (page 480)

PARSLEY ROOT
(*Petroselinum crispum* variety *tuberosum*)
also Rooted Parsley, Turnip-Rooted Parsley, Dutch Parsley,
Hamburg Parsley, Heimischer, Petoushka

A winter root that has long been stirred in the soup pots of Germany, Holland, and Poland, this Old World vegetable is raised almost exclusively in New Jersey, in our country, and in very small volume. It is an unusual member of the umbelliferous family in that it is cultivated for its root, rather than its leaves—although they may be

eaten as well, tasting rather like slightly bland flat-leaf Italian parsley. The small, irregularly shaped vegetable looks like a small parsnip (often double-rooted) attached to large, feathery parsley leaves. The taste, between celeriac and carrot, adds depth and aroma to braises, stews, and soups, particularly hearty main-course types.

SELECTION AND STORAGE: Although traditionally a winter vegetable, parsley root can be found almost year round in some markets, particularly those with a Central European clientele. Look for firm, creamy-beige roots of more or less the same size, with luxuriant leaves. Do not trim these off until you are ready to prepare the roots. Wrapped in plastic the parsley root should remain in good shape for about a week or more, but will be useful in soups and stews even after it has become somewhat flabby.

USE: Think of parsley root as you would parsnip or celeriac—aromatic, slightly aggressive, herbal-pungent. It combines beautifully with other roots and tubers, such as carrots, potatoes, turnips, onions. You can use it by itself—creamed, puréed, or simply steamed or boiled and buttered. Most will find its pleasantly pervasive taste works best in combination—in soups, stews, and vegetable mixes and purées.

PREPARATION: Clean parsley root by scrubbing it with a vegetable brush to remove all soil. Although the peel is most tasty, some prefer vegetables minus their jackets. Remove the leaves, wash them thoroughly, dry, and enclose in a plastic bag to use for flavoring and color, as you would leaf parsley. If small, you can keep the roots whole; or cut them into slices or dice.

NUTRITIONAL HIGHLIGHTS: Parsley root is low in calories, but rather high in sodium, for those watching their intake.

SOUP OF WINTER VEGETABLES AND DRIED MUSHROOMS

This sturdy pottage warms a nippy day and perfumes a winter kitchen. A light red wine, salad of dandelion with bacon dressing, and baked or stewed fruit make a casual good meal.

4 generous servings

⅓ cup dried *Boletus* mushrooms (porcini, cèpes, or Polish mushrooms)

1 cup hot water

½ pound very small leeks (4 leeks), halved lengthwise and cleaned

2 tablespoons bacon, duck, goose, chicken, or fresh pork fat

¾ pound parsley root (weighed without leaves, which should be reserved), peeled and diced

½ pound carrots (weighed without tops), peeled and diced

1 celery stalk with leaves, chopped small

1½ pounds potatoes, peeled and diced

6 cups hearty lamb, beef, or ham stock

Salt and plenty of pepper

1. Break mushrooms into small pieces, if necessary, and combine with hot water; let soak for 15–30 minutes.

2. Cut off very heavy upper leaves from leeks and reserve for another use. Slice leeks across in thin slices. Heat fat in a large flameproof casserole and stir in leeks, parsley root, carrots, and celery; cook over moderately low heat until softened, about 10 minutes.

3. Drain mushrooms and strain soaking liquid through cheesecloth, rinse mushrooms lightly. Add both to the casserole with potatoes and stock. Partly cover and simmer until tender—about 45 minutes. Add salt and pepper to taste and simmer a few minutes longer. Chop parsley tops to make about ¼ cup and sprinkle over the soup to serve.

Note: Like most thick soups, this one mellows with reheating.

MASHED POTATOES AND PARSLEY ROOT

Homey and delicious, this should please all lovers of mashed potatoes. Parsley root adds a sweet, slightly herbal flavor to the potatoes, a suggestion of celery, parsnip, celeriac, and parsley all at once. I like a purée with texture (one that is downright lumpy, as a matter of fact), which is why I prefer to retain the thin peel of the parsley root and why I mash rather than sieve the vegetables. If you prefer a fine, smooth purée, peel the parsley root and press both vegetables through a food mill.

4 servings

¾ pound parsley root (weighed with leaves)

1¼ pounds potatoes (not new), peeled and chunked

Butter to taste

Hot milk or cream to taste (a few tablespoons)

Salt and white pepper

1. Cut off parsley-root tops and reserve for another recipe. Scrub roots with a brush, then cut into ½-inch slices.

2. Drop parsley root and potatoes into a pot of boiling, salted water. Return to a boil and cook until tender—about 15 minutes. Drain well.

3. Add butter and hot milk, mashing (preferably with a potato masher) to desired consistency. Add salt and white pepper to taste.

PASSION FRUIT
(Passiflora edulis, Purple Passion Fruit;
Passiflora edulis forma flavicarpa, Yellow Passion Fruit)
also Passionfruit, Maracuja, Maracudja, Purple Granadilla

*N*ative to Brazil, the passion fruit has adapted to environments around the globe, the purple fruit thriving in temperate climates, the yellow and related red and violet forms in tropical and subtropical. Fruit fanciers in Australia, New Zealand, South America, Central America, Hawaii, Kenya, South Africa, New Guinea, Taiwan, and

India devour *Passiflora* species and the juice squeezed from them in substantial amounts (recent figures give world-wide annual production at roughly 8½ million pounds). Yet, despite the fact that passion fruit was introduced into Florida more than ninety years ago, and continues to be raised there and in California (though not on a commercial scale in either state), it is far from a household word in this country.

Recently, however, passion fruit has made considerable inroads into European and American restaurant kitchens of *haute* repute, at necessarily *haute* prices (since it is flown in from faraway places). If you're one who is susceptible to its tropical-paradise fragrance, you'll know why people are willing to pay up. Astonishingly intense—jasmine, honey, lemon—its freshness does not dissipate, whether the fruit is processed for juice, frozen, or mixed with other ingredients. You have to try it to understand. Like oysters or truffles or perfect raspberries, there is no fitting comparison.

While it is natural to assume that such a fruit is named for the sensual passion it evokes, the reference is to the Passion of Christ. The complex and remarkably beautiful flowers are the origin of this name, with the different parts of the bloom representing the wounds, crucifixion nails, crown of thorns, and the Apostles.

Aesthetically speaking, the ripe fruit is another matter entirely. The size and shape of a blunted egg, most commonly a dusty purple-brown (Florida's are rounder and pale violet, gold, or reddish), it looks like a partly deflated rubber ball left in the rain, then dried. When you saw open the cardboardy rind/shell with a paring knife you'll be faced with liquidy bits of mustard-yellow pulp the shape of teardrops. The whole gives the impression of a tablespoon of fish eggs about to hatch or paramecia gone mad. Each of the juicy capsules contains a tiny, crisp, dark seed (*granadilla* means "little pomegranate," by the way, a reference to the fruit's seediness), which you would do better to enjoy, since getting rid of them is a nuisance. The interior walls of the shell are pearly, similar to the inside of a milkweed pod.

SELECTION AND STORAGE: Look for passion fruit virtually all year: the dark and dusky fruit from New Zealand from early spring through early summer; the fruits from Florida in summer; and the California fruit takes over through fall. You'll have little choice at most markets, but if you do, seek fruits that are large and heavy (since they're usually sold by the piece, and weight promises an abundance of pulp). Deep purple passion fruit is ready to eat when it is creased (but not so far gone as to be cracked or squishy); its shell-like casing remains quite firm. Passion fruits keep amazingly well. I've never had one that was rotten—only underripe. If you find fruits that are firm, smooth, and rounded, take them home and keep them at room temperature for a few days until they become dimply and sound sloshy when shaken. The lighter-colored fruits are quite smooth when ripe, with a little "give."

Once sufficiently ripened, there are a number of ways to store the fruits. You can keep them in the refrigerator for about a week (I stick them in the rack with the eggs, where they look like Chinese thousand-year eggs). Or enclose them in plastic bags and freeze for months. When desired, simply pluck out and halve; the pulp will defrost quickly and taste bright-fresh. The freezing also breaks down the pulp a bit, making it easier to purée. Or scoop out the pulp, dump into individual ice-cube containers (generally 2 fruits per cube; one for the Florida variety) and freeze solid; then pop out into a plastic bag and keep frozen for months. You can stir a little sugar into the pulp before freezing.

USE: Most recipes that I have read come from places where the fruit is grown on a large scale. They begin: "Take a cup of pure, strained passion-fruit pulp." Today, in the United States, that could cost $25. Fortunately, however, passion fruit works best as a flavoring. There is so much perfume and so little pulp that you can think of it as you would vanilla, or Cognac, or a spoon of dense raspberry purée—something to aromatize a dish.

When you're planning a recipe for passion fruit, the less interference from other sources the better. In my opinion, the best way to use the lemony-tart fruit is as an instant sauce, simply scooped from its shell, sweetened (with sugar or a sweet liqueur), and poured over soft fruits; or spoon small amounts over vanilla or fruit ice creams, Bavarian creams, mousses, custards, puddings or rice puddings, or soufflés or frozen soufflés. For a richer sauce, blend passion fruit and sugar (about ½ tablespoon per fruit) until liquefied; fold this into whipped cream (figure 3–4 passion fruit per cup of cream).

Make glorious tropical drinks, alcoholic or not, with passion fruit. The most moon-light-tropical evocative quaff I know is passion-fruit pulp, white rum, and sugar syrup to taste—preferably chilled but not ice-cubed. If you make a batch of this and let it age, it improves—like many of us. (You can also steep seeds left over from sieved passion-fruit pulp; they remain astonishingly perfumed.) Fruit-juice drinks that include orange, pineapple, lime, or apricot or peach nectar, or pear or guava nectar (several or many) are transformed with the addition of passion fruit. It is the ideal punch ingredient.

If you enjoy experimenting with more elaborate preparations, passion fruit is un-equaled in ices and ice creams, as a flavoring for soufflés, mousses, and creamy concoctions of all persuasions.

PREPARATION: This means seeded or not. If yes, slice the shell tip, as you would a soft-cooked egg. Hold over a bowl (to save every precious drop), scoop out all the pulp; stir, adding a little sugar if you like, to help break up the pulp. Strain through a nonaluminum sieve, scraping to press through every golden drop. Or line a sieve with damp cheesecloth, then twist to extract as much juice as possible.

NUTRITIONAL HIGHLIGHTS: Passion fruit contributes small but appreciable amounts of vitamins A and C and high amounts of fiber (if not strained), and is very low in sodium.

Note: All recipes were tested with dark purple medium-sized fruit. If you can get the larger yellow or red or violet varieties, you will need fewer; but taste and adjust, as they are less intense. They usually have larger seeds, as well.

PASSION FRUIT CUP

Even a small quantity of passion fruit provides a concentrated amount of intense flavoring power. Liquefied, the golden pulp exhales an exotic perfume that develops the taste of other fruits. The seeds add a pleasant textural crunch, but if you don't fancy the sensation, sieve them out.

The following recipe is a guide. Stir up the simple sauce of passion fruit to fancify and aromatize any soft fruits—ripe pears, oranges, melons, strawberries, etc. The frozen pulp (see Selection and Storage) works perfectly here, so keep some in reserve.

2 servings

2 passion fruit
1 tablespoon fragrant honey
Lime juice
1 large kiwi, peeled, halved, and cut
    across into semicircles
1 small banana, sliced thin on the bias
¾–1 cup halved seedless red grapes (5–6
    ounces)

Cut top from each passion fruit; scoop out pulp. Combine with honey and lime juice to taste. Combine with the fruits, toss gently, and serve.

CHICKEN BREAST WITH PASSION FRUIT SAUCE

Mysterious, subtle, elegant, with a hint of maple, tropical flowers, lime, *je ne sais quoi*—in less than 10 minutes.

2 servings

¾ pound boned and skinned chicken
    breasts
2 tablespoons butter
1 tablespoon corn oil
Salt and pepper to taste
1 scant teaspoon sugar
2 tablespoons light rum
2 teaspoons lime juice
Pulp and seeds from 2 passion fruits

1. Remove tendons from chicken breasts. Pound meat to flatten to about ¼ inch. Heat 1 tablespoon butter and corn oil in heavy skillet over moderate heat. When foaming, add chicken breasts and brown, adjusting heat to prevent too quick darkening. When richly browned, remove to a cutting board and season generously with salt and pepper.

2. Pour out fat. Add sugar, rum, and lime juice to pan. Stir over low heat to dissolve all browned bits. Stir in passion fruit and barely heat through. Off heat stir in remaining butter. Season sauce.

3. Immediately slice chicken on diagonal in ¼-inch slices. Fan out on warmed plates. Spoon sauce evenly over each portion and serve at once.

PASSION FRUIT JUICE

Follow this method to extract as much flavorful juice as possible from passion fruits, which produce little of the precious liquid. It can be combined with lemon, orange, pineapple, lime, tangerine, apricot, or guava juice or nectar to make memorable punches, or with light rum, gin, brandy, fruit liqueurs, or eaux-de-vie for breathtaking mixed drinks.

Makes ⅔ cup

8 passion fruit
½ cup boiling water

Cut tops from passion fruits as you would soft-boiled eggs; scoop contents into nonaluminum sieve set over a small bowl. Scrape through as much pulp and juice as possible. Combine residue from sieve with boiling water; cover and let stand 5 minutes or longer. Strain and scrape through sieve, adding to juices in bowl. If not used within a few hours, cover and refrigerate or freeze.

JIM FOBEL'S PASSION FRUIT CUSTARD

Depending upon which ingredient you choose, this custard can be either firmish or pourable. If you stir in butter, you'll have a delectable filling for cakes, cream puffs, éclairs, napoleons and the fabulous trifle on page 224. If you opt for the cream, you have a thickish but liquid custard to adorn angel-food or sponge cake, poached pears, peaches, or apricots, or fresh raspberries.

Makes 1⅓ to 1⅔ cups

2 tablespoons cornstarch
2½ tablespoons sugar
Pinch salt
1 cup milk
⅓ cup Passion Fruit Juice (see preceding recipe)
1 egg yolk (be sure "string" to white is removed)
1 tablespoon butter (OR ¼ cup light cream or half-and-half)
½ teaspoon orange-flower water OR vanilla

1. Combine cornstarch, sugar, and salt in small, heavy saucepan. Gradually blend in 3 tablespoons milk. Add remaining milk. Stir constantly over moderately low heat until mixture thickens. As custard boils, whisk vigorously for 1 minute.

2. Remove from heat. Whisk in juice, blending completely. Blend yolk in small bowl; gradually whisk in half custard mixture. Scrape back into saucepan and return to low heat. Stir constantly until custard just begins to bubble and heave.

Remove from heat at once; if adding butter, stir it in at this point. Scrape into small bowl.

3. Add orange-flower water. Set bowl in another bowl half filled with ice and water. Whisk occasionally until cool. If adding cream, stir in now. Refrigerate until needed.

PASSION FRUIT CAKELETS

Little golden petits fours to grace an afternoon tray of lemonade, tea, or madeira. Be warned that this is only for those who like a seedy crunch (like big poppyseeds), in their sweets. If you want moister cakes, wrap and let mellow for a few hours or overnight; dust with confectioners' sugar at serving time.

Makes 20 small cakes

5 dark purple passion fruits
About 3 tablespoons passion fruit
    liqueur, or other fragrant fruit liqueur
    (see Note)
7 tablespoons butter, softened; plus
    additional butter for molds
½ cup sugar
1 extra-large egg
1 extra-large egg yolk
1 cup plus 2 tablespoons cake flour
½ teaspoon baking powder
¼ teaspoon salt
Confectioners' sugar

1. Scoop every bit of pulp from 3 halved fruits into nonaluminum sieve; press through all juice and pulp; discard seeds. Scoop out and add remaining pulp to sieved; combine with enough passion fruit liqueur to equal ⅓ cup. With softened butter, brush 20 tartlet molds of about 2-tablespoon capacity.

2. Cream butter in small bowl of electric mixer until light; gradually add sugar. Add egg and yolk and beat on high speed until light and fluffy. Gradually add passion fruit; beat a few minutes.

3. Sift cake flour (you should have 1⅓ cups). Resift with baking powder and salt. Gradually add to creamed mixture on lowest speed, beating to just barely blend.

4. Spoon into tartlet molds to fill about two-thirds. Smooth the tops. Set on baking sheet and place in center of 350-degree oven. Bake until lightly browned, about 25 minutes. Cool briefly, then unmold on a rack.

5. At serving time sprinkle with confectioners' sugar.

Note: La Grande Passion, a passion fruit and Armagnac blend, is well worth the investment, to my taste.

PASSION FRUIT—MELON ICE

Serve this fragrant ice alone, or along with Kiwi Sorbet (page 260), for a beautiful and exotic dessert. Use only the ripest, sweetest melon.

Makes about 1 quart

About ½ cup sugar
1½ cups water
2 cups 1-inch melon pieces (use whatever in season is best)
1 very small (or ½ medium) ripe banana, chunked
4 ripe passion fruit
4–6 tablespoons lime juice, to taste

1. Combine ½ cup sugar and water in saucepan; bring to a boil, stirring. Pour into a metal pan and cool, then chill.

2. Purée melon and banana in blender or processor. Cut off one end and scoop all pulp from 3 passion fruit. Press through a sieve to remove seeds, rubbing fruit through carefully to extract every bit of precious juice. Only clean, shiny seeds should be left in the sieve—no pulp. Blend with melon mixture. Scoop pulp from remaining passion fruit; add.

3. Stir fruit mixture into sugar syrup. Add lime juice and sugar to taste. Set on bottom of freezer and chill until mushy throughout.

4. Quickly scrape into a bowl and beat on high speed with electric mixer until fluffy and homogenized, but not liquefied. Immediately return to the pan, cover, and freeze until almost firm.

5. Repeat step 4.

6. Scrape into a container, close tightly, and freeze for at least a day. Soften slightly in the refrigerator before serving.

PASSION FRUIT MOUSSE

Palest pink from the touch of strawberries, melting in texture, this dessert cream has a pure fruit flavor—no eggs or thickeners or extracts in the way. If you do not have passion fruit liqueur, substitute 1 tablespoon Cognac or Armagnac and add more passion fruit to the mousse. For the sauce, substitute any sweet fruit liqueur that enhances the passion-fruit flavor.

6 servings

MOUSSE MIXTURE
1 envelope gelatine
3 tablespoons cold water
4 passion fruits
½ cup hulled, sliced strawberries
⅔ cup sugar
2½ teaspoons lime juice
2 tablespoons passion fruit liqueur (see Note)
1 cup heavy (or whipping) cream, preferably not ultrapasteurized
4 egg whites
Pinch salt

SAUCE AND GARNISH
2 passion fruits
2 tablespoons passion fruit liqueur
4 small strawberries
Tiny lime wedges or triangles of kiwifruit

1. Sprinkle gelatine over water in small saucepan; let stand 5 minutes. Slice off one end of each passion fruit and scrape every bit of juice and pulp into container of processor or blender; add berries and ⅓ cup sugar, then purée. Strain through nonaluminum sieve.

2. Stir gelatine on low heat until it dissolves. Stir in a few tablespoons of fruit purée. Scrape into a mixing bowl; add remaining purée, 2 teaspoons lime juice, and liqueur.

3. Set mixing bowl in bowl of ice and water, and stir now and then until almost jelled, but still liquid. Meanwhile, pin collar of folded waxed paper to extend 2 inches above rim of straight-sided glass or soufflé dish of about 4-cup capacity.

4. As gelatine mixture thickens up, remove from ice and stir vigorously. Beat cream until it just forms soft mounds; do not beat firm. Beat egg whites and remaining ½ teaspoon lime juice in small bowl of an electric mixer until soft, foamy billows form. Gradually beat in remaining ⅓ cup sugar and salt, beating only until soft, shiny rounded peaks form; do not beat stiff.

5. Whisk gelatine mixture to soften, if it has firmed up. At once whisk one-third of the whites into gelatine, blending completely. Fold in remainder. Fold in cream thoroughly. Gently scoop into prepared dish. Chill at least 4 hours.

6. To make sauce, scoop pulp from 2 remaining passion fruit (do not seed) and combine with remaining 2 tablespoons liqueur. Remove paper from dish. Halve berries lengthwise and press into mousse with lime or kiwi. Serve with sauce.

Note: La Grande Passion, a passion fruit and Armagnac blend, is worth the investment, to my taste.

PEPINO
(Solanum muricatum)
also Pepino Melon, Melon Pear, Melon Shrub, Mellowfruit

Given its multitude of conflicting common names, it's a wonder this poor creature has survived. Is it a *pepino*, which means cucumber in Spanish? An eggplant, which it slightly resembles and to which it is closely related? A melon or pear? I'm sorry to confuse by responding that it has a bit of the qualities of all, if you ask this taster. It is

as refreshing as a fresh summer cucumber. Its sleek skin, which has a golden ground that is dappled or striated with mauve or violet, is as flawless and satiny as that of eggplant; its shape can also resemble an eggplant's—as can its sometimes bitter aftertaste. The yellow-to-gold pulp compares to the finest-textured and juiciest melon— although it is much less sweet, while its aroma suggests a perfumed Bartlett pear blended with vanilla and honey.

A nursery catalogue states: "Here is a useful sub-tropical fruiting plant from Peru . . . which should have a place in every garden. The plant is a handsome, bushy evergreen shrub, becoming 3 feet or more in height, producing . . . quantities of oval, bright yellow fruits splashed with violet. . . . These delicious edible fruits are tender, aromatic and juicy and have a fine flavor which everyone seems to like." Written in California in 1937, these words may have taken fifty years to reach the right audience, if you judge from the present considerable interest among growers in that state.

Most of the fruit that is sold in American markets, though, comes from New Zealand (once again, it is difficult to comprehend why) and is meeting with little success, to generalize from what I have gleaned at random from soundings around the country. In Japan, however, people are willing to pay more for this fruit than just about any other. It is offered as a gift, as a dessert, as a showpiece, perfectly smooth in its glossy glory—unstuffed, unsweetened, unadorned. But the pepino's extremely pale flavor does not yet seem to fit in with American tastes, although many consider its aroma memorable. As the local Korean fruit man explained, when I marveled at how Japanese value the fruit: "Orientals understand deep tastes, not in the front." And this low-key beauty is anything but up front. Try for yourself. If you're intrigued, but unsure, keep experimenting, as the difference in quality from one fruit to another can be enormous.

SELECTION AND STORAGE: Pepino is erratically available somewhere between late winter and spring. Selection is everything with this elusive fruit, and even then there is no guarantee you will have the best. Fruits can range from the size and shape of a greengage plum to a baby football. The interior quality does not seem to change with size. Sniff the fruit deeply: it should smell lightly, but distinctly, sweet, almost like honeysuckle. Pressed, the flesh should feel like a partly ripe plum, not soft. No dents or bruises should be apparent. Most telling is the undercolor of the skin, which should be golden to pinky-apricot, not greenish or mustardy. If all but the color seems right, buy the pepino and keep at room temperature for a few days until more golden. Chill to serve. Try not to store longer, as the delicate qualities are fleeting.

USE: In South America and Japan the pepino is enjoyed straight: that's it. In New Zealand, where it is just coming into its own, it is served in every way imaginable: as a seafood and fruit salad component and container; sauced; with prosciutto; as a garnish for meats, fish, or soup; and in desserts.

PREPARATION: Although distributors' literature advises eating the skin, I find it tough and unpalatable. It pulls off quickly once you slice the fruit. The seeds are soft and pulpy and thoroughly edible. Simply spoon out or slice the refreshing, bland flesh.

NUTRITIONAL HIGHLIGHTS: Pepino is a fine source of vitamin C as well as being low in calories.

PEPPER, HOT
See Chili-Pepper

PERSIMMON
(Diospyros kaki)

*I*t should come as no surprise that the persimmon, as perfect as a gleaming, lacquered bud vase, is cultivated primarily in Japan, and is native to China. The species name, *kaki,* is also the Japanese name for the fruit (*Diospyros,* the genus, indicates that it belongs to the Ebony family). Thanks probably to Commander Perry's

expedition, it is this species that is raised today in the United States. And because of our growing Oriental population, there is an ever-increasing demand here.

While the Oriental fruit is the most familiar, it is the small native American *Diospyros virginiana* that gave us the word *persimmon*—from the Algonquin *putchamin* or *pessemin* (and a handful of other transliterations). The Algonquins collected the bite-sized treats jam-ripe from the ground where they fell and consumed them on the spot; or they dried the fruit and formed it into bricks for winter enjoyment. While most countries designate the fruit as *kaki,* Americans have held on to the Indian word despite the fact that few have tasted the difficult-to-obtain fruit from which the name derives.

Orchards of flame-orange, jelly-soft Japanese persimmon flourish in California, France, Spain, Italy, North Africa, and Chile. While many varieties are raised in these countries and 500 have been introduced into the United States—each with a slightly different color, texture, shape, and degree of tenderness and astringency (some have none)—it is the acorn-shaped Hachiya that makes up the majority of our plantings. When ripe, this large, showy fruit is unusually sweet (and firmer and more transportable than most), although experts tell me that other varieties can be more flavorful (persimmons can be faint in taste, but plums, honey, and pumpkin play parts in the whole). The smaller, rounded, light-colored Fuyu is becoming increasingly available, because it is tannin-free, even when crisp-hard, which is the way it is usually eaten. It is this non-astringent variety that is most commonly grown and enjoyed in Israel and Japan.

SELECTION AND STORAGE: You'll usually find persimmons in the market from late fall through the winter, but a few arrive at unlikely times in between (generally from Chile). Do not buy persimmons that are hard (except the aforementioned Fuyu); eating them will make your mouth pucker as though you had just downed the dregs of a bottle of undrinkably tannic wine. Look for fruit that is softer than baby cheeks (almost liquid), cradle it gently, and tote it home directly (or consume as nearby as possible). It should be sweetly luscious and messy.

Should you find too-firm persimmons, they will ripen if treated properly. A grower offers these pointers: Choose fruits that are deep, rich orange, with no trace of yellow or mustard. Place them in a plastic container stem side up, and pour a drop or two of rum, bourbon, brandy, or whatever liquor you fancy on each of the four green-brown sepals of the calyx. Close the container tightly and allow the ethylene fumes to work until the fruit is meltingly soft, which should take from three to six days. Or enclose the persimmons in a bag with a banana or apple. Eat when ripe, refrigerating only briefly, if necessary.

Although many sources advise freezing as a method of "ripening" persimmons, I find that, although they do soften, they remain bitter and become unpleasantly mushy.

USES (AND NON-USES): While freezing does not hasten ripening, it is ideal for preserving fruit that is becoming too ripe. Cut off a tiny piece of the pointed tip of the persimmon, wrap the fruit tightly, and freeze up to about 3 months.

Although recipes for puddings, cakes, muffins, breads, and pies abound in early books, the native American persimmon is the basis for these. To my taste, the creamy-soft Hachiya is virtually inedible once subjected to more than the briefest heating, becoming tough, tasteless, and astringent. I recommend eschewing all traditional recipes that hide the fruit in batter.

Generally, persimmons are at their best when least tampered with, as their unusual texture and delicate flavor are easily obscured. Press through a coarse nonaluminum sieve, adding extrafine sugar and lime juice to make a sauce for soft fruits, or cake (angel-food, sponge, pound, or génoise), pudding, gingerbread, or cornbread.

Carefully slice persimmons (preferably peeled) to combine with other subtle fruits for a dessert or salad. For such preparations the Fuyu is best; it has the texture of a plum inside, and slices neatly and easily. Halve and glaze quickly under the broiler as a simple main-course accompaniment.

PREPARATION: A rinse is about all persimmons usually need, but you may want to peel them for salads (directions are included in salad recipes). Or try the following fancy presentation from *Fruits* (the Good Cook Series of Time-Life) when you serve it as dessert. Sometimes extremely ripe fruit resists this treatment, but it is an attractive one to know. With a sharp knife cut around and into the leaf base to remove it, cone-like. Score the persimmon skin lengthwise from the tip almost to the base at 8 equal intervals. Carefully peel or pull back the skin to open out like the radiating petals of a flower or points of a star.

NUTRITIONAL HIGHLIGHTS: Persimmon is an outstanding source of vitamin A, high in fiber, and a good source of potassium. The fruit is moderately high in calories and is very low in sodium.

FROZEN PERSIMMONS

For keeping ripe persimmons out of season, or simply enjoying a new taste, try making "instant sherbet" this way:

Cut off a tiny piece of the pointed tip, then wrap the fruit tightly and freeze up to three months. When you're in the mood for a dense, sherbet-like sweet, partially thaw the persimmon in the refrigerator until just spoonable—about 4 hours; do not thaw completely or the fruit will be mushy. For an added nuance, insert the tip of a knife and dribble in a little fruit or nut liqueur. Serve the persimmon whole and let guests scoop the frozen pulp from the skin.

BROILED PERSIMMON HALVES WITH BROWN SUGAR

Serve this simple, beautiful fruit as part of a fall brunch, or alongside a main course of roast pork, duck, chicken, or ham. For each person:

1 ripe Hachiya persimmon
2 heaping teaspoons brown sugar
1½ teaspoons thinly shaved cold butter
Optional: Sour cream

1. Cut out leaf end of persimmon, then halve fruit lengthwise. Delicately slide a sharp paring knife around fruit close to the skin to free the flesh (but do not remove from skin).

2. Spread 1 heaping teaspoon brown sugar evenly on each half; dot both sides evenly with butter.

3. Set in a pan close to flame in preheated broiler. Heat only until sugar bubbles and glazes—about 1 minute—or fruit will become tough and astringent. Serve at once, with sour cream, if desired.

NUTTED PERSIMMONS

Enjoy this lush, yet simple dessert after a rich meal. Experiment with different liqueurs and nuts if you're passionate about persimmons and wish to devour them often during their short season. For each person:

1 tablespoon whole, unblanched almonds
1 ripe persimmon, preferably Hachiya
2–3 teaspoons hazelnut or almond liqueur
Very small bunch of small grapes, or a
   sliced fresh fig

1. Set almonds in pan in preheated 325-degree oven for 15 minutes, until lightly golden inside. Cool, then chop into coarse slivers.

2. Gently cut out leaf-stem end from each persimmon. Halve fruit lengthwise and set on a serving dish. With a sharp paring knife deeply score a diamond pattern into the flesh, reaching almost to the skin.

3. Drizzle liqueur slowly over each persimmon half, squeezing the fruit gently to open the interstices. Sprinkle with almonds. Set the grapes or fig in the leaf cavity and serve.

SPICE ROLL WITH PERSIMMON AND CREAM FILLING

This very tender, festive dessert has a taste reminiscent of both pumpkin pie and mango mousse—sweetly spicy, fruity, and creamy.
   8 servings

¾ cup confectioners' sugar
⅓ cup all-purpose flour
¼ teaspoon salt
1 teaspoon ground ginger
¼ teaspoon black pepper
1 teaspoon allspice
1 teaspoon cinnamon
1 teaspoon ground coriander
2 teaspoons unsweetened cocoa powder

5 eggs, separated
¼ teaspoon cream of tartar
2 tablespoons granulated sugar
2 tablespoons rum
3 very ripe medium persimmons
1 cup heavy (or whipping) cream
Confectioners' sugar or cocoa powder to
   sift over cake

1. Butter a 10-by-15-inch jelly-roll pan and line with a sheet of waxed paper to extend slightly over the short ends. Butter paper heavily.

2. Sift together ½ cup confectioners' sugar, flour, salt, ginger, pepper, allspice, cinnamon, coriander, and cocoa. Sift again.

3. In a large mixer bowl beat egg whites until foamy. Add cream of tartar and beat until soft peaks form. Sift in ¼ cup confectioners' sugar and beat until stiff peaks form.

4. Without washing beaters, whip yolks in a large bowl until pale and thick. On lowest speed, add flour mixture, beating just long enough to incorporate. With rubber spatula fold half the beaten whites into this, blending completely. Gently fold in remainder, in 2 batches.

5. Spread batter evenly in pan. Bake in center of preheated 350-degree oven for about 18–20 minutes, or until the cake springs back slightly when pressed in the center—it should no longer sound foamy-wet when pressed.

6. Sprinkle a thin layer of confectioners' sugar on a kitchen towel. Invert cake onto towel; carefully peel off paper. Starting at short end, roll up cake and towel to form neat cylinder. Cool completely.

7. Combine granulated sugar and rum in a small saucepan; cook until sugar dissolves and liquid is clear. Cool.

8. Halve persimmons lengthwise and scoop out flesh; chop roughly (there should be about 1½ cups). Whip cream to form peaks.

9. Carefully unroll cake. Paint with rum syrup; spread evenly with persimmon, leaving a 2-inch margin at one short end. Spread whipped cream evenly over persimmon. Starting at the short end that has filling up to the edge, gently but firmly roll cake. Set seam side down on a serving dish. Refrigerate, covered, for at least an hour, or up to 12.

10. To serve, trim away a very thin sliver from each end of roll to present pretty cream swirls. Sieve a thin layer of confectioners' sugar or cocoa over the roll.

ઌ *ADDITIONAL RECIPE*
Salad of Pomegranates, Persimmons, and Kiwis (page 372)

PHYSALIS
See Cape Gooseberry

PLANTAIN
(Musa X paradisiaca)
also Plátano, Plátano Macho, Cooking Banana

*I*n much of the southern hemisphere a good part of dinner is made up of cooking banana, not in a pudding or cake, but as a staple starch or main dish—whether crisply fried, baked tender, formed into spicy fritters or dumpling-like balls (kofta in India, fufu in Cuba), or simmered with a garlicky coconut-chili sauce. Northerners, just lately

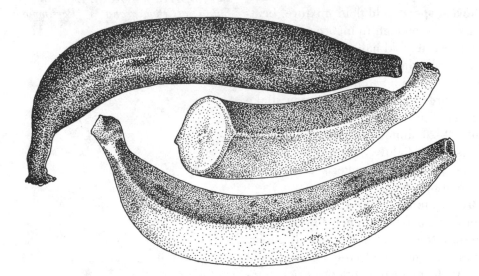

introduced to some of the members of the Musa family (which has been on earth longer than mere mortals), have begun to discover the banana's diversity, thanks to the Latin American, Caribbean, and Asian restaurants that have sprung up throughout the country. It is the cooking banana that is most popular in the tropics, the hard green or black fruit that is often passed over by many in North American markets, who believe it to be too green, too bruised, too large, or too black. Elsewhere the situation is reversed: it is the sweet dessert banana that we know so well that is eaten in moderation.

Dubbed *plantain* in North America, this vegetable-banana (called *banane-légume* in the French West Indies—where one type of banana is called a fig!) can be eaten, and tastes different, at every stage of development. The interior color of the fruit will remain creamy, yellowish, or lightly pink. When the plantain's peel is green to yellow, the flavor of the flesh is bland and its texture simply starchy, the uses similar to those for a potato. As the peel changes from yellow-brown through black, plantain plays the role of both fruit and vegetable, having a sweetness and banana aroma, but keeping a firm shape when cooked. Only experience can teach you which stages suit your taste, and consequently how you wish to incorporate the plantain in your meals.

Multiple personalities come naturally to the banana or plantain, which is, surprisingly, classified as a large berry. This botanical berry that certainly resembles no other hangs from an enormous herb, or so it is called. What appears to be a tree trunk is actually the sheathed bases of spirally arranged broad leaves, which form at ground level. The trunk-like tube of overlapping sheaths supports the mass of upper leaves and drooping clusters of fruit. The real stem is a large underground rhizome, a bulblike growth that extends massive roots from its underside. When the fruit is picked, the plant is cut down. It then develops suckers that become new "trunks," then flowers, then fruits—for up to fifty years in some areas.

SELECTION AND STORAGE: As far as I can tell, unless a plantain is dry-hard, squishy, moldy, or cracked, it's good for eating. Do not be put off by any amount of browning or blackening; that's the way plantains look. What state of ripeness you choose depends upon how you plan to cook the fruit. Kept at room temperature, it will slowly ripen through every phase and store for a considerable time, as well. (Occasionally plantains do not ripen properly, but harden instead; fully ripe black plantains should give like firm bananas. If they are hard, throw them out.) It pays to buy an oversupply if you don't regularly find plantains in your market.

Do not refrigerate plantains unless they are at the stage you wish to use them, or they will stop ripening. Even when ripe, they'll hold for a bit; so unless you have a mass of fruit and a heat wave, there's no reason to fill up the refrigerator with them.

Like bananas, plantains freeze well. When sufficiently ripe, peel, wrap each tightly in plastic, then freeze.

USE: Green or greenish plantains, which are very hard and starchy, have little banana flavor and no sweetness. They are generally cooked in the same ways as potatoes and require comparable cooking time. They are best when thin-fried as chips, made into tostones (see recipe), or boiled in chunks to be added to salty, spicy soups or stews.

Yellow-ripe plantains can be used in these same ways, and will have a lovely creamy texture and light banana scent, once cooked. They are more tender than green plantains, but nowhere near as soft as bananas. You can rinse them, cut in fairly wide crosswise sections, and boil; then peel and serve as a side dish. Add them to soups, stews, and vegetable mixtures—peeling before or after cooking, as you prefer (they hold their shape better with peel). Mash the cooked, peeled plantain, mixing with squash or apple or sweet potato. Make irresistible tostones (see recipe) and fritters. Sauté or deep-fry plantain slices—diagonals, rounds, or full lengths—to accompany roasts, stews, or broiled meat. Or rinse the plantain, trim the ends, and slit it lengthwise; bake about 45 minutes in a moderate oven and serve as you would a sweet potato.

An unusual and useful way to cook half-ripe plantains is to grill them. Cuban cook Maricel Presilla cooks the peeled and diagonally halved fruit over a low fire, basting with oil, or even better, with her delicious Mojo Agrio (see page 509). Grill slowly, turning and brushing often with oil, until tender and creamy within.

Black-ripe plantains are superb cooked as you would ripe bananas, because they hold their shape for a longer time and are therefore able to absorb more flavors and develop more complexity.

PREPARATION: If you wish to peel the plantain before cooking, the way you go about it depends on the particular fruit and its stage of ripeness. Black-ripe fruit can usually be peeled as you would a banana. Other stages are unpredictable; most require this treatment: Rinse the plantain and trim the ends. Cut fruit across in 2–4 sections, depending on size. The very thick, stiff peel is then cut lengthwise along its four ridges. Remove each strip of skin, starting at a corner and pulling slightly crosswise, rather than down the length of each strip. Remove woody fibers, if necessary, with a paring knife.

NUTRITIONAL HIGHLIGHTS: Plantain is relatively high in calories at 125 per cup. It is an excellent source of potassium, a good source of vitamin C, and low in sodium.

PLANTAIN BAKED IN ITS SKIN

For the simplest, most basic dish, plantain needs nothing more than to be baked in its skin, like a potato. Choose brown to black-ripe plantain for full flavor and softness. Baked without adornment, the plantain will be tender, not mushy, with a fruity sweetness. It is just firm enough to remove whole from the peel to be served as a vegetable accompaniment to roasted or fried meats or stews, with which it is particularly compatible. Or sprinkle over sugar, butter, and spices once the peel has baked enough to split open, then continue baking until caramelized: a truly no-fuss dessert.

Rinse and dry as many plantain as needed, usually figuring one medium-sized per person. Trim off tips. Cut lengthwise slit in each fruit. Set slit-side up in a foil-lined pan and bake in 375-degree oven until creamy-tender, about 40 minutes. When it is baked, you can peel and serve whole, or separate in lengthwise strips along the natural seed divisions, or slice crosswise in rounds or diagonals.

VARIATIONS FOR BAKED PLANTAIN:

- ☐ Cut in thin, diagonal slices and drizzle with melted butter.
- ☐ Slice in thick diagonals, sprinkle with lime juice, butter, and pure mild chili powder; heat through in the oven.
- ☐ Bake in the oven while you roast meat, then serve with pan juices or gravy.
- ☐ Prepare chili or meat sauce (figuring on ⅓–½ cup per ½ pound plantain). Pour over sliced fruit and bake at 375 degrees for about 20 minutes, until puffed and soft.
- ☐ Reheat in wide skillet with sweet dessert sauce, such as rum, caramel, or citrus.
- ☐ Slice and arrange in buttered baking dish; top with chopped pineapple, butter, brown sugar, and nuts or coconut. Bake in hot oven until bubbling.

SIMPLE SAUTÉED PLANTAIN

For an accompaniment that suits just about any dish that a fried potato might, sauté slightly sweet half-ripe plantain slices until golden brown. Rather dry, somewhat firm, they will taste like a cross between potatoes and bananas: easy, appealing, just a little out of the ordinary.

Figuring about ½ large plantain per person, peel the fruit (see Preparation). Slice in long diagonal slices about ¼ inch thick. Heat half oil and half butter in a skillet, preferably nonstick. Add the slices and sauté over moderate heat until deep gold on both sides—about 3–4 minutes per side. Lower heat as necessary so that center of each slice is tender when exterior is properly colored. Sprinkle with salt and pepper and serve.

MINERVA ETZIONI'S FRIED RIPE PLANTAIN STRIPS

Minerva Etzioni, raised in Mexico City, believed that there was no such thing as a classical preparation in her country, that each family prepared even the simplest dishes in slightly different ways. A good example of this is the standard fried ripe plantains, which in her mother's kitchen were treated to an unusual final fillip—a dip in lightly sugared water to retain the natural succulence and dispel greasiness. Mrs. Etzioni liked to arrange the golden plantain around a ring of molded Mexican rice, each piece topped with a spoonful of sour cream.

Fully ripe plantains
Vegetable oil
For each 4 plantains: 2 teaspoons sugar mixed with 1 cup boiling water.

Cut tips from each plantain, then slit skin lengthwise; unwrap from the fruit. Halve each plantain crosswise; cut each half into lengthwise slices about ¼ inch thick. Pour a thin layer of oil into a wide skillet (preferably nonstick) and heat until almost smoking. Place as many plantain strips in the pan as will fit in one layer. Fry very briefly, until just lightly golden. Turn gently and fry until lightly golden on the other side. Immediately dip each piece into the hot water and place on a baking sheet lined with paper toweling. Keep warm in a low oven while you fry the remaining plantain.

TOSTONES (FRIED PLANTAIN ROUNDS) WITH SALSA

A version of this crunchy, piquant appetizer is prepared by Gail Lewis at Sabor Restaurant in New York's Greenwich Village. The sweet, starchy *tostones*, crisp on the outside, soft in the center, are more addictive than potato chips, so be warned.

4–6 servings

SALSA

¼ pound Anaheim chilies (or other medium-hot green chili-peppers)
About ¼ cup corn oil
1 tiny onion, minced
1 small garlic clove, minced
About 3 tablespoons distilled white vinegar
About 3 tablespoons lime juice
About ½ teaspoon kosher salt
Black pepper

TOSTONES

4 half-ripe plantains, each about 8 ounces
3 cups water
1 tablespoon coarse kosher salt
1 pound solid vegetable shortening

1. Prepare sauce: Remove and discard stems (not seeds) from peppers; chop medium fine. Heat ¼ cup oil in skillet; add peppers, onion, and garlic. Cook over moderate heat until slightly softened, about 3 minutes. Off heat stir in oil, vinegar, lime juice, salt, and pepper to taste. (The sauce keeps at room temperature for a day.)

2. Cut each plantain crosswise into 3 or 4 sections. Cut lengthwise slits in skin, then pull off. Cut plantain across in ½-inch slices. Combine water and salt; soak plantains for about an hour.

3. Heat shortening in a wide skillet (about 11 inches), preferably an electric one, until it reaches 325 degrees. Drop in plantain (do not crowd) and fry until lightly golden, but not browned, turning once.

4. Remove slices with perforated spoon or spatula; place on a board, cut sides down, with plenty of space between the slices. Lay a sheet of waxed paper over the pieces; flatten each to an even thickness of ¼ inch, using a meat pounder or comparable device. Meanwhile, raise heat of fat to 375 degrees.

5. Drop in the slices, in batches if necessary. Fry until golden brown, turning once. Drain on paper towels. Serve hot with the dipping sauce.

—

MARICEL PRESILLA'S FLOWER TOSTONES

Using completely green plantains, the talented Cuban cook Maricel Presilla has devised her own decorative version of the traditional *tostones*. She cuts peeled plantain across in 1½-inch pieces and fries them in 325-degree corn oil until lightly golden. She then drains and dips into a salt-water solution. Maricel flattens the pieces as above between sheets of waxed paper; then, using a paring knife she cuts around the edge of the flattened plantain to make points or scallops. (Reshape if parts break or seem uneven, she says; the finished *tostones* will look fine.) Raise heat to 375 degrees and fry until nicely golden. Drain and serve hot with an Indian fresh coriander chutney, or the salsa in the preceding recipe, or almost any savory sauce you can imagine.

—

SUGAR-BAKED PLANTAINS

In this dessert, plantains both absorb and thicken their rich sauce, creating a deliciously sticky, brown-butter gloss. Called *plátanos en tentación* in some Latin cuisines—which translates roughly as plantain temptation—the sweet is one that can be assembled on a whim (provided you have the plantains).

4 servings

2 good-sized black-ripe plantains
2 tablespoons softened butter
1 cinnamon stick, broken up into
 smallish pieces
3 cloves
2 tablespoons lemon juice
4 tablespoons brown sugar
3 tablespoons rum
Optional: Sour cream

1. Slit plantain peel lengthwise; pull off. Halve fruit crosswise, then lengthwise. Spread half the butter in baking dish that will hold pieces closely. Arrange plantains, slightly overlapping. Scatter over cinnamon and cloves; spoon over lemon juice; top with butter, cut in small bits.

2. Bake 10 minutes in preheated 450-degree oven. Sprinkle with 2 tablespoons brown sugar. Gently turn over pieces; sprinkle with remaining sugar. Bake 10 minutes longer, or until plantain is tender-soft in center.

3. Add rum, baste, and bake 5 minutes longer, or until liquid thickens. Serve at once, with sour cream, if desired.

MINERVA ETZIONI'S SOUP OF LENTILS, HAM HOCKS, AND PLANTAINS

When Minerva Etzioni (political scientist and extraordinary cook and hostess) prepared this stick-to-the-ribs dish for her five sons and husband, the eminent sociologist Amitai Etzioni, it was merely an appetizer. For my family, this very thick soup (almost a stew) would serve as a main course, to be followed by a salad of bitter greens and crunchy sweet peppers.

Cooking the plantains *before* peeling helps retain their shape and mellow sweetness. You will soon find that you add them to other soups and stews in the way that you would potatoes.

6 servings

¼ cup corn oil
¼ cup chopped onion
1½–2 tablespoons minced garlic
2 cups crushed, peeled (see page 23) fresh or canned tomatoes
2 cups lentils, picked over and rinsed
2 small smoked ham hocks
¾ teaspoon thyme, crumbled
6–8 cups chicken or beef broth or water (my preference)
3 large plantains, half ripe
Salt and pepper to taste

1. Heat oil in a large casserole over moderate heat; add onions, then garlic, and stir briefly. Add tomatoes and cook for a few minutes to reduce slightly. Add lentils, ham hocks, thyme, and 6 cups broth.

2. Scrub plantains thoroughly with a brush, then cut into 1½-inch sections; add to soup. Bring to a boil, then turn heat to low and cover. Simmer until lentils are tender, about 50 minutes.

3. Transfer plantain sections and hocks to a board and let cool slightly. Remove skin, fat, and bones from hocks and cut meat into small bits. Add to soup and continue to simmer, uncovered. If too thick, add liquid, as desired. Add salt and pepper.

4. Peel plantains and return to soup. Simmer briefly, until the soup has reached the desired consistency.

Note: Most soup-stews will improve with a cool-down, then a day or two mellowing time in the refrigerator. This one is no exception.

RIPE PLANTAIN FRITTATA-CAKE
TORTILLA DE PLÁTANOS MADUROS

Sturdy, plain fare, this firm, sliceable melding of soft-fried plantains and eggs comes from Cuban cook Maricel Presilla. It is for those who enjoy the sweet starchiness of the fruit, for the flavor and texture of the dish *are* plantain, unembellished. The browned savory cake, sliced in wedges, can be served hot, warm, or at room temperature (which makes it a handy buffet item). Or accompany with Mardee Regan's Green Sauce (Salsa Verde) (page 469), Sauce of Dried Chili, Tomatillo, and Cilantro (page 471), or Mardee Regan's Chunky Poblano-Tomato Salsa (page 127) and salad, for a light lunch.

6 servings

4 small black-ripe plantains (about ½
    pound each)
Vegetable oil for deep-frying
8 eggs
About ½ teaspoon salt
1–2 tablespoons olive oil

1. Peel plantains; slant-cut to form slices ¼–½ inch thick and 3–4 inches long. Heat vegetable oil to 325 degrees; deep-fry slices until golden outside and soft inside, not browned, 2–4 minutes, depending on your fryer. Drain on paper towels and cool completely.

2. Blend eggs and salt in mixing bowl. Add plantains and mix.

3. Heat 1 tablespoon olive oil in 10-inch nonstick skillet (preferable); tip pan to coat sides. Pour in mixture and distribute plantain evenly so top is flat. Turn heat to moderate for a minute, until eggs form skin on underside.

4. Turn heat to lowest point. Cover and cook until not quite set through, about 15 minutes. Eggs must cook *very* slowly or they will be tough; if your heat does not turn low enough, use a flame tamer or set two burner grids together to lift pan from heat source.

5. Hold a large plate over tortilla; invert it and skillet. Slip flipped-over tortilla gently into pan (if your skillet is not non-stick type, add remaining oil and heat briefly before returning tortilla to pan). Without covering, cook on lowest heat until completely set (it will be firm, like a potato cake, not eggy), about 5 minutes. Slide onto serving plate. Serve hot, warm, or at room temperature, in wedges.

PLÁTANO
See Plantain

PLEUROTTE
See Oyster Mushrooms

POBLANO (PEPPER)
See Chile-Pepper, Poblano

POMEGRANATE
(Punica granatum)
also Chinese Apple

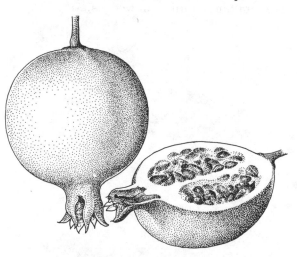

*S*cheherazade of the groves, inspiration for poets and fabulists, painters and sculptors; symbol of fertility in Chinese, Greek, Persian, Roman, and Hebrew lore, of hope in Christian art—the pomegranate has been naturalized for so long throughout the Old World that no one is quite sure where it originated (but Persia seems most likely).

Though still a constant in Eastern and Mediterranean life, the pomegranate has never grown deep roots in the culinary gardens of the New World. According to produce dealers in this country, Italians, Arabs, and children of any nationality are the best pomegranate customers. Perhaps they are in less of a rush than others, for the fruit must be consumed attentively if it is to be enjoyed. Other leisurely eaters and cooks in Spain, Italy, Central America, South America, and the Middle East—to name some of the homes of the pomegranate—happily incorporate the fruit into cooling drinks, vegetable salads, tart stews, soups, and colorful desserts. Its unique sweet-sour taste is part of everyday food, as lemon juice is in the United States.

The size of a smallish grapefruit, crowned with a turret-like calyx that gives the fruit a regal look, covered with a leathery skin, the pomegranate (from the Latin *pomum granatum*, meaning apple or fruit of many seeds) is so distinctive that it has a genus of its own. Its translucent, scarlet pulp surrounds myriad tiny seeds (each fleshy, glassy unit is called an *aril*) that are compartmentalized between shiny, tough white membranes. Working one's way through the indelible ruby juices and seeds is an act of devotion. Although many types are cultivated world-wide, running the gamut from golden to garnet, from tart to sweet, there is just one major market variety available in the United States. Humbly called "Wonderful" or "Red Wonderful," it is very red, very large, and sweet, with relatively large seeds.

SELECTION AND STORAGE: Pomegranates show up in the fall and early winter. Look for richly colored, large fruits, which will have a higher proportion of the clear red, juicy-crisp pulp. Heavy fruits promise more juice. If powdery clouds puff from the crown when it is pressed, move on: the pomegranate will be dusty dry. Although the skin is tough, it should be fairly thin, almost splitting from the full seeds within.

Pomegranates keep miraculously well. Whole, in the refrigerator, they'll last for up to three months. The seeds, packed tightly into an airtight container in the freezer, will keep about the same amount of time. To use, scrape them out of the container without defrosting and scatter the desired quantity over food.

USE: Once you've gotten the pomegranate habit, it's hard to stop. Just about any dish will be enhanced by a sprinkling of the tart, glistening seeds, a made-to-order size for garnishing dishes throughout a meal. They add texture, color, and a burst of flavor to vegetable or fruit salads; they provide a lovely finish for soups; point up the acidity of a sauce for meat or fowl; and look ravishing on fruit desserts, ices, ice creams, and tarts.

PREPARATION: In this case, preparation means separating the seeds, and although a laborious task, it is an aesthetically and culinarily rewarding one. To remove the arils from their rubbery white chambers: Cut out the blossom end of the fruit, removing with it some of the white pith, but taking care not to pierce the red seeds within. Lightly score the skin in quarters, from stem to blossom end. Gently break the fruit in half, following the score lines, then break each piece in half again. (Do not cut the fruit, or you will release the juices.) Bend back the rind and pull out the seeds. Although some recommend spitting out the seeds when you've finished eating the pulp, I can't imagine it worth the trouble of eating a pomegranate unless you enjoy the seed crunch.

Juicing is another matter. I have yet to find a satisfactory method for obtaining the juice and keeping it (see method following). (Although halving, then juicing the pomegranate on a reamer is often suggested, the results are usually unpleasantly tannic.) Here's a pleasurable way to drink up: Place the whole, unpeeled pomegranate on a hard surface: press the palm of your hand against the fruit, then roll gently to break all the juice sacs inside (you'll be able to hear when they've stopped rupturing). Prick a hole and suck out the juice; or poke in a straw and do the same, more tidily, pressing the fruit all the while to release the liquids.

NUTRITIONAL HIGHLIGHTS: Pomegranate has a stupendous quantity of potassium and more modest amount of vitamin C. It is relatively low in calories (105 per fruit) and very low in sodium.

POMEGRANATE SYRUP (GRENADINE)

Because this familiar drink mixer is generally marketed without pomegranate juice these days, it makes good sense to concoct your own homemade version, which will have a *raison d'être* in addition to color. The most popular brand of grenadine currently available in retail stores contains corn sweetener, sugar-cane syrup, water, citric acid, natural fruit flavors—not pomegranate, the manufacturer assured me haughtily—FD & C red dye 40, and sodium benzoate. The following product costs less, lasts as long, and adds sweetness, a slight pomegranate flavor, and a carmine hue to drinks, fruit mixtures (raw or cooked), and sauces.

Makes about 2 cups

2 large pomegranates, seeded (see
    Preparation), or 2 cups seeds
2 cups sugar

1. Combine seeds and sugar in a non-aluminum saucepan; stir to mix, crushing until you have a wet mass. Cover and let stand 12–24 hours.

2. Bring to a boil over moderate heat, stirring constantly. Lower heat and simmer 2 minutes.

3. Strain out seeds, pressing down to extract juice. Pour into a hot sterilized jar. Cover with a piece of cloth or clean towel until cooled. Remove cloth, cap tightly, then refrigerate.

SALAD OF POMEGRANATES, PERSIMMONS, AND KIWIS

Serve this exquisitely gaudy concoction to take the place of both fruit and salad courses, after a rich meal. Or offer it as the opening course for an unusual fall meal.

4 servings

1 large pomegranate, seeded (see
    Preparation), or 1 cup seeds
1 cup yogurt
About 1 tablespoon honey
About 1 tablespoon lemon juice
4 small ripe persimmons (Fuyu variety
    does well here)
4 kiwis, peeled, halved lengthwise, then
    sliced crosswise

1. Lightly crush ⅔ cup pomegranate seeds in a bowl to extract some juice. Stir in yogurt and honey and lemon juice to taste. Refrigerate for ½ hour or longer.

2. Cut out leaf base from the persimmons, then halve fruits lengthwise. With a sharp paring knife gently cut into the flesh as close to the skin as possible, to separate the two. (Alternatively, if you have one of the jelly-soft persimmons, you may have to first cut the fruit into lengthwise slices, then delicately pare off the skin from each slice.) Gently cut into slices.

3. Arrange persimmon and kiwi slices on 4 salad plates. Drizzle the dressing over each, then sprinkle the reserved pomegranate seeds over all.

SALAD OF WINTER SQUASH, POMEGRANATE, AND CHICORY

Colorful and festive, this salad makes a fine accompaniment to roasted pork or poultry. Look for pale, frizzly imported French chicory *(chicorée frisée)*, which is more tender and mild than the domestic.

6 servings

1 small butternut squash (about 1¾ pound) or a chunk of calabaza the same weight
1 tablespoon grated fresh ginger
½ teaspoon salt, or to taste
2 tablespoons lemon juice
2 tablespoons cider vinegar
½ cup corn oil
1 medium-small curly chicory (about ¾ pound), washed, dried, and cut into thin slivers
1 large pomegranate, seeded (see Preparation) or about 1 cup seeds

1. Halve squash and remove seeds; cut into 2-inch sections and pare off rind. Cut flesh into thin julienne strips. Drop into boiling salted water; return to a boil, then drain at once. Drop into a bowl of ice water, then drain. Spread on an absorbent towel to dry.

2. Combine ginger, salt, lemon juice, and vinegar in a jar; shake to blend. Add oil and shake again. Combine three-quarters of the dressing with squash. Toss and refrigerate until serving time.

3. To serve, toss remaining dressing with chicory; add squash and pomegranate seeds and mix gently.

SHERRIED GELATINE WITH GRAPES AND POMEGRANATE

If you've forgotten how subtle "real" gelatine can be, try this shimmering golden dessert, rich in winy-fruity flavor and dotted with sparkling garnet and russet morsels. Not only that, it's low-calorie.

6 servings

2 packets unflavored gelatine
3 cups white grape juice (24-ounce bottle)
½ cup medium-dry sherry (Amontillado)
1 cup seedless red grapes (about 6 ounces), halved across
3 tablespoons fresh pomegranate seeds (see Preparation)

1. Sprinkle gelatine over 1 cup of grape juice in small pan; let stand a few minutes to soften. Stir over low heat until gelatine dissolves completely.

2. Pour gelatine into a bowl. Add remaining grape juice and sherry. Set in a larger bowl of ice and water and stir occasionally until almost set—about 35–40 minutes; it should be lumpy and thick.

3. Fold in grapes and pomegranate seeds gently with a rubber spatula, distributing evenly. Pour into a glass serving dish and chill for several hours.

❧ *ADDITIONAL RECIPE*
Layered Fresh Kiwis, Oranges, and Pomegranates (page 258)

POMELO
See Pummelo

PORCINI
See Bolete

PRICKLY PEAR
See Cactus Pear

PUMMELO
(Citrus grandis and *Citrus maxima)*
also Shaddock, Chinese Grapefruit

*T*he first time I met up with pummelo was in a tiny family restaurant in Martinique. The menu included *conserve de chadec* (a French corruption of Shaddock or Chaddock, the captain who brought the fruit seed to the West Indies in the mid-seventeenth century). This turned out to be a few slim slices of peel preserved in thick

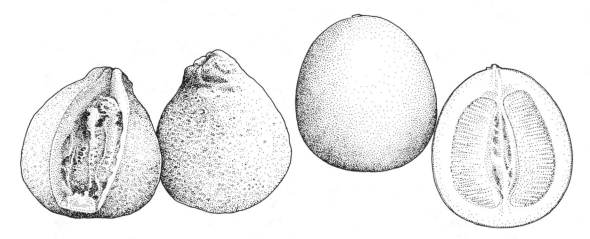

syrup, dropped unceremoniously on a dingy saucer. A standard dessert in the Antilles, it was absolutely delicious. The second meeting was at a Chinese New Year celebration in New York City, where the entire giant, grapefruit-like fruit was offered as part of a ceremony. (Unfortunately the role it played at the celebration was spiritual, not corporeal, so it went untasted.) The third was in Singapore, during pummelo season, when an entire block of markets is devoted to the fruit. Here, I tasted many.

Still enormously popular in the lands of its origin (the Malaysia-Indochina region), where it grows abundantly, it is also cultivated in China and Japan, where, unlike other citrus, it thrives in tropical lowlands, particularly around brackish water. Ranging from the size of a baby cantaloupe to near basketball size, slightly pear-shaped or round, greenish to yellow to pinkish, the pummelo is the largest citrus fruit. It has an enormously thick, rather soft pith and rind that begs to be conserved, as mentioned. The quality of the pale yellow to pink fruit within—which ends up being just slightly larger than a good-sized grapefruit, once peeled—differs dramatically from one variety to another: from pleasantly juicy to dryish, from slightly acid to very sweet, from enormously seedy to seedless, from insipid to spectacular. What all pummelos lack, unlike grapefruits, is bitterness of any kind, which makes them a likely candidate for development in this country where some small groves are doing well.

SELECTION AND STORAGE: Look for pummelos in Oriental markets and some supermarkets from mid-January through mid-February. Take what you can find, as they are scarce and much-prized. If you have a choice, look for what you would in a grapefruit: heaviness, filled-out skin, a rich aroma (which pummelos have in abundance). Store in the refrigerator. Since it's difficult to tell how long the pummelo has been on the road, I'd suggest using it fairly promptly.

USE: Once you've removed all pith and membrane (see below), you can use the pummelo as you would grapefruit sections. A light sugar syrup, poured warm over the sections, will enhance the fruit. Or, for a salad, marinate the divided sections in dressing for a while before serving. Serve pummelo in small bits in mixed fruit cup and fruit salad. Or pull the pulp into vermicelli-like strands, to serve as a refreshing side-dish, as is done throughout Asia.

PREPARATION: Every bit of the heavy pith and membrane must be removed from a pummelo before it is edible. Cut off the ends of the fruit, score the thick skin, and peel off pith and rind together in thick pieces, so you can candy it later on. Separate the segments and pull off the entire membrane covering from each. This is easy to do because the firm pulp stays compact and does not burst, as a grapefruit would. Slice or break the very large sections, or separate into small strands or vesicles.

NUTRITIONAL HIGHLIGHTS: Pummelo is an excellent source of vitamin C and potassium. It is low in sodium and contains 75 calories per cup.

PUMMELO MARMALADE

The generous quantity of pectin-rich peel makes a lustrous, honeyish marmalade with a pleasant bitterness. The preparation process for marmalade is easier than some realize—and is made even easier by the food-processor method below. Look for fruit that is firm and fresh, or even immature, which is fine for marmalade. With withered, older fruit you may have difficulty reaching a jelling point.

Makes about 8 half-pint jars

1 large pummelo (about 16 inches
  around, 1½–2 pounds)
1 quart water
About 7 cups sugar
⅓ cup lime juice
⅓ cup lemon juice

1. Score pummelo lengthwise to remove skin and attached white pith. Cut membranes from fruit and place them in nonaluminum saucepan with water. Separate flesh from seeds, placing seeds in pan. Chop flesh; place in large bowl.

2. Using shredding blade, process rind and pith pieces, pushing down hard so that you get good-sized shreds. Combine in saucepan with water to cover generously. Bring to a boil; boil 1 minute. Drain.

3. Gently simmer seeds and membrane, partly covered, for 45 minutes. Strain, pressing to extract all liquid; discard solids. Add enough water to this liquid to make 5 cups. Combine with pulp in mixing bowl; add shredded peel. Cover; let stand in a relatively cool place for about 24 hours.

4. Measure fruit mixture. Combine in a wide pot with an equal amount of sugar; add lime and lemon juices. Bring to a boil, stirring.

5. Continue boiling, stirring often as mixture thickens; then stir constantly as shreds begin to stick to bottom of pot. Continue boiling until marmalade reaches the jellying point. To test for this, dip a clean, cool metal spoon in the syrup (don't pick up shreds), move it away from the steam, then tilt so jelly runs out. If it forms a stream, or falls in two distinct drops, boil the marmalade a little longer. If the two drops travel slowly along the rim of the spoon and merge, remove the pot from the heat at once. Test often, using a clean spoon each time.

6. Ladle into hot, just-washed jars. Clean jar rims with a towel dipped in boiling water. Put the appropriate number of two-piece screw-type vacuum lids in a bowl and pour boiling water over them. Place flat lids on jars, then put on screw bands and tighten. Arrange jars on a rack in a large pot. Pour in hot water to cover by 2 inches. Bring to a boil, covered. Boil 10 minutes.

7. With tongs, remove jars (do not pick up by lids) to a towel. Do not disturb for 6 hours or more. Press centers of lids to be sure they remain depressed. (If they are flexible, refrigerate them, as they have not sealed.) Store in a dark cabinet up to a year.

CANDIED PUMMELO PEEL

Those who are fond of glacéed fruit peel will be delighted with this exquisite confection. Paler, more fruity, less bitter than grapefruit peel, the candy has a sugar-crusted exterior and transparent, unusually tender interior. The peel from one pummelo yields a full 1¼ pounds of candy. Serve with after-dinner coffee and brandy.

Makes about 1¼ pounds

1 large pummelo (about 16 inches in circumference)
1½ cups sugar
1½ cups water
⅓ cup light corn syrup
Additional sugar (about 1¼ cups) for coating peel

1. Deeply score pummelo skin and pith lengthwise in eighths. Pull off skin and thick white pith together. Wrap and reserve fruit for another use. Cut peel on the bias into strips ¼ inch wide or slightly less. There will be about 4 cups.

2. Cover peel with water and bring to a boil; boil a minute, then drain and rinse quickly. Repeat.

3. Cover again with cold water and bring to a boil. Lower heat and simmer until outer rind is barely tender—about 10 minutes. Drain.

4. Combine 1½ cups sugar, 1½ cups water, and corn syrup in a heavy, wide saucepan of 2–3-quart capacity. Bring to a boil; boil 1 minute. Add peel; boil gently until syrup gets thickish, stirring now and then. Continue boiling gently, stirring often, being careful not to break up peel. Boil until almost no liquid remains. Then stir constantly until no liquid remains visible in bottom of pot. (The whole operation will take about 40 minutes.)

5. Spread 1 cup sugar on large baking sheet. Lift pummelo strips onto this with a fork, a few at a time. Separate and straighten them as you proceed. Let cool slightly, then sprinkle with ¼ cup sugar. As strips cool, toss them gently to coat and separate.

6. When thoroughly cooled, spread strips on a rack. Dry until crunchy-crisp, which may take a day or more, depending on the weather. Pack in airtight containers.

PUMPKIN
See Calabaza, Kabocha

Q

QUINCE
(Cydonia oblonga)

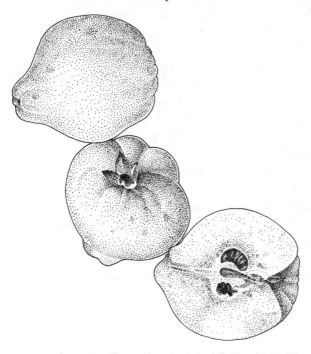

*T*he beautiful quince tree, its blossom a mainstay of Oriental art, bears fruit of several forms. It may be the color and size of a Comice pear, or golden and shaped more like a Delicious apple. The skin may be covered with a woolly down, or it may be smooth. You can pluck it in Greece or the United States, Argentina or New Zealand, France or Iran (its probable birthplace—although the name *Cydonia* derives from an area of Crete) and a host of other countries. The quince's only constant factor is its penetrating perfume, musky-wild as a tropical fruit, reminiscent of pineapple, guava, Bartlett pear, and apple—depending on the variety you have in hand.

Until recently, this aromatic fruit was considered a staple in kitchens all over the United States and the rest of the world, but it has now been demoted to a "specialty item." Perhaps it is because so many homemakers have given up preserving that the quince's popularity has faded, for it is the quintessential put-up fruit. It yields a remarkable amount of pectin, which makes it ideal for naturally jelled confections: jelly, jam, fruit leather, candy, conserves, and marmalade—the very word comes from the Portuguese word for quince, *marmelo*.

Quince requires cooking to be edible, unlike most fruits. Its very firm, dryish flesh seldom softens to eating texture or develops enough sugar to be enjoyed raw. But the hard, ivory interior, when slowly cooked, develops a rich flavor and appealing pale apricot to carnelian hue that make it a delight in sweet and savory dishes.

SELECTION AND STORAGE: Quinces are likely to appear—whatever variety chance

378

brings—in the fall, but they make odd appearances now and then at other times. Choose large, aromatic, smooth fruits, which are easier to peel and less wasteful than small, knotty ones. If only blemished fruits can be found, they'll be fine, once cooked.

If you wish to perfume a room, store quinces at room temperature for a week or so. For longer storage, wrap each fruit in a double layer of plastic and refrigerate where it won't be bumped. While quinces bruise easily, they last for months—so stock up.

USES: Poaching, stewing, baking, and braising bring out the unique flavor and dense but melting texture of this close-grained fruit. In addition to its world-wide confectionery role, in Persian, Balkan, Rumanian, and Moroccan cuisine, quinces are traditionally combined with meat in stews, or served as accompaniments to roasts. They are ideal in long-cooked dishes, as they hold their shape beautifully, neither becoming soft nor disintegrating, as apples would. Quinces are lovely when simply stewed, as a dessert, breakfast dish (with cream), or side dish for meats (with a sprinkling of nuts, or spices to suit). Or add a small proportion of peeled, sliced cooked quinces to pear and apple dishes for a surprising amplification of flavor. Include the same in pies and tarts or puddings. Purée to use as you would a full-bodied applesauce.

PREPARATION: Prepare quinces for cooking by peeling and coring thoroughly; protect your fingers as you hack out the rock-hard centers. (For purées, the fruit need not be cored beforehand.) Although it is not absolutely necessary to remove the peel, which cooks to an edible texture, I find that it usually adds an undesirable bitterness. If you won't be using the seeds, core, and peel for the dish you're making, tie them in a cheesecloth bag and cook with a batch of stewed fruit to add body and flavor.

NUTRITIONAL HIGHLIGHTS: Quinces are a good source of fiber, a fair source of vitamin C and potassium, and are low in calories.

HONEY-BAKED QUINCE SLICES

Baked to a rich pink-gold, this quince dish tastes like intensified apples, but less juicy. Serve the slices with cream, for dessert; or as an accompaniment to smoked meats, fowl, or pork. The fruit is at its best warm or at room temperature, not chilled.

4 or 5 servings

4 medium quinces, about 2 pounds
4 tablespoons fragrant, light honey
2 tablespoons lime juice
3 tablespoons water

1. Quarter and peel quinces. With melon-ball cutter or very sharp knife, remove the entire core area, being sure no hard bits remain. Cut each quarter lengthwise into 4 slices. Arrange the slices closely overlapping in a baking dish about 7–8 inches wide and 10–12 long.

2. Drizzle honey evenly over slices to coat them; sprinkle with lime juice and water. Cover closely with foil.

3. Bake in center of preheated 300-degree oven for about 40 minutes to an hour, until slices are very tender. Remove the foil, raise heat to 425 degrees, and bake about 10 minutes, until syrup is slightly thickened and slices are golden.

CHICKEN BAKED WITH QUINCES

In this simple and special dish, quinces show off their unusual ability to remain neatly intact, even as they become yielding with prolonged cooking. Subtly spicy and fruity, this combination produces a unique fall pleasure.

4 servings

4 medium quinces, about 2 pounds
1 cup apple juice
1 cup fruity, aromatic white wine
About 2 tablespoons light brown sugar
¼ cup flour
½ teaspoon salt
3–3½-pound chicken, in serving pieces
2 tablespoons butter
1 tablespoon vegetable oil
2 teaspoons ground coriander
White pepper

1. Quarter, peel, and core quinces. Combine in a nonaluminum pan with apple juice and wine; simmer, covered, until tender. (Timing varies, but 30–50 minutes is usual.) Add sugar to taste; sim-mer, uncovered, until pan liquid reduces to 1 cup—about 5–10 minutes.

2. Meanwhile, mix flour and salt; dredge chicken in this. Brown in very large skillet in butter and oil. Pour off fat. Sprinkle chicken with 1 teaspoon corian-der; turn over and sprinkle with remain-der. Transfer to wide baking dish and grind over the pepper.

3. Pour quince liquid into pan in which chicken browned; bring to a boil, stirring. Pour over chicken. Add quinces; cover. Bake in upper level of preheated 375-degree oven for 15 minutes. Baste thoroughly. Bake 15 minutes longer, bast-ing several times, until glazed and golden.

STEW OF QUINCES AND LAMB WITH SAFFRON AND SPLIT PEAS

Mrs. Simin Samiy of the Caspian Tea Room in Washington, D.C., prepares this dish in the comfortable restaurant and pastry shop that she runs with her husband, Fatola. In their native Iran, relatively small quantities of meat are cooked in combination with fruits, vegetables, and grains, serving more as a rich flavoring medium than a main ingredient. Thus, a dish such as the one that follows would contain more quince and split peas and less meat if prepared Iranian style and more meat if prepared in true American restaurant fashion. This version, somewhere between the two, is thick with slices of the fruit in a hearty gravy. The lightly sweet-tart flavor balance is typically Iranian.

Serve with a generous amount of fluffy, white long-grain rice, preferably imported basmati or an aromatic grain grown in the United States.

6 servings

1 large onion, coarsely diced
1 tablespoon light vegetable oil
2¼ pounds lean stewing lamb in large
    pieces
About 3 cups water
About 1½ teaspoons salt
Pepper to taste
3 fragrant quinces—1½–2 pounds
2 tablespoons butter
⅓ cup yellow split peas, picked over and
    rinsed
About ⅓ cup fresh lemon juice
About 1 tablespoon sugar
¼–½ teaspoon saffron threads in 2
    tablespoons boiling water

1. In a heavy flameproof casserole over moderate heat stir onion in oil until browned. Add meat and brown on all sides. Add water, 1¼ teaspoons salt, and pepper. Simmer gently, covered, for ½ hour.

2. Meanwhile, quarter quinces and cut out every bit of the cores and seeds. (Reserve this in the refrigerator to cook with stewed fruit for added body and flavor.) Cut into ⅛–¼-inch slices. Sauté over moderate heat in a very wide skillet in the butter until lightly colored—about 5–10 minutes.

3. Add quinces, split peas, ¼ cup lemon juice, and 2 teaspoons sugar to the lamb. Bring to a boil, then turn to lowest heat. Add saffron liquid. Cook, partly covered, until the peas and lamb are tender—about 1 hour, stirring gently every now and then. You may have to cook a little longer, or add a little water; keep testing.

4. Adjust lemon juice, sugar, salt, and pepper to taste. Cook, then cover and refrigerate until serving time.

Note: Like most stews, this one improves if allowed to mellow a day or two before serving. Skim off fat before reheating.

QUINCE CONSERVE WITH VANILLA

Slivers of melting quince in heavy, golden-pink syrup will embellish breakfast, brunch, or teatime loaves, buns, rolls, brioche, or croissants. Spoon a little of the soft vanilla-scented confection onto a thick layer of cream cheese- or butter-gilded bread, or savor a spoonful alongside strong tea, à la russe.

Makes 6 or 7 half-pints

About 4 pounds quinces, washed
¼ cup lemon juice
4 cups sugar
1 large, tender vanilla bean, cut into 7 pieces (see Note)

1. Quarter, peel, and core quinces, placing all peelings in a nonaluminum pot. Add water to barely cover; simmer, covered, until very tender, about 45 minutes or more.

2. Meanwhile, halve each quince quarter lengthwise. Using medium (4 millimeter) slicing blade of processor, cut thin crosswise slices. Combine with lemon juice and water to cover.

3. When peelings are tender, strain cooking liquid and return to pan. Drain and add quince slices. Simmer, covered, until not quite tender—15–30 minutes.

4. Add sugar; stir until dissolved. Add vanilla. Boil gently until quince is very tender and translucent—about 45 minutes.

5. Lift out fruit slices with slotted spoon, draining completely over pan. Place in hot, just-washed half-pint jars, leaving 1–1½ inches headspace. Check that there is a vanilla piece in each jar.

6. Boil syrup until it reaches the jelly stage. Check for this as follows: Dip a clean metal spoon in syrup. Move it away from the steam, then tilt so jelly runs off. If it forms a stream or falls in 2 distinct drops, continue boiling. If two drops travel slowly along the rim and merge, remove pot from heat at once. Test often, using a clean spoon each time. Pour syrup into each jar to reach within ¼ inch of the top.

7. Wipe jar rims with a towel dipped in boiling water. Place appropriate number of two-piece screw-type vacuum lids in a bowl and pour boiling water over them. Set lids on filled jars, then place bands on these and screw shut. Arrange jars on a rack in a large pot; pour in hot water to cover by at least 1½ inches. Bring to a boil, covered. Process 10 minutes for half-pints, keeping at a full boil. Using tongs, remove jars and set on a towel. Do not disturb for 12 hours. Press centers of lids to be sure they remain depressed; if any remain flexible, or pop up, refrigerate. The conserve can be stored for a year in a dark place.

Note: If you can get the gloriously fragrant large Tahitian vanilla beans, I recommend them wholeheartedly.

QUINCE MARMALADE WITH LEMON AND GINGER

I think it worthwhile to make a healthy amount of any preserve—particularly this luscious quince—but you can halve this recipe if you prefer. The quince mixture sits for 12 hours or so before canning, so plan accordingly.

Makes 12 half-pints

3 pounds quinces
2 lemons
Large chunk fresh ginger, about 5 inches
   long
About 10 cups sugar

1. Peel and core quinces, reserving cores in a small saucepan. Shred quince coarse or cut into fine julienne strips, using a processor or vegetable shredder. Combine with water to not quite cover in a large, heavy nonaluminum pot.

2. Halve lemons lengthwise. Remove seeds, if any, and add them to quince cores. Slice lemon thin and add to quince. Peel and coarsely grate ginger; add to lemon and quince. Boil this mixture gently for 5 minutes, then remove from heat.

3. Add water to cores and seeds to cover by a few inches. Boil gently for 30 minutes, adding water as needed to keep covered. Strain the pectin-rich liquid into quince mixture. Cover seeds and cores with fresh water and boil gently for another 30 minutes, to extract more pectin. Strain into quince. Cover the pot with a clean towel and let stand about 12 hours.

4. Measure mixture and divide between 2 heavy, nonaluminum pots. Add same amount of sugar as there is fruit to each (about 10 cups of each total). Bring to a boil, stirring often. Continue boiling and stirring until mixture becomes thick and sticky. Stir constantly to prevent scorching as mixture reaches the jelly stage. To test for this, dip a clean metal spoon into syrup (don't pick up shreds). Move away from steam, then tilt spoon so jelly runs off. If it forms a stream or falls in 2 distinct drops, continue boiling. If 2 drops travel slowly along the rim and merge, remove the pot from the heat at once. Test often, using a clean spoon.

5. Ladle into hot, just-washed jars. Proceed as in step 6 of Quince Conserve with Vanilla (preceding recipe).

QUINCE AND ALMOND TART

An abundance of smooth, intense quince slices are cooked in brown-sugar syrup, then arranged prettily over an almond filling baked in a flaky pastry case.

8 servings

1½ pounds quinces (preferably small
    ones, about 4)
1 cup light brown sugar
1 small piece vanilla bean

PASTRY
1¼ cups flour
¼ teaspoon salt
1 teaspoon sugar
5 tablespoons chilled unsalted butter, cut
    in small bits
2½ tablespoons chilled vegetable
    shortening, cut in small bits
About 3 tablespoons ice water, as needed

FILLING
1 cup plus 2 tablespoons almonds (not
    blanched), lightly toasted
2 tablespoons sugar
1 egg, lightly beaten
¼ cup milk
⅛ teaspoon almond extract
Pinch of salt

1. Halve and peel quinces, reserving peelings. With melon-ball cutter, remove seeds and cores. Combine with peelings in large, nonaluminum pot. Add quince halves and water to cover. Simmer, partly covered, until almost tender, 30–45 minutes. Add sugar and vanilla and simmer, uncovered, until fruit is soft (which can vary from ½ to 1½ hours; test often). With slotted spoon transfer quinces to a dish; cool, cover, then chill. Strain out peels and cores. Reserve cooking syrup.

2. Make pastry: Blend flour, salt, and sugar in processor. Add butter and shortening and process just until the mixture resembles oatmeal flakes. Scrape into a bowl. Gradually sprinkle in ice water, tossing with a fork until dough can be massed together easily into a ball. Form a disk ½ inch thick; wrap and refrigerate 30 minutes or more.

3. Roll dough on lightly floured surface to form a circle 12–13 inches in diameter. Fit into a fluted 9½-inch tart pan with a removable bottom. Trim edge, leaving a 1-inch overhang: turn this in; press to form slightly raised border. Line shell with foil and fill with dried beans or other weights. Bake in preheated 400-degree oven until edge is set—about 8 minutes. Carefully lift out foil and beans, prick crust here and there with skewer, and bake until lightly browned—about 10 minutes. Set on a rack to cool. Lower oven heat to 375 degrees.

4. Prepare filling: combine 1 cup almonds with sugar in processor. Whirl until finely ground. Add egg, milk, almond extract, and salt, and whirl to a smooth, light purée. Spread in pastry shell.

5. Cut quinces on a slant into ¼-inch slices. Arrange, closely overlapping, with wide ends against tart rim. Fill in spaces with quince slices. Bake in lower third of oven 30 minutes.

6. Meanwhile, boil reserved quince syrup until reduced to a thick, syrupy glaze. When tart has baked 30 minutes, brush with glaze. Bake 15 minutes longer.

7. Remove tart from oven and paint generously with glaze. Sliver remaining 2 tablespoons almonds; scatter over tart.

QUINCE PASTE CANDY

This sweet, a time-honored favorite in France, where it is called *cotignac*, is also familiar as *membrillo* in Spain. It makes a charming old-fashioned gift.

Because it takes a long time to reduce to the proper consistency, I'd suggest a few helping hands for stirring—but not little ones, as the hot paste splutters dangerously.

Makes about 1¾ pounds, or about 96 pieces

2 pounds quinces
About 3 cups sugar
Granulated sugar for coating candies, preferably vanilla-flavored
A few cinnamon sticks and bay leaves

1. Quarter and peel quinces (I find the peel adds bitterness, although it is often included); do not core. Slice fruit roughly and combine in a heavy pot with water to barely cover. Simmer, covered, for 1 hour, or until very tender. Let cool, then cover with a clean towel and let stand overnight.

2. Press mixture through medium disk of a food mill, leaving only seeds. Simmer in a heavy pan, stirring occasionally, to reduce by about one-quarter and thicken slightly (about 3 cups purée is average).

3. Measure the purée and add an equal amount of sugar. Cook over moderate heat, stirring occasionally as mixture begins to thicken; then stir more often to prevent scorching. Toward the end you will be stirring constantly. It should take an hour or more to produce a paste thick enough to leave a neat trench when a spoon is pulled through it.

4. Spread purée evenly in 3 *very, very* lightly oiled 8-by-8-inch pans, or thereabouts. Leave mixture overnight, or as long as necessary to become dry enough to turn over; the surface should not be sticky. This can take from 12 to 48 hours, depending on the weather. Flip the slabs onto a rack and let dry until no longer very sticky to the touch.

5. With a fluted pastry cutter (or knife), cut the slabs into 2-by-1-inch strips. Toss them in sugar. Set on a rack to dry overnight.

6. Pack candy in airtight containers, separating the layers with waxed paper. Break up a cinnamon stick or two and a couple of bay leaves and place in each tin for added aroma.

QUINCE CORDIAL

This makes a strong, golden, rather spicy liqueur. I like it iced, in tiny glasses.
Makes about 3 cups

1 medium quince
3 whole cardamom pods
1 clove
2 cups white rum
⅓ cup sugar
⅓ cup water

1. Peel and roughly chop quince; do not core. Combine with cardamom, clove, and rum in a clean, wide-mouthed 1-quart jar. Cover with plastic, then cap tightly.

2. Let stand in a dark place for a month or more, shaking the jar whenever you think of it.

3. Boil sugar and water for 3 minutes; cool completely. Strain out and discard solids from the liqueur. Strain through several thicknesses of fine cheesecloth. Add sugar syrup gradually, to taste.

4. Pour liqueur into a bottle that will hold it with little air space. Kept this way, in a dark place, the cordial will last a year.

R

RADICCHIO
(Cichorium intybus)
also Red Chicory, Red-Leafed Chicory

*F*ive years ago few in this country were familiar with the stunning red-leafed chicory that became the darling of American chefs, and later quietly part of the home cook's domain. Probably no other vegetable has done as much to decorate, enliven, and refresh the American salad plate—and it tastes absolutely wonderful cooked, as

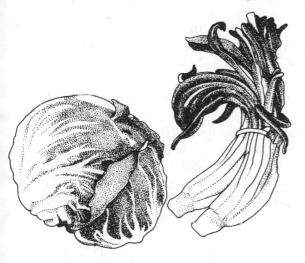

well. When I first became aware of the bittersweet, satiny, crisp chicory, it cost $6 per half pound and was available only at the fanciest imported produce shops. This summer I bought it at a supermarket on Cape Cod for $2 per half pound (after having nobly—and foolishly—explained to the reluctant and stubborn checkout girl that it was not baby red cabbage, for which she would have charged 39 cents a pound).

Radicchio (rahd-EEK-ee-o), the Italian name for chicory, reveals the provenance of the glamorous and useful vegetable that has been part of the European salad bowl, in its wild form, since salads in bowls became part of the repertoire. In fact, much of the most beautiful, deep-colored radicchio is still imported from Italy. All cultivated red chicories, which much resemble their wild grandparents, are unpredictable growers. They begin life as bright green leaves, then turn deeper green, then red as the weather cools. Some, however, never turn red, and the chameleon act also includes changing the shape of both leaves and head as the plant matures, which means any type may end up with characteristics of the others. But all have a typical firmness of leaf and distinct bittersweet flavor that is very similar to that of their close relatives escarole and Belgian endive.

The varieties, named after their growing regions, look quite different from one another. The round deep-burgundy to red-bronze *radicchio rosso* (also called *radicchio di Verona, rosso di Verona,* or *red Verona chicory*) is shaped rather like a cabbage rose and has shiny, smooth leaves with white central ribs. It may range from Bibb to Boston lettuce size. Radicchio di Treviso or red Treviso chicory has spear-shaped leaves, which are pink to deep red. It resembles a sharp-petaled, narrow tulip and may be as small as baby endive or large as a small romaine. It has been cultivated in Italy since the sixteenth century and is probably the forebear of the other varieties. Radicchio di Castelfranco and radicchio di Chioggia both have variegated leaves (whether pink, green, or red flecked and swirled), looser heads, and a slightly crinkly texture; in size and shape they are similar to Verona chicory.

SELECTION AND STORAGE: Radicchio is available virtually year round, whether from Italy, Mexico, California, or New Jersey (so far, the domestic chicory has been far less flamboyantly colored). You can usually be sure of finding a perfect specimen if the white core at the base is firm, unblemished, and free of holes, but occasionally one will be brown inside. Leaves should exhibit no browning at the edge and should seem spunky, not tired; the Treviso variety should be crisply sleek, like endive. However, should only slightly rusty heads be available, the tired leaves can be removed; the layer beneath will usually be just fine. Choose smaller heads than you usually do for head lettuce. Radicchio leaves are closely wrapped and extremely flavorful; and there is rarely any waste.

In terms of storage, the aristocratic-looking leaves turn out to be surprisingly sturdy. Although I don't recommend doing the same, I have accidentally kept unwashed radicchio, loosely wrapped, for more than 2 weeks in the refrigerator. For optimum crispness and flavor, use within a week.

USE: You can substitute radicchio in most recipes that call for Belgian endive or escarole. Think of it primarily as a salad-bowl and garnish leaf par excellence. For flavor, color, and texture it can't be beat. Radicchio holds its own in all kinds of salads —from the simplest greens assortment to a grand concoction of cooked meat or fish. Of the many compatible partners, mushrooms, ham, cooked dried or fresh shell beans, oranges, game, cheese, red bell peppers, nuts, capers, olives, anchovies, and many complementary salad leaves make for splendid munching. Or sauté the leaves very briefly for a warm salad, enriched with ham slivers or wild mushrooms or slivers of cheese and olives.

Radicchio (particularly the Verona type) makes a charming basket to hold cooked vegetable salads or meat, fish, or pasta salads. The firm, leakproof leaves make handy bowls—and each head is composed of graduated sizes. Enclose soft cheese, or olives, or fruit. Or cup individual salads for a barbecue or picnic, as the solid little leaf prevents juices from seeping through it. Set in a cupcake tin to transport.

Quartered or halved, coated with olive oil or butter, red chicory can be grilled, baked, or sautéed until just tender, accented with herbs or garlic, as you like. Shredded radicchio, sautéed in oil, transforms pasta, rice, and beans. The same pairing makes for an earthy, sweetly bitter soup with a curious, wine-brown color.

PREPARATION: Cutting from the base, remove the white central core. Separate the leaves and trim as necessary. Rinse and spin-dry or blot dry with an absorbent towel. Wrap and chill, if using for salad. Slice the leaves as you need them, not beforehand.

NUTRITIONAL HIGHLIGHTS: Chicories are considered an excellent source of vitamin A and vitamin C.

SPAGHETTI WITH RADICCHIO, ANCHOVIES, AND GARLIC

When I first saw cooked radicchio, I was taken aback: where was the gorgeous garnet leaf with its sturdy crispness? But after a few tastes I began to understand the subtle changes the escarole-like leaf underwent when subjected to heat: an intensification of flavor and a broadening of range reveal its bitter-to-mellow-to-sweet spectrum. Although its brilliant red is lost once sautéed, radicchio gains an altogether new taste coloring.

4 servings

1 pound spaghetti
⅓ cup full-flavored olive oil
2–3 teaspoons finely minced garlic, to taste
1 pound radicchio (preferably 2 heads), cored, rinsed, and slivered
2-ounce can anchovies in olive oil, sliced (do not discard oil)
2 tablespoons minced chives
¼ cup minced flat-leaf parsley
Black pepper to taste
1 cup finely grated provolone (about 2 ounces)

1. Drop spaghetti into a large kettle of well-salted boiling water; stir until water returns to a boil. Cook until just barely tender.

2. Meanwhile, heat oil in a large skillet; stir in garlic; cook over moderately low heat until just golden. Add radicchio and toss for a few minutes over high heat, until just wilted.

3. Drain pasta and toss in a heated bowl with the anchovies and oil. Add radicchio, chives, parsley, and plenty of pepper and toss well. Add half the cheese and toss. Serve at once with the remaining cheese on the side.

SALAD OF RADICCHIO, RED PEPPER, AND AVOCADO

Brilliant-colored, this refreshing salad of bitter chicory, crisp red bell pepper, and creamy avocado spotlights radicchio's unique qualities.

4–6 servings

2 small heads radicchio (about ½ pound)
2 medium red bell peppers
1 medium avocado
2 tablespoons lime juice
¼ teaspoon salt, or to taste
Pepper to taste
4 tablespoons olive oil

1. Core, rinse, and thoroughly dry radicchio (see Preparation). Cut into bite-sized pieces. Stem and seed peppers, then cut into thin julienne strips. Quarter and peel avocado, then cut across into thin slices or dice. Combine all in a serving bowl.

2. Blend lime juice, salt, and pepper. Gradually beat in oil. Pour over the salad and toss gently to coat the leaves. Serve.

SAUTÉED RADICCHIO, MUSHROOMS, AND FENNEL

This quickly prepared dish, which becomes an all-over autumnal brown, suits any roasted, grilled, or fried meat, poultry, or fish. The dried mushrooms emphasize the earthiness, but the sauté will be delicious even if they are omitted, or if fresh are substituted.

4 servings

5 large dried Oriental mushrooms
   (shiitake, or forest mushrooms)
2 tablespoons olive oil
1 pound fennel (weighed without stalks)
½ pound radicchio rosso (the round kind)
2 tablespoons butter
Salt and pepper to taste

1. Pour 1 cup hot water over dried mushrooms, add 1 tablespoon oil, and soak for 30 minutes or more. Lift out, dry, then cut caps into strips; reserve stems and liquid for another use.

2. If necessary, remove heavy strings from fennel. Cut crosswise into slices about ¼ inch wide and 2 inches long. Rinse and core radicchio. Quarter lengthwise, then cut across into thin slivers.

3. Heat butter and remaining tablespoon oil in a large skillet. Add fennel and toss over moderately high heat until tender, about 5 minutes. Add radicchio, mushrooms, and salt and pepper, and toss until wilted and tender, about 3 minutes.

GRILLED RADICCHIO

When you're grilling lamb, chicken, spareribs, or beef, you might consider a side dish of radicchio. Although the red leaves turn tawny, they soften and sweeten, more than compensating for the loss.

For this you'll want the round-headed radicchio. If it is tiny, halve it; if larger, divide into quarters. Brush liberally with olive oil and set on the grill for about 5 minutes, turning once, until pleasantly softened but not limp. Timing can vary considerably, depending on the variety and thickness of leaves; check frequently. Meanwhile heat a little minced garlic in olive oil; drizzle onto the cooked radicchio, grind over some pepper, and serve at once.

🍃 *ADDITIONAL RECIPES*
Salad of Arugula, Endive, and Radicchio (page 24)
Salad of Chayotes, Sugar Snap Peas, and Radicchio (page 114)

RADISH, BLACK
(Raphanus sativus)

*W*hen you savor your way through one of those irresistible cold spreads that keep appearing in nineteenth-century Russian novels, the black radish is one of the *zakuski* you would expect to find—along with the pickled mushrooms, sausage, beet salad, herring and onions, sturgeon, black bread, and vodka. It would probably have been

coarsely grated, then mixed with a generous amount of thick sour cream and chives or scallions—just as it would be now if you were to encounter it in many parts of Russia or in Russian (particularly Jewish) households throughout the world. But if those are not your origins, you may be at a loss when you spy black radishes in the marketplace, which becomes more likely as produce stands overflow with "ethnic" specialties such as these.

Black radishes can be almost as pungent as horseradish, and are firm and rather dry; in short, nothing like the juicy-crisp ladylike scarlet beauties that sit prettily in crystal and porcelain bowls to be consumed as delicate pre-meal appetite stimulants. These sturdy characters, clearly of ancient origin (they have a downright primeval aspect), are the shape and size of turnips (ranging from about 2–6 inches in diameter), sooty black or matte black-brown on the outside and white within. They are cold-climate favorites, originally grown for winter storage, as their compact flesh permits extended keeping without sprouting or becoming pithy. At present the American marketplace offers two black radish varieties—Long Black Spanish and Round Black Spanish (weighing from about 2 ounces to a pound). They can be found in an unpredictable selection of American markets, often where there are shoppers of Russian, Polish, German, Hungarian, Ukrainian, Lithuanian (and probably other Central European countries, I've not been able to corroborate) and/or Jewish heritage.

SELECTION AND STORAGE: Look for black radishes primarily in winter and early spring, although they can appear in the market year round. Select very firm, comparatively heavy dark globes that show no flabbiness, pitting, sponginess, or cracks. They should have been topped and tailed (that is, have had the leaves and roots, which draw moisture from them, removed), or be closely trimmed.

Store the unwashed radishes (trim off leaves, if present) in the vegetable crisper, wrapped in perforated plastic. They will keep longer than just about anything you've ever had, unless you let them become dried out or too damp, when they mold. Check for moisture every now and then. They mellow as they store and are dandy for grating and shredding after months of refrigeration.

USE: Use black radishes to make amazing garnishes. If to be used just for show (to which I object), scrub the radish and carve away, leaving designs of black and white. For eating, follow directions for Striped Radishes.

In most of the countries that serve them, black radishes are enjoyed as an appetizer (but not eaten straight, in the small-radish manner) and receive more or less the same treatment. They are either coarsely shredded or sliced thin, salted to mellow the bite, then rinsed, drained, and bound with sour cream or chicken fat; or radish slices are dipped into the latter. This unlikely and delicious duo is usually offered with pumpernickel or chewy sour rye bread. (Another traditional preparation that may seem unusual is the Jewish preserve *Eingemachts*, made of shredded radish cooked with sugar and honey until transparent, then mixed with ground ginger and almonds.)

But there is no reason to limit any radishes to an appetizer role. Use them as Orientals do their many large, sturdy radish varieties, throughout a meal. When they are cut in fine julienne or coarsely shredded, their peppery bite works well in mixed slaws or as cooked vegetable strips in a remoulade dressing. Or chop the radish and combine with soft cheeses, sour cream, or chopped chicken liver.

Black radishes taste like firm, rather strong turnips when cooked, but their cooking time is less predictable, ranging from 10–25 minutes, depending on how long the radish has been stored or how dense its flesh. Sliced, diced, or shredded, they add a piquancy to soups, stews, braises, or stir-fries. Or chop fine to add to meatball or meatloaf mixtures.

PREPARATION: Black radishes need a hearty scrubbing and trimming before peeling, which is always recommended by the sources I have consulted. However, upon further discussion with farmers, breeders, and old-time radish aficionados, I have decided that the decision is purely aesthetic, and sometimes not even that. For example, in a stir-fry or soup, when the well-scoured radish is diced or cut into julienne, the black edging, tiny and tidy, is most attractive. Boiled radish quarters or halves look fabulous stripe-peeled with a citrus zester. Whether to peel or not ought really to depend on the toughness of the skin and the way the dish is being prepared.

If you are going to serve the radishes raw, they need a preliminary salting to tame the bite and harshness. Using about 1 teaspoon salt per 1¼ cups chopped, shredded, sliced, or julienned radish, toss the two together to mix well. Cover the surface of the vegetable (not the bowl) closely with plastic, then overlap and seal the edges of the container (the smell is fierce). Set a weight on top of the radish and let stand for an hour or longer. Rinse, drain, and dry.

NUTRITIONAL HIGHLIGHTS: Black radishes are very low in calories at about 20 calories per ½ cup. They are low in sodium.

STRIPED BLACK RADISHES

When served whole, black radishes do best with some of the thickish skin pared off. Using a zester (the small tool designed to remove strips of peel from citrus fruit), you can zip stripes of skin from each radish, leaving a sharply delineated black-and-white decoration. And the black neither grays out nor peels off when the radish is boiled.

HOT BUTTERED RADISHES

Select small radishes (about 2 inches in diameter). Scrub them well with a brush to remove soil and tiny rootlets. Cut off the fibrous turnip-like tip of each, then slice across the stem end to remove it. Working carefully, remove thin vertical strips of the radish skin with the zester, leaving a design of sharply black stripes. Place the radishes in a pot with plenty of cold water to cover generously. Bring to a boil, add salt, and boil until tender throughout, testing with a sharp knife or cake tester; this can take 15–30 minutes, depending on the age of the radishes. Drain and serve at once, well buttered.

COLD SCALLOPED RADISH SLICES FOR CANAPÉS OR SALADS

Follow the directions above, using larger radishes and retaining a bit more of the black skin. Undercook very slightly, so the radishes will remain firmish when sliced. Drain and drop into ice water to cool. Drain again and dry. Slice into rounds or half-rounds about ¼ inch thick. Include the scalloped, black-edged radishes in a composed salad. Or use the slices as the base for canapés or as cocktail dippers: they are particularly well suited to creamy fish or egg spreads.

BLACK RADISHES IN CREAM SAUCE

Although they resemble turnips in taste and shape, black radishes are usually firmer, stronger, earthier. Even mellowed by a slightly sweet sauce, the vegetable retains its pungency, which allies most admirably with roast lamb, pork, turkey, or ham; or flavorful grains such as kasha (buckwheat groats), cracked wheat, brown rice, or whole-wheat or buckwheat noodles.

4 servings

1 pound smallish black radishes, about 3 ounces each
1 quart water
½ teaspoon salt
1 tablespoon butter
1 tablespoon flour
1 teaspoon sugar
¼ cup heavy (or whipping) cream
¼ cup milk
Additional salt and pepper to taste
Optional: Parsley

1. Cut off radish tips and trim stem ends. Peel, then quarter lengthwise. Combine radishes, water, and salt in saucepan. Boil until tender throughout; timing can vary from 15 to 25 minutes, so test often.

2. Drain and reserve liquid. Set radishes aside. Heat butter in saucepan; stir in flour. Cook over low heat until golden, 2 minutes. Meanwhile heat ½ cup cooking liquid, sugar, cream, and milk. Add to flour mixture and stir vigorously with whisk until boiling. Simmer 2 minutes, stirring occasionally.

3. Gently place radishes in cream; simmer 2–3 minutes. Taste and season. Serve sprinkled with parsley, if desired. (Can be reheated.)

BLACK RADISH RELISH

Strong, biting, yet refreshing, grated radish makes a welcome foil for smoky or fatty meats, used in the way that you might horseradish, but more generously. Try it with duck, roast pork, sausages, or smoked fish. I like it on avocado or cream-cheese sandwiches, as well.

Makes about 2 cups

About 10 ounces (2 medium) black radishes
2 teaspoons coarse kosher salt
¼ cup rice vinegar (or another mild vinegar)
2 teaspoons sugar
2 tablespoons corn oil

1. Scrub radishes thoroughly with a brush. Peel or not, to taste. Grate in coarse shreds. Combine in bowl with salt; toss to mix well. Cover surface of radish closely with plastic, then seal edges of bowl (the smell is overpowering). Set a heavy weight in the bowl. Let stand at least an hour, preferably more.

2. Drain, then rinse the radish. Drain again, pressing dry. Mix vinegar and sugar; add oil. Toss with radish. Cover tightly; refrigerate for several hours.

SOUP OF PORK, BLACK RADISH, AND NOODLES

Pungent radish mingles with sweet pork in a meal-in-broth reminiscent of Japanese *nabe mono* (one-pot meals). The soup is unusually flavorful for a soup that has no mellowing time, thanks to the aggressive black radish—which is quickly tamed by cooking in broth.

Small packets of cellophane noodles (also called *saifun, silver noodles*, or *bean threads*) can usually be found in Oriental groceries or in the Oriental section of the supermarket.

4 or 5 main-course servings

3 medium scallions, plus greens of 3 more scallions

12 ounces chilled, well-trimmed lean pork, cut into 1-inch pieces

4 teaspoons cornstarch

2 tablespoons sake or dry sherry

About 1 tablespoon soy sauce

⅛ teaspoon nutmeg

1 packet (3⅞ ounces, approximately) cellophane noodles

1 pound well-scrubbed, trimmed black radishes

8 cups pork, chicken, veal, or light beef stock

1 medium carrot, sliced in paper-thin rounds

1. Mince 3 scallions in processor; add pork and chop until coarse. Add cornstarch, sake, 2 teaspoons soy sauce, and nutmeg, and chop medium-fine. Let stand while you prepare the rest of the soup.

2. Pour boiling water over whole bundle of noodles and let stand about 10–15 minutes. Using the fine julienne blade or coarse grating blade of a processor or vegetable cutter, shred the black radish. Form meat mixture into 40–50 very small balls (they needn't be neat; cooking shapes them up).

3. Combine radish and stock in a large pot; bring to a simmer. Meanwhile, with scissors cut noodles into 4–5-inch lengths; cut off binding, if necessary, then drain. Add to soup with meatballs. Cook, keeping broth under a simmer, for 4 minutes, until the meat is firm.

4. Add carrots and barely simmer until tender, about 3 minutes. Taste and add soy sauce, if necessary. Slice scallion greens and add to the soup.

RADISH, ORIENTAL, OR DAIKON
(Raphanus sativus, cv. 'Longipinnatus')
also Japanese Radish, Chinese Radish (but *not* Chinese Turnip), Loh Baak or Lo Pak

*U*ntil very recently reserved for Oriental markets, these large radishes are gradually becoming familiar in the general American marketplace. While size, color, and textural differences exist among the many radishes that are cultivated for the tables of the Orient (the probable birthplace of all of them), when it comes to culinary use, they

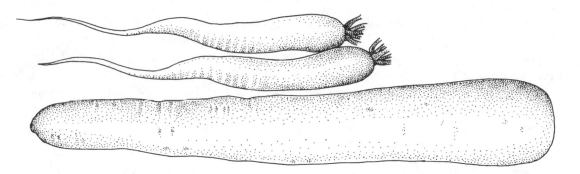

have more in common than not. Botanically, all are members of the same group as our cheery red ball of a radish (the vast Crucifer, or Mustard, family), even if they don't look as though they should be.

Throughout the East the relatively mild, juicy-crisp root is a staple that appears raw or cooked in nearly all meals. The Oriental radish most commonly available in American markets is a sweet, juicy, pearly white variety that is about a foot long, cylindrical, and tapered at the tip like a carrot. In Chinese markets shorter, rounder, slightly more irregular and greenish varieties are usual, although it is possible to encounter rose, black, and other shades. While the Oriental radish will grow to a weight of fifty pounds or so, what you're likely to see will range between one-half and two pounds, or thereabouts. Sometimes Oriental markets will sell radishes with the peppery, nutritious green tops attached, or even sell the greens separately; in American markets they are most often removed.

SELECTION AND STORAGE: Oriental radishes are available year round, with fall and winter roots most flavorful and mild, the spring and summer ones somewhat hotter and weaker in flavor. Choose very firm, smooth roots, which have a luminous gleam, not a flat opacity, which indicates a long storage time. Although giant daikons may be somewhat spongy, the general range available is of equal consistency, whether one or three inches in diameter, whether eight or eighteen inches long.

Despite its appearance, from which one might infer an association with long-stored root vegetables, Oriental radishes are not keepers, as they quickly lose moisture and become flabby and flavorless. For raw eating, buy only enough of the root to last two or three days (either a cut chunk, plastic-wrapped, or a small whole radish). For braises and soups, you can use the root for a week or so. Keep it closely wrapped in plastic in the vegetable crisper (having first removed green tops, if any).

USE: Raw daikon can be slivered, diced, or sliced to add its crunch and zip to relishes, salads, crudité platters (it makes neat, perfect wafers for dips). For salads, thin-sliced daikon is particularly nice in the company of carrot and of sesame—toasted seeds or oil. Chopped radish, with additional hot and aromatic seasonings, can be blended with yogurt for a dressing or side dish or relish—particularly when enhanced by cilantro.

Grated daikon, formed into a pretty heap, is the traditional accompaniment to Japanese raw fish dishes, such as sashimi; it is equally good with broiled fish. Mixed with lemon juice or vinegar, grated radish is a traditional and useful Japanese dressing for vegetables, poultry, and seafood.

As a garnish for fish, meat, soup, vegetables—you name it—daikon is unequaled, a carver's delight, slivered in ribbons, turned into flowers, or carved into ornamental fantasies.

Oriental radish is an important vegetable for pickling in much of the Far East, particularly China, Japan, and Korea. It appears in long-fermented, smelly (and delicious) pickles, such as the garlicky, hot Korean kimchee, the simple salt-cured Chinese pickles, and quick-seasoned sweet and/or sour Japanese pickles. Cookbooks from any of these countries will offer a wide range of the easily prepared pickles, none of which require special processing or canning, simply time to develop and a place where they can do that.

Stir-fried daikon slices, strips, or cubes are turnipy-sweet, but milder, and cook quickly. Chunks or roll-cut pieces added to stews and braises will season and sweeten the whole while absorbing some of the cooking liquid; but be careful not to overcook. Diced or julienne-cut radish flavors soup stocks and becomes tender and tasty in moments; try it with dried mushrooms for a warm, earthy brew. Briefly cook daikon and root vegetables, then purée for a subtle, light-bodied soup.

Shredded, salted, drained, and rinsed radish makes an unusual filling for breads and pastries, such as the spicy parathas of India and flaky pastries of China. Shredded radish combined with rice flour, fish, pork, mushrooms, and sausage makes up a famous steamed savory pudding (Lo Baak Go) in China. Chopped daikon adds moisture, texture, and flavor to meatball and meatloaf mixtures.

In addition to the root, the tops can be braised, steamed, blanched, or made into soup. The seeds, when sprouted (see Radish Sprouts, page 401) make an attractive, peppery garnish, sandwich component, or salad green.

PREPARATION: Depending upon the quality of the skin, you may want to simply scrub the radish with a bristly brush; or it may be removed with a swivel peeler. There is never any need to pare deeply, as you would most other root vegetables: Daikon skin is thin and fine.

NUTRITIONAL HIGHLIGHTS: Oriental radish is very, very low in calories—at about 10 per ½ cup. It provides a small amount of vitamin C.

SAUTÉED ORIENTAL RADISH (DAIKON) SLICES

All the bite disappears when radish is cooked, and a taste somewhere between broccoli stems and baby turnips takes its place, making this basic dish a natural for pairing with pork, lamb, and beef. Tossed over moderately high heat, the slices keep their pretty white translucence.

2 servings

¾ pound firm, slender daikon
1 tablespoon vegetable oil
½ teaspoon sugar
About ⅛ teaspoon salt
1 tablespoon minced parsley
2 teaspoons minced fresh chives or dill

1. Scrub daikon and remove any rootlets. Cut across into thin slices (if the radish is wide, halve lengthwise before slicing across).

2. Heat wok and pour oil around the edge. Add daikon and toss to coat all slices. Add sugar and salt to taste. Toss over moderately high heat until daikon has lost its raw crunch, about 5 minutes.

3. Scoop into a heated dish, toss with parsley and chives. Serve hot.

CHILLED DAIKON-POTATO CREAM SOUP

The daikon base of this soup is not identifiable but serves to lighten and freshen the creamy white soup, making it more delicate and smooth than a potato cream soup. The crunchy, raw daikon bits are the only clue to the unusual purée's components.

4 servings

1 pound Oriental radish (daikon), scrubbed and peeled
¾ pound russet baking potatoes, peeled
3 cups light chicken stock or vegetable stock
About ¼ cup heavy (or whipping) cream
White pepper to taste
Salt to taste
¼ cup radish sprouts (see page 401) or 2 tablespoons minced dill

1. Cut up enough daikon to make ⅔ cup fine dice; cover and refrigerate. Slice remaining radish ½ inch thick and place in saucepan. Slice potatoes thin and add to radish with stock. Simmer, covered, until very tender, about 20 minutes.

2. Purée solids in processor or blender, adding cooking liquid as necessary. When smooth, pour into a bowl. Stir in all liquid. Add cream, white pepper, and salt to taste. Cool, then cover and refrigerate until serving time.

3. Ladle into 4 chilled bowls. Top each portion with diced daikon and sprouts or dill.

RED-COOKED BEEF AND ORIENTAL RADISH (DAIKON)

Barbara Spiegel included this easy variation on a Shanghai classic in a summer cooking class she taught called a "No-Last-Minute Chinese Feast." She advises that, like most stews, it improves with age. It can be made 2 days before serving.

6 servings

2 pounds beef rump or chuck
2 tablespoons peanut oil
1½ teaspoons minced garlic
1 tablespoon chopped fresh ginger
3 scallions, sliced
¼ cup soy sauce, preferably dark or
    black (see Note)
½ cup dry or medium-dry sherry
1½ cups water
5 "petals" (pointed pieces, not whole
    "flowers") star anise (see Note)
1 tablespoon molasses
2 pounds daikon

1. Trim beef and cut into 1-inch cubes. Heat oil in flameproof casserole or Dutch oven; add beef, garlic, and ginger. Toss for a moment.

2. Add scallions, soy sauce, sherry, water, star anise, and molasses. Cover and bake in preheated 350-degree oven 1½ hours, until nearly tender.

3. Peel daikon and cut into cubes or half-rounds slightly larger than beef. Mix thoroughly into stew. Cover and simmer about 30 minutes longer, until beef and radish are tender. If there is too much liquid for your taste, uncover and cook briefly over high heat to reduce.

Note: Dark soy sauce and star anise are available in Oriental groceries, as well as many supermarkets.

🕊 *ADDITIONAL RECIPE*
Salad of Glasswort, Oriental Radish, and Cucumber (page 208)

DOUBLE RADISH AND CARROT SLAW

For a refreshing salad, crunchy and forceful, try this pungent combination. If you can't find radish sprouts, substitute trimmed watercress leaves.

4 servings

1 pound daikon (Oriental radish), peeled
½ pound carrots, peeled
1½ teaspoons coarse kosher salt
1 tablespoon sugar
1 tablespoon sharp mustard
½ cup white wine vinegar, rice vinegar, or cider vinegar
¼ cup sour cream
¼ cup heavy (or whipping) cream
1 thinly sliced scallion green
1 packet radish sprouts, preferably kaiware (see page 401)

1. With a processor, vegetable mill, or mandoline cut daikon and carrots into fine julienne strips (or grate coarse shreds).

2. Stir together salt, sugar, mustard, and vinegar; toss with vegetables. Blend together sour cream and cream. Cover both containers and refrigerate for 1 hour or more.

3. Drain vegetables thoroughly, pressing out as much liquid as possible. Add creams and scallions and stir to blend. Serve, or refrigerate until serving time. Surround with radish sprouts.

ORIENTAL RADISH (DAIKON), SQUASH, AND SWEET PEPPER SALAD

Colorful, sweet with a radishy bite, this is an easy and unusual salad for any time of year.

4 servings

2 small zucchini or yellow summer squash (about ¾ pound), scrubbed
½ pound slender daikon, scrubbed
1 small sweet yellow or red bell pepper, in tiny dice
¼ teaspoon salt, or to taste
½ teaspoon sugar
2 tablespoons rice vinegar
2 tablespoons peanut oil
2 tablespoons Oriental sesame oil (dark oil)

1. Drop squash into a large pot of boiling, salted water. Boil about 4 minutes, or until pressure of fingers leaves indentation. Drop in ice water; cool. Drain. Cut across into thin coins.

2. Cut daikon into thin rounds (halve lengthwise, if wide). Combine in serving dish with squash and sweet pepper.

3. Combine salt, sugar, and vinegar; blend. Add peanut and sesame oils. Toss with vegetables; chill until serving time.

RADISH SPROUTS
(Raphanus sativus)
**including Kaiware, Tsumamina, Clover Radish, Spicy Sprout mixtures—and any other
sprouted radish seeds alone or in combination**

*R*adish sprouts and other peppery miniatures have been on and off the market for years. But, with America's new love for "hot" foods and the acceptance of sprouts as delicious and "real," not mere rabbit nibbles for health foodies, there may be a good chance of keeping them in the stores. (Them, and what promises to be a whole new world of sproutables, for fennel, coriander, mustard, fenugreek, caraway, and other full-flavored sprouted seeds are just around the corner.) If you have ever had the pleasure of English mustard cress, the ubiquitous duo *(Sinapis alba* and *Lepidium sativum)* that is snipped over egg salad, tucked into buttered bread, or strewn about slabs of meat, you have an idea of how good these little tidbits can be.

What is available at present (although erratically) ranges from a tangle of bland sprouts seasoned with 10–20 percent radish and poufed into little plastic bags to hot sprouts that stand neatly upright, a forest of clover-like leaflets on skinny legs rooted on pads of blotter material, the whole enclosed in a see-through box. The upright sprouts, currently marketed as kaiware (one firm, deceased, called them *2-mamina* after another Japanese word for the sprouts, *tsumamina*), are quite large, more seedlings than sprouts, with their long (4-inch), silky stems. They are the extremely pungent week-old growth of seeds of a white Oriental radish (Osaka 45-day). In between the long-stemmed beauties and the fluffy, squiggly heap of radish with alfalfa and company is a changing brigade of deliciously sharp, highly nutritious baby greens that become indispensable once you have enjoyed their zesty kick. Only by sniffing about the marketplace, looking, and asking will you know what is to be found in your area (and asking creates a demand).

SELECTION AND STORAGE: Sprouts are available, if at all, year round. They are particularly susceptible to heat, however, and are less likely to show up in summer unless produced nearby. Look for green (not yellowing), clean, perky sprouts—which they almost always are. If bagged, not planted, check for a minimum of loose, unsprouted seeds, which decay—or worse, an already slimy swamp.

Store sprouts in the refrigerator. How long they last depends on the variety; the rooted ones may be snippable for about a week. The more delicate tousled packets may lose their snap in a few days. If this happens, soak in ice water for 10 minutes, then drain well. Dry thoroughly. Rewrap and chill.

USE: Think of radish sprouts as miniature watercress with mere threads of stems and you'll have an idea of what to do with them and their affiliates. As a garnish the larger strong varieties can't be beat: beautiful nosegays with a peppery punch for raw or cooked fish, shrimp, chicken, eggs, potatoes, noodles, lamb, hamburgers—just about anything that would take parsley, pepper, or watercress. Or float on clear soup, snip into dips, fold into omelets. Do not cook beyond a moment, or the pungency and texture will be lost.

Mild mixtures, particularly the pretty clover and radish blend, make a puffy, tasty cushion for roasted meat or grilled fish. Or stuff into sandwiches as a pepper-upper and filler.

PREPARATION: One of the handy things about sprouts is that they are grown in water that is constantly refreshed (like brook water around cress). They are packed clean, so you need do nothing more than snip them from their roots, if planted; or fluff and untangle the mass in the bag.

NUTRITIONAL HIGHLIGHTS: Radish sprouts are very low in calories, with about 10 per ½ cup. They are a source of folic acid and of vitamin A, and are low in sodium.

WARM SPROUTS WITH AVOCADO

Clover-radish sprouts become sweeter and greener when subjected to a quick toss over high heat, and although they will wilt, they retain their crunch. Serve as a first-course salad or as a vegetable side dish.

2 servings

1 very small avocado, peeled and cubed (or ½ medium)
1 tablespoon lime or lemon juice
2 tablespoons full-flavored olive oil
1 large garlic clove, peeled and quartered
6-ounce package clover-radish sprouts
Salt and pepper
Optional: Slivered red radish for garnish

1. Set a serving dish in a low oven to heat. Combine avocado and lime juice in a bowl; toss to coat.

2. Heat oil and garlic in wide skillet, holding the pan tipped so garlic "deep-fries." Cook until golden, then discard garlic.

3. Fluff sprouts to untangle slightly, then add to pan; with two spoons pick up and toss sprouts over high heat until just barely wilted, but hot—about 30 seconds. Scoop into the warm serving dish, add avocado, salt, and pepper. Toss and serve immediately, garnished with radish.

CLOVER-RADISH SPROUT AND CARROT SALAD OR GARNISH

Too simple to really be called a salad, this fresh toss of tiny blush-tipped sprout tendrils and carrots makes an attractive bed for grilled fish or chicken, fills out a sandwich, combines deliciously with cold shrimp for a lunch dish, and garnishes almost anything. As variations, add thin-sliced scallion greens, or snipped chives or mint if you like. Or include a handful of chopped nuts.

4 servings

6 ounces (4 cups) clover-radish sprouts, fluffed to separate
4 medium carrots, in coarse shreds
¼ cup lemon juice
1 tablespoon sugar
¼ teaspoon salt

Toss together sprouts and carrots in a serving dish. Stir together lemon juice, sugar, and salt to dissolve crystals. Combine with vegetables, toss, then serve.

FINE NOODLE SALAD WITH DAIKON SPROUTS

Great for a buffet, picnic, or barbecue, this dish plays both starch and salad roles. Rounded, cleft leaves (*kaiware* means "split shell" in Japanese) and a confetti of crisp red-pepper bits are tossed with a silky tangle of delicate Japanese noodles called *somen*. If you prefer your salad chilled, this can be assembled beforehand; but I find the velvety noodles most delicious at room temperature, freshly tossed with perky sprouts.

4 servings

½ pound somen (see Note)
2 tablespoons lemon juice
2 tablespoons peanut oil
1½ tablespoons soy sauce
1 tablespoon dark (Oriental) sesame oil
¼ teaspoon finely grated lemon zest
2 packages (about 4 ounces each) kaiware (Oriental radish sprouts)
1 small red or yellow bell pepper, minced fine

1. Drop somen in boiling salted water; boil until tender, about 2 minutes, Drain; rinse in cold water.

2. Combine lemon juice, peanut oil, soy sauce, sesame oil, and lemon zest. Pour over noodles and toss with your hands, gently coating all strands thoroughly. Leave at room temperature until serving time.

3. To serve, cut sprouts to suit your taste. Add to noodles with minced pepper and toss to mix thoroughly. Adjust seasoning.

Note: Somen (fine, white Japanese wheat noodles) are readily available in all Oriental groceries and in many supermarkets and most specialty stores. If you must substitute, use *very* thin noodles, such as angel hair.

SALAD OF RADISH SPROUTS, ENDIVE, PEPPER, AND MUSHROOMS

Full-flavored and colorful, this blue cheese–dressed salad makes a lively first course for a light meal; or serve it with a hamburger, chop, or steak for a fast, good dinner.

4 generous servings

¼ cup crumbled or chopped blue cheese

Small piece minced garlic (or 2 teaspoons finely minced scallion)

About 2 teaspoons red wine vinegar

Pepper to taste

6 tablespoons heavy (or whipping) cream

2 medium red peppers, cut into small dice

4 medium Belgian endive (½ pound), bases cut out, then sliced into julienne strips 2–3 inches long

½ pound small white mushrooms, sliced thin (see Note)

1 pack radish sprouts (about 4 ounces), roots trimmed

1. Using a fork, mash together blue cheese, garlic or scallion, vinegar, and pepper; gradually stir in the heavy cream.

2. Combine red peppers, endive, mushrooms, and sprouts in a bowl; toss to mix. Divide among 4 plates, drizzle with the dressing. Serve.

Note: You can substitute enoki mushrooms (trimmed and separated) for the common button mushrooms.

RAMP
See Wild Leek

RAPINI
See Broccoli Raab

ROCKET
See Arugula

S

SALAD SAVOY
See Flowering Kale

SALSIFY	SCORZONERA
(Tragopogon porrifolius)	*(Scorzonera hispanica)*
also called Oyster Plant, Vegetable Oyster, White Salsify	also Black Salsify, Black Oyster Plant, Viper Grass

Salsify is a word used to describe two plants, both of which belong to the vast (20,000-species) Compositae family.

Tragopogon means "goat's beard" and refers to the milky white seed filaments (like dandelion fluff) that distinguish members of the genus. *Porrifolius* means leek-

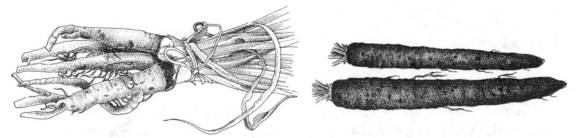

leaved and describes to a degree the grassy, flat greens of this plant, which is the only cultivated member of the group. The root vegetable itself is shaped like an irregular parsnip and has relatively thin, pale-tan skin (the flesh is off-white), the whole covered with tiny rootlets.

The word *scorzonera* (skort-soh-NAIR-a) comes from either *escorzo nera*, Spanish for black bark, or from *escorço*, the Catalan word for viper, so named because the plant's juices were thought to provide an antidote to snakebite. The plant was introduced to European culture through Spanish seed; hence *hispanica*. This most edible root is nothing great to look at, resembling in appearance a muddy brown (cream beneath the skin), nontapering, petrified carrot. It is usually more regularly shaped, longer, and smoother than white salsify.

From horticultural and culinary points of view, there are fairly good reasons to group these vegetables together, as their growth patterns and kitchen uses are almost identical. Both were latecomers to cultivation, becoming part of kitchen gardens in Europe in the late sixteenth and early seventeenth centuries. They are particular favorites in Belgium (from whence comes all our scorzonera at present) but the British,

French, and Italians have been known to wax lyrical about them as well. Salsify in general has long been a popular winter vegetable for home gardeners (Thomas Jefferson planted more salsify than other crops that we now consider common, as did many farmers through the nineteenth century), but has just recently begun to appear in specialty shops.

In recipes, white salsify and scorzonera are virtually interchangeable, as far as techniques and timing go (although the taste and texture are slightly different). Culinary literature tells us that the flavor of the vegetables is exactly or somewhat like oysters depending on what you're reading, or like asparagus. I will confuse matters further by saying that I find no oysters therein, but the flavor and consistency of very soft-cooked artichoke heart with a touch of coconut. This is most often true of the scorzonera, which I have found preferable on all counts, since it is fleshier, less fibrous, easier to peel, and has a more pronounced taste. Expect both kinds of salsify to be subtle and delicate—too bland for some tastebuds.

SELECTION AND STORAGE: Look for both the domestic white salsify and Belgian scorzonera from late fall through early spring, although some filters in at odd times. White salsify is generally sold in bunches, with its flowing tops attached; scorzonera is sold virtually leafless, in perforated plastic bags. In either case, look for medium-sized even roots, with no obvious flabbiness. Although not as firm as carrots, neither should be soft. Very large roots tend to be fibrous; very small ones wind up more waste than flesh.

If oyster plant is in good shape when you buy it, you can keep it up to two weeks in the refrigerator, wrapped in plastic. Just check to be sure it isn't drying out.

USE: Whichever culinary technique you choose, go gently with flavoring, as salsify's charm is low-key. And beware of overcooking, as the roots change quickly from succulent and soft to mushy.

Because salsify breaks easily, I find steaming preferable to boiling. Follow directions for cleaning and steaming (see Salsify in Cream); or, if you're using white salsify, steam the whole, scrubbed root, then peel after cooking. Once cooked, the vegetables can be cut to suit, and gently heated in butter touched with a little sugar, salt, and lemon juice. Or combine the oyster plant in a shallow baking dish with a light béchamel or cheese sauce and bake in the upper part of a hot oven until just lightly browned. Or bathe the cooked salsify in vinaigrette sauce and let cool to room temperature.

Add peeled, diagonally cut salsify to stews and braises during the last forty-five minutes or so of cooking. Or brown first, then braise with fowl or veal. Add salsify to chunky vegetable soups, as well; or simmer salsify in light stock, then purée for a delicate soup.

White salsify is usually sold with its luxuriant, grasslike greens. The palest parts of these (or even better, baby shoots, if you grow salsify) make a nice addition to salads, rather like retiring Belgian endive; the whole green makes a pleasant, if vague, contribution to puréed soups. The young leaves of scorzonera are edible, too, but do not appear on the vegetable as sold at present.

PREPARATION: When salsify is peeled, it darkens immediately and unevenly. It is best to place it in a bowl of water and lemon juice (about 2 tablespoons per quart) as you work. You can wear rubber gloves to prevent discoloring your hands as you work, if a temporary rusty-brown stain will bother you.

Scorzonera is generally evenly shaped, and is simple to peel before cooking. However, white salsify often has a crazy conformation, forked and tentacled, that makes peeling wasteful and time consuming. Therefore, it is easier to cook, cool slightly, then slip off the peel, being careful not to break up the roots.

NUTRITIONAL HIGHLIGHTS: Salsify is low in calories, with about 35 calories per ½ cup.

Note: Salsify has been known to cause gastric grumbling, sometimes volcanic, in some poor souls (even if Louis XIV is said to have included it in his meals as a digestive aid). If you are subject to such miseries, or have not eaten it before, enjoy it in moderation until you've figured out your tolerance.

SALSIFY-FISH CHOWDER

Warmly satisfying, this combination suggests more complexity than you might imagine—hints of mushrooms, artichoke hearts, potatoes—thanks to the soft, mysterious salsify.

4 servings

1 meaty fish skeleton (1–1½ pounds)
5 cups water
3 small onions, sliced thin (1 cup)
2 tablespoons butter
1 pound scorzonera (or substitute white salsify)
Lemon juice
2 tablespoons flour
1 pound thick, lean fish fillets (cod, hake, haddock), cut into 1-inch pieces
About ¾ cup light cream or half-and-half
Salt and white pepper

1. Remove gills if any, from fish head; chop skeleton into manageable pieces; combine with water and simmer, partly covered, for 2 minutes. Remove meat from bones and reserve. Skim broth; return bones to pot and simmer gently for 20 minutes, partly covered. Strain and reserve stock. Discard bones.

2. In a heavy flameproof casserole cook onions in butter over moderately low heat until very soft. Meanwhile, scrub salsify, then peel and cut into 1-inch sections. Drop into bowl containing water and 2 tablespoons lemon juice. Add flour to casserole and stir and scrape for a few minutes.

3. Add fish stock and bring to a boil, stirring. Add salsify and simmer, covered, until tender—about 10 minutes. Add raw and cooked fish; cook over low heat until just opaque—about 2 minutes. Stir in cream. Add salt, pepper, and lemon juice to taste. Serve hot.

CREAMY SALSIFY SOUP

Reserve this luxurious purée for lovers of reticent tastes; it is not at all assertive. However, even less-sensitive souls will enjoy the silky texture of what might appear to be extra-fancy potato cream soup. Like most soups, this improves with reheating.

6 servings as a first course

2 tablespoons butter
1 medium carrot, chopped
1 small leek, dark green removed, rinsed
  and sliced thin
2 medium celery stalks, strings pared off,
  chopped
2 pounds scorzonera (or substitute white
  salsify)
Lemon juice
¾ pound potatoes
4 cups veal or chicken stock
2 cups water, approximately
1 cup light cream or half-and-half,
  approximately
Salt and white pepper
Nutmeg
Minced celery leaves for garnish

1. Melt butter in a flameproof casserole and stir in the carrot, leek, and celery. Stir over low heat until softened, about 10 minutes.

2. Scrub, trim, and peel salsify (you need not be meticulous; dark bits will be strained out later). Cut into 1–2-inch pieces. As you work, drop roots into water acidulated with a few tablespoons lemon juice. Peel and chunk potatoes.

3. Add drained salsify and potatoes to casserole. Add stock and water. Simmer, partly covered, for 30 minutes, or until soft.

4. Purée to a very fine consistency in processor or blender, then strain through a sieve. Add cream to taste. Season with lemon juice, salt, pepper, and a generous grating of nutmeg.

5. Allow to cool completely, then cover and chill. To serve, reheat slowly and season to taste, adding more light cream, if desired. Serve in warmed soup plates, sprinkled with celery leaves.

CHICKEN BRAISED WITH SALSIFY

There are some dishes in which ingredients seem to give and take, in equal quantities, as do salsify and chicken here: each lends its special flavor to the other to make a new but familiar taste. For an easy, change-of-pace meal, add this to your repertoire.

4 servings

3½-pound chicken, cut in serving pieces (giblets reserved for another use)
2 tablespoons flour
2 tablespoons butter
1 tablespoon peanut or corn oil
1½ pounds scorzonera or white salsify
1 medium onion, chopped (¾ cup)
Big pinch each pepper, nutmeg, cinnamon, and thyme
½ cup dry vermouth or white wine
1 cup chicken stock or broth
Salt

1. Trim fat from chicken; sprinkle with flour. Heat butter and oil in a large skillet and brown chicken on both sides over moderate heat. Transfer to a casserole.

2. Scrub, trim, and peel salsify. Cut into 2-inch lengths (see Note). Brown slowly in skillet; it takes about 10 minutes. Add to casserole.

3. Add onion to skillet; stir. Cover and cook over moderately low heat until somewhat softened, about 5 minutes. Add pepper, nutmeg, cinnamon, and thyme. Add vermouth and broth and bring to a simmer, stirring. Add salt to taste.

4. Cover; bake in preheated 350-degree oven until tender, about 45 minutes.

Note: If you want to prevent salsify from darkening as you peel, drop into a quart of water mixed with 2 tablespoons lemon juice.

SCORZONERA VINAIGRETTE

Delicate sticks of tender, mild black salsify coated in a creamy mustard dressing are a pleasing first course or salad. The texture and flavor combination is fairly rich, so plan moderate portions.

6 servings

¼ cup lemon juice
6 cups water, approximately
1 teaspoon salt
2 pounds scorzonera, scrubbed

DRESSING
1 egg yolk, at room temperature
1 teaspoon sharp, smooth mustard
1 tablespoon finely minced scallion
    greens
White pepper to taste
1½ tablespoons lemon juice
Salt to taste (about ¼ teaspoon)
3 tablespoons olive oil
3 tablespoons corn oil
Minced parsley, basil, or chervil to taste

1. Combine lemon juice, water, and salt in a saucepan large enough to hold sliced scorzonera. Peel a scorzonera root. Cut it in 3-inch lengths, then cut each into 2 or 4 slices lengthwise, depending on thickness. Drop into the saucepan. Continue until all scorzonera is sliced. Add water, if necessary, to cover.

2. Bring to a boil. Cover, lower heat, and barely simmer until tender throughout, testing often, from 20–30 minutes; vegetable should be tender, but not mushy. Drain. Cool to lukewarm.

3. Prepare dressing: Combine yolk, mustard, scallion, pepper, lemon juice, and salt; blend. Gradually beat in the oils with a whisk. Pour over scorzonera. Serve at room temperature or chilled.

4. Sprinkle with herb of your choice to serve.

SALSIFY IN CREAM

There are some simple combinations that are just plain right—like salsify and cream.

4 servings

1½ pounds scorzonera (or use large, even-shaped white salsify)
Few tablespoons lemon juice
⅔ cup heavy (or whipping) cream

1 tablespoon finely minced shallot
Big pinch dried tarragon
Big pinch dried thyme
Salt

1. Scrub and peel roots. As you proceed, place each immediately in a bowl of water acidulated with a few tablespoons lemon juice.

2. Drain, place on rack of steamer, set over boiling water. Cover and steam until just tender throughout; timing can vary from 10 to 20 minutes. Check smaller roots first, and withdraw from steamer as they become tender; do not overcook or they will be mushy.

3. Meanwhile, combine cream, shallot, and herbs in a small, heavy saucepan; simmer gently until shallots are soft, about 3–4 minutes.

4. Cut salsify into 2-inch lengths and add to cream with salt to taste. Simmer gently until most cream is absorbed—about 2 minutes.

SALSIFY IN LEMON SAUCE

Virtually all early American cookbooks contained recipes for stewed salsify, a much-favored vegetable and presentation. Some recommended cooking the salsify in vinegar, water, butter, and a little sugar and salt, to which egg yolks were added at the end as thickener and enrichment. The sauce that follows is between that and the Greek avgolemono, stabilized with a little starch to permit final cooking with the salsify without curdling.

3 servings

1 pound white salsify or scorzonera
2 tablespoons lemon juice
8 tablespoons water
1¼ teaspoons sugar
About 1 tablespoon butter
About ¼ teaspoon salt
2 scant teaspoons cornstarch
1 egg yolk
2 tablespoons heavy (or whipping) or light cream
White pepper to taste

1. Scrub salsify hard with a brush. Boil, covered, in a skillet of salted water until tender, 5–12 minutes, testing often. Remove smaller pieces (if any) as they become tender; do not overcook or roots become mushy and *impossible* to peel.

2. Drain and cool slightly. Gently slip off skins and trim roots. Cut into ½-inch pieces (there should be about 2 cups).

3. Combine lemon juice, 6 tablespoons water, sugar, 1 tablespoon butter, and ¼ teaspoon salt. Blend cornstarch and remaining 2 tablespoons water and add. Bring to a boil, stirring constantly.

4. Blend yolk and cream in a small bowl. Whisk in a few spoons of the sauce. Return this mixture to the pot and stir briskly to blend over low heat.

5. Add salsify and cook over low heat, covered, for a few minutes. If the sauce becomes too thick, add a little more butter. Season to taste and serve.

SAMPHIRE
See Glasswort

SANTA FE GRANDE (PEPPER)
See Chili-Pepper, Santa Fe Grande

SAPOTE, WHITE
(Casimiroa edulis)
also Zapote Blanco, Zapote, and two incorrect forms—Sapote and Sapota

*W*ith only a few acres planted in California and Florida, it may be a bit premature to discuss this silky, creamy, utterly confusing (in name only) fruit. But its market potential looks so promising that making a place for it on greengrocers' shelves seems more a matter of time than of question.

The white sapote's (sah-PO-tay) pale cream flesh is unusually soft, juicy, and light-textured, truly the consistency of fine flan—devoid of fiber or granules. It has a very sweet, mild flavor (sometimes downright bland) that may hint of peaches, lemons, mango, coconut, caramel, or vanilla, depending upon the variety. The size of an orange or grapefruit, its very thin skin may be bright green to canary yellow, and everything in between. The white sapote has 2–5 seeds that may be flat and chiplike or the size and shape of orange seeds (the fruit, like Citrus, is a member of the Rutaceae or Rue family). They are embedded at random (or so it appears to me) in the delicate custardy flesh of this apparently coreless fruit.

Growers and distributors in the two states where the white sapote is grown in this country agree on its virtues and future prospects—most unusual when consulting with competing growing areas. Although the fruit is a native of the highlands of Mexico and Central America, it has grown well in California since the early 1800s. Several severe problems have prevented it from becoming a commercial crop; the main one has been the sorting out of innumerable varieties and grafts in order to concentrate on several strains that might bear predictably. (The quantity poses no problem, for as white sapote trees develop—and they get huge and old—they may produce as much as 2–3 tons per tree annually.) Further problems have been too large fruits (which fall to the ground), too large seeds, skin that blemishes, flavor loss after harvesting, and ripening that occurs too rapidly after picking (the fruit is gathered when hard, like an avocado, then softens). Happily, it seems that most of the drawbacks have been eliminated and that it is only a matter of time before *some* strain of this likable fruit becomes familiar.

Now to the confusing part. A number of fruits called simply *sapote* or *sapota* by produce handlers show up now and then in the market (although the white sapote is the most likely). There is the black sapote, a rather leathery green-skinned member of the Diospyros clan (the same as the persimmon) which has flesh the color and texture of chocolate pudding (truly) when fully ripe. There is the increasingly popular mamey sapote *(Pouteria sapota)* which is football-shaped, uncommonly large, and covered with a rough brown skin. Its flesh, when ripe, is very sweet and creamy, bright salmon in color, and contains a giant avocado-like central pit. Then there are the green sapote and the yellow sapote (neither yet sampled by this writer), some half-dozen others not available in the United States—and finally there is the entire family heading, *Sapota-ceae*, under which others huddle. This overlapping use of *sapote* makes more sense than it might appear to at first when you realize that all these fruits originated in the same part of the world where the ancient word *tzapotl* (*zapote* in modern Mexican) means no more than a soft fruit. So do not drop the modifying color, in this case white, since different "sapotes" have little in common.

SELECTION AND STORAGE: It is impossible to say what time of year the white sapote will be on the market, but thus far, fall and winter fruit have been superior. Many consider the yellow-skinned white sapote to be most flavorful; if a green variety, look for yellowy green. Select hard fruits, leave at room temperature—but don't go away for the weekend. I have never seen fruit soften as quickly as this: from rock-hard to persimmon-tender in 3 days.

When the fruit is soft as a ripe plum (it looks much like a Greengage or Kelsey plum), chill it briefly before serving. Refrigerate for a day or two, if necessary.

Most varieties freeze quite well, although a few become bitter. Wrap the whole fruit and tuck into the freezer. Half-thaw in the refrigerator, then spoon from the skin like sherbet. Or scoop out the pulp and freeze in a small container. Although the flesh will not be as seamlessly perfect as when fresh, the thawed fruit is pleasant for purées, drinks, parfaits, sauces.

USE: Treat the white sapote more or less as you would a ripe persimmon—very simply. Spoon the light pulp from the skin (which adds nothing and can be bitter) and enjoy it plain, or with a few drops of lime or lemon. Or halve the fruit, remove the seeds, then sprinkle the surface with lemon and sugar; let stand briefly. Cover with cream, whipped cream, or a combination of sour cream and cream, or crème fraîche. Or purée the white sapotes to make a fluffy fruit sauce. Or peel and pit the fruit, then scoop neat balls with a melon-ball cutter.

NUTRITIONAL HIGHLIGHTS: White sapote is a fairly good source of vitamin C and fiber, and is low in calories.

WHITE SAPOTE, KIWI, AND STRAWBERRY SALAD

White sapote whips into a frothy, low-calorie sauce to serve with melting-soft fruits. Look for fragrant, small strawberries. If these are difficult to find, substitute very ripe apricots. juicy raspberries, or sweetest papaya. The light flavors are best suited to those who enjoy delicate dishes.

4 servings

3 white sapotes, each 8–10 ounces
1 pint small, very ripe strawberries, rinsed and hulled
About 1 tablespoon fragrant honey
About 1 tablespoon fruit liqueur or sweet fruit brandy, as desired—strawberry, raspberry, or apricot
2 large kiwis

1. Halve the largest sapote. Remove peel and any green, bitter flesh close to it. Slice the fruit, extracting large and small seeds. Combine in a processor with 4 strawberries, honey, and fruit liqueur. Purée to a very fine, light texture; adjust liqueur and honey to taste. Chill until serving time.

2. Halve remaining sapotes. With small melon-ball cutter, scoop tiny balls of the flesh into a bowl with strawberries. Halve kiwis crosswise and scoop out pulp in the same way and add to the mixture. Chill.

3. To serve, either heap fruit mixture on a plate and ladle a puddle of sauce alongside; or pile in a dish and top with sauce.

SERRANO (PEPPER)
See Chili-Pepper, Serrano

SHADDOCK
See Pummelo

SHIITAKE
(Lentinus edodes)
also Forest Mushroom, Black Forest Mushroom, Golden Oak Mushroom, Oriental Black Mushroom, Chinese Black Mushroom

Swarthy and handsome, with a cream-colored interior, lightly garlic-pine aroma, the supple-firm shiitake (shee-TAH-kay) is among the most popular of the "exotic" mushrooms—particularly in restaurants that offer new-style French, Oriental, Italian, and American cuisine. The subtle scent and appealing feel of the mushroom are made even more attractive by the fact that it can be cultivated in captivity.

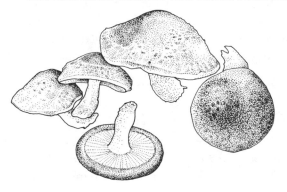

The fleshy, gold to brown, flavorful shiitake has been raised successfully in a number of states, although just a few years ago this treasure was to be found only in the Orient. The fungus that is now marketed represents several strains of shiitake cultivated in one of two ways. For both methods, spawn (the threadlike root filaments produced by germinating spores) is grown in a laboratory from material that comes from the Orient. Most shiitake farms culture the spawn in a temperature-controlled environment in artificial logs composed of sterilized plant matter. A few farms on the East Coast "plant" the spawn outdoors in oak logs. Depending upon the shiitake strain and the way it is cultivated, maturity can be reached at five weeks—or up to eighteen months. Consequently, there is enormous variation in quality, and there should be in cost. Unfortunately, flimsy, fast-grown, bland shiitake and dense, slow-raised, rich-flavored ones are often the same price. Because farming techniques are new, and rapidly improving, you can expect a large increase in volume for this mushroom (the Campbell Soup Company has even entered the competition), and hopefully a subsequent decrease in price at all levels.

SELECTION AND STORAGE: While shiitake are available to some extent year round, they are most plentiful during spring and autumn. They should be firm, dryish (but not leathery or wizened), and plumply meaty, with a distinct aroma; skimpy, odorless ones are not worth the luxury price. Look for fleshy, large mushrooms with domed and dappled caps, their edges curled under. Parasol-flat specimens are not fresh. Stems should be small.

You can store fresh shiitake longer than other mushrooms, but they will lose their special scent and lush texture (even though they do not appear to spoil). Spread them in one or two layers in a basket or dish and cover with a single layer of barely damp cheesecloth. Refrigerate, sprinkling a few drops of water on the cloth when mushrooms appear dry. If bought in optimum condition, the mushrooms will stay in good shape for a week.

USE: Although you can cook shiitake in just about any way that you would button mushrooms *(Agaricus bisporus)*, you'll do best to let them star in whatever preparation you chose. Like so many mushrooms, shiitake's taste is obscured by a great deal of butter or heat, and benefits from a combination of sautéing and braising. Or braised in the traditional way, shiitake holds its own without losing flavor. Grilled or broiled shiitake needs a generous supply of oil.

PREPARATION: Trim the bases of the stems, then clean the caps with a soft paint-brush or damp paper towel. Shiitake stems are considerably tougher and woodier than those of common mushrooms and require special attention. Slice thin or chop them and cook separately in a little stock until soft. Either combine them with the dish you're preparing, or use with sautéed vegetables, or as part of a soup, stew, or duxelle preparation.

NUTRITIONAL HIGHLIGHTS: Shiitake are a good source of fiber and the B vitamins niacin, thiamine, and riboflavin. They are low in calories and sodium.

SAUTÉED-BRAISED SHIITAKE MUSHROOMS

Woodsy shiitake respond well to meaty stocks and sauces. They may need longer cooking than other mushrooms, so plan accordingly. If wine doesn't suit the meal, add a second installment of stock.

4 servings

1 pound shiitake
1 cup beef, turkey, chicken, or duck or
    game stock
3 tablespoons butter
2 tablespoons minced shallots
⅓ cup dry white wine or dry vermouth
Salt and pepper
Optional: Minced parsley, thyme, lemon
    thyme, or rosemary

1. Cut shiitake stems in thin slivers and combine in a small saucepan with stock. Simmer, covered, until tender—about 10 minutes. Wipe caps with a damp cloth or brush with a soft paintbrush. Break into large bite-sized pieces, if necessary—or leave whole.

2. Heat butter in a large skillet; add shallots and stir for a moment. Add mushroom caps and sauté over moderate heat until barely softened.

3. Add stock and stems and cook over moderately high heat until most liquid has evaporated, about 5 minutes. Add wine and toss over high heat until almost evaporated. Season and serve, sprinkled with herbs if desired.

SHIITAKE WITH RED WINE AND GARLIC

The firm texture and full flavor of shiitake are underscored here by strong seasoning that would overwhelm many other mushrooms.

4 servings

1 pound shiitake
¾ cup strong beef stock
Pinch each thyme and allspice
3 tablespoons olive oil or goose or bacon fat
1 teaspoon minced garlic
½ cup red wine
Salt and pepper
Minced parsley

1. Clean shiitake caps with soft paintbrush or damp towel. Slice stems thin and combine in a small pot with stock, thyme, and allspice, and 1 teaspoon fat or oil. Simmer, partly covered, until tender—about 10 minutes. Cut caps into generous mouthfuls, or leave whole, if small.

2. Heat remaining oil in a large skillet; stir in garlic and toss a moment. Add shiitake caps and toss to coat. Add contents of saucepan and stir over moderately high heat until liquid evaporates, 5–6 minutes. Add wine and toss until it nearly evaporates, about 2 minutes.

3. Season with salt and pepper, sprinkle with parsley, and serve.

CROSTINI OF CHICKEN LIVERS AND SHIITAKE

Crostini—slices of toasted crusty bread spread with an intensely flavored savory topping—are among the most blessed of Italian culinary inventions. The unorthodox combination that follows can open a rustic meal or accompany a hefty vegetable soup.

12 toasts, to serve 6 as an appetizer, 3 or 4 with a meal

¼ pound shiitake
4 tablespoons full-flavored olive oil
6 juniper berries, crushed
2 tablespoons chopped onion
5 ounces chicken livers, cleaned and quartered
Salt and pepper
About 12 slices firm country-style Italian whole-wheat or white bread cut ¼–½ inch thick

1. Wipe the mushroom caps clean; remove stems and slice thin. Heat 2 tablespoons oil in a skillet and stir in stems, juniper berries, and onion; cook over moderately low heat, covered, for 5 minutes.

2. Chop caps coarse and add with 1 tablespoon more oil. Cook over moderate heat, uncovered, until tender—5–10 minutes. Scrape into a processor container.

3. Add remaining tablespoon oil to pan; in it sauté livers until just cooked—still pink in the center. Sprinkle with salt and pepper and add to processor.

4. Toast bread in preheated broiler as close to flame as possible, turning when lightly browned—about 1 minute per side; check often. Process liver mixture in quick pulses to coarse texture. Spread on warm toast and serve immediately.

NOODLES WITH SHIITAKE, TOMATOES, AND ROSEMARY

This combination of soft noodles, piny rosemary, sweet-acid tomato bits, and earthy shiitake slivers is the kind of fresh-tasting simple dish I love.

4 servings

1 pound shiitake
¼ cup dry vermouth mixed with 2 tablespoons water
1 pound tomatoes, peeled (page 23) and seeded
4 tablespoons full-flavored olive oil
1 teaspoon minced garlic
1 teaspoon fresh rosemary (or ½ teaspoon dried), chopped
About ½ teaspoon salt
½ pound wide egg noodles
Pepper to taste
Minced parsley

1. Wipe the shiitake caps clean with soft paintbrush or damp towel; reserve. Slice stems thin and combine in a small pan with vermouth and water. Simmer gently, covered, until tender—about 10 minutes.

2. Cut tomatoes in strips about ¼ inch wide and 2 inches long. Slice shiitake caps into strips about the same size as tomatoes.

3. Heat 2 tablespoons oil in a large skillet; add garlic, rosemary, and ¼ teaspoon salt. Toss for 1 minute over moderate heat. Add stems and liquid, tomatoes, and caps; toss gently over moderate heat until tomatoes and mushrooms soften and juices thicken a bit—about 5 minutes. Add 1 tablespoon more olive oil.

4. As sauce finishes, boil noodles until just tender; drain. Toss with remaining tablespoon oil in a hot serving dish. Pour the sauce over all; season with salt and pepper; sprinkle with parsley.

 ADDITIONAL RECIPES
Richard Sax's Chicken with Celeriac and Mushrooms (page 100)
Warm Salad of Two Mushrooms, Celery, and Parmesan (page 105)

SNOW PEA
See Sugar Pea

SORREL
Garden or Common Sorrel (*Rumex acetosa*) and
Round or French Sorrel (*Rumex scutatus*); also Sour Grass

*A*mericans seem to have an on-again off-again affair with the sharply acid green leaves to which the French have been devoted as long as there has been France. Most likely the fickleness is due to the fact sorrel *is sour*. A relative of rhubarb, its name derives from the Old French *surele*, through the Germanic *sur*, meaning sour. Happily,

for the moment fashion dictates "on" again —probably because sophisticated diners have sampled deliciously tart sorrel in Europe, or in American restaurants in which chefs have been inspired by continental cuisine.

In Britain the situation is similar. A revered medicinal herb, spring elixir, and culinary ingredient throughout England's history, sorrel was a particular favorite in soups, sauces, and custards, both sweet and savory. So popular was the sweet-sour "greensauce," a relish served with meats and fowl, that almost every kitchen garden until the nineteenth century contained some form of the green, its main ingredient. (The use of the sauce was so common that sorrel itself came to be called *greensauce* in many English towns.) Yet by 1861 Mrs. Beeton had this to say on the subject: "At the present day, English cookery is not much indebted to this plant" (*The Book of Household Management*). She offered one recipe for sorrel—green sauce (this version a puckery-sharp pleasure of gooseberries, sorrel juice, sherry, sugar, and butter)—followed by this note: "We have given this recipe . . . thinking that some of our readers might sometimes require it; but, at the generality of fashionable tables, it is now seldom or never served." Such is fickle fashion!

Fortunately, the tables of France and Belgium and many in Holland, Scandinavia, Hungary, and Russia are more constant in their affections for the soft, bright green leaves, so we can turn to them for supplies when we change our minds again.

SELECTION AND STORAGE: Sorrel now appears to be available from greenhouses year round in the United States, with spring and summer peak seasons for availability. The large (6–8 inch long) arrow-shaped cultivated leaves are very bright green and smooth, less sharp-flavored than the smaller wild ones, should you encounter them. Choose bright, firm leaves with no limpness or yellowing. Look for the most delicate, least fibrous stems.

Store in the vegetable drawer of the refrigerator in a plastic bag for a few days at most. Although you can make a purée and freeze it quite successfully, there is no reason to do so if you can get fresh sorrel in the first place, as the same market will carry it practically year round.

USE: Sorrel leaves, stripped of their stems and slivered, can be used as an acid accent in mixed green salads or a fresh garnish to soups or cooked vegetables.

For the most part, however, sorrel is used as a flavoring purée, a state it assumes naturally the moment it is cooked, without sieving or the addition of liquids or thickeners. You can simply simmer the cleaned, shredded leaves in a tiny amount of water for a few minutes to achieve this, or stir them into a pan of butter or a little cream. However you make the purée, count on considerable reduction—even more than spinach. But the result will be a remarkably tart, velvety flavoring medium.

With no additional ingredients, the purée adds verve to puréed root vegetables or creamy bean dishes. Or use a dollop to enliven a lightly sweet vegetable or egg dish.

Mellowed with cream or eggs, sorrel purée becomes a sauce that pairs spectacularly with pheasant, chicken, veal, and rich fishes. (Although the French classic pairing of shad and sorrel is delicious indeed, I think half of the fun is saying *alose à l'oseille* —pronounced ahLOZ-ah-lozay.) Or spoon the sauce over or inside an omelet, or set poached eggs on a thick reduction of sorrel and cream. Thickened with flour, and seasoned with onion, goose fat, lard, or bacon, the purée becomes a vegetable-sauce combination.

A thinned purée, based on stock or water, thickened with egg yolks, makes a soup that is served around the world, hot or chilled. Particularly well-known versions of this are the Jewish *schav* and French *potage germiny*. Sorrel transforms lentil, pea, and bean purées in the Middle East, sharpening the impact of the bland legumes.

Or add the purée to quiches and custard mixtures for timbales, as they did during the Middle Ages.

PREPARATION: Clean sorrel by dunking it up and down in a sink filled with water; then lift out gently and drain. To use raw, dry in a salad spinner or on soft, absorbent towels. For most preparations, you'll need to strip the leaves from the stems: hold each folded leaf in one hand, then simply pull the stem from it with the other. Roll or stack the leaves, then sliver with a stainless-steel knife. Do not cook sorrel in aluminum or iron.

NUTRITIONAL HIGHLIGHTS: Sorrel is an excellent source of fiber and of vitamins A and C, as well as a good source of iron.

SORREL CREAM SAUCE FOR VEGETABLES

This astonishingly simple sauce provides tart and complex dressing for asparagus, yellow or green beans, cauliflower, summer squash, or other quite crisp, not-too-strong vegetables. The amount provided below will enrich about 1 pound of vegetables.

Makes about ¾ cup sauce

About 3 ounces fresh sorrel, rinsed and stripped (see Preparation)
About ⅓ cup heavy (or whipping) cream
Big pinch salt

1. With stainless-steel knife, cut the leaves into thin strips, slivering enough to make about 1¾ cups light packed leaves. (Save one or two for garnish.)

2. Combine ⅓ cup cream and salt in a small, nonaluminum saucepan and bring to a boil. Add sorrel; simmer, stirring and mashing the leaves until the sauce is thickened slightly and sorrel incorporated evenly, which takes about 4–5 minutes. Adjust seasoning and cream, as desired.

3. Serve hot over steaming blanched vegetables; garnish with a few strips of slivered sorrel leaves.

PURÉED POTATOES, PARSNIPS, AND SORREL

This unusual combination of tastes—mild, starchy potato, sweet parsnip, and sour-herbal sorrel—is freshly appealing. The balance of flavors is such that none of the vegetables is in the foreground; instead the purée seems to be made of one creamy, mysterious root.

4 servings

1 pound rather starchy potatoes (not new potatoes), peeled
¾ pound parsnips (2 good-sized ones), peeled
6 ounces sorrel, rinsed and stripped (see Preparation)
2–3 tablespoons butter
About ¾ cup heavy (or whipping) cream
Salt and pepper

1. Cut potatoes and parsnips in large chunks. Drop into boiling salted water; cook until tender throughout—about 15 minutes.

2. Bunch sorrel leaves together and cut in thin strips, using a stainless-steel knife. Heat 2 tablespoons butter in a non-aluminum skillet. Add sorrel; stir over moderate heat until it forms a soft, purée-like mass—about 3–4 minutes.

3. Drain potatoes and parsnips. Press through medium disk of a food mill. Stir in sorrel and cream to taste. Reheat over very low heat, stirring. Add more butter, if desired, and season to taste.

SALAD OF SORREL, ENDIVE, AND MUSHROOMS
WITH WALNUT DRESSING

Woodsy and wild, with a green and earthy aroma. The sourness of sorrel and bitterness of the endive are offset by the sweetness of balsamic vinegar and walnuts.

6 servings

⅓ cup walnuts
1 tablespoon balsamic vinegar
1 tablespoon cider vinegar
½ teaspoon sugar
¼ teaspoon salt
3 tablespoons imported walnut oil
2 tablespoons peanut oil
½ pound small sorrel leaves, rinsed and well dried
½ pound Belgian endive, rinsed
½ pound mushrooms, cleaned
Pepper to taste

1. Toast nuts in preheated 375-degree oven (or toaster oven) for 5 minutes, until barely crisped. With a towel rub off as much of the husks as possible. Cool and chop in coarse pieces; reserve.

2. Combine vinegars, sugar, and salt; mix. Gradually beat in the oils. Set aside.

3. Strip off and discard sorrel stems. Cut leaves in narrow strips. Trim bases and cores from endive, then slice in julienne strips 2–3 inches long. Slice mushrooms thin.

4. Combine sorrel, endive, and mushrooms in a serving bowl; add walnuts and pepper. Pour dressing over and toss gently.

CHILLED SORREL-AND-PEA SOUP

Smooth, grassy-fresh, with a light sweetness, this delicate purée makes a refreshing first course for a summer soirée.

4–6 servings as a first course

3½ cups water
3 tablespoons white rice
1 medium onion, coarsely chopped
1 tablespoon light vegetable oil
2 pounds fresh peas, shelled (2 cups peas)
2 teaspoons sugar
1½ teaspoons kosher salt
¾ pound fresh sorrel, rinsed, stripped (see Preparation)
½–1 cup buttermilk
¼–½ cup heavy (or whipping) cream
White pepper

1. Combine 3 cups water and rice in a pot; simmer, covered, until very soft—about 20 minutes. Meanwhile, cook onion over low heat in oil in a saucepan until slightly soft. Add peas and toss for a minute; add rice with its cooking liquid, sugar, and salt.

2. Simmer, covered, until tender—about 8–10 minutes. Press soup through medium disk of a food mill.

3. Slice sorrel with a stainless-steel knife, reserving a handful for garnish. Combine in a nonaluminum pot with the remaining ½ cup water; stir over moderate heat until "melted." Add sorrel to purée; press all through a fine sieve. Add ½ cup buttermilk and ¼ cup cream. Adjust seasoning and add white pepper.

4. Refrigerate at least 4 hours. To serve, add buttermilk and cream to taste. Season, then garnish with reserved sorrel leaves, slivered.

COLD POACHED SALMON IN SORREL CREAM SAUCE

For an elegant buffet, serve this tender salmon blanketed in a rich sauce—a surprising alternative to mayonnaise. Although the coating could not be simpler to prepare (you simply simmer sorrel and cream together for 5 minutes), it tastes as though you've spent hours refining and balancing the flavors and texture.

When you use hothouse sorrel, which is large-leafed and sold in big bunches, the amount below should do; if you have wild sorrel, which can be more adamantly tart, use a bit less and boil down the sauce a little longer to mellow and thicken it.

If you've never oven-poached a fish, try it. You'll be converted, as I was when my friend Richard Sax showed me the way in *Cooking Great Meals Every Day* (Random House).

6–8 main-course servings

½ tablespoon softened butter
2 tablespoons chopped shallots
2 tablespoons chopped celery
2½ pounds boned center-cut salmon fillet
Salt and white pepper
About ½ cup dry white wine or dry vermouth
About ½ cup water
½ pound sorrel, rinsed, stripped (see Preparation)
1 cup heavy (or whipping) cream

1. Poach fish: Spread butter in a large flameproof utensil slightly larger than the salmon measured with its boned flaps opened outward. Sprinkle shallots and celery in pan and set salmon on top, skin side down; sprinkle lightly with salt and white pepper. Add enough wine and water to reach three-quarters up the sides of the fish. Cover with a sheet of buttered waxed paper to just fit inside container. Bring to a simmer.

2. Set in preheated 375-degree oven. Bake until fish loses its raw pinkness on top. Do not overcook; fish continues to poach in liquid when removed from oven. Timing varies, but 10–15 minutes is usual for a center-cut fillet.

3. Remove paper; let cool 15 minutes. Very carefully lift fish from broth onto a platter and turn so skin side is up. When cool enough, peel off skin. Cool completely, then cover and chill. (Strain and freeze cooking stock for another use.)

4. Prepare sauce: With stainless-steel knife sliver as many sorrel leaves as needed to equal 3 lightly packed cups; wrap and refrigerate the remainder. Combine cream and ¼ teaspoon salt in skillet (not aluminum or iron); bring to a boil. Add sorrel; lower heat. Simmer, stirring and mashing, for about 5 minutes, until sauce is thickened and sorrel well blended with cream; it should be quite thick. Scrape into a dish and cool, stirring occasionally to prevent a skin from forming. Cover and chill until serving time.

5. To serve, pour juices that have accumulated around salmon into sorrel sauce. Stir and season with salt and pepper. Spoon sauce over salmon. Sliver about 1 cup remaining sorrel leaves and arrange a loose, scattered wreath of them around salmon. Serve chilled, or cream will soften and lose its mayonnaise-like consistency.

SOUR CHERRY
(Prunus cerasus)
also Pie Cherry, Red Cherry, Tart Cherry

*T*he cherry's botanical designation places it in the family of Roses, the genus of stone fruits, the species *cerasus* (through Greek from *karsu*, cherry, the word used by the Assyrians and Babylonians, who were probably the first to cultivate the fruit). Because the sour cherry had by prehistoric times already taken root in the area it now

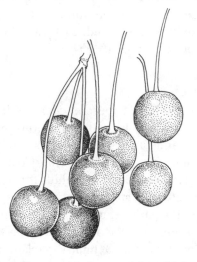

occupies (temperate Europe, Asia, and North America), there has been considerable disagreement among botanists (and etymologists) about its origin. It was one of the first trees to be cultivated by the colonists in Massachusetts, being easier to raise than its sister sweet cherry *(Prunus avium)*, as it is much smaller and self-fruitful (most sweet cherries require pollinators).

What then is the sour cherry doing in this book, tucked in among relative newcomers to the American marketplace? The answer is that it is making a *re*appearance.

For it is only recently, with the advent of greenmarkets and demand for old-fashioned American specialties that such a delicate fruit—thin-skinned, bursting with juice, unsuitable for long-distance shipping—has become available to us. For years it has been hiding in cans under the name pie cherries, afraid to venture out raw for fear that some consumer might reject it for its blemishes, which are relatively unknown in the dark-hued, tough-hided Bings and their allies. Well, they've finally come out of the pantry and into the marketplace (albeit rarely and briefly), either trucked from nearby, or to be gathered at a pick-your-own orchard.

Crisp, deep-garnet, sweet cherries simply do not compare with sour cherries when it comes to cooking. Although some sour cherries are good raw, all are best cooked. Their soft skins and pulp become creamy tender when subjected to heat, and the flavor blooms, delightfully fresh and acid. Nor will the flesh exude a discoloring ink—only a clear or pale pink juice. While several sour cherry varieties are grown here, the Montmorency is virtually the sole kind produced for the fresh market: light to dark red skin (cherry red that is, not burgundy or maroon), with creamy tan flesh, lots of juice, and a medium-tart taste. Other varieties are grown primarily for canning—which, you may be surprised to know, accounts for the cultivation of almost as many tart cherries as sweet. The United States, to my amazement, is the leading cherry-producing country in the world, followed by Rumania, Italy, and Germany. Two-thirds of the American crop comes from Michigan, with the next most-productive state being New York; Utah, Wisconsin, Oregon, Pennsylvania, and Colorado also grow goodly quantities.

SELECTION AND STORAGE' Keep an eye out for sour cherries (usually sold in pint or quart wooden baskets) during June and July, after sweet cherries have come into the markets. The cherries should be soft and juicy as dead-ripe plums. It is impossible to find them unbruised, so don't bother to try. Look for containers with as few browned fruits as possible.

Do not even attempt to keep a supply of the fragile cherries, which will be even more bruised when you get them home from the market. If the weather is sultry, keep in the refrigerator, uncovered. Plan to cook them within a day or two, at the most.

Sour cherries freeze well: Stem and pit them (figure a pound will yield about two cups, pitted), then simply freeze in small containers. Or place in freezer containers, sprinkling lightly with sugar as you go. Let stand, stirring a few times, until the sugar has dissolved and produced a syrup. Cover and freeze.

USE: Sour cherries are used, in the countries that grow them, in every course of the meal, from soup though after-dinner liqueur. Cold cherry and mixed-fruit soups (spiced or not), shiny red or pinked with cream, are part of the northern and central European repertoire from Denmark down through Rumania.

Sauces of sour cherries, barely sweetened or thick and rich, enliven poultry, game, and even fish in parts of Russia, Poland, Hungary, Germany, Rumania, Denmark, France. In Persian cuisine the cherries are cooked with lamb or chicken, or combined with rice, creating their own sauce as they cook. In France and Belgium cherries are pickled in aromatic vinegar to be served with pâtés and game dishes, an unexpected and delicious sensation.

Almost every familiar dessert that calls for cherries would do better with sour ones —pies, tarts, cakes, fritters, dumplings, strudel, crêpes. Black Forest torte and cherry cobbler were invented with the sour cherry, the reasons for which will be clear the first time you've tasted either made with the real thing. Jams, preserves (a spoon of cherry preserves, savored Russian-style with fine black tea, is a treat worth discovering), confections (cherries in brandy, chocolate-covered, and the like), and most cordials began life with sour, not sweet, cherries as their base. Any good recipes that call for cherries will require no changes, save an increase in sugar, when you substitute sour cherries.

PREPARATION: For most dishes you'll need to pit the cherries. Rinse them first, then pluck out the stems. Set each cherry in a pitter, press firmly, and discard the stone. You can use a hairpin, if you're handy, but a tong-shaped pitter works best.

For some understanding cherry lovers the fruits need not be pitted. Retaining the stone helps keep in both flavor and juice, but will frustrate and worry most diners, so gauge your company. For some recipes in which the fruit is steeped or macerated or poached, you can stone the cherries, crush the pits slightly, and knot in cheesecloth to add their bitter-almond flavor to the dish.

NUTRITIONAL HIGHLIGHTS: Sour cherries are low in calories. They are a fair source of vitamin A. They provide a fairly good quantity of vitamin C and some potassium.

SOUR CHERRY CLAFOUTIS

Clafoutis, a custardy pancake of the Limousin area of France, is most often made with dark, sweet cherries, usually unpitted. I can't imagine it could be better than this beguiling variation: pink sour cherries, puffed by cooking, their almondy flavor underscored by puréed pine nuts, are clustered in an eggy batter, then baked until golden. I like it best for Sunday breakfast, with big cups of café au lait, but it won't hurt for dessert.

2 generous brunch servings

½ pound sour cherries, stemmed and pitted (see Preparation), 1 cup

3 tablespoons sugar, preferably vanilla-flavored

2 tablespoons kirsch or marasquin

2½ tablespoons pine nuts (pignolia)

½ cup milk

1 egg

¼ teaspoon vanilla

Pinch salt

⅛ teaspoon ground cardamom (or cinnamon)

1 tablespoon melted butter

⅓ cup plus 1 tablespoon flour

Confectioners' sugar

1. Combine cherries, sugar, and liquor, and macerate briefly—about 15 minutes or so.

2. Meanwhile, whirl 2 tablespoons nuts in processor or blender to make a paste. Add milk; blend. Drain in juice from cherries; add egg, vanilla, salt, cardamom, and butter; blend. Sift in flour. Mix for 15 seconds, or just until combined. Adjust thickness, if necessary, to that of heavy cream.

3. Pour ¼ inch of batter into well-buttered 7–8-inch round cake pan or baking dish. Spread cherries on this; top with remaining batter. Sprinkle with remaining ½ tablespoon nuts.

4. Bake on lower shelf of preheated 400-degree oven until puffed in center and lightly browned—about 30 minutes. Dust with confectioners' sugar and serve at once.

SOUR CHERRY RATAFIA

Cherries flavor many of the most aromatically appealing liqueurs and eaux-de-vie made—ratafia, marasquin, and kirsch. For home-made cordials, the fruit works remarkably well, thanks to the intense almondy kernel flavor, which is quickly imparted without complicated techniques or machinery.

The somewhat old-fashioned term *ratafia* is used to describe liqueurs or cordials made by steeping or infusing, particularly stone fruits. The drink has been around since the Renaissance, when it was served upon the ratification of treaties and pacts —or so say the majority of authorities on spirits. The Oxford English Dictionary calls this conjecture; but it remains a most appealing derivation. Although the word is still used today in France, England, and some older American cookbooks, the meaning has expanded to include biscuits, puddings, creams, cakes, and cookies that taste of ground almonds or apricot pits or other kernel flavors.

Serve this cherry-bright liqueur over ice, or combined with white wine or sparkling water for an apéritif; or offer it well chilled, in small glasses for dessert.

Makes about 1 quart

1 pound sour cherries, *plus ½ pound a week or two later*
2 cups white rum
1–2-inch piece vanilla bean
12 peppercorns
½ cup water
½ cup sugar

1. Stone 1 pound cherries, reserving pits. Enclose these in a bag, wrap in a towel, then crack with meat pounder or hammer.

2. Rinse a quart canning jar with boiling water. In it combine pits, pitted cherries, rum, vanilla, and peppercorns. Cover with baking parchment, cap tightly, and shake. Let stand in a dark place for a week or two, shaking occasionally.

3. Pour liqueur through a cheesecloth-lined sieve, then squash cherries in cheesecloth to extract most juice. Discard pulp; save vanilla and return it to the jar.

4. Prick the fresh ½ pound cherries with a clean needle. Combine in jar with liqueur. Cover as before. Leave another week or so, shaking now and then.

5. Combine water and sugar and boil for a minute; cool. Repeat squeezing and straining of ratafia as in step 3, but finish up by straining the cordial through several layers of fine cheesecloth.

6. Pour liqueur through a coffee filter in small batches, removing the filter occasionally to rinse off solids. (This is a slow job, but necessary.)

7. Gradually add cooled sugar syrup to taste. Decant into a bottle to just fit. Once you have used a good portion, transfer the cordial to a smaller bottle to prevent discoloration and loss of flavor.

SOUR CHERRIES IN RUM

Although the ingredients for this heady, rosy concoction are almost the same as those for the ratafia, the result is quite different. If you're a fan of fruits steeped in brandy or Armagnac—those gorgeous, expensive jars stacked in luxury shop cases— you'll be delighted with this simple version of same, a recipe that is still part of many a good home in France, England, and Italy.

I like the fuller cherry flavor and the color that the white rum allows, but brandy is the traditional steeping medium. Make a few jars if you have a windfall of cherries, so that holiday time finds you rich in spirituous pleasures.

For about 1 quart

1 pound sour cherries
½ cup sugar
Optional: 1-inch piece vanilla
About 2 cups white rum

1. Stem cherries; discard ones with discolored flesh. Prick each all over with a clean needle. Place cherries in a sieve; pour a kettle of boiling water over them to clean and soften skin.

2. Rinse a 1-quart canning jar with boiling water. Put cherries in the jar, sprinkling in sugar as you proceed. Add optional vanilla, then pour in rum to reach top of jar.

3. Place a piece of baking parchment over jar top so metal cap will be covered by it; then screw the cap on tightly. Shake to dissolve most sugar.

4. Leave jar in a dark place to age for a month or more.

5. Serve both liqueur and a few cherries as dessert or after-dinner cordial.

AROMATIC RICE WITH SOUR CHERRIES

Light and soft, this fresh-tasting dish of palest rice and tart cherries will be adored by some, considered strange by others. The fluffy grains, particularly tender in this treatment, are tinted party pink and yellow from the cherries and saffron. It is a festive complement to poultry and vegetable main courses.

6 servings

2 cups long-grain white rice (see Note)
1 tablespoon salt
¼ cup sugar
¼ cup water
1 small cinnamon stick, broken in three
Optional: 3 crushed cardamom pods
1 pound sour cherries, pitted (2 cups, approximately)
3 tablespoons butter
¼ teaspoon saffron threads
2 tablespoons hot water

1. Wash rice by swishing in a bowl of water. Drain and repeat twice. Dissolve salt in enough water to cover rice by an inch. Soak 1 hour or longer.

2. Bring 6 cups water to a boil. Stir in rice and soaking water. Bring to a boil, stirring. Boil about 5 minutes, or until kernels are cooked on outside but still firm in center. Drain rice in sieve. Rinse with cold water and fluff a few times.

3. Combine sugar, water, and cinnamon (and optional cardamom) in small nonaluminum pot. Bring to a boil, stirring.

Cover and simmer 3 minutes. Uncover and add cherries; stir. Cook on low heat, uncovered, for 2 minutes, or until puffed.

4. In heavy flameproof casserole of about 2½-quart capacity, heat 1½ tablespoons butter and half cherry liquid. Add half drained rice. Top with half cherries. Cover with remaining rice.

5. Add remaining butter to cherries and liquid; heat until melted. Pour over rice, tucking cinnamon sticks in center. Turn heat to high. When sizzling, place clean dish towel over casserole, cover tightly, then pick up ends onto cover to keep away from flame.

6. Turn heat to low and cook 15 minutes. Remove from heat and let stand 10–20 minutes. Meanwhile, crumble saffron and combine with 2 tablespoons hot water.

7. Toss rice a few times with spatula, then drizzle saffron over top.

Note: If you can find imported basmati rice, it is delightful, preferable, and authentic for this dish.

Chicken and Rice with Sour Cherries

The dish above is based (very loosely) on a traditional Iranian chicken dish. To convert the side dish to a meaty main dish is straightforward: Halve, bone, and skin 3 medium chicken breasts (about 2½–2¾ pounds before trimming). Sprinkle evenly with ¼ teaspoon each salt, cardamom, white pepper, and cinnamon. Brown lightly in 2 tablespoons butter. Place chicken between the rice layers in step 4 and proceed.

SOUR GRASS
See Sorrel

SPAGHETTI SQUASH
See Vegetable Spaghetti

SQUASH
See Buttercup, Calabaza, Chayote, Delicata, Golden Nugget, Kabocha, Sweet Dumpling

SQUASH FLOWERS
or SQUASH BLOSSOMS
(Cucurbita Pepo)

*A*lthough these natural appurtenances precede every squash that comes into the world, they are usually difficult to find without a garden. Golden-yellow, fleeting, fragile, they are picked just before they open and must be used shortly thereafter, or they will wilt to the consistency of used Kleenex. Blossoms can be plucked from any

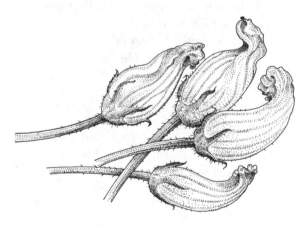

squash, whether a summer or winter variety, but zucchini, which has particularly luxuriant blooms, is most often the source.

Despite the fact that American Indians have long cooked squash blossoms (and celebrated them in their art and rituals), most contemporary North Americans familiar with the flowers have learned about their charms in Mediterranean dishes.

While it is most likely that you will find the radiant blossoms at an Italian-American market, colorful California cuisine and the restaurateurs' lust for the unusual have helped the squash-blossom cause—as has an increasing Mexican-American population. Because a majority of squash is native to Mexico, the flowers are part of everyday dishes there.

SELECTION AND STORAGE: Squash blossoms show up during the summer months. They may appear in fancy vegetable markets, in greenmarkets, or in Latin or Italian stores. Select only those that are closed and fresh-looking, taking into consideration that petals are softish and somewhat limp by nature. Although they will be expensive, you get a surprisingly large quantity for your money.

If you are picking the flowers from a garden, you will want to collect the male flowers only (leaving a few to continue the good work), so that your squash (the females) will develop. The male flowers appear earlier in the season than females, and continue blossoming until enough squash have set. They are easily distinguished by their narrow stems; the females attach to an enlarged base that bulges and resembles a baby squash, which in fact it is.

Do not try to store squash flowers longer than a day, at most. Keep them in a basket in the refrigerator if it is very hot out.

USE: At their simplest—cleaned, sliced, and sautéed—squash flowers make a beautiful garnish for steamed, mashed zucchini, fried tomatoes, thick creamy soups, or vegetable purées. Or fold the sautéed blooms, seasoned with shallots or chives, into omelets or crêpes, or add chilis and tuck into *quesadillas* (fried tortilla turnovers). Or toss with strips of ham, poultry, or shrimp, for an unusual light lunch.

The French and Mexicans sliver squash blossoms into soups, in concert with a diversity of summer vegetables. In Nice the chopped blossoms are combined with chard leaves, rice, cheese, basil, and egg in a lovely gratin called *tian*. In Greece the vegetable medley that includes the glowing petals is thick and stewlike.

All who cook squash blossoms seem to favor frying, and no wonder: Lightly battered, the surprisingly meaty petals, which taste like a pale version of whichever squash they produce, make one of the most appealing appetizers ever invented. The Niçoises and Italians fry them neat, or stuff the expandable blossom packets with mixtures that may contain cheese, meat, herbs, nuts, eggs, crumbs, rice, or potatoes. Or the flowers may enclose a morsel of softish cheese, such as fontina or mozzarella, with or without a pinch of herbs or garlic. The stuffed party favors are then batter-dipped and fried.

PREPARATION: Cookbooks recommend removing the stamenate portions (the filaments that stand upright in each blossom) from the blooms, but I see no reason for this unless you are stuffing the flower or unless the section is unusually large or, slimy (which can happen). Trim the stems to about an inch. Open the petals very carefully and dunk the flower in and out of a bowl of water. Or hold open the flower and run a gentle stream of water into it, which facilitates the opening process. Gently dab on a towel and set to dry. If you are stuffing the flowers, pinch out the stamen from each, open the petals wide, and place stem side up, like an upside-down umbrella, to dry somewhat.

NUTRITIONAL HIGHLIGHTS: Squash flowers are very low in calories (about 20 calories per cup, cooked). They contain vitamin A and calcium. They are high in fiber and low in sodium.

SAUTÉED SQUASH FLOWERS

Sautéed this way squash blossoms have a delicate woodsy flavor—rather like summer squash crossed with chanterelle.

Select about 8 medium flowers per person for a side dish, 4 to be part of another dish. Halve the rinsed and dried blossoms (see Preparation). Sauté for a minute in butter until wilted. Top with a sprinkle of minced chives and serve as a side dish. Or fill an omelet with the delicate blossoms; or strew over risotto or fresh pasta. Alternatively, you can slice up the flowers before sautéing them, if smaller pieces are desirable —as they would be for sprinkling over steamed summer squash or zucchini.

DEEP-FRIED SQUASH FLOWERS

When soft, summery squash blossoms appear in greenmarkets around town, I am forced to change my mind about my dislike of deep-frying in order to prepare these golden appetizers—a familiar estival antipasto in Italy, where they appreciate vegetables that are simply (or not at all) seasoned.

6 generous servings as an appetizer

1¼ cups cold water
¼ teaspoon salt
1 cup all-purpose flour
About 30 medium-sized squash flowers, rinsed, opened, trimmed, and dried (see Preparation)
Vegetable oil for deep-frying
Additional salt

1. Combine water and salt in a small bowl. Sift in flour, beating rapidly with a fork until blended. Cover with a towel and let stand an hour or longer.

2. When ready to serve, pour about an inch of oil into a wide, deep skillet (preferably electric) and heat to 375 degrees. Stir batter; coat a blossom thoroughly, then drop into the hot oil. Repeat quickly 4 or 5 times, dipping just enough flowers to allow plenty of "swimming" room in the oil. Fry until golden on one side—about 30 seconds; then flip each blossom and fry until golden on the other side.

3. Drain on paper towels, salt to taste, and serve at once.

Note: These are at their best straight from the skillet, but you can also keep a batch warm in a low oven. Or use 2 skillets to fry more flowers at once.

FRIED CHEESE-STUFFED SQUASH BLOSSOMS

For a special summer meal, offer this opener of bright squash blossoms plumped with herbed ricotta and pine-nut kernels, then fried in a light batter. Although it is possible to hold the flowers in a warm oven for a short period after frying, they are at their best fresh from the pan; so you might plan to serve them casually, as they are completed, while your guests have a drink.

4 servings as an appetizer

½ cup plus 2 tablespoons water
⅛ teaspoon salt
½ cup flour
½ pound ricotta
3 tablespoons pine nuts (pignolia)
2 tablespoons minced parsley
3 tablespoons minced basil
⅓ cup finely grated Parmesan cheese
Additional salt to taste
Pepper
20 good-sized squash blossoms, opened, rinsed, dried, with stamens removed (see Preparation)
Vegetable oil for deep-frying

1. Prepare batter: Combine water and salt in a small bowl. Sift in flour, beating rapidly with fork or whisk until just mixed. Cover with a towel and let stand at least 1 hour.

2. Meanwhile, place ricotta in a sieve over a bowl to drain and reach room temperature—about an hour. Toast nuts in a 325-degree oven until golden, about 10 minutes. Watch carefully: they burn quickly.

3. Combine parsley, basil, Parmesan, nuts, and drained ricotta in small bowl. Add salt and pepper to taste. Gently fill each blossom with a heaping teaspoon of the mixture, pushing it in carefully, so as not to break the flower. Twist petals closed to seal in filling.

4. Heat an inch of vegetable oil in a wide skillet (preferably an electric one, which maintains the temperature of oil automatically) to 375 degrees. Stir batter and coat 5 blossoms with it. Fry until golden, 30–45 seconds; turn over and fry until golden. Drain on paper towels, sprinkle with salt, and serve at once. Continue until all flowers have been fried.

—

SQUASH AND SQUASH FLOWER PUDDING

This adaptation of a traditional Niçois specialty includes yellow summer squash, squash blossoms, and a thickening of rice, eggs, and cheese. The saffron-golden dish is sunny, casual, straightforward—ideal for a rustic buffet. The soft bites of squash flower hidden in the rather firm, moist pudding lend a sweet, fresh flavor.

6 servings

2 pounds small yellow summer squash, scrubbed

⅓ cup white rice

2 tablespoons olive oil

1 large onion, coarsely chopped

1 large garlic clove, minced

3 eggs

3 ounces Parmesan cheese, grated (¾ cup)

¾ teaspoon salt

White pepper

8 large basil leaves, slivered (about 2 tablespoons), plus sprigs for garnish

15 large or 20 medium squash flowers (5–6 ounces), cleaned (see Preparation)

Optional: A few small squash flowers for garnish

1. Drop squash into boiling salted water; continue boiling until just tender, about 4–5 minutes. Lift out with tongs; drop in cold water. Add rice to boiling water and cook until tender, about 10 minutes. Drain rice and trim squash.

2. Heat oil in skillet over moderate heat and sauté onions until softened, about 5 minutes. Add garlic and stir for a minute. Transfer to processor.

3. Blend eggs in a mixing bowl. Add rice, cheese, salt, and pepper; blend well. Roughly purée onion mixture. Add basil and squash, chunked; roughly purée, in batches, keeping some texture. Add to egg mixture.

4. Slice blossoms across into ½-inch slices (you should have about 2 cups). Add to bowl and blend well.

5. Scrape into oiled shallow 8-cup baking-serving dish. Set in middle of preheated 350-degree oven. Bake 45 minutes, until set in center and very lightly browned. Cool to lukewarm or room temperature; garnish with small basil leaves. Garnish with pretty, fresh squash flowers —or if they are less than perfect, fry them.

STAR FRUIT
See Carambola

S U G A R   P E A (both SUGAR SNAP PEA and SNOW PEA)
(*Pisum sativum* variety *macrocarpon*)
also Edible-Podded Pea; Snow Pea is also called Mangetout,
Chinese Snow Pea, and Chinese Pea

*S*now peas and sugar snap peas (although *Sugar Snap*, properly speaking, only applies to one cultivar, the term is now used to mean any pea of this type) are both edible-podded (or sugar) peas. They differ from shelling peas in that the pods do not develop a tough, supportive lining (an alternative French name for the group is *pois sans parchemin*, or peas without parchment). As a result, the entire vegetable is

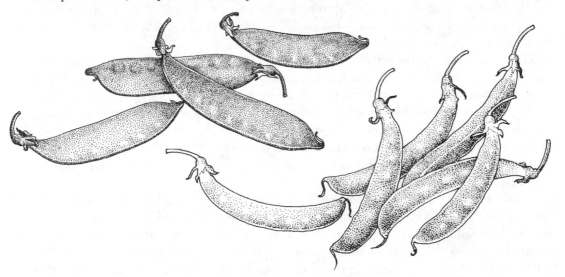

tender-edible. Ribbon-flat snow peas must be harvested when the immature peas are the size of peppercorns and the translucent straight-sided pods show only a suggestion of bumps within, or the whole will be fibrous and starchy. Sugar snap peas develop fat peas that tightly fill the curved, thick-walled pods, but both remain sweet and tender when mature.

Although relatively new in the American marketplace, edible-podded peas are no upstarts, having been fashionable in Europe as early as the sixteenth century (shelling peas have been around since ancient times).

Snow peas, generally assumed to be Chinese in origin, were most likely first cultivated in Europe, according to many sources. I have read that the Cantonese name for the vegetable, *ho laan* (as in Holland), is a likely clue to the source of the variety first planted. In support of this theory is the fact that French horticulturalists of the seventeenth century described the "Dutch pea" as a straight-podded sugar pea, probably introduced into France around 1600 by the French ambassador to Holland. The date 1954 that accompanied the entry for "snow pea" in Webster's Collegiate Dictionary (9th edition) led me to an article of that year entitled "An Exotic Vegetable" that appeared in the *New York Times*. The author, Anthony Lewis, wrote that "growing snow peas in the home is a worthwhile trick for the Chinese food fancier because the vegetable is not available . . . in ordinary stores. . . . Exotic as they sound, snow peas . . . are neither particularly mysterious, nor exclusively Chinese." Why *snow* (which is certainly a recent change), I cannot tell. It grows no earlier in the season than other peas, many of which can be surprised by a late snowfall.

The sugar snap pea is a horticultural refinement, not brand-new, as some claim. A thick-podded snap pea called the butter pea, which was similar to today's sugar snap, was described at length in *The Vegetable Garden*, published in English in 1885, and six types of "butter sugar peas" appeared in a report of the New York State Agricultural Experiment Station at Geneva in 1928. The Agway seed company introduced such a pea in 1950, then again in 1967 with the announcement: "Round Pod Sugar. Here it is again—the edible-podded variety that so many have asked for since it was discontinued 3 years ago. The snap bean of the pea family."

But it was only as recently as 1979 that the sugar snap type pea was perfected and marketed, primarily by one man, Calvin Lamborn. While tackling the problem of snow peas that buckled in processing (at the Gallatin Valley Seed Company in Twin Falls, Idaho), he crossed a thick-podded mutant green pea with a snow pea—and made breeding history. The resulting offspring, dubbed the *Sugar Snap*, won the coveted gold medal from All-America selections in the year of its release and an unprecedented response from home gardeners—a bit ironic, in that the cross was intended to solve a problem in commercial harvesting.

SELECTION AND STORAGE: Snow peas are available year round in Oriental markets, fancy groceries, and some supermarkets; sugar snap peas at the latter two. Look for relatively small pods that are crisp (snow peas are always soft and flexible, however). Even coloring, with no sign of yellow, indicates freshness, as does the condition of the stem, which should be bright, perky, and clean-dry. Dehydration, wetness, and flabbiness all indicate excessive storage.

Peas lose flavor and tone from the minute they are picked, so try not to purchase until you're ready to use them. But they will last in the refrigerator in a plastic bag, even if the stay doesn't improve their quality. Snow peas get tired within a day or two; sugar snaps should last a few days longer.

USE: Although both snow peas and sugar snaps are often nibbled raw, I find that brief cooking underscores sweetness, flavor, and color.

Generally speaking, you might consider both peas as comparable to asparagus, in terms of flavoring and cooking methods. Whether warm or chilled, they are best suited to few and light-tasting accompaniments—lemon; ginger; shallots or green onions; cream or butter; herbs such as basil, mint, marjoram, lemon balm; seafood; slivers of ham, chicken, or pork; julienne of carrot or mushrooms. Sauces that suit might be a hollandaise or maltaise, a chilled cream-based sauce, or Nutmeg Cream for Fiddlehead Ferns (page 206), or a very delicate vinaigrette.

Do not overcook sugar peas! Fast steaming, boiling, and stir-frying are the methods that best retain the bright green, crispness, and sweetness. Cook only until the peas lose their raw bite, not a second longer, or the whole point is lost. Figure about 1½ minutes' boiling time for snow peas, about 3 for steaming; about 2 minutes' boiling for sugar snaps, about 4 minutes' steaming.

Snow peas make an enchanting cocktail nibble. Split and string the straighter side of chilled barely cooked peas. With a small star tube pipe a soft mixture (creamy cheese, fish-roe spread) the length of the little canoes. Beware of overfilling.

For stir-fried dishes, snow peas should be added with 2–3 minutes' tossing time left. Sugar snaps should be blanched, then added to the stir-fry just long enough to heat through. If you are serving the peas cold, cook a few seconds less than you would for cooked dishes, and let cool to room temperature before refrigerating; or drop into ice water, drain, dry, and refrigerate.

PREPARATION: Although some stringless varieties may show up in the market, most snow peas and sugar snaps need to be strung. Do not be tempted to overlook this, as the fiber does not soften during cooking. The task is a pleasant one, considerably faster and easier than pea shelling.

Many snow peas require attention to the thicker seam only, the one to which the peas attach. To remove this, break or cut the stem end of the pea from the side opposite this, then pull to zip off the thicker, upper side. Try the lower side as well, in case you have a pod that requires double stringing. If you are serving the peas chilled, string them *after* cooking. As crazy as it may sound, when I compared methods, peas from the same batch tasted sweeter this way.

Sugar snaps generally require removal of the string from both seams. If you have very fresh young pods, this can sometimes be done in one move, by snapping the stem end, then gently pulling down both sides of the pea at once to remove the "backbones." If one side is stubborn, you'll have to zip it off, starting at the other end.

NUTRITIONAL HIGHLIGHTS: Sugar peas are low in calories. They provide a good dose of vitamin C, vitamin K, and fiber.

CLEAR SOUP WITH CHICKEN AND VEGETABLE JULIENNE

Cooking teacher Mary Beth Clark enjoys light and beautiful dishes, which this is. Poached for seconds, the slivers of snow pea, dried mushrooms, and chicken retain their textural integrity and color. Mary Beth stresses that the ingredients are meant to contrast, not blend; so be careful not to overcook. Duck stock and meat are delicious alternatives to the chicken.

4 servings as a first course

6 medium-sized dried black Oriental
    mushrooms (shiitake)
8 snow peas, strings removed (see
    Preparation)
4 cups chicken stock, skimmed of fat
Salt to taste
1 large chicken thigh, boned and
    skinned, cut in very thin slivers
1 teaspoon finely slivered ginger

1. Cover mushrooms with warm water and soak for 20 minutes. Drain; lightly press out moisture. Remove stems (reserve for stock making). Slice caps in ⅛-inch-wide strips.

2. Split snow peas along their straight sides, then slip in your finger and run it along the length of the pod to detach any teeny peas (which do not suit the look of the soup—so eat them if any lurk within). Slice pods lengthwise in ⅛-inch julienne.

3. Bring stock to a boil on high heat; add salt to taste. Add meat; stir 10 seconds. Add mushrooms; lower heat to medium and cook 30 seconds. Add snow peas; cook 10 seconds. Off heat stir in ginger.

4. Distribute evenly among small bowls and serve at once.

SUGAR SNAP PEAS FOR HORS D'OEUVRES—WITH TWO DIPS

Bright sugar snaps are just the right size and texture for scooping softly creamy dips—preferably rather mild ones, that will allow the clean taste of the peas to come through. Although you can serve the peas raw, a brief steam bath brings out the flavor and enhances the texture. The cream and mayonnaise dips that follow are merely beginnings: either one might be flavored in many ways to complement the sugar snaps.

About 6 servings as an hors d'oeuvre

1¼ pounds sugar snap peas, strings
    removed (see Preparation)

1. Set peas on a rack over boiling water. Cover and steam only until the raw flavor disappears, but the peas are still crispy—about 3 minutes.

2. Dip in a bowl of ice water to stop the cooking; drain and dry well.

3. Chill until serving time. Serve with one of following dips.

Lime Mint Cream Dip

Makes about ¾ cup, enough for 1¼ pounds peas

About 2 tablespoons finely chopped mint
¼ teaspoon salt, approximately
½ teaspoon sugar
About 1½ tablespoons lime juice
⅔ cup heavy (or whipping) cream,
 preferably not ultrapasteurized

1. Crush together 1 tablespoon mint with salt and sugar. Gradually stir in 1½ tablespoons lime juice, mashing mint. Cover and let stand at least 30 minutes.

2. Press in a sieve to extract juice; discard mint. Slowly stir cream into lime-mint juice, then add remaining chopped mint. Season to taste, adding more lime juice and mint if desired.

3. Cover and chill for several hours to mellow and thicken (the dip will have the consistency of sour cream).

Tarragon Mayonnaise Dip

Makes about 1 cup mayonnaise, enough for about 1¼ pounds peas

1 egg
2 teaspoons vinegar
½ teaspoon salt
1 teaspoon prepared mustard
½ cup plus 2 tablespoons vegetable oil
½ cup olive oil
About 2 teaspoons finely minced tarragon
About 1 tablespoon minced chives
Lemon juice to taste
1–2 tablespoons boiling water

1. Blend together the egg, vinegar, salt, mustard, and 2 tablespoons vegetable oil in container of blender or processor. With motor running, slowly add remaining vegetable and olive oils.

2. Add tarragon, chives, and lemon juice to taste. Adjust seasonings to suit, then stir in boiling water to blend and soften mixture. Chill several hours or longer.

SUGAR SNAP (OR SNOW) PEAS WITH CARROTS AND MINT

A slight twist on an old standby—this time using the crunchy, gleamingly verdant sugar snap (or snow) pea, instead of the traditional green pea. Although any mints go well with this, you might consider other fresh alternatives: basil, lemon thyme, marjoram, chives, or dill.

6 servings

1 pound carrots (weighed without tops), peeled
2 tablespoons butter
¼ teaspoon salt, or to taste
1 cup water
1 pound sugar snap (or snow) peas, strings removed (see Preparation)
About ¼ cup freshly chopped mint

1. Cut carrots into strips about ¼ inch wide and 3 inches long. Combine in a heavy skillet with 1 tablespoon butter, salt, and water. Simmer, covered, until just barely tender, 6–8 minutes.

2. Drop peas into a pot of boiling salted water; boil until not quite tender—about 2 minutes. Drain.

3. Uncover carrots and shake pan over high heat until liquid has reduced to a glaze. Add peas and remaining tablespoon butter and heat through. Serve at once, sprinkled with mint.

SAUTÉED SUGAR SNAP (OR SNOW) PEAS, HAM, CUCUMBERS, AND DILL

Assembled in minutes, this bright, flavorful dish demands little attention. It more than fills the bill when you're in a hurry and want a refreshing and satisfying combination of colors, flavors, and texture. Serve with egg noodles.

2 servings

6 ounces sugar snap (or snow) peas, strings removed (see Preparation)
1 large cucumber
1 tablespoon butter
6–8 ounces sliced ham (not too thin), cut into 1-inch squares
1 tablespoon finely minced dill
1 teaspoon snipped chives

1. Cut peas in 1-inch pieces. Peel cucumber and cut into quarters lengthwise; scoop out seeds. Cut crosswise into thin slices.

2. Melt butter in a large skillet. Toss in peas and cucumbers; sauté over moderately high heat until vegetables just begin to lose their raw taste—about 2 minutes.

3. Add ham and toss until heated through. Add dill and chives and sauté for a minute.

➢ *ADDITIONAL RECIPES*
Salad of Chayotes, Sugar Snap Peas, and Radicchio (page 114)
Aromatic Broth with Vegetable Slivers (page 278)

SUGAR SNAP PEA
See Sugar Pea

SUNCHOKE
See Jerusalem Artichoke

SWEET DUMPLING SQUASH
(Cucurbita pepo)

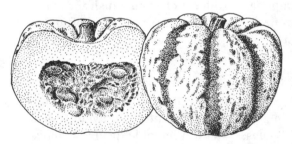

*L*ooking like a porcelain-perfect French soup tureen or tufted hassock, this small, rounded squash (the size of a hearty apple) weighs under a pound, usually about ½. The sweet dumpling is colored a solid cream (or, less often, orangy beige) and prettily scalloped with regular, shallow lobes, its indented areas striped in mottled ivy-green.

The pale yellow flesh is smooth-textured, fine and dry as a potato, richly starchy, with a light to medium sweetness and slight corn flavor. The appearance is of a winter squash (usually *Cucurbita maxima*), rather than *pepo*, which covers the summer varieties.

Developed in Japan about twenty years ago by that same productive seed company Sakata that brought us the kabocha and vegetable spaghetti (spaghetti squash), this squash is simply dubbed "vegetable gourd" in their catalogue. I have not been able to track down when and by whom its humble name was changed to sweet dumpling. Oddly, something called the "White-striped Flat Fancy Gourd," described and engraved in *The Vegetable Garden* of Vilmorin-Andrieux (1885), is remarkably similar to the sweet dumpling: "The peculiar shape and regular markings of this Gourd give it quite a unique appearance, and would lead one to think at first sight, that it belonged to some species very different from *Cucurbita Pepo*."

SELECTION AND STORAGE: Look for sweet dumplings from summer into early winter. They should have a creamy or lightly orange background color and clearly defined stripes with no tinge of green. Pick solid squash free of pitting or softening. Store these rather fragile hard-shelled squash for a shorter time than others: about two weeks at room temperature—preferably cool. Do not refrigerate.

USE: Once again, simplicity is best. The delicious pulp, of which there is usually a generous proportion, is heavenly when steamed or baked; how long this takes will depend on how thick it is, but 15 minutes' steaming and 50 minutes' baking time for a whole squash are average. Smaller squash make as appealing an individual presentation as you're likely to see. To prepare them, cut a little cap from the stem end, then scoop out all seeds and fibers. Add butter, salt and pepper; recap and bake about ¾–1 hour, until tender. Serve as is, or fill with tiny vegetables or vegetable dice. Try the steamed squash cold, sliced, then seasoned with lemon juice, grated ginger, and oil.

PREPARATION: One of the special qualities of this diminutive vegetable is its obliging coloring. Because the forest-green stripes are inset, you can run a vegetable peeler lightly over the surface, leaving the pretty stripes intact. All the skin is relatively tender for a hard-shelled squash and can be eaten; in other words, peel, partially peel, or leave unpeeled, as you wish.

NUTRITIONAL HIGHLIGHTS: No nutritional information is available for this squash. Extrapolating from similar varieties, it is most likely an excellent source of vitamin A and has substantial amounts of vitamin C, iron, and potassium. It is probably modest in calories and low in sodium.

STEAMED SWEET DUMPLING SQUASH WITH LIME AND BUTTER

Pared and cut as follows, the sweet dumpling provides a charming dish for every day—or special occasions. The bright yellow flesh, dressed in green stripes, softens to just the right moist, rich consistency when steamed. The simple and attractive presentation looks Oriental.

2 servings

1 sweet dumpling squash, about 1 pound
1½ tablespoons butter
About 1½ teaspoons lime juice
Pinch sugar
Cayenne pepper or ground pure chili powder to taste

1. Cut squash in half lengthwise, slicing slightly off center to avoid tough "poles." With vegetable peeler remove most of skin, leaving the indented green stripes. Halve each piece again, to make lengthwise quarters.

2. Set pieces on steamer rack over boiling water, skin side up. Cover and steam until tender, about 15 minutes.

3. Meanwhile, melt butter, stir in lime juice, sugar, and cayenne or chili powder to taste.

4. Spoon sauce over squash and serve at once.

SWEET DUMPLING SQUASH BAKED WITH CREAM

Another absurdly simple treatment that works perfectly for this flavor-rich, tender-fleshed squash. Figure on one small sweet dumpling per person. The cornlike aroma can be enhanced by using mace and nutmeg, as you would in a corn pudding. Or you might try a provençal approach with garlic, fennel, and thyme.

For each person

1 small sweet dumpling squash, about ½ pound

Salt and white pepper

Pinch herbs: either savory, thyme, basil, or sage

Pinch sweet spice, such as fennel, anise, cardamom, coriander, nutmeg, mace, or ginger

1 tablespoon heavy (or whipping) cream

Optional: Small unpeeled garlic clove or small shallot, peeled

Rinse squash and cut a neat cap, working carefully; the squash is quite hard. With melon-ball cutter scrape out all seeds and fibers. Sprinkle squash generously with salt and white pepper. Add herb, spice, and cream (and optional garlic or shallot). Recap, setting cap slightly askew. Place squash in baking dish; pour in ½ inch water. Bake in center of 350-degree oven until soft inside when pierced with a toothpick, about 35 minutes. Do not undercook; squash should be creamy. Remove garlic or shallot.

SWEET POTATO, WHITE
See Boniato

SWISS CHARD
(Beta vulgaris subspecies *cicla)*
also called Chard, Leaf Beet, Seakale Beet, Silver Beet, White Beet, Spinach Beet

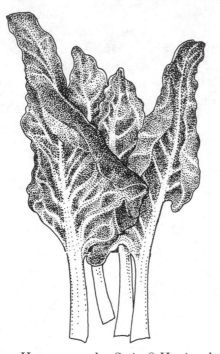

*A*part from its infuriatingly unfathomable name, Swiss chard is just about perfect, if you ask this cook: unusually versatile, mild yet earthy, sweet with a slightly bitter undertone, and texturally variable to suit your needs. If you like spinach and beets you'll adore Swiss chard. It is, in fact, a beet that has been encouraged by plant breeders to grow up (while its twin grows down) and produces large leaves and fleshy stalks, rather than a bulbous root. These stalks resemble thin, flattened celery and may be a pale celadon color or vivid scarlet (in the variety called *rhubarb* or *ruby chard*). The leaves have a texture and color similar to spinach, but are considerably wider and usually quite flat. The two parts are generally cooked separately, each in numerous ways.

Now, about that name: the word *chard* derives from the Latin and French words for thistle, which chard isn't, but cardoon (see page 88) is. It eventually came to mean the stalk or ribs of some vegetables, such as chard and cardoon. Some nineteenth-century seed catalogues used *Swiss* chard to distinguish the vegetable from French *charde* or *chardon*, which referred to cardoon. However, *why Swiss?* Having been on a wild goose chase of extended proportions, I still don't have a satisfactory answer. My guess is that Swiss may simply have been one of several seed varieties offered, but whether it came from Switzerland or not I cannot say. The *cicla* in the vegetable's scientific name makes more sense, as it derives from *sicula*, which refers to Sicily, one of the places where chard first grew— although it may have been equally well distributed throughout the Mediterranean and Near East. It is in the Mediterranean area that the plant is most popular today, although it is also farmed in northern Europe and South America. But the heart of chard country is Provence, specifically Nice, where the vegetable is cooked as regularly as we cook spinach.

SELECTION AND STORAGE: Look for Swiss chard from spring through fall, although it may pop in at other times, with peak supply from June through October. Some markets always carry it; some never do. It is easily obtained through distributors, so ask your greengrocer to stock it. Choose crisp-stalked bunches with firm, bright leaves. Because chard is extremely perishable, avoid limp bunches, seeking only the freshest specimens.

Some uninformed produce handlers trim off the stalks, thinking only the leaves are edible; tell them this is not the case. In fact, the stems are considered the choice part in most countries. Writes Richard Olney in *Simple French Food* (Atheneum, 1977): "Outside of meridional France . . . the green leafy parts of the chard are usually fed to the rabbits and the ducks."

Wrapped in plastic and kept in the coolest part of the refrigerator chard will remain fresh for about 2 days. The stalks, if separated from the leaves, will keep a few days longer.

Swiss chard greens, once blanched, freeze very well, as spinach does. Wash thoroughly, then separate green tops from stems. Drop tops into plenty of boiling water, return to boil, stirring. Boil 2 minutes; drain. Chill in ice water. Drain and pack in airtight containers. Although stems can be frozen (blanch 3 minutes), they become soggy, losing their special textural appeal.

USE: Raw Swiss chard, when young and small, adds a pleasant beet-like flavor and spinachy texture to combination salads, but should be added in moderation, as its flavor dominates.

When thinly sliced leaves and/or stems are stirred into soups during the last part of cooking they lend a most appealing flavor and texture, similar to that of bok choy.

Small and medium-sized Swiss chard can be quickly sautéed to make one or two side dishes, depending on whether you separate the leaves and stems or cook them together. Sautéing retains the delicate flavor more effectively than boiling, to my taste. (In Spain and Portugal deliciously strong olive oil, garlic, pine nuts, and sometimes raisins are added to the sauté.) Served cold with a squeeze of lemon and perhaps additional oil, chard makes a succulent salad/vegetable.

For older, larger chard you may want to boil the stems in salted water and lemon juice or simmer in stock or a court bouillon. In Nice the stalks are cooked in a bouillon that is later thickened with an oil-based roux and seasoned with garlic and mashed anchovies. For boiled or simmered chard you may want to add one or more of the usual basic vegetable embellishments: butter, lemon, cream, garlic, onions, shallots, vinaigrette, béchamel or mornay sauce, etc. Any treatment that suits spinach will suit chard leaves, but they must be cooked longer. Serve hot or at room temperature with the same kinds of sauces as the stems, from cream to vinaigrette.

Incorporate blanched, sliced chard into stuffings, savory custards, and frittata-style egg dishes. In Italy chard is packed into fat tortelli; or it is puréed for inclusion in pasta dough and gnocchi, in the way that spinach is. In France it is an indispensable part of the luscious pork sausage patties called *caillettes* or *gayettes*, as well as the unusual provençal *tourte de blette*, a pastry filled with chard, pine nuts, cheese, sugar, currants, apples, and usually perfumed with alcohol of some kind.

fleshy chard leaves, which make more delicious and easily handled packets than do grape leaves. Or line a dish with the leaves to form a "pastry" for a custardy or starchy filling. Or layer the leaves, chopped stems, cheese, ham, custard mixture to be baked and turned out, torta-style.

PREPARATION: Chard needs thorough washing. Dunk it in a sink filled with tepid water and swish the leaves around. Lift out gently so debris sinks to the bottom. Repeat until completely sand-free. Unless you have minute baby chard, separate the stems from the leaves with a knife or scissors (which better trim the fine upper midrib). If stems are fibrous, zip off the strings as you would from celery. Trim the bases if they are at all wilted or ragged. Like spinach, Swiss chard discolors if cooked in aluminum or unlined iron.

NUTRITIONAL HIGHLIGHTS: Swiss chard is a strong source of vitamin A, as well as a good source of vitamin C, potassium, and fiber. One cup cooked chard contains only 35 calories. However, the vegetable is naturally high in sodium—with about 315 milligrams in that same cup.

SIMPLEST SWISS CHARD

While this is an easy and thoroughly rewarding way to prepare either green or ruby Swiss chard, the ribs of the latter turn a garnet-russet that looks particularly appealing among the velvety green leaves.

4 servings

1¾–2 pounds Swiss chard (see Note), washed, trimmed, leaves and stems separated (see Preparation)
3 tablespoons flavorful olive oil
Optional: Salt and pepper, balsamic vinegar

1. Slice stems across on the diagonal about ½ inch wide (if wider than an inch or so, halve lengthwise before you slice). Coarsely slice leaves.

2. Heat 2 tablespoons oil in a wide, heavy, noncorrodible casserole. Stir in stems, cover, and cook over low heat until tender—about 15 minutes (but timing can vary from 5 to 25 minutes, so check often). Stir occasionally.

3. Add leaves and stir. Cover and cook over moderate heat until tender, about 5–10 minutes (but, again, timing varies), stirring a few times. Remove to a serving dish with a slotted spoon. Add remaining oil and, if desired, salt, pepper, and/or balsamic vinegar.

Note: Medium-sized Swiss chard (ribs about 1 inch wide) with full leaves are best for this dish, but all shapes and sizes will do.

—

SWISS CHARD WITH LEMON, OIL, AND PINE NUTS

This simple side dish could just as well be made with a range of delicious alternatives: butter or nut oil for the olive oil, balsamic vinegar for the lemon, and walnuts, pecans, or macadamia nuts for the pine nuts.

4–6 servings

3 tablespoons pine nuts (pignolia)
2 pounds Swiss chard (ruby or green), washed, trimmed, leaves and stems separated (see Preparation)
1 cup water
About 2 tablespoons lemon juice
About 2 tablespoons olive oil

1. Bake pine nuts in pan in preheated 325-degree oven (or toaster oven) until lightly golden—about 10 minutes. Set aside.

2. Cut chard stems on slant in 1-inch slices. Cut leaves in slices about 1 inch wide.

3. Combine stems, water, and 1 tablespoon lemon juice in a deep, wide skillet or Dutch oven (not iron or aluminum). Boil gently, covered, until very tender, 10–15 minutes (check often: timing can vary from 5 to 25 minutes). Lift out with slotted spoon; toss with 1 tablespoon oil, or to taste. Arrange in center of platter.

4. Add leaves to liquid in pan; simmer, uncovered, until tender—about 10 minutes (timing varies), stirring often. (Add water if necessary during cooking.) Drain. Toss with 1 tablespoon each lemon juice and oil, or to taste. Sprinkle with nuts. Serve warm or cool.

SWISS CHARD WITH DRIED MUSHROOMS

This bosky Swiss chard and wild mushroom combination is surprisingly subtle and easy to assemble. Accompanied by simple roasted chicken, new potatoes boiled with fresh rosemary, and a light-bodied Bordeaux, it should please admirers of foresty flavors.

2 or 3 servings

¼ cup dried *Boletus* mushrooms (cèpes, porcini, Polish mushrooms)
1 cup very hot water
1½ pounds Swiss chard, cleaned, trimmed, leaves and stems separated (see Preparation)
1 tablespoon butter
1 tablespoon olive oil
2 small shallots, minced
Salt and pepper

1. Combine mushrooms and hot water; soak about ½ hour. Lift out mushrooms and rinse lightly. Strain soaking liquid through fine cheesecloth or paper towel.

2. Cut chard stems in 1-inch pieces, the leaves in smaller slices.

3. Heat butter and oil in flameproof, noncorrodible casserole over moderate heat; stir in shallots and soften slightly. Add chard stems and ½ cup mushroom liquid; cover and simmer until tender—about 10 minutes, but timing varies; check often.

4. Add leaves and mushrooms. Cover and simmer until tender. Uncover and raise heat to evaporate some liquid. Season with salt and pepper.

Note: I prefer narrow-stemmed chard for this dish.

MOLDED SWISS CHARD, HAM, AND LEEK CUSTARD

Large, beautiful, tender Swiss chard leaves enclose a smoky and satisfying filling to form a broad, flat cake. Serve as a lunch or light supper entrée, or as the first dish of a multi-course dinner.

4 servings as a main course, 8 as a first course

1½ pounds Swiss chard with broad
    leaves, cleaned (see Preparation)
2 medium leeks
2 tablespoons butter
¼ teaspoon saffron threads, or ¼
    teaspoon marjoram
¼ teaspoon ground cinnamon
2 tablespoons very hot water
1 tablespoon flour
¾ cup milk
2 eggs
About ½ teaspoon coarse kosher salt
Pepper
1 medium potato (about 6 ounces)
4 ounces firm, smoky ham, in one piece,
    cut in ¼-inch dice

1. Cut apart Swiss chard stems and leaves, setting aside the dozen prettiest, smoothest, and largest of the latter. Stack these leaves flat in a colander. Pour a kettle of boiling water over them to soften, then spread flat on a towel to dry. Slice remaining leaves and set aside. Cut stems into ¼–½-inch pieces.

2. Trim darkest green part from leeks and reserve for another use. Split leeks and wash meticulously, then slice thin. Melt butter in large, nonaluminum skillet; stir in chard stems and leeks and sauté for a minute. Cover and cook over low heat, stirring occasionally, until tender—about 10 minutes (timing varies). Uncover and add slivered leaves; toss over high heat until most liquid has evaporated.

3. Steep together saffron, cinnamon, and hot water for a few minutes. In a bowl blend flour with 1 tablespoon milk; gradually add remainder and stir to make a smooth liquid; add eggs, ½ teaspoon salt, and pepper to taste. Add saffron infusion; blend. Taste for salt.

4. Line buttered 9-inch cake pan or dish (preferably not aluminum) with reserved whole leaves. Overlap them so points meet in center and wide ends are draped over pan. Place a few extra leaves in center to cover holes.

5. Spread one-third of the vegetable mixture in pan. Grate ½ potato fine over this; top with half of the ham. Ladle a third of the custard mixture over this. Spread half of the remaining vegetables over this, then grate remaining potato over all; sprinkle with rest of ham. Ladle half of the remaining custard over this, spread with remaining vegetables; then pour on the last of the custard.

6. Place any remaining leaves on top, then turn in the overhanging leaves to cover the mixture. Cover with foil; set on a rack in a pan. Pour in boiling water to reach halfway up side of cake pan.

7. Bake in preheated 375-degree oven for about an hour, until the custard is set.

8. Cool 15 minutes. Run knife around edge; invert cake onto a serving plate. Serve warm, lukewarm, or at room temperature.

SWISS CHARD STUFFED WITH SAFFRON RICE, RAISINS, AND WALNUTS

For an unusual appetizer, offer Swiss chard leaves stuffed with spicy-sweet rice, raisins, and nuts, a combination of Arabic origin that appears in various forms in the cuisines of Nice, Spain, and Italy. Or enjoy the packets as a light lunch.

6 servings as an appetizer

4 tablespoons olive oil
¾ cup minced onions
⅔ cup long-grain white rice
Scant cup water, plus 2 tablespoons
½ teaspoon salt
¼ teaspoon cinnamon
Big pinch saffron threads
2 pounds Swiss chard with large leaves, cleaned (see Preparation)
¼ cup golden raisins
¼ cup coarsely chopped walnuts
Salt and pepper to taste
2 tablespoons lemon juice
Lemon wedges for garnish

1. Heat 2 tablespoons oil in small pan; stir in onions, and cook over low heat until softened. Add rice; stir until opaque. Add scant cup water, salt, and cinnamon; bring to a rolling boil. Turn to lowest heat, stir in saffron, cover, and cook 20 minutes. Remove from heat; keep covered.

2. Cut 15 largest, most perfect chard leaves from stems; stack in a colander. Pour over a kettle of boiling water to soften them. Spread flat on a towel.

3. Chop remaining leaves and stems; reserve 1 cup. Sauté remainder in 1 tablespoon oil in large skillet (not iron or aluminum) for 2 minutes. Cover and cook on low heat until tender, 5–10 minutes (timing varies). If moisture remains, uncover and stir over high heat to evaporate. Combine with rice, raisins, walnuts, and salt and pepper.

4. Spread 2 tablespoons stuffing in center of 1 leaf, toward wide end. Turn that end over the stuffing, fold in the sides to enclose it, then form a tight cylinder, rolling from the base. Spread reserved raw chard in the skillet; set the leaf package on the raw chard, seam side down. Fill remaining leaves and set in skillet.

5. Drizzle remaining tablespoon oil, lemon juice, and 2 tablespoons water over packets. Cover skillet tightly and cook on lowest heat 30 minutes. Transfer stuffed chard carefully to a serving dish.

6. Cool to lukewarm, then cover and refrigerate. Remove from refrigerator about ½ hour before serving. Set a small wedge of lemon on each packet.

🌿 *Swiss chard can be substituted in Spicy Collards, page 152, and for the combination of spinach and turnip greens in Turnip Greens and Spinach in Coconut-Peanut Sauce, page 477.*

T

TAMARILLO
(Cyphomandra betacea)
also Tree Tomato, Tomate de Arbol

*T*hat tamarillos are brazenly beautiful most will agree: satin-skinned as eggplants (a family member), glossy scarlet or golden yellow, they are as perfectly formed as eggs (but pointier). The fruit sports an elegant stem, and is equally stunning within—lush, deep apricot flesh with two purple whorls of seeds. Most would concur that the aroma is unusual and attractive. That the flavor is what you might expect from the other characteristics? Well . . .

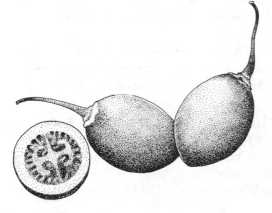

Such hesitation is unlikely in a good part of the rest of the world. Although probably native to the Peruvian Andes and parts of Chile, Ecuador, and Bolivia, the tree tomato is so popular that the small, fast-growing evergreen is now cultivated all over South and Central America, in Jamaica, Puerto Rico, Haiti, southern Asia, the East Indies, New Guinea, Australia, and New Zealand—from whence comes the majority of our fruit. (A small crop is growing in California.) And the plant is well-loved in even more places as a generously flowering, sweet-scented ornamental for garden or pot.

The tamarillo is a fruit that will need habituating time in the United States, where it has an ambiguous identity: Does it taste like a sweet vegetable or a bitter fruit? Does it smell like an apricot or a tomato? Does it have the consistency of a firm plum or a soft eggplant? Part of the problem may be in the promotion. The New Zealand posters of the fruit displayed at greengrocers and supermarkets show it atop ravishing tarts and ice-cream sundaes—but the tamarillo isn't very sweet (although a sweeter variety is expected soon in the marketplace), nor can it be simply sliced and served, as pictured. In fact, it's really not a fruit to eat out of hand at all, as the peel, albeit ravishing, is tough and acrid. The pleasantly bitter, almost meaty flesh is, however, very well suited for cooking. Tree tomato, the English name used until the 1967 New Zealand promotion began, most aptly suits tamarillo's culinary as well as its botanical status. The flavor is more like tomatoes than plums, bananas, or apples, as advertisements promise, although desserts are certainly part of the repertoire. Try tamarillo in a few ways suggested below, then decide for yourself.

SELECTION AND STORAGE: Look for firm, heavy fruits from early summer through fall. Let them ripen at room temperature until they yield slightly to pressure and become fragrant. At that point you can refrigerate tamarillos for a week, some even longer. Yellow fruit is often milder and sweeter than red.

There are a few ways to preserve tamarillos for extended periods. They can be frozen if peeled, wrapped individually in plastic, then several together in freezer paper; or peeled, sliced, sugared, and frozen; or puréed, cooked, and frozen. They can be made into jams, chutneys, and relishes and processed in jars.

USE: No matter what dish you prepare, tamarillos tend to require the addition of sugar and acid to display their full flavor. Uncooked, they need a heavier dose of both, as well as some time marinating in dressing or syrup, depending on whether they'll be part of a vegetable or fruit salad.

In most instances, tamarillos are at their best when cooked. They can be sliced and baked to accompany roast meat or fowl, or simmered in sugar syrup to become part of a fruit compote. When combined with other fruits, tamarillo develops a mysterious spicy flavor that blends the whole. But use in moderation or it will dominate loudly.

Because of its dense texture and assertive flavor, tamarillo holds its own particularly well in highly seasoned preparations such as chutneys, salsas, relishes, and sweet and savory sauces. In the South American highlands, many dishes that we prepare with tomato are made with tamarillos.

PREPARATION: A tamarillo must be peeled before you eat it, whether raw or cooked. This is easily accomplished with a vegetable peeler; or pierce the fruit with a long-handled fork and hold directly in flames for ½ minute, until skin splits and bubbles. To skin a large batch, pour a kettle of boiling water over the lot and let stand for a minute. Drain, then peel from the stem end. When you slice the red fruits, beware of indelible purple stains.

NUTRITIONAL HIGHLIGHTS: Tamarillos are low in calories, with about 50 calories per ½ cup. They are a source of vitamin A and vitamin C.

—

BAKED TAMARILLOS IN SYRUP

Tart-sweet, with a vivid color and fruity-spicy aroma, tamarillos prepared in this fashion hold their shape well, so can be combined with cooked fruits, dried or fresh, for an intriguing flavor mélange. Serve with roast meat, as a condiment or side dish, or for dessert, topped with ice cream or cream.

For *each* person, peel 1 tamarillo; use a peeler for a few, the blanching method if you're feeding many (see Preparation). Cut fruit across into ¼-inch rounds. Arrange in a baking dish and sprinkle 1 teaspoon sugar, a pinch of salt, a pinch of pepper, and ½ teaspoon lemon juice over each tamarillo. Bake in preheated 375-degree oven about 20 minutes, or until tender, basting once with the syrup.

—

TAMARILLO CHUTNEY

Serve this garlicky, hot, deep-purple relish with fried foods, roast duck or pork, or ham. Its lush texture and intense taste make a little go a long way.

About 2½ cups

4 large tamarillos, peeled (see Preparation)
¼ cup sugar
½ teaspoon cinnamon
⅛ teaspoon cloves
1 tablespoon peanut or corn oil
4 large garlic cloves, chopped (1½ tablespoons)
2 small jalapeño or serrano chili-peppers, seeded and minced
2 medium onions, diced coarse (about 1¼ cups)
1 large, tart apple, peeled and diced
½ teaspoon salt
3 tablespoons cider vinegar

1. Slice tamarillos lengthwise, then across into ¼-inch half-rounds. Combine in a bowl with sugar, cinnamon, and cloves; toss.

2. Heat oil in a flameproof casserole; stir in garlic, chilies, and onions. Cook over low heat until softened slightly—about 5 minutes. Add apple, tamarillo mixture, salt, and vinegar; stir over moderate heat until mixture thickens slightly and apples are tender—about 15 minutes.

3. Cool, then cover and chill up to two weeks. (Can also be frozen.)

ANNABEL LANGBEIN'S SOUTH SEAS HOLLANDAISE SAUCE

New Zealand food authority Annabel Langbein prepares this rich sauce for poached or broiled fish, although it's equally delicious on new potatoes or other plain vegetables. Speedy and unusual, the soft pink topping retains a full, buttery savor, while the tamarillo adds overtones of nutmeg, raspberry, and allspice. Quite a remarkable transformation—and a good beginning for the tamarillo-shy.

Makes about 1½ cups

3 egg yolks
1 teaspoon lemon juice
½ teaspoon salt
1¼ sticks (5 ounces) unsalted butter
1 medium red tamarillo, peeled and roughly chopped (see Preparation)

Combine yolks, lemon juice, and salt in processor container. Heat butter on low until bubbling (do not brown). Turn on processor and slowly add hot butter. Once incorporated and thick, scrape down sides and add tamarillo. Process until smooth and pink.

BASIC TAMARILLO-BANANA PURÉE

Grace Kirschenbaum, a food consultant and freelance writer who specializes in foods from New Zealand, has devised this simple, all-purpose tamarillo recipe to be used in a variety of ways:
☐ Spoon over fresh or cooked fruit, vanilla pudding, or rice or tapioca pudding.
☐ Spread in jelly rolls or between cake layers.
☐ Layer with whipped cream or crème fraîche as a parfait.
☐ Blend with light cream cheese for a pretty pink spread for the brunch table.
The thick, full-flavored concoction—with its raspberry-strawberry flavor and look of strawberry-rhubarb purée—appeals to even the least adventurous eaters.

Makes about 2 cups

2 large red tamarillos, peeled (see Preparation)
About ⅓ cup lemon juice
2 medium bananas, peeled and sliced
⅓ cup sugar

1. Slice tamarillos; combine in a bowl with lemon juice, bananas, and sugar; toss. Let stand for about ½ hour.

2. Purée fruit in processor or blender until smooth. Scrape into a small pot. Bring to a boil, stirring.

3. Cool, then cover and refrigerate.

GOLDEN TAMARILLO SALAD/RELISH

Although I am not fond of most uncooked tamarillo preparations, this simple combination works well with the more diminutive golden tamarillos, which have smaller seeds and a milder flavor than the red. The recipe couldn't be easier.

Slice crosswise as many peeled tamarillos (see Preparation) as you want, figuring 1–1½ per person. Season heavily with sugar and salt, then *drench* with lime juice. Strew with finely snipped mint and serve.

TAMARILLO, BANANA, ORANGE SHERBET

Pastel pink (or yellow, if you use golden tamarillos), soft and fine-textured, this musky and intriguing sherbet harmonizes with Middle Eastern and Oriental meals. Its ambiguous flavor will not be for all palates—but then neither is the tamarillo.

Makes about 5 cups

1 large navel orange
½ small cinnamon stick, broken up
¼ teaspoon allspice berries
¾ cup sugar
Pinch salt
1½ cups water
2 good-sized tamarillos, peeled (see Preparation)
1 large banana, chunked
Lemon juice to taste
Optional: Kirsch or other eau-de-vie

1. Combine rind of ½ orange with cinnamon, allspice, sugar, salt, and water; bring to a boil. Simmer, covered, 10 minutes. Cool, strain, and chill.

2. Cut tamarillo in chunks; press through medium disk of food mill. Peel and chunk orange (both halves); combine in processor with banana; whirl to a fine purée. Sieve.

3. Stir purée into tamarillo; add chilled syrup. Add lemon juice (and optional eau-de-vie) to taste. Pour into cream can of an ice-cream machine. Chill thoroughly.

4. Freeze according to manufacturer's directions. Scoop into a container and mellow in freezer for half a day or longer. Soften slightly in refrigerator to serve.

❧ *ADDITIONAL RECIPE*
Annabel Langbein's Apple and Cape Gooseberry Picnic Cake (page 80, see Note)
Tamarillos can be substituted for tomatoes in the salsa recipes on pages 126 and 127.

TANNIA
See Malanga

TARO, DASHEEN
(Colocasia esculenta, Colocasia antiquorum, Colocasia esculenta variety antiquorum)
**also Tannia, Eddo, Eddoes, Malanga, Tannier, Malanga Isleña, Coco, Sato Imo,
Woo Tau, Hung Nga Woo Tau (Red-budded Taro)**

*T*he extraordinary number of similar varieties of this plant and related *Xantho-soma* species (see Malanga) make generalizations and classification a nightmare. As Alex Hawkes wrote, somewhat desperately for an otherwise methodical and lucid botanist: "Taro is a sort of all-encompassing term for a small yet diverse, botanically

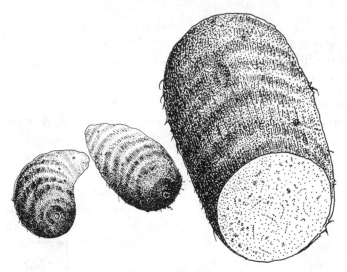

confused group of primarily tropical plants with edible tubers and, in some instances, foliage" (*A World of Vegetable Cookery,* Simon & Schuster, 1985). But, since man has been collecting names for about a thousand types of this vegetable for three times that number of years (and probably nine times, judging from recent evidence in Papua New Guinea), it is not surprising that there is little common usage.

Although some members of the Arum family are toxic or irritating (and some are old friends, such as philodendron and dieffenbachia), the genus *Colocasia* offers deliciously edible immature leaves, tuberous growths that flourish below ground, and blanched young shoots forced from these corms. An Old World vegetable that probably originated in the East Indies, the sweetly nutty, floury tubers have been welcomed throughout the Pacific Islands, much of the Orient, the Caribbean, North Africa, and small areas of South and Central America.

Of the many dense, starchy tubers that I have tasted (leaves and shoots are difficult to obtain), taro varieties are the ones I find most delightful, and most likely to be acceptable to American taste (with the exception of the Hawaiian dish *poi*, a paste made of water-thinned pounded cooked taro that has never been much of a hit with most tourists). With a distinct artichoke-heart and chestnut flavor, and the texture of the latter, the vegetable can be made into a subtle puréed soup, soufflé, hearty stew, crunchy chips and fritters, or even dessert.

Taro has two distinct forms: by far most common (and for me most useful and flavorful) is one that ranges from turnip to rutabaga-size. It is brown, shaggy, barrel-shaped (one tip may have a topknot), circled with distinct rings; snaggly rootlets usually twist from one end. It is often cut to expose smooth, very white, cream, or lilac-gray flesh, sometimes speckled with what looks like grated chocolate. The other type is small, about the size of a little new potato, and elongated in form. Shaped like a kidney bean, it has a much smoother form, is quite "hairy," and may sprout a pinkish bud at the tip. This cormel, which attaches laterally to the larger corm (described above), is favored by the Chinese and Japanese, and in a few Caribbean islands, where it is called *eddo*.

SELECTION AND STORAGE: Taro is available year round in Latin-American and Oriental markets, and in some supermarkets. Choose large corms for dishes in which you want a dry, nutty, sweet effect. They generally run from about ½ to 2 pounds, but can be larger. The small ones, which weigh from 2 to 6 ounces or so, are more moist and smooth, best for steaming and boiling whole. In either case, choose very firm, full taro with no sign of shriveling or molding. Good markets will usually slice off a piece to show you how bright and coconutty-firm the flesh is. The cut surface should smell fresh and look juicy.

Store in a basket in a single layer in a cool, well-ventilated place—not in the refrigerator. When the taro becomes the slightest bit soft, use it at once. Although I have heard that it is possible to keep taro for a while, mine has never lasted more than a few days.

USE: Before you are surprised, you should know that taro turns from bright white or cream to a dappled grayish or purplish when cooked. Also know that it must be served *piping* hot, or it becomes unpleasantly dense and waxy.

When you plan recipes with taro, think of it as a combination of chestnuts and potatoes, in terms of both flavor and texture. Small or large, it can be steamed or boiled. It takes well to stews, absorbing rich and fatty juices without disintegrating, and at the same time adding its nutty thickening. Or it can be chunked and cooked in hefty soups.

While its flavor becomes intensified and meaty when baked, taro dries out considerably; so plan to serve it very hot and doused with butter or meat juices. Similarly, it can be parboiled and roasted, but must be basted constantly with fat or it becomes hopelessly dry (roast with whole garlic cloves, turning occasionally for about 25 minutes, and drizzling with more fat than you can imagine).

Less sticky than other tropical roots (such as yuca, yam, and malanga), taro can be cooked, then puréed with enrichments for croquettes, fritters, soufflés, and mixtures to be piped and browned. Do not plan to simply boil and purée or mash, however, as the vegetable will be gluey without the additional baking or frying that aerates, dries, and flavors the mixture.

Pan-fried or deep-fried taro is heavenly. It has more texture and flavor than most fried starches, crisping while keeping its identity. Fry it in thin chips or strips or grated in pancakes. Or assemble the spectacular nest of shredded taro that you may have tasted, seafood-filled, in a Chinese restaurant, made exactly as the French do their bird's-nest potatoes.

In some Latin countries taro is cooked in chunks, in syrup, to be enjoyed as a lush confection—like *marrons glacés*. This can then be puréed and pressed through a colander to make a sweet heap of wiggly vermicelli, just like Mont Blanc aux Marrons.

PREPARATION: All taro contains an acrid juice that can irritate the skin (and worse, if you make the mistake of eating it raw). Oil your hands or wear gloves if you find the sticky substance bothers you. Slice off the ends of the taro, then pare deeply to remove all skin and discolored spots. Place at once in cold water. (Taro can be peeled hours before cooking.)

NUTRITIONAL HIGHLIGHTS: Taro is moderate in calories at 100 calories per ½ cup. It is an excellent source of potassium and a fairly good source of fiber. It is very low in sodium.

——

STIR-FRIED BEEF, TARO, AND CABBAGE

For a delicious one-dish meal in under half an hour, try this balanced combination of juicy meat, chestnutty taro, and crisp greens.

2 servings

¾ pound taro root (1 piece)
¼ teaspoon kosher salt
1 tablespoon Scotch or bourbon
1 tablespoon soy sauce
2 teaspoons Oriental sesame oil
Big pinch cayenne
1 medium garlic clove, peeled and flattened (or minced, if you like more garlic flavor)
¾ pound top round of beef or flank steak, sliced very thin on the diagonal
1 tablespoon peanut oil
½ pound Chinese cabbage, washed, then cut into 1-inch pieces

1. Peel taro and quarter lengthwise; cut each quarter across into ¹⁄₁₆-inch slices. Set over boiling water on a steamer rack; sprinkle with salt. Cover; steam taro until tender, about 15–20 minutes.

2. Combine Scotch, soy sauce, sesame oil, cayenne, and garlic. Add beef and toss. Marinate for 15 minutes or more, tossing now and then.

3. Heat a wok over moderate heat; pour peanut oil around rim and tip to distribute. Add garlic clove from marinade and toss for a moment. Add meat and brown slightly, tossing. Add cooked taro and cabbage and toss constantly until cabbage is crisp-tender—about 2 minutes. Remove whole garlic, if you are using it. Serve at once.

BASIC TARO, STEAMED OR BOILED

I love the delicate sweetness and dry, fluffy texture of steamed or boiled taro, especially with sauces, stews and meat juices or gravy.

Small taro can be boiled or steamed with or without skin (always well scrubbed). Cooked with the skin (which slips right off when tender) it will be somewhat more moist, but the flesh may be purplish or grayish. Peeled, then cooked, the flesh is drier, more flaky-potatoish, and a fairly even cream color. I prefer the large root peeled and cut into 4-ounce chunks, approximately.

Whatever you decide, the small corms will need about 25 minutes' steaming time to become tender, the chunks of larger taro about 40 minutes. Boiled, the small taro takes about 15 minutes, the large about 30. However you decide to treat the taro, be sure to serve it *boiling* hot (it can be reheated in a steamer) or it will be waxy and unpleasantly dry.

SOUFFLÉED TARO

Imagine a soufflé composed of potatoes and chestnuts and you have the color and flavor of this delicious dish (at half the price). The combined techniques of boiling, puréeing, and baking transform the heavy vegetable into a light side dish that is puffed and delicate, smooth and melting—without the fragility of a real soufflé. You'll find the taro to be a delightful accompaniment for chicken, lamb, veal, pork, duck, quail, and squab.

4 servings

1 pound large taro, peeled and cut in 2-inch chunks (see Preparation)

About ¾ teaspoon salt

About 1¼ cups milk

About 1¼ cups water

1½ tablespoons butter

1 egg, lightly beaten

⅛ teaspoon ground cardamom

White pepper to taste

1. Combine taro in a heavy saucepan with ¾ teaspoon salt and equal parts of milk and water to cover. Simmer, uncovered, until tender, about 30 minutes.

2. Drain, reserving liquid. Press taro through medium disk of food mill. Strain cooking liquid. Stir in enough to make a smooth medium-bodied purée (you'll probably have ½ cup or so left). Stir in butter, egg, cardamom, and salt and pepper to taste.

3. Scoop into a buttered 1-quart baking dish. (This can be left several hours at room temperature.) Bake in upper level of preheated 400-degree oven until puffed evenly, lightly browned, and firm on the surface—about 30 minutes. Serve hot.

PURÉED TARO SOUP

Taro absorbs astonishing amounts of liquid, forming thick, smooth, and dense purées, rather like creamy split-pea soup in texture. This substantial soup is warm with spices, nutty and rich.

4 servings

2 tablespoons butter
1 medium onion, chopped
2 medium carrots, chopped
2 or 3 tender inner celery stalks with
    leaves, chopped
1-inch chunk ginger, peeled and minced
1 pound large taro, peeled, in 1-inch
    chunks
¼ teaspoon thyme
¼ teaspoon mace
2–3 cups chicken or duck stock or broth
2 cups beef or ham stock or broth
About 1¼ cups milk
About 2 tablespoons rum
Salt and white pepper to taste
Garnish: Julienne of carrot and minced
    celery leaves or croutons

1. Heat butter in flameproof casserole over low heat; stir in onion, carrots, celery, and ginger. Cook until very soft, about 10 minutes, stirring often.

2. Add taro, thyme, mace, 2 cups chicken broth and the beef broth to casserole. Bring to a boil, stirring. Lower heat and simmer, covered, until taro is tender—about 30 minutes.

3. Purée soup thoroughly, in small batches, in processor or blender. Return to rinsed-out casserole. Stir in additional stock and milk, as needed, adjusting viscosity to suit. Gradually stir in rum, salt and pepper to taste. Warm soup and serve, garnished as desired (can be prepared ahead and reheated).

Note: You can substitute any malanga variety for the taro for an earthier, denser, muskier flavor.

SANDRA ALLEN'S CHUNKY TARO-SAUSAGE SOUP

Following these proportions, adapted from the recipe of a Brazilian cooking teacher, you can assemble a casual soup-stew based on taro, rather than potatoes. It is well suited to such treatment, as it can be long-simmered without disintegrating and imparts a nutty sweetness.

6–8 servings

1 pound fresh hot sausage links, or one large sausage (see Note)
1 tablespoon lard or vegetable oil
2 medium onions, chopped
2 medium garlic cloves, minced
2 medium tomatoes (1 pound), peeled (page 23), seeded, and chopped
2 pounds taro, peeled and cut in ¾-inch cubes (see Preparation)
6 cups beef stock
½ teaspoon dried sage
Tabasco or other hot pepper sauce to taste
Salt to taste
Cilantro or fresh sage for garnish

1. Prick sausages: cook in lard over moderate heat in heavy casserole until browned (they needn't cook through). Transfer to dish. If more than 2 tablespoons fat remain in pan, discard excess.

2. Add onions to remaining fat; cook over moderate heat until soft. Add garlic and tomatoes; stir for a few minutes. Add taro, stock, and sage. Simmer, covered, for ½ hour, until taro is partly tender.

3. Cut sausage in ¾-inch slices. Add to soup and simmer, covered, until taro is very tender, about ½ hour.

4. Season with Tabasco and salt to taste. To serve, sprinkle with cilantro or fresh sage.

Note: If you prefer to use cooked or partly cooked sausage, such as kielbasa or linguiça, it will add a more pronounced flavor. You can cut this up before browning, then put into the soup for the last 15 minutes of cooking.

ELIZABETH ANDOH'S "TUMBLE-ABOUT" TARO

In Elizabeth Andoh's cookbook, *An American Taste of Japan*, she includes a recipe for *Jagaimo No Nikkorogashi*, or potatoes cooked first by steaming, ingeniously peeled, then finished in broth, soy sauce, and mirin (sweetened rice wine). She writes: "The Japanese language is very onomatopoetic and the name of this dish, *nikkorogashi*, is taken from the sound of small whole potatoes being shaken about in a pan as they cook." While her recipe was adapted for American cooks who want to use potatoes, the traditional ingredient is *sato imo*, or taro.

Use only the baby corms, which run about ten to a pound and are available in Oriental markets. Elizabeth suggests sprinkling the finished taro with a half-and-half mixture of *ao nori* (a Japanese seaweed seasoning) and dried parsley flakes. I have substituted toasted sesame seeds, as I like the crunch on the tacky taro.

4 servings

1¼ pounds small taro (about 12), scrubbed with a brush

1 cup chicken stock

1½ tablespoons soy sauce

1½ tablespoons mirin (see Note)

1 tablespoon hulled sesame, toasted in tiny pan until golden

Optional: Snipped chives, minced celery leaves, or scallion greens

1. Score each taro around its "equator" with a knife, making a neat, shallow cut. Set on a rack over boiling water and steam until a toothpick will just pass easily through the center—about 12 minutes; do not overcook. Holding each taro lightly with a kitchen towel, twist one hand clockwise, the other counterclockwise. The skins will slip off. Discard them.

2. Combine stock, soy sauce, and *mirin* in pan to fit taro in single layer.

Bring to boil; add taro. Cook over moderately high heat about 10 minutes, shaking the pan ("tumbling") as liquid reduces. Continue cooking until liquid has nearly evaporated and taro is red-brown. Sprinkle with sesame and optional chives and serve hot.

Note: Mirin or aji-mirin (with flavoring added) is a Japanese syrupy wine made for cooking. It is available in all Oriental markets and in most supermarkets in the Oriental section.

🎋 *ADDITIONAL RECIPES*
Malanga Fritters from the Ballroom (page 292)
Malanga Fritters from Sabor (page 293)
Malanga-Yam Pancakes (page 294)
Maricel Presilla's Yams in Garlic-Citrus Sauce (page 509)
Maricel Presilla's Escabeche de Ñame (page 511)

TOMATILLO
(Physalis ixocarpa)
also Mexican Green Tomato, Jamberry, Mexican Husk Tomato, Tomate Verde, Tomate de Cascara, Fresadilla, Tomatito Verde, Miltomate, Tomate de Bolsa
(Note: These common names are shared by other Physalis species.)

*T*his star of Mexican salsas is one of about a hundred *Physalis* species, among which the best-known edibles are the ground cherry and Cape gooseberry. Commonly called *Chinese lantern plants*, because of their unusual formation, this group has fruits that are enclosed in papery calyxes that cover them like Oriental lampshades. Dry as

antique leaves, parchment-colored, the web-like enclosure is easily peeled off to reveal the fruit. The tomatillo (toe-mah-TEE-yo), which ranges from an inch in diameter to plum-sized, resembles a green cherry tomato (both are members of the Nightshade family) but is more lustrous and firm. Although it may be purplish, and may ripen to yellow, it is commonly used green.

Tomatillos are almost always cooked to develop their lemony-herbal flavor and soften their rather solid hides; but they can be used raw, for a more sharply acid flavor. They have become familiar, and celebrated, as the base for a number of memorable Mexican, and now New Mexican, dishes; their unique, slightly gelatinous texture and citric edge lend body and freshness to sauces both fiery and fragrant.

It was not until Americans discovered the glories of Mexican and Tex-Mex dishes in the late 1970s and early '80s that a tomatillo appeared outside a can—but that's where it seems to begin and end, much to this researcher's frustration! How can it be that a delicacy cultivated since ancient Aztec times is still grown only in Mexico and now, through Mexican migration, in southern California? The plant is easy to grow. Friends have raised their own from the seeds of tomatillos purchased in supermarkets. Just about every other fruit or vegetable that started out in that part of the world has been carried to some area of Asia or the South Pacific, and closely related species, most notably the Cape gooseberry *(Physalis peruviana)*, have spread to several continents. Yet, although I have read of cultivation in India (but nowhere else) I have not been able to turn up a single snippet of culinary literature to corroborate use outside of Mexico and the United States.

SELECTION AND STORAGE: Look for tomatillos year round, with no predictable season. It is one of those foods that you must ask for to create a regular demand, as it is widely available and well distributed in many areas—in supermarkets, greengrocers, or Latin shops. Choose fruits that are firm and dry with clean, close-fitting husks that show no blackness or mold. They should be hard; they do not have give like tomatoes.

Tomatillos can be stored in the refrigerator for an astonishing length of time; I have kept good ones for close to a month with no signs of deterioration. Place them in a paper-lined dish or basket and simply let them be.

For longer storage, tomatillos freeze extremely well, once cooked. Husk, wash, and stem them. Combine with water to barely cover; keep at under a simmer until softened, but not squishy. Cool in the liquid, then freeze in cooking liquid in 1-cup containers for handy sauce-making (use both fruit and liquid for this; do not drain).

USE: Although traditionally the tomatillo is not used raw, you might like to try it chopped in salad, in gazpacho or guacamole, or slivered or diced as a garnish for cold soups and a sandwich ingredient. You can make the tomatillo into a spectacular garnish by merely pulling back the husk, which will give the effect of a missile in motion, a comet's tail.

Like red tomatoes, tomatillos have great sauce-ability. Chopped or puréed, they make a tart dressing; cooked and puréed, the flavor is fuller, more mellow, and takes to all kinds of spicing and herbing.

The traditional uses for tomatillos are hard to beat: In *salsa cruda* the barely cooked fruits are combined with chili-peppers, onion, garlic, cilantro, and optional seasonings for an all-purpose sauce that seems to go with everything that can be dipped or dressed. The cooked sauce enlivens tacos, cheese dishes, potatoes, huevos rancheros, or chicken enchiladas. Blended with herbs, or pumpkin seeds, stock, or other sauce components, tomatillos are the basis for a wealth of green sauces in which chicken, turkey, fish, or vegetables are simmered.

My friend Joseph Schultz, gifted cook, says that tomatillos are great in apple pie (I have tried the closely related Cape gooseberry this way, and it is delicious).

PREPARATION: Tomatillos must be husked before use. Peel off the crackly husk, then thoroughly wash the fruits to remove the sticky resinous material near the stems (also removed, obviously). I've never found a reason to be meticulous about this cleansing, but many cooks say it is important.

To cook or precook the tomatillo, choose one of these methods, depending upon whether you wish a liquidy, saucy result (the first method) or a firmer, drier one.

☐ Barely cover husked tomatillos with cold water; poach gently, without simmering, until tender, 2–15 minutes, depending on the tomatoes—so keep tabs.

☐ Roast unhusked, rinsed tomatillos in a dish in a preheated 450–500-degree oven until tender, 10–15 minutes. Watch closely that they do not burst. Remove and let cool until you can handle easily. Pull back and twist off the husks. Rinse the tomatillos gently.

NUTRITIONAL HIGHLIGHTS: Tomatillos are quite low in calories, with 100 per cup. They are a fairly good provider of vitamin C and vitamin K.

ENDIVE AND AVOCADO WITH TOMATILLO-BASIL DRESSING

Difficult-to-identify flavors make this bright-green dressing a pleasing surprise: lemony, herbal, fruity, with a slight bite. Although the sauce neatly coats bittersweet endive and suave avocado, it enhances other foods as well—poached and chilled fish, cooked vegetables, or poultry. The dressing yield is 1 generous cup, or enough for four servings.

4 servings

2 small shallots, sliced
3 tablespoons slivered fresh basil leaves
1 teaspoon grated ginger
½ teaspoon sugar
¼ teaspoon salt
6 medium tomatillos, roasted and husked (see Preparation)
1 tablespoon lime juice, or to taste
⅓ cup corn oil
4 medium Belgian endive (about ¾ pound)
2 medium avocados, halved, pitted, and peeled

1. Combine shallots, basil, ginger, sugar, and salt in processor. Whirl to chop fine. Add tomatillos and 1 tablespoon lime juice and buzz to crush slightly. Add corn oil with motor running and whirl to blend, but do not make a completely smooth purée. Adjust seasoning. Cover and chill if not using at once; but do not keep much more than an hour, or the shallot and basil become dominant and somewhat bitter.

2. Core endive; cut in longish diagonal shards. Arrange on 4 plates. Thinly slice avocado crosswise over endive. Spoon dressing over all.

DICED GAZPACHO SALAD

This is not really a gazpacho salad, but the vegetables have much in common with the ingredients for that favorite cold soup—and the title would be too long if all were included. The colorful combo gets its refreshing tang from fresh tomatillos, which replace vinegar or lemon juice and add a crispy texture, as well.

4 servings

7 medium tomatillos (about 7 ounces),
    husks removed, rinsed
¼ teaspoon salt
½ teaspoon oregano (fresh or dried)
¼ cup (1 handful) parsley, not chopped
Black pepper to taste
⅓ cup full-flavored olive oil
½ cup diced red onion
1 medium cucumber, seeded and cut into
    ¼-inch dice (1 cup)
1 large red bell pepper, cut into ½-inch
    squares (1½ cups)
1 small avocado, cut into ½-inch dice

1. Slice 2 tomatillos and combine in processor with salt, oregano, parsley, and pepper; chop fine. Add oil and blend. Cut remaining tomatillos into ¼-inch dice.

2. Combine diced tomatillos, onion, cucumber, and red pepper in a serving dish; toss with dressing. Add avocado and toss gently. Cover and chill for about an hour before serving.

—

MARDEE REGAN'S GREEN SAUCE (SALSA VERDE)

Mardee—friend, editor, and endless source of information—devised this chunky, assertive version of Mexican green tomato sauce. In addition to incorporating it in traditional dishes, she suggests that you serve it with sliced avocado and sweet pink grapefruit sections; or combine it with mashed avocado for "instant guacamole" (adding some diced tomato and more cilantro); or spoon over soft flour tortillas topped with melted jack cheese and sprinkle with crumbled bacon.

Line up the gorgeously green ingredients and you'll understand why *salsa verde* can be called nothing else.

Makes 1–1½ cups

½ pound (8 medium-small) tomatillos
1 very small onion, quartered
1 large medium-hot chili-pepper, such as New Mexican or poblano, seeded and chopped coarse
1 garlic clove (size to taste), chopped
Big pinch sugar
½ teaspoon ground cumin
1–2 tablespoons lime juice
2–3 tablespoons minced fresh cilantro

1. Remove and discard tomatillo husks; wash tomatillos to rid them of sticky residue. Combine in small saucepan with water to cover. Bring to boil on high heat; lower heat and simmer until not quite soft, 3–6 minutes, depending on size.

2. Meanwhile, combine onion, chili-pepper, and garlic in processor or blender. Drain tomatillos; add to processor container. Whirl to chunky texture, not purée. Scoop into a bowl. Stir in sugar and cumin, then gradually add lime juice to taste. Stir in cilantro. Serve at room temperature.

Note: If you fancy fiery salsa, add some minced very hot chilies—such as serrano, jalapeño, or Fresno. If you prepare the salsa ahead, cover and refrigerate without adding the cilantro. To serve, bring to room temperature, then add cilantro.

CORNISH HENS WITH AROMATIC GREEN SAUCE

This richly fragrant, savory dish has its origins in the Mexican *mole verde* (an herbal green sauce) and *pollo en pipián* (chicken in squash or pumpkin-seed sauce). I have combined the two to my taste to make a dish that is at once spicy and herbal, leafy and lemony—and quick to prepare. If you don't fancy heat, eliminate the jalapeño; if you're a passionate pepper fan, use a whole instead of half.

4 servings

1¾ cups chicken broth

¼ cup sliced cilantro stems

2 Rock Cornish hens, quartered, loose fat removed from under skin

3 medium-hot medium-sized green chili-peppers (such as poblano or New Mexico)

2 slices whole-wheat sandwich bread

⅓ cup roasted cashew nuts

Green part of 4 large scallions, sliced (¾ cup)

1 cup, packed, coarsely chopped cilantro leaves (about 2 bunches)

½ cup, packed, coarsely chopped mint leaves

1 pound tomatillos, husked and rinsed

Optional: ½ seeded, minced jalapeño pepper (or more, to taste)

½ teaspoon sugar

Salt to taste

Cilantro sprigs for garnish

1. In a large skillet bring chicken broth to a simmer with cilantro stems; add hens and simmer, covered, for 8 minutes. Turn over pieces, cover, and simmer 8 minutes longer.

2. Meanwhile, blister and blacken chili-peppers directly in flame (or as close to broiler as possible); wrap in wet paper towel or plastic bag and let stand briefly —about 5 minutes. Remove skin, stem, and seeds; chop coarse. Taste, deciding at this point whether you want to add the jalapeño (figure that the chilies will be much milder when combined with sauce ingredients).

3. In processor or blender whirl bread to make coarse crumbs. Add cashews; whirl to a fine texture. Add scallions, cilantro, and mint; chop fine.

4. Remove hens from skillet; add tomatillos, optional jalapeño, and sugar; simmer, covered, until not quite tender— about 8–10 minutes. Turn occasionally to cook evenly.

5. With slotted spoon transfer all solids in skillet to the processor; add chopped peeled chili-peppers. Purée. Add 1 cup broth and whirl smooth. Add salt to taste.

6. Return to skillet with hens. Simmer 5 minutes, stirring now and then. Turn hens and simmer 5 minutes longer. Season to taste. Garnish with cilantro sprigs.

TOMATILLO, DRIED CHILI, AND CILANTRO SAUCE

This easy-to-make sauce is one of those special creations that become complex and mysterious, that taste greater than the sum of their parts—although its parts are certainly nothing less than wonderful.

Combine the dark, aromatic blend with browned, cut-up chicken, pork, lamb, or beef, or with large fish fillets or salt cod (see following recipe), then braise gently.

Makes about 2 cups sauce

2 large, dried New Mexico chilies *(ristra chiles, chiles colorados)*
1 cup boiling water
¾ pound fresh tomatillos, husked and rinsed
2 very large garlic cloves, sliced
1 medium-large bunch cilantro, about 3–4 ounces

1. Stem and seed chilies; break up pods. Combine in a saucepan with the boiling water; let stand for at least 15 minutes.

2. Add tomatillos and garlic to saucepan. Separate cilantro stems and leaves. Chop stems (and well-scrubbed roots, if present); add to pan.

3. Bring to a simmer, then lower heat and cook, covered, until tomatillos are soft, 10–20 minutes, turning them occasionally. Transfer contents of pan to blender or processor.

4. Add cilantro leaves to container; whirl to a coarse purée. Cool completely; refrigerate or freeze.

Note: For variety, you can substitute other fleshy dried chilies, such as guajillo, ancho, pasilla.

SALT COD WITH TOMATILLO, DRIED CHILI, AND CILANTRO SAUCE

For salt cod lovers, this dish is it. Easy to assemble, the assertive sauce with its herbal aroma, acid edge, and chili bite complements the firm, strong-flavored cod. A starchy accompaniment—such as plantain, yam, taro, hominy, polenta, or rice—will turn this into a distinctive sturdy meal.

4 servings

1 pound thick, boneless salt cod
4 tablespoons strong olive oil, preferably Spanish
2 large white onions (1¼ pounds), halved and sliced ¼ inch thick
Flour for dredging
1 cup (½ recipe) Tomatillo, Dried Chili, and Cilantro Sauce (preceding recipe)
10 oil-cured black olives

1. Soak cod in cold, slightly dripping water for about 6 hours; or soak in bowl in refrigerator, changing water 4 times during a 12–24-hour period. Taste for saltiness and soak longer, if required.

2. Heat 2 tablespoons oil in a large skillet, preferably nonstick. Gently cook onions until slightly colored, then transfer to a shallow earthenware baking dish large enough to hold fish in a single layer.

3. Drain cod and dry well. Cut in 8–10 pieces of roughly equal size. Dredge each piece with flour, shaking off excess. Heat remaining 2 tablespoons oil in skillet and lightly brown cod on both sides. Arrange pieces close together in dish with onions.

4. Add sauce to pan in which fish cooked; bring to a simmer, stirring. Pour over fish; dot with olives. Bake in upper level of preheated 400-degree oven about 20 minutes, until hot and bubbling.

TREE TOMATO
See Tamarillo

TURNIP GREENS
(*Brassica rapa* subspecies *rapifera*)
also Turnip Tops, Turnip Salad

*T*he strong flavors of the Mustard family have never made it big in the United States, although they are great favorites throughout Europe and the Orient, where vigorous vegetable bitterness and bite are valued. With a particularly harsh heat and rough-textured leaves (like those of a coarse radish), turnip greens are not a loved

vegetable in America, except to those who have been raised on them.

Despite the fact that the vegetable was sowed in Virginia as early as 1609, it has just begun to move beyond its residence in the South, thanks to the recent and passionate interest in regional cuisine. Turnip greens are cooked as they have been since slaves combined them with whatever pork parts were not used in the Great House, then stewed them until there was time to eat. As it happens, this is one of the most delicious ways to prepare the sharply assertive green, and it was eventually adopted in many not-so-humble homes (although it is still primarily plain folks' food).

Unusual for such a simple food was its appearance in cookbooks from quite early on. In 1824 Mary Randolph wrote in *The Virginia Housewife* that turnip tops "are the shoots which grow out, (in the spring) from the old turnip roots." She recommended that they be boiled in plenty of water, to prevent bitterness. "They are still better boiled with bacon in the Virginia style," she added. Elaborating on the style in *Housekeeping in Old Virginia* (1879), the editor, Marion Cabell Tyree, wrote this typical recipe for Turnip Salad: "Pick early in the morning . . . add to a pot of boiling water in which a piece of bacon has boiled several hours, and the amount of water become much reduced. Take out the bacon, put in the salad, put the bacon back on top of the salad and boil till very tender. Dip from the pot with a perforated skimmer, lay in a deep dish, skim the fat from the liquor and pour over the salad. Cover with nicely poached eggs."

Nor did Escoffier omit the sturdy peasant food nearly a century later, noting that it should be cooked "à l'anglaise" (that is, boiled; the term has always sounded like a French euphemism to me). I was surprised to see the same treatment recommended in *Paul Bocuse's French Cooking* (1977), a book that focuses on rather *haute cuisine*. While simple treatments are fine, it will probably be the new Americans from Asia and the Orient, with their myriad modes of saucing, slicing, and spicing, who will put all bitter greens back on the map.

SELECTION AND STORAGE: Turnip greens can be found in markets erratically year round, with peak availability from November through March. Turnip tops do not come attached to the familiar root, so do not look for it. (In fact, most varieties that are marketed never develop the turnip, although a few are dual purpose.) They are surprisingly perishable for such a tough-looking plant, so don't buy them unless they'll be used within a few days, at most. Look for relatively small, tender leaves that are moist and well cooled; if kept in a warm place the greens dry out and get bitter and tough. Avoid heavy stems and yellowed leaves. Often the greens are packed in plastic, which will make the selection process more difficult, but not impossible.

Wrap the greens in damp towels, then a plastic bag and keep in the vegetable crisper or the bottom of the refrigerator. Or freeze them, which works very well, by blanching for a few minutes in boiling water. Cool well in ice water, drain, then chop and pack into freezer containers. Freeze for about 6 months.

USE: First of all, what not to do is use turnip greens as a salad vegetable, although it is sometimes recommended. They are much too bitter and chewy-tough. Nor should they be cooked in aluminum or iron pans.

For a pleasantly sharp flavor, similar to that of mustard greens, cook turnip tops in an Oriental manner, by stirring slivered leaves into wok-braised dishes. Or add to soups, as they do in much of the Orient, Portugal, and Spain.

Cook in the traditional Southern way, with fatty pork pieces as seasoning. Combine with a variety of greens—such as chard, spinach, mustard greens, kale—for an equally traditional, less bitter, and more complex flavor. Accompany with hot pepper sauce, if desired. If the tops are particularly tender and young, sauté them with garlic and oil, Italian-style.

Blanched in boiling water, greens will be milder, suitable for baking or simmering with cream and cheese sauces or for layering in casseroles with noodles, grains, cooked meat, and sauce (as you would spinach). Less common, but even more succulent, stew greens in coconut milk (see page 55 for preparation) lightly or heavily spiced.

If you can buy the fashionable "new" baby vegetables (or better, if you grow your own), choose tiny turnips about 1 inch in diameter with perky tops. Wash and separate them. Sauté the roots in butter and a sprinkle of sugar until colored, then cover and cook on low heat until tender, 5–10 minutes. Arrange in a warm dish. Sliver the leaves and sauté in more butter until tender, a few minutes. Arrange alongside the turnips and serve.

PREPARATION: Turnip greens need a careful bath. Dunk them up and down in a sink filled with tepid water, then lift out so debris sinks. Repeat. Taste and check for sand. Repeat as needed. Shake the leaves, then strip from the stems (which are discarded). For many dishes, you may want to blanch the leaves to mellow them.

NUTRITIONAL HIGHLIGHTS: Turnip greens are low in calories, with only 30 per cup, cooked. They are an excellent source of vitamin A and folic acid. They are a very good source of vitamin C, and contribute small amounts of calcium, iron, riboflavin, and B_6. (You can see why you're supposed to eat your greens!)

"TURNIP SALLAD"

Apparently what was good for Virginia (see quotes in general introduction to turnip greens) was fine for Kentucky, too. In *The Kentucky Housewife* (1839) Mrs. Lettice Bryan gives this explicit and delicious recipe for Turnip Sallad. Although I have not picked my own tops, I have happily cooked store-bought greens this way:

Cut the young, tender tops that shoot forth from the turnips in the spring, pick them carefully, as the under leaves are apt to have little roots and dry leaves sticking to them. Wash them clean in at least two waters, and if they have been gathered more than a few hours, soak them for an hour or two in fresh water, which will make them fresh and lively, and boil tender with greater facility. They should always be boiled with bacon, it being the only good way they can be prepared. Let your bacon be more than half done; have a good quantity of water; if they are boiled in a small quantity, they will be tough and yellow, and to put them in the water when it is cold has the same effect. Having skimmed the pot, raise the bacon with a fork, put in the tops, lay the bacon on, and boil them till they will mash easily; then drain off the liquor, make them smooth in the dish, skin the bacon, lay it on the sallad, and send it up warm. Have salt, pepper, and vinegar to season it at table. It is a plain dish, but when well prepared it is a very good one. (From facsimile edition printed by Collector Books, no date.)

CREAMED TURNIP GREENS

One of the standard treatments for turnip greens is also one of the simplest and best. Creamed greens are a lovely accompaniment to broiled or roast lamb, pork, turkey, or liver.

4 servings

1½ pounds turnip greens, cleaned, stripped (see Preparation)
1 tablespoon butter
½ cup minced onions
1 cup broth or stock
1 tablespoon flour
½ cup milk
¼–½ cup heavy (or whipping) cream, to taste
Salt and pepper

1. Drop leaves into a large pot of boiling water; return to a boil. Drain leaves and chop fine.

2. Melt butter in skillet (not iron or aluminum); add onions and cook until slightly softened. Add greens and broth and simmer, partly covered, until greens are tender, 20–25 minutes.

3. Uncover and stir over high heat until moisture evaporates. Sprinkle in flour and stir 2 minutes. Add milk and ¼ cup cream; bring to a simmer, stirring. Cover and cook on lowest heat (adding cream to taste) until you have the desired flavor and consistency—about 5–10 minutes. Season and serve.

TURNIP GREENS AND SPINACH IN COCONUT-PEANUT SAUCE

In a recipe based on a number of Southeast Asian vegetable preparations, turnip greens and spinach are stewed together in a seasoning and enriching medium of coconut milk and ground peanuts. The creamy sweetness of the coconut, the heat of the chili-pepper, and the meaty flavor of the nuts give the greens unusual depth.

4 servings

¾ pound turnip greens, rinsed and stripped (see Preparation)

¾ pound spinach, rinsed and stripped (as for turnip greens; see Preparation)

1 tablespoon butter

1 medium onion, coarsely diced

1 hot chili-pepper, such as jalapeño or Fresno, seeded and diced

1 cup coconut milk (see Note)

½ cup roasted peanuts, very finely ground

1. Cut turnip greens and spinach leaves in thin slivers.

2. Heat butter in a 2–3-quart non-reactive casserole. Stir in onion and chili; cook for a few minutes to soften slightly. Stir in greens over high heat, adding gradually until they are all reduced sufficiently to fit easily into the pot.

3. Add coconut milk and peanuts. Simmer gently, partly covered, until greens are very soft and velvety and the sauce is thickened and creamy—about 30 minutes.

Note: You can buy unsweetened coconut milk in some specialty stores, or prepare your own, as described on page 55.

🍂 *ADDITIONAL RECIPES*
Braised Collards with Ginger and Chili-Pepper (page 150)
Soup of Collards and Sausage (page 151)

U

UGLI FRUIT
(cross between *Citrus reticulata* and *Citrus paradisi* or *Citrus grandis*)

Ugli Fruit is a trademarked name, which supposedly originated in response to the initial marketing foray of this Jamaican citrus fruit (which Jamaicans tell me is pronounced OO-gli). Canadians to whom it was first introduced, and who still consume it eagerly, demanded more of that "ugly fruit." As if that weren't precious enough, the

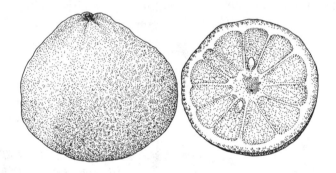

spelling was registered with an "i" and the advertisements bear a slavering bulldog and the slogan "but the affliction is only skin deep."

As far as I am concerned, these are the only points against the fruit. The somewhat puffy, thick, slightly loose-fitting skin, which may form a furrowed collar or neck on the rounded or slightly pear-shaped fruit, seems to be the reason for the ugliness campaign. This skin, which ranges from lime-green to light orange (and any combination in between, sometimes mottled), is certainly not unsightly; it is simply not as sleek and regularly painted as more common citrus fruits. The loosely adhering coat is a cinch to peel, and the pulp is relatively free of seeds. Uglis vary from the size of a healthy navel orange to that of a mammoth grapefruit. The pulp is a sunshiny yellow-orange and composed of atypically large, tender juice sacs (vesicles) that give it an unusually soft succulence for a citrus. Once cut, the fruit fairly overflows with juice that is generally of considerable flavor and distinction. Brightly acid-sweet, under-scored by a zesty pungency, ugli fruit at its best reveals the influence of its ancestors, probably a mandarin and a grapefruit.

No one seems to be sure just who the parents of this strange citrus (classified as a natural tangelo) might be. The ugli was discovered in Jamaica, a chance seedling, where it was propagated by F. G. Sharp at Trout Hall, then exported in 1934 by his son. Shippers today claim it is a cross between a bitter orange, a mandarin (or tangerine, as we call some mandarins in the United States), and a grapefruit. Citrus authorities all agree on the mandarin as a source but some offer a pummelo in lieu of the grapefruit and withdraw the bitter orange, more often than not.

In 1985, very small amounts of ugli fruit were available in forty of the fifty states, with a concentration in the Midwest. Britain and Canada are the main markets for the relatively small crop (15,000 to 20,000 cases) that is shipped from Jamaica—only.

SELECTION AND STORAGE: Ask for ugli fruit from January on (I have seen it turn up in the stores as late as June), prodding your produce dealer to get some. Heft fruits to find ones heavy for their size, with no sign of drying at the stem end. Any amount of mottling, bronzing, surface scarring, or uneven coloring is perfectly normal. Like a grapefruit, the ugli should have a little bit of give, indicating that the interior is juicy. Choose small or large according to how you will use the fruit. Small fruits are not less mature than large ones, and, in fact, often have a more pronounced flavor and sweetness, with less tendency to wateriness—which occasionally shows up in ugli fruits.

The ugli's thick natural wrapping keeps it safe and sound for quite some time. If I am to believe the dealer who swore to me that he had kept his for a month, I can report that the fruit was sprightly in flavor and brimming with juice. Unless you'll be using the fruit within a few days, store it in the refrigerator.

USE: Enjoy the easily peeled fruit out of hand as a habit-forming treat. For heavenly breakfast fare, halve the ugli, sprinkle sparingly with sugar, and let rest a minute or two to get the juices flowing—and they will. Scoop out with a grapefruit spoon—and forget grapefruit while uglis are in season. (For lovers of broiled grapefruit: broiling ugli fruit results in a loss of both flavor and juice.)

Or section the fruit, as you would oranges or grapefruit, and serve in fruit or vegetable salads. Like other citrus, ugli is particularly pleasant in the company of avocado, sweet onion, endive, chicory, radicchio, and other bitter leaves. It also shines with bananas, grapes, strawberries—and any other fruits that usually complement oranges. Use in compotes and gelatine desserts. The grated rind makes a particularly pungent flavoring. Or follow the instructions for Candied Pummelo Peel (page 377) for a lovely after-dinner confection.

PREPARATION: You can peel and segment ugli fruit as you would grapefruit or orange, but when you cut it into rounds the soft sections, which separate easily, tend to come apart. When dishes are prepared ahead, remember to adjust liquids for the enormous amount of juice the ugli exudes.

NUTRITIONAL HIGHLIGHTS: Ugli fruit is a good source of vitamin C and is high in fiber.

UGLI FRUIT, PAPAYA, AND STRAWBERRIES

Although no one really needs a *recipe* for a simple fruit cup, this tasted lovely one sunny brunch and might serve as an idea shaper. Blueberries and mango would do nicely in place of strawberries and papaya, orange-flower water instead of liqueur.

4 servings

1 pint very ripe strawberries, rinsed
½ full-ripe medium papaya (about ¾ pound)
2 medium ugli fruits
Sugar to taste
About 1 tablespoon orange liqueur

1. Hull berries and slice thin; place in serving dish. Remove papaya seeds; peel and cut into slivers about same size as strawberries. Add to dish.

2. Peel ugli fruits, shaving off all pith and membrane to expose flesh. Holding ugli over fruit bowl, slice down to the core on either side of each membrane partition to free each section; let drop into dish. Squeeze emptied ugli "carcass" into fruits to extract the considerable amount of juice therein.

3. Sprinkle with sugar, add liqueur. Chill briefly to blend flavors. Toss gently to serve.

SALAD OF UGLI FRUIT AND FENNEL

Refreshing, clean, and simple, this combination of crispy fennel strips and tender ugli fruit segments keeps both in the forefront. Serve during a rich meal.

3 or 4 servings

2 medium ugli fruits (about 10 ounces each), rinsed and dried
1 tablespoon lemon juice
⅛ teaspoon salt, or to taste
1 tablespoon light olive oil
1 fennel bulb of about 10 ounces (weighed without stalks)

1. Grate enough rind from 1 ugli fruit to yield about ½ teaspoon. Place in a bowl. Peel ugli fruits. With very sharp knife sliver off all white pith and membrane. Working over the bowl to catch juice, slice along each membrane partition to remove all fruit segments; set them aside. Squeeze the remaining emptied structure over a small bowl to extract all juice—which should be a good deal. Add lemon juice, salt, and oil.

2. Trim fennel bulb; pull off any coarse "strings" if necessary. Cut the bulb into very thin julienne strips about 1½ inches long. Place in serving dish. Top with ugli fruit segments. Cover and chill until serving time. Chill dressing separately.

3. To serve, pour dressing over fennel and ugli fruit. If fennel leaves are available, snip some and sprinkle over the top. Toss gently and serve.

ROCK CORNISH HENS WITH UGLI FRUIT

Essential flavors and simple presentation: roasted hens with a sauce of reduced stock flavored with ugli fruit peel, juice, caramelized sugar, and vinegar, and garnished with the fresh fruit. Gauge the servings by knowing your diners. While we never have more than half a bird each in my home, we do complement the bird with a large quantity of vegetables—our way of eating, but not everyone's.

If you want a crisp bird, you'll need to plan a day in advance (see step 1).

2–4 servings

2 large Rock Cornish hens, about 1½ pounds each
About 2 teaspoons coarse kosher salt
About ½ teaspoon ground white pepper
2 medium ugli fruits
1½ tablespoons softened butter
3 tablespoons sugar
About 3 tablespoons red wine vinegar
1 cup strong chicken stock (not canned broth)
Lemon juice to taste

1. Remove loose fat from hens. Combine 2 teaspoons salt and ½ teaspoon pepper; sprinkle about one-third inside hens; rub remainder all over them. Set hens on cake rack on plate. Refrigerate 1–2 days, as convenient. (Although you can ignore this step, it dries the skin so that you have a crisp, browned bird instead of a rather soft-skinned one.)

2. Let hens rest at room temperature about an hour before roasting. Rinse one ugli fruit. With swivel peeler remove rind (but no pith). Place half of peel in cavity of each hen. Truss hens. Rub with butter. Place breast side down on rack.

3. Set in center of preheated 400-degree oven and roast 20 minutes. Turn over carefully, being careful not to tip juice into pan. Roast about 30 minutes longer, until golden.

4. Meanwhile combine sugar and 3 tablespoons vinegar in small, heavy non-aluminum saucepan. Boil, swirling pan occasionally, until liquid becomes golden brown and syrupy—a matter of a few minutes. Add stock, being careful of splatters. Stir to blend. Boil gently, swirling pan now and then, until liquid has reduced to a syrupy ⅓–¼ cup or thereabouts. Reserve.

5. Working over a bowl to catch juice, remove all rind and pith from ugli fruits. Slicing along interior membranes, free segments and place in a bowl. Squeeze emptied fruit "carcass" into reduced stock; there will be abundant juice.

6. Remove hens from oven. Carefully tip each over the stock so all interior juices fall into it. Set hens to rest a few minutes before carving. Boil sauce, stirring often, to reduce to a lightly syrupy consistency. Season with lemon juice, additional vinegar, salt, and pepper.

7. Quarter hens and arrange on warmed plates. Divide ugli fruit sections among plates and arrange alongside hens. Spoon sauce over all and serve at once.

VEGETABLE SPAGHETTI, SPAGHETTI SQUASH
(*Cucurbita pepo*)

Although none of the scientists with whom I spoke knew when and where this curious squash came on the scene, I can tell you who put it on the American map: Frieda Caplan of Frieda's Finest Produce Specialties, Inc., a Los Angeles–based distributor of fruits and vegetables who has changed our larder with her adventurous spirit and smart marketing techniques. Suddenly every market in the country has these hard, cream-to-yellow oval vegetables, shaped like a cross between a football and a small pumpkin, that Frieda has designated *spaghetti squash* (the true seed name is *vegetable spaghetti*).

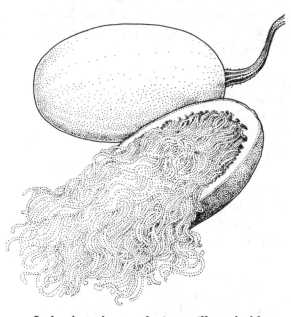

Talking to geneticists, farmers, and botanists has not helped me discover vegetable spaghetti's story before it came to the attention of the Queen of Produce. Most authorities agree that the squash is a cultivar of an American native, like all the Cucurbit family, but in just what part of North or Central America it first vined and twined they cannot say. Nor does anyone agree on the squash's journey after it left. Some say it moved to China, others say definitely Italy, but the confusion will probably continue because of the existence of another member of the Cucurbit clan, *Lagenaria siceraria*, which unfortunately includes spaghetti gourd among its many common names (although it is usually known as *cucuzzi*). Because both squash are filled with long fibers that suggest noodles, and may have traveled in the same circles, the historical strands get twisted. We do know that the breeding work for the present market varieties of vegetable spaghetti was done in Japan over the last thirty years or so. Our current fall-winter crop comes from California, Arizona, Colorado, Texas, Georgia, Michigan; the early crop from Mexico.

People who love the squash seem to be charmed with its novelty, above all. There is no doubt that it is just plain fun to cook a vegetable the shape of a watermelon, open it up, and pull out what appear to be miles of crisp-tender, golden strands. You wind up with a mountain of swirly strings and a thin squash shell (it all seems as unlikely as the little car from which emerges a crowd of circus clowns). Fans also love the idea that anything pastalike can be so very very low in calories. The taste is quite bland, lightly sweet, and fresh, a perfect saucing medium. A new cultivar, Orangetti, is a deeper yellow-orange and may be sweeter, firmer, and a bit more moist.

SELECTION AND STORAGE: Although vegetable spaghetti stores well, and is therefore marketed virtually year round, the squash that comes into the market from early fall through the winter is the most flavorful. Look for very hard, smooth, evenly yellow, cream, or tan squash without ridges, spots, or bumps. Avoid greenish, honeydew-colored squash, which may be immature or have sprouting seeds. Choose the size according to your needs, but be aware that the larger the vegetable, the better the flavor—and the thicker the strands. A tiny squash will have the equivalent of fedelini, while a larger one will have fully spaghetti-sized fibers. The squash can be stored for weeks at room temperature, if purchased in good condition.

USE: Cook vegetable spaghetti by one of the basic methods suggested, then combine the hot squash with a full-flavored but not overpowering sauce, such as white clam, cheese, pesto, a light and fresh tomato, or garlic and herbs. Serve as you would spaghetti—with the unspaghetti-like advantage of being able to keep the dish warm for a while in a low oven. Or cool and refrigerate the squash for later use in a gratin or salad.

For a gratin, mix the squash with a comparatively thick, creamy, cheesy, or mushroomy sauce, top with crumbs and cheese, and bake briefly to heat through in a hot oven. Combine with sautéed ground meat or sliced sausages. To make pancakes, blend with flour, grated onion, and egg.

Cool the squash and dress as you would potatoes, with a creamy sauce, mayonnaise, or a zesty vinaigrette. Season assertively and chill to blend flavors.

Spaghetti squash is also used to make a traditional Spanish sweet, *cabellos de ángel* (angel hair). The squash is cooked, separated into strands, then simmered in a heavy sugar syrup until richly sweet. One of the reasons I've not tried the recipe is that the old version I have begins this way (freely translated): "First you take your squash, please not picked recently, preferably a year ago, and throw it on the floor and smash it (you may use a table instead of the floor), then you cook it, then you separate the fibers with a fork. . . ."

NUTRITIONAL HIGHLIGHTS: One cup cooked spaghetti squash contains a very low 45 calories. It is an excellent source of folic acid, is quite high in fiber, and contributes a fair amount of potassium and small amounts of vitamin A and niacin, as well as being very low in sodium.

COOKING VEGETABLE SPAGHETTI (SPAGHETTI SQUASH)

Do not overcook this vegetable: it gets watery and loses its fresh sweetness. When properly cooked, it retains crispness, without tasting raw. For the average squash, which weighs 2–2½ pounds the following timing and methods should do. Although all books seem to recommend boiling the squash whole, I find this the least satisfactory method, as it is the messiest and produces wetter strands.

TO STEAM

Halve the squash lengthwise. Scoop out and discard seeds. Halve each piece lengthwise again, then place flesh side down on a steamer rack, well above the boiling water. Cover and steam until your finger leaves an indentation in the skin, from 20 to 30 minutes, depending on the state of maturity. Gently pull strands from shell until only a thin skin remains.

TO BAKE

Prick the squash through with a sharp knife or fork in 2–3 places to prevent bursting. Place in a pan in a 350–375-degree oven (to suit whatever else you may be cooking) and bake until easily depressed by a finger, about 45 minutes to an hour. Remove from oven and halve at once, or squash will continue cooking. Let cool briefly, then scoop out and discard seeds. With fork "comb" strands from each half until only shell remains.

TO BOIL

Bring a large pot of water to a boil. Boil squash until it can be depressed quite easily with a fingertip, about 30 minutes. Remove from water and halve at once, to prevent further cooking. Remove and discard seeds. With fork fluff out all the strands in the squash until only the shell remains.

VEGETABLE SPAGHETTI WITH RED PEPPER, PINE NUTS, AND BASIL

Bright strips of red bell peppers, shreds of fresh basil, and crunchy toasted pine nuts add flavor, texture, and color to simply baked, golden spaghetti squash.

6 servings

¼ cup pine nuts (pignolia)
2-pound spaghetti squash (vegetable spaghetti)
2 medium red peppers, very thinly sliced
3 tablespoons butter, or more to taste
⅓ cup slivered fresh basil
Salt and pepper to taste

1. Put nuts in a pan and place in pre-heated 375-degree oven to toast until golden—about 8 minutes; reserve. Bake squash as directed in Cooking Vegetable Spaghetti (preceding recipe).

2. Meanwhile, sauté peppers over moderate heat in 2 tablespoons butter until slightly softened. When squash is cooked, cut it in half crosswise, scoop out seeds, then pull out strands with a fork; fluff them into a hot dish.

3. Combine sweet peppers and squash. Add remaining tablespoon butter (or more, to taste), basil, pine nuts, and salt and pepper. Toss to mix well.

SALAD OF VEGETABLE SPAGHETTI, TOMATOES, PEPPER, AND ONION

Bake spaghetti squash some evening while you're making dinner, then assemble this easy salad for the next day. Slightly chewy, a little like tabbouleh, it makes a pleasant side dish on a bed of chicory or radicchio; or stuff into pita for a delicious sandwich.

4 servings

2½-pound spaghetti squash (vegetable spaghetti)
1¼ teaspoon coarse kosher salt
Pepper to taste
3 tablespoons red wine vinegar
¼ teaspoon minced garlic
⅓ cup olive oil
1 medium red onion, chopped
1 large red bell pepper, chopped
1 bunch parsley, minced (⅓ cup)
½ pint cherry tomatoes, halved

1. Cook squash by whichever method you prefer (see Cooking Vegetable Spaghetti, page 484.)

2. Pull out strands with fork into a colander; toss with ¾ teaspoon salt. Let cool, draining.

3. Mix remaining salt with pepper, vinegar, and garlic; add oil and blend. Toss in a bowl with cooled, drained squash, onion, red pepper, and parsley. Season to taste and chill, covered.

4. At serving time add the tomatoes.

VEGETABLE SPAGHETTI WITH TOMATO-CHILI SAUCE

Serve this fresh, simple dish as a side dish or main course, depending on your love of vegetables, in general, and spaghetti squash in particular.

4 servings

2-pound spaghetti squash (vegetable spaghetti)

4 tablespoons full-flavored olive oil, preferably Spanish

1 teaspoon minced garlic

1 or 2 jalapeño (or serrano or Fresno) chili-peppers, seeded and minced

1½ pounds very ripe plum tomatoes, peeled (page 23), seeded, and coarsely diced

About ½ teaspoon salt

1–2 teaspoons balsamic vinegar

Pepper to taste

3 tablespoons chopped cilantro

1. Bake squash as directed in Cooking Vegetable Spaghetti (page 484).

2. Heat 3 tablespoons oil; add garlic and jalapeño; stir for a minute over moderate heat. Add tomatoes and cook for about 5 minutes, stirring occasionally, until slightly thickened. Add ½ teaspoon salt and balsamic vinegar to taste.

3. When squash is cooked, halve and cool slightly. Scoop out seeds. With a fork, pull out strands into a serving dish. Toss with the remaining tablespoon oil and salt and pepper to taste.

4. Spoon the tomato mixture over the squash, then sprinkle with the cilantro. Toss gently at the table.

VEGETABLE SPAGHETTI BAKED WITH HERBED CHEESE SAUCE

Delicately flavored spaghetti squash takes well to a creamy sauce seasoned with garlic and herbs, and a light crumb-cheese crust. The strands remain distinct and slightly crisp as they absorb the sauce.

4 servings

2-pound vegetable spaghetti (spaghetti squash)
1½ tablespoons butter
1½ tablespoons flour
1 teaspoon minced garlic
1½ cups milk
½ teaspoon dried thyme, or ¾ teaspoon mixed *herbes de Provence*, or similar herb mixture
½ cup grated firm cheese—such as Gruyère or Cheddar or Parmesan
½ teaspoon salt, approximately
½ cup dry bread crumbs

1. Bake squash as directed in Cooking Vegetable Spaghetti (page 484). Let cool briefly. Halve crosswise, then scoop out seeds. With fork pull out strands, leaving only shell. There should be about 4 cups. Set in a sieve to drain.

2. Heat butter in small, heavy pot over low heat; add flour and garlic; stir over lowest heat for 3 minutes. Meanwhile, combine milk and herbs in a small pot and bring to a boil. Pour into flour mixture; continue stirring over low heat until mixture is thickened and reduced— about 10 minutes. Stir in ¼ cup cheese.

3. Press squash to extract moisture. Gently mix with sauce in baking-serving dish; season to taste. Combine remaining cheese and bread crumbs and sprinkle evenly over squash; pat down gently.

4. Bake in upper level of a 400-degree oven until mixture is bubbling and lightly browned. (Can be prepared ahead and reheated.)

VIDALIA ONION
See Onions, Sweet

WALLA WALLA ONION
See Onions, Sweet

WATER CHESTNUT
(Eleocharis dulcis)
**also Chinese Water Chestnut, to distinguish it from *Trapa bicornis*,
which shares the common name water chestnut**

*I*t can only be the fresh water chestnut's rarity that has prevented it from becoming a staple in the American market, for even those who have tasted only the virtually flavorless canned ones seem to come back for more. Sweet, juicy, and versatile, the water chestnut has crisp white flesh that looks and tastes a bit like a cross between a

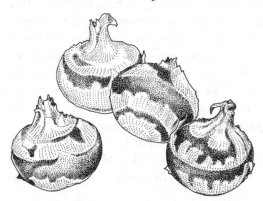

McIntosh and a jícama—but really like neither. Cooked, the sweet vegetable smells and tastes remarkably like baby summer sweet corn.

Water chestnuts in their fresh form look like muddy little tulip bulbs or bulbous chocolate kisses—and, of course, like chestnuts. They come dressed in shabby brown-to-black coats decorated with frayed leaf scales, not because they have been poorly tended, but because they grow in mud along the edges of ponds, lakes, and marshes (in China, where they are cultivated on a large scale, they also thrive in flooded fields). Corms planted along sludgy banks send out underground root stems (rhizomes) that develop rushlike tubular stalks above the water, then small flowers. New corms develop soon after, maturing from a starchy to a sweet vegetable. This process requires a relatively lengthy time in a frost-free environment, which is notably lacking in the United States. Although almost all of our market chestnuts are from China at present, a good deal of experimentation is taking place in this country. Small farms in Georgia, Florida, Alabama, and California have had some success (and considerable failure; water chestnuts are tricky to harvest), and domestic production will probably increase in the near future.

SELECTION AND STORAGE: Water chestnuts are irregularly available year round, primarily in Oriental markets. They bruise and spoil easily, and thus require careful selection. It is reasonable to buy a bit more than you think you'll need, as there is a large amount of waste in peeling, and there will usually be a few bad specimens in any collection. Press each chestnut all over to check for soft spots, which denote decay; each should be rock-hard. Those that look somewhat shiny are best, but rather scruffy specimens are fine, provided they have not begun to shrivel.

You can place the unwashed chestnuts in a jar of water in the refrigerator for up to two weeks. They stay crisp and fresh, although they lose a tiny bit of flavor. Or enclose the unwashed chestnuts in a paper bag and keep for about the same time in the coldest part of the refrigerator. They may begin to shrivel, so check occasionally. Or freeze the peeled water chestnuts in a resealable container or bag and withdraw as you need them.

Although storing the peeled chestnuts in water is frequently recommended, I find they lose almost all flavor and spoil rapidly if kept this way.

USE: To my taste, all water chestnuts are improved with cooking (see Basic Water Chestnuts), but many people enjoy them raw. In China water chestnuts are served as a refreshing street snack, each skewered, lollipop-fashion, and kept cool in water. Try them as between-meal nibbles, straight from the refrigerator, or as part of a crudité platter, whether you're a dieter or plain old food lover.

Chinese water chestnuts add an inimitable crunch and sweetness to cold or hot mixed salads. You don't need many, as the texture and flavor are defined and satisfying. Add slices, strips, or dice to salads of fresh fruit, vegetables, rice, noodles, seafoods, or poultry—dressed Western, Chinese, or Southeast Asian style.

Water chestnuts need no precooking when combined with raw ground meat or seafood: Deep-fry for appetizers, or make balls for soup or patties for steaming or frying. Cut the chestnuts in tiny dice and simply mix in; they'll stay crunchy and separate. Some time ago, rumaki, a delicacy from Hawaii, was a favorite American cocktail food. The combination of grilled (or deep-fried) bacon-wrapped water chestnuts skewered with marinated chicken livers deserves a revival.

Sautés and stir-fries are the ideal spot for water chestnuts. Quarter, slice, dice, or julienne precooked water chestnuts to toss with any vegetable, meat, or fish you can imagine; or add to bean curd (tofu), where the crunch is particularly welcome. Try a few discreet snippets in savory custards and quiches for a surprising lift. Add slices to sukiyaki or other broth-simmered dishes, or to light soups as a garnish.

PREPARATION: Rinse and scrub water chestnuts well to rid them of mud. Peel them and place in lightly acidulated water. Or, for smoother shape and less loss of flesh, follow directions for Basic Water Chestnuts, cooking before you peel. Peeling is slow work, no matter how you do it. A razor-sharp paring knife works best for me, although the Chinese use a narrow cleaver. Cut out any brown spots; the rest of the chestnut is usually fine—but have a sniff to be sure (you will know *at once* if it is gone; spoiled chestnuts smell fiercely alcoholic or sour). Then halve, quarter, slice, dice, julienne, or cut julienne into confetti-like squares (which I find easier and neater than mincing).

NUTRITIONAL HIGHLIGHTS: Water chestnuts are low in calories, at 35 calories per cup, cooked.

BASIC WATER CHESTNUTS

Although raw water chestnuts are a common recipe ingredient, I find that cooking improves them immeasurably. They gain sweetness, lose raw starchiness and fiber—but not crunch. In fact, it is surprisingly difficult to overcook a chestnut. For dishes in which they'll receive some further cooking, boil unpeeled or peeled chestnuts for 5 minutes or steam for a few minutes longer. (When you peel is really a question of preference; peeling after cooking results in less waste, as the softened flesh carves more easily—though the color may change from cream-white to beige when they are cooked in the jacket.) Drop in ice water, then drain. Peel (if you have not already done so) and sliver, dice, or cut to suit the dish they'll be enhancing.

For water chestnuts that will receive no further cooking, 10 minutes' boiling (or about 15 minutes' steaming) will give a nuttier flavor and more compact texture. For an exquisite treat, serve these whole or halved chestnuts hot, with nothing more than butter, as you would the finest summer corn. For salads, chill in ice water. Cut in whatever size suits the other ingredients.

SHRIMP AND WATER CHESTNUTS IN LIGHT CREAM SAUCE

Succulent pink shrimp and crisp, sweet water chestnuts are briefly simmered in a light cream-enriched stock. The dusting of spices highlights the natural flavors, rather than adds new tastes.

3 servings

1 pound small shrimp in the shell
Salt and white pepper to taste
⅛ teaspoon ground cardamom
⅛ teaspoon nutmeg
¾ cup chicken stock
½ pound water chestnuts, peeled (see
 Preparation)
¼ cup heavy (or whipping) cream
2 scallions
1 tablespoon butter
1 teaspoon sherry, preferably medium
 dry
1 teaspoon cornstarch

1. Shell and devein shrimp, placing shells in medium saucepan. Toss shrimps in bowl with salt and pepper, cardamom, and nutmeg; set aside.

2. Add stock to shells; boil 5 minutes. Strain; discard shells. Cut water chestnuts in fairly thick slices and add to stock. Simmer 5 minutes. Lift out with slotted spoon and set aside.

3. Add cream to stock and boil until reduced to ½ cup. Mince scallion white and green parts separately.

4. Heat butter in medium skillet or moderate heat. Add 2 tablespoons scallion whites; stir until softened. Add shrimp and chestnuts; toss. Add cream-stock mixture; simmer, stirring, until shrimps turn pink.

5. Stir sherry into cornstarch. Add to shrimp and stir over moderate heat until mixture boils. Scrape into a warmed serving dish, sprinkle with 1 tablespoon scallion greens, and serve at once.

SALAD OF SUMMER SQUASH, WATER CHESTNUTS, AND HAM

Crunchy and summery, this colorful salad can serve as first course, side-dish salad, or part of a buffet. Although ham is included, it functions as a flavoring, not a main ingredient.

4 servings

¾ pound water chestnuts, scrubbed (see Note)
2 very small yellow summer squash (½ pound)
2 very small zucchini (½ pound)
4 ounces firm ham cut in thick slice, then into tiny confetti dice
1–2 tablespoons finely snipped dill (or dill, chives, and parsley)
About 1½ tablespoons rice vinegar
About ¼ teaspoon salt
1½ tablespoons yogurt
White pepper to taste
4 tablespoons corn oil

1. Set water chestnuts on steamer rack over boiling water. Cover and steam 5 minutes. Scrub both kinds of squash; place alongside chestnuts. Cover and steam until squash dents easily when pressed—5 minutes.

2. Place squash and chestnuts in ice water; cool. Drain thoroughly. Slice squash in thin coins. Peel chestnuts and do the same. Combine in serving dish with ham and 1 tablespoon dill.

3. Mix together 1½ tablespoons rice vinegar and ¼ teaspoon salt. Add yogurt and white pepper to taste. Gradually beat in corn oil, a tablespoon at a time. Season to taste with salt, pepper, and vinegar.

4. Blend half dressing with cooled salad. Cover and chill at least 1 hour. To serve, whisk remaining dressing, pour over salad, and toss. Season with remaining dill, salt, pepper, and vinegar.

Note: You can peel chestnuts before steaming, as you prefer.

SIMPLEST STUFFED WATER CHESTNUTS

Beginning with fresh water chestnuts and soft, fresh cream cheese (American or imported), you have the base for a delectable cocktail presentation to be seasoned and decorated as whimsically as you like. Select a light garnish or herb to transform the simple nibble; top with a tiny shrimp, a fragment (cutouts are fun) of grilled sweet pepper, a curl of smoked salmon, a dusting of *fines herbes*, salmon roe, snippets of ham, minced chives, shreds of pickled pink ginger—or all of the above, for a really festive platter.

About 20 stuffed chestnuts

1 pound (20–24) large fresh water chestnuts, well scrubbed

About 4 ounces softened cream cheese, without preservatives, vegetable gum, or the like

Cream as needed

Optional: White pepper and lemon juice

Topping to taste (see suggestions above)

1. Either boil chestnuts for 6 minutes or steam for 10. Drop into ice water and cool. Drain.

2. Peel chestnuts carefully with *very* sharp knife. With small melon-ball cutter (or knife) gently hollow as large a cavity as you can without breaking chestnut. When all are scooped, chill chestnuts.

3. Chop scooped-out parts fine. Mash and soften cream cheese, adding a little cream if stiff. Mix in chestnuts; blend thoroughly. Season to taste with pepper and lemon.

4. With teaspoon form neat, smoothed mounds of filling in chilled chestnuts. Chill, covered. At serving time, top to taste.

Note: You can peel water chestnuts before cooking, if you prefer, but they break more easily when hollowed.

WILD LEEK
(Allium tricoccum)
also Ramp

*T*he wild leek, with a scallion-slim stalk streaked with violet and graceful leaves resembling those of lily of the valley, has a wild and woodsy aroma and ferocious onion-garlic flavor despite its ladylike appearance. It flourishes in rich forest soil, generally within sugar-maple groves, from Canada through New England to Georgia and as far west as Minnesota. In the southern Appalachians it is called *ramp*, and its appearance is the cause of spring celebrations throughout the area—notably the Ramp Romp in West Virginia. Wild leek is unusual for an onion: it has uncharacteristically broad and tapering leaves that emerge in the early spring, then die back soon after; and it is not until midsummer that the stalk, leafless at the time, begins to bloom.

SELECTION AND STORAGE: Depending on the weather, you ought to be able to smell out wild leeks in your market from late March to June. Choose ones that are firm, springy, bright green—not yellowing or flabby, or they may have an off-taste. The roots should always be intact, and downright dirty; if the leeks have been trimmed or washed they develop an unpleasant smell and lose their fresh flavor.

Store fresh wild leeks very tightly wrapped in several layers of plastic, or everything in your refrigerator will smell leek-like. If the leaves are fresh and dry, the plants should keep for about a week under refrigeration.

USE: Cook wild leeks in just about any way that you would cultivated ones, but with discretion, as they are stronger. Simmer them in soups; blanch and serve in a vinaigrette; incorporate into quiches, pies, or custards; or parboil them and serve hot, with butter or Hollandaise sauce or Nutmeg Cream (page 206). Although I am told that they are commonly consumed raw in ramp country, I would guess that their pungency would be too much for all but the most devoted.

PREPARATION: Clean wild leeks by slipping off the first layer of skin from the bulbs, then trimming off the roots. Remove any yellowing or wilted leaves, then rinse the leeks in several changes of water, swishing them about vigorously.

No nutritional information is available for wild leeks.

WILD LEEKS VINAIGRETTE

While the potent, earthy aroma of raw wild leeks can be overpowering, the plants become sweet and gentle when tamed by a few minutes in boiling water.

4 servings as a first course

12 ounces wild leeks (or about 3 dozen), cleaned (see Preparation)
1 tablespoon lemon juice
1 tablespoon red wine vinegar
1 teaspoon sharp mustard
¼ teaspoon salt, or to taste
3–4 tablespoons olive oil, to taste

1. Cut apart leek bulbs and leaves. Drop bulbs into a skillet of boiling, lightly salted water. Cook until tender—about 2 minutes. Lift out with slotted spoon, then lay on a towel to dry. Place leaves gently in water; boil 30 seconds. Drain and dry on towel.

2. Combine lemon juice, vinegar, mustard, and salt in a small jar; shake to blend. Add oil and shake.

3. Spread leeks in serving dish and pour dressing over them. Chill until serving time, covered.

SHAD STUFFED WITH ITS ROE AND WILD LEEKS

This smoky, springtime recipe has been adapted from one served by Paul Neuman, who with his vibrant wife Stacy Bogdonoff runs a take-out and catering place on Manhattan's Upper East Side (Neuman & Bogdonoff, natch).

4 servings

¼ pound sliced bacon
½ pound wild leeks, cleaned (see Preparation)
1 pair shad roe (about ¾ pound)
1 large, boned shad fillet (about 1¼ pounds)
Salt and pepper
Melted butter
Lemon

1. Cook bacon in large skillet until lightly browned, not crisped. Drain and reserve fat. Halve bacon crosswise, then cut into very thin lengthwise strips.

2. Cut apart leek leaves and bulbs. Wrap and refrigerate three-quarters of the leaves for another use (such as vinaigrette). Slice thin the remaining leaves and bulbs. (There should be about 1¼ cups.)

3. Heat 1 tablespoon bacon fat in skillet; add leeks and cook just until softened, not browned or transparent; reserve.

4. Heat 2 tablespoons bacon fat in skillet. Over moderately low heat cook roe, covered, until nicely browned on both sides—about 6 minutes. Do not cook on high heat or cook through; roe should remain mushy in center when pressed; it should be soft and pink. Cool slightly; remove heavy central connective tissue. Slice diagonally into medallions about ¾ inch thick.

5. Set shad on buttered pan that can go into broiler. Slip 6 strings under the fish. Open out the flaps ("like a toolbox," says Paul); season lightly with salt and pepper. Spread half leeks, then half bacon over center section, not flaps. Cover with roe medallions, distributing evenly. Cover with remaining leeks and bacon. Season.

6. Fold over flaps. Cover central gap with long strip of foil folded just to fit. Tie strings to hold fish firmly. Brush flesh with melted butter.

7. Set in upper level of preheated 375-degree oven for 12 minutes, until just barely cooked through. Set under broiler to brown. Remove foil, squeeze lemon over top. Snip and remove strings. Serve, cut into wide slices.

Note: The fish can be prepared through step 6, then refrigerated. Bring to room temperature (this takes about an hour) before baking.

WILD LEEK AND SEAFOOD TIMBALES
WITH LIME SABAYON SAUCE

This is an elegant presentation, lovely for the first course of a spring dinner party. Although time-consuming to prepare, the dish can be almost entirely made ahead (through step 6).

8 servings as a first course

2 bunches small wild leeks (about 3 dozen, or 11–12 ounces), cleaned (see Preparation)
1½ tablespoons butter
2 cups plus 1 tablespoon water
¾ pound shrimps in the shell, chilled
1½ teaspoons tomato paste
½ pound scallops, chilled
¼ teaspoon salt
1 egg plus 1 egg white, chilled
½ cup heavy (or whipping) cream, chilled

SAUCE

1 egg, plus 2 yolks
About 2 tablespoons lime juice
About ¼ teaspoon salt
Reserved shrimp stock
About 1 tablespoon finely minced fragrant fresh mint

Mint sprigs for garnish

1. Cut apart leaf and bulb-stem sections of leeks, leaving no stem on the leaves. Place leaves flat in a skillet of simmering, salted water. Simmer 2 minutes; drain and refresh in cold water. Spread on a towel. Reserve 8 prettiest, tiniest bulbs and drop into simmering water. Boil until barely tender, about 1 minute. Refresh in cold water.

2. Slice remaining bulbs; stew gently in butter and 1 tablespoon water until very tender—about 15 minutes. Cool and chill.

3. Peel, devein, and halve shrimp crosswise, placing shells in a small pot. Add 2 cups water to the shells; boil gently, partly covered, for 20 minutes. Uncover and boil until liquid is reduced to about ⅓ cup. Strain out shells, pressing hard. Add tomato paste and boil to reduce to ¼ cup. Reserve for sauce.

4. Butter eight 6-ounce custard cups. Line with leek leaves, overlapping slightly and letting them overhang edges of cups. Cut large and broad leaves in half crosswise to fit without doubling.

5. Combine shrimp, scallops (halved, if large) and ¼ teaspoon salt in processor; purée fine. Add 1 egg and 1 egg white; process 10 seconds. Scrape down sides and process about 5 seconds. Turn off machine and add stewed leeks. Turn on machine; pour in cream.

6. Divide mousse mixture among custard cups. With wet hands even mixture and tap dishes to settle it. Fold over leaves. Set dishes on a rack in a large roasting pan. (Can be prepared ahead to this point. Cover and refrigerate until 20 minutes before serving time.)

7. Pour boiling water into roasting pan to come halfway up custard cups. Set in oven center and bake 15 minutes.

8. Meanwhile, prepare sauce: Beat remaining whole egg and 2 yolks in top of a double boiler with 1½ tablespoons lime juice and ¼ teaspoon salt until light and fluffy. Heat the reserved shrimp stock and add it, beating. Set over barely simmering water and beat until slightly thickened and hot throughout. Season with lime juice and salt. Fold in mint, adjusting to taste.

9. Divide sauce among 8 warmed plates. Immediately unmold a timbale on each. Garnish with the reserved leek bulbs and mint sprigs.

SOUP OF WILD LEEKS AND POTATO WITH CHEESE TOASTS

Smoky, earthy, warming, and homey. Lovers of a strong onion-garlic flavor should double the amount of wild leeks.

4 servings

3 ounces thick-sliced bacon
1 bunch wild leeks, about ¼ pound, cleaned (see Preparation)
2 medium parsnips, about 8–10 ounces, peeled and chopped
2 stalks tender celery, sliced thin
5 cups rich stock—duck, ham, turkey, chicken, lamb, or beef
1½ pounds potatoes, peeled and cut in ½-inch dice
1 cup milk
12 slices French bread (1 small, thin loaf), about ½ inch thick
2–3 ounces sharp Cheddar cheese, shredded (½ cup)
Minced celery leaves or parsley
Pepper and salt to taste

1. Cut bacon across in ¼-inch strips. Cook in heavy flameproof casserole over moderate heat until lightly colored. Meanwhile, slice leeks thin. Add to pot with parsnips, and celery.

2. Cook over moderately low heat, covered, until very soft—about 15 minutes. Uncover and cook 5 minutes longer.

3. Add stock and potatoes and simmer, partly covered, until potatoes are very tender—about 20–25 minutes.

4. Remove 2 cups soup from pot; purée thoroughly. Return to pot with milk. Add pepper and salt. Cool, cover, and chill (like many soups, this needs mellowing).

5. At serving time, reheat soup. Make cheese toasts: Heat bread on baking sheet in preheated 375-degree oven 15 minutes, until golden. Divide cheese over toast; return to oven to melt. Place in soup dishes and pour soup over. Sprinkle with celery leaves or parsley.

WINGED BEAN
(Psophocarpus tetragonolobus)
also Goa Bean, Asparagus Bean, Four-Angled Bean, Manila Bean, Princess Pea

*T*he winged bean is not exactly a household word in this country, nor is it likely to be soon, having just recently arrived and being very sensitive to cold. But, given the virtues of the plant, and its phenomenal growth world-wide, we would do well to get to know it. In 1975 the National Academy of Science published a report on the vegetable,

at that time a tropical legume grown almost exclusively in Papua New Guinea and a few areas in Southeast Asia. Since then, the plant has been introduced into seventy or more countries as far-flung as Colombia and Czechoslovakia, with the most substantial production in Papua New Guinea, Bangladesh, India, Sri Lanka, Burma, Thailand, Vietnam, Laos, Cambodia, and the Philippines. The interest is such that a computerized Winged Bean Information and Documentation Service Center has been set up by the Agricultural Information Bank for Asia.

The winged bean is receiving this kind of response because it is as variously bountiful as Al Capp's shmoo: It produces shoots, leaves, flowers, tubers, pods, seeds (and a cooking oil from these) that are all tasty, nutritious, and comparatively high in protein. Not only that, the parts of the plant most generally eaten—the pods and flowers—are beautiful. The former are usually deep green, but may be red, pink, or purple. Each one has four slightly ruffled, equally spaced wings or fins (of a material reminiscent of the wings of maple seeds) that run its length, so slices resemble a tapered cross. These pods are larger than string beans, but lightweight. Cooked, their flavor is between that of a shell bean and a pod bean: meatier, blander, and starchier-tasting than string beans, but crunchier and greener-flavored than a shell bean. I have not seen or eaten the flowers, but have been told that they taste sweetly mushroomy when cooked.

As if all that weren't sufficient reason for cultivating winged beans, they are also disease-resistant, high-yielding and quick-growing—but only in the tropics, where they thrive. They won't tolerate temperatures below forty, no matter how briefly, which means that in the continental United States only the southernmost parts of Florida, California, and Texas are possible growing sites. But researchers have been working on development of a strain that will suit our temperate climate, with promising results.

498

SELECTION AND STORAGE: Pick the smallest pods, in which seeds have not yet developed (open a couple and have a look, if necessary) or the flavor will be tinny and waxy, like canned stringbeans. Keep them tightly wrapped in plastic in the upper part of the refrigerator, not the colder crisper. Plan to use them quickly: Winged beans store miserably, wilting and collapsing within a few days or less.

USE: Winged beans can be used in any way that you would string beans, but they taste more beany, less greeny. If you season them quite boldly with plenty of hot and spicy or oniony-garlicky or acid and sweet flavors (as you might dried legumes), you'll be surprised at how much flavor and texture the delicate-seeming vegetable has. Add thin slices to soups or stir-fries (my favorite place for them; they remain crunchy, a bit chewy, and absorb flavors quickly). Or add thicker cross-cuts or diagonal slices to wok braises. Or boil (I find they steam less successfully) and serve as a side dish, topped with sesame oil, scallions, and cilantro, or sweet-hot or sweet-sour sauce, or garlic and oil. Or chill cooked beans and marinate in a full-bodied dressing.

Dip ½-inch-wide cross-cut pieces of winged beans in tempura batter and deep-fry. Serve with a dipping sauce of grated ginger, soy sauce, and sugar for an unusual appetizer or first course.

Winged beans make a delicious pickle, using the same kind of piquant mixture you would for Jerusalem artichokes (see page 239) or a dill-pickling liquid as you would for string beans. Pickling is a favorite use for the vegetable in southern India and Sri Lanka.

PREPARATION: Dunk the beans in a sink filled with water, then lift out and drain. Unless the winged beans are overmature (with sizable beans inside), they don't need to be stringed. For most recipes, you'll want to slice the beans, either on a slant or straight across; remove the tip as you proceed. If boiling the beans, cook them whole; slices often come apart. When the beans are cooked and cooled, check again to see if the strings are sufficiently tender; if not, zip them off.

NUTRITIONAL HIGHLIGHTS: Dried mature winged beans are a good source of protein. The small green pods are sources of vitamin A, and small amounts of thiamine and riboflavin. They are very low in sodium and calories (only 25 calories per cup, cooked).

WINGED BEANS STIR-FRIED WITH SESAME AND GARLIC

Stir-fried winged beans keep their crunch, color, and flavor. Toss together this dish to accompany grilled or broiled fish or chicken. If you don't have Oriental sesame paste, substitute twice the amount of tahini (sesame paste or cream) or creamy peanut butter. If you don't stock Chinese chili-garlic paste, substitute minced garlic and hot pepper flakes to suit.

2 servings

½ pound winged beans, rinsed
2 tablespoons peanut oil
1 small onion, diced
1 tablespoon soy sauce
½ teaspoon Oriental sesame-seed paste (see Note)
⅛–¼ teaspoon chili paste with garlic (see Note)
Water, as needed

1. Slice winged beans across in ½-inch pieces, discarding the ends as you cut. Heat wok; pour oil around rim and tilt pan to distribute. Immediately add beans and onion and stir-fry over moderate heat until crunchy, but cooked—about 5–8 minutes. If beans appear to be drying out, add a few tablespoons of water.

2. Blend together soy sauce and sesame and chili pastes. Add to beans and toss to coat. Season and serve hot.

Note: Oriental sesame paste, darker and thicker than the Middle Eastern paste (or cream, or butter) and chili paste with garlic are available in Oriental groceries and many supermarkets.

JIM FOBEL'S WINGED BEANS WITH SPICY BEEF SAUCE

Jim Fobel (author of *Beautiful Food*) is an imaginative cook who is always ready to experiment. When I gave him some of the winged beans I had been working with, he couldn't help getting right to the kitchen and presented me with two delicious recipes a few days later. Jim urges that this dish not be limited to Oriental accompaniments but served alongside macaroni and cheese or other pasta dishes.

4 servings as a main course

1 pound winged beans, washed
½ cup beef broth
1 tablespoon cornstarch
2 tablespoons dry sherry
1 tablespoon soy sauce
2 teaspoons cider vinegar
1 teaspoon sugar
½ teaspoon ground coriander
½ teaspoon curry powder
Optional: ¼ teaspoon cayenne pepper
2 tablespoons vegetable oil
1 tablespoon minced ginger
1 garlic clove, minced
½ pound lean ground beef

1. Cut beans on bias into 1-inch lengths, discarding about ¼ inch from each end as you work.

2. In small bowl stir broth gradually into cornstarch. Add sherry, soy sauce, vinegar, sugar, coriander, curry powder, and cayenne.

3. Heat wok over high heat; drizzle 1½ tablespoons oil around rim, then tip to distribute. Add winged beans and stir-fry until edges are browned and beans just tender—about 5–8 minutes. Remove with slotted spoon.

4. Add remaining ½ tablespoon oil to wok. Add ginger and garlic; stir over moderate heat 30 seconds. Add ground beef and stir-fry, breaking it up, until just cooked through—about 2 minutes. Stir spice mixture; add with winged beans. Stir constantly as sauce thickens and boils. Serve hot.

WINGED BEAN AND TOMATO SALAD WITH DILL AND MINT

Although I prefer the distinct crunch of stir-fried winged beans, boiled beans pair particularly well with dressings, plumping slightly with the absorption of oil. The texture will not be as crisp as that of string beans, nor will the flavor be as freshly green, but the look can't be beat: graceful, green, four-pointed stars tossed with bright cherry-tomato halves.

4 servings

1 pound winged beans, the smaller the better
About 1½ tablespoons minced dill
About 1½ tablespoons minced mint
½ teaspoon salt
½ teaspoon sugar
Pepper to taste
Optional: Garlic to taste
2 tablespoons white wine vinegar
5 tablespoons olive oil
1 pint cherry tomatoes, halved

1. Drop beans into a very large kettle of boiling salted water. Return to a boil over highest heat and cook until barely tender—from 3 to 5 minutes. Drain, then drop into a bowl of ice water. When cool, drain and dry. If strings along sides are tough, pull them off; if not, simply proceed by slicing beans crosswise in ½-inch slices. Combine in a serving dish with 1½ tablespoons each minced dill and mint.

2. Combine salt, sugar, pepper, optional garlic, and vinegar in a jar; shake to blend. Add oil; shake. Toss with beans. Chill until serving time.

3. At serving time, gently mix cherry tomatoes into beans. Season salad with additional salt, pepper, dill, and mint.

🐟 *Winged bean can be substituted in recipes for yard-long beans, pages 514–516.*

JIM FOBEL'S WINGED BEANS WITH BACON

Sweet, sour, and smoky, this crisp bean dish deserves to be included in your repertoire—even if you must substitute yard-long beans or green beans.

4 servings

1 pound winged beans, rinsed
5 slices bacon, cut into ½-inch pieces
2 medium onions, cut lengthwise into thin slivers
1 medium garlic clove, minced
3 tablespoons tomato paste
1 cup water
½ teaspoon basil
½ teaspoon salt
¼ teaspoon pepper
1 tablespoon cider vinegar
2 teaspoons sugar

1. Cut beans across (on slant or straight) into ½-inch lengths, cutting away and discarding about ¼ inch from each end as you work.

2. Stir bacon in large skillet (not iron or aluminum) over moderate heat until golden and almost crisp. Remove with slotted spoon. Add onions to fat and sauté until soft and translucent. Add garlic and stir 1 minute. Add tomato paste, water, basil, salt, and pepper.

3. Return bacon to skillet; add winged beans. Simmer, partly covered, stirring occasionally, until beans are tender—about 10 minutes. Stir in vinegar and sugar. Serve hot.

WOOD EAR

**(*Auricula polytricha*) is the most commonly marketed of the Auriculariaceae family,
but one finds other members and common names, such as Cloud Ear, Tree Ear,
Mo-Ehr, Silver Ear, Black Fungus, Judas Ear, Jew's Ear, Kikurage, Mook Yee
(all either *Auricularia polytricha* or *Auricularia auricula*).**

*O*nce sold in dried form only, in Chinese groceries, the fresh form of wood ear is becoming somewhat more widely available, thanks to our large Oriental-American population and an enormous interest in Oriental food. In addition to its culinary virtues, wood ear is thought to be instrumental in preventing heart disease and beneficial

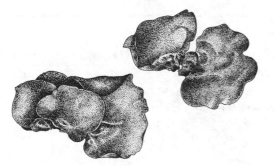

for other health reasons, which has made it even more widely respected in the Orient. (Wood ear does not, however, meet the claims of one grower, who states that it consists of over 50 percent protein and will prevent cancer.) Currently cultivated and primarily available on the West Coast, the market for this unique specialty is growing, as it is for all kinds of exotic mushrooms.

The dry wood ear, although remarkable in its ability to rehydrate to its dark translucent original form (even years after desiccation), reveals little of the delicate, foresty aroma of the fresh, nor its springy-soft consistency. It is the latter quality for which it is loved in the Orient but which makes American cooks uneasy. Slightly gelatinous, almost crunchy, cartilaginous, it feels as though its place of origin might lie somewhere between the ocean floor and the woods. Like the dried, the fresh caps—really flattened plates, with occasional whorls and ruching (similar, indeed, in form and veining to an ear)—can be the size of a quarter or a saucer.

SELECTION AND STORAGE: At this writing, there is little choosing to be done with wood ears. Erratically available year round, they are usually sold in plastic bags or clear plastic containers, generally in Oriental markets. This barely matters, as the shelf life is unparalleled among fungi and quality does not change with size or color. Just watch out for very mushy-soft specimens; but do not be wary of wet-looking ones, since the mushrooms have a damp, jellyish look. Although a month's refrigerator time is promised by distributors, I prefer to use the wood ears within a week. Or freeze the amazing fungus (in the package) for months.

USE: Wood ears are best utilized as textural and visual enhancers, either to stress or complement certain smooth or rough qualities and colors. Think of the fungus as a lively accentuating device, rather than a lone vegetable to be served as a side dish. Include it with other vegetables, grains, noodles, fowl, meat, or seafood in stir-fried dishes, casseroles, soups, or braises. It does not lose its distinctive texture when subjected to lengthy cooking, but softens somewhat and pleasantly absorbs the surrounding liquid.

PREPARATION: Although I have read of using raw wood ears, I find their virtues best displayed when cooked. Clean by rinsing vigorously under running water. (The bag will smell foul no matter what state the mushrooms are in; this odor dissipates at once, if the fungus is fresh.) Discard mushy, gummy pieces, if any. For dishes in which you want a particularly springy-firm texture, slice (there should be no trimming needed) and add to the dish as is. Or you can drop the wood ears into boiling water for 1 minute, then drain and slice to size. This step brings out the pleasant aroma of the mushrooms and makes them highly amenable to sauce absorption, as well as slightly more tender.

NUTRITIONAL HIGHLIGHTS: Wood ear mushrooms are very, very low in calories, with 15 per ½ cup. They contribute small amounts of the B vitamins thiamine, niacin, and riboflavin, and a goodly amount of fiber.

CHICKEN BREAST WITH WOOD EAR MUSHROOMS

A cross-cultural main dish, this blends elements from several cuisines to produce a light, speedy, balanced main course of tender, lemony chicken strips and crunchy-thin dark mushroom ribbons.

2 or 3 servings as a Western-style main course
4 or 5 servings at an Oriental meal

1 teaspoon Hungarian sweet paprika
¼ teaspoon salt
¼ teaspoon sugar
½ teaspoon grated lemon zest
⅛ teaspoon cayenne pepper
4 teaspoons cornstarch
1 tablespoon lemon juice
1 pound skinned and boned chicken breast, tendons removed
¼ pound fresh wood ear mushrooms
3 tablespoons sherry, preferably medium-dry, such as Amontillado
⅔ cup chicken stock
2 tablespoons oil
2 tablespoons minced white of scallion
1 tablespoon finely slivered scallion green
Finely minced dill to taste

1. Blend paprika, salt, sugar, lemon zest, and cayenne pepper in bowl that can fit chicken. Combine 2 teaspoons cornstarch and lemon juice; add to bowl and mix. Slice chicken breast in strips about ¼ inch wide and 2 inches long. Toss with marinade; let stand ½–1 hour.

2. Drop mushrooms into boiling water; boil 1 minute. Drain. Cut into strips about ½ inch wide and 2 inches long. Blend together remaining 2 teaspoons cornstarch and sherry; add stock and stir.

3. Heat wok; pour oil around rim. Add scallion whites and toss 30 seconds. Add chicken and toss until almost opaque. Add mushrooms and blended sauce ingredients. Stir over moderate heat until thickened, about 2 minutes.

4. Turn into hot serving dish. Top with scallion greens and dill.

JIM FOBEL'S FRIED RICE WITH SLIVERED WOOD EARS

Chewy wood ears, soft scrambled eggs, firm rice grains, and crunchy vegetables create an appealing textural play. Add slivers of cooked meat just before you stir-fry the rice, for variation. If you have about 3½ cups cooked, cold rice, it works even better than freshly prepared. Jim recommends toting along the colorful dish to a picnic, as it is delicious at room temperature.

6 servings as a side dish or part of a Chinese meal
3 or 4 servings as a main dish

1 cup long-grain white rice
1¾ cups water
6 ounces fresh wood ear mushrooms
4 eggs
1 tablespoon Oriental sesame oil
3 tablespoons vegetable oil
2 tablespoons minced fresh ginger
1 large clove garlic, minced
3–4 celery ribs, strings removed, cut in
    ¼-inch dice (to make 1½ cups)
1 medium red bell pepper
1 medium onion, chopped
3 tablespoons soy sauce

1. Combine rice and water in heavy 1–2-quart saucepan; bring to rolling boil, stirring occasionally. Turn heat to lowest point; cover. Cook 20 minutes; remove from heat, and let stand 10–15 minutes. Fluff into a dish. Toss occasionally with fork until cooled.

2. Rinse wood ears well. Cut out and discard any very tough, knotty stem-like parts, if necessary. Slice into long, pointed slivers about ¼-inch wide.

3. Combine eggs and sesame oil in bowl; blend well with fork. Heat wok; pour 1 tablespoon vegetable oil around edge, rotating pan to coat well. Add eggs and quickly scramble until just barely set. Scoop onto a plate. Wipe out wok with paper towels.

4. Heat remaining oil in wok on moderately high heat. Add ginger, garlic, and wood ears; stir-fry one minute. Remove a tablespoon of this for garnish. Add celery, red pepper, and onion; stir-fry 2 minutes, or until lightly cooked but still crunchy. Add cooled rice and stir-fry until lightly colored, 2–3 minutes. Chop up eggs and add with soy sauce. Toss with rice until just hot.

5. Pack lightly into 6–8-cup round-bottomed bowl (heat bowl first with boiling water for 5 minutes, if you're serving rice hot). Cover with a towel and let stand about 15 minutes, to blend flavors. Place a serving dish over bowl and invert. Garnish with wood ears. Serve warm or at room temperature.

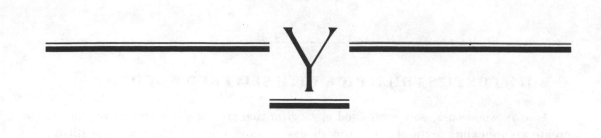

YAM OR ÑAME (pronounced nyAH-may)
(*Dioscorea* species)
also Igname (pronounced EE-nyahm), and many other Oriental and Caribbean names

*W*hat we in the United States call a yam is actually a sweet potato, a misnomer that has existed since slaves arrived and used a word like *yam* to designate the American vegetable. Yams grown by Africans do *very* superficially resemble sweet potatoes (which are part of another family; see BONIATO, page 46). No one outside the United

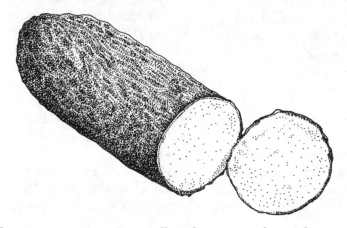

States calls sweet potatoes "yams," and anyone who wishes to continue doing so should know that the majority is overwhelming: 25 million tons of yams are produced annually, by most countries in the tropics and subtropics, making them one of the most important food crops in the world.

Not only do yams have value as sustenance for a vast number of people, they are also revered as religious objects and given ceremonial status—as was life-giving corn for some American Indians. The Trobriand Islanders build intricately decorated wooden "yam houses" where the splendid tubers are ensconced to be viewed by neighbors. In Cuba, yams are considered festival food, to be saved for special occasions. Because they can stay in the ground longer than just about any other tuber, they can be hauled out and appreciated whenever important celebrations occur—and for these, the bigger the better. It may well be that yams are worshiped because they can become awesomely huge. In the Pacific Island of Ponape, the size of yams is described as 2-man, 4-man, or 6-man, designating the number needed to lift the tuber. One would be tempted to dismiss this as exaggeration were it not for the fact that 600-pound yams 6 feet long have been recorded.

Volumes have been written about the probable origins and dispersal of the yam, but the definitive word has not yet been spoken. Chances arc best that it originated in the East, moved to the West, and evolved independently in both hemispheres. What we know for sure is that this beautiful, shiny-leafed, twisting vine and its tuberous offspring are presently cultivated throughout the tropics, with the majority grown in West Africa and Indonesia and a lesser but considerable quantity in China, Korea, the South Pacific, the Caribbean, and India.

Although there are 600 species of yam, what we are most likely to encounter in the United States is a brown, black-brown, or rusty-tan shaggy-coated tuber that may be shaped like a log, an elongated sweet potato, a distorted mitten, or a rhinoceros foot. The raw flesh is crisp, slippery, mucilaginous; either white, ivory, or yellow. A cooked yam's taste will be more potato-like than any of the other tropical starches, but the texture is looser, coarser, and drier, the flavor blander. Yam can have a pleasant nuttiness and firm, chewy texture, and be floury-light, or have virtually no taste—at least to my palate, which is not well educated in tubers.

In the lands that cultivate it, the yam is rarely eaten unadorned, and is almost always a foil for something strong, salty, fatty, oily, or piquant. It is boiled, baked, fried as chips or fritters, grated and dried, and grated and steamed for bread and cakes with sweetening and coconut. In Europeanized areas, it is treated to all the standard potato modes as well—scalloped, creamed, souffléd, etc.

SELECTION AND STORAGE: Look for yams year round, primarily in Latin markets. Select regularly shaped ones that are very hard, with no cracks or soft or shrunken spots. I'm told that of the mitten-shaped variety, the hand end, rather than the opposite "head" or "knot" is tastiest. In good markets, cut yams will be displayed to show the smooth interior. In the best, a fine *viandero* (a Latin American produce man, particularly one versed in the ways of tubers and roots, collectively referred to as *viandas*) will split one to show you the quality. If you have no such guide, prick the yam with a fingernail to be sure that it is juicy and slippery; if it is dry, reject it.

Yams can be stored, at room temperature, for longer periods than other tropical tubers, upward of a week. If you want to use part of the yam, just cut it off. The latex-like juice will seal the cut, as if cauterized.

USE: Yam works particularly well fried, whether grated or in chips. Baked, it becomes fluffy and as dry as toasted meal (do not imagine serving without *loads* of sauce), with a surprisingly meaty flavor. When boiled, it is waxy and bland, and takes to salty, spicy, and hot sauces. It can be grated and incorporated into cakes and breads, or boiled and puréed for the same, as well as for puddings. The only use for which it is unsatisfactory is in simple purées or soufflés, where it is tasteless and gluey.

PREPARATION: Scrub the yam with a brush. Cut into large but manageable chunks —preferably about a pound each. With a paring knife, cut deeply to remove both skin and underlayer. Rinse and place in a bowl of water to which you've added lemon juice. Many cooks advise oiling your hands when you peel yam, as it may be an irritant.

NUTRITIONAL HIGHLIGHTS: Yam provides an excellent supply of potassium and zinc. It is moderate in calories, with 80 per cup.

BASIC YAMS (ÑAME) WITH VARIATIONS

In most countries that enjoy them, yams are merely a foil for salty fish and meat stews, richly spiced soups, and pungent sauces. The technique for cooking yam at its simplest follows.

Figuring 6–8 ounces per person, rinse yams and pare off skin and underlayer, placing vegetable in cold water as you peel. Keep pieces whole, or at least large, as yam cooks unevenly. Drop into boiling salted water and keep at a gentle simmer (do not boil) until just tender when pierced with a toothpick or cake tester; this can vary from 30 to 40 minutes, so test frequently. Once your yam is cooked, serve it boiling hot (it can stay in the water for ¼–½ hour) with:

☐ Tomatillo, Dried Chili, and Cilantro Sauce (page 471)
☐ Chunky Tomato Horseradish Salsa (page 231), heated
☐ Garlic Sauce from Michael Rose's Yuca con Mojo (page 522)
☐ Mardee Regan's Chunky Poblano-Tomato Salsa (page 127)

Alternatively, cook the yam, then cut into logs of a hefty French-fry size. Fry these gently in plenty of garlic and olive oil, sprinkle with cilantro. Or deep-fry.

MARICEL PRESILLA'S YAMS IN GARLIC-CITRUS SAUCE

Mojo agrio, the intensely flavored sauce that follows, is made traditionally with the juice of sour (or bitter) oranges—to be preferred if they are available to you. The blend of pungent garlic and sharp citrus adds zest (and moisture) to all bland vegetables.

Definitely a food for garlic lovers only, the sauce is even more powerful if prepared in more authentic fashion: Add lemon and orange juices to mashed garlic and salt, then stir into the oil and onions. Heat through and serve.

6 servings

2 pounds yams (ñame), peeled, in large pieces (see Preparation)

½ head garlic (about 6 very large cloves)

1½ teaspoons coarse salt

¼ cup full-flavored olive oil, preferably Spanish

1 small, sweet white onion, cut in medium slices, separated in rings

½ cup sour orange juice (or 3 tablespoons lemon juice plus 5 tablespoons orange juice)

1. Drop yams into boiling salted water and keep at a gentle simmer until just tender when pierced with a toothpick or cake tester; this can vary from 30 to 40 minutes, so test frequently.

2. Meanwhile, crush garlic and salt in mortar to a coarse paste (if you have no mortar, use side of heavy knife to crush on a cutting board). Combine with olive oil and onion in small pan. Cook over lowest heat, stirring often, until garlic colors just slightly (about 5 minutes).

3. When yams are cooked (they can remain in water for up to 15 minutes to keep hot), drain and place in heated dish. Cut carefully in large, neat serving chunks. Add citrus juices to hot oil and bring to a simmer, stirring. Pour over yams. Serve hot.

Note: The recipe above is intended as a general guide, for which all types of malanga, yuca, and taro are equally well suited.

SMOKY YAM-CELERY SOUP

Used as you would potatoes, yams make a bland, warming winter soup. This basic formula is just that, to be augmented with whatever lurks in your larder: leek, carrot, parsnip, parsley root, turnip, cabbage, shell beans, squash. Substitute bacon or meaty ham bone for the hock.

4–6 servings

1 meaty ham hock (about 1 pound)
A few chicken wings or necks
2 quarts water
¼ cup chopped ham fat or bacon
2 medium onions cut in ½-inch dice (2 cups)
1½ cups diced celery and leaves (3 large stalks, strings removed)
1½–1¾ pounds yam, scrubbed ferociously
½ teaspoon dried thyme
1 teaspoon ground cardamom
¼ teaspoon ground pepper
Celery leaves for garnish

1. Combine ham hock and chicken in water; bring to a simmer. Continue simmering for a few minutes, skimming. Cover and simmer 1 hour. Remove and cool meats; reserve stock. Remove and discard ham rind. Chop ham and reserve. Pick chicken from bones (discard these) and reserve.

2. Heat fat until crisp in large pot or Dutch oven; add onions and celery. Stir over moderate heat until softened and colored, about 10 minutes.

3. Peel skin and underlayer from yam; cut flesh in ½-inch dice. Add to vegetables with thyme, cardamom, pepper, and stock. Simmer, partly covered, until soft—about 20 minutes.

4. Cool pot in sink filled with cold water. Chill, covered.

5. To serve, skim off as much fat as you wish. Reheat slowly. Season, then sprinkle with a generous amount of celery leaves.

MARICEL PRESILLA'S ESCABECHE DE ÑAME
(YAMS, PEPPERS, AND ONIONS VINAIGRETTE)

When dynamic Maricel Presilla is not working on her doctorate in medieval Spanish literature, traveling with her cardiologist husband, or cooking in restaurants, she is preparing copious meals for a never-ending stream of visitors from all over the world —and around the corner.

This traditional dish is one that adapts easily to whatever starchy tubers you find in best condition. The firm, pale, coarse-textured yams keep their shape neatly when tossed with the generous amounts of dressing (and garlic, which is typical of many Cuban dishes)—and drink up most of it, so don't stint.

6 servings

2–2¼ pounds yam, peeled (see Preparation), in large pieces

½ head garlic

1 cup full-flavored olive oil, preferably Spanish

1 medium green pepper, cut in rings or strips

1 large red pepper, cut in rings or strips

1 medium sweet white onion (½ pound), sliced, separated into rings

1 bay leaf, crumbled

1 teaspoon oregano

Big pinch cumin

1 teaspoon salt

½ cup distilled white vinegar or white wine vinegar

Optional: Olives for garnish

1. Drop yams in abundant boiling salted water. Simmer (do not boil) until easily pierced in center with cake tester or toothpick; timing will vary, but 35 minutes is average.

2. When yams are just about cooked, turn off heat and let stand a few minutes while you prepare dressing. Crush garlic cloves slightly wth one side of heavy knife; remove skins. Combine in skillet with oil and cook gently over moderately low heat until golden, about 5 minutes.

3. Add peppers and onion and toss on high heat for 1 minute to soften just a tiny bit. Add bay leaf, oregano, cumin, salt, and vinegar. Stir and remove from heat.

4. Immediately drain yams. Cut into pieces about ½ inch thick and 1 inch square. Arrange in a shallow serving dish. Pour over the hot dressing. Let stand until cool, gently turning with rubber spatula now and then. If not serving that day, cover and refrigerate. Return to room temperature before serving, or yams will be cardboardy.

Note: Maricel suggests plantain (green, boiled), yuca, malanga, or calabaza (preferred in the Dominican Republic) as alternatives to the yam in this versatile dish. I liked a malanga-yam combo, as well. Breadfruit should work well, too.

511

YAM BEAN
See Jícama

YARD-LONG BEAN
(Vigna unguiculata, subspecies *sesquipedalis)*
Also Long Bean, Asparagus Bean, Dau Gok

All cooking references that I have consulted describe the yard-long bean as a string bean extended, more or less. Well, it isn't; not botanically or culinarily. It is in fact sister to the cowpea or black-eyed pea, which does not belong to the same genus as common bush or pole beans. Probably native to southern Asia (its culture is so

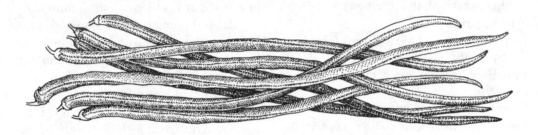

ancient that none are sure), it is sensitive to cold, while the beans with which it is compared fare as well in a temperate environment. The yard-long bean is still cultivated for the most part in Asia, but also thrives in Indonesia, China, parts of Africa, some Pacific Islands, and into the Caribbean, where it is called *bodi* or *boonchi*. In northern China it is allowed to mature and produce peas that are similar to its black-eyed sibling of the American South. Its leaves are also edible, and extremely protein-rich. However, it is most often harvested early on for its pencil-slim, flexible, lengthy pods, which are generally picked when about 1½ feet long—although they may reach as much as 3 feet. (Their Latin subspecies name, by the way, means 1½ feet, while *Vigna* refers to a seventeenth-century Italian scientist, not a vine.)

Culinarily, the yard-long bean's virtues are distinctly more bean than green. Its special characteristics distinguish it from the green bean. It is perfect for frying, stewing, and braising, becoming chewy and firm. Its crunch is solid, but not juicy, its flavor leguminous, intensifying with cooking. It is not crisp or sweet, like a fresh common green bean. In fact, when treated as a green bean—steamed or boiled—it is pleasant, though hardly worth bothering with, to my taste. But, once you have stir-fried this bean, you won't bother with others for this cooking method.

SELECTION AND STORAGE: Yard-long beans are available year round, primarily in Asian and Oriental markets. Look for very thin, smallish specimens (they cannot be too small, only too large) in which the peas have not matured, or the taste may be somewhat oily and the texture fibrous. Since long beans do not contain as much moisture as green beans, they will be comparatively flexible, not snappy-crisp—but they should not appear dry, rusty, or overly limp. Do not choose beans that have become yellow (do not confuse this with the more yellow variety, below) or whitish.

The pale-green and dark-green beans marketed have slightly different qualities. The paler bean, usually limper and less vivacious, cooks up to become somewhat sweeter and meatier than the deeper-colored, which tends to be a bit more fibrous and less delicate. For quick-cooking dishes I prefer the pale bean; for dishes in which a certain firmness and strength are desirable, such as a braise, I like the spruce-green beans.

Yard-long beans languish quickly. They will become limp very soon after purchase, then develop rusty patches. Keep them in the least cold part of your refrigerator and use them within a few days, at most.

USE: If you think of treating yard-long beans as you might green peppers and dried beans, you'll get the most from them. Rich flavors and textures seem to bring out the best in the beans: pork, ginger, nuts, fermented black beans, garlic, assertive herbs, soy and fish sauce, chili-peppers, sausages, or plenty of oil and vinegar.

Frying (whether sautéing, stir-frying, shallow-frying, or deep-frying) gives you long beans at their best. You can even tie them into loose pretzly knots, dip them in tempura batter, and fry for an amusing appetizer. Trim, cut up, and stir-fry yard-long beans to develop the dryish, chewy-crunchy texture that makes them so special—the quality you will recognize if you have eaten Szechuan-style dry-sautéed beans in a Chinese restaurant. Cook until the beans lose their raw flavor—about 5 minutes. Chinese friends also suggest blanching, then stir-frying yard-long beans, which is juicy-delicious indeed, if you prefer a moister, more string bean quality.

If you are boiling or steaming the beans to eat as you would string beans, figure 2–5 minutes for boiling, 3–7 for steaming. The timing depends on the size and maturity of the beans.

Braising and stewing are also suited for yard-long beans, as they retain their firm texture and absorb juices. Add them to whatever vegetable or meat combination you are slow-cooking about 20 minutes before the dish is completed. Meaty, spicy, garlicky, oniony braising liquids are delicious, as is coconut milk.

Although I have not tried it, in the Caribbean yard-long beans are bound around skewered meat and vegetables to keep them in shape, the ends being fastened around the skewer with vines or twisted foil.

PREPARATION: Since one yard-long bean equals 5 or 6 stringbeans, they are faster and easier to prepare than string beans, with considerably less waste. Line up a batch of beans at the stem end. Cut these off, then proceed to slice the beans into desired lengths (generally 1–2 inches) on the diagonal or straight. Occasionally the other end of the beans will also need a bit of trimming.

NUTRITIONAL HIGHLIGHTS: Yard-long beans are low in calories, at about 45 calories per cup. They are a rich soure of vitamin A, a fair one of vitamin C and potassium, and very low in sodium.

SWEET-SOUR YARD-LONG BEANS WITH PEANUTS

Tart-sweet, briskly gingery and garlicky, this quick side dish will make a meal with any plain-broiled meat, poultry, or fish.

4 servings

3 tablespoons peanut oil

1¼ pounds yard-long beans (preferably the lighter-green variety), trimmed and cut in 1-inch diagonal lengths

2 medium garlic cloves, minced or grated (1½ teaspoons)

1½ tablespoons finely grated fresh ginger (no need to peel)

2 tablespoons soy sauce

3 tablespoons lime juice

1½ tablespoons brown sugar

⅓ cup chopped, salted, roasted peanuts

1. In large skillet or wok heat oil. Add beans and toss over moderate heat until almost tender—about 5–6 minutes; beans will be slightly wrinkled and lightly browned. Add garlic; toss for a minute.

2. Combine ginger, soy sauce, lime juice, and sugar in a cup; stir to mix. Add to beans and toss over high heat until liquid evaporates. Season and serve hot, sprinkled with peanuts.

YARD-LONG BEANS WITH PORK

Mary Beth Clark ran a cooking school in New York in which she taught Chinese and Southeast Asian cuisines, among several subjects. She has adapted this Szechuan dish of chewy beans to fit the needs of this book, and of an American audience that steers away from deep-fat frying.

2 servings as a main course, 4 as part of a Chinese meal

4 ounces coarse-ground pork (preferably rather fatty)

3 teaspoons soy sauce

¼ teaspoon sugar

2 tablespoons peanut oil, approximately

½ pound yard-long beans, trimmed and cut in 3-inch lengths

½ teaspoon minced garlic

1. Blend pork well with 1½ teaspoons of the soy sauce. Combine remaining soy sauce and sugar and stir to mix.

2. Heat a wok and pour 1 tablespoon oil around the rim. Toss beans over moderate heat until slightly wrinkled, lightly browned, and tender—about 5 minutes. Transfer to a dish

3. Add oil to the wok as needed. Stir-fry pork until deeply browned and crisp; add garlic and toss 5 seconds. Add soy-sauce mixture and toss 30 seconds; add beans and toss 30 seconds longer. Serve hot.

STIR-FRIED YARD-LONG BEANS WITH BEEF AND MUSHROOMS

A fast, delicious, substantial, well-balanced meal in a wok. The reason for cooking yard-long beans, not the usual string beans, is clear when you prepare this simple dish: the beans stay firm, intensely green, and crunchy and chewy at the same time—and they require no precooking. Serve with brown rice.

4 servings

4 tablespoons peanut oil

1 pound yard-long beans, in 1½-inch diagonal lengths

2½ tablespoons soy sauce

1 tablespoon Oriental sesame oil

2 teaspoons brown sugar

10 ounces firm medium-sized mushrooms, in ½-inch slices (halve or quarter first, if large)

2 medium-large onions, quartered and sliced vertically

¾ pound ground beef or lamb

⅛–¼ teaspoon crushed hot pepper flakes

1. Heat wok. Pour 2 tablespoons oil around rim; tilt to distribute. Over moderately high heat toss beans until they are slightly wrinkled and have lost their raw flavor—about 3 minutes. Transfer to a dish. Stir together soy sauce, sesame oil, and sugar, mixing to dissolve sugar.

2. Add remaining 2 tablespoons oil to wok and toss mushrooms and onions until browned, about 3 minutes. Add meat and red pepper flakes and toss and break up until meat loses most of its redness.

3. Return beans to wok and toss to heat through. Add soy-sauce mixture and continue tossing and stirring until beans are cooked through and no liquid remains in pan, about 1 minute. Serve at once.

YARD-LONG BEAN, EGGPLANT, AND TOMATO STEW WITH MINT AND DILL

Another example of long beans' unusual texture: braised with other vegetables, the bean remains firm and full-flavored. While the eggplant softens to a velvety texture and the tomatoes melt into a sauce, the beans intensify and keep their crunch, becoming almost nut-like. As with ratatouille, which this dish closely resembles, a mellowing period develops and knits together the several flavors. Leftovers know no limits: casseroles, omelet and sandwich fillings, pasta sauce, seasoning for other vegetables.

4 servings as a side dish

1-pound eggplant, rinsed, stem end removed
3 tablespoons olive oil
1 medium onion, diced
2 tablespoons coarsely chopped mint
2 tablespoons coarsely cut dill
1 medium garlic clove
About ¾ teaspoon salt
4 medium plum tomatoes (10 ounces), rinsed and cut in small chunks
Pepper to taste
About 1 teaspoon sugar
About 1 tablespoon vinegar
½ pound yard-long beans, trimmed, cut in 1-inch diagonals
Garnish: 1 plum tomato diced small; 1 tablespoon each minced dill and mint

1. Cut eggplant in 1-inch dice. Heat oil in heavy casserole. Add eggplant and onion and toss to coat. Cook over moderate heat until lightly browned, about 8 minutes, tossing occasionally.

2. Meanwhile combine mint, dill, garlic, and ¾ teaspoon salt in processor; mince fine. Add tomatoes, pepper, 1 teaspoon sugar, and 1 tablespoon vinegar. Purée mixture.

3. Add beans to eggplant-onion mixture and toss 1 minute. Add purée and bring to a boil, stirring. Cover and cook at a low simmer until eggplant is soft, about 20 minutes. Beans should remain somewhat crunchy.

4. Cool mixture, stirring occasionally with rubber spatula. Season with sugar, salt, pepper, and vinegar, as desired. Cover and chill, preferably 12 hours or more.

5. Serve warm, hot, at room temperature, or chilled, sprinkled with diced tomato and minced dill and mint.

YAUTIA
See Malanga

YUCA, CASSAVA
(Manihot esculenta)
Manioc, Tapioca, Mandioca

*L*ike oatmeal, nopales (cactus pads), okra, cornmeal mush, even gumdrops, tapioca is unbearable to some poor souls. If you are one of them, chances are good that the tacky, waxy, tasty blandness of cassava (the source of that thickener we call tapioca) will not make you happy. Dense, softly fibrous, so starchy it becomes almost translucent when cooked, it is certainly sticky—and to some that means no good. But it has a sweetness, butteriness, and a glutinous chewiness that is much appreciated by about half the world—so you might at least sample it for the sake of worldliness.

Native to Brazil (the scientific name, *Manihot*, is the Indian word for the root), cassava is now cultivated throughout South and Central America, the Caribbean, Africa, Asia, the South Pacific—and Florida, for immigrants from all those places who have come to the United States. The swollen roots of this handsome shrub (a relative of poinsettia) are shaped like long, narrow sweet potatoes and covered with what looks like bark. Market specimens may weigh ½–3 pounds and measure 1½–4 inches in diameter. Beneath the rough, brown coat, through which may be visible rosy or tan patches, is flesh that is as hard, dense, and white as coconut.

Yuca—pronounced YOO-ka, not yukka—(the Spanish name is most common in the United States, where the vegetable is cooked primarily by people of Hispanic origin) appears throughout the meal, from soup through dessert, in the many countries in which it is cultivated. At its simplest, it is boiled or baked, and almost always sauced (for most, this is not a vegetable that is eaten "neat"). Or it is fried as fritters and chips, particularly throughout the Caribbean.

In stews, yuca both thickens and absorbs juices. In an East African dish, it is simmered with beef in a rich sauce of onions, tomato, coconut milk, chili-pepper, and spices. In Nigeria, its blandness is offset by cooking with salt herring. In the extremely complex vegetable stews or "boils" of Venezuela, Cuba, Colombia, Brazil, and Puerto Rico—particularly *sancocho*, *ajiaco*, and *cocido*—yuca/cassava is the constant, as potatoes are in many of our stews. One of the more unusual traditional stews is the

Caribbean pork pepperpot, which is flavored with the juice of grated cassava that has been boiled down with spices and brown sugar.

If the main dish does not contain yuca, accompaniments will: unleavened rounds of *cassabe*, a hard flatbread made of dried cassava meal, absorb rich gravies in the Caribbean; toasted cassava meal *(farinha de mandioca)* is served with Brazilian food; grated fresh cassava is steamed or baked in pone, dumplings, and breads that are staples throughout the Pacific and Caribbean islands.

Tapioca-style sweets are commonplace in the South Pacific, usually cooked with grated coconut or coconut milk. These puddings are topped with mango, papaya, or pineapple. Or the grated tuber is combined with coconut and sweetening, then baked or steamed to make chewy, glutinous cakes in Asia and the Caribbean.

SELECTION AND STORAGE: Choosing good-quality yuca (available year round in Hispanic markets and many supermarkets) is more crucial to its success than the way you cook it. Nothing can be done to help it along if it is not superb. Always buy a bit extra, for even if you select well, there may be some waste.

Look for yuca that is as completely bark-covered as possible, although it is always patchy. There should be no sliminess or mold, nor should there be hairline cracks, which indicate dryness. Yuca should smell clean and fresh, not at all sour or ammonia-like. Several cut pieces should display the interior, which is perfectly, pristinely white. Do not buy tubers that show any grayish-blue fibers or even the slightest darkening near the skin. Since the rubbery juices seal over soon after cutting, you will probably need to see freshly cut tubers to check their quality. Most good markets expect to cut the yuca for you.

Do not plan to store cassava, which spoils rapidly. If you must keep it, store in the coolest place you can find other than the refrigerator; it will probably keep for a few days. If you have a very large amount and wish to use a bit each day, slice off what you need and leave the yuca to seal up its cut surface (do not cover). Or peel, cover with water, and refrigerate up to a day. (Although yuca will keep for a longer time than this without spoiling, it loses all its flavor and cooks to a gummy mass.) Or boil, then drain and keep for a few days, closely wrapped and refrigerated.

Yuca freezes well. Simply peel the chunks and freeze for several months, tightly wrapped (it is sold this way in many Latin markets).

USE: Yuca is suited to boiling, frying, sautéing, and use in stews. Being bland and tacky, it takes well to salty, spicy, and *picante* sauces. It can be grated and incorporated into cakes and breads, or boiled and puréed for the same, as well as for puddings. The only way it is unpalatable (for most) is in simple purées or soufflés, where glueyness prevails.

PREPARATION: Yuca is easy to peel, but only if you know how. Do not hack at the bark with a peeler or paring knife. Instead, scrub each tuber, then cut (be careful: it is *hard*) into 2–3-inch sections. Incise a lengthwise slit in each. You will see an underskin beneath the bark; place your paring knife inside the slit and under this, then pull off both bark and underlayer, unwrapping. Some pieces will resist and you'll need to cut off the layers instead. Rinse well, then place in cold water. If you are not cooking the tubers whole, you can halve them lengthwise and pull out the central fibrous cord. If left whole, pull out this fiber after cooking.

NUTRITIONAL HIGHLIGHTS: Yuca is high in calories, about 135 per ½ cup. It is a good source of iron, and contains small amounts of niacin and calcium.

Note: You may have heard of the cyanide-laden wild cassava which has been concentrated for tipping murderous arrows and blowguns in South America (yes, this is true), but the vegetable that is cultivated for our markets is not harmful when cooked. Some very sensitive people, however, develop upset stomachs from yuca. If you are prone to such distress, go easy if you are eating the food for the first time. Yuca is *not* Yucca, a genus of the bayonet-leaved, showy plants of the Agave family.

BASIC YUCA (CASSAVA)

Although cassava is roasted in embers in parts of South America and the South Pacific, the most common mode of cooking is boiling—which is easier than coming up with embers, for many of us. But boiling this vegetable takes some care and attention, for it can become a sticky mass of fibers if unattended (or if you did not take care when choosing it, in which case it will never cook properly). I have been told that in Cuba, if the yuca is in top shape, virtually all other parts of the meal go unpraised at company dinners, so important is the quality of this simply-cooked vegetable.

Figure about ½ pound per person, or less (yuca is extremely dense and filling); rinse, peel, and pare (see Preparation). Keep the pieces whole, or halve them lengthwise and remove the fibrous cord. Combine in a large pot with abundant cold water (and lemon juice and garlic and herb flavorings, as you like). Bring to a boil, add salt, then lower the heat a bit. Each time the liquid threatens to boil, add cold water to keep it at a simmer and "shock it," as they say in Cuba. (Less traditionally, simply simmer the yuca.) Start testing with a cake tester or toothpick after 20 minutes, piercing the pieces in the center. When the tester slips through easily, gently lift out the piece and set aside. Check often, as the pieces rarely finish cooking at the same time. None will be as neat as potatoes. Some will separate lengthwise (there are 4 sections to each whole tuber). Do not undercook and do not cook to a mush.

Once your yuca is cooked, drain and serve it boiling hot (it can stay in the water for an hour) with:

☐ Garlic-Citrus Sauce from Maricel Presilla's Yams recipe (page 509)
☐ Tomatillo, Dried Chili, and Cilantro Sauce (page 471)
☐ Mardee Regan's Chunky Poblano-Tomato Salsa (page 127)

Alternatively, cook the yuca, then cut into logs. Fry these gently in plenty of garlic and olive oil; sprinkle with cilantro. Or undercook the yuca slightly, cut into logs, and deep-fry.

MARTHA WASHINGTON'S BOBO DE CAMARÃO
SHRIMP IN YUCA [CASSAVA] AND COCONUT SAUCE

Martha Washington, a jazzy Brazilian caterer, cooked this Bahian dish for me one steamy summer afternoon in New York City. I fell in love with it at once—but I happen to love tapioca pudding *and* cream of wheat, both of which the sauce resembles.

If you're still here, you can look forward to a dense, creamy, pink sauce (almost a soup, if you measure in quantity) made of yuca, fresh tomatoes, coconut milk, and sparked with sweet shrimps, lime, and plenty of garlic and hot pepper oil. Martha served it with rice that had been gently cooked with onion, garlic, and olive oil until golden, then simmered in a combination of coconut milk and water.

6 servings

1½ pounds medium shrimp in the shell

Juice of 4–6 limes, as needed

1 pound yuca, peeled and cut in 2-inch sections (see Preparation)

¼ cup olive oil

1½ tablespoons chopped garlic

1 medium onion, coarsely chopped

2 tablespoons water

¼ cup coarsely chopped flat-leaf parsley

Hot pepper or chili oil (Brazilian or Oriental; see Note)

Salt to taste

5 medium tomatoes

6.76-ounce bottle (or ¾ cup) pure coconut milk

1 tablespoon oil of palm (dendê oil; see Note)

1. Combine shrimp in saucepan with lime juice and water to cover generously, adjusting amount to use slightly more water than lime juice. Simmer 2 minutes. Drain and reserve liquid.

2. Combine yuca in saucepan with drained shrimp liquid; add water to cover by an inch. Simmer until soft, about 30 minutes, adding water if needed. Meanwhile, shell and devein shrimp.

3. Heat oil in large skillet; add garlic and stir over low heat until lightly golden; add onion and continue stirring over low heat until softened. Add shrimp, 2 tablespoons water, and parsley; add a few drops hot oil and salt to taste. Remove from heat and stir a minute.

4. Bring tomatoes to a simmer in cold water to cover; simmer gently 4 minutes. Drain, peel, halve, then squeeze out seeds. Purée; reserve.

5. Drain yuca, reserving liquid. Remove fibrous central core and any other fibrous parts. Purée yuca in blender or processor, adding cooking liquid as needed. Blend tomato purée, yuca, and coconut milk in batches. Scoop into a pot; add salt to taste and more cooking liquid, if needed, to obtain a thick, pourable consistency.

6. Add shrimp and palm oil. Heat through, stirring. Season to taste and serve hot, over rice.

Note: Chili oil or hot pepper oil is available in supermarkets and Oriental and Latin groceries. Dendê (palm oil) is available in markets that stock South American products. If you cannot obtain it, leave it out. If coconut milk is not obtainable, prepare your own, following directions on page 55.

MARICEL PRESILLA'S BOLITAS DE YUCA

Cuban cook Maricel Presilla adds a subtle undertaste of fennel to this irresistible deep-fried yuca appetizer—gumdrop-chewy inside, firm and crunchy-dry outside. Because of their dense texture, these yuca balls stay warm longer than most fried tidbits.

Makes about 40 small balls

¼ pound firm aged Cheddar or Gouda, grated or finely shredded

1 tablespoon melted butter

¼ teaspoon ground fennel (or anise or Chinese five-spice powder)

2 extra-large or jumbo eggs, lightly blended

½ teaspoon coarse kosher salt

½ teaspoon sugar

1 pound yuca, scrubbed, cut in 3-inch sections, peeled (see Preparation)

Corn oil for deep frying

1. Combine cheese, butter, fennel, eggs, salt, and sugar in small mixing bowl. Grate yuca on medium opening of standing hand grater (you should have about 3 cups, loosely packed). Add to bowl and blend thoroughly.

2. Heat at least 1 inch oil to 350–375 degrees (preferably in electric frying pan). Form mixture in 1–1¼-inch balls. Drop into fat. Fry until golden, about 5 minutes, turning occasionally. Drain on towels. Serve piping hot.

MICHAEL ROSE'S YUCA CON MOJO
(CASSAVA WITH GARLIC SAUCE)

Michael Rose, chef at the Ballroom Restaurant and Tapas Bar in New York, grew up in that melting-pot city, where he "learned as much as from travelling around the world." In the Spanish neighborhood near the old site of the High School of Music and Art, which he attended, he tasted many versions of this standard of the Latin repertoire —and came up with his own.

4 servings

1 whole head garlic
2 bay leaves
2 tablespoons plus ¾ teaspoon coarse kosher salt
3 quarts water
1¼–1½ pounds yuca, scrubbed, peeled (see Preparation)
2 medium garlic cloves, minced
Juice of ½ lemon, approximately
Pinch pepper
Big pinch oregano, rosemary, or thyme, crumbled
1 serrano chili-pepper, seeded and minced (or other hot pepper to taste)
1½ tablespoons vegetable oil
2 tablespoons olive oil
Vegetable oil for frying

1. Combine garlic head, bay leaves, 2 tablespoons salt, and water in a saucepan; bring to a boil. Add yuca; simmer until cake tester or toothpick can pierce center of each piece, but not until soft; it should be a little too firm. You may have to remove chunks at different times, as yuca cooks unevenly. Check often, but 30–40 minutes should do.

2. Meanwhile, prepare sauce: combine minced garlic, lemon juice, ¼ teaspoon salt, pepper, oregano, and serrano; blend. Add vegetable and olive oils and mix well. Reserve.

3. Drain yuca thoroughly and dry on paper towels. Cut into strips the size of French fries. Heat a skillet with a shallow layer of oil, or half fill with oil (heat to 375 degrees)—depending on whether you wish to pan-fry or deep-fry the yuca. Sprinkle with the remaining ½ teaspoon salt and toss. Drop into hot fat and fry on both sides until golden, but not browned. Serve hot, with sauce.

> *Yuca can be used in the recipe on page 294, Malanga-Yam Pancakes, Maricel Presilla's Yams in Garlic-Citrus Sauce, page 509, and Maricel Presilla's Escabeche de Ñame, page 511.*

BIBLIOGRAPHY

Many books and articles were consulted in the writing of this work. Those listed below were particularly helpful:

Alexander, D. McE., P. B. Scholefield, and A. Frodsham. *Some Tree Fruits for Tropical Australia*. Australia: Commonwealth Scientific and Industrial Research Organization, 1983.

Andrews, Jean. *Peppers: The Domesticated Capsicums*. Austin: University of Texas Press, 1984.

Angell, Madeline. *A Field Guide to Berries and Berrylike Fruits*. Indianapolis and New York: Bobbs-Merrill, 1981.

Bailey, Liberty M. *Hortus Third: A Concise Dictionary of Plants Cultivated in the United States and Canada*. New York: Macmillan, 1976

————. *Manual of Cultivated Plants*, rev. ed. New York: Macmillan, 1949.

Beutel, James A. "Asian Pears." Photocopied. University of California, Davis, 1984.

Biondi, Lisa. *Il cucinafunghi*. Milan: Editrice Erpi, n.d.

Bittenbender, H. C. *Handbook of Tropical Vegetables*. East Lansing: Michigan State University, 1983.

Brackett, Babette, and Maryann Lash. *The Wild Gourmet*. Boston: David R. Godine, 1975.

Chin Hoon Fong, and Yong Hoi-Sen. *Malaysian Fruits in Colour*. Kuala Lumpur: Tropical Press Sdn. Bhd., 1982.

Composition of Foods: Fruits and Fruit Juices. Washington, D.C.: USDA Handbook No. 8–9, rev. August 1982.

Composition of Foods: Vegetables and Vegetable Products. Washington, D.C.: USDA Handbook No. 8–11, rev. August 1984.

Dahlen, Martha, and Karen Phillipps. *A Popular Guide to Chinese Vegetables*. New York: Crown, 1983.

David, Elizabeth. "Concerning Coriander." *Petits Propos Culinaires 2*, Prospect Books, August 1979.

de Candolle, Alphonse. *Origin of Cultivated Plants*. 2d ed., 1886. Reprint, New York: Hafner Press, 1967.

Duke, James A. *Handbook of Legumes of World Economic Importance*. New York: Plenum Press, 1983.

Fruit and Vegetable Facts and Pointers (series of 78 booklets). Washington, D.C.: United Fresh Fruit and Vegetable Association, n.d.

Grigson, Jane. *Jane Grigson's Fruit Book*. New York: Atheneum, 1982.

————. *Jane Grigson's Vegetable Book*. Harmondsworth and New York: Penguin Books, 1981.

————. *The Mushroom Feast*. Harmondsworth and New York: Penguin Books, 1983.

Harrington, Geri. *Grow Your Own Chinese Vegetables*. Pownal, Vt.: Garden Way Publishing, 1984.

Hawkes, Alex D. *A World of Vegetable Cookery*. New York: Simon and Schuster, 1985.

Hedrick, U. P., ed. *Sturtevant's Edible Plants of the World*, 1919. Reprint, New York: Dover Publications, 1972.

Herklots, Geoffrey A. C. *Vegetables in South-East Asia*. London: George Allen & Unwin, 1972.

Hill, Lewis. "The Appeal of Currants and Gooseberries." *Horticulture*, September 1982, pp. 36–45.

Indoor Citrus & Rare Fruit Society Newsletter. Issues 1–14.

Kaye, Geraldine C. *Wild and Exotic Mushroom Cultivation in North America*. Cambridge: Farlow Reference Library and Herbarium of Cryptogamic Botany, Harvard University, 1984.

Kennedy, Diana. *Recipes from the Regional Cooks of Mexico*. New York: Harper & Row, 1978.

Knight, Robert J., Jr. *The Longan: A Subtropical Fruit Potential for Florida*. South Miami: Rare Fruit Council of South Florida, 1969.

———. "The Potential for Florida of Hybrids Between the Purple and Yellow Passionfruit." *Proceedings of the Florida State Horticultural Society* 85 (1972): 288–292.

———, and Carl W. Campbell. "The Florida Mango Industry and Its Cultivars." Abstract., K.p.: USDA, n.d.

Larkcom, Joy. *The Salad Garden*. New York: Viking Press, 1984.

Les Champignons au Fil des Saisons. Paris: L'Ami des Jardins et de la Maison, 1984.

Lincoff, Gary H. *The Audubon Society Field Guide to North American Mushrooms*. New York: Knopf, 1981.

Magness, J. R., G. M. Markle, and C. C. Compton. *Food and Feed Crops of the United States*. New Brunswick: Rutgers University, 1971

Martin, Franklin, ed. "Breeding New Sweet Potatoes for the Tropics." *Proceedings of the American Society for Horticultural Science, Tropical Region* 27 (1983): 35–41.

———. *CRC Handbook of Tropical Food Crops*. Boca Raton: CRC Press, 1984.

Miller, Carey D., Katherine Bazore, and Mary Bartow. *Fruits of Hawaii*. Honolulu: University Press of Hawaii, 1981.

Morash, Marian. *The Victory Garden Cookbook*. New York: Knopf, 1982.

Morton, Julia F. "The Chayote, a Perennial, Climbing, Subtropical Vegetable." *Proceedings of the Florida State Horticultural Society* 94 (1981): 240–245.

———. "Cocoyams *(Xanthosoma caracu, X. atrovirens* and *X. nigrum)*, Ancient Root- and Leaf-Vegetables, Gaining in Economic Importance." *Proceedings of the Florida State Horticultural Society* 85 (1972): 85–94.

———. "Ornamental Plants with Toxic and/or Irritant Properties II." *Proceedings of the Florida State Horticultural Society* 75 (1962).

———. "The Sturdy Seminole Pumpkin Provides Much Food with Little Effort." *Proceedings of the Florida State Horticultural Society* 88 (1975).

———. "The Tree Tomato, or 'Tamarillo,' a Fast-Growing, Early-Fruiting Small Tree for Subtropical Climates." *Proceedings of the Florida State Horticultural Society* 95 (1982): 81–85.

———. "Yellow Passionfruit Ideal for Florida Home Gardens." *Proceedings of the Florida State Horticultural Society* 80 (1967).

———, and O. S. Russell. "The Cape Gooseberry and the Mexican Husk Tomato." *Proceedings of the Florida State Horticultural Society* 67 (1954): 261–266.

Mowry, Harold, L. R. Toy, and H. S. Wolfe. *Miscellaneous Tropical and Subtropical Florida Fruits*. Gainesville: Agricultural Extension Service, University of Florida, 1958.

Nagy, Steven, Phillip E. Shaw, eds. *Tropical and Subtropical Fruits*. Westport, Conn., AVI Publishing, 1980.

Niethammer, Carolyn. *American Indian Foods and Lore*. New York: Collier Books, 1974.

O'Hair, Stephen K., George H. Snyder, and Loy V. Crowder, Jr., eds. *Taro and Other Aroids for Food, Feed and Fuel*. Gainesville: Center for Tropical Agriculture, International Programs, Institute of Food and Agricultural Sciences, University of Florida, 1983.

————, ————, and Julia F. Morton. "Wetland Taro: A Neglected Crop for Food, Feed and Fuel." *Proceedings of the Florida State Horticultural Society* 95 (1982): 367–374.

Ortiz, Elisabeth Lambert. *The Book of Latin American Cooking*. New York: Knopf, 1979.

Oster, Gerald, and Selmaree Oster. "The Great Breadfruit Scheme." *Natural History*, March 1985, pp. 35–40.

Oxford Book of Food Plants, The. Oxford University Press, 1982.

Pacioni, Giovanni. *Simon and Schuster's Guide to Mushrooms*. American edition edited by Gary Lincoff. New York: Simon and Schuster, 1981.

"Oriental Herbs and Vegetables," *Plants & Gardens, Brooklyn Botanic Garden Record*, vol. 39, no. 2 (July 1983).

Popenoe, Wilson. *Manual of Tropical and Subtropical Fruits*. 1920. Reprint, New York: Hafner Press, 1974.

Purseglove, J. W. *Tropical Crops*. 2 vols. N.p.: Longman, 1979.

Rare Fruit Council International, Inc. 1985 Yearbook. Miami: Rare Fruit Council International, 1985.

Ray, Richard, and Lance Walheim. *Citrus: How to Select, Grow and Enjoy*. Tucson: H. P. Books, 1980.

Reuther, Walter, Herbert John Webber, and Leon Dexter Batchelor, eds. *The Citrus Industry*. vol. 1. Berkeley: University of California, 1967.

Root, Waverley. *Food*. New York: Simon and Schuster, 1980.

————. "Lamb's-Lettuce." *Gourmet*, May 1982, pp. 50–62.

Skinner, Gwen. *The Cuisine of the South Pacific*. Auckland, New Zealand: Hodder and Stoughton, 1983.

Smith, Janell, et al. "Utilization Potential for Semi-Tropical and Tropical Fruits and Vegetables in Therapeutic and Family Diets." *Proceedings of the Florida State Horticultural Society* 96 (1983): 241–244.

Stobart, Tom. *Herbs, Spices and Flavourings*. Harmondsworth and New York: Penguin Books, 1979.

Sturrock, David. *Fruits for Southern Florida*. Stuart, Fla.: Horticultural Books, 1980.

Swain, Roger. "Skototropism: *Monstera's* Shady Behavior." *Horticulture*, October 1978, pp. 10–12.

Tatum, Billy Joe. *Billy Joe Tatum's Wild Foods Cookbook and Field Guide*. Edited by Helen Witty. New York: Workman Publishing, 1976.

Tee, George. "Samphire." *Petits Propos Culinaires* 15 (1983): 40–44.

Terrell, Edward E. *A Checklist of Names for 3,000 Vascular Plants of Economic Importance*. Washington, D.C.: USDA Agriculture Handbook No. 505, 1977.

Thomson, Paul H. "The Sapote." *California Rare Fruit Growers Quarterly Newsletter* vol. 4, no. 3 (August 1972).

Thorndike, John. "The Making of the 'Sugar Snap' Pea." *Horticulture*, January 1983, pp. 14–22.

Tropical Legumes: Resources for the Future. Washington, D.C.: National Academy of Sciences, 1979.

Underexploited Tropical Plants with Promising Economic Value. Washington, D.C.: National Academy of Sciences, 1975.

Vegetable Gardening in the Caribbean Area. Washington, D.C.: USDA Agriculture Handbook No. 323, n.d.

Vilmorin-Andrieux, MM. *The Vegetable Garden.* 1885. Reprint. Berkeley: Ten Speed Press, n.d.

Walheim, Lance, and Robert L. Stebbins. *Western Fruits, Berries and Nuts.* Tucson: H. P. Books, 1981.

Whealy, Kent, ed. *The Garden Seed Inventory.* Decorah, Iowa: Seed Saver Publications, 1985.

Winged Bean, The. Washington, D.C.: National Academy Press, 1981.

Yamaguchi, Mas. *World Vegetables.* Westport, Conn.: AVI Publishing Co., 1983.

INDEX